Mobil
Travel Guide

Southern
Great Lakes

2005

Illinois

Indiana

Ohio

ExxonMobil
Travel Publications

Acknowledgements

We gratefully acknowledge the help of our representatives for their efficient and perceptive inspections of the lodging and dining establishments listed; the establishments' proprietors for their cooperation in showing their facilities and providing information about them; and the many users of previous editions who have taken the time to share their experiences. Mobil Travel Guide is also grateful to all the talented writers who contributed entries to this book.

Printing Acknowledgement: North American Corporation of Illinois

www.mobiltravelguide.com

Front cover photo: Rock and Roll Hall of Fame and Museum on Lake Erie, Cleveland, Ohio.

ISBN: 0-7627-3591-0

ISSN: 1550-0063

Manufactured in the United States of America.

10 9 8 7 6 5 4 3 2 1

Contents

MAP SYMBOLS

TRANSPORTATION

CONTROLLED ACCESS HIGHWAYS

Freeway
Tollway
Under Construction
Interchange and Exit Number

OTHER HIGHWAYS

Primary Highway
Secondary Highway
Divided Highway
Other Paved Road
Unpaved Road
Check conditions locally

HIGHWAY MARKERS

Interstate Route
U.S. Route
State or Provincial Route
County or Other Route
Trans-Canada Highway
Canadian Provincial Autoroute
Mexican Federal Route

OTHER SYMBOLS

Distances along Major Highways
Miles in U.S.; kilometers in Canada and Mexico
Tunnel; Pass
Auto Ferry; Passenger Ferry

OTHER MAP FEATURES

Time Zone Boundary
Mt. Olympus Mountain Peak; Elevation
7,985 in Feet
Perennial; Intermittent River

RECREATION

National Park
National Forest; National Grassland
Other Large Park or Recreation Area
Small State Park
with and without Camping
Military Lands
Indian Reservation
Trail
Ski Area
Point of Interest

CITIES AND TOWNS

National Capital
State or Provincial Capital
Cities, Towns, and Populated Places
Type size indicates relative importance
Urban Area
State and province maps only
Large Incorporated Cities
City maps only

ALASKA

HAWAII

© MAPQUEST

0   150   300 mi
0   150   300 km

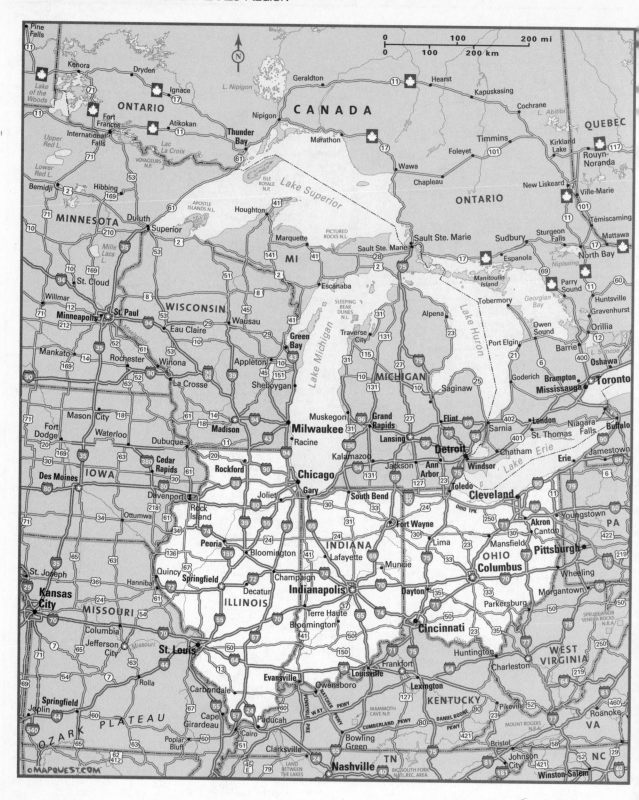

©MAPQUEST.COM

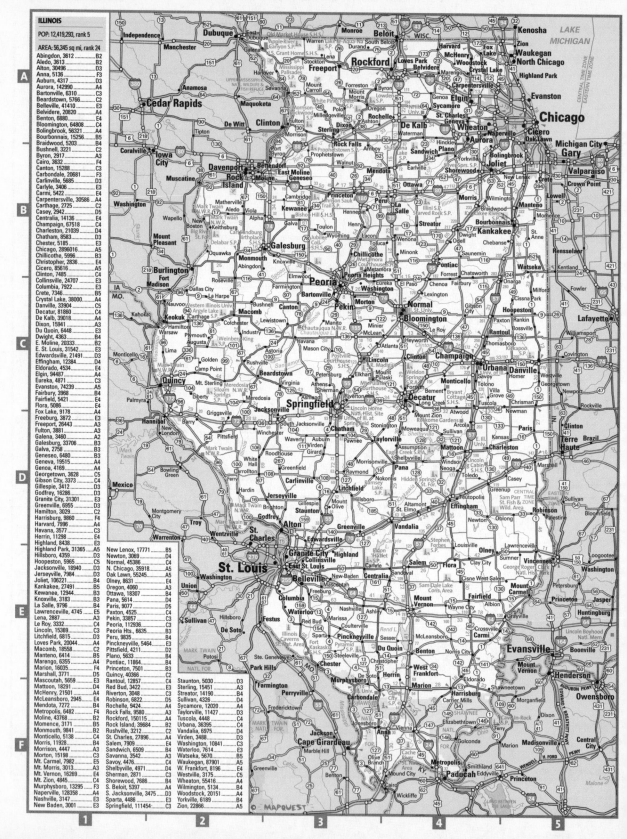

ILLINOIS
POP: 12,419,293, rank 5
AREA: 56,345 sq mi, rank 24

Abingdon, 3612 .... B2
Aledo, 3613 .... B2
Alton, 30496 .... D3
Anna, 5136 .... F3
Auburn, 4317 .... D3
Aurora, 142990 .... A4
Bartonville, 6310 .... C3
Beardstown, 5766 .... C2
Belleville, 41410 .... E3
Belvidere, 20820 .... A4
Benton, 6880 .... E4
Bloomington, 64808 .... C4
Bolingbrook, 56321 .... A4
Bourbonnais, 15256 .... B5
Braidwood, 5203 .... B4
Bushnell, 3221 .... C2
Byron, 2917 .... A3
Cairo, 3632 .... F4
Canton, 15288 .... C3
Carbondale, 20681 .... F3
Carlinville, 5685 .... D3
Carlyle, 3406 .... E3
Carmi, 5422 .... E4
Carpentersville, 30586 .... A4
Carthage, 2725 .... C2
Casey, 2942 .... D5
Centralia, 14136 .... E4
Champaign, 67518 .... C4
Charleston, 21039 .... D4
Chatham, 8583 .... D3
Chester, 5185 .... E3
Chicago, 2896016 .... A5
Chillicothe, 5996 .... B3
Christopher, 2836 .... E4
Cicero, 85616 .... A5
Clinton, 7485 .... C4
Collinsville, 24707 .... E3
Columbia, 7922 .... E3
Crete, 7346 .... B5
Crystal Lake, 38000 .... A4
Danville, 33904 .... C5
Decatur, 81860 .... C4
De Kalb, 39018 .... A4
Dixon, 15941 .... A3
Dwight, 4363 .... B4
E. Moline, 20333 .... B2
E. St. Louis, 31542 .... E3
Edwardsville, 21491 .... D3
Effingham, 12384 .... D4
Eldorado, 4534 .... E4
Elgin, 94487 .... A4
Eureka, 4871 .... C3
Evanston, 74239 .... A5
Fairbury, 3968 .... C4
Fairfield, 5421 .... E4
Flora, 5086 .... E4
Fox Lake, 9178 .... A4
Freeburg, 3872 .... E3
Freeport, 26443 .... A3
Fulton, 3881 .... A3
Galena, 3460 .... A2
Galesburg, 33706 .... B3
Galva, 2758 .... B3
Geneseo, 6480 .... B3
Geneva, 19515 .... A4
Genoa, 4169 .... A4
Georgetown, 3628 .... C5
Gibson City, 3373 .... C4
Gillespie, 3412 .... D3
Godfrey, 16286 .... D3
Granite City, 31301 .... E3
Greenville, 6955 .... D3
Hamilton, 3029 .... C2
Harrisburg, 9860 .... E4
Harvard, 7996 .... A4
Havana, 3577 .... C3
Herrin, 11298 .... E3
Highland, 8438 .... D3
Highland Park, 31365 .... A5
Hillsboro, 4359 .... D3
Hoopeston, 5965 .... C5
Jacksonville, 18940 ...... D3
Jerseyville, 7984 .... D3
Joliet, 106221 .... B4
Kankakee, 27491 .... B5
Kewanee, 12944 .... B3
Knoxville, 3183 .... B3
La Salle, 9796 .... B4
Lawrenceville, 4745 ..... E5
Lena, 2887 .... A3
Le Roy, 3332 .... C4
Lincoln, 15369 .... C3
Litchfield, 6815 .... D3
Loves Park, 20044 ...... A4
Macomb, 18558 .... C2
Manteno, 6414 .... B5
Marengo, 6355 .... A4
Marion, 16035 .... F4
Marshall, 3771 .... D5
Mattoon, 18201 .... D4
McHenry, 21501 .... A4
McLeansboro, 2945 .... E4
Mendota, 7272 .... B4
Metropolis, 6482 .... F4
Moline, 43768 .... B2
Momence, 3171 .... B5
Monmouth, 9841 ...... C2
Monticello, 5138 ...... C4
Morris, 11928 .... B4
Morrison, 4447 .... A3
Morton, 15198 .... C3
Mt. Carmel, 7982 ..... E5
Mt. Morris, 3013 ...... A3
Mt. Vernon, 16269 .... E4
Mt. Zion, 4845 .... C4
Murphysboro, 13295 .. F3
Naperville, 128358 ... A4
Nashville, 3147 ...... E3
New Baden, 3001 .... E3

New Lenox, 17771 .... B5
Newton, 3069 .... D4
Normal, 45386 .... C4
N. Chicago, 35918 .... A5
Olney, 8631 .... D4
Oregon, 4060 .... A3
Ottawa, 18307 .... B4
Pana, 5614 .... D4
Paris, 9077 .... D5
Paxton, 4525 .... C4
Pekin, 33857 .... C3
Peoria, 112936 .... C3
Peoria Hts., 6635 ...... B3
Peru, 9835 .... B4
Pinckneyville, 5464 .... E3
Pittsfield, 4211 .... D2
Plano, 5633 .... A4
Pontiac, 11864 .... C4
Princeton, 7501 .... B3
Quincy, 40366 .... C2
Rantoul, 12957 .... C4
Red Bud, 3422 .... E3
Riverton, 3048 .... D3
Robinson, 6822 ...... D5
Rochelle, 9424 ...... A4
Rock Falls, 9580 .... A3
Rockford, 150115 ... A4
Rock Island, 39684 .. B2
Rushville, 3212 ..... C2
St. Charles, 27896 .. A4
Salem, 7909 .... E4
Sandwich, 6509 .... B4
Savanna, 3542 ..... A3
Savoy, 4476 .... C4
Shelbyville, 4971 .. D4
Sherman, 2871 .... D3
Shorewood, 7686 . B4
S. Beloit, 5397 .... A4
S. Jacksonville, 3475 D3
Sparta, 4486 ...... E3
Springfield, 111454 . C3

Staunton, 5030 .... D3
Sterling, 15451 .... A3
Streator, 14190 .... B4
Sullivan, 4326 .... D4
Sycamore, 12020 ...... A4
Taylorville, 11427 ..... D3
Tuscola, 4448 .... D4
Urbana, 36395 .... C4
Vandalia, 6975 .... D4
Virden, 3488 .... D3
Washington, 10841 .. C3
Waterloo, 7614 ...... E3
Watseka, 5670 .... C5
Waukegan, 87901 .... A5
W. Frankfort, 8196 .. E4
Westville, 3175 ...... C5
Wheaton, 55416 .... A4
Wilmington, 5134 .. B4
Woodstock, 20151 .. A4
Yorkville, 6189 ..... B4
Zion, 22866 .... A5

© MapQuest

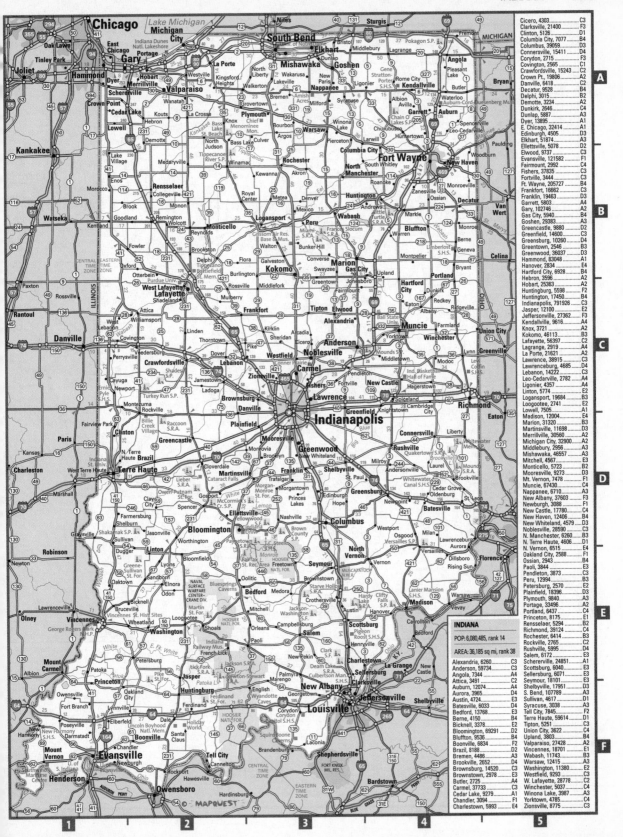

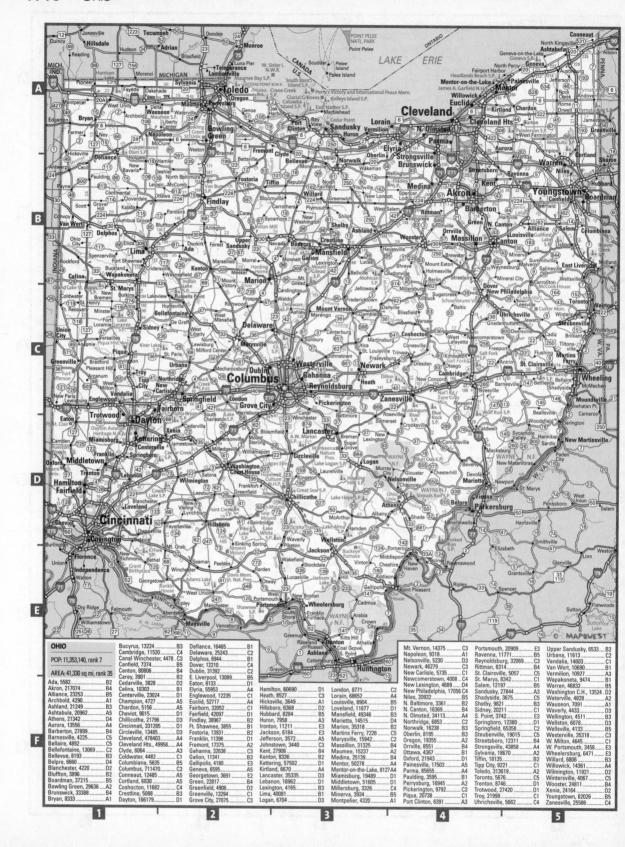

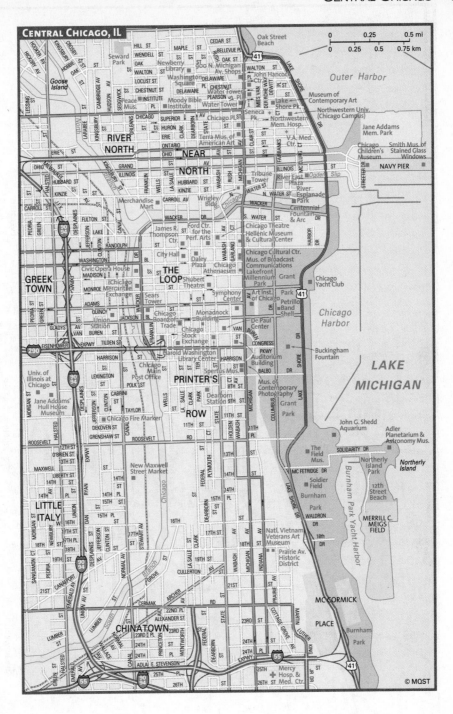

CENTRAL CHICAGO, IL

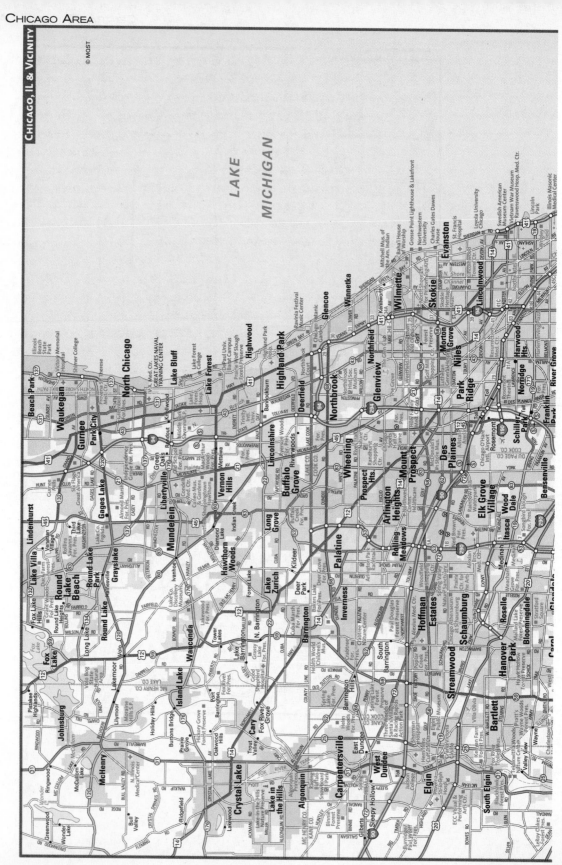

CHICAGO, IL & VICINITY

© MOST

LAKE MICHIGAN

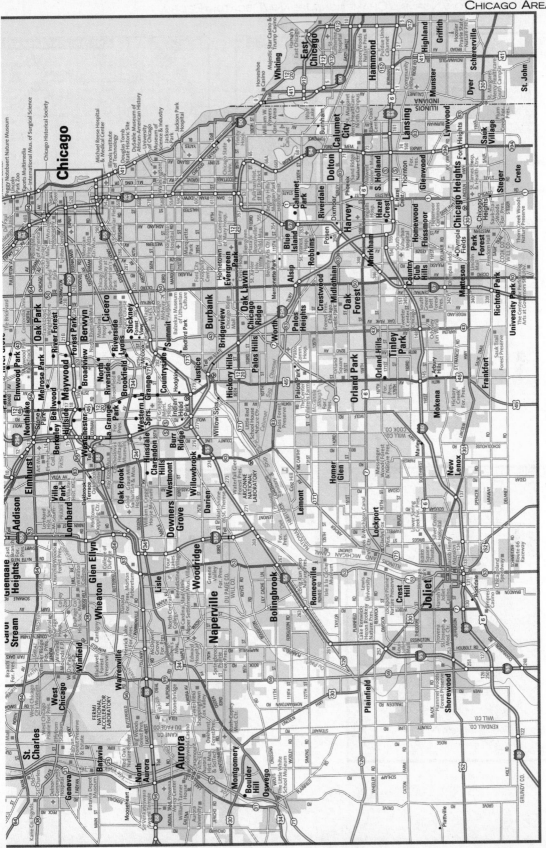

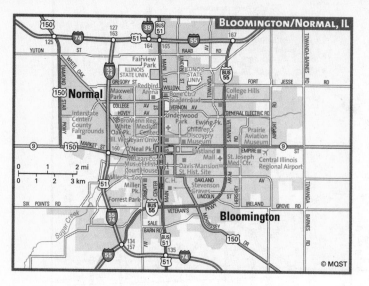

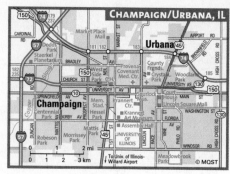

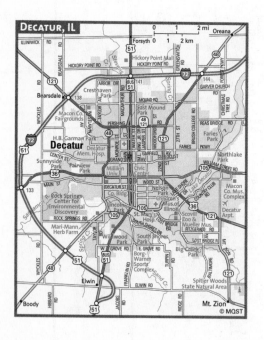

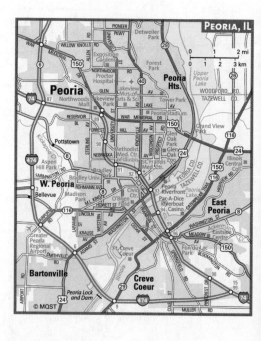

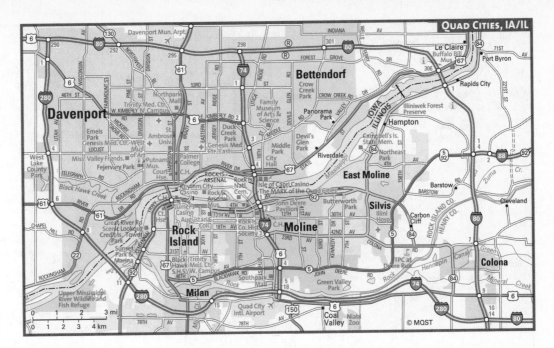

Quad Cities, IA/IL

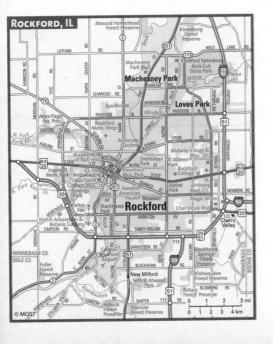

Rockford, IL

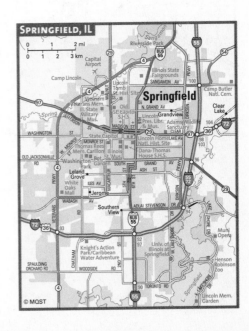

Springfield, IL

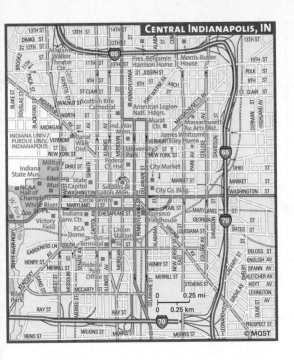

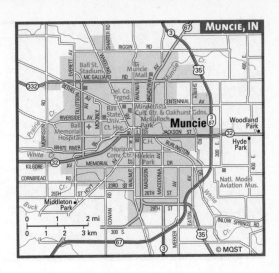

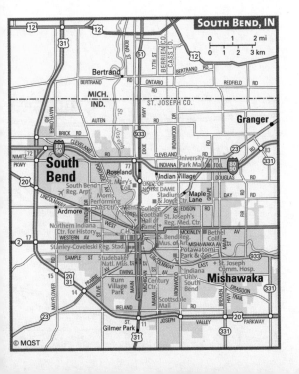

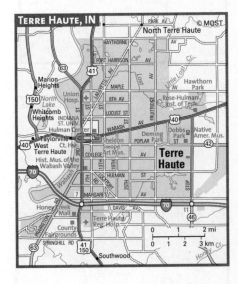

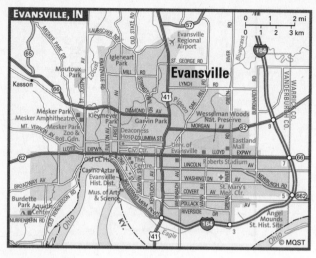

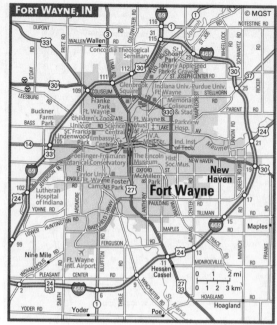

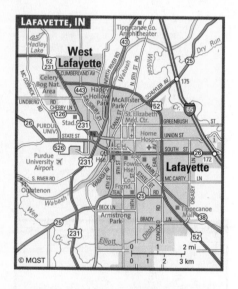

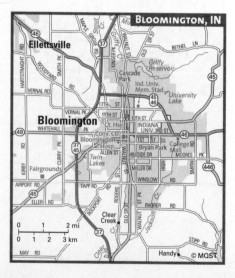

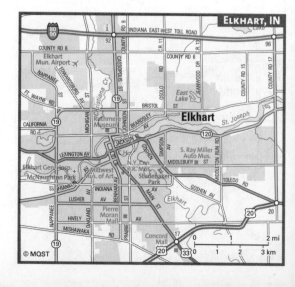

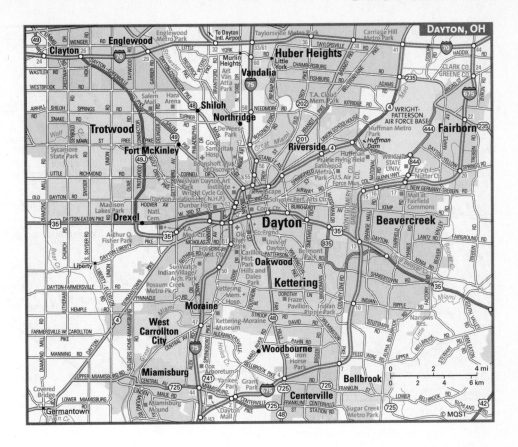

DAYTON, OH

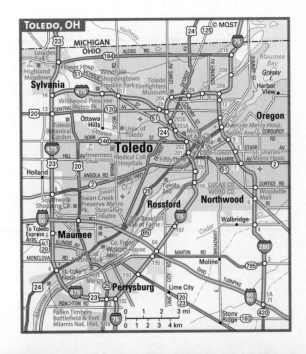

TOLEDO, OH

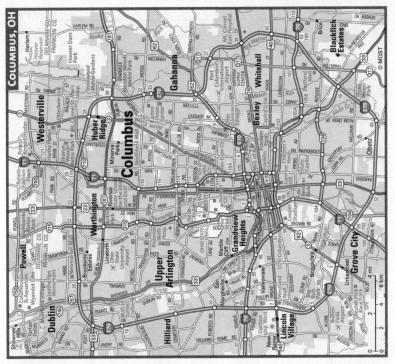

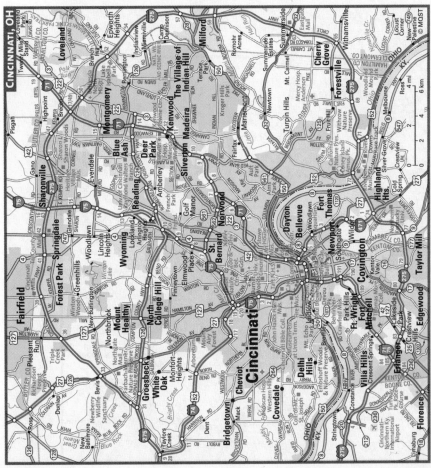

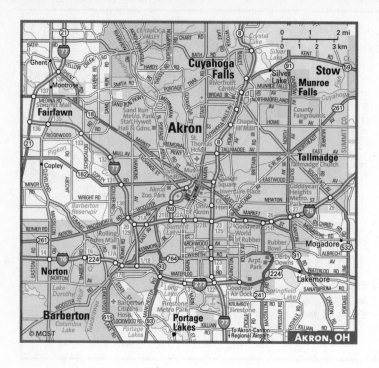

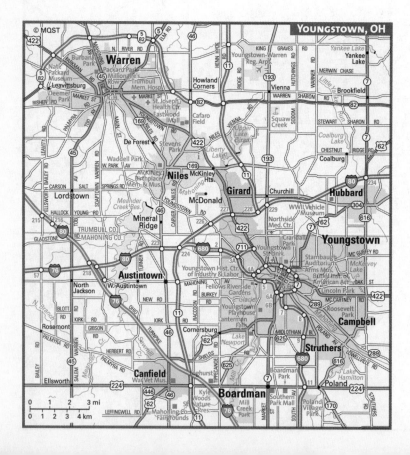

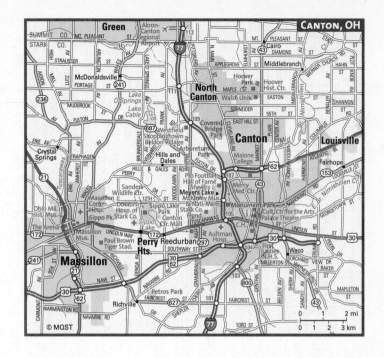

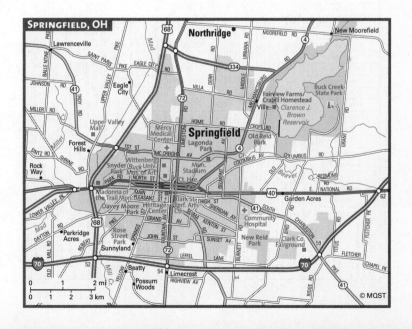

Mileage Chart

Distances in chart are in miles. To convert miles to kilometers, multiply the distance in miles by 1.609

Example:
New York, NY to Boston, MA = 215 miles or 346 kilometers (215 x 1.609)

	ALBUQUERQUE, NM	ATLANTA, GA	BALTIMORE, MD	BILLINGS, MT	BIRMINGHAM, AL	BISMARCK, ND	BOISE, ID	BOSTON, MA	BUFFALO, NY	BURLINGTON, VT	CHARLESTON, SC	CHARLESTON, WV	CHARLOTTE, NC	CHEYENNE, WY	CHICAGO, IL	CINCINNATI, OH	CLEVELAND, OH	DALLAS, TX	DENVER, CO	DES MOINES, IA	DETROIT, MI	EL PASO, TX	HOUSTON, TX	INDIANAPOLIS, IN	JACKSON, MS	KANSAS CITY, MO	LAS VEGAS, NV	LITTLE ROCK, AR	LOS ANGELES, CA	LOUISVILLE, KY	MEMPHIS, TN	MIAMI, FL	MILWAUKEE, WI	MINNEAPOLIS, MN	MONTRÉAL, QC	NASHVILLE, TN	NEW ORLEANS, LA	NEW YORK, NY	OKLAHOMA CITY, OK	OMAHA, NE	ORLANDO, FL	PHILADELPHIA, PA	PHOENIX, AZ	PITTSBURGH, PA	PORTLAND, ME	PORTLAND, OR	RAPID CITY, SD	RENO, NV	RICHMOND, VA	ST. LOUIS, MO	SALT LAKE CITY, UT	SAN ANTONIO, TX	SAN DIEGO, CA	SAN FRANCISCO, CA	SEATTLE, WA	TAMPA, FL	TORONTO, ON	VANCOUVER, BC	WASHINGTON,DC	WICHITA, KS
ALBUQUERQUE, NM		1490	1902	991	1274	1333	966	2240	1808	2178	1793	1568	1649	538	1352	1409	1619	754	438	1091	1608	263	994	1298	1157	894	578	900	806	1320	1033	2155	1426	1339	2172	1248	1276	2015	546	973	1934	1954	466	1670	2338	1395	841	1020	1876	1051	624	818	825	1111	1463	1949	1841	1597	1896	707
ATLANTA, GA	1490		679	1889	150	1559	2218	1100	910	1158	317	503	238	1482	717	476	726	792	1403	967	735	1437	800	531	386	801	2067	528	2237	419	389	661	813	1129	1241	242	473	869	944	989	440	782	1868	676	1197	2647	1511	2440	527	549	1916	1000	2166	2618	2705	455	958	2838	636	989
BALTIMORE, MD	1902	679		1959	795	1551	2401	422	370	481	583	352	441	1665	708	521	377	1399	1690	1031	532	2045	1470	600	1032	1087	2445	1072	2705	602	933	1109	805	1121	564	716	1142	192	1354	1168	904	104	2366	246	520	2830	1626	2623	152	841	2100	1671	2724	2840	2775	960	565	2908	38	1276
BILLINGS, MT	991	1889	1959		1839	413	626	2254	1796	2181	2157	1755	2012	455	1246	1552	1597	1433	554	1007	1534	1255	1673	1432	1836	1088	965	1530	1239	1547	1625	2554	1175	839	2093	1648	1955	2049	1227	904	2333	2019	1199	1719	2352	889	379	960	2053	1341	548	1500	1302	1176	816	2348	1762	949	1953	1067
BIRMINGHAM, AL	1274	150	795	1839		1509	2170	1215	909	1241	466	578	389	1434	667	475	725	647	1356	919	734	1292	678	481	241	753	1852	381	2092	369	241	812	763	1079	1289	194	351	985	729	941	591	897	1723	763	1313	2599	1463	2392	678	501	1868	878	2021	2472	2657	606	958	2791	758	838
BISMARCK, ND	1333	1559	1551	413	1509		1039	1846	1388	1773	1749	1347	1604	594	838	1144	1189	1342	693	675	1126	1597	1582	1024	1548	801	1378	1183	1702	1139	1337	2224	767	431	1685	1315	1734	1641	1136	616	2003	1611	1662	1311	1944	1301	320	1372	1645	1053	960	1599	1765	1749	1229	2018	1354	1362	1545	934
BOISE, ID	966	2218	2401	626	2170	1039		2697	2239	2624	2520	2182	2375	737	1708	1969	2040	1711	833	1369	1977	1206	1952	1852	2115	1376	760	1808	1033	1933	1954	2883	1748	1465	2535	1976	2234	2491	1506	1234	2662	2462	993	2161	2795	432	930	430	2496	1628	342	1761	1096	646	500	2677	2204	633	2395	1346
BOSTON, MA	2240	1100	422	2254	1215	1846	2697		462	214	1003	741	861	1961	1003	862	654	1819	2004	1326	741	2465	1890	940	1453	1427	2757	1493	3046	964	1353	1529	1100	1417	313	1136	1563	215	1694	1463	1324	321	2706	592	107	3126	1921	2919	572	1181	2395	2092	3065	3135	3070	1380	570	3204	458	1616
BUFFALO, NY	1808	910	370	1796	909	1388	2239	462		375	899	431	695	1502	545	442	197	1393	1546	868	277	2039	1513	508	1134	995	2299	1066	2572	545	927	1425	642	958	397	716	1254	400	1262	1005	1221	414	2274	217	560	2667	1463	2460	485	749	1936	1665	2632	2677	2612	1276	106	2745	384	1184
BURLINGTON, VT	2178	1158	481	2181	1241	1773	2624	214	375		1061	782	919	1887	930	817	567	1763	1931	1253	652	2409	1916	878	1479	1366	2684	1437	2957	915	1297	1587	1027	1343	92	1086	1588	299	1632	1390	1383	371	2644	587	233	3052	1848	2845	630	1119	2322	2036	3020	3062	2997	1438	419	3130	517	1554
CHARLESTON, SC	1793	317	583	2157	466	1749	2520	1003	899	1061		468	204	1783	907	622	724	1109	1705	1204	879	1754	1110	721	703	1102	2371	900	2554	610	760	583	1003	1319	1145	543	783	773	1248	1290	379	685	2184	642	1101	2948	1824	2741	428	850	2218	1310	2483	2934	2973	434	1006	3106	539	1291
CHARLESTON, WV	1568	503	352	1755	578	1347	2182	741	431	782	468		265	1445	506	209	255	1072	1367	802	410	1718	1192	320	816	764	2122	745	2374	251	606	994	601	918	822	395	926	515	1022	952	790	454	2035	217	839	2610	1422	2403	322	512	1880	1344	2393	2620	2571	845	537	2705	346	953
CHARLOTTE, NC	1649	238	441	2012	389	1604	2375	861	695	919	204	265		1637	761	476	520	1031	1559	1057	675	1677	1041	575	625	956	2225	754	2453	464	614	730	857	1173	1003	397	713	631	1102	1144	525	543	2107	438	959	2802	1678	2595	289	704	2072	1241	2405	2759	2827	581	802	2960	397	1145
CHEYENNE, WY	538	1482	1665	455	1434	594	737	1961	1502	1887	1783	1445	1637		972	1233	1304	979	100	633	1241	801	1220	1115	1382	640	843	1076	1116	1197	1217	2147	1012	881	1799	1240	1502	1755	773	497	1926	1725	1004	1425	2059	1166	305	959	1760	892	436	1046	1179	1176	1234	1941	1468	1368	1659	613
CHICAGO, IL	1352	717	708	1246	667	838	1708	1003	545	930	907	506	761	972		302	346	936	1015	337	283	1543	1108	184	750	532	1768	662	2042	299	539	1382	89	409	841	474	935	797	807	474	1161	768	1819	467	1101	2137	913	1930	802	294	1406	1270	2105	2146	2062	1176	510	2196	701	728
CINCINNATI, OH	1409	476	521	1552	475	1144	1969	862	442	817	622	209	476	1233	302		253	958	1200	599	261	1605	1079	116	700	597	1955	632	2215	106	493	1141	398	714	815	281	820	636	863	736	920	576	1876	292	960	2398	1219	2191	530	350	1667	1231	2234	2407	2368	935	484	2501	517	785
CLEVELAND, OH	1619	726	377	1597	725	1189	2040	654	197	567	724	255	520	1304	346	253		1208	1347	669	171	1854	1328	319	950	806	2100	882	2374	356	742	1250	443	760	588	531	1070	466	1073	806	1045	437	2085	136	751	2469	1264	2262	471	560	1738	1481	2437	2478	2413	1101	303	2547	370	995
DALLAS, TX	754	792	1399	1433	647	1342	1711	1819	1393	1763	1109	1072	1031	979	936	958	1208		887	752	1218	647	241	913	406	554	1331	327	1446	852	466	1367	1010	999	1772	681	525	1589	209	669	1146	1501	1077	1246	1917	2140	1077	1933	1309	635	1410	271	1375	1827	2208	1161	1441	2342	1362	367
DENVER, CO	438	1403	1690	554	1356	693	833	2004	1546	1931	1705	1367	1559	100	1015	1200	1347	887		676	1284	701	1127	1088	1290	603	756	984	1029	1118	1116	2069	1055	924	1843	1162	1409	1799	681	541	1847	1744	904	1460	2102	1261	404	1054	1688	855	531	946	1092	1271	1329	1862	1512	1463	1686	521
DES MOINES, IA	1091	967	1031	1007	919	675	1369	1326	868	1253	1204	802	1057	633	337	599	669	752	676		606	1283	992	481	931	194	1429	567	1703	595	720	1632	378	246	1165	725	1117	1121	546	136	1411	1091	1558	791	1424	1798	629	1591	1126	436	1067	1009	1766	1807	1822	1426	834	1956	1025	390
DETROIT, MI	1608	735	532	1534	734	1126	1977	741	277	652	879	410	675	1241	283	261	171	1218	1284	606		1799	1338	318	960	795	2037	891	2310	366	752	1401	380	697	564	541	1079	622	1062	743	1180	592	2074	292	838	2405	1201	2198	627	549	1675	1490	2373	2415	2350	1194	233	2483	526	984
EL PASO, TX	263	1437	2045	1255	1292	1597	1206	2465	2039	2409	1754	1718	1677	801	1543	1605	1854	647	701	1283	1799		758	1489	1051	1085	717	974	801	1499	1112	1959	1617	1530	2363	1328	1118	2235	737	1236	1738	2147	432	1893	2563	1767	1105	1315	1955	1242	864	556	730	1181	1944	1753	2032	2087	2008	898
HOUSTON, TX	994	800	1470	1673	678	1582	1952	1890	1513	1916	1110	1192	1041	1220	1108	1079	1328	241	1127	992	1338	758		1033	445	795	1474	447	1558	972	586	1201	1193	1240	1892	801	360	1660	449	910	980	1572	1188	1366	1988	2381	1318	2072	1330	863	1650	200	1487	1938	2449	995	1561	2583	1433	608
INDIANAPOLIS, IN	1298	531	600	1432	481	1024	1852	940	508	878	721	320	575	1115	184	116	319	913	1088	481	318	1489	1033		675	485	1843	587	2104	112	464	1196	279	596	872	287	826	715	752	618	975	655	1764	370	1038	2280	1101	2073	641	239	1549	1186	2122	2290	2249	990	541	2383	596	674
JACKSON, MS	1157	386	1032	1836	241	1548	2115	1453	1134	1479	703	816	625	1382	750	700	950	406	1290	931	960	1051	445	675		747	1735	269	1851	594	211	915	835	1151	1514	423	185	1223	612	935	694	1135	1482	988	1550	2544	1458	2337	914	505	1813	644	1780	2232	2612	709	1183	2746	996	771
KANSAS CITY, MO	894	801	1087	1088	753	801	1376	1427	995	1366	1102	764	956	640	532	597	806	554	603	194	795	1085	795	485	747		1358	382	1632	516	536	1466	573	441	1359	559	932	1202	348	188	1245	1141	1360	857	1525	1805	710	1598	1085	252	1074	812	1695	1814	1872	1259	1028	2007	1083	192
LAS VEGAS, NV	578	2067	2445	965	1852	1378	760	2757	2299	2684	2371	2122	2225	843	1768	1955	2100	1331	756	1429	2037	717	1474	1843	1735	1358		1478	274	1874	1611	2733	1808	1677	2596	1826	1854	2552	1124	1294	2512	2500	285	2215	2855	1188	1035	442	2444	1610	417	1272	337	575	1256	2526	2265	1390	2441	1276
LITTLE ROCK, AR	900	528	1072	1530	381	1183	1808	1493	1066	1437	900	745	754	1076	662	632	882	327	984	567	891	974	447	587	269	382	1478		1706	526	140	1190	747	814	1446	355	455	1262	355	570	969	1175	1367	920	1590	2237	1093	2030	983	416	1507	600	1703	2012	2305	984	1115	2439	1036	464
LOS ANGELES, CA	806	2237	2705	1239	2092	1702	1033	3046	2572	2957	2554	2374	2453	1116	2042	2215	2374	1446	1029	1703	2310	801	1558	2104	1851	1632	274	1706		2126	1839	2759	2082	1951	2869	2054	1917	2820	1352	1567	2538	2760	369	2476	3144	971	1309	519	2682	1856	691	1356	124	385	1148	2553	2538	1291	2702	1513
LOUISVILLE, KY	1320	419	602	1547	369	1139	1933	964	545	915	610	251	464	1197	299	106	356	852	1118	595	366	1499	972	112	594	516	1874	526	2126		386	1084	394	711	920	175	714	739	774	704	863	678	1786	394	1062	2362	1215	2155	572	264	1631	1125	2144	2372	2364	878	589	2497	596	705
MEMPHIS, TN	1033	389	933	1625	241	1337	1954	1353	927	1297	760	606	614	1217	539	493	742	466	1116	720	752	1112	586	464	211	536	1611	140	1839	386		1051	624	940	1306	215	396	1123	487	724	830	1035	1500	780	1451	2382	1247	2175	843	294	1652	739	1841	2144	2440	845	975	2574	896	597
MIAMI, FL	2155	661	1109	2554	812	2224	2883	1529	1425	1587	583	994	730	2147	1382	1141	1250	1367	2069	1632	1401	1959	1201	1196	915	1466	2733	1190	2759	1084	1051		1478	1794	1671	907	874	1299	1609	1654	232	1211	2390	1167	1627	3312	2176	3105	954	1214	2581	1401	2688	3140	3370	274	1532	3504	1065	1655
MILWAUKEE, WI	1426	813	805	1175	763	767	1748	1100	642	1027	1003	601	857	1012	89	398	443	1010	1055	378	380	1617	1193	279	835	573	1808	747	2082	394	624	1478		337	939	569	1020	894	880	514	1257	865	1892	564	1198	2063	842	1970	899	367	1446	1343	2145	2186	1991	1272	607	2124	799	769
MINNEAPOLIS, MN	1339	1129	1121	839	1079	431	1465	1417	958	1343	1319	918	1173	881	409	714	760	999	924	246	697	1530	1240	596	1151	441	1677	814	1951	711	940	1794	337		1255	886	1337	1211	793	383	1573	1181	1805	881	1515	1727	606	1839	1216	621	1315	1257	2014	2055	1654	1588	924	1788	1115	637
MONTRÉAL, QC	2172	1241	564	2093	1289	1685	2535	313	397	92	1145	822	1003	1799	841	815	588	1772	1843	1165	564	2363	1892	872	1514	1359	2596	1446	2869	920	1306	1671	939	1255		1094	1632	383	1625	1300	1466	454	2637	607	282	2963	1758	2756	714	1112	2232	2043	2931	2972	2907	1522	330	3041	600	1547
NASHVILLE, TN	1248	242	716	1648	194	1315	1976	1136	716	1086	543	395	397	1240	474	281	531	681	1162	725	541	1328	801	287	423	559	1826	355	2054	175	215	907	569	886	1094		539	906	703	747	686	818	1715	569	1234	2405	1269	2198	626	307	1675	954	2056	2360	2463	701	764	2597	679	748
NEW ORLEANS, LA	1276	473	1142	1955	351	1734	2234	1563	1254	1588	783	926	713	1502	935	820	1070	525	1409	1117	1079	1118	360	826	185	932	1854	455	1917	714	396	874	1020	1337	1632	539		1332	731	1121	653	1245	1548	1108	1660	2663	1643	2431	1002	690	1932	560	1846	2298	2731	668	1302	2865	1106	890
NEW YORK, NY	2015	869	192	2049	985	1641	2491	215	400	299	773	515	631	1755	797	636	466	1589	1799	1121	622	2235	1660	715	1223	1202	2552	1262	2820	739	1123	1299	894	1211	383	906	1332		1469	1258	1094	91	2481	367	313	2920	1716	2713	342	956	2189	1861	2839	2929	2864	1150	507	2998	228	1391
OKLAHOMA CITY, OK	546	944	1354	1227	729	1136	1506	1694	1262	1632	1248	1022	1102	773	807	863	1073	209	681	546	1062	737	449	752	612	348	1124	355	1352	774	487	1609	880	793	1625	703	731	1469		463	1388	1408	1012	1124	1792	1934	871	1727	1331	505	1204	466	1370	1657	2002	1403	1295	2136	1350	161
OMAHA, NE	973	989	1168	904	941	616	1234	1463	1005	1390	1290	952	1144	497	474	736	806	669	541	136	743	1236	910	618	935	188	1294	570	1567	704	724	1654	514	383	1300	747	1121	1258	463		1433	1228	1440	928	1561	1662	525	1455	1263	440	932	927	1630	1672	1719	1448	971	1853	1162	307
ORLANDO, FL	1934	440	904	2333	591	2003	2662	1324	1221	1383	379	790	525	1926	1161	920	1045	1146	1847	1411	1180	1738	980	975	694	1245	2512	969	2538	863	830	232	1257	1573	1466	686	653	1094	1388	1433		1006	2169	963	1422	3091	1955	2884	750	993	2360	1180	2467	2918	3149	82	1327	3283	860	1434
PHILADELPHIA, PA	1954	782	104	2019	897	1611	2462	321	414	371	685	454	543	1725	768	576	437	1501	1744	1091	592	2147	1572	655	1135	1141	2500	1175	2760	678	1035	1211	865	1181	454	818	1245	91	1408	1228	1006		2420	306	419	2890	1686	2683	254	895	2160	1774	2779	2900	2835	1062	522	2968	140	1330
PHOENIX, AZ	466	1868	2366	1199	1723	1662	993	2706	2274	2644	2184	2035	2107	1004	1819	1876	2085	1077	904	1558	2074	432	1188	1764	1482	1360	285	1367	369	1786	1500	2390	1892	1805	2637	1715	1548	2481	1012	1440	2169	2420		2136	2804	1335	1308	883	2343	1517	651	987	358	750	1513	2184	2307	1655	2362	1173
PITTSBURGH, PA	1670	676	246	1719	763	1311	2161	592	217	587	642	217	438	1425	467	292	136	1246	1460	791	292	1893	1366	370	988	857	2215	920	2476	394	780	1167	564	881	607	569	1108	367	1124	928	963	306	2136		690	2590	1386	2383	341	611	1859	1519	2494	2599	2534	1019	321	2668	240	1046
PORTLAND, ME	2338	1197	520	2352	1313	1944	2795	107	560	233	1101	839	959	2059	1101	960	751	1917	2102	1424	838	2563	1988	1038	1550	1525	2855	1590	3144	1062	1451	1627	1198	1515	282	1234	1660	313	1792	1561	1422	419	2804	690		3223	2019	3016	670	1279	2493	2189	3162	3233	3168	1478	668	3301	556	1714
PORTLAND, OR	1395	2647	2830	889	2599	1301	432	3126	2667	3052	2948	2610	2802	1166	2137	2398	2469	2140	1261	1798	2405	1767	2381	2280	2544	1805	1188	2237	971	2362	2382	3312	2063	1727	2963	2405	2663	2920	1934	1662	3091	2890	1335	2590	3223		1268	578	2925	2057	771	2322	1093	638	170	3106	2633	313	2824	1775
RAPID CITY, SD	841	1511	1626	379	1463	320	930	1921	1463	1848	1824	1422	1678	305	913	1219	1264	1077	404	629	1201	1105	1318	1101	1458	710	1035	1093	1309	1215	1247	2176	842	606	1758	1269	1643	1716	871	525	1955	1686	1308	1386	2019	1268		1151	1720	963	628	1335	1372	1368	1195	1970	1429	1328	1620	712
RENO, NV	1020	2440	2623	960	2392	1372	430	2919	2460	2845	2741	2403	2595	959	1930	2191	2262	1933	1054	1591	2198	1315	2072	2073	2337	1598	442	2030	519	2155	2175	3105	1970	1839	2756	2198	2431	2713	1727	1455	2884	2683	883	2383	3016	578	1151		2718	1850	524	1870	642	217	755	2899	2426	898	2617	1568
RICHMOND, VA	1876	527	152	2053	678	1645	2496	572	485	630	428	322	289	1760	802	530	471	1309	1688	1126	627	1955	1330	641	914	1085	2444	983	2682	572	843	954	899	1216	714	626	1002	342	1331	1263	750	254	2343	341	670	2925	1720	2718		834	2194	1530	2684	2934	2869	805	660	3003	108	1274
ST. LOUIS, MO	1051	549	841	1341	501	1053	1628	1181	749	1119	850	512	704	892	294	350	560	635	855	436	549	1242	863	239	505	252	1610	416	1856	264	294	1214	367	621	1112	307	690	956	505	440	993	895	1517	611	1279	2057	963	1850	834		1326	968	1875	2066	2125	1008	782	2259	837	441
SALT LAKE CITY, UT	624	1916	2100	548	1868	960	342	2395	1936	2322	2218	1880	2072	436	1406	1667	1738	1410	531	1067	1675	864	1650	1549	1813	1074	417	1507	691	1631	1652	2581	1446	1315	2232	1675	1932	2189	1204	932	2360	2160	651	1859	2493	771	628	524	2194	1326		1419	754	740	839	2375	1902	973	2094	1044
SAN ANTONIO, TX	818	1000	1671	1500	878	1599	1761	2092	1665	2036	1310	1344	1241	1046	1270	1231	1481	271	946	1009	1490	556	200	1186	644	812	1272	600	1356	1125	739	1401	1343	1257	2043	954	560	1861	466	927	1180	1774	987	1519	2189	2322	1335	1870	1530	968	1419		1285	1737	2275	1195	1714	2410	1635	624
SAN DIEGO, CA	825	2166	2724	1302	2021	1765	1096	3065	2632	3020	2483	2393	2405	1179	2105	2234	2437	1375	1092	1766	2373	730	1487	2122	1780	1695	337	1703	124	2144	1841	2688	2145	2014	2931	2056	1846	2839	1370	1630	2467	2779	358	2494	3162	1093	1372	642	2684	1875	754	1285		508	1271	2481	2601	1414	2720	1531
SAN FRANCISCO, CA	1111	2618	2840	1176	2472	1749	646	3135	2677	3062	2934	2620	2759	1176	2146	2407	2478	1827	1271	1807	2415	1181	1938	2290	2232	1814	575	2012	385	2372	2144	3140	2186	2055	2972	2360	2298	2929	1657	1672	2918	2900	750	2599	3233	638	1368	217	2934	2066	740	1737	508		816	2933	2643	958	2834	1784
SEATTLE, WA	1463	2705	2775	816	2657	1229	500	3070	2612	2997	2973	2571	2827	1234	2062	2368	2413	2208	1329	1822	2350	1944	2449	2249	2612	1872	1256	2305	1148	2364	2440	3370	1991	1654	2907	2463	2731	2864	2002	1719	3149	2835	1513	2534	3168	170	1195	755	2869	2125	839	2275	1271	816		3164	2577	140	2769	1843
TAMPA, FL	1949	455	960	2348	606	2018	2677	1380	1276	1438	434	845	581	1941	1176	935	1101	1161	1862	1426	1194	1753	995	990	709	1259	2526	984	2553	878	845	274	1272	1588	1522	701	668	1150	1403	1448	82	1062	2184	1019	1478	3106	1970	2899	805	1008	2375	1195	2481	2933	3164		1383	3297	916	1448
TORONTO, ON	1841	958	565	1762	958	1354	2204	570	106	419	1006	537	802	1468	510	484	303	1441	1512	834	233	2032	1561	541	1183	1028	2265	1115	2538	589	975	1532	607	924	330	764	1302	507	1295	971	1327	522	2307	321	668	2633	1429	2426	660	782	1902	1714	2601	2643	2577	1383		2711	563	1217
VANCOUVER, BC	1597	2838	2908	949	2791	1362	633	3204	2745	3130	3106	2705	2960	1368	2196	2501	2547	2342	1463	1956	2483	2087	2583	2383	2746	2007	1390	2439	1291	2497	2574	3504	2124	1788	3041	2597	2865	2998	2136	1853	3283	2968	1655	2668	3301	313	1328	898	3003	2259	973	2410	1414	958	140	3297	2711		2902	1977
WASHINGTON, DC	1896	636	38	1953	758	1545	2395	458	384	517	539	346	397	1659	701	517	370	1362	1686	1025	526	2008	1433	596	996	1083	2441	1036	2702	596	896	1065	799	1115	600	679	1106	228	1350	1162	860	140	2362	240	556	2824	1620	2617	108	837	2094	1635	2720	2834	2769	916	563	2902		1272
WICHITA, KS	707	989	1276	1067	838	934	1346	1616	1184	1554	1291	953	1145	613	728	785	995	367	521	390	984	898	608	674	771	192	1276	464	1513	705	597	1655	769	637	1547	748	890	1391	161	307	1434	1330	1173	1046	1714	1775	712	1568	1274	441	1044	624	1531	1784	1843	1448	1217	1977	1272	

© MapQuest.com, Inc.

Simplify your life with Speedpass.

Weekday to weekend, you are constantly on the move. That's why there's *Speedpass.*™ It's more convenient than cash and faster than a credit card, because Speedpass lets you pay for gas, food, and other items without ever slowing down to reach for your wallet or purse. Plus, *Speedpass* is free and links directly to a major credit or check card you already have. To get yours, enroll online at speedpass.com or call toll free 1-87-SPEEDPASS (1-877-733-3727). Everything in life should be this easy. Speedpass gets you in, out, and on your way. How do we know? We're drivers too.

We're drivers too.

Make every tankful count for college.

You need gas. So why not save for college every time you do? ExxonMobil is working with Upromise to help you save for college. You can join for FREE at upromise.com/xom17 and register your check card or credit card. Then every time you buy gas at an Exxon or Mobil location with the card registered with Upromise, ExxonMobil will contribute toward your child's college education. And be sure to link that same card to your *Speedpass.*™ That way, all your Speedpass gasoline purchases can contribute to your Upromise account. If you don't have a Speedpass device, you can get one, free. Just go to speedpass.com or call toll free 1-87-SPEEDPASS (1-877-733-3727). Upromise is an easy way to help you save for your child's education. How do we know you'd like to make every tankful count? We're drivers too.

We're drivers too.

Welcome

Dear Traveler,

Since its inception in 1958, Mobil Travel Guide has served as a trusted advisor to auto travelers in search of value in lodging, dining, and destinations. Now in its 47th year, the Mobil Travel Guide is the hallmark of our ExxonMobil family of travel publications, and we're proud to offer an array of products and services from our Mobil, Exxon, and Esso brands in North America to facilitate life on the road.

Whether you're looking for business or pleasure venues, our nationwide network of independent, professional evaluators offers their expertise on thousands of travel options, allowing you to plan a quick family getaway, a full-service business meeting, or an unforgettable Mobil Five-Star celebration.

Your feedback is important to us as we strive to improve our product offerings and better meet today's travel needs. Whether you travel once a week or once a year, please take the time to contact us at www. mobiltravelguide.com. We hope to hear from you soon.

Best wishes for safe and enjoyable travels.

Lee R. Raymond
Chairman and CEO
Exxon Mobil Corporation

A Word to Our Readers

Travelers are on the roads in great numbers these days. They're exploring the country on day trips, weekend getaways, business trips, and extended family vacations, visiting major cities and small towns along the way. Because time is precious and the travel industry is ever-changing, having accurate, reliable travel information at your fingertips is critical. Mobil Travel Guide has been providing invaluable insight to travelers for more than 45 years, and we are committed to continuing this service well into the future.

The Mobil Corporation (known as Exxon Mobil Corporation since a 1999 merger) began producing the Mobil Travel Guide books in 1958, following the introduction of the US interstate highway system in 1956. The first edition covered only five Southwestern states. Since then, our books have become the premier travel guides in North America, covering all 50 states and Canada.

Since its founding, Mobil Travel Guide has served as an advocate for travelers seeking knowledge about hotels, restaurants, and places to visit. Based on an objective process, we make recommendations to our customers that we believe will enhance the quality and value of their travel experiences. Our trusted Mobil One- to Five-Star rating system is the oldest and most respected lodging and restaurant inspection and rating program in North America. Most hoteliers, restaurateurs, and industry observers favorably regard the rigor of our inspection program and understand the prestige and benefits that come with receiving a Mobil Star rating.

The Mobil Travel Guide process of rating each establishment includes:

- Unannounced facility inspections
- Incognito service evaluations for Mobil Four-Star and Mobil Five-Star properties
- A review of unsolicited comments from the general public
- Senior management oversight

For each property, more than 450 attributes, including cleanliness, physical facilities, and employee attitude and courtesy, are measured and evaluated to produce a mathematically derived score, which is then blended with the other elements to form an overall score. These quantifiable scores allow comparative analysis among properties and form the basis that we use to assign our Mobil One- to Five-Star ratings.

This process focuses largely on guest expectations, guest experience, and consistency of service, not just physical facilities and amenities. It is fundamentally a relative rating system that rewards those properties that continually strive for and achieve excellence each year. Indeed, the very best properties are consistently raising the bar for those that wish to compete with them. These properties proactively respond to consumers' needs even in today's uncertain times.

Only facilities that meet Mobil Travel Guide's standards earn the privilege of being listed in the guide. Deteriorating, poorly managed establishments are deleted. A Mobil Travel Guide listing constitutes a positive quality recommendation; every listing is an accolade, a recognition of achievement. Our Mobil One- to Five-Star rating system highlights its level of service. Extensive in-house research is constantly underway to determine new additions to our lists.

- The Mobil Five-Star Award indicates that a property is one of the very best in the country and consistently provides gracious and courteous service, superlative quality in its facility, and a unique ambience. The lodgings and restaurants at the Mobil Five-Star level consistently and proactively respond to consumers' needs and continue their commitment to excellence, doing so with grace and perseverance.

- Also highly regarded is the Mobil Four-Star Award, which honors properties for outstanding achievement in overall facility and for providing very strong service levels in all areas. These award winners provide a distinctive experience for the ever-demanding and sophisticated consumer.

- 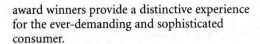 The Mobil Three-Star Award recognizes an excellent property that provides full services and amenities. This category ranges from exceptional hotels with limited services to elegant restaurants with a less-formal atmosphere.

- A Mobil Two-Star property is a clean and comfortable establishment that has expanded amenities or a distinctive environment. A Mobil Two-Star property is an excellent place to stay or dine.

- A Mobil One-Star property is limited in its amenities and services but focuses on providing a value experience while meeting travelers' expectations. The property can be expected to be clean, comfortable, and convenient.

Allow us to emphasize that we do not charge establishments for inclusion in our guides. We have no relationship with any of the businesses and attractions we list and act only as a consumer advocate. In essence, we do the investigative legwork so that you won't have to.

Keep in mind, too, that the hospitality business is ever-changing. Restaurants and lodgings—particularly small chains and stand-alone establishments—change management or even go out of business with surprising quickness. Although we make every effort to double-check information during our annual updates, we nevertheless recommend that you call ahead to make sure the place you've selected is still open and offers all the amenities you're looking for. We've provided phone numbers; when available, we also list fax numbers and Web site addresses.

We hope that your travels are enjoyable and relaxing and that our books help you get the most out of every trip you take. If any aspect of your accommodation, dining, or sightseeing experience motivates you to comment, please drop us a line. We depend a great deal on our readers' remarks, so you can be assured that we will read your comments and assimilate them into our research. General comments about our books are also welcome. You can write to us at Mobil Travel Guide, 1460 Renaissance Drive, Suite 401, Park Ridge, IL 60068, or send an e-mail to info@mobiltravelguide.com.

Take your Mobil Travel Guide books along on every trip you take. We're confident that you'll be pleased with their convenience, ease of use, and breadth of dependable coverage.

Happy travels!

How to Use This Book

The Mobil Travel Guide Regional Travel Planners are designed for ease of use. Each state has its own chapter, beginning with a general introduction that provides a geographical and historical orientation to the state and gives basic statewide tourist information, from climate to calendar highlights to seatbelt laws. The remainder of each chapter is devoted to travel destinations within the state—mainly cities and towns, but also national parks and tourist areas—which, like the states, are arranged in alphabetical order.

The following sections explain the wealth of information you'll find about those travel destinations: information about the area, things to see and do there, and where to stay and eat.

Maps and Map Coordinates

At the front of this book in the full-color section, we have provided state maps as well as maps of selected larger cities to help you find your way around once you leave the highway. You'll find a key to the map symbols on the Contents page at the beginning of the map section.

Next to most cities and towns throughout the book, you'll find a set of map coordinates, such as C-2. These coordinates reference the maps at the front of this book and help you find the location you're looking for quickly and easily.

Destination Information

Because many travel destinations are close to other cities and towns where travelers might find additional attractions, accommodations, and restaurants, we've included cross-references to those cities and towns when it makes sense to do so. We also list addresses, phone numbers, and Web sites for travel information resources—usually the local chamber of commerce or office of tourism—as well as pertinent statistics and, in many cases, a brief introduction to the area.

Information about airports, ground transportation, and suburbs is included for large cities.

Driving Tours and Walking Tours

The driving tours that we include for many states are usually day trips that make for interesting side excursions, although they can be longer. They offer you a way to get off the beaten path and visit an area that travelers often overlook. These trips frequently cover areas of natural beauty or historical significance.

Each walking tour focuses on a particularly interesting area of a city or town. Again, these tours can provide a break from everyday tourist attractions. The tours often include places to stop for meals or snacks.

What to See and Do

Mobil Travel Guide offers information about nearly 20,000 museums, art galleries, amusement parks, historic sites, national and state parks, ski areas, and many other types of attractions. A white star on a black background ★ signals that the attraction is a must-see—one of the best in the area. Because municipal parks, public tennis courts, swimming pools, and small educational institutions are common to most towns, they generally are not mentioned.

Following an attraction's description, you'll find the months, days, and, in some cases, hours of operation; the address/directions, telephone number, and Web site (if there is one); and the admission price category. The following are the ranges we use for admission fees, based on one adult:

- ✪ **FREE**
- ✪ **$** = Up to $5
- ✪ **$$** = $5.01-$10
- ✪ **$$$** = $10.01-$15
- ✪ **$$$$** = Over $15

Special Events

Special events are either annual events that last only a short time, such as festivals and fairs, or longer, seasonal events such as horse racing, theater, and summer concerts. Our Special Events listings also include infrequently occurring occasions that mark certain dates or events, such as a centennial or other commemorative celebration.

Side Trips

We recognize that your travels don't always end where state lines fall, so we've included some side trips that fall outside the states covered in this book but that travelers frequently visit when they're in the region. Nearby national parks, major cities, and other prime tourist draws fall into this category. You'll find side trips for a particular state at the end of that state's section.

Listings

Lodgings, spas, and restaurants are usually listed under the city or town in which they're located. Make sure to check the related cities and towns that appear right beneath a city's heading for additional options, especially if you're traveling to a major metropolitan area that includes many suburbs. If a property is located in a town that doesn't have its own heading, the listing appears under the town nearest it, with the address and town given immediately after the establishment's name. In large cities, lodgings located within 5 miles of major commercial airports may be listed under a separate "Airport Area" heading that follows the city section.

LODGINGS

Travelers have different wants and needs when it comes to accommodations. To help you pinpoint properties that meet your particular needs, Mobil Travel Guide classifies each lodging by type according to the following characteristics.

Mobil Rated Lodgings

○ **Limited-Service Hotel.** A limited-service hotel is traditionally a Mobil One-Star or Mobil Two-Star property. At a Mobil One-Star hotel, guests can expect to find a clean, comfortable property that commonly serves a complimentary continental breakfast. A Mobil Two-Star hotel is also clean and comfortable but has expanded amenities, such as a full-service restaurant, business

center, and fitness center. These services may have limited staffing and/or restricted hours of use.

○ **Full-Service Hotel.** A full-service hotel traditionally enjoys a Mobil Three-Star, Mobil Four-Star, or Mobil Five-Star rating. Guests can expect these hotels to offer at least one full-service restaurant in addition to amenities such as valet parking, luggage assistance, 24-hour room service, concierge service, laundry and/or dry-cleaning services, and turndown service.

○ **Full-Service Resort.** A resort is traditionally a full-service hotel that is geared toward recreation and represents a vacation and holiday destination. A resort's guest rooms are typically furnished to accommodate longer stays. The property may offer a full-service spa, golf, tennis, and fitness facilities or other leisure activities. Resorts are expected to offer a full-service restaurant and expanded amenities, such as luggage assistance, room service, meal plans, concierge service, and turndown service.

○ **Full-Service Inn.** An inn is traditionally a Mobil Three-Star, Mobil Four-Star, or Mobil Five-Star property. Inns are similar to bed-and-breakfasts (see below) but offer a wider range of services, most significantly a full-service restaurant that serves at least breakfast and dinner.

Specialty Lodgings

Mobil Travel Guide recognizes the unique and individualized nature of many different types of lodging establishments, including bed-and-breakfasts, limited-service inns, and guest ranches. For that reason, we have chosen to place our stamp of approval on the properties that fall into these two categories in lieu of applying our traditional Mobil Star ratings.

○ **B&B/Limited-Service Inn.** A bed-and-breakfast (B&B) or limited-service inn is traditionally an owner-occupied home or residence found in a residential area or vacation destination. It may be a structure of historic significance. Rooms are often individually decorated, but telephones, televisions, and private bathrooms may not be available in every room. A B&B typically serves only breakfast to its overnight guests, which is included in the room rate. Cocktails and refreshments may be served in the late afternoon or evening.

✪ **Guest Ranch.** A guest ranch is traditionally a rustic, Western-themed property that specializes in stays of three or more days. Horseback riding is often a feature, with stables and trails found on the property. Facilities can range from clean, comfortable establishments to more luxurious facilities.

Mobil Star Rating Definitions for Lodgings

✪ ★ ★ ★ ★ ★ : A Mobil Five-Star lodging provides consistently superlative service in an exceptionally distinctive luxury environment, with expanded services. Attention to detail is evident throughout the hotel, resort, or inn, from bed linens to staff uniforms.

✪ ★ ★ ★ ★ : A Mobil Four-Star lodging provides a luxury experience with expanded amenities in a distinctive environment. Services may include, but are not limited to, automatic turndown service, 24-hour room service, and valet parking.

✪ ★ ★ ★ : A Mobil Three-Star lodging is well appointed, with a full-service restaurant and expanded amenities, such as a fitness center, golf course, tennis courts, 24-hour room service, and optional turndown service.

✪ ★ ★ : A Mobil Two-Star lodging is considered a clean, comfortable, and reliable establishment that has expanded amenities, such as a full-service restaurant on the premises.

✪ ★ : A Mobil One-Star lodging is a limited-service hotel, motel, or inn that is considered a clean, comfortable, and reliable establishment.

Information Found in the Lodging Listings

Each lodging listing gives the name, address/location (when no street address is available), neighborhood and/or directions from downtown (in major cities), phone number(s), fax number, total number of guest rooms, and seasons open (if not year-round). Also included are details on business, luxury, recreational, and dining facilities at the property or nearby. A key to the symbols at the end of each listing can be found on the page following the "A Word to Our Readers" section.

For every property, we also provide pricing information. Because lodging rates change frequently, we list a pricing category rather than specific prices. The pricing categories break down as follows:

✪ **$** = Up to $150

✪ **$$** = $151-$250

✪ **$$$** = $251-$350

✪ **$$$$** = $351 and up

All prices quoted are in effect at the time of publication; however, prices cannot be guaranteed. In some locations, short-term price variations may exist because of special events, holidays, or seasonality. Certain resorts have complicated rate structures that vary with the time of year; always confirm rates when making your plans.

Because most lodgings offer the following features and services, information about them does not appear in the listings:

✪ Year-round operation

✪ Bathroom with tub and/or shower in each room

✪ Cable television in each room

✪ In-room telephones

✪ Cots and cribs available

✪ Daily maid service

✪ Elevators

✪ Major credit cards accepted

Although we recommend every lodging we list in this book, a few stand out—they offer noteworthy amenities or stand above the others in their category in terms of quality, value, or historical significance. To draw your attention to these special spots, we've included the magnifying glass icon to the left of the listing, as you see here.

SPAS

Mobil Travel Guide is pleased to announce its newest category: hotel and resort spas. Until now, hotel and resort spas have not been formally rated or inspected by any organization. Every spa selected for inclusion in this book underwent a rigorous inspection process similar to the one Mobil Travel Guide has been applying to lodgings and restaurants for more than four decades. After spending a year and a half researching more than 300 spas and performing exhaustive incognito inspections of more than 200 properties, we narrowed our list to the 48 best spas in the United States and Canada.

Mobil Travel Guide's spa ratings are based on objective evaluations of more than 450 attributes. Approximately half of these criteria assess basic expectations, such as staff courtesy, the technical proficiency and skill of the employees, and whether the facility is maintained properly and hygienically. Several standards address issues that impact a guest's physical comfort and convenience, as well as the staff's ability to impart a sense of personalized service and anticipate clients' needs. Additional criteria measure the spa's ability to create a completely calming ambience.

The Mobil Star ratings focus on much more than the facilities available at a spa and the treatments it offers. Each Mobil Star rating is a cumulative score achieved from multiple inspections that reflects the spa management's attention to detail and commitment to consumers' needs.

Mobil Star Rating Definitions for Spas

✪ ★ ★ ★ ★ ★ : A Mobil Five-Star spa provides consistently superlative service in an exceptionally distinctive luxury environment with extensive amenities. The staff at a Mobil Five-Star spa provides extraordinary service above and beyond the traditional spa experience, allowing guests to achieve the highest level of relaxation and pampering. A Mobil Five-Star spa offers an extensive array of treatments, often incorporating international themes and products. Attention to detail is evident throughout the spa, from arrival to departure.

✪ ★ ★ ★ ★ : A Mobil Four-Star spa provides a luxurious experience with expanded amenities in an elegant and serene environment. Throughout the spa facility, guests experience personalized service. Amenities might include, but are not limited to, single-sex relaxation rooms where guests wait for their treatments, plunge pools and whirlpools in both men's and women's locker rooms, and an array of treatments, including at a minimum a selection of massages, body therapies, facials, and a variety of salon services.

✪ ★ ★ ★ : A Mobil Three-Star spa is physically well appointed and has a full complement of staff to ensure that guests' needs are met. It has some expanded amenities, such as, but not limited to, a well-equipped fitness center, separate men's and women's locker rooms, a sauna or steam room, and a designated relaxation area. It also offers a menu of services that at a minimum includes massages, facial treatments, and at least one other type of body treatment, such as scrubs or wraps.

RESTAURANTS
All Mobil Star rated dining establishments listed in this book have a full kitchen and offer seating at tables; most offer table service.

Mobil Star Rating Definitions for Restaurants

✪ ★ ★ ★ ★ ★ : A Mobil Five-Star restaurant offers one of few flawless dining experiences in the country. These establishments consistently provide their guests with exceptional food, superlative service, elegant décor, and exquisite presentations of each detail surrounding a meal.

✪ ★ ★ ★ ★ : A Mobil Four-Star restaurant provides professional service, distinctive presentations, and wonderful food.

✪ ★ ★ ★ : A Mobil Three-Star restaurant has good food, warm and skillful service, and enjoyable décor.

✪ ★ ★ : A Mobil Two-Star restaurant serves fresh food in a clean setting with efficient service. Value is considered in this category, as is family friendliness.

✪ ★ : A Mobil One-Star restaurant provides a distinctive experience through culinary specialty, local flair, or individual atmosphere.

Information Found in the Restaurant Listings
Each restaurant listing gives the cuisine type, street address (or directions if no address is available), phone and fax numbers, Web site (if available), meals served, days of operation (if not open daily year-round), and pricing category. Information about appropriate attire is provided, although it's always a good idea to call ahead and ask if you're unsure; the meaning of "casual" or "business casual" varies widely in different parts of the country. We also indicate whether the restaurant has a bar, whether a children's menu is offered, and whether outdoor seating is available. If reservations are recommended, we note that fact in the listing. When valet parking is available, it is noted in the description. In many cases, self-parking is available at the restaurant or nearby.

Because menu prices can fluctuate, we list a pricing category rather than specific prices. The pricing categories are defined as follows, per diner, and assume that you order an appetizer or dessert, an entrée, and one drink:

- ✪ **$** = $15 and under
- ✪ **$$** = $16-$35
- ✪ **$$$** = $36-$85
- ✪ **$$$$** = $86 and up

Again, all prices quoted are in effect at the time of publication, but prices cannot be guaranteed.

Although we recommend every restaurant we list in this book, a few stand out—they offer noteworthy local specialties or stand above the others in their category in terms of quality, value, or experience. To draw your attention to these special spots, we've included the magnifying glass icon to the left of the listing, as you see here.

SPECIAL INFORMATION FOR TRAVELERS WITH DISABILITIES

The Mobil Travel Guide 🅳 symbol indicates that an establishment is not at least partially accessible to people with mobility problems. When the 🅳 symbol follows a listing, the establishment is not equipped with facilities to accommodate people using wheelchairs or crutches or otherwise needing easy access to doorways and rest rooms. Travelers with severe mobility problems or with hearing or visual impairments may or may not find the facilities they need. Always phone ahead to make sure that an establishment can meet your needs.

AMERICA'S BYWAYS™

Mobil Travel Guide is pleased to announce a new partnership with the National Scenic Byways Program. Under this program, the US Secretary of Transportation recognizes certain roads as National Scenic Byways or All-American Roads based on their archaeological, cultural, historic, natural, recreational, and scenic qualities. To be designated a National Scenic Byway, a road must possess at least one of these six intrinsic qualities. To receive an All-American Road designation, a road must possess multiple intrinsic qualities that are nationally significant and contain one-of-a-kind features that do not exist elsewhere. The road or highway also must be considered a destination unto itself.

America's Byways are a great way to explore the country. From the mighty Mississippi to the towering Rockies to the Historic National Road, these routes take you past America's most treasured scenery and enable you to get in touch with America's past, present, and future. Bringing together all the nationally designated Byways in the South, this bonus section of the book is a handy reference whether you're planning to hop in the car tomorrow or you're simply looking for inspiration for future trips. Look for it at the end of the front section, before page 1.

Understanding the Symbols

What to See and Do

★	=	One of the top attractions in the area
$	=	Up to $5
$$	=	$5.01 to $10
$$$	=	$10.01 to $15
$$$$	=	Over $15

Lodgings

$	=	Up to $150
$$	=	$151 to $250
$$$	=	$251 to $350
$$$$	=	Over $350

Restaurants

$	=	Up to $15
$$	=	$16 to $35
$$$	=	$36 to $85
$$$$	=	Over $85

Lodging Star Definitions

★★★★★   A Mobil Five-Star lodging establishment provides consistently superlative service in an exceptionally distinctive luxury environment with expanded services. Attention to detail is evident throughout the hotel/resort/inn from the bed linens to the staff uniforms.

★★★★   A Mobil Four-Star lodging establishment is a hotel/resort/inn that provides a luxury experience with expanded amenities in a distinctive environment. Services may include, but are not limited to, automatic turndown service, 24-hour room service, and valet parking.

★★★   A Mobil Three-Star lodging establishment is a hotel/resort/inn that is well appointed, with a full-service restaurant and expanded amenities, such as, but not limited to, a fitness center, golf course, tennis courts, 24-hour room service, and optional turndown service.

★★   A Mobil Two-Star lodging establishment is a hotel/resort/inn that is considered a clean, comfortable, and reliable establishment, but also has expanded amenities, such as a full-service restaurant on the premises.

★   A Mobil One-Star lodging establishment is a limited-service hotel or inn that is considered a clean, comfortable, and reliable establishment.

Restaurant Star Definitions

★★★★★   A Mobil Five-Star restaurant is one of few flawless dining experiences in the country. These restaurants consistently provide their guests with exceptional food, superlative service, elegant décor, and exquisite presentations of each detail surrounding the meal.

★★★★   A Mobil Four-Star restaurant provides professional service, distinctive presentations, and wonderful food.

★★★   A Mobil Three-Star restaurant has good food, warm and skillful service, and enjoyable décor.

★★   A Mobil Two-Star restaurant serves fresh food in a clean setting with efficient service. Value is considered in this category, as is family friendliness.

★   A Mobil One-Star restaurant provides a distinctive experience through culinary specialty, local flair, or individual atmosphere.

Symbols at End of Listings

- Facilities for people with disabilities not available
- Pets allowed
- Ski in/ski out access
- Golf on premises
- Tennis court(s) on premises
- Indoor or outdoor pool
- Fitness room
- Major commercial airport within 5 miles
- Business center

Making the Most of Your Trip

few hardy souls might look back with fondness on a trip during which the car broke down, leaving them stranded for three days, or a vacation that cost twice what it was supposed to. For most travelers, though, the best trips are those that are safe, smooth, and within budget. To help you make your trip the best it can be, we've assembled a few tips and resources.

Saving Money

ON LODGING

Many hotels and motels offer discounts—for senior citizens, business travelers, families, you name it. It never hurts to ask—politely, that is. Sometimes, especially in the late afternoon, desk clerks are instructed to fill beds, and you might be offered a lower rate or a nicer room to entice you to stay. Simply ask the reservation agent for the best rate available. Also, make sure to try both the toll-free number and the local number. You may be able to get a lower rate from one than from the other.

Timing your trip right can cut your lodging costs as well. Look for bargains on stays over multiple nights, in the off-season, and on weekdays or weekends, depending on the location. Many hotels in major metropolitan areas, for example, have special weekend packages that offer leisure travelers considerable savings on rooms; they may include breakfast, cocktails, and/or dinner discounts.

Another way to save money is to choose accommodations that give you more than just a standard room. Rooms with kitchen facilities enable you to cook some meals yourself, reducing your restaurant costs. A suite might save money for two couples traveling together. Even hotel luxury levels can provide good value, as many include breakfast or cocktails in the price of a room.

State and city taxes, as well as special room taxes, can increase your room rate by as much as 25 percent per day. We are unable to include information about taxes in our listings, but we strongly urge you to ask about taxes when making reservations so that you understand the total cost of your lodgings before you book them.

Watch out for telephone-usage charges that hotels frequently impose on long-distance, credit-card, and other calls. Before phoning from your room, read the information given to you at check-in, and then be sure to review your bill carefully when checking out. You won't be expected to pay for charges that the hotel didn't spell out. Consider using your cell phone if you have one; or, if public telephones are available in the hotel lobby, your cost savings may outweigh the inconvenience of using them.

Here are some additional ways to save on lodgings:

- Stay in B&B accommodations. They're generally less expensive than standard hotel rooms, and the complimentary breakfast cuts down on food costs.

- If you're traveling with children, find lodgings at which kids stay free.

- When visiting a major city, stay just outside the city limits; these rooms are usually less expensive than those in downtown locations.

- Consider visiting national parks during the low season, when prices of lodgings near the parks drop by 25 percent or more.

- When calling a hotel, ask whether it is running any special promotions or if any discounts are available; many times reservationists are told not to volunteer these deals unless they're specifically asked about them.

- Check for hotel packages; some offer nightly rates that include a rental car or discounts on major attractions.

- Search the Internet for travel bargains. Web sites that allow for online booking of hotel rooms and travel planning, such as *www.mobiltravelguide.com*, often deliver lower rates than are available through telephone reservations.

ON DINING

There are several ways to get a less expensive meal at an expensive restaurant. Early-bird dinners are popular in many parts of the country and offer considerable savings. If you're interested in visiting a Mobil Four- or Five-Star establishment, consider going at lunchtime. Although the prices are probably still relatively high at midday, they may be half of those at dinner, and you'll experience the same ambience, service, and cuisine.

ON ENTERTAINMENT

Although many national parks, monuments, seashores, historic sites, and recreation areas may be visited free of charge, others charge an entrance fee and/or a usage fee for special services and facilities. If you plan to make several visits to national recreation areas, consider one of the following money-saving programs offered by the National Park Service:

- **National Parks Pass.** This annual pass is good for entrance to any national park that charges an entrance fee. If the park charges a per-vehicle fee, the pass holder and any accompanying passengers in a private noncommercial vehicle may enter. If the park charges a per-person fee, the pass applies to the holder's spouse, children, and parents as well as the holder. It is valid for entrance fees only; it does not cover parking, camping, or other fees. You can purchase a National Parks Pass in person at any national park where an entrance fee is charged; by mail from the National Park Foundation, PO Box 34108, Washington, DC 20043-4108; by calling toll-free 888/467-2757; or at www.nationalparks.org. The cost is $50.

- **Golden Eagle Sticker.** When affixed to a National Parks Pass, this hologram sticker, available to people who are between 17 and 61 years of age, extends coverage to sites managed by the US Fish and Wildlife Service, the US Forest Service, and the Bureau of Land Management. It is good until the National Parks Pass to which it is affixed expires and does not cover usage fees. You can purchase one at the National Park Service, the Fish and Wildlife Service, or the Bureau of Land Management fee stations. The cost is $15.

- **Golden Age Passport.** Available to citizens and permanent US residents 62 and older, this passport is a lifetime entrance permit to fee-charging national recreation areas. The fee exemption extends to those accompanying the permit holder in a private noncommercial vehicle or, in the case of walk-in facilities, to the holder's spouse and children. The passport also entitles the holder to a 50 percent discount on federal usage fees charged in park areas, but not on concessions. Golden Age Passports must be obtained in person and are available at most National Park Service units that charge an entrance fee. The applicant must show proof of age, such as a driver's license or birth certificate (Medicare cards are not acceptable proof). The cost is $10.

- **Golden Access Passport.** Issued to citizens and permanent US residents who are physically disabled or visually impaired, this passport is a free lifetime entrance permit to fee-charging national recreation areas. The fee exemption extends to those accompanying the permit holder in a private noncommercial vehicle or, in the case of walk-in facilities, to the holder's spouse and children. The passport also entitles the holder to a 50 percent discount on usage fees charged in park areas, but not on concessions. Golden Access Passports must be obtained in person and are available at most National Park Service units that charge an entrance fee. Proof of eligibility to receive federal benefits (under programs such as Disability Retirement, Compensation for Military Service-Connected Disability, and the Coal Mine Safety and Health Act) is required, or an affidavit must be signed attesting to eligibility.

A money-saving move in several large cities is to purchase a **CityPass.** If you plan to visit several museums and other major attractions, CityPass is a terrific option because it gets you into several sites for one substantially reduced price. Currently, CityPass is available in Boston, Chicago, Hollywood, New York, Philadelphia, San Francisco, Seattle, southern California (which includes Disneyland, SeaWorld, and the San Diego Zoo), and Toronto. For more information or to buy one, call toll-free 888/330-5008 or visit www.citypass.net. You can also buy a CityPass from any participating CityPass attraction.

Here are some additional ways to save on entertainment and shopping:

- Check with your hotel's concierge for various coupons and special offers; they often have two-for-one tickets for area attractions and coupons for discounts at area stores and restaurants.

- Purchase same-day concert or theater tickets for half-price through the local cheap-tickets outlet, such as TKTS in New York or Hot Tix in Chicago.

- Visit museums on their free or "by donation" days, when you can pay what you wish rather than a specific admission fee.

ON TRANSPORTATION

Transportation is a big part of any vacation budget. Here are some ways to reduce your costs:

- If you're renting a car, shop early over the Internet; you can book a car during the low season for less, even if you'll be using it in the high season.

- Rental car discounts are often available if you rent for one week or longer and reserve in advance.

- Get the best gas mileage out of your vehicle by making sure that it's properly tuned up and keeping your tires properly inflated.

- Travel at moderate speeds on the open road; higher speeds require more gasoline.

- Fill the tank before you return your rental car; rental companies charge to refill the tank and do so at prices of up to 50 percent more than at local gas stations.

- Make a checklist of travel essentials and purchase them before you leave; don't get stuck buying expensive sunscreen at your hotel or overpriced film at the airport.

FOR SENIOR CITIZENS

Always call ahead to ask if a discount is being offered, and be sure to carry proof of age. Additional information for mature travelers is available from the American Association of Retired Persons (AARP), 601 E St NW, Washington, DC 20049; phone 202/434-2277; www.aarp.org.

Tipping

Tips are expressions of appreciation for good service. However, you are never obligated to tip if you receive poor service.

IN HOTELS

- Door attendants usually get $1 for hailing a cab.

- Bell staff expect $2 per bag.

- Concierges are tipped according to the service they perform. Tipping is not mandatory when you've asked for suggestions on sightseeing or restaurants or for help in making dining reservations. However, a tip of $5 is appropriate when a concierge books you a table at a restaurant known to be difficult to get into. For obtaining theater or sporting event tickets, $5 to $10 is expected.

- Maids should be tipped $1 to $2 per day. Hand your tip directly to the maid, or leave it with a note saying that the money has been left expressly for the maid.

IN RESTAURANTS

Before tipping, carefully review your check for any gratuity or service charge that is already included in your bill. If you're in doubt, ask your server.

- Coffee shop and counter service waitstaff usually receive 15 percent of the bill, before sales tax.

- In full-service restaurants, tip 18 percent of the bill, before sales tax.

- In fine restaurants, where gratuities are shared among a larger staff, 18 to 20 percent is appropriate.

- In most cases, the maitre d' is tipped only if the service has been extraordinary, and only on the way out. At upscale properties in major metropolitan areas, $20 is the minimum.

- If there is a wine steward, tip $20 for exemplary service and beyond, or more if the wine was decanted or the bottle was very expensive.

- Tip $1 to $2 per coat at the coat check.

AT AIRPORTS

Curbside luggage handlers expect $1 per bag. Car-rental shuttle drivers who help with your luggage appreciate a $1 or $2 tip.

Staying Safe

The best way to deal with emergencies is to avoid them in the first place. However, unforeseen situations do happen, so you should be prepared for them.

IN YOUR CAR

Before you head out on a road trip, make sure that your car has been serviced and is in good working order. Change the oil, check the battery and belts, make sure that your windshield washer fluid is full and your tires are properly inflated (which can also improve your gas mileage). Other inspections recommended by the vehicle's manufacturer should also be made.

Next, be sure you have the tools and equipment needed to deal with a routine breakdown:

- Jack
- Spare tire
- Lug wrench
- Repair kit
- Emergency tools
- Jumper cables
- Spare fan belt
- Fuses
- Flares and/or reflectors
- Flashlight
- First-aid kit
- In winter, a windshield scraper and snow shovel

Many emergency supplies are sold in special packages that include the essentials you need to stay safe in the event of a breakdown.

Also bring all appropriate and up-to-date documentation—licenses, registration, and insurance cards—and know what your insurance covers. Bring an extra set of keys, too, just in case.

En route, always buckle up! In most states, wearing a seatbelt is required by law.

If your car does break down, do the following:

- Get out of traffic as soon as possible—pull well off the road.
- Raise the hood and turn on your emergency flashers or tie a white cloth to the roadside door handle or antenna.
- Stay in your car.
- Use flares or reflectors to keep your vehicle from being hit.

IN YOUR HOTEL

Chances are slim that you will encounter a hotel or motel fire, but you can protect yourself by doing the following:

- Once you've checked in, make sure that the smoke detector in your room is working properly.
- Find the property's fire safety instructions, usually posted on the inside of the room door.
- Locate the fire extinguishers and at least two fire exits.
- Never use an elevator in a fire.

For personal security, use the peephole in your room door and make sure that anyone claiming to be a hotel employee can show proper identification. Call the front desk if you feel threatened at any time.

PROTECTING AGAINST THEFT

To guard against theft wherever you go:

- Don't bring anything of more value than you need.
- If you do bring valuables, leave them at your hotel rather than in your car.
- If you bring something very expensive, lock it in a safe. Many hotels put one in each room; others will store your valuables in the hotel's safe.
- Don't carry more money than you need. Use traveler's checks and credit cards or visit cash machines to withdraw more cash when you run out.

For Travelers with Disabilities

To get the kind of service you need and have a right to expect, don't hesitate when making a reservation to question the management about the availability of accessible rooms, parking, entrances, restaurants, lounges, or any other facilities that are important to you, and confirm what is meant by "accessible."

The Mobil Travel Guide 🅓 symbol indicates establishments that are not at least partially accessible to people with special mobility needs (people using wheelchairs or crutches or otherwise needing easy access to buildings and rooms). Further information about these criteria can be found in the earlier section "How to Use This Book."

A thorough listing of published material for travelers with disabilities is available from the Disability Bookshop, Twin Peaks Press, Box 129, Vancouver, WA 98666; phone 360/694-2462; disabilitybookshop.virtualave.net. Another reliable organization is the Society for Accessible Travel & Hospitality (SATH), 347 Fifth Ave, Suite 610, New York, NY 10016; phone 212/447-7284; www.sath.org.

Important Toll-Free Numbers and Online Information

Hotels

Adams Mark 800/444-2326
www.adamsmark.com

AmericInn 800/634-3444
www.americinn.com

AmeriHost Inn 800/434-5800
www.amerihostinn.com

Amerisuites 800/833-1516
www.amerisuites.com

Baymont Inns 877/BAYMONT
www.baymontinns.com

Best Inns & Suites 800/237-8466
www.bestinn.com

Best Value Inn 888/315-BEST
www.bestvalueinn.com

Best Western 800/780-7234
www.bestwestern.com

Budget Host Inn 800/BUDHOST
www.budgethost.com

Candlewood Suites 888/CANDLEWOOD
www.candlewoodsuites.com

Clarion Hotels 800/252-7466
www.choicehotels.com

Comfort Inns and Suites 800/252-7466
www.choicehotels.com

Country Hearth Inns 800/848-5767
www.countryhearth.com

Country Inns & Suites 800/456-4000
www.countryinns.com

Courtyard by Marriott 800/321-2211
www.courtyard.com

Cross Country Inns (KY and OH) 800/621-1429
www.crosscountryinns.com

Crowne Plaza Hotels and Resorts 800/227-6963
www.crowneplaza.com

Days Inn 800/544-8313
www.daysinn.com

Delta Hotels 800/268-1133
www.deltahotels.com

Destination Hotels & Resorts 800/434-7347
www.destinationhotels.com

Doubletree Hotels 800/222-8733
www.doubletree.com

Drury Inn 800/378-7946
www.druryinn.com

Econolodge 800/553-2666
www.econolodge.com

Embassy Suites 800/362-2779
www.embassysuites.com

ExelInns of America 800/FOREXEL
www.exelinns.com

Extended StayAmerica 800/EXTSTAY
www.extstay.com

Fairfield Inn by Marriott 800/228-2800
www.fairfieldinn.com

Fairmont Hotels 800/441-1414
www.fairmont.com

Four Points by Sheraton 888/625-5144
www.starwood.com/fourpoints

Four Seasons 800/545-4000
www.fourseasons.com

Hampton Inn 800/426-7866
www.hamptoninn.com

Hard Rock Hotels, Resorts, and Casinos . . 800/HRDROCK
www.hardrock.com

Harrah's Entertainment 800/HARRAHS
www.harrahs.com

Hawthorn Suites 800/527-1133
www.hawthorn.com

Hilton Hotels and Resorts (US) 800/774-1500
www.hilton.com

Holiday Inn Express 800/465-4329
www.hiexpress.com

Holiday Inn Hotels and Resorts 800/465-4329
www.holiday-inn.com

Homestead Studio Suites 888/782-9473
www.homesteadhotels.com

Homewood Suites 800/225-5466
www.homewoodsuites.com

Howard Johnson 800/406-1411
www.hojo.com

Hyatt 800/633-7313
www.hyatt.com

Ian Schrager . . . . Contact individual hotel
www.ianschragerhotels.com

Inns of America 800/826-0778
www.innsofamerica.com

InterContinental 888/567-8725
www.intercontinental.com

Joie de Vivre 800/738-7477
www.jdvhospitality.com

Kimpton Hotels 888/546-7866
www.kimptongroup.com

Knights Inn 800/843-5644
www.knightsinn.com

La Quinta 800/531-5900
www.laquinta.com

Le Meridien 800/543-4300
www.lemeridien.com

Leading Hotels of the World 800/223-6800
www.lhw.com

Loews Hotels 800/235-6397
www.loewshotels.com

MainStay Suites 800/660-6246
www.choicehotels.com

Mandarin Oriental 800/526-6566
www.mandarin-oriental.com

Marriott Hotels, Resorts, and Suites 800/228-9290
www.marriott.com

Microtel Inns & Suites 800/771-7171
www.microtelinn.com

Millennium & Copthorne Hotels 866/866-8086
www.mill-cop.com

Motel 6 . . . . 800/4MOTEL6
www.motel6.com

Omni Hotels 800/843-6664
www.omnihotels.com

Pan Pacific Hotels and Resorts 800/327-8585
www.panpac.com

Park Inn & Park Plaza 888/201-1801
www.parkhtls.com

The Peninsula Group . . . . Contact individual hotel
www.peninsula.com

Preferred Hotels & Resorts Worldwide 800/323-7500
www.preferredhotels.com

Quality Inn 800/228-5151
www.qualityinn.com

Radisson Hotels 800/333-3333
www.radisson.com

Raffles International Hotels and Resorts . . . 800/637-9477
www.raffles.com

Ramada Plazas, Limiteds, and Inns 800/2RAMADA
www.ramada.com

Red Lion Inns 800/733-5466
www.redlion.com

Red Roof Inns 800/733-7663
www.redroof.com

Regal Hotels 800/222-8888
www.regal-hotels.com

Regent International 800/545-4000
www.regenthotels.com

Relais & Chateaux 800/735-2478
www.relaischateaux.com

Renaissance Hotels 888/236-2427
www.renaissancehotels.com

Residence Inn 800/331-3131
www.residenceinn.com

Ritz-Carlton 800/241-3333
www.ritzcarlton.com

Rockresorts 888/FORROCKS
www.rockresorts.com

Rodeway Inn 800/228-2000
www.rodeway.com

Rosewood Hotels & Resorts 888/767-3966
www.rosewood-hotels.com

Select Inn 800/641-1000
www.selectinn.com

Sheraton 888/625-5144
www.sheraton.com

Shilo Inns 800/222-2244
www.shiloinns.com

Shoney's Inn 800/552-4667
www.shoneysinn.com

Signature/Jameson Inns 800/822-5252
www.jamesoninns.com

Sleep Inn 800/453-3746
www.sleepinn.com

Small Luxury Hotels of the World 800/525-4800
www.slh.com

Sofitel 800/763-4835
www.sofitel.com

SpringHill Suites 888/236-2427
www.springhillsuites.com

SRS Worldhotels 800/223-5652
www.srs-worldhotels.com

St. Regis Luxury Collection 888/625-5144
www.stregis.com

Staybridge Suites 800/238-8000
www.staybridge.com

Summerfield Suites by Wyndham 800/833-4353
www.summerfieldsuites.com

Summit International 800/457-4000
www.summithotels.com

Super 8 Motels 800/800-8000
www.super8.com

The Sutton Place Hotels 866/378-8866
www.suttonplace.com

Swissôtel 800/637-9477
www.swissotel.com

TownePlace Suites 888/236-2427
www.towneplace.com

Travelodge 800/578-7878
www.travelodge.com

Vagabond Inns 800/522-1555
www.vagabondinns.com

W Hotels 888/625-5144
www.whotels.com

Wellesley Inn and Suites 800/444-8888
www.wellesleyinnandsuites.com

WestCoast Hotels 800/325-4000
www.westcoasthotels.com

Westin Hotels & Resorts 800/937-8461
www.westin.com

Wingate Inns 800/228-1000
www.wingateinns.com
Woodfin Suite Hotels 800/966-3346
www.woodfinsuitehotels.com
Wyndham Hotels & Resorts 800/996-3426
www.wyndham.com

Airlines

Air Canada 888/247-2262
www.aircanada.ca
AirTran 800/247-8726
www.airtran.com
Alaska Airlines 800/252-7522
www.alaskaair.com
American Airlines 800/433-7300
www.aa.com
America West 800/235-9292
www.americawest.com
ATA 800/435-9282
www.ata.com
Continental Airlines 800/523-3273
www.flycontinental.com
Delta Air Lines 800/221-1212
www.delta.com
Frontier Airlines 800/432-1FLY
www.frontierairlines.com
Jet Blue Airways 800/JET-BLUE
www.jetblue.com
Midwest Express 800/452-2022
www.midwestexpress.com
Northwest Airlines 800/225-2525
www.nwa.com
Southwest Airlines 800/435-9792
www.iflyswa.com

Spirit Airlines 800/772-7117
www.spiritair.com
United Airlines 800/241-6522
www.ual.com
US Airways 800/428-4322
www.usairways.com
Vanguard Airlines 800/VANGUARD
www.flyvanguard.com

Car Rentals

Advantage 800/777-5500
www.arac.com
Alamo 800/327-9633
www.goalamo.com
Avis 800/831-2847
www.avis.com
Budget 800/527-0700
www.budgetrentacar.com
Dollar 800/800-4000
www.dollarcar.com
Enterprise 800/325-8007
www.pickenterprise.com
Hertz 800/654-3131
www.hertz.com
National 800/227-7368
www.nationalcar.com
Payless 800/729-5377
www.800-payless.com
Rent-A-Wreck.com 800/535-1391
www.rent-a-wreck.com
Thrifty 800/847-4389
www.thrifty.com

Meet the Stars

Mobil Travel Guide 2005 *Five-Star* Award Winners

CALIFORNIA
Lodgings
The Beverly Hills Hotel, *Beverly Hills*
Chateau du Sureau, *Oakhurst*
Four Seasons Hotel San Francisco,
    San Francisco
Hotel Bel-Air, *Los Angeles*
The Peninsula Beverly Hills, *Beverly Hills*
Raffles L'Ermitage Beverly Hills, *Beverly Hills*
The Ritz-Carlton, San Francisco, *San Francisco*

Restaurants
The Dining Room, *San Francisco*
The French Laundry, *Yountville*
Gary Danko, *San Francisco*

COLORADO
Lodgings
The Broadmoor, *Colorado Springs*
The Little Nell, *Aspen*

CONNECTICUT
Lodging
The Mayflower Inn, *Washington*

FLORIDA
Lodgings
Four Seasons Resort Palm Beach, *Palm Beach*
The Ritz-Carlton, Naples, *Naples*
The Ritz-Carlton, Palm Beach, *Manalapan*

GEORGIA
Lodgings
Four Seasons Hotel Atlanta, *Atlanta*
The Lodge at Sea Island Golf Club,
    St. Simons Island

Restaurants
The Dining Room, *Atlanta*
Seeger's, *Atlanta*

HAWAII
Lodging
Four Seasons Resort Maui at Wailea, *Wailea,
    Maui*

ILLINOIS
Lodgings
Four Seasons Hotel Chicago, *Chicago*
The Peninsula Chicago, *Chicago*
The Ritz-Carlton, A Four Seasons Hotel, *Chicago*

Restaurants
Charlie Trotter's, *Chicago*
Trio, *Evanston*

MASSACHUSETTS
Lodgings
Blantyre, *Lenox*
Four Seasons Hotel Boston, *Boston*

NEW YORK
Lodgings
Four Seasons Hotel New York, *New York*
The Point, *Saranac Lake*
The Ritz-Carlton, New York, Central Park,
    New York
The St. Regis, *New York*

Restaurants
Alain Ducasse, *New York*
Jean Georges, *New York*
Masa, *New York*

NORTH CAROLINA
Lodging
The Fearrington House Country Inn, *Pittsboro*

OHIO
Restaurant
Maisonette, *Cincinnati*

PENNSYLVANIA
Restaurant
Le Bec-Fin, *Philadelphia*

SOUTH CAROLINA
Lodging
Woodlands Resort & Inn, *Summerville*

Restaurant
Dining Room at the Woodlands, *Summerville*

TEXAS
Lodging
The Mansion on Turtle Creek, *Dallas*

VERMONT
Lodging
Twin Farms, *Barnard*

VIRGINIA
Lodgings
The Inn at Little Washington, *Washington*
The Jefferson Hotel, *Richmond*

Restaurant
The Inn at Little Washington, *Washington*

Mobil Travel Guide has been rating establishments with its Mobil One- to Five-Star system since 1958. Each establishment awarded the Mobil Five-Star rating is one of the best in the country. Detailed information on each award winner can be found in the corresponding regional edition listed on the back cover of this book.

Four- and Five-Star Establishments in the Southern Great Lakes

Illinois

★ ★ ★ ★ ★ Lodgings

Four Seasons Hotel Chicago, *Chicago*
The Peninsula Chicago, *Chicago*
The Ritz-Carlton, A Four Seasons Hotel, *Chicago*

★ ★ ★ ★ Lodging

Park Hyatt Chicago, *Chicago*

★ ★ ★ ★ ★ Restaurants

Charlie Trotter's, *Chicago*
Trio, *Evanston*

★ ★ ★ ★ Restaurants

Ambria, *Chicago*
Crofton on Wells, *Chicago*
The Dining Room, *Chicago*
Everest, *Chicago*
Les Nomades, *Chicago*
Seasons, *Chicago*
Spring, *Chicago*
Tru, *Chicago*

Ohio

★ ★ ★ ★ Lodgings

The Cincinnatian Hotel, *Cincinnati*
The Ritz-Carlton, Cleveland, *Cleveland*

★ ★ ★ ★ ★ Restaurant

Maisonette, *Cincinnati*

America's Byways™ are a distinctive collection of American roads, their stories, and treasured places. They are roads to the heart and soul of America. In this section, you'll find the nationally designated Byways in Illinois, Indiana, and Ohio.

The Great River Road

ILLINOIS

Experiencing the Mississippi River for the first time is a memory few can forget. The awe that many people feel toward this river may come from the power of a flood or the beauty of a golden sunset that reflects off the still winter waters and turns graceful steel bridges into shimmering lines of color.

Looking out over the river, it is almost impossible to comprehend the complex layers of history that have been acted out along its banks. From the large communities of the Hopewell Indian culture (the most complex society in North America that existed from approximately AD 700 to 1400) and early French colonial settlements and fortifications to the frightened, cautious, and optimistic eyes of slaves seeking freedom on the Underground Railroad, this corridor has played a role in many of this continent's most dramatic hours. Today, 15 percent of the nation's shipping passes through the river's complex system of locks and dams, yet such commercial activity occurs under the spreading wings of the newly thriving American bald eagle.

Length: 557 miles.

Time to Allow: 4 or 5 days.

Best Time to Drive: Fall months are the best due to the beautiful colors of the foliage. High season is late spring to early fall.

Byway Travel Information: Western Illinois Tourism Development Office: phone 309/837-7460, toll-free 877/477-7007.

Special Considerations: Gas, food, and lodging are available at various cities along the Byway.

Restrictions: Generally, the entire route of Illinois' portion of the Great River Road is within the 100-year flood plain. While flooding does not occur regularly, roads are closed and detours are marked when flooded.

Bicycle/Pedestrian Facilities: The Great River Road accommodates bicycle and pedestrian traffic. A 62.5-mile bike path is under construction along the route from Mississippi Palisades State Park in Savanna to Sunset Park in Rock Island, where it meets with the American Discovery Trail crossing. At this time, approximately 42 miles have been built. This portion of the bike path is primarily a two-lane, off-road trail winding through the trees and over specially constructed bridges following the route of the Great River Road in Illinois.

It is from the Great River Road that most visitors and residents understand and define their relationship with the Mississippi. It is from this road that the historic sites and cultural artifacts of the area can be accessed, from Native American mounds to the Mormon (Church of Jesus Christ of Latter-Day Saints) temple. The beautiful Mississippi bluffs tower over the Byway as permanent sentinels for the great river. Whether directly along the banks of the river or winding through the vast flood plain miles from the water, the Great River Road links resources, people, and history.

The Byway Story

The Great River Road tells archaeological, cultural, historical, natural, recreational, and scenic stories that make it a unique and treasured Byway.

ARCHAEOLOGICAL

A little-known treasure trove of archaeological sites, the Illinois Great River Road has several places for visitors to discover pieces of the past. Among the archaeological qualities that can be found along this road are burial mounds of native tribes that lived along the river. The mounds, many of which were built more than 2,000 years ago, are representative of Native American religious practices and reverence for their ancestors. Cahokia Mounds near East St. Louis and Collinsville has been designated as a United Nations World Heritage Site. Among the most fascinating of the archaeological structures on the Great River Road is Monk's Mound, a 100-foot-tall, four-tiered platform that took 300 years to build.

In addition to Native American sites, many villages on the Byway offer a taste of archaeology in their preservation of the not-so-distant past. Many villages, like Maeystown, Galena, and Nauvoo, are listed on the National Register of Historic Places. These villages often re-create the lifestyles of the first settlers along the Great River Road for visitors who want to know more about the nation's past. With both Native American heritage sites and historic sites of the earliest European settlers, the Great River Road offers opportunities for you to discover America's archaeology all along the way.

CULTURAL

Some of the first people to settle along the banks of the Mississippi River were Native American tribes. These tribes were embedded in a culture that held the utmost respect for nature and the resources of the land. Their inextricable connection to the land can be seen in the burial mounds they left behind, as well as in museums and monuments.

Since the habitation of the first cultures in the area, several other cultures have passed through the Illinois Great River Road area, and some have stayed permanently. During the 1800s, the now-historic communities along the Great River Road were settled for reasons that ranged from gold rushes to religious freedom. The people who live in these communities maintain a distinct place on the Byway, with their styles of architecture and inventiveness. Today, the culture of the Great River Road embodies the relaxed hometown pace. The towns and villages along the Byway offer you a change of scenery and a chance to slow down. These towns are often small and full of rich historical detail that influences cultures even today.

HISTORICAL

As an area that has enraptured American Indians, explorers, and settlers, the Illinois Great River Road holds pieces of the past that are intriguing to today's visitors. Since 1938, the road has been protected and enhanced in order to preserve the scenic and historical qualities found along it. The heritage of the native tribes of the Sauk and Fox Indians remains prevalent in many places along the Byway.

You can find historic architecture in several of the historic towns along the road: Nauvoo, Quincy, Alton, Belleville, and Cairo allow you to experience the Great River Road as the settlers of nearly 200 years ago did. These cities all have their share of historic places and buildings that are full of Civil War tales and pioneer stories. As a passage on the Underground Railroad, the river represents a piece of African-American history as well. The river itself holds a story of steamboats chugging up the river. It represents the ingenuity of inventors and engineers in the earliest days of travel. The river is the lifeblood of the area that has drawn so many people to its shores.

NATURAL

Among the bluffs and rolling hills of the Illinois Great River Road area, you can observe wildlife and nature at its fullest. The lands surrounding the Byway are home to white-tailed deer, wild turkeys, ducks, and geese. Supported by the rich natural resources that abound in the river area, these creatures can be seen throughout the drive. During the fall, the trees along the Byway exhibit a beautiful spectrum of color, providing a fringe of brightness along the river. By the time winter sets in, there is a new visitor to the Great River Road. The American bald eagle arrives in late November, and by late December, hundreds of these magnificent birds are roosting in the rocky walls of the bluffs overlooking the river. Travelers come from miles around to watch them dive and soar in the air above the bluffs.

All along the banks and bluffs of the river, you will enjoy many interesting sights. At one point on the Illinois Great River Road, you will see a formation known as Tower Rock. This formation is an isolated mass of limestone that divides the river in half. In the areas surrounding the river, you'll also find lakes, wetlands, and swamps that provide their own style of natural beauty.

RECREATIONAL

On and around the river, you have places to go and different ways to get there. Hikers and bikers find riverside trails attractive, while other travelers may prefer to enjoy a pleasant afternoon on a riverboat. Ferries, canoes, and even old-fashioned steamboats give you a closer view of the greatest river in the nation. To see more of the communities on the Byway, you may enjoy a trolley tour or a park area, as well as museums and historical buildings. Museums and monuments to the past are sprinkled along the road to give you a sense of what came before on the Great River Road.

Other forms of fun can be found on the Byway as well. More than 75 golf courses help you track your progress along the Byway by greens. Travelers who would like to test their luck can try a riverboat casino. Communities all along the Byway offer numerous stops for antique shoppers who are looking for a piece of Illinois' past to take home with them, and if antiques aren't enough, plenty of novelty shops and gift shops abound. For the hungry traveler, many restaurants along the Byway are sure to suit your fancy. Entertainment is an element of the Byway's recreational offerings, too. Many towns host musicals, dinner shows, and old-fashioned theater experiences.

Chances to enjoy the outdoors along the Great River Road come often. In addition to the Shawnee National Forest, 29 state recreation and/or conservation areas are available along the route of the Great River Road. The Mississippi Palisades State Park and National Landmark offers phenomenal views to and from the bluffs (palisades) along the Mississippi River. The facilities for tent and trailer camping, fishing, cross-country skiing, and ice fishing are top notch.

The Big River State Forest is a 2,900-acre facility dedicated to demonstrating sound forestry practices. Fire breaks and a fire tower afford breathtaking views and hikes. Nearby, camping, hiking, and river and lake fishing are available at Delabar State Park. In the south, Horseshoe Lake Conservation Area is one of the loveliest places to hike, camp, hunt, and boat. Horseshoe Lake is a quiet, shallow lake lined with cypress and tupelo gum and wild lotus. You can find places for bird-watching and exploring wetlands, and canoeing along the river is a widely recognized source of recreation all along the Byway.

SCENIC

The Mississippi River itself is a natural phenomenon that few visitors will forget. This body of moving water presents a picture of the forces of nature at work with their surroundings. Perhaps one of the prettiest sights you will see along the Byway is the great waters of the Mississippi River flanked by the glacier-carved bluffs at the river's edge. Along the Byway, observe scenic vistas and bluffs that overlook the river: erosion from glacial movement has left unique formations of rock in the riverside

topography. Feast your eyes on the rich architecture that has been a part of this area's history. From grand courthouses to historic bridges, sights all along the Byway complement the natural beauty of the Great River Road. In the summer, the fields along the Byway are adorned with wildflowers. During the fall, several communities host festivals celebrating the season, and the drive along the Byway becomes even more scenic with every leaf that dons its fall color. And keep in mind that a sunset on the Mississippi River is a sight not to be missed.

Highlights

When traveling the Moline-to-Nauvoo section of the Illinois Great River Road, consider using the following itinerary.

⊙ Both the past and present of the world-famous John Deere & Company operations are centered in Moline, where you begin your tour. At the **John Deere Commons,** catch historic trolleys to other Deere sites, tour the John Deere Pavilion with interactive displays of historic and modern farm equipment, and visit the John Deere Store. The Deere Administrative Center, Deere corporate headquarters, lies on the outskirts of Moline. This building, designed by Eero Saarinen, and grounds are widely regarded as masterworks of architecture and landscape architecture. The Deere-Wiman House and Butterworth Center are mansions built in the late 1800s by Charles Deere. Guided tours of the homes and gardens are available.

⊙ **Rock Island Arsenal** lies on spectacular Rock Island in the Mississippi River directly in front of the John Deere Commons. Visitors to the island can visit Historic Fort Armstrong (1812), the Rock Island Arsenal Museum (with exhibits of military equipment and small firearms), and other historic structures. The Rock Island Arsenal is the largest weapons manufacturing arsenal in the country. Located next to Lock and Dam 15, the largest roller dam in the world, the US Army Corps of Engineers **Mississippi River Visitor Center** features an observation deck for tow boats and birds. The visitor center includes displays about Upper Mississippi geography, ecology, and the lock-and-dam system. It is also a designated Great River Road interpretive center.

⊙ Two miles south of Rock Island lies the next stop on the tour, **Black Hawk State Historic Site**—a wooded, steeply rolling 208-acre tract. Prehistoric Indians and 19th-century settlers made their homes here, but the area is most closely identified with the Sauk nation and the warrior-leader whose name it bears—Black Hawk. The site, which is also noted for its many natural features, is managed by the Illinois Historic Preservation Agency. The **Hauberg Indian Museum,** located in the lodge constructed by the Civilian Conservation Corps in 1939, interprets the culture of the Sauk and the Mesquackie. Nearly 175 species of birds and 30 species of wildflowers, as well as a prairie restoration, can be observed here. Dickson Pioneer Cemetery is where many early settlers are buried. Picnicking and hiking are also available.

⊙ Following the Byway along the Mississippi River for another 50 miles, you arrive at the 2,900-acre **Big River State Forest.** The forest lies in Henderson County, 6 miles north of Oquawka, where gas and food are available. The area's oldest pine plantation, the **Milroy Plantation,** with towering red, white, and jack pines lies within. The forest is a remnant of a vast prairie woodland border area that once covered much of Illinois. Two endangered plants, penstemon and Patterson's bindweed, are found here. A prominent landmark in the forest is its fire tower, located at the headquarters area and accessible to the public at non-emergency times. Sixty miles of firebreaks interlace Big River State Forest, which are used by hikers, horseback riders, and snowmobilers. Tent, trailer, and equestrian camping sites, boat launch, picnic areas, hunting, stables, and scenic drives are available.

⊙ Located on the Mississippi River about 4.5 miles south of Big River State Forest and 1.5 miles north of Oquawka, the 89-acre **Delabar State Park** offers quality outdoor experiences for anglers, hikers, campers, and picnickers. More than 50 species of birds have been sighted in the park, making it a destination for bird-watching, too. Picnic areas, playground facilities, tent and trailer camping, trailer dumping, hiking trails, river and lake fishing, boat launching, ice fishing, and ice skating are available in the area.

⊙ This tour of a short section of the Byway terminates about 45 miles south of Delbar State Park in **Nauvoo.** The town is located at a picturesque bend in the river at Hancock County. Nauvoo was settled by Joseph Smith and members of the Church of Jesus Christ Latter-Day Saints (LDS) and served as the religious, governmental, and cultural center of the church from 1839 until Joseph Smith's death in 1846. Two visitor centers interpret the remaining town sites. The LDS Visitor Center features costumed hosts, interpretive displays, a sculpture garden, and tours of 25 Nauvoo town sites. The Joseph Smith Visitor Center, run by the Reorganized Church of Jesus Christ of Latter-Day Saints (RLDS), features displays, an informative video, and access to the gravesite and homes of Joseph Smith and family. In late 1999, the LDS church began rebuilding the historic limestone temple destroyed in the late 19th century. Nearby Nauvoo State Park features recreational opportunities. The wine and cheese traditions of the French Icarians, who came to Nauvoo after the LDS church, are still pursued.

The Historic National Road

ILLINOIS   An All-American Road

Part of a multistate Byway; see also IN, OH.

The Historic National Road crosses the state of Illinois from near the Wabash River to the great Mississippi River. The rolling countryside, prairie fields, and small towns along the old trail whisper of an earlier time. Each of the seven counties of the old trail weaves its own story.

The route of the Historic National Road is a road of history. Nineteenth-century river transportation and commerce, along with historic cemeteries, tell of the struggles of the early settlers on the western frontier. County fairs and main-street storefronts speak of small towns where you can still find soda fountains, one-room schools, and old hotels where travelers stopped to rest.

Small and large museums, a National Register Historic District, and National Register Historic Sites are found all along the Byway. Prehistoric Native American life is evident here as well, along with giant earthwork mounds that took 300 years to build. This old trail still beckons as it did more than a century and a half ago, with lakes, streams, wildlife refuges, nature preserves, and trails where white-tailed deer play. The atmosphere of old-fashioned travel is stored in the little shops and towns along the way. The western end of the Byway takes you to Eads Bridge and the gateway to the West.

QUICK FACTS

Length: 165 miles.

Time to Allow: 12 hours.

Best Time to Drive: All seasons have their unique attractions on this Byway. High season is during the fall.

Byway Travel Information: Effingham Convention & Visitors Bureau: phone toll-free 800/772-0750; Collinsville Convention & Visitors Bureau: phone 618/345-4999; Cahokia Mounds State Historic Site: phone 618/346-5160; Byway local Web site: www.nationalroad.org.

Restrictions: Some delays may be experienced during severe weather, and seasonal storms may increase driving times.

Bicycle/Pedestrian Facilities: All counties, except for Madison (which is on the western end of the Byway), rate the route as suitable for bicycles. In Madison County, bicyclists are urged to be cautious; bicycling is not advisable due to high traffic.

The Byway Story

The Historic National Road tells archaeological, historical, natural, recreational, and scenic stories that make it a unique and treasured Byway.

ARCHAEOLOGICAL

The Cahokia Mounds State Historic Site, an archaeological site with worldwide recognition, bisects the Historic National Road. This remarkable World Heritage Archaeological Site consists of the largest mound buildings built by Native Americans on the North American continent. As you pass the site while driving the Byway, you see Monks Mound rising out of the ground on the north side of the Byway, covering 14 acres and rising 100 feet into the air. You may also notice a large circle of wooden posts, known as Woodhenge, next to the road. The visitor center is the pride of the Illinois Historic Preservation Agency and provides more information on the site and the people who created it.

HISTORICAL

In 1806, Congress appropriated funds to construct a National Road that would run westward from Cumberland,

Maryland, to the Mississippi River. It was the first federally funded road system in this great new country. The Illinois section was surveyed in 1828 by Joseph Schriver, and construction was started in 1831 under the supervision of William C. Greenup. The section to Vandalia was completed in 1836. However, the western section was never funded due to high costs and waning interest in road building. With the coming of the Terre Haute-Vandalia-St. Louis Railroad that paralleled the road, the National Road fell into disrepair, only to be resurrected in the early 1920s when it was hard surfaced and designated Highway 40. Today, most of the original alignment of the 1828 surveyed National Road is still in place and is in public hands.

The route passes through many historic towns and villages that were established in the mid-1800s along this great road. On the eastern end of the Byway is Marshall, a town that sports the oldest continuously operating hotel. Also on the eastern end is the village of Greenup, with its unique business section decorated with original overhanging porches. This village was designated as a Historic Business District on the National Register of Historic Places. In the central section is Vandalia, the second capital of Illinois, its original business district intact. The Capitol Building, in which Abraham Lincoln passed his test to practice law, is now a State Historic Site and sits on the Historic National Road.

The Illinois Historic National Road ends at the historic Eads Bridge, just across the river from the Jefferson Memorial Expansion National Park and the St. Louis Arch, the gateway to the West.

NATURAL

The Historic National Road in Illinois is dominated at each end of the Byway by rivers. The Wabash River is on the east end, and the mighty Mississippi River lies on the west end. Rivers and lakes are interspersed throughout the middle area, with flat prairies and hilly landscapes combining to create many natural features along the Byway. Different species of wildlife make their homes all along the route, and fish are plentiful in the many lakes and rivers.

The topography along the Byway was created by glaciers that advanced and retreated over the land during the Pleistocene Period, leaving behind moraines and glacial deposits that created regions of undulating landscape in some areas and flat prairies in other

areas. The landscape of the Byway is defined by three major areas: the Embarras River Basin on the east side, the Wabash River Basin in the central area, and the Sinkhole Plain on the west side (which is contained in the Mississippi River Basin).

The Mississippi River is the third-largest river in the world, and as a result of its size, this river has played an important part in the lives of those who have called this area home. From flooding to fertile land, the river has shaped the lives of Native Americans, pioneers, settlers, and current residents of the many cities that dot the banks of the river. The river, through irrigation, has been the lifeblood of farmers, and also has been a recreational destination for many. In addition, over 400 species of wildlife—including ancient lineages of fish—live on and near the Mississippi River. In fact, 40 percent of North America's duck, goose, swan, and wading bird populations use the Mississippi as a migration corridor.

RECREATIONAL

The Historic National Road in Illinois offers many recreational opportunities. You can bike or hike on the various trails that are accessible from the Byway. Numerous state parks allow you to enjoy the natural characteristics of the Byway; many of the towns have city parks and recreational facilities. From camping to bird-watching, there is something for everyone along this Byway.

At Lincoln Trail Lake State Park, you can travel in the route Abraham Lincoln took from Kentucky to Illinois. This park is on part of that route, and today, it is a place where you can enjoy hiking, fishing, boating, or camping. Summer is not the only time to enjoy this area, however; wintertime sports include ice fishing, ice skating (when the lake allows it), and cross-country skiing.

Many lakes, rivers, and streams provide recreational opportunities. Carlyle Lake is a 26,000-acre multi-purpose lake known for its great fishing and water-fowl hunting. You can catch bass, bluegill, crappie, catfish, walleye, and sauger fish. At Eldon Hazlet State Park, controlled pheasant hunting is available, and bird-watching is also a popular activity at the lakes. Carlyle Lake is well known among sailors, and you can rent a houseboat at the park. Camping and golf courses are available here as well.

Numerous small towns are spread across the Byway, providing a variety of activities. If more adventurous activities are what you are looking for, you can board the *Casino Queen,* a riverboat casino that is docked in East St. Louis. At Collinsville, the Gateway International Raceway hosts motor sports in a state-of-the-art facility.

SCENIC

Diverse and changing, the landscape of the Historic National Road in Illinois offers many scenic views to the Byway traveler. The route is dotted with towns and rural communities, interspersed with rural lands and farms. The large metropolitan area of the western edge of the Byway, in Collinsville and East St. Louis, provides a different kind of scene. From historic buildings and bridges to gently rolling hills, this Byway exemplifies a scenic drive.

The natural layout of the land is one of variation. In the east, the rolling hills and interspersed forests provide a different view than the flat, unbroken views presented on the western edge of the Byway. In between, cultivated fields, distant barns, farmhouses, and grazing livestock all speak of the nature of the land. Small communities were developed around the agriculture of the area, and now these towns beckon visitors with historic buildings and one-of-a-kind features, such as Greenup's historic porches.

Many features of the Byway revolve around transportation because of the importance of the National Road. Bridges, such as the S-bridge, remain to provide visitors a chance to glimpse these engineering feats. Picturesque stone bridges, as well as covered bridges, may be seen on the Byway. In addition, the Eads Bridge stands in East St. Louis on the Mississippi, giving the metropolitan skyline a distinct look.

Highlights

The Illinois National Road Museum Tour takes you through some of the museums located on the National Road in Illinois. The tour begins in Martinsville and goes to Collinsville (east of St. Louis).

- **Lincoln School Museum:** This quality museum is located in Martinsville, about 18 miles west of the Indiana state line. The building itself was built in 1888, and the school is open to groups for an interpretation of early pioneer days.

- **Franciscan Monastery Museum:** Dating to 1858, this historic monastery has a wonderful museum that displays artifacts from early settlers as well as the Franciscan Fathers. Visitors can view pioneer items such as toys and kitchen utensils, and religious items such as Bibles and vestments. There are also antique legal documents on display, such as marriage licenses. The monastery is located about 5 miles east of Effingham.

- **My Garage Corvette Museum:** This museum, located in Effingham, about 30 miles west of Martinsville, is a must for automobile lovers. On display are vintage Corvettes from the 1950s and 1960s—a perfect museum for the National Road.

- **Collinsville Historical Museum:** Located about 90 miles west of Effingham in Collinsville, this museum offers visitors a unique glance into the region's residents all the way back to John Cook, the first settler in 1810. Many interesting artifacts are on display, including a variety of Civil War objects and miners' tools. No museum tour would be complete without a visit to this high-quality museum.

Lincoln Highway

ILLINOIS

The innovative development of the Lincoln Highway was the prototype of roadways as we know them today. This historic Byway follows the original alignment of the Lincoln Highway, the first paved transcontinental highway in the United States and the forerunner of the modern interstate transportation system as it was origi-nally conceived in 1913.

The 179-mile route crosses the width of northern Illinois, starting in Lynwood on the Indiana border. The route travels through eight counties and 31 cities to Fulton at the Iowa border. The Illinois portion of the Lincoln Highway, located near the center of the 3,389-mile transcontinental route, was the site of the first seedling mile of paved roadway constructed to demonstrate the superiority of pavement over dirt roads. The Lincoln Highway was also the first instance in which transportation principles such as directional signs and urban bypasses were employed.

Not only does the Lincoln Highway tell the story of early automobile travel and highway design, but it also ties together the histories, economies, and identities of the cities and towns of northern Illinois. Be sure to stop at a few of the Byway communities to find out what makes each one unique. The highway winds its way through the downtowns of many of the towns along its length, and you may visit a newly constructed windmill, go on a scenic river walk, or visit a bustling downtown area near Chicago.

QUICK FACTS

Length: 179 miles.

Time to Allow: 5 to 6 hours.

Best Time to Drive: Early summer.

Byway Travel Information: Illinois Lincoln Highway Coalition: phone toll-free 866/455-4249; Byway local Web site: www.lincolnhwyil.com.

Special Considerations: This Byway is long and may be difficult to follow as it winds its way through and around the Illinois interstate system and countryside. To experience all that the Lincoln Highway has to offer, you may want to spend two days driving the route.

Bicycle/Pedestrian Facilities: Pedestrian travel is accommodated by sidewalks along the majority of the Byway. Although bicycle travel along the Lincoln Highway is not advised, many biking and hiking trails/routes can be found intersecting the highway or in the communities along the route.

The Byway Story

The Lincoln Highway tells cultural, historical, recreational, and scenic stories that make it a unique and treasured Byway.

CULTURAL

The culture of the Lincoln Highway centers around its communities, and these communities all share a pride in being part of the history and future of transportation. In most of the Lincoln Highway communities, you find at least one defining characteristic—one aspect that makes the community unique. In Dixon, it is the Victory Arch that spans the highway; in Chicago Heights, it is the Arche Fountain commemorating Abraham Lincoln; in Batavia, it is the unique architecture.

The people of the Lincoln Highway allow this historic road to string them all together and bring them to the threshold of history. But with this historical remembrance, the communities of the Lincoln Highway continue to grow and change.

HISTORICAL

In 1913, a core group of automobile industrialists and enthusiasts established an organization to promote the development of "good roads" and conceived a route for a paved, transcontinental road. This group sought, initially without government assistance, to secure private funding to build a road that would serve the needs of industry, particularly the automobile industry. They had the notion of paving 1-mile stretches of road along the Lincoln Highway route with concrete to lay the groundwork for the future. They called these stretches seedling miles. They purposely placed them away from major cities so that motorists drawn by publicity would have to struggle over unimproved dirt roads to reach them. The first such seedling mile was completed in Malta, Illinois, just west of DeKalb, in September of 1914. Four more seedling miles were constructed in 1915. These prototypes immediately became popular motorist destinations. The stark contrast between these smooth patches of pavement and the bumpy or muddy roads leading up to them created a groundswell of public opinion in favor of good roads.

This clamor for action was directed at local, state, and federal officials and resulted in the passage of the Federal Aid Road Act of 1916, which authorized and appropriated $75 million for the construction of what were called post roads. This amount was to be matched by the states seeking to build the roads, thus starting the practice of federal-state grant matching for road construction. Additionally, many segments were constructed by volunteer labor, such as the Mooseheart segment of the Lincoln Highway, which was built by area businessmen, manual laborers, and others to demonstrate their support of their community and of local businesses.

Shortly thereafter, America became involved in World War I, shifting national attention onto the war effort and away from the road-building effort. However, interest in good roads resumed in earnest shortly after the war ended in November 1918. In 1919, Lincoln Highway Association leader Harry Ostermann persuaded the War Department to conduct a transcontinental motor convoy trip from the East Coast to San Francisco on the marked route of the Lincoln Highway. A 76-vehicle convoy combining public and private vehicles took off from the White House on July 7, 1919. The convoy, primarily following the Lincoln Highway route, finally arrived in San Francisco, but not after considerable difficulty on the dirt roads traveled en route. The seedling miles of concrete made a strong impression. Among those participating in the convoy was Lt. Colonel Dwight D. Eisenhower, who much later applied his experiences on the Lincoln Highway, along with his experiences with World War II and the German Autobahn system, to conceive of an interstate road system to aid the movement of troops, goods, and people across the country.

Various aspects of the Lincoln Highway's early development predated and predicted some of the technical and fundamental elements of current US transportation policy. These aspects went beyond those of paved roadways and transcontinental travel. They included directional signage, a system of concrete markers designed to assist travelers determining their location along a given roadway. The markers included a small coin-like bust of Lincoln with the inscription, "This highway dedicated to Abraham Lincoln." Never before had a consistent road signage system been employed. Another new concept was the urban bypass: the Lincoln Highway was purposely routed 25-30 miles south and west of Chicago to avoid the congestion and time delays associated with traveling through the city.

With much of its original (and modified) objectives achieved, the Lincoln Highway Association was dissolved in 1935. Its legacy for America has been the prominent role it played in the development of the roadway system in place today in the United States. Since 1935, much of the original Lincoln Highway has been paved over, bypassed, or converted to numbered US, state, and county highways or municipal streets. Very few of the 1928 cement markers still exist. However, the name Lincoln is still attached to much of the route in the form of roadway and street names, local Lincoln businesses and brochures, articles, and artifacts preserved in museums and historical societies along the route.

The Lincoln Highway was designated a National Scenic Byway in 2000 and presents many opportunities to enjoy the culture and history of Illinois. Most of all, the Lincoln Highway offers a unique opportunity to relive the days of the cross-country road trip and the sights of a developing nation.

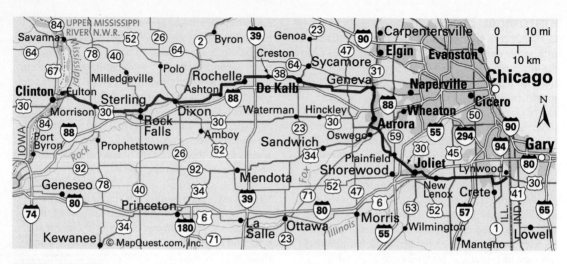

RECREATIONAL

Recapture the adventure of the open road, just as avid motorists of nearly a century ago braved the elements to heed the call of wanderlust to travel the Lincoln Highway. From the rolling hills of western Illinois and the Mississippi River Valley to the sights and sounds of the Chicago metropolitan area, the Lincoln Highway includes an impressive collection of diverse recreational opportunities.

Near Franklin Grove, stop at Franklin Creek State Natural Area to enjoy a picnic by the edge of Franklin Creek. Hiking, skiing, horseback riding, and snowmobiling trails are available there. As you near Chicago, you'll find increased shopping opportunities in places like Chicago Heights and Joliet. In Geneva, tour the Japanese Gardens or go biking on the Riverwalk. While touring each community, you are sure to come across several enticing activities.

Whether for an overnight getaway trip or for an extended stay to enjoy northern Illinois' hospitality and charm, the Lincoln Highway beckons travelers of all ages to experience firsthand the history, sights, and stories of the highway.

SCENIC

Although the scenic qualities of the Lincoln Highway may differ from those of other Byways, the highway is scenic nonetheless. Several architectural treats await you. Often, this architecture is combined with elements of nature for a scenic effect. Many of the most interesting sites on the Byway can be seen from the car, but you will likely want to get out and try some of the biking trails or river walks.

Highlights

This tour begins in North Aurora, Illinois, and travels west across the state. If you wish to take the tour traveling east, read this list from the bottom and work your way up.

○ **Mooseheart:** Just north of North Aurora on Illinois Route 31, you'll find Mooseheart. This lodge is an important piece of history for the Lincoln Highway, because members of the Moose Lodge raised $12,000 to fund the initial paving of the Lincoln Highway. Members of the lodge from all over the country then traveled to Illinois and helped grade the road using picks and shovels. In appreciation for the efforts of the lodge, the state later paved an extra 10-foot strip, which is still visible today, in front of Mooseheart.

○ **DeKalb Memorial Park:** Traveling west from Mooseheart on SR 60, you come to the city of DeKalb. The Memorial Park in DeKalb is famous for its memorial clock called Soldiers and Sailors, which was originally dedicated in 1913. The clock was restored completely in 1996, and in 1999, a community mural was painted on the side of the old Chronicle building, located behind the park. The mural highlights the history of DeKalb and can be seen from the Byway.

○ **First Seedling Mile:** Cement companies donated the cement to pave seedling miles on the highway. These paved miles of road were meant to show travelers what they had to look forward to when highways would be paved with a hard surface. Seedling miles were set in rural areas so that travelers wanting to see them would have to drive over a length of unpaved road and would quickly understand the advantages of the hard surface. The first seedling mile in the country is located west of Malta on SR 38.

○ **Railroad Park:** Located in Rochelle, west of Malta and the first seedling mile, is Railroad Park, one of two X rail crossings in the country. People come from all over the world to watch the rail traffic of the Union Pacific and the Burlington Northern Santa Fe Railroads, the two major rail carriers in the western United States.

Meeting of the Great Rivers Scenic Route

ILLINOIS

QUICK FACTS

Length: 57 miles.

Time to Allow: 2 hours.

Best Time to Drive: In the fall, people come from miles around to see the colors of the leaves and to enjoy harvest in the orchards and vineyards. During the spring, the dogwoods and redwoods are in bloom. In the summer, recreational activities are abundant on the Byway. In the winter, look for eagles swooping near the bluffs.

Byway Travel Information: Greater Alton/ Twin Rivers Convention and Visitors Bureau: phone 618/465-6676.

Special Considerations: One of the only gas stations along the entire Byway is located in Grafton.

Restrictions: Roads can be closed during the spring due to flooding and during the winter due to ice. When this happens, alternate routes are provided. Also, ferries cannot operate when the river freezes. During these times, use the Joe Paige Bridge at Hardin to connect with Kampsville in Calhoun County.

Bicycle/Pedestrian Facilities: Touted as the longest and perhaps the most picturesque bicycle path in the region, the 25-mile Vandalabene (Great River Road) Bicycle Trail runs parallel to the Meeting of the Great Rivers Scenic Route from Alton to the north of Pere Marquette State Park. The trail provides walking and bicycling opportunities, and it is the non-motorized, interconnecting link to 80 percent of the attractions along the Byway. There are also pedestrian trails within Pere Marquette State Park.

Within a 25-mile expanse, the Mississippi, Missouri, and Illinois rivers meet to form a 35,000-acre floodplain. This confluence is the backdrop for the Meeting of the Great Rivers Scenic Route. The river systems have been vital transportation routes as long as there has been human habitation, moving people and goods to world markets.

The Meeting of the Great Rivers Scenic Route offers a dramatic composite of the Mississippi River. Beneath white cliffs, the Byway runs next to the Mississippi, beginning in an industrial, urban setting and changing to a scenic, natural area. The area is so magnificent that the Illinois legislature called it "the most beautiful stretch of the entire Mississippi River." As though moving back through time, expanses of pastoral countryside and stone houses are reminders of a time long ago in the Lower Illinois River Valley.

The Meeting of the Great Rivers Scenic Route crosses the Illinois River on a ferry to the Kamp Store Museum in Kampsville. Artifacts of the earliest aboriginal people in America reside here, and the Byway's rich historical and archaeological qualities unfold. The road then travels to Alton, where history converges with present developments in the engineering wonder of the Clark Bridge and the memory of the last Lincoln-Douglas debate. Little towns along the Byway seem almost forgotten by time, giving travelers a look at historic architecture and small-town life along the Mississippi River.

The Byway Story

The Meeting of the Great Rivers Scenic Route tells archaeological, cultural, historical, natural, recreational, and scenic stories that make it a unique and treasured Byway.

ARCHAEOLOGICAL

Despite present-day development, archaeological remains are largely intact along the Meeting of the Great Rivers Scenic Route. For example, the Koster Site, located south of Eldred, is world renowned because of the evidence found that shows that humans lived on the site 8,000 years ago. Structures dating back to 4200 BC are considered to be the oldest such habitations found in North America, and villages flourished here circa 3300 BC, 5000 BC, and 6000 BC. More than 800 archaeological sites have been inventoried along the route. Experts believe that the Mississippi and Illinois rivers, known as the Nile of North America, nourished the development of complex and sophisticated Native American cultures. So complete are cultural records that archaeologists term the area "the crossroads of prehistoric America."

CULTURAL

Visitors discover real river towns along this Byway. For example, the historic town of Alton has a solid Midwestern appeal. Legends and folklore of the past have formed the communities along the Byway into the unique places they are today. From the Piasa Bird to riverside amusements, things to do and see are plentiful along the Meeting of the Great Rivers Scenic Route. The people of the Byway are aware of the area's role in the past and have restored and preserved many of the places and sights along the Byway that represent the evolving culture of the Meeting of the Great Rivers. Monuments and museums stand as a tribute to the past that present visitors can enjoy.

Many important cultural events have occurred along this Byway. For example, Lewis and Clark trained the Corps of Discovery, Lincoln and Douglas had their final debate, and Elijah Lovejoy was martyred here while defending the freedom of the press and fighting slavery. The tallest man in history, Robert Wadlow, called Alton home. Also, spanning the Mississippi River at Alton is the famous Clark Bridge, a suspension marvel that was featured in a two-hour PBS Nova documentary entitled "Super Bridge." It is a beautiful structure that proves that intelligent and compassionate engineers can marry function and form.

To celebrate each unique aspect of their culture, many of the communities on the Byway have established their own museums. In addition, the region displays an appreciation of high culture through orchestras, theaters, galleries, institutions of higher learning, and many diverse festivals that celebrate the arts. Throughout the year, more than 50 festivals and fairs celebrate the history, art, music, and crafts of this region. As you explore these cultural venues, the unique flavor of the communities along the Byway will permeate your senses.

HISTORICAL

The Mississippi River is internationally famous. Father Marquette and Louis Joliet first made their expedition down the Mississippi in 1673. Later, when the Illinois Territory was formed, the Missouri River was the gateway to the unexplored West, and the Illinois River led to the Great Lakes and was also a connection to the East. Early American explorers began in the confluence area. Lewis and Clark, for example, embarked from Fort Dubois near the mouth of the Missouri. Eventually, towns were settled on the shores of the rivers, providing a secure way for travel and commerce using the rivers. The buildings that these towns were composed of still stand, many of them dating to the early 1800s.

As the nation grew and developed, many of the towns along the Byway were growing and developing as well. Although many of the towns that stand today seem to be nestled somewhere in history, some of the Byway's communities have been at the edge of new ideas. During pre-Civil War times, the Underground Railroad ran through this area, bringing escaped slaves to the safety of the north. The city of Alton was also the site of the last Lincoln-Douglas debate. Confederate prison ruins found on the Byway are another testament to this corner of Illinois' involvement in the Civil War.

By the 19th century, Mark Twain's Mississippi River stories had inspired an ideal of Mississippi legends, history, and culture in the minds of Americans. Meanwhile, as the river and its uses were also evolving, paddleboats gave way to barges and tows. River traffic increased as industries grew, and Lock and Dam 26 was built. Today, historic 18th-century river towns, islands, bars, points, and bends create beautiful scenery beneath limestone bluffs, which are covered by forests that extend nearly 20,000 acres. Historical and cultural features in the 50-mile corridor have received national recognition, with seven sites presently registered on the National Register of Historic Places.

NATURAL

Nature abounds along the Meeting of the Great Rivers Scenic Route. The wetlands from three different waterways, the rock bluffs, and the stately trees all harbor native creatures and provide lovely views along the Byway. The palisade cliffs and towering bluffs provide a characteristic drive along the riverside where visitors can see the results of this great channel of water carving its way through post-glacial terrain. You may want to enjoy the nature of the Byway from the car, look for hikes along the way, or get out and explore a wildlife refuge.

Located right in the middle of the United States is Piasa country, a bird-watcher's heaven. Migratory flyways using the Mississippi, Illinois, and Missouri rivers converge within a 25-mile zone from Alton to Grafton. This offers amazing opportunities to see many species of birds that pass through this choke-point region, from the American bald eagle to the white pelican. Deer, otters, and beavers are present, as well as raccoons, opossums, and squirrels. Fishing enthusiasts will discover many species in the local waters.

Many natural points of interest dot this Byway. For example, Pere Marquette State Park is one of Illinois' largest state parks. It is nestled along the banks of the Illinois River on the Byway near Grafton. Here, a myriad of trails take you within the wild forests and up to spectacular viewing areas along the bluff line above.

The Riverlands Environmental Wetlands Area is another natural point of interest. Located near Alton, this US Army Corps of Engineers site provides a fertile wetland that attracts all types of wildlife. Early-morning travelers frequently see wildlife making their way to the river. The Mark Twain Refuge is located near Pere Marquette State Park and is often open to the public. The preserve offers sanctuary to rare and endangered migratory birds on their long flights up and down the Mississippi and Illinois rivers.

All the stunning views that can be enjoyed from a vehicle can also be enjoyed on foot or by bike. The Sam Vadalabene Trail, a bicycle and walking trail, winds more than 25 miles from Alton to Pere Marquette State Park on the Byway, making this a Byway that encourages and accommodates hikers and bikers.

RECREATIONAL

After you have seen the sights on the Meeting of the Great Rivers Scenic Route, you may decide to enjoy the surroundings on a closer level. Trails and paths along the Byway offer excitement for hikers and bikers. Also, forests that line the roadsides are perfect places for camping, picnicking, or simply enjoying the peaceful solitude that nature affords. Be sure to tour the historic districts of the Byway communities and stop at the museums and visitor centers that provide a closer look at the Byway and its characteristics.

There is always fun to be found on the Mississippi River. Visitors enjoy the water in every way, from parasailing to jet skiing. Sailboats and riverboats keep the river alive with movement year-round. During the summer, families stop at one of the two water parks along the Byway or travel on one of the four free river ferries located in the area. The Meeting of the Great Rivers Scenic Route is one of the most accommodating to bikers, with a bicycle path that goes directly along the Byway.

Shopping for crafts and antiques in the historic riverside towns along the Byway is a pleasant pastime, and golfers enjoy the ten courses in the region. There's a theater in Wood River and an amphitheater in Grafton for musical productions, stage productions, and other kinds of entertainment. It is hard to miss the *Alton Belle* Riverboat Casino on a leisurely cruise down the river. In addition to the attractions along the Byway, festivals, fairs, and events are always occurring in its communities.

SCENIC

The Mississippi River is like a chameleon. Depending on weather conditions, sun angles, and the color of the sky, the waters can turn from serene pale blue to dark navy to muddy brown. Insiders' favorite time for viewing the river is early in the morning as the sun is rising. Often, the river is glass-like, creating a mirror of the sky above. The blue is sweet and clear, and the reflections of the bluffs and trees are remarkable. Majestic bluffs tower above the Byway, creating a stunning wall of trees, rocky cliffs, and soaring birds. The meandering curves of the river provide amazing views, and you can see up and down the river for miles. The bluffs, which are imposing when immediately adjacent to the road, diminish into the far horizon at several viewing areas.

Note the unusual sunsets along these parts. Most think of the Mississippi as a southbound river that cuts up and down the center of the nation. This is not true here. In Piasa country, the Mississippi River makes a distinct turn and the current flows from west to east. In Alton, Grafton, and Elsah, the sun rises and sets in the long stretch of the water. On many evenings at dusk, the fiery reds, yellows, and oranges run nearly the entire length of the river. One of the great pastimes along this Byway is celebrating these glorious and unique sunsets.

Along the road to Eldred, the bluffs give way to rolling hills, farms, and forests. Depending on the season, roadside stands with fruits and vegetables may entice you to stop. The apples and peaches in Jersey, Calhoun, and Greene counties are legendary. In Eldred, an old-fashioned Illinois town full of Americana, most travelers stop for a slice of pie and get out to smell the crisp, fresh air. Eldred is a small town, but the smiles are big. Moving northward, you see the great Illinois farmlands that bring the bounty of food to both America's and the world's dinner tables. Soon the road branches westward, and the journey ends with another free ferry over the Illinois River into Kampsville.

This Byway is a must-see destination during all four seasons. In the spring, the trees and shrubs turn the bluffs and countryside into a wonderful tapestry of colorful buds and blossoms. Summer brings festivals, fairs, and river recreation. Autumn hosts the Fall Color Caravan and some of America's most amazing foliage, accented by the nearby rivers. Finally, the winter brings the American bald eagle by the hundreds to winter along the bluffs and feed along the banks of the rivers. The rivers, majestic bluffs, fantastic trees and wildlife, quaint villages, and rolling farmlands all make this Byway a wonderful adventure.

© MapQuest.com, Inc.

Highlights

This must-see tour of the Meeting of the Great Rivers Scenic Route begins at the northernmost point (Kampsville) and concludes at the southernmost point (Alton). If you're traveling in the other direction, simply read this itinerary from the bottom and work your way up.

- **Kampsville:** In Calhoun County on the Illinois River. Free ferry ride (drive east on Highway 108 approximately 5 miles to Eldred). Home of the **American Center for Archaeology;** site of **Old Settlers Days** with Lewis and Clark, Civil War, and other reenactments. Gas, food, shops.

- **Eldred:** In Greene County at Highway 108 and Blacktop Road. Wonderful Illinois village with gas, food, shops. The **Eldred Home** shows a glimpse of life in the 1800-1900s. Turn south (right) onto

Blacktop Road. Drive approximately 15 miles to the intersection of Blacktop Road, Highway 100, and Highway 16; continue straight ahead and onto Highway 100 southbound. Continue approximately 10 miles to Pere Marquette State Park.

☺ **Pere Marquette State Park:** In Jersey County on Route 100. This 7,895-acre preserve overlooks the Mississippi and Illinois rivers. Nature trails, prehistoric sites, horseback riding, camping, fishing, boating, and hiking. Wonderful lodge built in the 1930s by the Civilian Conservation Corps. The fireplace alone soars 50 feet into the grand hall, and the great room is rich with massive timber beams and stone. Continue southward (left) out of Pere Marquette State Park onto Highway 100. Continue approximately 3 miles to Brussels Ferry.

☺ **Brussells Ferry:** On the Illinois River. Take a free ride across the Illinois River (it's okay to turn around and come right back!) and get a feel of the river under the wheels of your vehicle. Nearby is the **Mark Twain Wildlife Refuge,** the seasonal home for hundreds of thousands of migratory birds (American bald eagles, herons, owls, pelicans, geese, ducks, and many rare species) on the Mississippi Flyway. Return to Highway 100 (where you boarded the ferry) and turn eastbound (right) for approximately 2 miles.

☺ **Grafton:** On Highway 100 in Jersey County. All but wiped out by the Great Flood of 1993, this amazing river town bounced back and is now considered one of the most important stops on the Byway. Bed-and-breakfast inns, antiques and specialty shops, casual family dining, riverside entertainment, summer outdoor family amphitheater, a small museum, a visitor center, parasailing, jet skiing, pontoon boats, fishing, hunting, hiking, bike trails, cottages, horseback riding, a mystery dinner theater, and much more. Festivals abound throughout the spring, summer, and fall. Continue southbound approximately 1/2 mile to the bluffs running along the Mississippi River.

☺ **Scenic bluffs:** Without question, the most spectacular view anywhere along this route is from just outside Grafton, approximately 15 miles southeast to Alton. The bluffs tower above the river with the Byway road surface immediately between the peaks and the riverbank. The ever-flowing Mississippi is alive with commercial traffic, sailboats, and wildlife,

in contrast to the majestic bluffs soaring overhead. Any time is good viewing, but late afternoon and sunset are very rewarding. Because the river runs west to east, the sun illuminates the geologic structures, creating a vista unlike anywhere else on the Mississippi. Be careful: many people stop along the highway to take pictures of the bluffs and river. Try to remain in your car to photograph the scenery. Also exercise caution because of many bicyclists and fast-moving traffic at all times. Continue eastbound on Highway 100 about 5 miles from Grafton to Elsah. Be prepared to make an abrupt northward turn (left).

☺ **Village of Elsah:** In Jersey County. Considered by many national travel writers as the river town that time forgot. This adorable village contains more than two dozen homes built in the 1800s, when Elsah was an important riverboat stop. Because the town has almost no contemporary structures, you immediately feel like you have been transported back into the mid-1800s. Bed-and-breakfasts and small shops abound. Continue eastbound (left from Elsah) onto Highway 100 about 10 miles to the Cliffton Terrace Park.

☺ **Cliffton Terrace Park:** In Madison County in Godfrey. Pleasant roadside park with facilities for picnics, seasonal wildlife viewing, comfort station, and playground. Continue eastbound (left from Cliffton Terrace Park) onto Highway 100 about 5 miles to the legendary Piasa Bird. Be alert for an abrupt turn northward (left) as you begin seeing riverside barges tied up along the banks.

☺ **Piasa Bird:** In Madison County in Alton. This mythical creature was seen by American Indian tribes and early European explorers. Today, a gigantic bluff painting depicts the half-dragon, half-cat creature. Restored from early sketches and photography of the 1800s, the site is being developed into an interpretive park and wetlands area. Continue southeasterly (left from Piasa Bird) about 1 mile on Highway 100 and enter Alton.

☺ **Alton:** In Madison County. The community dates to the early 1800s as a major river port just north of St. Louis and can best be summed up by the word "historic." The Reverend Elijah Lovejoy was martyred here in his stand against slavery and for freedom of the press. It was also the site of the last Lincoln-Douglas debate. Nearby in Hartford-

Wood River, Lewis and Clark built Camp Dubois, assembled the Corps of Discovery, and set off on their monumental expedition. The world's tallest man, Robert Wadlow, called Alton home. During the Civil War, thousands of Confederate soldiers were held at the Federal Penitentiary; today, a solemn monument and cemetery honors the dead. Alton has fantastic recreational facilities, including golf courses and ball fields that welcome national championship tournaments. The city has unique casual and fine restaurants, bed-and-breakfasts, inns, hotels, an antique shopping district, a shopping mall, parks, riverboat gaming, and other leisure activities throughout the year. Continue eastbound on Highway 100, going approximately 3 miles to the stoplight. Turn north (right) into the Melvin Price Locks and Dam Complex and National Great Rivers Museum site.

⊙ **Melvin Price Locks and Dam, National Great Rivers Museum:** About 2 miles past the Clark Bridge, on Highway 100, is the Melvin Price Locks and Dam and the site of the **National Great Rivers Museum.** This colossal structure tames the mighty river and aids in flood control and navigation. A wonderful riverfront walkway surrounds the dam and museum. Watch long strings of barges full of fuel and grain pass through the locks to be lowered or raised as the river winds down to the delta. It offers a wonderful view of the Alton skyline and Clark Bridge.

Ohio River Scenic Byway

ILLINOIS
Part of a multistate Byway; see also IN, OH.

QUICK FACTS

Length: 188 miles.

Time to Allow: 8 to 10 hours.

Best Time to Drive: Year-round; high season is summer.

Byway Travel Information: Southernmost Illinois Tourism Bureau: phone 618/845-3777.

Special Considerations: There are no regular seasonal limitations on the Ohio River Scenic Byway in Illinois. In general, the route location and flood control systems allow the route to be traveled during ordinary periods of high water. Also, passenger vehicles are easily accommodated on the Byway in southern Illinois. The roads are well surfaced and in good condition. A narrow and hilly segment of the Byway near Tower Rock in Hardin County is not advised for RVs or tour buses. An alternate route has been identified for these vehicles along the roadside.

Restrictions: During periods of significant flooding, segments of the route may be closed, especially the terminus of the route in Cairo.

Bicycle/Pedestrian Facilities: The Ohio River Scenic Byway in Illinois offers hiking in the Shawnee National Forest, along the River to River Trail and along the proposed southern route of the American Discovery Trail—sharing several segments of the eastern Byway route. Officially designated bike routes exist along the Byway within the Shawnee National Forest and along Illinois State Route 146 between Cave-in-Rock and Golconda. Pedestrians are easily accommodated at all identified sites in the Byway corridor and in all communities along the route.

This Byway's history is closely tied to the Ohio River, which it follows. For example, many forts from the Civil War and the French and Indian War were placed strategically along this route, and the Underground Railroad had many stops along this Byway. This is where you can find the Cave-in-Rock, an enormous cave that was once home to river pirates. It is now a great vantage point from which to watch today's river traffic.

The outstanding scenery found along this Byway is largely due to the river, which offers winter homes to thousands of Canadian geese. Also, because of the river and the Shawnee National Forest (which the Byway goes through), you'll find plenty of places to picnic, camp, boat, fish, hike, and hunt.

The Byway Story

The Ohio River Scenic Byway tells archaeological, cultural, historical, natural, and recreational stories that make it a unique and treasured Byway.

ARCHAEOLOGICAL
Archaeological digs were conducted at Fort Massac State Park in Metropolis from 1939 to 1942, and again in 1966 and 1970. From these digs, reconstruction of the 1970s fort was started. A museum houses artifacts from the original excavations.

CULTURAL
The spirit of those who live along the Ohio River can be seen at Fort Defiance Park in the town of Cairo. This park, located south of Cairo on Route 51, was once called "probably the ugliest park in America, the park that no one wants," by the *Chicago Tribune*.

A grassroots organization of Cairo citizens, Operation Enterprise, leased the park from the state to renovate and maintain it. The park is now a beautiful place to watch the constant meeting of the Ohio and Mississippi rivers that refuse to merge. The Ohio River waters become a blue ribbon, rippling far down the brown Mississippi currents. Gulls wheel above the placid barges and tugs navigate the point.

Because all this magnificent scenery is found along the Ohio River, there is much evidence in Cairo of the people's desire for beauty. For example, located in the Halliday Park at Washington and Poplar is *The Hewer*, a statue that was made in 1906. Sculpted by George Grey Barnard and exhibited at the St. Louis World's Fair, this original bronze statue was declared by Laredo Taft to be one of the finest nudes in America.

You can also experience many annual cultural events and celebrations along this Byway. The Superman Celebration happens the second weekend in June. The Massac County Youth Fair takes place each year in July. The Superman Jet Rally is held the first weekend in October, and the Fort Massac Encampment occurs the third weekend in October.

The Living History Weekends in Fort Massac State Park happen throughout the year. Also consider visiting during the Labor Day Celebration or the Home Town Christmas Light Display from Thanksgiving through New Year's Eve.

HISTORICAL

Many historical sites are situated along the Ohio River Scenic Byway. These sites cover everything from early Native American cultures to Civil War sites. Kinkaid Mounds, a designated Byway site, is a monument to the Native American people who once inhabited this region.

The cities of Old Shawneetown and Golconda have numerous historic structures from the 1820s and 1830s. Cairo, positioned at the confluence of the Ohio and Mississippi rivers, was a thriving port city and an important strategic site during the Civil War. Fort Massac State Park in Metropolis is a reconstructed fort from the French and Indian War.

The Ohio River has been a river of both opportunity and tragedy. While the state of Illinois possesses many Underground Railroad sites, the Byway also passes near the Slave House, where captured fugitive slaves and even freed blacks were incarcerated before being returned to the South. This constituted the little-known Reverse Underground Railroad.

In addition, the Trail of Tears crossed the Ohio River in Golconda. At the Buel House (certified by the National Park Service as an official Trail of Tears designated site), the Cherokee were offered food and hospitality.

You'll find many historic buildings and structures along this Byway, starting in Cairo. For example, St. Patrick Catholic Church was built in 1894 and is located on 9th and Washington. The present church is a stately Romanesque structure of Bedford stone. It has three bells and numerous stained-glass windows. It is the oldest church in Cairo, and parishioners celebrated the church's 160th anniversary in 1998.

St. Mary's Park Pavilion was built in 1876 and is located on 28th Street between Magnolia Drive and Park Place West in Cairo. It was built as a memorial to the centennial. This pavilion was the site of President Roosevelt's address during his visit to Cairo in 1907. The pavilion was also the center for numerous Victorian celebrations.

The US Custom House was built in 1872 and is located on 14th and Washington in Cairo. This building is a rare example of Romanesque architecture. The monumental limestone structure was completed for a costly $225,000 at the time. It is one of the few remaining works of noted government architect A. B. Mullet and is currently under renovation. Within the Custom House is the flagpole from General Grant's flagship, the *Tigress*. As a river packet commandeered by the Union Army, the *Tigress* carried Grant up the Tennessee to the battle of Shiloh on April 6, 1862. A year later, the *Tigress* was sunk while running the shore batteries at Vicksburg. Her crew survived and returned the flag staff to Cairo. A Civil War cannon on the outside of the building complements Grant's standard.

NATURAL

The natural features of the Ohio Valley in Illinois represent some of the most dramatic features along the entire Ohio River. For example, the Garden of the Gods in the Shawnee National Forest preserves a grouping of unique limestone features with such names as Camel Rock and the Devil's Smokestack. Nearby Rim Rock and Pounds Hollow are also linked by the Byway route. Along the Byway, the Spur to Cave-in-Rock State Park is a great limestone cavern on the Ohio River. The enormous cave, once home to river pirates, provides a vantage point from which you can watch today's river traffic. Farther west, the designated Cache River Spur takes visitors to a rare wetland ecosystem, designated by the United Nations as a Wetland of International Importance.

The Horseshoe Lake Conservation Area in Miller City, 7 miles north of Cairo, has 10,645 acres, including a 2,400-acre lake. The first 49 acres of the park were purchased by the Department of Natural Resources in 1927 for development as a Canadian goose sanctuary. Additional tracts of land, including Horseshoe Island, continued to be purchased in order to create the conservation area that greets visitors today. Canadian geese began wintering at the site in 1928. The original 1,000 birds increased to a population of more than 40,000 by 1944, but this number dropped to 22,000 by 1947. Today, however, more than 250,000 Canadian geese winter at this site, thanks to improved refuge management and harvest controls.

RECREATIONAL

Horseshoe Lake Conservation Area resembles Louisiana bayous with its swamp cypress and wading herons. As the winter home of thousands of Canadian geese, Horseshoe Lake is a biologist's and birder's paradise throughout the year; with its large stands of trees around its 20-mile shoreline, it is a beautiful body of water. Since 1930, when a concrete, fixed spillway was constructed, the lake has maintained a fairly constant 4-foot depth. Four picnic areas are found in the park, and each site includes tables, park stoves, and parking. Children appreciate the playground that is located at the picnic area near the spillway. Drinking water is available at hydrants and fountains located conveniently throughout the park. For more information, call 618/776-5689 or 618/776-5215.

You can enjoy camping in both the Fort Massac State Park and throughout the Shawnee National Forest. The Shawnee National Forest in Illinois has 338 miles of equestrian/hiking trails, 454 campsites, 16 designated campgrounds, and 27 designated picnic areas. Recreational opportunities range from primitive make-your-own campsites and trails to developed campsites with beaches, showers, and electricity. For more information, call the Shawnee National Forest toll-free at 800/699-6636. Seven wilderness areas in the Shawnee National Forest are available for wilderness study, including Bald Knob, Burden Falls, Garden of the Gods, Panther Den, Bay Creek, Clear Springs, Lust Creek, and Ripple Hollow (conditionally).

In the tradition of the Mississippi steamships that featured gambling, drinking, and Old West living, a casino steamship still leaves the port of Metropolis. It takes visitors for two-hour cruises on the river during the hours of 9 am to 11 pm. For further information, call toll-free 800/929-5905 or 800/935-1111. Along the Metropolis riverfront is the Merv Griffin Theater, which presents a range of entertainers on special dates throughout the year (phone toll-free 800/949-5740).

Highlights

The Ohio River Scenic Byway must-see tour begins in Cairo, Illinois, and runs to the Indiana border. If you're traveling the opposite way, simply read this list from the bottom and work your way up.

○ **Fort Defiance Park** is right on the Byway. Stop and view the confluence of the Ohio and Mississippi rivers, where you can see tugs working. There are picnic tables and the Boatmens Memorial, which affords great photo opportunities at the spot where the nation's largest rivers meet.

○ Taking Highway 51 right through Cairo (on Washington Avenue), travel 1 1/2 miles to **The Hewer** statue in Halliday Park on the corner of Washington and Poplar avenues. About 1/2 mile later, you can see the **Safford Memorial Library,** where you can pick up a 50-cent book out of the "treasure bin" to read in bed that night. Across the street is the **US Custom House Museum.**

○ Where Highway 51 and Washington Avenue split, you can take a short detour following Washington Avenue along **Millionaire's Row** to see turn-of-the-century mansions such as River Lore and Magnolia Manor, which is open for tours. Then turn right on 28th Street to rejoin Byway.

○ Heading north on Highway 51 out of Cairo, about 5 miles at the junction of Highway 51 and Highway 37, is the **Mound City National Cemetery.** From Mound City, the Byway route goes onto Highway 37.

○ Traveling north on Highway 37, about 5 miles later is the **Olmstead Lock and Dam project,** which offers a lookout pavilion and rest rooms. The route then goes up Highway 37 about 5 miles to the Grand Chain Joppa Blacktop, and then it runs into Highway 45.

○ Highway 45 goes south into Metropolis, where you can see **Superman Square** in the center of town. A casino is located in Metropolis along the Ohio River.

○ **Fort Massac State Park** is the next stop (2 miles south of Superman Square), located on Highway 45, with picnic tables, a museum, and a variety of events that occur throughout the year. Follow the Byway out through Brookport, Unionville, and Liberty up through Baycity to Golconda (about 45 miles from Metropolis), where you will find the **Golconda Marina,** the **Buel House,** and many antique and novelty shops.

○ Continue on Highway 46 and go through Elizabethtown and on to **Cave-in-Rock State Park,** with a lodge, a restaurant, picnic tables, trails, and much more.

○ North of Cave-in-Rock, you can stop by **Garden of the Gods Wilderness Area** in the Shawnee National Forest to enjoy the hiking trails and picnic tables. Then continue on the Byway until it joins Indiana's portion of the Ohio River Scenic Byway.

The Historic National Road

INDIANA   An All-American Road
Part of a multistate Byway; see also IL, OH.

One of America's earliest roads, the National Road was built between 1828 and 1834 and established a settlement pattern and infrastructure that is still visible today. Nine National Register Districts are found along the route, as are 32 individually designated National Register Sites offering education and entertainment. As you travel Indiana's Historic National Road, you find a landscape that has changed little since the route's heyday in the 1940s.

Historic villages with traditional main streets and leafy residential districts still give way to the productive fields and tranquil pastures that brought Indiana prosperity. From the Federal-style architecture of an early pike town (a town that offered traveling accommodations and little else) to the drive-ins and stainless-steel diners of the 1940s, you can literally track the westward migration of the nation in the buildings and landscapes that previous generations have left behind.

Along the way, you will find many of the same buildings and towns that were here during the earliest days of westward expansion. A visit to Antique Alley gives you a chance to do some antique shopping and exploring along this historic road. The Indiana Historic National Road is a unique way to experience the preserved pike towns along the route, such as Centerville and Knightstown.

QUICK FACTS

Length: 156 miles.

Time to Allow: 3 to 9 hours.

Best Time to Drive: High seasons are spring and fall. In the spring, poppies, irises, and wildflowers are spread along the roadside. Black locusts and redbuds are also in bloom. During September and October, community festivals occur all along the Byway.

Byway Travel Information: Indiana National Road Association: phone 765/478-3172.

Bicycle/Pedestrian Facilities: In rural portions of the Historic National Road, you will not find sidewalks for pedestrians or shoulders specifically designated for bicycles. However, in rural portions of the Byway where traffic is often light, bicyclists and pedestrians can travel many stretches of the route in relative safety and comfort.

The Byway Story

Indiana's portion of the Historic National Road tells archaeological, cultural, historical, natural, recreational, and scenic stories that make it a unique and treasured Byway.

ARCHAEOLOGICAL

Eastern Indiana was the home of two groups of Native Americans identified by scholars as the Eastern Woodland Societies, who made their homes in the area following the retreat of the glaciers. One group occupied the area around 7000 to 1000 BC, the other from approximately 1000 to 700 BC. Many of their campsites have been found in the area of the Whitewater River Gorge. The Whitewater River Gorge was an important area after glacier movement and activity had stopped in the area. The area was excellent for hunting and fishing, with flowing streams and an abundance of resources.

CULTURAL

The National Road brought the nation to Indiana. The lure of limitless opportunities and the romance of the West drew tens of thousands of pioneers through Indiana between 1834 and 1848. Many stayed and settled in the Hoosier State, thus creating a new culture—the foundation for our national culture. This is because religious and economic groups left the distinctive colonial societies of the eastern seaboard and merged in the Midwest. Settlers to Indiana brought with them their own particular mix of customs, languages, building styles, religions, and farming practices. Quakers, European immigrants, and African Americans looking for new opportunities all traveled the National Road. Evidence of this mix of cultural influences can be seen along the corridor today in the buildings and landscapes. It can also be learned at the Indiana State Museum's National Road exhibit, and it can be experienced on a Conestoga Wagon at Conner Prairie or at a Civil War encampment along the route.

As the region matured, the culture continued to evolve under the influence of the nation's primary east-west route. Richmond was home of the Starr Piano Company, and later the Starr-Gennet recording studios, where jazz greats like Hoagy Carmichael and Louis Armstrong made recordings in an early jazz center. The Overbeck sisters, noted for their Arts and Crafts pottery, lived and worked in Cambridge City. The poet James Whitcomb Riley, author of "Little Orphant Annie" and "Raggedy Man," lived in Greenfield. Also, Indianapolis, the largest city on the entire Historic National Road, became an early center for automobile manufacturing. Today, visitors experience such attractions as the Children's Museum of Indianapolis (the largest in the world) and the Eiteljorg Museum of American Indian and Western Art, as well as a variety of other museums and cultural institutions.

The Historic National Road in Indiana represents one segment of the historic National Road corridor from Maryland to Illinois. The historic and cultural resources within Indiana are intimately tied to traditions and customs from the eastern terminus of the road in Cumberland, Maryland, and are built on goals and expectations of a nation looking west.

HISTORICAL
The National Road was the first federally funded highway in the United States. Authorized by Thomas Jefferson in 1803, the road ran from Cumberland, Maryland, west to Vandalia, Illinois. Designed to connect with the terminus of the C&O Canal in Cumberland, the National Road gave agricultural

goods and raw materials from the interior direct access to the eastern seaboard. It also encouraged Americans to settle in the fertile plains west of the Appalachians. For the first time in the United States, a coordinated interstate effort was organized and financed to survey and construct a road for both transportation purposes and economic development.

Built in Indiana between 1828 and 1834, the National Road established a settlement pattern and infrastructure that is still visible today. The historic structures along the National Road illustrate the transference of ideas and culture from the east as the road brought settlement and commerce to Indiana. The National Road still passes through well-preserved, Federal-style pike towns and Victorian streetcar neighborhoods, and it is lined with early automobile-era structures, such as gas stations, diners, and motels.

NATURAL
The topography of Indiana was created by glaciers that advanced and retreated over the land during the Pleistocene Period. Leaving behind moraines and an undulating landscape, the glaciers also helped to create the Whitewater River Gorge, where fragments of limestone, clay, and shale bedrock can be seen. The gorge and surrounding region is known internationally among geologists for its high concentration of Ordovician Period fossils.

RECREATIONAL
You can find many opportunities for recreation along the Historic National Road in Indiana, as well as in nearby cities. Golf is a popular sport along the highway, as evidenced by the many golf courses, such as the Glen Miller Public Golf Course, the Hartley Hills Country Club, the Highland Lake Public Golf Course, and the Winding Branch Public Golf Course. Biking and hiking are other extremely popular sports along the Byway. Local park and recreation facilities are often directly accessible from the Byway or can be found nearby.

Professional sports can be enjoyed along the Byway as well. White River State Park in Indianapolis offers you an opportunity to enjoy a Triple-A baseball game at Victory Field (or to visit the Indianapolis Zoo). Just off the Historic National Road in downtown Indianapolis are the RCA Dome, home of the Indianapolis Colts, and Conseco Fieldhouse, home of the Indiana Pacers.

© MapQuest.com, Inc.

SCENIC

The Historic National Road is a combination of scenes from rural communities, small towns, and a metropolitan city. This combination makes the Byway a scenic tour along one of the most historically important roads in America. Small-town antique shops and old-fashioned gas pumps dot the Byway, making the Historic National Road a relaxing and peaceful journey. Broad views of cultivated fields, distant barns and farmhouses, and grazing livestock dominate the landscape. In other areas, courthouse towers, church steeples, and water towers signal approaching communities that draw you from the open areas into historic settlements. The topography of the land affords vistas down the corridor and glimpses into natural areas that sit mostly hidden in the rural landscape. This repeating pattern of towns and rural landscapes is broken only by metropolitan Indianapolis.

Highlights

The following are just some of the points of interest available to you when traveling west across the Indiana portion of this Byway from the western border of Ohio. If you're traveling east, read this list from the bottom up.

○ **Historic Richmond:** As one of Indiana's oldest historic towns (founded in 1806), Richmond has one of the Hoosier State's largest intact collections of 19th-century architecture. You can visit four National Register Historic Districts; **Hayes Regional Arboretum;** a bustling historic downtown full of unique shops and restaurants; and a fascinating collection of local museums, including the **Wayne County Museum,** the **Richmond Art Museum,** the **Gaar Mansion,** the **Indiana Football Hall of Fame,** the **Joseph Moore Museum** at Earlham College, and the **Rose Gardens** located along the road on the city's east side.

○ **Centerville:** One of the historic highway's most intact and quaint National Road-era pike towns is listed in the National Register of Historic Places for its fine collection of architecture. Centerville also has a noteworthy collection of small antique and specialty shops and is home to the world's largest antique mall, just several blocks north of the National Road.

○ **Pike towns and Antique Alley (Richmond to Knightstown):** You can meander along the National Road and enjoy the tranquil agricultural landscape interspersed with pike towns that recall the early years, when travelers needed a place to rest every 5 miles or so. This route is also heralded as Antique Alley, with more than 900 antique dealers plying their trade in and between every community along the route.

○ **Huddleston Farmhouse Inn Museum, Cambridge:** A restored National Road-era inn and farm tells the story of the historic highway and the people who formed communities along its length. The museum is owned and operated by the Historic Landmarks Foundation of Indiana and is the home office of the Indiana National Road Association, the National Scenic Byway management nonprofit group. The museum displays the way of life of an early Hoosier farm family and the experience of westward travelers who stopped for food and shelter. Cambridge City is also listed in the National Register of Historic Places and has unique historic buildings that are home to diverse shops and local eateries.

○ **Knightstown:** Knightstown grew because of its location on the National Road between Richmond and Indianapolis. The town has retained its significant collection of 19th- and 20th-century architecture; a large section of the town is listed in the National Register of Historic Places. Today, you can visit four antique malls, watch a nationally known coppersmith, and stay in one of two bed-and-breakfasts. Also available is the **Big Four Railroad Scenic Tour.**

☉ **Greenfield: James Whitcomb Riley's Old Home and Museum** on the National Road in Greenfield tells the story of the Hoosier poet and allows you to experience his life and community with guided tours. The town also is rich in small-town local flavor, with many shops and restaurants to satisfy you.

☉ **Irvington:** A classic 1870s Indianapolis suburb was developed as a getaway on the city's east side. Irvington has since been swallowed by the city but retains its stately architecture and peaceful winding cul-de-sacs. Listed in the National Register of Historic Places, Irvington recalls turn-of-the-century progressive design principles and allows the modern visitor a glimpse into the city's 19th-century development.

☉ **Indianapolis:** The center of Indiana's National Road is also its state capital. Downtown Indianapolis offers a growing array of activities and amenities, from the state's best shopping at **Circle Centre Mall,** an unprecedented historic preservation development that incorporates building façades from the city's past into a state-of-the-art mall experience, to gourmet dining and an active nightlife and sports scene. Along Washington Street just east of downtown, you can visit the **Indiana Statehouse,** the **Indianapolis Zoo,** the **Eiteljorg Museum of American and Indian Art,** and **White River State Park.** The **Indianapolis Colts** play at the RCA Dome, and the **Indiana Pacers** continue the ritual of Hoosier Hysteria at Conseco Fieldhouse downtown.

☉ **Plainfield:** Twentieth-century automobile culture dominates this area. Motels and gas stations remain from the early days and are interspersed with the sprawl and development of the modern city. The Diner, on the east side of Plainfield, is a remnant from the early days of travel, a stainless-steel café with an atmosphere reminiscent of the 1940s, an atmosphere that is quickly disappearing. From Plainfield to Brazil, look for roadside farmers' markets.

☉ **Brazil:** The western extension of the National Road was surveyed through what is now Brazil in 1825; today, its National Register-listed Meridian Street remains a classic example of how the historic highway promoted the growth of communities along its length. The village is also full of curios and collectibles.

☉ **Terre Haute:** The western edge of Indiana's National Road is anchored by Terre Haute, a community offering historic points of interest and cultural experiences of various kinds. The **Rose-Hulman Institute of Technology** on the city's east side was founded in 1874 and is an exceptionally beautiful college campus; just west of the city on State Road 150, the **St. Mary-of-the-Woods College** campus offers a touch of European elegance in the Indiana forest. Its campus is in a beautiful wooded setting and has several buildings dating to its 1841 founding. You can choose National Road restaurants along the city's **Wabash Avenue,** located in historic buildings. **Dobbs Park,** 1/2 mile south of the highway at the intersection of Highways 46 and 42, is home to a nature center and **Native American Museum. The Sheldon Swope Art Museum** at 25 South 7th Street features 19th- and 20th-century artworks in a 1901 Renaissance Revival-style building with an Art Deco interior. The **Children's Science and Technology Museum** at 523 Wabash Avenue houses rooms full of hands-on learning displays and special exhibits. Larry Bird fans can see memorabilia at **Larry Bird's Boston Connection** (55 South 3rd Street) and view a museum of his career keepsakes, including his Olympic medal, MVP trophies, photographs, and other mementos. Continue on Indiana's Old National Road to the Illinois portion of the road.

Ohio River Scenic Byway

INDIANA

Part of a multistate Byway; see also IL, OH.

This winding, hilly route follows the Ohio River, which has had a tremendous impact on this area's history. The route offers a pleasant escape from suburban concerns as it passes villages, well-kept barns, vineyards, and orchards. Historic architecture along the way retains a charm that is often missing from modern development.

Here, tucked away in the very toe of southwestern Indiana, are swamps full of water lilies and rare birds. The most rugged part of this Byway features rock outcroppings, forested hills, caves, and scenic waterways. The limestone bluffs (dotted with cave entrances) are abundant with wildlife.

QUICK FACTS

Length: 303 miles.

Time to Allow: 2 days.

Best Time to Drive: This route is a beautiful drive in any season. High season is July through October.

Byway Travel Information: Chamber of Commerce: phone 812/838-3639; Historic Southern Indiana: phone toll-free 800/489-4474; Byway local Web site: www.ohioriverscenicroute.org.

Special Considerations: Some areas along this Byway are prone to flooding during the fall and spring, causing occasional closures. The road can become slippery in the winter or when it rains. The road is also narrow in some spots, and sometimes it is winding and hilly.

Bicycle/Pedestrian Facilities: This Byway has narrow shoulders and winding roads, so only off-road biking and hiking are recommended. The new bicycle trail along the Byway includes Perry and Crawford counties. There are also many hiking and walking trails near the Byway in the Angel Mounds State Historic Site, the Hoosier National Forest, Clifty Falls State Park, and along the Ohio River. Just off the Byway, cyclists and hikers will find the American Discovery Trail, a nationally designated trail that will reach from the East Coast to the West Coast when it is completed.

The Byway Story

The Ohio River Scenic Byway tells archaeological, historical, natural, recreational, and scenic stories that make it a unique and treasured Byway.

ARCHAEOLOGICAL

Angel Mounds State Park is located on the banks of the Ohio River near Evansville. It is one of the best-preserved Native American sites in North America, where an advanced culture lived between AD 900 and 1600. These people were named Mississippian by archaeologists. The town served as an important center for religion, politics, and trade. Noted archaeologist Glenn A. Black directed excavation of the site from 1938 until his death in 1964. At the park is an interpretive center, where artifacts are displayed and explained.

HISTORICAL

The 981-mile Ohio River goes through six states. In the early days, the river was used by those living along its shores to transport their goods, and the Ohio River was the primary way west for early settlers of the frontier. Later, with the coming of the steamboat, the Ohio River became the center of the transportation and industrial revolution. Prior to the Civil War, the river had great significance as the boundary between slave and free states. Today, the river is still used to transport coal to generating plants, but mostly it is used for recreation.

Newburgh, once a large commercial port between Cincinnati and New Orleans, is now a historic district. This quaint town overlooks the Ohio River and offers a multitude of unique shopping and dining opportunities in its downtown district.

Abraham Lincoln's family built a farmstead along Little Pigeon Creek, not far from the Ohio River. At the Lincoln Boyhood National Memorial, you can see and help with the daily chores the Lincoln family performed on the Indiana frontier. Log farm buildings are staffed during the summer months by costumed interpreters who assist those delving into history to make butter, split wood, or break flax.

Corydon was the place where the Indiana State Constitution was drafted in 1816. The Corydon Capitol State Historic Site preserves the state's first capitol building, constructed of Indiana limestone.

The Culbertson Mansion State Historic Site in New Albany preserves a 22-room French Second Empire home built in 1869. It was built by one of the merchants whose wealth was derived from this location.

The Howard Steamboat Museum in Jeffersonville is housed in the mansion of the founder of the largest inland shipyard in the United States. It depicts the fascinating history of riverboats and their construction.

Madison, a prosperous town in the 19th century, is now a venue for historic homes. The Lanier Mansion State Historic Site found in this town is a Greek Revival home designed by architect Francis Costigan, who also designed other historic homes in Madison. While in Madison, stop by the Early American Trades Museum to view demonstrations on wheel wrighting, carpentry, blacksmithing, and other trades common to the 19th century.

Vevay, originally settled in 1802 by the Swiss, transformed the area into the first commercial vineyards and winery in the United States. Also, Rising Sun holds the oldest continuously operating courthouse in Indiana. A trolley runs through the town, offering a tour of all the historic sites.

The Levi Coffin House in Fountain City was the place where over 2,000 freedom seekers found refuge. Levi Coffin, known to many as the President of the Underground Railroad, opened the doors to his Newport home to offer food, shelter, and clothing to runaway slaves on their journey to freedom.

NATURAL

As a traveler of this route, you will enjoy agricultural countryside dotted with well-kept barns, vineyards, and orchards. Vistas of rural villages dominated by church spires and historic courthouses span the Byway, and thriving cities with imposing architecture can be seen as well. Tucked away in southwestern Indiana, you can find cypress swamps, water lilies, and rare birds.

One of the natural features that is found along the Ohio River Scenic Byway is the Hovey Lake State Fish and Wildlife Area. This area is a 4,300-acre wetland. Adjoining the lake is the Twin Swamps Nature Preserve, the highest-quality cypress swamp in Indiana.

In Evansville, nature can be found even in the middle of the city at the Wesselman Woods Nature Preserve, a 200-acre stand of virgin timber. Hoosier National Forest offers 80,000 acres of forest, along with four lakes, scenic drives, river overlooks, and Ohio River access sites. You'll find plenty of opportunities for camping, fishing, hiking, swimming, horseback riding, or just enjoying the shade and scenery.

The Harrison-Crawford State Forest includes Wyandotte Woods, with its breathtaking natural escarpments overlooking the Ohio River, and Wyandotte Caves. Here, you can tour the caverns used by past settlers for chert mining.

The Needmore Buffalo Farm is home to a sizeable North American bison herd. Visitors can discover the role of the buffalo in southern Indiana and purchase buffalo meat and craft items.

RECREATIONAL

The Hoosier National Forest offers plenty of opportunities for camping, fishing, hiking, swimming, and horseback riding. The Falls of the Ohio in Clarksville (phone 812/280-9970) offers many nature hikes where you can look at fossil beds and various aquatic habitats. There are also picnic areas and a museum.

SCENIC

The beauty of the Ohio River Scenic Byway is unmatched, especially in the fall when the forests surrounding the Byway change to red and golden tones. These beautiful colors are reflected in the blue serenity of the Ohio River. You can also take a side trip

off the Byway that leads to breathtaking views and opportunities for exciting sightseeing in the national and state forests surrounding the Byway.

Also, you don't want to overlook the charm of the Indiana towns with their historic districts that stand proud with regal Victorian homes.

Highlights

Heading east to west on the Byway, consider using the following itinerary. If you're traveling in the other direction, simply read this list from the bottom and work your way up.

⊙ **Hillforest Mansion:** Begin at Hillforest Mansion in Aurora and sightsee. Travel along Highway 56 and continue on Highway 156 to Madison. This stretch is approximately 60 miles, but it's on very curvy roads and will take longer than you may expect.

⊙ **J. F. D. Lanier State Historic Site:** The J. F. D. Lanier State Historic Site is located in Madison, and Clifty Falls State Park, with its many trails (many of them rugged), is located just outside the town on Highway 56. The town of Madison also has several historic sites open to the public as well as a wonderful Main Street.

⊙ **Howard Steamboat Museum and The Falls of the Ohio State Park:** Follow Highway 56 out of Madison and head south on Highway 62, just past the town of Hanover. Highway 62 will take you into Jeffersonville, Clarksville, and New Albany. These are also known as the Falls Cities and are directly across the Ohio River from Louisville, Kentucky. The Howard Steamboat Museum and The Falls of the Ohio State Park are located here.

⊙ **Corydon Capitol State Historic Site:** Continue on Highway 62 out of New Albany to Corydon. This is where the Corydon Capitol State Historic Site is

located—Indiana's first state capitol. Other historic sites and a Civil War battle memorial are also located in Corydon. Corydon is approximately 20 miles from New Albany.

⊙ **Wyandotte Caves and Woods:** About 10 miles west of Corydon on Highway 62, you come to the Wyandotte Caves and Wyandotte Woods. A variety of cave tours are available, and Wyandotte Woods offers hiking, camping, and picnic areas. Just past the town of Leavenworth, about 8 miles from the Wyandotte area, take Highway 66. Around this area, you'll enter the Hoosier National Forest, where you will find a variety of activities.

⊙ **Lincoln Boyhood National Memorial:** Stay on Highway 66 through the Ohio River towns of Cannelton, site of the Cannelton Cotton Mill (a National Register site), Tell City, and Grandview. As a side trip, take Highway 231 north just past Grandview to Lincoln Boyhood National Memorial. This national park celebrates the life of Abraham Lincoln. He lived in a cabin at this site from the ages of 7 to 21.

⊙ **Angel Mounds Historic Site:** Back at Grandview, stay on Highway 66 to Newburgh. Angel Mounds State Historic Site is between Newburgh and Evansville.

⊙ **The Reitz Home Museum:** The Reitz Home Museum is located in the historic downtown Riverside District of Evansville. This is just a short distance from the Ohio River. Take Highway 62 west out of Evansville. It's about 25 miles to the Illinois border and the end of the Indiana portion of the Ohio River Scenic Route.

Amish Country Byway

OHIO

QUICK FACTS

Length: 76 miles.

Time to Allow: 4 to 6 hours.

Best Time to Drive: Early autumn means harvest season (which brings produce stands) and stunning fall foliage.

Byway Travel Information: Chamber of Commerce/Travel and Tourism Bureau of Holmes County: phone 330/674-3975; Byway local Web site: www.visitamishcountry.com.

Special Considerations: Please respect the privacy and religious beliefs of the Amish and don't take pictures of them. Because of the unique agriculture and culture of Amish Country, you must share the road with Amish buggies, agriculture equipment, cyclists, etc. The two-lane state routes and Highway 62 should be traveled at a somewhat slower pace than most paved roads. Keep in mind that while rest areas, public rest rooms, and some gas stations remain open on Sundays, many services are not available on that day.

Restrictions: Roads are sometimes bad in the winter because of ice or snow. Every ten years or so, spring and summer bring flooding, but rarely are the major highways closed.

Bicycle/Pedestrian Facilities: The Great Ohio Bicycle Adventure has included the Amish Country Byway on its route numerous times. Many bicycling groups meander the Byway. In most areas frequented by bicycles and buggies, the curbs or road berms have been widened enough to allow slower travelers, including buggies, to move to the side of the road and let vehicles pass by.

In this 21st century of cell phones, computers, fast cars, multiple and demanding appointments, and time commitments, there is a community within America that holds steadfast to its traditional beliefs and customs. The Amish people in Holmes County, Ohio, make up the largest concentration of Amish communities in the world, and they provide a unique look at living and adapting traditional culture. Traditional but not old-fashioned, the Amish continue to live simply, the way they always have.

When the Amish and others first settled and explored this northern Appalachian region, many depended on agriculture-based professions, and this profession continues today. The growing and harvest season in this area is particularly exciting because of the large produce auction held along the Byway. Holmes County is a strong dairy-producing region, and cheese and specialty meat products are made locally by both the Amish and non-Amish residents.

Part of this simple living is inherent in the religious tradition of the Amish people. This community is a living reminder of the principles of religious freedom that helped shape America. With a devout sense of community and adherence to beliefs, the Amish Country is a rare opportunity to witness a different way of life that will remind you that life can be simple.

The Byway Story

The Amish Country Byway tells cultural, historical, natural, recreational, and scenic stories that make it a unique and treasured Byway.

CULTURAL

One of the most important features of the Amish Country Byway is seen in the visible aspects of culture along the Byway. The Amish have established themselves in the Holmes County area, and it is estimated that one in every six Amish in the world live in this area. The Amish choose to live a simple way of life, which is clearly evident by the presence of horses and buggies, hand-made quilts, and lack of electricity in Amish homes. Entrepreneurial businesses owned by the Amish add to the friendly atmosphere along the Byway while creating a welcomed distance from the superstores of commercial America. In the 21st century, the Amish Country Byway is an important example of a multicultural community, as both the Amish and English (that is, non-Amish) traditions are strong in the region. These two cultures have built on similarities while still respecting differences. By working together, they have created a thriving, productive community that is a wonderful experience for all who visit it.

The Amish, as a branch of the Anabaptist people, are traditionally devout and religious. Like so many other immigrants, they came to America in search of religious freedom. In Europe, the Anabaptists had been persecuted for their beliefs, but today, Amish beliefs are more accepted and laws have been passed protecting their rights in regard to education, Social Security, and military service. Horses and buggies, plain dress, independence from electricity, plain window curtains, homemade quilts, spinning tops, and lots of reading materials are some of the things you might find in an Amish home—all evidence of their simple living. A community event, such as a barn raising, helps build relations among neighbors and is an efficient way to get work done.

Another important aspect of the Amish Country Byway is the influence of early Native American Indians and Appalachian folklore. The presence of both is felt along the Byway, as festivals and parades, such as the Killbuck Early American Days Festival, celebrate these early settlers. Coal fields and stone quarries drew settlers from the east, and today, this influence is manifested in the strong mining and manufacturing industries in the area.

Agriculture is the economic heart of Amish Country, and visitors to the area are likely to see rows of haystacks or fields being plowed. Holmes County boasts the second-largest dairy production in the state, the largest local produce auction during the growing season, and weekly livestock auctions in the communities along the Byway. The Swiss and German heritage of the early settlers in the county is evident in the many specialty cheese and meat products and delicious Swiss/Amish restaurants. A variety of festivals and local produce stands along the Byway allow visitors to taste a part of Amish Country. Agriculture-based weekly auctions are held at the Mount Hope, Farmerstown, and Sugarcreek sale barns, and specialty sales are held throughout the year at various times.

When the Amish settled in the area, most depended on agriculture as their profession, but others who were not farmers worked instead in blacksmith shops, harness shops, or buggy shops. In addition, many specialties sprang up, such as furniture-making. Today, shops are scattered throughout the Byway, specializing in everything from furniture to gazebos. Artists and craftsmen have made the Amish Country Byway home, and travelers can see cheese-makers, bakers, quilters, potters, and a variety of other artisans at work.

HISTORICAL

The story of the Amish Country Byway is the story of the movement and settlement of people. The Byway serves as a reminder of why people came to America and the struggles that many had in settling new and uncharted lands. Holmes County settlers came from the east, but even before that, many had come from Europe.

Today, roads forged by the early settlers in the area have been upgraded to highways, and while Amish farmers still use horses and buggies as transportation, the roads have improved their journey. The historic nature of the Byway is felt from these roads to the numerous buildings that stand on the National Historic Register.

The Amish branch of the Anabaptist faith began in Switzerland in the 16th century with the Swiss Brethren movement. The Reformation in Europe had created a new Europe in which the Catholic Church was not the only church. As a result, persecutions developed as people of different faiths conflicted with one another. To escape some of these persecutions, many Anabaptists immigrated to America and settled primarily in southeastern Pennsylvania. Because many who settled in the area were of the Swiss Brethren and Mennonite movements, there remains a strong influence of Swiss and German food and culture in the area.

In 1807, three Amish men began the uncertain and dangerous task of scouting out additional lands, yet unknown to them. Long before the Amish came to call Holmes County home, bison herds crisscrossed the state, led by instinct down the valleys and along the terminal moraine. Indians later used the trails left by the bison. Eventually, these trails became the main paths of the Amish. Today, those paths make up State Route 39, one of the main arteries of the Amish Country Byway. In the 1830s, before the railroad, Amish and English farmers would drive their fattened pigs along well-worn paths to the Ohio Erie Canal at Port Washington from Millersburg. This walk to the canal was referred to as a three-day drive. Today, along the Byway, Amish and English neighbors continue to work together, making Holmes County an important agricultural, furniture-manufacturing, and cheese-producing region of Ohio and the nation.

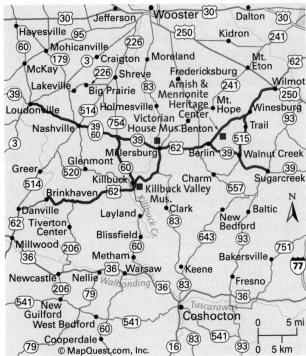

Visiting any of the places of interest along the Byway is only one way to experience the historical nature of the Byway. The majority of the historic buildings are located in Millersburg, and the entire downtown district has been designated a historical area. The entire Byway speaks of the past, and the many people living along the Byway still engage in the activities and livelihoods in which their ancestors participated.

NATURAL

The Amish Country Byway may be known primarily for its distinctive cultural and historical aspects; however, many natural features in the area make this a place where people would naturally choose to settle. The area is diverse in its natural features, and you can enjoy them from your car or by exploring various regions along the Byway. From natural passageways created by the earth forces to forests and wildlife, the area is rich in resources and natural beauty.

The Amish Country Byway is literally the product of being at the upper edge of the terminal moraine, making it the northwest gateway to Appalachia. (A terminal moraine marks the farthest point to which a glacier has advanced.) Because of this terminal moraine, natural paths developed, one of which has

become the Byway as it is known today. This activity causes arc- or crescent-shaped ridges to form, and this is what has happened along the Byway. The terminal moraine runs west to east, paralleling State Route 39 with visible formations along the road. Large rock cliffs and small, deep lakes in the northwest portion of the Amish Country Byway are the products of this geological process. Briar Hill Stone Quarry is the largest sandstone quarry in operation in the United States and is located just off the Byway near Glenmont. This quarry has provided an important natural resource, and many Amish farms and schools have been established in this area.

Another important industry along the Byway is drawn from the forests of large oak and cherry trees. Rich soil and available water tables underneath the ground have made this a rich area for timber to grow. There has been an increase in the demand for hardwood over the past few years, and the Amish Country Byway is known for its good timber. The Amish often use this timber as they make their furniture, and you can see the finished products for sale along the Byway.

The natural wonders found at the Killbuck Marsh Wildlife Area are mainly the wildlife of the wetland region. This area is home to birds and other wildlife. Most notably, the American bald eagle has roosting nests in the marsh area. Local bird-watchers, especially the Amish, have formed groups and organizations to document the birds and provide educational activities to inform others about the value of birds and wildlife as a resource in the area.

RECREATIONAL

From leisurely drives to hiking and biking, recreational opportunities exist for everyone traveling the Amish Country Byway. Every season can be enjoyed, with hiking, biking, rodeos, horseback riding, tennis, golfing, and hunting in the summer months. You can also enjoy numerous water activities, such as canoeing, swimming, fishing, and boating. Winter can be a memorable experience, with activities such as cross-country skiing and snowmobiling.

The Amish Country Byway is not one for speed demons. By slowing down, you get to experience the many recreational opportunities that are unique to this Byway. There are carriage rides, hay rides, and sleigh rides that reflect the agricultural traditions of the area, while unique activities, such as hot air balloon rides and airplane rides, may also be enjoyed. Because of the high aspects of culture and history along the Byway, one of the most popular activities is visiting Amish homesteads and farms, antique shops, and museums. In addition, you can find many places to stop and enjoy some good cooking or shopping.

More traditional recreational activities abound along the Amish Country Byway. The Holmes County Trail goes through Millersburg and links the Byway with the northern part of the county and state. This trail is open to bicycles, hikers, and buggies. The local Amish citizens who sit on the Rails to Trails board provide valuable insight into how to make this a success for the Amish, their English neighbors, and visitors. This trail travels through beautiful Amish Country and is a good way to get off of the main Byway route.

Another way to get off the main Byway route is to use the area's river and creek network. These rivers and creeks were critically important to the transportation and commerce of the past, and today, they provide a great opportunity for visitors to go canoeing, swimming, boating, or fishing. The Killbuck Creek feeds into Killbuck Marsh, which also provides excellent bird-watching opportunities. Tucked away on the western edge of the Byway, the Mohican River is the basis for making this one of the most popular recreational retreats in the state of Ohio. Canoeing is especially popular along the river—this area has been coined the Camp and Canoe Capital of Ohio.

SCENIC

The view on the Amish Country Byway is one of rolling hills; undisturbed marshland and forests; beautiful trees and landscapes; well-kept farmhouses, barns, and ponds; neat rows of agricultural crops and vegetables; brilliant displays of flowers; and bucolic scenes of Amish farmers/laborers with their families and children.

The simple living of the Amish and the gentle hospitality of the residents of Holmes County make the Amish Country Byway a scenic trip indeed. The gently rolling farmlands of the Byway give you a chance to experience the area's grand agricultural tradition. Bales of hay, freshly plowed fields, barn raisings, and locally grown produce sold at the roadside are some of the scenes that will greet you.

Red barns, buggies, and laundry hung out neatly on the line to dry are some of the unique scenes along the Byway. The Amish idea of simple living is reflected in the balance and harmony with nature. The friendly and hospitable nature of those who live along the Byway may be lacking in other big cities and thus makes this Byway unique.

Highlights

The following itinerary gives you an idea for spending a day on the eastern half of State Road 62.

○ Enjoy the peace of the early morning at the **Killbuck Marsh Area.** Fish or hike while the sun rises. Have a picnic breakfast while enjoying the birds and scenery.

○ Head north to **Millersburg.** If you're interested in historic buildings, you're in luck. Downtown Jackson, Clay, and Washington streets are a Historic District. There are plenty of National Register of

Historic Places homes to see, like the G. Adams House, the G. W. Carey House, and the Victorian House and Museum. There are also a lot of neat shops downtown, like Maxwell Brothers and the Three Feathers Pewter Studio/Gallery. Take time to look around and see what else you can discover. You can find plenty of places to eat in Millersburg, so this is a perfect place to have lunch before you head off to the Rolling Ridge Ranch.

◎ The **Rolling Ridge Ranch** is a good place for families to visit. Kids love the petting zoo and playground. You can take wagon rides and see many kinds of animals there.

◎ **Behalt-Mennonite Information Center** is an essential next stop, because you can learn about the Amish and Mennonites and why they live the way they do. See the historical mural. This is interesting, free education.

◎ Just about the time you're done at the Information Center, you'll be ready for dinner. The **Alpine Alpa Restaurant** is just up the road from the Information Center. It's famous not only for its food but also for the interesting things you can see and buy there. You can also experience a bit of Swiss culture.

CanalWay Ohio Scenic Byway

OHIO

The construction of the Ohio and Erie Canal in 1825 drastically changed the people and pace of this region. Many Byway visitors travel this route to learn about the development of the pre- and post-canal eras. The route also offers an impressive display of historical sites, along with many opportunities for hiking, biking, and water sports.

The Byway Story

The CanalWay Ohio Scenic Byway tells archaeological, cultural, historical, natural, recreational, and scenic stories that make it a unique and treasured Byway.

ARCHAEOLOGICAL

The CanalWay Ohio Scenic Byway boasts more than 500 archaeological sites; seven are listed on the National Register of Historic Places. With all possibility, many more sites exist, because a systematic, corridor-wide archaeological survey has not yet been made.

One site, Irishtown Bend, is located in Cleveland's Flats. This is where an early settlement of Irish canal workers lived. While visitors can't see very much at this site because the house foundations that have been semi-excavated have been covered up for protection, the findings at this site are significant. They show that people in this particular settlement were drinking alcohol less than those in surrounding Irish settlements, thus dispelling in part the working-class Irish myth. Artifacts from Irishtown Bend are displayed periodically.

The locations of these archaeological sites are not advertised in order to protect them from ransacking and vandalism.

CULTURAL

The influences on area culture can be classified into four elements: the resilience of farming communities, life during the canal period, the gumption of immigrants, and the accomplishments of wealthy industrialists.

Farming is still important to area culture, and the strength of past and present farmers is reflected in the sturdiness of the farms themselves: many farms from the mid-19th century are still standing and working. The village of Zoar, which was founded in 1817 by a German religious sect, the Zoarites, is still working according to many of its old agricultural practices. Burfield Farm (near Bolivar) is another durable example of early area farming and its influences.

The sway of the canal era on area culture is apparent because its flavor is still potent in the historic cities of Clinton, Canal Fulton, Boston, Everett, and Peninsula.

QUICK FACTS

Length: 110 miles.

Time to Allow: 4.5 hours.

Best Time to Drive: Spring and summer.

Byway Travel Information: Byway local Web site: www.canalwayohio.com.

Special Considerations: Be sure to allow plenty of time to savor each of the many points of interest found along the Byway.

Restrictions: Riverview Road in south Cuyahoga County is occasionally closed due to flooding. This happens only during major storms and doesn't last for very long. Fort Laurens, Towpath, and Dover Zoar roads also lie in the flood path.

Bicycle/Pedestrian Facilities: The Towpath Trail is excellent for bicycle and pedestrian travel. It runs parallel to the Byway in many places. The Towpath Trail is currently 44 miles long and will eventually be extended to 88 miles in length.

The neighborhoods that immigrants developed retain their special foreign flavor, creating small pockets of spice that add verve to the Byway. Particularly, these National Register historic neighborhoods near Cleveland are based on Archwood-Dennison Avenue, Broadway Avenue, Ohio City, and Warszawa.

The ambitions of early wealthy industrialists are represented in the homes they built. Some of the more notable are the Stan Hywet Hall (Goodyear founder Frank A. Seiberling's home) and the Anna Dean Farm (Diamond Match founder O. C. Barber's estate).

Replete with continuous high-culture events, the larger cities on the route (Cleveland, Akron, Barberton, and Strongsville) retain several historic and well-known venues. The area's local culture is manifested in locally produced festivals and entertainment.

One of Cleveland's most prominent venues is Playhouse Square Center, which recently celebrated its 75th anniversary and is the hub of the region's performing-arts scene. Akron, Barberton, and Strongsville are similarly awash in cultural activities.

HISTORICAL

People have lived in the CanalWay Ohio area for nearly 12,000 years. The area was an important transportation route for American Indians, and it was deemed neutral territory so that all might travel safely from the cold waters of the Great Lakes to warmer southern waters. European explorers and trappers arrived in the 17th century, and immigrants slowly moved in to farm over the centuries. The modern catalyst for area development was the Ohio and Erie Canal, which gave way to the area's industrial era. The CanalWay Ohio Scenic Byway takes you through places that still show evidence of the early inhabitants and the effects of industrial development.

The countryside north of Dover consists of wooded ravines and hillsides. It is separated by tilled croplands and isolated farms. This setup comes from early settlement of the Pennsylvania Germans and the Moravians. The Zoar Historic Village represents the Zoarites, the religious group that helped settle this former western frontier.

The newly constructed Indigo Lake Visitor Shelter is a stop on the old railroad. Here, visitors can fish in the adjacent lake, access the canal towpath, or walk to Hale Farm. This farm is a 19th-century farm, presented to visitors through a full program of living history.

Towns such as Dover, Bolivar, Navarre, Barberton, Canal Fulton, and Clinton show the influence of the canal with their early 19th-century architecture, original canal-oriented street patterns, locks and spillways, and towpath trails along the historic canal route. Tours on the *St. Helena II* Canal Boat in Canal Fulton give visitors firsthand experience of canal life. The Canal Visitors Center is housed in an 1852 canal tavern.

Waters from the Summit Lakes provided the cooling needed for the industrial rubber boom, which created the prosperous Akron of the 1920s. Brick factories that were four and five stories high illustrate life in industrial-era Akron. These buildings were capped by tall clock towers rimmed by rail lines, and they were surrounded by neighborhoods for industry workers.

Close to the Byway is the National Historic Landmark Stan Hywet Hall. This used to be the home of F. A. Seiberling, the founder of the Goodyear Rubber Company. Visitors will enjoy viewing the home's superb landscape (designed by Warren Manning), as well as taking tours of the house itself. These modest homes are distinct from the large Tudor Revival mansions created by the wealth of the industrial boom economy of the 1920s.

Overhead train trestles, interstate pipelines, fields of oil tanks, and aluminum and steel works tell the story of industrial might created by the marriage of Great Lakes iron ore and Appalachian coal—brought together by the Ohio and Erie Canal.

NATURAL

The CanalWay Ohio Scenic Byway is a biological crossroad because it transects three regions: lake plains, glaciated plateau, and unglaciated plateau. This results in a great diversity of plants and animals, textbook examples of forest communities and habitats.

The primary trees in the glaciated plateau region are beech-maple (the most common), oak-hickory, and hemlock-beech. Ice Age hemlock-beech forests are found in ravines, while oak-hickories are found atop ridges and in drier areas. The Tinkers Creek Gorge National Landmark has a rare settlement of hemlock-beech on the moist valley floor.

Rolling hills and steep valleys characterize the unglaciated plateau region. Oak-hickory is common in this southern part of the route. Many of these lands are public and are being preserved by public agencies.

RECREATIONAL

There is plenty to do along the CanalWay Ohio Scenic Byway. Towpath Trail is extremely popular; over 3 million users enjoy the trail in a typical year. Other recreation includes skiing, golfing, picnicking, hiking, fishing, and boating, and water excursions are available along the Cuyahoga and Tuscawaras rivers as well. Also, the route passes through several entertainment districts.

SCENIC

The scenery found along the CanalWay Ohio Scenic Byway is interestingly diverse. It ranges from the heavy industry of the Cleveland Flats (and the resulting immigrant neighborhoods) to rolling hills and farmland. You can also see the remnants of the towns and villages associated with the canal, as well as samples of 200-year-old architecture. You will find hundreds of varied vistas along the route.

Highlights

This itinerary takes you through Cuyahoga Valley National Park and into Akron. Although it does not cover the entire distance of the Byway, it gives you a taste of how you can drive a portion of this road.

○ Start with a dawn picnic breakfast at the **Cuyahoga Valley National Park (CVNP).** The CVNP is on the Byway, and its entrance is about 8 miles south of Cleveland. In this gorgeous 33,000-acre region, you can do just about anything outdoorsy (hiking, golfing, bicycling, horseback riding, and so on). Admittance is free. After breakfast, go biking along the Towpath Trail, which runs through the park for about 44 miles. Take an hour or two to enjoy a bike ride along any part of the trail.

○ For another two (or three) hours before lunch, stop at **Hale Farm,** which is at the southern end of the CVNP. There is an admittance fee for this living-history farm, where you can wander the grounds and talk to the artisans who make the impressive wares for sale there. The buildings and history here are fascinating. Eat lunch and head south to Akron.

○ Akron is a buzzing city with much to do. One possibility is to stop at the **Akron Art Museum.**

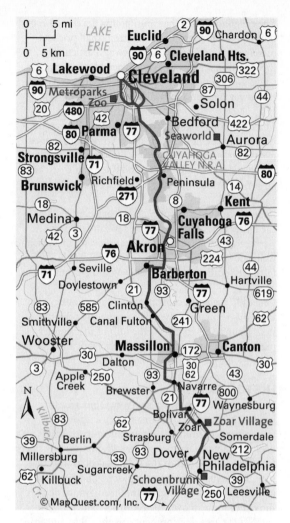

Admission and parking here are free for visitors, and the museum always has engaging exhibits.

○ After your visit at the museum, go to the **Cascade Locks Park** (also in Akron). Admittance is free here as well. This park has 15 canal locks in a 1-mile stretch (all necessary to climb over the Continental Divide), and you can follow them along on a trail; signs along the trail explain the locks and the history of the canal. There are also two historic buildings to visit in this park.

○ Have dinner in Akron and round off your evening with a concert or a play at one of the many famous and popular performing arenas and halls. Check local event calendars for details.

The Historic National Road

OHIO   An All-American Road

Part of a multistate Byway; see also IL, IN.

The story of the Ohio Historic National Road is the story of our nation's aspirations and desires. The National Road literally paved the way west through the newly formed states of Ohio, Indiana, and Illinois and provided a direct connection to the mercantile and political centers of the East Coast, helping to secure the influence and viability of these new settlements. As much as the road's boom times during the early and mid-19th century signified its importance to national commerce and expansion, its decline during the late 19th and early 20th centuries reveal the meteoric rise of the railroad as the primary means of transport and trade across the nation. Likewise, the renaissance of the National Road in the mid-20th century reflects the growing popularity of the automobile.

QUICK FACTS

Length: 228 miles.

Time to Allow: 4 days.

Best Time to Drive: Summer and fall, depending on which end (east or west) you will be spending most of your time. Summer is high season for festivals in Ohio. On the western section of the Byway, you find more agriculture, so summer and late summer have the most picturesque fields. The eastern section of the Byway offers hills and fall colors.

Byway Travel Information: Ohio Historic Preservation Office: phone 614/298-2000.

Special Considerations: Excessive and heavy snow or rain falls occasionally in this part of the country. It may impair drivability but does not result in long-lived road closures.

Bicycle/Pedestrian Facilities: In rural areas, on-road bicycling is feasible because of relatively low traffic volumes and generally wide shoulders. Similarly, small towns accommodate both pedestrians and bicyclists because of low traffic volumes, slow traffic speeds, and sidewalks. The large urban areas along the Byway all provide pedestrian sidewalks, and some have dedicated bicycle lanes.

Today, the Byway is a scenic journey across Ohio. The steep, wooded hills and valleys of the eastern edge of the Byway give way to the gently rolling farmland of the western part of the Byway. Picturesque farms, hiking trails, craft industries, and historic sites and museums await you along this portion of the Historic National Road.

The Byway Story

The National Historic Road tells archaeological, cultural, historical, natural, recreational, and scenic stories that make it a unique and treasured Byway.

ARCHAEOLOGICAL

Prehistoric civilizations once dominated the land surrounding what is now known as the Historic National Road in Ohio, and today, remnants of these early people can be found just off of the Byway. One important aspect for these early cultures was making tools and weapons. They found flint for these tools at what is known today as Flint Ridge State Memorial. The Hopewell Culture frequented Flint Ridge because of the quality and beauty of the flint found there. This flint would have been a very important resource to that culture, the way that coal and iron ore are in Ohio today. Flint from Ohio has been found from the Atlantic seaboard to Louisiana. Flint was so important, in fact, that it has become the state gem of Ohio.

Located near Newark, the Moundbuilders State Memorial and Ohio Indian Art Museum tell about the Hopewell Indian civilization, which is most remembered for the large earthworks that were constructed there. Exhibits show the artistic achievements of these prehistoric cultures that lived in the area from around 10,000 BC to AD 1600. The Octagon Earthworks and Wright Earthworks are also located near Newark.

CULTURAL

The Historic National Road in Ohio hosts a rich tradition of culture. Museums, festivals, and other cultural facilities offer a chance to both explore more of the National Road's history and seek diversions from it. Outstanding performing arts venues are well represented along the Byway. In addition to these cultural features, the eastern section of the Byway is known for its selection of traditional and modern crafts.

HISTORICAL

The history of the Historic National Road in Ohio highlights the importance of this road in terms of development and settlement that it brought to the Ohio area. The history of the construction of the National Road is significant because it serves as an example of larger events that were transpiring in America simultaneously. Early pioneer settlement gave way to railroads, and finally the automobile became the most frequent traveler along the National Road.

NATURAL

While traveling the Historic National Road in Ohio, you are treated to a diverse Byway that traverses steep wooded hills and valleys in the east and gently rolling farmland in the west. This diversity of natural features offers refreshing and contrasting views along the Byway. The changing landscape determined how the National Road was constructed, as well as the types of livelihoods settlers engaged in throughout the history of the road.

RECREATIONAL

A tremendous network of large state parks, regional metropolitan parks, local parks, and privately run facilities provide a bountiful array of outdoor recreational facilities that give you a chance to enjoy the area's natural beauty. For the most part, the state parks are located on the eastern half of the Byway, and over 50,000 acres of state parks, forests, and wildlife areas are easily accessible from the Ohio Historic National Road. Along portions of the Byway, you can hike, camp, fish, hunt, and picnic while relishing the various species of local flora and fauna.

SCENIC

The Historic National Road in Ohio is full of variation and diversity. Changing topography and landscapes provide scenic views for travelers of the Byway, from hilly ridges to long, unbroken views of the horizon. Small towns, unique and historic architecture, and stone bridges all provide scenes from the past along the Byway. Farms, unspoiled scenery, and large urban landscapes give you a sense of the great diversity of this Byway.

Ohio River Scenic Byway

OHIO

Part of a multistate Byway; see also IL, IN.

QUICK FACTS

Length: 452 miles.

Time to Allow: 2 days.

Best Time to Drive: Spring and summer

Byway Travel Information: Ohio River Trails, Inc.: phone 513/553-1500.

Special Considerations: Storms seldom force road closings on rural state and federal highways like those utilized by the Ohio River Scenic Byway. However, delays are possible in heavily traveled areas around towns and cities during such storms. Also, although flooding along the Ohio River is a rare event, it is most likely to occur between November and April, and the Byway route could be affected due to its proximity to the river. In addition, short sections along the route may experience annual or bi-annual flooding, including the portion of Highway 52 east of Cincinnati known as Eastern Avenue. The Ohio Department of Transportation works with county managers to mitigate the effects of floods and other events that force road closings by temporarily redirecting traffic to alternate routes. Snowstorms are possible, particularly from mid-December through mid-March, and can cause road closures.

Bicycle/Pedestrian Facilities: The Ohio Department of Transportation keeps the Byway in excellent condition. Where the Byway passes through towns and cities, sidewalks accommodate pedestrian use. Some towns, such as Marietta, have made provisions for bicyclists as well. In addition, a portion of the American Discovery Trails System, which runs from California to Maryland, parallels the Ohio River Scenic Byway in western Hamilton County.

This Byway passes through 14 counties and encompasses the birthplaces of three US presidents. The Byway also includes the grand and historic Highway 52, known as the Atlantic and Pacific Highway and the US Grant Memorial Highway.

This scenic route follows the Ohio River, so you can enjoy majestic river views for the entire drive. The Ohio River is a historical American icon. Native Americans and early European settlers used it heavily, especially to access the West. It marked the boundary between the North and South during the slavery era and was later the gateway to freedom for many slaves. The river was also the means of progress for industrialists and merchants.

The Byway Story

The Ohio River Scenic Byway tells archaeological, cultural, historical, natural, recreational, and scenic stories that make it a unique and treasured Byway.

ARCHAEOLOGICAL

Several archaeological sites and museums are found along the Ohio River Scenic Byway. These include several Native American cultural sites in Tiltonsville, as well as the Mound Cemetery Chester.

The town of Portsmouth, which hosts the Southern Ohio Museum and Cultural Center, is where many travelers learn about the history of this area. There are also Native American cultural sites near here.

CULTURAL

The Ohio River has been a center of human activity for centuries and, therefore, is a cultural hotbed. Academic and historical organizations recognize this fact and have made the river and the immediate area (the Byway's territory) the focus of their cultural studies. One such organization is the University of Kentucky's Ohio River Valley Series. This intercollegiate project specifically studies how the state's history (which is inextricable from culture) has been affected by the social use of the Ohio River.

Numerous grassroots organizations also investigate the river's role in the development of their towns and cities. One such group is the Ohio Historical Society's Ohio River Museum, which specifically examines how artifacts and technological improvements associated with the river affected area culture. Another of these organizations is Ohio River Trails, Inc., which focuses on the shoreline and scenic route in relation to area culture.

HISTORICAL

The Ohio River is most significant for its historical importance to the region. Described both as a river of beauty (the Iroquois named the river Oyo, which the French interpreted as *la belle riviere*) and a river of opportunity, the Ohio River symbolized a new future. Its history is a powerful reflection of the American experience; one of the valleys surrounding it was even called the Valley of Democracy.

The region's rich history includes the migration of people along the river into the four states that border it (Kentucky, Ohio, Indiana, and Illinois), as well as the three states that are located within the river's basin (Tennessee, Mississippi, and Alabama). The industry and technology of the area were important to the Ohio River as well. They changed the river's influence on the region through the development of steamboat travel and shipping, the creation of locks and dams to control navigation and flooding, the establishment of industries such as steel and coal plants and their associated landing docks, and the development of large chemical and electrical power generating facilities.

NATURAL

This Byway contains many natural features that surround both the Ohio River and the forests along the Byway. Many native animals and plants add to the scenic quality of the Byway. Natural sites along the Byway include Fernwood State Forest, located near the Mingo Junction on State Route 151; the Quaker

Meeting House, located near Mount Pleasant on State Route 647; and Barkcamp State Park. This park has historical significance and is located by a lake just off the Byway turning from Bellaire on State Route 149 (65330 Barkcamp Park Road, Belmont, phone 614/484-4064). Campsites are available.

Other natural sites include Sunfish Creek State Forest, located past Powhatan Point on State Route 7, and Wayne National Forest, located right along the Byway, starting past the city of Hannibal covering the area to Marietta. Two rustic covered bridges are located in this forest.

Travelers also enjoy visiting Shade River State Forest and Forked Run State Park, both of which are located right next to each other just past the city of Belpre. There is camping available at Forked Run State Park. Also, the Wayne National Forest begins again near the town of Gallipolis and ends near Hanging Rock along the Byway. Camping is available at the Vesuvius Recreation Area in the forest.

Finally, the Shawnee State Forest is located along the Byway past Portsmouth. Camping is available in the nearby Shawnee State Park to the west of the forest.

RECREATIONAL

Several state forests and parks along this Byway offer opportunities for outdoor recreation and camping. Camping is available at the Barkcamp State Park, in the Forked Run State Park near Belpre, and in the Shawnee State Park near Portsmouth. The Wayne National Forest begins near the town of Gallipolis and ends near Hanging Rock along the Byway. You can camp at the Vesuvius Recreation Area in the forest as well.

SCENIC

This scenic Byway leads travelers through the colorful tapestry surrounding the Ohio River and also through many national and state parks. During the fall, the golden leaves of the forests reflect in the shining waters of the Ohio River, giving travelers a sense of serenity as they drive the Byway. Families coming in the summer feel the energy of nature's fresh, green growth as their children play along the banks of the Ohio.

Highlights

Starting from Cincinnati, you can travel alongside the Ohio River without flood walls obstructing your view. Here, you see a more pastoral life of the Ohio, with no industry or other large buildings to interrupt the flow of fields, nature, and water.

⊙ **North Bend:** Your first stop is at the nation's great monument, the **Harrison Tomb,** located off Cliff Road, west of Highway 50, North Bend. The 60-foot marble obelisk in this 14-acre park pays tribute to William Henry Harrison, the ninth US president.

⊙ **Cincinnati:** Continue to Cincinnati and visit the historic **Harriet Beecher Stowe House.** It was here that Stowe learned of the injustices of slavery and wrote her famous novel, *Uncle Tom's Cabin.*

⊙ **Point Pleasant:** On the way to New Richmond, the scenery changes from the cityscape of Cincinnati to lush green forests, blue skies, and a rolling river. You are going on to Point Pleasant, the birthplace of the 18th US president, Ulysses S. Grant (Highway 52 and State Route 232): a one-story, three-room cottage.

⊙ **Georgetown:** Follow Grant's life back on Highway 52, heading north, taking State Route 231 to historic Georgetown, where you can visit **Grant's boyhood home** on 219 East Grant Avenue. From Georgetown, head south again on State Route 68 to State Route 62, back to the Byway (Highway 52).

⊙ **Ripley:** Stop in the town of Ripley and visit the **Ripley Museum** (219 N Second Street; call 513/392-4660 for group tours) and **Rankin House** (Rankin St, off State Route 52; call 513/392-1627 for group tours). Abolitionists John and Jean Rankin hid some 2,000 escaped slaves in this way

station on the Underground Railroad. Harriet Beecher Stowe stopped here to speak with Rankin about the problems of slavery before writing her novel; she used some of the stories she heard in her book. The **Parker home,** also in Ripley, was another home involved in the Underground Railroad; Parker was himself a former slave, inventor, and businessman. His home, located on 330 N Front Street (phone 937/392-4004), is in the process of being restored.

⊙ **Portsmouth:** Continue on Highway 52 to the town of Portsmouth, where you'll see artistic flood-wall murals that beautify the Byway and protect the city from the rising waters of the Ohio River.

⊙ **Gallipolis:** Continue to the **French Art Colony** of Gallipolis. Here, you can learn about the rich history of the local area and state. While traveling through, note the French-style homes along the riverbanks.

⊙ **Pomeroy:** Traveling farther east along the Byway, you come upon the city of Pomeroy, which has been featured on *Ripley's Believe It or Not* for its unusual **courthouse,** which is built into the side of a cliff and is accessible on all three levels from the outside.

⊙ **Marietta:** Continue on the Byway to Marietta, the place where Ohio began, the first city founded in the Northwest Territory. The early days of Marietta are remembered at the **Campus Martius Museum,** which offers displays of riverboats and other antiquities. You can also stop at the **Ohio River Museum** next to the Martius Museum. Be sure to tour the historic town itself—beautiful old buildings and antiques are waiting to be discovered.

○ **Steubenville:** Heading north up the river, you run into the town of Steubenville, where you witness the **Old Fort Steuben** reconstruction (100 S Third Street, phone 614/264-6304). This fort was under the command of Captain John Francis Hamtramck for the protection of the surveyors of the Northwest Territory. Demonstrations, land office tours, and food are available here. In downtown Steubenville, you'll see murals depicting the 1850s and 1920s city life of the town. The murals are painted on the sides of many of the great buildings in the area. While here, explore the historic bed-and-breakfasts and unusual paddleboat restaurant dedicated to river living. Also, in late August, check out the Steubenville Marina off State Route 7, for the Steubenville Regatta and Racing Association's Rumble on the River. Call ahead to check for times at the Steubenville Convention & Visitors Bureau, phone toll-free 800/510-4442.

○ **Wellsville:** Continuing on State Route 7, you come to Wellsville and the **Wellsville River Museum,** a three-story building constructed in 1870. Period furniture and paddlewheel displays are featured in the various rooms.

○ **East Liverpool:** Continue on the Byway to the **Museum of Ceramics** in the town of East Liverpool. The town has been called Crockery City and is known for its artistic place settings. The city's ceramics museum operates out of the former post office. From here, you can continue following the Byway into Pennsylvania if you wish.

Illinois

Illinois extends from Chicago, on the shores of Lake Michigan, to the vast woodlands of the Shawnee National Forest. It is a major transportation center, and its resources include wheat, corn, soybeans, livestock, minerals, coal, oil, and an immense diversity of manufactured goods. The growth of this industrial-agricultural giant has been remarkable. In less than two centuries, it has evolved from a frontier to a vast empire of cities, farms, mines, and mills. The state is home to nearly 1 million factory workers; more than 90 percent of the land is cultivated, producing more than 40 different crops with an annual value of $4.2 billion. Livestock value averages more than $1 billion annually.

Population: 12,419,293
Area: 57,918 square miles
Elevation: 279-1,235 feet
Peak: Charles Mound (Jo Daviess County)
Entered Union: December 3, 1818 (21st state)
Capital: Springfield
Motto: State Sovereignty, National Union
Nickname: Land of Lincoln
Flower: Violet
Bird: Cardinal
Tree: White Oak
Fair: Mid-August in Springfield
Time Zone: Central
Web site: www.enjoyillinois.com

The state takes its name from the confederated tribes who called themselves the Iliniwek ("superior men") and inhabited the valley of the Illinois River. In 1673, the first known white men entered the land of the Iliniwek. Pére Jacques Marquette and Louis Jolliet paddled down the Mississippi, returned up the Illinois, and carried their canoes across the portage where Chicago now stands. Five years later, Robert Cavelier Sieur de La Salle established Fort Crévecoeur, near Peoria Lake. French interest then shifted to the area around Cahokia and Kaskaskia. Fort de Chartres was built in 1720, and trappers and traders soon followed. The district was designated Illinois, the first official use of the name.

French rule ended when the British seized Fort de Chartres in 1765, but the British stayed in Illinois only briefly. The region was important to the American cause and was won by George Rogers Clark in 1778-1779. For a while, Illinois was claimed as a county by Virginia, but it was ceded to the federal government; in 1787, it became part of the Northwest Territory. This territory was variously subdivided; Illinois, first part of Indiana Territory, became Illinois Territory in 1809, with Ninian Edwards as its first governor. Nine years later, it was admitted into the Union as the 21st state.

Through the early years of the 19th century, the Sauk (or Sac) and Fox tribes struggled to retain their lands. They were moved across the Mississippi by a treaty that touched off the Black Hawk War of 1832. The defeat of the Sauk and Fox, and a later treaty forcing the Potawatomie to cede their lands, virtually removed Native Americans from the state. Settlers then surged into the fertile country.

A young backwoods lawyer named Abraham Lincoln returned from the Black Hawk War and entered politics. As leader of the Sangamon County delegation in the state legislature, he successfully moved the capital from Vandalia to Springfield. Lincoln supported projects for waterway improvements, which resulted in canals and interstate railroads. The new transportation

Calendar Highlights

FEBRUARY

Chicago Auto Show (*Chicago*). *McCormick Place. Phone 312/744-3370.* Hundreds of foreign and domestic cars are displayed.

MARCH

St. Patrick's Day Parade (*Chicago*). *Phone 312/744-3370.* The Chicago River is dyed green in honor of the Irish saint. The city parade takes place on the Saturday before the holiday; the South Side parade occurs on the Sunday before the holiday.

JUNE

Swedish Days (*Geneva*). *Phone 630/232-6060.* Six-day festival with parade, entertainment, arts and crafts, music, and food. Also includes the state's largest music competition and Swedish rosemaling (painting).

JULY

Bagelfest (*Mattoon*). *Phone 217/235-5661.* The world's biggest bagel breakfast. Bagelfest Queen Pageant, Beautiful Bagel Baby Contest. Parade, talent show, and music.

Illinois Shakespeare Festival (*Bloomington*). *Ewing Manor. Phone 309/438-2535.* Shakespearean performances preceded by Elizabethan-era music and entertainment.

Taste of Chicago (*Chicago*). *Grant Park. Phone 312/774-6630. egov.cityofchicago.org.* Showcase of Chicago's diverse culinary scene. Selected Chicago restaurants offer sample-size specialties. Also concerts by well-known musical acts.

Western Open Golf Tournament (*Lockport*). *Cog Hill Golf Course. Phone 630/257-5872.* A major tournament on the PGA Tour.

AUGUST

Illinois State Fair (*Springfield*). *Illinois State Fairgrounds. Phone 217/782-6661.* Baking contests, livestock competitions, agricultural displays, food, and entertainment.

OCTOBER

Scarecrow Festival (*St. Charles*). *Lincoln Park. Phone 630/377-6161 or toll-free 800/777-4373. www.scarecrowfest.com.* Display of up to 100 scarecrows; entertainment, food, and crafts.

Spoon River Scenic Drive (*Havana and Peoria*). *Phone 309/547-3234.* A 140-mile autumn drive through small towns and rolling, wooded countryside noted for fall color; 19th- and early-20th-century crafts, exhibits, and demonstrations; antiques, collectibles; produce, food.

---

system helped build commercial centers and contributed to the state's eventual industrialization. The Civil War sparked broad industrialization and rapid growth that, together with vast agricultural riches, have carried the state through many economic crises.

Illinois stretches 385 miles from north to south. As a vacation area, it offers lakes and rivers with excellent fishing, beautiful parks and recreation areas, historical and archaeological sites, landmark buildings, prairie lands, and canyons. The attractions in

Chicago and the surrounding area are endless, as are the hundreds of festivals and events sponsored by cities and towns year-round throughout the state.

When to Go/Climate

Illinois weather can be unpredictable. Winters can bring heavy snows; summers are often hot, hazy, and humid. Summer thunderstorms are frequent and magnificent. Tornadoes have been recorded from spring through fall.

AVERAGE HIGH/LOW TEMPERATURES (° F)

Chicago

Jan 29/13	**May** 70/48	**Sept** 75/54
Feb 34/17	**June** 80/58	**Oct** 63/42
Mar 46/29	**July** 84/63	**Nov** 48/32
Apr 59/39	**Aug** 82/62	**Dec** 34/19

Springfield

Jan 33/16	**May** 75/52	**Sept** 79/56
Feb 37/20	**June** 84/62	**Oct** 67/44
Mar 50/32	**July** 87/66	**Nov** 52/34
Apr 64/43	**Aug** 84/63	**Dec** 37/22

Parks and Recreation

Water-related activities, hiking, riding, various other sports, picnicking, and visitor centers are available in many of Illinois's parks and recreational areas. Camping is permitted in more than 60 areas ($8-$15 per site per night) only by permit from the park ranger, obtainable for overnight or a maximum of 14 nights. Pets on leash only. State parks are open daily, weather permitting, except January 1 and December 25. For full information about state parks, tent camping, and other facilities, contact the Department of Natural Resources, Division of Land Management & Education, 600 N Grand Ave W, Springfield 62706, phone 217/782-6752.

FISHING AND HUNTING

Lakes, streams, and rivers provide fishing to suit every freshwater angler. The Illinois shoreline of Lake Michigan is 63 miles long. A nonresident season fishing license costs $26.50; a ten-day license costs $15; a 24-hour fishing license costs $7.50; and a resident season license costs $15. Licenses and further information may be obtained from the Department of Natural Resources, License Section, 524 S 2nd St, Springfield 62701-1787, phone 217/782-7305, or from department vendors throughout the state.

Many areas of the state provide good hunting, with Canadian geese, ducks, quail, rabbits, and squirrels plentiful. Deer and turkey hunting is by permit only. A nonresident season hunting license costs $55.75, and a five-day license costs $32.75. Additional stamps are required for waterfowl ($12.50) and habitat game ($7.50).

The Department of Natural Resources maintains shooting areas at numerous places throughout the state. For more information concerning fishing and hunting in Illinois, contact the Department of Natural Resources, 524 S 2nd St, Springfield 62701-1789, phone 217/782-6302. Licenses may be obtained from department vendors throughout the state.

Driving Information

Safety belts are mandatory for all persons in the front seat of a vehicle. Children under 7 years anywhere in a vehicle must be in approved passenger restraints; children age 4 and under must use approved child safety seats.

INTERSTATE HIGHWAY SYSTEM

The following alphabetical listing of Illinois towns shows that these cities are within 10 miles of the indicated interstate highways. Check a highway map for the nearest exit.

Highway Number	Cities/Towns within 10 Miles
Interstate 39	Peru, Rockford.
Interstate 55	Bloomington, Brookfield, Chicago, Cicero, Collinsville, Downers Grove, Edwardsville, Hinsdale, Joliet, La Grange, Lincoln, Lockport, Naperville, Oak Lawn, Springfield.
Interstate 57	Arcola, Benton, Cairo, Champaign/Urbana, Charleston, Chicago, Effingham, Homewood, Kankakee, Marion, Mattoon, Mount Vernon, Oak Lawn, Salem.
Interstate 64	Belleville, Collinsville, Edwardsville, Effingham, Greenville, Marshall, Vandalia.
Interstate 70	Altamont, Collinsville, Edwardsville, Effingham, Greenville, Marshall, Vandalia.
Interstate 72	Champaign/Urbana, Decatur, Springfield.
Interstate 74	Bloomington, Champaign/Urbana, Danville, Galesburg, Moline, Perioa.
Interstate 80	Chicago, Homewood, Joliet, Lockport, Moline, Morris, Ottawa, Peru, Rock Island.

Interstate 88 (E-W tollway)	Aurora, Brookfield, Chicago, Chicago O'Hare Airport Area, Cicero, De Kalb, Dixon, Downers Grove, Elmhurst, Geneva, Glen Ellyn, Hillside, Hinsdale, Itasca, La Grange, Moline, Naperville, Oak Brook, Oak Park, St. Charles, Wheaton.
Interstate 90	Arlington Heights, Chicago, Chicago O'Hare Airport Area, Cicero, Elgin, Elmhurst, Hillside, Itasca, Oak Park, Rockford, Schaumburg, Union.
Interstate 94	Chicago, Chicago O'Hare Airport Area, Evanston, Glenview, Grayslake, Gurnee, Highland Park, Highwood, Libertyville, Northbrook, Skokie, Waukegan, Wheeling, Wilmette.
Interstate 290	Arlington Heights, Chicago, Chicago O'Hare Airport Area, Cicero, Elmhurst, Glen Ellyn, Hillside, Itasca, Libertyville, Northbrook, Oak Brook, Oak Park, Schaumburg.
Interstate 294	Arlington Heights, Chicago, Chicago O'Hare Airport Area, Cicero, Elmhurst, Evanston, Glen Ellyn, Glenview, Highland Park, Highwood, Hillside, Itasca, Libertyville, Northbrook, Oak Brook, Oak Park, Skokie, Wheeling, Wilmette.
Interstate 355 (N-S tollway)	Chicago O'Hare Airport Area, Downers Grove, Elmhurst, Glen Ellyn, Hillside, Hinsdale, Itasca, La Grange, Lockport, Naperville, Oak Brook, Schaumburg, Wheaton.

Additional Visitor Information

For specific information about Illinois attractions, activities, and travel counseling, contact the Illinois Bureau of Tourism, phone toll-free 800/226-6632 or 800/406-6418 (TTY).

Illinois tourist information centers (April-October) can be found in the following locations: off I-80 (eastbound) near Rapid City; off I-57 near Monee; off I-24 (westbound) near Metropolis; off I-57 near Whittington; off I-57 (northbound) near Anna; off I-64 (eastbound) near New Baden; off I-70 (eastbound) near Highland; off I-70 (westbound) near Marshall; off I-74 (westbound) near Oakwood; off I-80 (eastbound) near South Holland; and off I-90 (southbound) near South Beloit.

THE GREAT RIVER ROAD

Illinois has over 500 miles of distinctive state, county, and US highways comprising its Great River Road, which runs along the Mississippi River from East Dubuque to Cairo. One of the most scenic drives in Illinois, the Great River Road entices travelers with a glimpse into laid-back life along Old Man River. Natural beauty alternates with river history; something is always on the offer. The route is meandering to say the least; it winds back and forth over the river, changes direction frequently, and wanders in and out of towns long-since forgotten. That being said, this is the perfect trip for those looking to get lost for a little while. However, you don't have to worry about getting too lost. The portion of the route that runs through Illinois (the Great River Road also runs through nine other states) is particularly well marked. Keep your eyes peeled for the green-and-white signs with a steamboat design in the middle, and you're sure to stay on the right road. You also can contact the Mississippi Parkway Commission (Pioneer Building, Suite 1513, 336 North Robert Street, St. Paul, MN 56101) for a detailed map (a $1 donation is requested).

From Rockford, take Highway 20 to Route 84, the starting point for this tour. If you're looking for a little action, East Dubuque has paddleboat gambling. Otherwise, head first to Galena, one of Illinois's most treasured historic towns. When it comes to tourist attractions, Galena has much to satisfy a range of interests. Spend some time exploring the many mansions and buildings listed on the National Historic Register, poke through tiny antique stores, or take a guided walking tour. If these options don't inspire you, try a tour and wine tasting at the Galena Cellars Winery, a river cruise, or a visit to the Galena-Jo Daviess County History Museum (see). Farther south on our route along the Big Muddy is the historic Mormon town of Nauvoo. Architecture is the big draw here; you'll find 25 historic sites (circa 1840) to explore. Heading south once again, you eventually will come upon the town of Grafton, home to Père Marquette (see), Illinois's largest state park. Grafton is also where you'll find some of the prettiest stretches of the Great River Road. If you are traveling during the winter, you'll want to stop next in nearby Alton to do some eagle-watching. About 200 to 400 bald eagles winter in this area every year. The Cahokia Native American village reconstruction (a World Heritage Site) near Collinsville is also worth a stop. South of Carbondale, the cool woods of Shawnee National Forest provide a welcome respite from the dead heat of an Illinois summer. Acres of hiking trails are available if you're interested in stretching your legs a bit. When you are ready to return to Rockford, keep in mind that sticking to main interstates and highways (rather than returning via the Great River Road) will allow for a much speedier trip. **(Approximately 500 miles)**

Altamont (D-4)

See also Effingham, Vandalia

Population 2,283
Elevation 619 ft
Area Code 618
Zip 62411
Information Chamber of Commerce, PO Box 141; phone 618/483-5714

Limited-Service Hotel

★ **SUPER 8.** *RR2, Box 296, Altamont (62411). Phone 618/483-6300; toll-free 800/800-8000; fax 618/483-3323. www.super8.com.* 25 rooms, 2 story. Pets accepted; fee. Check-out 11 am. **$**

Alton (D-3)

See also Cahokia, Collinsville, Edwardsville, Père Marquette State Park

Population 30,496
Elevation 500 ft
Area Code 618
Zip 62002
Information Greater Alton/Twin Rivers Convention & Visitors Bureau, 200 Piasa St; phone 618/465-6676 or toll-free 800/258-6645
Web site www.altoncvb.org

Alton is located on the bluffs just above the confluence of the Mississippi and Missouri rivers. It has three historic districts, four square blocks of antique stores, and many opulent houses, the former residences of steamboat captains, industrialists, and railroad barons. Here, in 1837, Elijah Lovejoy, the abolitionist editor, died protecting his press from a proslavery mob. In the Alton Cemetery, there is a 93-foot monument to Lovejoy. A sandbar in the river was the scene of the projected Lincoln-Shields duel of 1842, which was settled without bloodshed. The final Lincoln-Douglas debate was held in Alton on October 15, 1858. Alton was the home of Robert Wadlow, the tallest man in history; a life-size 9-foot statue of Wadlow is on College Avenue.

What to See and Do

Alton Belle Riverboat Casino. *1 Front St. On the waterfront. Phone toll-free 800/711-4863.* Entertainment complex includes slots, showrooms, lounges, and restaurants. (Daily)

Alton Museum of History and Art. *2809 College Ave. Phone 618/462-2763.* Displays on local history and culture, including an exhibit on Alton's Robert Wadlow, the world's tallest man. **$**

Brussels Ferry. *20 miles W on Great River Rd (Hwy 100), near Grafton. Phone 618/786-3636.* Ferry boat navigates the Illinois River at the confluence of the Mississippi River. (Daily) **FREE**

Confederate Soldiers' Cemetery. *Rozier St. W of State St. Phone toll-free 800/258-6645.* Monument lists names of soldiers who died in Illinois's first state prison, which was a prisoner-of-war camp during the Civil War.

Père Marquette State Park. *Approximately 23 miles W on Hwy 100. Phone 618/786-3323.* (see)

Piasa Bird Painting Reproduction. *On bluffs NW of town, best seen from the river and Hwy 100. Phone toll-free 800/258-6645.* According to Native American legend, a monster bird frequented these bluffs and preyed on all who came near. When Marquette sailed down the Mississippi in 1673, he saw "high rocks with hideous monsters painted on them" at this spot. The paintings, destroyed by quarrying in the 19th century, were reproduced in 1934. These reproductions in turn were destroyed by the construction of Great River Road. They were reproduced a second time on a bluff farther up the river.

Village of Elsah. *Great River Rd, Elsah. 11 miles W on Great River Rd (Hwy 100). Phone 618/374-1059.* Many buildings are more than 100 years old. Museum (Apr-Nov, Thurs-Sun afternoons). **FREE**

Limited-Service Hotel

★ ★ **HOLIDAY INN.** *3800 Homer Adams Pkwy, Alton (62002). Phone 618/462-1220; toll-free 800/465-4329; fax 618/462-0906.*

www.holiday-inn.com. 137 rooms, 4 story. Complimentary continental breakfast. Check-out noon. Restaurant, bar. Fitness room. Indoor pool, whirlpool. Airport transportation available. **$**

Antioch

See also Gurnee, Waukegan

Settled 1836
Population 8,788
Elevation 772 ft
Area Code 847
Zip 60002
Information Chamber of Commerce, 884 Main St; phone 847/395-2233
Web site www.lake-online.com/antioch

What to See and Do

Chain O'Lakes Area. Year-round recreational facilities; includes boating, fishing, ice fishing, cross-country skiing, and snowmobiling.

Hiram Butrick Sawmill. *790 Cunningham Dr. At Gage Brothers Park on Sequoit Creek. Phone 847/395-2160.* Replica of water-powered sawmill (1839) around which the community grew. Tours (by appointment). **FREE**

Wilmot Mountain. *Wilmot, WI (53192). 3 miles N on Rte 83, then W on WI County C; 1 mile S of Wilmot, WI, near the IL state line.* Quad, three triple, four double chairlifts, three rope tows; patrol, school, rentals, snowmaking; restaurant, cafeteria, bar. Snowboarding. Longest run 2,500 feet; vertical drop 230 feet. Night skiing. (Mid-Nov-Mar, daily; closed Dec 24 evening)

Limited-Service Hotel

★ **BEST WESTERN REGENCY INN.** *350 Hwy 173, Antioch (60002). Phone 847/395-3606; toll-free 800/780-7234. www.bestwestern.com.* 68 rooms, 3 story. Pets accepted, some restrictions; fee. Complimentary continental breakfast. Check-in 3 pm, check-out 11 am. Bar. Indoor pool, whirlpool. **$**

Arcola

See also Champaign/Urbana, Charleston, Decatur, Mattoon

Population 2,652
Elevation 678 ft
Area Code 217
Zip 61910
Information Chamber of Commerce, 135 N Oak, PO Box 274; phone 217/268-4530 or toll-free 800/336-5456
Web site www.arcola-il.org

Arcola is located in Illinois's Amish Country, where it is not unusual to see horse-drawn carriages traveling the highways.

What to See and Do

Illinois Amish Interpretive Center. *111 S Locust St (61910). Phone 217/268-3599; toll-free 888/452-6474. www.amishcenter.com.* Museum dedicated to central Illinois's Amish community, the first museum of its kind. Exhibits include antique buggies, quilts, and handicrafts. Local tours available. (Apr-Nov, Mon-Sat; Dec-Mar, Wed-Sat) **$$**

Rockome Gardens. *125 N County Rd 425E (61910). 5 miles W on Hwy 133. Phone 217/268-4106.* Native rocks inlaid in concrete to form fences, arches, ornamental designs; landscaped gardens, ponds; petting zoo; train and buggy rides; lookout tower, treehouse; Amish-style restaurant, shops; replica of Amish house. Re-creation of Illinois frontier village on 15 acres, including craft guild shop, blacksmith shop, old country store, calico shop, bakery, and furniture and candle shops; antique museum; special weekend events. Admission includes all attractions except buggy ride. (Memorial Day-Oct, daily; mid-Apr-Memorial Day, days vary) **$$$**

Special Event

Raggedy Ann Festival. *135 N Oak St, Arcola (61910). Phone 217/268-4530.* Honors local man Johnny Gruelle, creator of Raggedy Ann and Andy. Includes carnival and petting zoo. Third week in May.

Limited-Service Hotel

★ **COMFORT INN.** *610 E Springfield Rd, Arcola (61910). Phone 217/268-4000; toll-free 800/228-5150;*

fax 217/268-4001. www.comfortinn.com. 41 rooms, 2 story. Complimentary continental breakfast. Check-out 11 am. Outdoor pool. **$**

Restaurants

★ **DUTCH KITCHEN.** 127 E Main, Arcola (61910). Phone 217/268-3518. Amish, American menu. Breakfast, lunch, dinner. Closed two weeks in Jan. Children's menu. **$$**

★ **ROCKOME FAMILY STYLE.** 125 N County Rd, Arcola (61910). Phone 217/268-4106; fax 217/268-4226. Amish, American menu. Lunch, dinner. Closed Nov-mid-Apr. Children's menu. **$**

Arlington Heights

See also Chicago O'Hare Airport Area, Schaumburg, Wheeling

Settled 1836
Population 76,031
Elevation 700 ft
Area Code 847
Information Chamber of Commerce, 180 N Arlington Heights Rd, 60004; phone 847/253-1703
Web site www.arlingtonhtschamber.com

What to See and Do

Historical Museum. 110 W Fremont St. Phone 847/255-1225. Complex consists of 1882 house, 1907 house, a coach house, and a reconstructed log cabin. (Sat-Sun, also first Fri of month; closed holidays) Also here is a heritage gallery (Thurs-Sun). **$**

Kemper Lakes Golf Club. Old McHenry Rd, Long Grove (60049). Phone 847/320-3450. www.kemperlakesgolf.com. A regular host of PGA events in the Chicago area is Kemper Lakes, which was the site of the 1989 PGA Championship, as well as several Champions Tour and LPGA events. Located in Long Grove, northwest of the hustle and bustle of the city, the course plays 7,217 yards long, a challenging length for almost any golfer. The $135 greens fee may seem steep, but the course's twilight rates can save you a bundle, and you can still make use of the course's state-of-the-art global positioning system that helps judge yardage to a given hole from every golf cart. **$$$$**

Long Grove Village. Rtes 83 and 53, Long Grove (60047). 1 mile N, at jct Rtes 53, 83. Phone 847/634-0888. www.longgrove.net. Restored 19th-century German village with more than 120 antique shops, boutiques, and restaurants. Seasonal festivals. (Daily) **FREE**

Full-Service Hotel

★ ★ ★ **SHERATON CHICAGO NORTHWEST.** 3400 W Euclid Ave, Arlington Heights (60005). Phone 847/394-2000; toll-free 800/325-3535; fax 847/394-2095. www.sheraton.com. The hotel is conveniently located near Woodfield Mall (see SCHAUMBURG) and Arlington International Race Track, to which complimentary transportation is provided. 429 rooms, 13 story. Pets accepted. Check-in 3 pm, check-out 11 am. Restaurant, bar. Fitness room. Indoor pool, whirlpool. Tennis. Business center. **$**

Restaurants

★ ★ ★ **LE TITI DE PARIS.** 1015 W Dundee Rd, Arlington Heights (60004). Phone 847/506-0222; fax 847/506-0474. www.letitideparis.com. With more than 800 selections, the wine list at this fantastic French restaurant is about as long as a Norman Mailer novel. Chefs Pierre Pollin and Michael Maddox serve marvelously innovative cuisine with nearly impeccable service. Signatures include such delights as sautéed salmon with cider sauce and Asian spiced duck. If you can, save room for one of the creatively presented desserts. French menu. Dinner. Closed Sun-Mon; holidays. Casual attire. **$$$**

★ ★ **PALM COURT.** 1912 N Arlington Heights Rd, Arlington Heights (60004). Phone 847/870-7770; fax 847/870-8586. www.palmcourt.net. In an area that offers mostly chain restaurants, Palm Court is a refreshing option. Serving fresh seafood, steaks, lamb, and veal, this family-owned restaurant caters to businesspeople as well as to casual diners. Nightly live piano music adds a romantic touch to the good-sized bar area. American menu. Lunch (Mon-Fri), dinner. Closed July 4, Dec 25. Bar. Children's menu. Casual attire. Reservations recommended. **$$**

★ ★ **RETRO BISTRO.** 1746 W Golf Rd, Mt Prospect (60056). Phone 847/439-2424. French menu. Lunch, dinner. Closed Sun; holidays. Bar. Children's menu. **$$**

Aurora (A-4)

See also DeKalb, Geneva, Joliet, Naperville, St. Charles

Settled 1834
Population 142,990
Elevation 676 ft
Area Code 630
Information Aurora Area Convention & Tourism Council, 44 W Downer Pl, 60507; phone 630/897-5581 or toll-free 800/477-4369
Web site www.ci.aurora.il.us

Potawatomi chief Waubonsie and his tribe inhabited this area on the Fox River when, in the 1830s, pioneers arrived from the East. Water power and fertile lands attracted more settlers, and two villages united as Aurora. Today, the city prospers because of its location along a high-tech corridor.

What to See and Do

Aurora Historical Museum. *20 Downer Pl. Phone 630/897-9029.* In the restored Ginsberg building, the museum contains displays of 19th-century life, a collection of mastodon bones, a history center and research library, and public art displays. (Wed-Sun afternoons) **$$**

Blackberry Farm and Pioneer Village. *Galena Blvd and Barnes Rd. W on I-88 (E-W tollway) to Orchard Rd, S to Galena Blvd, then W to Barnes Rd. Phone 630/892-1550. www.foxvalleyparkdistrict.org.* An 1840s-1920s living history museum and working farm. Exhibits include a children's animal farm, discovery barn, and train. Visitors enjoy craft demonstrations, wagon and pony rides, and a farm play area. (Late Apr-Labor Day, daily 10 am-4:30 pm; Labor Day-Oct, Fri-Sun) **$$**

Fermi National Accelerator Laboratory. *Kirk Rd and Pine St, Batavia (60510). 2 miles N on Hwy 31, 2 1/2 miles E on Butterfield Rd (Hwy 56), then N on Kirk Rd. Phone 630/840-3351.* World's highest energy particle accelerator is on a 6,800-acre site. Also on the grounds are hiking trails and a buffalo herd. Obtain brochures for self-guided tours (if permitted by current security conditions) in the atrium of 15-story Wilson Hall. Art and cultural events, films in auditorium. Call for hours. **FREE**

Michael Jordan Golf Center. *4523 Michael Jordan Dr. 2 miles S of I-88, W of Rte 59. Phone 630/851-0023.* Facilities include covered and heated tee stations, a short-game area, a three-tiered putting green, and 18-hole miniature golf. Clinics, youth programs, lessons, and golf schools. Clubhouse with golf shop, equipment, and video imaging; restaurant. (Daily)

Paramount Arts Centre. *23 E Galena Blvd. Along river. Phone 630/896-7676. www.paramountarts.com.* (1931) Theater designed by Rapp and Rapp to compete with the opulent movie palaces of the area; restored to its original appearance, it stages a variety of productions throughout the year. Guided backstage tours. (Mon-Fri) **$**

Schingoethe Center for Native American Cultures. *347 S Gladstone Ave. Phone 630/844-5402.* Private collection, thousands of Native American artifacts; jewelry, textiles, pottery, baskets. (Tues-Fri, Sun; closed holidays; also Aug) **DONATION**

SciTech—Science and Technology Interactive Center. *18 W Benton. Phone 630/859-3434. www.scitech.mus. il.us.* In a historic post office building, this interactive center provides more than 150 hands-on learning exhibits using motion, light, sound, and fun-to-teach science principles. (Mon-Sat 10 am-5 pm, Sun noon-5 pm) **$$**

Limited-Service Hotel

★ **COMFORT INN.** *111 N Broadway, Aurora (60505). Phone 630/896-2800; toll-free 800/517-4000; fax 630/896-2887. www.comfortsuites.com.* 82 rooms, 3 story, all suites. Complimentary continental breakfast. Check-in 4 pm, check-out 11 am. Fitness room. Indoor pool. Business center. **$$**

🏃 🚶 ♨

Restaurant

★ **WALTER PAYTON'S ROUNDHOUSE.** *205 N Broadway Ave, Aurora (60506). Phone 630/264-2739. www.walterpaytonsroundhouse.com.* Located in a former railroad roundhouse and originally owned by the late football star Walter Payton. American menu. Lunch, dinner. **$**

Barrington

Restaurants

★ ★ **BARRINGTON COUNTRY BISTRO.**
*700 W Northwest Hwy, Barrington (60010).
Phone 847/842-1300; fax 847/842-1315. www.
barringtonbistro.com.* French menu. Lunch, dinner.
Closed holidays. Bar. Casual attire. Outdoor seating. **$$**

★ ★ **MILLROSE.** *45 S Barrington Rd, South
Barrington (60010). Phone 847/382-7673; fax 847/304-
6619. www.millroserestaurant.com.* American menu.
Lunch, dinner, Sun brunch. Closed Dec 25. Bar.
Children's menu. Casual attire. Outdoor seating. **$$**

Belleville (E-3)

See also Cahokia, Collinsville, Edwardsville

Founded 1814
Population 42,785
Elevation 529 ft
Area Code 618
Information Belleville Tourism, Inc, 216 East A St,
62220; phone 618/233-6769 or toll-free 800/677-9255

Named Belleville (beautiful city) by its early French
settlers, the city today is largely populated by people
of German descent. The governmental, financial, and
medical center of southern Illinois, Belleville is also
the headquarters of Scott Air Force Base.

What to See and Do

National Shrine of Our Lady of the Snows. *442 S
Demazenod Dr. Phone 618/397-6700.* Unique architecture and imaginative landscaping on 200 acres;
features replica of Lourdes Grotto in France. Visitor
center, restaurant, lodging, gift shop. (Daily) **FREE**

Limited-Service Hotels

★ **HAMPTON INN.** *150 Ludwig Dr, Fairview
Heights (62208). Phone 618/397-9705; toll-free 800/
426-7866; fax 618/397-7829. www.hamptoninn.com.*
55 rooms, 3 story. Complimentary continental breakfast. Check-out noon. Indoor pool, whirlpool. **$**

★ ★ **RAMADA INN.** *6900 N Illinois, Fairview
Heights (62208). Phone 618/632-4747; toll-free 888/298-
2054; fax 618/632-9428. www.ramada.com.* 159 rooms,
5 story. Pets accepted; fee. Complimentary continental
breakfast buffet. Check-out noon. Restaurant. Fitness
room. Indoor pool, outdoor pool, whirlpools. **$**

Restaurants

★ **FISCHER'S.** *2100 W Main St, Belleville (62226).
Phone 618/233-1131; fax 618/233-1135.* American
menu. Lunch, dinner. Closed July 4, Dec 24 evening.
Bar. Children's menu. **$**

★ **LOTAWATA CREEK.** *311 Salem Pl, Fairview
Heights (62208). Phone 618/628-7373; fax 618/628-0665.
www.lotawata.com.* Steak menu. Lunch, dinner. Closed
Thanksgiving, Dec 25. Bar. Children's menu. **$$**

Benton (E-4)

See also Du Quoin, Marion, Mount Vernon

Population 6,880
Elevation 470 ft
Area Code 618
Zip 62812
Information Benton/West City Area Chamber of
Commerce, 500 W Main St, PO Box 574; phone 618/
438-2121

What to See and Do

Rend Lake. *12220 Rend City Rd. 5 miles N via I-57,
exit Hwy 154. Phone 618/724-2493.* Created from
the Big Muddy and Casey Fork rivers, the Y-shaped
Rend Lake covers 19,000 acres adjacent to 21,000
acres of public land with six recreation areas. Two
beaches; fishing for bass, crappie, and catfish; boating
(launches, marina); hiking, biking, and horseback rid-
ing trails; hunting, trap range; golf course. Restaurant.
Five campgrounds; amphitheaters, programs. Visitor
center at main dam. (Apr-Oct) Fee for some activities.
On the east shore, off I-57 exit 77, is

Wayne Fitzgerrell State Recreation Area.
11094 Ranger Rd, Benton. Phone 618/629-2320.
Approximately 1/3 of the 3,300 acres used for
hunting and dog field trial grounds. Swimming,
water-skiing, fishing, boating (ramps, dock).
Hiking and bridle trails, hunting, picnicking (shel-
ters), camping, tent and trailer sites (dump station,

hookups), cabins, playground, grocery, restaurant. Standard hours, fees.

Southern Illinois Arts & Crafts Marketplace. *14967 Gun Creek Trail (62897). 6 miles N on I-57, then W on Hwy 154.* Phone 618/629-2220. Houses Illinois artisan shops and galleries. Special events, demonstrations. (Daily; closed holidays) **FREE**

Special Event

Rend Lake Water Festival. *12220 Rend City Rd, Benton.* Phone 618/724-2493. Second week in May.

Limited-Service Hotels

★ **DAYS INN.** *711 W Main St, Benton (62812).* Phone 618/439-3183; toll-free 800/329-7466; fax 618/435-4184. www.daysinn.com. 57 rooms, 2 story. Pets accepted, some restrictions; fee. Check-out noon. Restaurant, bar. **$**

★ ★ **REND LAKE RESORT.** *11712 E Windy Ln, Whittington (62897).* Phone 618/629-2211; toll-free 800/633-3341; fax 618/629-2584. www.dnr.state.il.us/ lodges/rendlake.htm. 112 rooms. Check-out 11 am. Restaurant. Pool, children's pool. Tennis. **$**

Bishop Hill (B-3)

See also Galesburg, Kewanee

Settled 1846
Population 125
Elevation 780 ft
Area Code 309
Zip 61419

What to See and Do

⭐ **Bishop Hill State Historic Site.** *200 S Bishop Hill St (61419).* Phone 309/927-3345. www.bishophill.com. Settled in 1846 by Swedish immigrants seeking religious freedom, the communal-utopian colony was led by Erik Jansson until his assassination in 1850. In 1861, communally owned property was divided and the colony dissolved. Descendants of the settlers still live in the community. The state-owned Colony Hotel and Colony Church still stand, as do 15 of the original 21 buildings. (Daily 9 am-5 pm; closed holidays) **FREE** Among the restorations are

Bishop Hill Museum. *103 N Bishop Hill St, Bishop Hill.* Houses collection of paintings by Olof Krans, whose primitive folk art depicts the Bishop Hill colony of his childhood.

Colony Blacksmith Shop. *203 N Bishop Hill St, Bishop Hill.* Phone 309/927-3390. Traditional craftsmen selling and demonstrating crafts.

Colony Church. *N Bishop Hill St and Maiden Ln, Bishop Hill.* Phone 309/927-3345. (1848) This gambrel-roofed building houses a collection of Bishop Hill artifacts. Second floor features restored sanctuary with original walnut pews.

Colony Store. *101 W Main St, Bishop Hill.* Phone 309/927-3596. (1853) Restored general store with original shelving and counters. (Daily; closed Thanksgiving, Dec 25)

Steeple Building. *103 N Bishop Hill St, Bishop Hill.* Phone 309/927-3899. (1854) This three-story Greek Revival edifice is of handmade brick covered with plaster. The clock, in its wooden steeple, was designed with only one hand. Heritage Museum houses displays of the community's history. The Bishop Hill Heritage collection of late-19th-century Bishop Hill memorabilia is here; slide show daily in season. (Apr-Dec, daily; closed Thanksgiving, Dec 25) **DONATION**

Village tours. *103 N Bishop Hill St.* Phone 309/927-3899. The Bishop Hill Heritage Association conducts tours of the village (Apr-mid-Dec, by appointment). **$$**

Special Events

Bishop Hill Jordbruksdagarna. *110 N Olson St, Bishop Hill (61419).* Phone 309/927-3345. Agricultural celebration features harvesting demonstrations, children's games, "colony stew," hayrack rides. Late Sept.

Julmarknad. *Bishop Hill.* Phone 309/927-3345. Christmas market with decorated shops; Swedish foods; "Juletomte" (Christmas elf) and "Julbok" (Christmas goat) roam the village. Late Nov-early Dec.

Lucia Nights. *Bishop Hill.* Phone 309/927-3345. Festival of lights. "Lucia" girls with candle crowns serve coffee and sweets to guests; choral programs, carolers; sleigh rides. Mid-Dec.

Midsommar. *Village Park, center of town, Bishop Hill (61419).* Phone 309/927-3345. Sun afternoon concerts. June.

Bloomington-Normal (C-4)

See also Lincoln, Peoria

Founded 1843
Population 64,808
Elevation 829 ft
Area Code 309
Information Bloomington-Normal Area Convention and Visitors Bureau, 210 S East St; phone 309/829-1641 or toll-free 800/433-8226
Web site www.visitbloomingtonnormal.org

Bloomington, the McLean County seat, took its name from the original settlement of Blooming Grove. The Illinois Republican Party was formed here in 1856 at the Anti-Nebraska convention, at which Abraham Lincoln made the famous "lost speech," spelling out the principles that were to elect him president. Bloomington was also the home of Adlai E. Stevenson, vice president under Grover Cleveland. His grandson, Illinois Governor Adlai E. Stevenson II, twice Democratic candidate for president and United States Ambassador to the United Nations, is buried here.

Along with agriculture, the founding of Illinois Wesleyan University (see) and the selection of North Bloomington (now the twin city of Normal) as the site for Illinois State University (see) helped determine the town's economic future.

What to See and Do

Funk Prairie Home. *RR 1. Call for directions. Phone 309/827-6792.* (1863) Built by LaFayette Funk with lumber and timber felled in Funk's Grove, the large Italianate house with wraparound porches features an elaborately decorated parlor with a Chickering piano, an Italian marble fireplace, and gold valance boards above windows. Guided tours (allow 1 1/2-2 hours; reservations advised) includes the adjacent Gem and Mineral Museum. (Mar-Dec, Tues-Sat; closed holidays) **FREE**

Illinois State University. *220 N Main St, Normal (61701). 1 mile S of jct Hwy 51, I-55. Phone 309/438-2181. www.ilstu.edu.* (1857) (22,000 students) The first state university in Illinois. Tours arranged. On campus is

Adlai E. Stevenson Memorial Room. *School and North sts, Bloomington. Phone 309/438-5669.* Contains personal memorabilia, photographs. (Mon-Fri) **FREE**

Illinois Wesleyan University. *104 E University St (61701). North side residential area on Hwy 51, I-55 Business, and Hwy 9. Phone 309/556-3034. titan.iwu.edu.* (1850) (2,000 students) Liberal arts college. On campus is

Sheean Library. *East and Beecher sts, Bloomington. Phone 309/556-3350.* Contains the papers of former United States Congressman Leslie Arends and the Gernon Collection of 19th- and 20th-century literature. Also on display is a collection of Native American pottery of Major John Wesley Powell, former faculty member at Wesleyan and credited with the first exploration of the Colorado River and Grand Canyon. **FREE**

Miller Park Zoo. *1020 S Morris, Bloomington (61701). 1/2 mile N of I-55 Business. Phone 309/434-2250.* Big cats, river otters in natural settings; sea lions; tropical rain forest; children's zoo. Other activities in Miller Park include swimming, fishing, boating; picnicking; tennis, miniature golf (some fees). There is a playground and a steam locomotive display. Band concerts are held in season. (Daily) **$**

Old Courthouse Museum. *200 N Main St. Phone 309/827-0428.* Maintained by McLean County Historical Society and housed in 1903 courthouse. Exhibits include area history, farming, an authentic courtroom, hands-on displays, and a research library. Museum store. (Mon-Sat; closed holidays) **$**

Special Events

The American Passion Play. *Scottish Rite Temple. 110 E Mulberry St, Bloomington (61701). Phone 309/829-3903.* A cast of more than 300; presented annually since 1924. Sat-Sun, late Mar-mid-May.

Illinois Shakespeare Festival. *Ewing Manor, Emerson and Towanda sts, Bloomington. Phone 309/438-2535.* Shakespearean performances preceded by Elizabethan-era music and entertainment. June-early Aug.

Limited-Service Hotels

★ **BEST WESTERN UNIVERSITY INN.** *6 Traders Cir, Normal (61761). Phone 309/454-4070; toll-free 800/780-7234; fax 309/888-4505. www.*

bestwestern.com. 102 rooms, 2 story. Pets accepted. Complimentary continental breakfast. Check-out 11 am. Fitness room. Indoor pool. Airport transportation available. **$**

⊠ 🏋 🐾 ≈

★ **EASTLAND SUITES LODGE.** *1801 Eastland Dr, Bloomington (61704). Phone 309/662-0000; fax 309/663-6668. www.eastland-suites.com.* 88 rooms, 3 story. Complimentary continental breakfast. Check-out noon. Fitness room. Indoor pool, whirlpool. Airport transportation available. Business center. **$**

⊠ 🏋 🐾 ≈

★ **HAMPTON INN.** *604 1/2 IAA Dr, Bloomington (61701). Phone 309/662-2800; toll-free 800/426-7866; fax 309/662-2811. www.hampton-inn.com.* 108 rooms, 3 story. Complimentary continental breakfast. Check-out noon. Outdoor pool. Airport transportation available. **$**

≈

★ ★ **HOLIDAY INN.** *8 Traders Cir, Normal (61761). Phone 309/452-8300; toll-free 800/465-4329; fax 309/454-6722. www.holiday-inn.com.* 160 rooms, 5 story. Pets accepted; fee. Check-out noon. Restaurant, bar. Fitness room. Indoor pool, whirlpool. Airport transportation available. Business center. **$**

🏋 🐾 ≈

Full-Service Hotel

★ ★ ★ **THE CHATEAU.** *1601 Jumer Dr, Bloomington (61704). Phone 309/662-2020; toll-free 800/285-8637; fax 309/662-6522. www.jumers.com.* Located just minutes away from Illinois State University (see), this hotel features an indoor pool, sauna, and whirlpool. Dining is made easy with an on-site restaurant and lounge. 180 rooms, 5 story. Pets accepted; fee. Check-out noon. Restaurant, bar. Fitness room. Indoor pool, whirlpool. Airport transportation available. **$**

⊠ 🏋 🐾 ≈

Restaurants

 ★ ★ **CENTRAL STATION CAFE.** *220 E Front St, Bloomington (61701). Phone 309/828-2323. www.centralstation.cc.* In a former fire station (1902). American menu. Lunch, dinner. Closed Sun-Mon. Bar. **$$**

★ ★ **JIM'S STEAK HOUSE.** *2307 E Washington St, Bloomington (61704). Phone 309/663-4142.* Steak menu. Lunch, dinner. Closed Dec 25. Bar. **$$**

Brookfield

See also Cicero, Hinsdale, La Grange, Oak Brook

Population 19,085
Elevation 620 ft
Area Code 708
Zip 60513
Information Chamber of Commerce, 3724 Grand Blvd; phone 708/485-1434

What to See and Do

⭐ **Brookfield Zoo.** *3300 Golf Rd (60513). 31st St and 1st Ave. Phone 708/485-0263. www.brookfieldzoo.org.* Located just 14 miles west of downtown, the Brookfield Zoo is a world-class, 216-acre facility that houses more than 2,800 animals. Long known for its progressive approach to wildlife, the zoo was the first in the country to go "barless," installing animals in near-natural habitats instead of in cages. Visitors can experience this approach firsthand in many of the habitats, such as the African Savannah, the African Forest, the Swamp, the Living Coast, and the Salt Creek Wilderness. A favorite is Tropic World, with its rain forest exhibit complete with waterfalls and thunderstorms. Children get special attention here: a 2-acre, 300-animal Family Play Zoo enables kids and their families to interact with the animals, and a separate Children's Zoo includes the Walk-In Farmyard and the Pet and Learn Circle. The zoo also features botanical gardens, a dolphin show, several restaurants, a store, roving naturalists and docents offering on-the-spot lessons, and ongoing special programming. (Daily) **$$**

Cahokia

See also Alton, Belleville, Collinsville, Edwardsville, Père Marquette State Park

Founded 1699
Population 16,391
Elevation 411 ft
Area Code 618
Zip 62206
Information Cahokia Area Chamber of Commerce, 905 Falling Springs Rd; phone 618/332-1900

Cahokia, the oldest town in Illinois, was once the center of a vast French missionary area that included what is now Chicago, more than 260 miles northeast. The first church in Illinois was built here by Father St. Cosme in 1699, and a trading post developed around the mission. Cahokia came under the British flag in 1765 and under the American flag in 1778.

What to See and Do

Cahokia Courthouse State Historic Site. *107 Elm St. Just off Hwy 3. Phone 618/332-1782.* Believed to be the oldest house (circa 1735) in the state. Former house of François Saucier, son of the builder of Fort de Chartres. Sold in 1793, it was used as a territorial courthouse and jail until 1814. Museum display of courtroom and period lifestyle; interpretive program. (Tues-Sat) **FREE**

★ **Cahokia Mounds State Historic Site.** *30 Ramey St, Collinsville (62234). I-255 exit 24, W on Collinsville Rd. Phone 618/346-5160.* This site preserves the central section of the only prehistoric city north of Mexico. Archaeological finds indicate that the Cahokia site was first inhabited around AD 700. Eventually, a very complex community developed; the city of Cahokia covered 6 square miles and had a population of tens of thousands. The earthen mounds, used primarily for ceremonial activities of the living, originally numbered more than 100. Only 68 are currently preserved. Monks Mound, the great platform mound named for Trappist monks who once lived near it (1809-1813), is the largest mound north of Mexico and also the largest prehistoric earthen construction in the New World. Its base covers 14 acres, and it rises in four terraces to a height of 100 feet. Two other types of mounds, conical and ridgetop, are also found here. Archaeological excavations have partially uncovered remains of four circular sun calendars, which once consisted of large, evenly spaced log posts probably used to predict the changing seasons. One has been reconstructed in the original location. The 2,000-acre site has a resident archaeologist. Activities include hiking and picnicking. Self-guided tours available. A museum displays artifacts from the nearby mounds and village areas. (Daily; closed holidays) **FREE**

Historic Holy Family Mission Log Church. *116 Church St. At jct Hwy 3, 157. Phone 618/337-4548.* Completed in 1799; restored in 1949; the original walnut logs stand upright in Canadian fashion. The old cemetery is behind the church. (June-Aug, daily 10 am-4 pm) **DONATION**

Cairo (F-4)

See also Carbondale

Settled 1837
Population 3,632
Elevation 314 ft
Area Code 618
Zip 62914
Information Chamber of Commerce, 220 8th St; phone 618/734-2737

Farther south than Richmond, Virginia, Cairo (CARE-o), a city of magnolia trees, is located at the confluence of the Ohio and Mississippi rivers. Settlement was attempted in 1818 by a St. Louis merchant who named the site Cairo because he thought it resembled the Egyptian capital. Cairo and the southern tip of Illinois are still locally referred to as "Little Egypt."

Dominating rail and river traffic, spearheading the thrust of free territory into the South, and harboring citizens with Southern sympathies, strategic Cairo was immediately fortified after the outbreak of the Civil War. Cairo served as headquarters, fortress, supply depot, and hospital for Grant's Army of the Tennessee. After the Civil War, the town had the highest per capita commercial valuation in the United States. Rich with war profits, citizens lavished money on both public and private building projects that, according to the National Register of Historic Places, remain as "individual works of architectural brilliance."

Bridges at Cairo connect three states: Illinois, Missouri, and Kentucky. Local legend has it that a penny tossed into the confluence of the rivers at Point Cairo will bring one back again. The levee, rising from the river delta, and the streets along it retain the flavor of the steamboat era.

What to See and Do

Custom House Museum. *1400 Washington Ave.* This 19th-century federal building contains artifacts and replicas from Cairo's past. (Mon-Fri) **FREE**

Fort Defiance State Park. *On Hwy 51 at the S edge of town. Phone 618/734-3015.* Splendid view of the confluence of Ohio and Mississippi rivers on 39 acres; site of a Civil War fort.

Horseshoe Lake State Conservation Area. *RR 3, Olive Branch. 7 miles NW on Hwy 3.* Phone 618/776-5689. Large flocks of Canada geese migrate to these 10,336 acres in winter. Fishing, boating (ramp; 10-hp motor limit mid-Mar-mid-Nov); hunting; hiking; picnicking, concession; camping.

Magnolia Manor. *2700 Washington Ave.* Phone 618/734-0201. (1869) Italianate Victorian mansion (14 rooms) built for wealthy flour merchant contains period furnishings, items of local historical interest. View of Mississippi and Ohio rivers from tower. (Daily; closed holidays) **$$**

Carbondale (F-3)

See also Cairo, Du Quion, Fort Kaskaskia State Historic Site, Marion

Founded 1852
Population 20,681
Elevation 415 ft
Area Code 618
Zip 62901
Information Convention and Tourism Bureau, 1245 E Main St, Suite A32; phone 618/529-4451 or toll-free 800/526-1500
Web site www.cctb.org

Carbondale is surrounded by lakes and rivers, including Crab Orchard and Little Grassy lakes and the Big Muddy River. Railroad yards, Southern Illinois University (see), and surrounding coal fields give the community a unique personality.

What to See and Do

Bald Knob. *3630 Bald Knob Rd, Alto Pass (62905). 16 miles S on Hwy 51 to Cobden, then 4 miles W to Alto Pass.* Phone 618/529-4451; toll-free 800/248-4373. View of three states from this high point in the Illinois Ozarks.

Ferne Clyffe State Park. *Hwy 37 S, Goreville.* Phone 618/995-2411. Hawk's cave, a shelter bluff, gorges, canyons on 1,125 acres. Fishing; hunting; hiking and riding trails; picnicking; camping, equestrian camping. Nature preserve. (Daily) **FREE**

Giant City State Park. *336 S Church St, Makanda. 10 miles S on Hwy 51, then E on Old Rte 51.* Phone 618/457-4836. Picturesque rock formations and a prehistoric "stone fort" on 4,055 acres. Fishing; hunting; hiking and riding trails; picnicking, concession, lodge, dining room. Camping, cabins, horse campground. (Daily) **FREE**

Southern Illinois University. *Communications Bldg #1259. S on Illinois Ave, Hwy 51.* Phone 618/453-2121. *www.siu.edu.* (1869) (19,500 students) On campus is

> **University Museum.** *Lincoln Dr and Illinois Ave, Carbondale. N end of Faner Hall.* Phone 618/453-5388. Exhibits include southern Illinois history, nationally known artists, local collections; changing exhibits. Gift shop. (Tues-Sat by appointment; Sun 1-4 pm; closed school holidays) **FREE**

Limited-Service Hotels

★ **BEST INN.** *1345 E Main St, Carbondale (62901).* Phone 618/529-4801; toll-free 800/237-8466; fax 618/529-7212. www.bestinn.com. 82 rooms, 2 story. Complimentary continental breakfast. Check-out 1 pm. Pool. **$**

★ **SUPER 8.** *1180 E Main St, Carbondale (62901).* Phone 618/457-8822; toll-free 800/800-8000; fax 618/457-4186. www.super8.com. 63 rooms, 3 story. Pets accepted. Check-in 2 pm, check-out 11 am. **$**

Restaurants

★ **MARY LOU'S GRILL.** *114 S Illinois Ave, Carbondale (62901).* Phone 618/457-5084. American menu. Breakfast, lunch. Closed Sun-Mon; holidays. **$**

★ **TRES HOMBRES.** *119 N Washington St, Carbondale (62901).* Phone 618/457-3308; fax 618/549-2106. Mexican menu. Lunch, dinner. Closed holidays. Bar. **$**

Centralia (E-4)

See also Edwardsville, Mount Vernon, Salem

Founded 1853
Population 14,136
Elevation 499 ft
Area Code 618
Zip 62801
Information Chamber of Commerce, 130 S Locust St; phone 618/532-6789

Centralia, named for the Illinois Central Railroad, and its neighbors, Central City and Wamac, form a continuous urban area that is the trading center and labor pool for four counties in south central Illinois.

What to See and Do

Centralia Carillon. *114 N Elm. At Noleman. Phone 618/533-4381.* This 160-foot tower houses 65 bells. Concerts; tours (by appointment). **FREE**

Fairview Park. *Broadway and Buena Vista. W on Hwy 161, at W Broadway. Phone 618/532-6789.* Site of Engine 2500. One of the largest steam locomotives ever built (225 tons), the engine was donated to the city by the Illinois Central Railroad. Swimming; picnicking; playgrounds. (Daily)

Lake Centralia. *Green Street Rd. 8 miles NE on Green Street Rd.* Swimming, fishing, boating; picnicking.

Raccoon Lake. *3 miles E on Hwy 161, then 1/2 mile N on Country Club Rd.* Fishing, boating (ramp). (Apr-Oct)

Special Event

Balloon Fest. *Foundation Park, 130 S Locust St, Centralia (62801). Phone 618/532-6789.* Hot air balloon races, crafters, food, children's activities, cardboard boat races. Mid-Aug.

Restaurant

★ ★ **CENTRALIA HOUSE.** *111 N Oak St, Centralia (62801). Phone 618/532-9754.* Turn-of-the-century elegance. Cajun, American menu. Dinner. Closed Sun; holidays. Bar. **$$**

Champaign/ Urbana (C-4)

See also Arcola, Danville

Settled Champaign, 1855; Urbana, 1822
Population 67,518
Elevation Champaign, 742 ft; Urbana, 727 ft
Area Code 217
Zip Champaign, 61820; Urbana, 61801
Information Convention and Visitors Bureau, 1817 S Neil St, Suite 201, Champaign 61820-7234; phone 217/351-4133 or toll-free 800/369-6151
Web site www.cupartnership.org

Champaign and Urbana, separately incorporated, are united as the home of the University of Illinois. Champaign started as West Urbana when the Illinois Central Railroad ran its line 2 miles west of Urbana, the county seat. Defying annexation by Urbana in 1855, the new community was incorporated in 1860 as Champaign and prospered as a trade center. Today, the two communities are geographically one; Champaign continues as a commercial and industrial center, with the larger part of the university falling within the boundaries of Urbana.

Urbana became the seat of Champaign County in 1833, but its anticipated growth was interrupted when the railroad bypassed it. In 1867, the Industrial University opened in Urbana. Now the University of Illinois, it extends into the "twin city" of Champaign. Lincoln Square, the second downtown covered mall in the United States, is a forerunner in the revitalization of downtown districts.

What to See and Do

Champaign County Historical Museum. *102 E University Ave, Champaign. Phone 217/356-1010.* Located in the Historical Cattle Bank (1857); many original items. (Wed, Sun; closed holidays) **$**

Lake of the Woods County Preserve. *405 N Lake of the Woods Rd, Mahomet (61853). 10 miles W on I-74, then 1/4 mile N on Hwy 47. Phone 217/586-3360 (park).* Swimming, boating (rentals), fishing; golf (fee); picnicking; playground. Also Early American Museum and botanical gardens (Memorial Day-Labor

Day, daily; after Labor Day-early Oct, weekends). Visitor center. Park (daily). **FREE**

Orpheum Children's Science Museum. *346 N Neil St, Champaign (61820). Phone 217/352-5895.* Located in historic Orpheum Theatre. Hands-on exhibits include Dino Dig, Kinderblocks, water tornado, and ghost images. (Wed-Sun, afternoons) **$$**

University of Illinois. *919 W Illinois St (61801). Information desk at Illini Union, Wright and Green sts. Campus Visitors Center, Levis Faculty Center (Mon-Fri). Phone 217/333-0824. www.uiuc.edu.* (1867) (37,000 students) Included among the 200 major buildings on campus are the main library, the third-largest academic library in the United States (daily); the undergraduate library, built underground to prevent throwing a shadow on the Morrow Plots, the oldest experimental plot of land still in use; Mumford House, the oldest building on campus (1870); Altgeld Hall with a carillon that plays tunes periodically throughout the day; Krannert Center for the Performing Arts; the 69,200-seat Memorial Stadium; and the domed Assembly Hall, which hosts basketball games and concerts. Campus walking tour available. Also on campus are

Krannert Art Museum. *500 E Peabody Dr, Champaign. Peabody St, between 4th and 6th sts. Phone 217/333-1860.* (Tues-Sat, also Sun afternoons) **DONATION**

Museum of Natural History. *1301 W Green St, Urbana. Adjacent to Illini Union. Phone 217/333-2517.* (Mon-Sat, also Sun afternoons) **FREE**

World Heritage Museum. *Lincoln Hall, 702 S Wright St, Urbana. Phone 217/333-2360.* (Academic year, Mon-Fri, also Sun afternoons) **FREE**

William M. Staerkel Planetarium. *Parkland College Cultural Center, 2400 W Bradley Ave, Champaign (61821). Phone 217/351-2446.* Second-largest planetarium in Illinois projects 7,600 visible stars on a 50-foot dome. Multimedia shows, lectures. (Thurs-Sat) **$$**

Limited-Service Hotels

★ **BEST WESTERN PARADISE INN.** *1001 N Dunlap St, Savoy (61874). Phone 217/356-1824; toll-free 800/780-1234; fax 217/356-1824. www.bestwestern .com.* 62 rooms, 2 story. Pets accepted, some restrictions; fee. Complimentary continental breakfast. Check-out 11 am. Pool, children's pool. Airport transportation available. **$**

★ **CHANCELLOR INN.** *1501 S Neil St, Champaign (61820). Phone 217/352-7891; fax 217/352-8108.* 224 rooms, 7 story. Pets accepted, some restrictions; fee. Complimentary continental breakfast. Check-out 1 pm. Indoor pool, outdoor pool, children's pool. Airport transportation available. Dinner theater. **$**

★ **COMFORT INN.** *305 W Marketview Dr, Champaign (61821). Phone 217/352-4055; toll-free 800/228-5150; fax 217/352-4055. www.comfortinn.com.* 67 rooms, 2 story. Complimentary continental breakfast. Check-out 11 am. Indoor pool, whirlpool. **$**

★ **EASTLAND SUITES.** *1907 N Cunningham Ave, Urbana (61802). Phone 217/367-8331; toll-free 800/253-8331; fax 217/384-3370. www. eastlandsuitesurbana.com.* 127 rooms, 2 story. Pets accepted; fee. Complimentary full breakfast. Check-out 11 am. Bar. Fitness room. Indoor pool. Airport transportation available. **$**

★ **LA QUINTA INN.** *1900 Center Dr, Champaign (61820). Phone 217/356-4000; toll-free 800/531-5900; fax 217/352-7783. www.laquinta.com.* 122 rooms, 2 story. Pets accepted; fee. Complimentary breakfast. Check-out noon. Pool. **$**

Full-Service Hotel

★ ★ **HISTORIC LINCOLN HOTEL.** *209 S Broadway, Urbana (61801). Phone 217/384-8800; fax 217/384-9001.* Upon entering the grand lobby, guests will feel the elegance and style of a time gone by. Guest rooms are beautifully decorated with artwork, fireplaces, and woodwork. 130 rooms, 4 story. Pets accepted, some restrictions; fee. Check-out noon. Restaurant, bar. Indoor pool, whirlpool. Airport transportation available. **$**

Restaurants

★ **NED KELLY'S.** *1601 N Cunningham Ave, Urbana (61801). Phone 217/344-8201. www. nedkellyssteakhouse.com.* Steak menu. Lunch, dinner. Closed Dec 25. Bar. Children's menu. **$$**

★ ★ **TIMPONE'S.** *710 S Goodwin Ave, Urbana (61801). Phone 217/344-7619.* Italian, American menu. Lunch, dinner. Closed Sun; holidays. Bar. **$$**

Charleston (D-4)

See also Arcola, Mattoon

Population 20,398
Elevation 686 ft
Area Code 217
Zip 61920
Information Charleston Area Chamber of Commerce, 501 Jackson St, PO Box 77; phone 217/345-7041
Web site www.charlestonchamber.com

One of the great Lincoln-Douglas debates was held here on September 18, 1858. As an itinerate lawyer riding the circuit, Abraham Lincoln practiced law in the area. His father, Thomas Lincoln, and stepmother once lived in a cabin 8 miles south of Charleston.

What to See and Do

Coles County Courthouse. *651 Jackson Ave #8.* (1898) Courthouse sits on Charleston Square, where Lincoln practiced law in an earlier courthouse and where the Charleston Riot took place; riot involved 300 men in armed conflict during the Civil War.

Eastern Illinois University. *600 Lincoln Ave (61920). Phone 217/581-2787. www.eiu.edu.* (1895) (10,000 students) Tarble Arts Center on South 9th Street at Cleveland Avenue houses visual arts exhibits; changing displays. (Tues-Sun; closed holidays) (See SPECIAL EVENTS) **FREE**

Fox Ridge State Park. *18175 State Park Rd, Charleston. 8 miles S on Hwy 130. Phone 217/345-6416.* A rugged area of 1,500 acres with Ridge Lake maintained by Illinois Natural History Survey. Fishing (permit from Survey required), boating (no motors); hiking; picnicking; camping (fee).

Lincoln Log Cabin State Historic Site. *400 S Lincoln Hwy Rd, Lerna. 8 miles S of Charleston on 4th St.* *Phone 217/345-1845.* This 86-acre site contains the Thomas Lincoln Log Cabin, reconstructed on the original foundation as it was when Abraham Lincoln's father built it in 1840; a reconstructed 1840s farm surrounds the cabin. In nearby Shiloh Cemetery are the graves of Thomas Lincoln and Sarah Bush Lincoln, the president's stepmother. Interpretive program offered May-October. Picnicking. (Daily; closed Jan 1, Thanksgiving, Dec 25) (See SPECIAL EVENTS) **FREE**

Moore Home State Historic Site. *400 S Lincoln Hwy Rd, Lerna. 7 miles S of Charleston on 4th St. Phone 217/345-1845.* Before leaving for his inauguration, Lincoln ate his last meal here with his stepmother and her daughter, Matilda Moore. (June-Aug, limited hours) **FREE**

Special Events

Celebration: A Festival of the Arts. *Eastern Illinois University, 600 Lincoln Ave, Charleston (61920). Phone 217/581-2113.* Exhibits include paintings, crafts, pottery, and sculptures; plays, music, dancing; foods from around the world; children's activities. Late Aug.

Coles County Fair. *Fairgrounds, 416 W Madison Ave, Charleston (61920). Phone 217/345-2656.* Late July.

Harvest Frolic and Trades Fair. *Lincoln Log Cabin State Historic Site, 400 S Lincoln Hwy Rd, Lerna (62440). Phone 217/345-1845.* Festival based on central Illinois's agricultural history; exhibits, entertainment. First weekend in Oct.

Limited-Service Hotel

★ ★ **BEST WESTERN WORTHINGTON INN.** *920 W Lincoln Ave, Charleston (61920). Phone 217/348-8161; toll-free 800/528-8161; fax 217/ 348-8165. www.bestwestern.com.* 67 rooms, 2 story. Pets accepted, some restrictions. Complimentary continental breakfast. Check-out 11 am. Restaurant. Outdoor pool. Airport transportation available. **$**

Chicago (A-5)

See also Chicago O'Hare Airport Area, Cicero, Evanston, Highland Park, Itasca; Hammond, IN

Settled 1803
Population 2,896,016
Elevation 596 feet
Area Code 312, 773
Information Chicago Office of Tourism, Chicago Cultural Center, 78 E Washington St, 60602; phone 312/744-2400 or toll-free 800/226-6632
Web site www.choosechicago.com
Suburbs *North*: Evanston, Glenview, Gurnee, Highland Park, Highwood, Northbrook, Skokie, and Wilmette; *Northwest*: Arlington Heights, Itasca, Schaumburg, and Wheeling; *South*: Homewood and Oak Lawn; *West*: Brookfield, Cicero, Downers Grove, Elmhurst, Geneva, Glen Ellyn, Hillside, Hinsdale, La Grange, Naperville, Oak Brook, Oak Park, St. Charles, and Wheaton.

Rudyard Kipling wrote of Chicago, "I have struck a city—a real city—and they call it Chicago." For poet Carl Sandburg, it was the "City of the Big Shoulders"; for writer A. J. Liebling, a New Yorker, it was the "Second City." Songwriters have dubbed it a "toddlin' town" and "my kind of town." Boosters say it's "the city that works"; and to most people, it is "the Windy City." But over and above all the words and slogans is the city itself and the people who helped make it what it is today.

The people of Chicago represent a varied ethnic and racial mix. From the Native Americans who gave the city its name—Checagou—to the restless Easterners who traveled west in search of land and opportunity to the hundreds of thousands of venturesome immigrants from Europe, Asia, and Latin America who brought with them the foods and customs of the Old World to the Southern blacks and Appalachians who came in hopes of finding better jobs and housing, all have contributed to the strength, vitality, and cosmopolitan ambience that make Chicago a distinctive and unique experience for visitors.

Chicago's past is equally distinctive, built on adversity and contradiction. The first permanent settler was a black man, Jean Baptiste Point du Sable. The city's worst tragedy, the Great Chicago Fire of 1871, was the basis for its physical and cultural renaissance. In the heart of one of the poorest ethnic neighborhoods, two young women of means, Jane Addams and Ellen Gates Starr, created Hull House, a social service institution that has been copied throughout the world (see Jane Addams Hull House Museum). A city of neat frame cottages and bulky stone mansions, it produced the geniuses of the Chicago school of architecture (Louis Sullivan, Daniel Burnham, Dankmar Adler, William LeBaron Jenney, and John Willborn Root), whose innovative tradition was carried on by Frank Lloyd Wright and Ludwig Mies van der Rohe. Even its most famous crooks provide a study in contrasts: Al Capone, the Prohibition gangster, and Samuel Insull, the financial finagler whose stock manipulations left thousands of small investors penniless in the late 1920s.

Chicago's early merchants resisted the intrusion of the railroad, yet the city became the rail center of the nation. Although Chicago no longer boasts a stockyard, its widely diversified economy makes it one of the most stable cities in the country. Metropolitan Chicago has more than 12,000 factories with a $20 billion annual payroll and ranks first in the United States in the production of canned and frozen foods, metal products, machinery, railroad equipment, letterpress printing, office equipment, musical instruments, telephones, housewares, candy, and lampshades. It has one of the world's busiest airports, the largest grain exchange, and the biggest mail-order business. It is a great educational center (58 institutions of higher learning); one of the world's largest convention and trade show cities; a showplace, marketplace, shopping, and financial center; and a city of skyscrapers, museums, parks, and churches, with more than 2,700 places of worship.

Chicago turns its best face toward Lake Michigan, where a green fringe of parks forms an arc from Evanston to the Indiana border. The Loop is a city within a city, with many corporate headquarters, banks, stores, and other enterprises. To the far south are the docks along the Calumet River, used by ocean vessels since the opening of the St. Lawrence Seaway and servicing a belt of factories, steel mills, and warehouses. Behind these lies a maze of industrial and shopping areas, schools, and houses.

Although Louis Jolliet mapped the area as early as 1673 and du Sable and a compatriot, Antoine Ouilmette, had established a trading post by 1796, the real growth of the city did not begin until the 19th century and the onset of the Industrial Revolution.

Chicago Fun Facts

- The world's first skyscraper was built in Chicago in 1885.
- The Hostess Twinkie was first produced in Chicago in 1930.
- The abbreviation ORD for Chicago's O'Hare Airport comes from its old name, Orchard Field.
- The Chicago Public Library is the world's largest public library with a collection of more than 2 million books.
- Chicago is home to the world's longest street: Western Avenue.
- Chicago is home to the world's largest food festival—the Taste of Chicago (see SPECIAL EVENTS)—every summer in Grant Park.

In 1803, the fledging US government took possession of the area and sent a small military contingent from Detroit to select the site for a fort. Fort Dearborn was built at a strategic spot on the mouth of the Chicago River; on the opposite bank, a settlement slowly grew. Fort and settlement were abandoned when the British threatened them during the War of 1812. On their way to Fort Wayne, soldiers and settlers were attacked and killed or held captive by Native Americans who had been armed by the British. The fort was rebuilt in 1816; a few survivors returned and new settlers arrived, but there was little activity until Chicago was selected as the terminal site of the proposed Illinois and Michigan Canal. This started a land boom.

Twenty thousand Easterners swept through on their way to the riches of the West. Merchants opened stores; land speculation was rampant. Although 1837—the year Chicago was incorporated as a city—was marked by financial panic, the pace of expansion and building did not falter. In 1841, grain destined for world ports began to pour into the city; almost immediately, Chicago became the largest grain market in the world. In the wake of the grain came herds of hogs and cattle for the Chicago slaughterhouses. Tanneries, packing plants, mills, and factories soon sprang up.

The Illinois and Michigan Canal, completed in 1848, quadrupled imports and exports. Railroads fanned out from the city, transporting merchandise throughout the nation and bringing new produce to Chicago. During the slump that followed the panic of 1857, Chicago built a huge wooden shed (the Wigwam) at the southeast corner of Wacker and Lake to house the Republican National Convention. Abraham Lincoln was nominated Republican candidate for president here in 1860. The Civil War doubled grain shipments from Chicago. In 1865, the mile-square Union Stock Yards were established. Chicago was riotously prosperous; its population skyrocketed. Then, on October 8, 1871, fire erupted in a cow barn and roared through the city, destroying 15,768 buildings, killing almost 300 people, and leaving a third of the population homeless. But temporary and permanent rebuilding started at once, and Chicago emerged from the ashes to take advantage of the rise of industrialization. The labor unrest of the period produced the Haymarket bombing and the Pullman and other strikes. The 1890s were noteworthy for cultural achievements: orchestras, libraries, universities, and the new urban architectural form for which the term "skyscraper" was coined. The Columbian Exposition of 1893, a magnificent success, was followed by depression and municipal corruption.

Chicago's fantastic rate of growth continued into the 20th century. Industries boomed during World War I, and, in the 1920s, the city prospered as never before—unruffled by dizzying financial speculation and notorious gang warfare, an outgrowth of Prohibition. The stock market crash of 1929 brought down the shakier financial pyramids; the repeal of Prohibition virtually ended the rackets; and a more sober Chicago produced the Century of Progress Exposition in 1933. Chicago's granaries and steel mills helped carry the country through World War II. The past several decades have seen a reduction of manufacturing jobs in the area and an increase of jobs in service industries and in the fields of finance, law, advertising, and insurance. The 1996 relocation of Lake Shore Drive made it possible to create the Museum Campus, a 57-acre extension of Burnham Park. The Museum Campus provides an easier and more scenic route to the Adler Planetarium, Field Museum of Natural History, and Shedd Aquarium and surrounds these three institutions with one continuous park featuring terraced gardens and broad walkways.

Art Deco the Chicago Way

Chicago is a textbook of Art Deco design. Look up at the façades of historic high rises, peek into the lobbies of landmark office buildings, ride an elevator or two. Begin at the Chicago Board of Trade (141 W Jackson Blvd), home to the world's oldest and largest futures exchange, formed in 1848. Ceres, the Roman goddess of grain and harvest, receives due homage with a 31-foot-tall statue atop the original 1930 building and a monumental mural in the atrium, added in the 1980s. A massive clock is ornamented with a distinctive agrarian motif. The three-story lobby, a dazzling Art Deco masterpiece, gleams with contrasting black- and buff-colored marble trimmed with silver; the elevator doors are silver and black. Light fixtures behind translucent panels throw out a diffused glow, and stylized figures are abundant.

Walk a couple of blocks west for breakfast at Lou Mitchell's Restaurant (565 W Jackson Blvd), known for egg dishes served in sizzling skillets. The restaurant presents boxes of Milk Duds to waiting female patrons. Then head north to the American National Bank Building (1 N LaSalle St). This 49-story limestone building, with typical Art Deco setbacks and dominant vertical lines, occupies an entire block of Chicago's financial district. A stunning Art Deco lobby features dark marble contrasted by gleaming metalwork and exquisite carved wood sconces. Outside, at the fifth-floor level, relief panels chronicle the 17th-century explorations of René-Robert Cavelier, Sieur de La Salle (Vitzhum & Burns, 1930).

Turn east to the former Chicago Daily News Building (400 W Madison St). The careers of Horace Greeley, Joseph Pulitzer, and other famous journalists, as well as events from Chicago's rich newspaper history, are chronicled with stylized bas-relief figures carved by Alvin Meyer. Originally, the limestone building with dramatic setbacks and an open riverfront plaza was designed to house the newspaper's offices and plant. Inside are ornate metal elevator doors, grillwork, and terrazzo floors in a geometric pattern. Travel north to the Carbide and Carbon Building (230 N Michigan Ave). This Art Deco skyscraper is as dramatically dark as its eponymous minerals. Offsetting piles of black polished granite are dark green masonry and gold terra-cotta trim. The stunning two-story lobby features marble walls, elegant bronze grillwork, gold-and-white plaster, and recessed lights of frosted glass. Just a block or two southwest, Heaven on Seven is tucked away on the seventh floor of the Garland Building (111 N Wabash St). Notable Cajun and Creole cooking includes gumbo, po' boy sandwiches, spicy jambalaya, sweet potato pie, and bread pudding.

Divert your attention to the fifth floor of the limestone building at 343 North Michigan Avenue. Seven-foot-high carved panels depicting settlers and Native Americans commemorate the site of Fort Dearborn, which overlooked the Chicago River at this spot. The lobby has terrazzo floors of black, russet, and green and brass elevator doors decorated with stylized figures. Farther north on the Magnificent Mile (see), look up above chic storefronts at the former Palmolive/Playboy Building (919 N Michigan Ave). Notice the dark bas-relief designs between the windows of this massive, stepped building. Turn the corner onto Walton and check out the lobby. It features Art Deco lights and handsome walnut elevator doors sculpted with bas-relief figures. Ride an elevator and note that the ornate carvings continue inside. The Saloon (200 E Chestnut) (see) is a warm, cheery steakhouse with high-quality, flavorful meat, suitably marbled and dry-aged. Be sure to try a side of bacon-scallion mashed potatoes. Décor features stenciled earth-tone walls, parchment sconces, and Native American murals.

Although, in the eyes of some, Chicago evokes the image of an industrial giant, it is also a city in which the arts flourish. Chicagoans are proud of their world-famous symphony orchestra, their Lyric Opera, and their numerous and diverse dance companies. Since 1912, Chicago has been the home of *Poetry* magazine. Chicago's theater community is vibrant, with more than 100 off-Loop theaters presenting quality drama. The collections at The Art Institute of Chicago, Museum of Contemporary Art, and many galleries along Michigan Avenue and in the River North area (see RIVER NORTH GALLERY DISTRICT) are among the best in the country.

Other museums are equally renowned: the Museum of Science and Industry, the Field Museum of Natural History, the Chicago Children's Museum, and the various specialty museums that reflect the ethnic and civic interests of the city.

The zoos, planetarium, and aquarium, as well as many parks and beaches along the lakefront, afford pleasure for visitors of all ages. Chicago's attractions are many, and sightseeing tours can be taken by boat, bus, car, bicycle, or foot.

Buses and rapid transit lines are integrated into one system—the most extensive in the nation—with interchangeable transfers. Elevated lines run through the Loop. Subway trains run under State and Dearborn streets and run on elevated structures to both the north and south. Rapid transit lines also serve the West Side, as well as O'Hare and Midway airports. Commuter trains stretch out to the far western and southern suburbs and near the Wisconsin and Indiana borders.

Driving and parking in Chicago are no more or less difficult than in any other major city. There are indoor and outdoor parking areas near and in the Loop; some provide shuttle bus service to the Loop or to the Merchandise Mart.

The attractions decribed under CHICAGO are arranged alphabetically, and most contain neighborhood designations following their addresses. The Loop is considered the center of the city, with State Street running north and south and Madison Street east and west as the baselines. The eastern border of the city is Lake Michigan. In addition, some attractions in outlying areas are listed.

Additional Visitor Information

For a few more attractions and accommodations, see CHICAGO O'HARE AIRPORT AREA, which follows CHICAGO.

When available, half-price, day-of-performance tickets are offered, with a slight service charge, at Hot Tix ticket booths: 78 W Randolph St, Chicago; 163 E Pearson St, Chicago; and 9501 N Skokie Blvd, Skokie. Hot Tix booths also are at these Tower Records: 214 S Wabash Ave, Chicago; 2301 N Clark St, Chicago; 1209 E Golf Rd, Schaumburg; and 383 W Army Trail Rd, Bloomingdale. (Tues-Sat; Sun tickets sold on Sat) For available tickets, check www.hottix.org.

Chicago magazine is helpful for anyone visiting Chicago; it's available at most newsstands. *Key-This Week in Chicago* and *Where*, at major hotels, provide up-to-date information. For additional information, see any of the daily newspapers; special sections to look at are "Friday" in the Friday *Chicago Tribune*, the "Arts & Entertainment" section in the Sunday *Chicago Tribune*, and the "Weekend Plus" section of the Friday *Sun-Times*. A free weekly newspaper, *The Reader*, provides information about local events, art, and entertainment.

There are five Illinois Travel Information Centers: 310 S Michigan Ave, the Sears Tower (233 S Wacker Dr), the James R. Thompson Center (100 W Randolph St), and at Midway and O'Hare airports. (Mon-Fri)

The Pumping Station (see OLD CHICAGO WATER TOWER AND PUMPING STATION), at the corner of Chicago and Michigan avenues, houses a visitor information center that provides brochures and information about points of interest and transportation. (Daily)

Contact the Chicago Office of Tourism, Chicago Cultural Center, 78 E Washington St, 60602, phone 312/744-2400 or toll-free 800/226-6632. The Office of Tourism distributes an event calendar, maps and museum guides, and hotel and restaurant guides, plus other information about the Chicago area. (Mon-Sat, also Sun afternoons)

Public Transportation

Chicago Transit Authority (CTA)/Regional Transit Authority (RTA). Public buses. Phone 312/836-7000

What to See and Do

Adler Planetarium & Astronomy Museum.
1300 S Lake Shore Dr (60605). On a peninsula in Lake Michigan. Phone 312/322-0300. www. adlerplanetarium.org. One of the oldest observatories in the Western Hemisphere, the Adler Planetarium offers a high-tech look at the night sky. In May 2003, schoolchildren were able to videoconference with astronauts and cosmonauts aboard the International Space Station, and astronomers are studying meteorite fragments that landed in Chicago's suburbs that same month. The planetarium works closely with scientists at The University of Chicago (see) and is linked via computer with the Apache Point observatory in New Mexico. Exhibits commemorate the Space Race of the 1960s, as well as new techniques to learn more about the Milky Way. Tours of the facility are available, and shows are included with the price of admission. If you want a bargain, go September-December on Mondays-Tuesdays, when admission is free. (Mon-Fri 9:30 am-4:30 pm, Sat-Sun 9 am-4:30 pm; closed Thanksgiving, Dec 25) **$$$**

American Girl Place. *111 E Chicago Ave (60611). Phone 312/943-9400; toll-free 877/247-5223. www. americangirl.com.* If you're strolling around downtown Chicago, you're bound to see legions of girls toting red shopping bags from American Girl Place. Dolls are the major draw here, but the store also sells clothing and accessories (for dolls and their owners) and doll furniture and toys. American Girl Place also features a café (reservations recommended), various special events, and a Broadway-style show ($$$$), *Circle of Friends: An American Girls Musical*, at the on-site theater. **FREE**

American Sightseeing Chicago. *27 E Monroe St (60603). Phone 312/251-3100; toll-free 800/621-4153. www.americansightseeing.org/chicago.htm.* Tours depart from the Palmer House hotel (see) and range from two to eight hours. Options include a historic Oak Park (see OAK PARK) and Frank Lloyd Wright tour and a dinner tour of Chinatown (see). **$$$**

Apollo Theatre. *2540 N Lincoln Ave (60614). Phone 773/935-6100. www.apollochicago.com.* An intimate theater in Chicago's Lincoln Park (see) neighborhood, the Apollo has been home to both famous and infamous productions over the years. The year 2003 saw a run of Eve Ensler's *The Vagina Monologues,* and previous years have included productions of the plays of Neil Simon, Clifford Odets, and many others. Built in 1978, the theater saw many productions by the Steppenwolf Theater Company (see) (including *Balm in Gilead* with Gary Sinese and John Malkovich), as well as native Chicagoan Jim Belushi starring in David Mamet's *Sexual Perversity in Chicago.* It is a great setting in which to see a show, with small crowds filling the seats and big names on the stage.

Arie Crown Theater. *2301 S Lake Shore Dr (60616). Phone 312/791-6000. www.ariecrown.com.* This recently renovated theater near McCormick Place (see) hosts an irregular lineup of plays, concerts, and conferences. It seats 5,000.

⭐ **The Art Institute of Chicago.** *122 S Michigan Ave (60603). Phone 312/443-3600. www.artic.edu.* No visit to Chicago is complete without a stop at The Art Institute of Chicago, a local treasure with an international reputation. Adjacent to Millennium Park on South Michigan Avenue, this 1879 Beaux Arts building, originally part of the Columbian Exposition, houses more than 300,000 works of art within its ten curatorial departments. The museum has what's considered the finest and most comprehensive modern and contemporary art collection in the world, one of the largest arms collections in America, and one of the two finest collections of Japanese woodblock prints. Highlights include Georges Seurat's *A Sunday on La Grande Jatte—1884,* Grant Wood's *American Gothic,* Edward Hopper's *Nighthawks,* 33 Monet paintings, Marc Chagall stained-glass windows, a reconstructed Adler and Sullivan Chicago Stock Exchange trading room, and significant photo and architectural drawing collections. You also can attend free daily lectures, visit the well-stocked gift shop, dine at one of three restaurants, including a summertime garden, and take a special tour for the visually impaired. (Daily; closed Thanksgiving, Dec 25) Free admission Tues. **$$**

Auditorium Building. *430 S Michigan Ave (60605). In the Loop.* (1889) Landmark structure designed by world-renowned architects Louis Sullivan and Dankmar Adler. The interior is noted for its intricate system of iron framing, breathtaking ornamentation, and near-perfect acoustics. Now houses Roosevelt University (see).

Auditorium Theatre. *50 E Congress Pkwy (60605). Phone 312/922-2110. www.auditoriumtheatre.org.* The Auditorium Theatre building, designed by world-

Books and Movies That Feature Chicago

Add a little atmosphere to your Chicago journey with books and movies to set the stage. Here are some ideas to get you started.

Books

The Adventures of Augie March, by Saul Bellow (1953). A coming-of-age novel about growing up in a working-class Jewish neighborhood in Chicago in the first half of the 1900s. Bellow's novel follows the intelligent but unfocused Augie through a variety of jobs as he attempts to make a living during the Great Depression. The book was among the first of Penguin's Great Books of the 20th Century series.

The Bishop Goes to the University, by Andrew M. Greeley (2003). Bishop Blackie Ryan, assistant to the Chicago Cardinal, is asked to look into the mob-style execution of a visiting Russian Orthodox monk found murdered in his University of Chicago office. Father Greeley puts his Irish crime-solver into a caper that involves the CIA, the former KBG, the Church, and, of course, a body double.

Blacklist, by Sara Paretsky (2003). Secrets and betrayals—political, social, sexual, and financial—that deal with the aftermath of the 9/11 terrorist attacks and the ghosts of the 1950s House Un-American Activities Committee play out against a Chicago backdrop. This is the 11th novel in Paretsky's series starring that hard-boiled detective dame, V. I. Warshowski.

The Devil in the White City: Murder, Magic, and Madness at the Fair That Changed America, by Erik Larson (2003). The White City is the 1893 Chicago World's Fair; the devil is H. H. Holmes, a serial killer responsible for scores of deaths around the same time. Larson weaves anecdotes about Thomas Edison, Susan B. Anthony, and Buffalo Bill Cody into this true story while alternating chapters about architect Daniel Burnham, who built the White City, and the sinister Holmes, who built the World's Fair Hotel complete with crematorium and gas chamber for his victims. The book is nonfiction but reads like a can't-put-down novel.

The Time Traveler's Wife, by Audrey Niffenegger (2003). Henry DeTamble is a librarian at Chicago's Newberry Library (see). Because he is inflicted with "chrono displacement," he suddenly jumps into the past or the future—always without warning—and meets his wife at certain times in their lives. The novel's scenes take place throughout the city.

Others Chicago-related books include *Ordinary People*, by Judith Guest; *The Deep End of the Ocean*, by Jacquelyn Mitchard; *The House on Mango Street*, by Sandra Cisneros; *Lieberman's Law*, by Stuart Kaminsky; *Maxwell Street Blues*, by Michael Raleigh; and *Nowhere Man*, by Aleksandar Hemon. Chicago authors who use Chicago settings include Nelsen Algren and Scott Turow.

Movies

The Blues Brothers (1980). James Brown, Aretha Franklin, Ray Charles, and Cab Calloway sing backup for John (Jake "Joliet" Blues) Belushi and Dan (Elwood Blues) Aykroyd's antics, car crashes, and special effects as the duo try to put together their old band to save the Catholic home where they were raised. The movie was filmed throughout Chicago and its suburbs.

His Girl Friday (1940). Howard Hawks directed this screwball romantic comedy about newspaper editor Walter Burns (Cary Grant), whose ace reporter and former wife Hildy Johnson (Rosalind Russell) is about to leave the paper to marry another man. Authors Charles MacArthur and Ben Hecht originally wrote Hildy as a male character who was leaving the paper because he was tired of the grind (*The Front Page*); other versions have remained truer to the story, but *His Girl Friday* is a Grant-Russell classic.

Hoop Dreams (1994). Many viewers and Oscar voters alike thought that *Hoop Dreams* should have been nominated for Best Picture. Alternatively funny, sad, poignant, and always interesting, this documentary—filmed over several years—follows the lives of two inner-city Chicago high school basketball players on their quest to become hoops superstars.

My Best Friend's Wedding (1997). A comedy wtih Julia Roberts, Dermot Mulroney, Cameron Diaz, and Rupert Everett about what happens when a woman (Roberts) decides that she's in love with her best friend (Mulroney) on the day he announces his engagement. The wedding was filmed at Chicago's beautiful Fourth Presbyterian Church (see) just off Michigan Avenue on Chestnut Street.

The Untouchables (1987). It's a tough image to suppress, and many Chicagoans have given up trying. The decade: the 1920s. The stage: Prohibition.

The characters: Al Capone and Elliot Ness. You can't get much more Chicago than that. You'll get a real appreciation for Chicago's Union Station after seeing this movie, starring Kevin Costner and Sean Connery (who won a Best Supporting Actor Oscar for the film).

Other movies set in the Windy City include *About Last Night* (1986), *Call Northside 777* (1948), *Chicago* (2002), *City That Never Sleeps* (1953), *Eight Men Out* (1988), *Ferris Bueller's Day Off* (1986), *The Fugitive* (1993), *Risky Business* (1983), *Running Scared* (1986), and *The Sting* (1973).

renowned architects Louis Sullivan and Dankmar Adler, underwent a face-lift in 2003, getting a new state-of-the-art stage and orchestra pit. The stage was returned to its original height, as designed in the 1880s. The building has been host to many different types of performances in its history, from large-scale musical productions like *Les Misérables* to its function in the 1960s and 1970s as the premier concert venue in Chicago, hosting names like Jimi Hendrix and Janis Joplin. The Joffrey Ballet opened the new stage in late 2003, and the historic building begins yet another era as one of the premier places to watch a show of any kind in the City of Big Shoulders.

Balmoral Park Race Track. *26435 S Dixie Hwy, Crete (60417). 25 miles S on I-94 to Hwy 394, continue S to Elmscourt Ln. Phone 708/672-1414. www.balmoralpark.com.* Harness racing. (All year, days vary)

Balzekas Museum of Lithuanian Culture. *6500 S Pulaski Rd (60629). South Side. Phone 773/582-6500.* Antiques, art, children's museum, memorabilia, and literature spanning 1,000 years of Lithuanian history. Exhibits include amber, armor and antique weapons, rare maps, textiles, dolls, stamps, coins; research library. (Daily; closed Jan 1, Thanksgiving, Dec 25) Free admission Mon. **$$**

Bloomingdale's Home + Furniture Store. *600 N Wabash Ave (60611). Phone 312/324-7500.* Set in the historic Medinah Temple, formerly the home of Chicago's Shriners, this four-level wonder is filled with both architectural and commercial treasures. If the store's ample selection of high-end kitchenware,

linens, and home furnishings doesn't grab your attention, the magnificently restored stained-glass windows, soaring dome, and shining façade are sure to have you oohing and aahing. (Mon-Sat 10 am-8 pm, Sun 11 am-7 pm)

Briar Street Theatre. *3133 N Halsted St (60657). Phone 773/348-4000.* The Briar Street Theatre has been the Chicago home of the national sensation Blue Man Group, which incorporates everyday objects like metal drums and pipes into a musical experience rife with color and comedy. Prior to men in blue body paint entertaining the crowds, the 625-seat venue hosted long-running renditions of *Driving Miss Daisy* and Steve Martin's *Picasso at the Lapin Agile*. It's easily accessible by CTA rapid transit, and tickets are less pricey than at many other theaters in the city. The theater sits on the old site of the horse stables of Marshall Field's department store, having been used as a theater only since 1985.

Blue Man Group. *3133 N Halsted St, Chicago. In the Briar Street Theatre. Phone 773/348-4000. www.blueman.com.* Blue Man Group is a percussion (drums) band and performance group that's literally blue—all three members cover themselves in blue body paint. The group performs by thumping on drums, banging on barrels, and pounding on pipes. The heart-pounding, entertaining, dramatic performance includes audience members (although no one is forced to participate against his will); if you so choose, you may even get painted, too! Performances last just over two hours. **$$$$**

Cadillac-Palace Theater. *151 W Randolph St (60601). Phone 312/977-1700.* This theater is a Chicago landmark inspired by the decadence of the palace at Versailles in France. It originally played first-run movies during the 1920s and 1930s and was converted to a live theater in the 1950s. It was purchased by the Bismarck hotel in the 1970s and turned into a banquet hall. In 1999, the theater reopened in its original role and hosted performances of Giuseppe Verdi's *Aida* (as adapted by Elton John and Tim Rice), as well as the hit theatrical production of Disney's *The Lion King*.

Carson Pirie Scott. *1 S State St (60603). At Madison St. In the Loop. Phone 312/641-7000. www.carsons .com.* (1899) This landmark department store building is considered architect Louis Sullivan's masterpiece. Extraordinary cast-iron ornamentation on the first and second floors frames display windows like paintings. (Mon-Sat, select Sun; closed holidays)

⭐ **Chicago Architecture Foundation tours.** *224 S Michigan Ave (60604). Phone 312/922-8687. www. architecture.org.* For an interesting and informative introduction to Chicago, sign up for a Chicago Architecture Foundation tour. This not-for-profit organization dedicated to raising public awareness of architecture features 65 different tours given by more than 450 volunteer (but extraordinarily well trained and knowledgeable) docents. The two-hour Loop and Historic Skyscraper walking tours give an excellent general history of the city and how it grew, while other tours cater to more specialized interests, such as Art Deco buildings, the Theater District, modern skyscrapers, and Loop sculpture, as well as individual city neighborhoods like Old Town, River North, Printers Row, the Gold Coast, and the Sheffield Historic District. One of the most popular tours is the 90-minute Architecture River Cruise that passes more than 50 architecturally significant sights. Bus tours, bike tours, and even "L" train tours are also available (on specific dates only). You can purchase tickets and meet for tours at one of two tour centers on Michigan Avenue. **$$$** Among the tours offered are

Chicago Highlights Bus Tour. *224 S Michigan Ave, Chicago. Phone 312/922-3432.* This four-hour bus tour covers the Loop, the Gold Coast, Hyde Park, three historic districts, and three university campuses; includes interior of Frank Lloyd Wright's Robie House (see). Reservations required. (Sat-Sun) **$$$$**

Chicago River Boat Tour. *455 E Illinois St, Chicago. Phone 312/942-3432.* This 1 1/2-hour tour covers the north and south branches of the Chicago River, with views of the city's celebrated riverfront architecture; historic 19th-century railroad bridges and warehouses, 20th-century bridgehouses, and magnificent Loop skyscrapers. (May-Sept, daily; Oct, Tues, Thurs, Sat-Sun; no tours Labor Day) Reservations required. **$$$$**

Graceland Cemetery Tour. *4001 N Clark St, Chicago. Phone 773/525-1105.* Walking through Graceland Cemetery on the city's North Side is like taking a step back into Chicago's early history. Not only will you recognize the names of the movers and shakers who put Chicago on the map—Philip Armour, Mayor Joseph Medill, Cyrus McCormick, George Pullman, Potter Palmer, and Marshall Field, to name a few—but you'll also find memorials to the people who helped build it: architects Louis Sullivan, Daniel Burnham, John Root, and Mies van der Rohe. Established in 1860, Graceland, with its winding pathways and gorgeous old trees, is perfect for solo exploration any time of the year. Throughout the cemetery, you'll discover varied and artistic memorials, from Greek temples and Egyptian pyramids to Celtic crosses and ethereal angels. Highlights include Louis Sullivan's tomb for Carrie Eliza Getty, a landmark described as the beginning of modern architecture in America; Daniel Burnham's island resting place in the middle of the lake; and Mies van der Rohe's elegantly understated grave marker. (Daily) **FREE**

Loop Walking Tours. *224 S Michigan Ave, Chicago. Depart from Tour Center. Phone 312/922-3432.* Each tour is two hours long. Early Skyscrapers traces the origins of the Chicago school of architecture and the skyscrapers built from 1880 to 1940. The tour includes the Monadnock (see) and Rookery buildings (see). Modern & Beyond reviews important newer buildings, including the Federal Center, the IBM Building, and the James R. Thompson Center; also public murals and sculptures by Calder, Chagall, Miro, Picasso, Henry Moore, and Dubuffet. (Daily) **$$$**

The Chicago Athenaeum: Museum of Architecture and Design. *307 N Michigan Ave (60601). Phone 312/372-1083. www.chi-athenaeum.org.* This museum honors the history of design in all apsects of civilization, from fashion to urban development. (Wed-Sun) **$**

Chicago Cultural Center. *78 E Washington St (60602). In the Loop. Phone 312/744-6630. www. cl.chi.il.us/tourism/culturalcenter.* If you have a couple of hours free, you may want to wander into the Chicago Cultural Center on Michigan Avenue between Randolph and Washington, a gem of a building that offers a wealth of free daily programming and ongoing exhibits. The landmark building, formerly a library, features Tiffany glass domes, mosaics, and marble walls and stairs. The center itself often offers exhibitions of groundbreaking art, as well as frequent performances by renowned poets and musicians. On weekdays during the summer, you can catch "Lunchbreak," a program designed to infuse lunch in the bustling city with good music in a great setting. (Mon-Sat 10 am-4:30 pm; Sun noon-5 pm; archives closed Sun; closed holidays) **FREE**

Chicago Fire Academy. *558 W DeKoven St (60607). West Side. Phone 312/747-8151.* Built on the site where the Great Chicago Fire of 1871 is believed to have started. Legend has it that it was a cow in Mrs. O'Leary's barn knocking over a lantern that began the fire, but recent investigations suggest this story may be fictitious. The fire academy pays tribute to those who serve the Windy City and donate their lives to the safety of Chicago's citizens. **FREE**

Chicago Historical Society. *1601 N Clark St (60614). Clark St at North Ave. Near North Side. Phone 312/ 642-4600. www.chicagohs.org.* Changing exhibits focus on the history and development of Chicago. Selected aspects of Illinois and United States history, including galleries devoted to costumes, decorative arts, and architecture. Pioneer craft demonstrations; hands-on gallery. (Daily; closed Jan 1, Thanksgiving, Dec 25) Free admission Mon. Additional charges for special exhibits. **$$**

⭐ **Chicago lakefront.** *Phone 312/742-7529. www. chicagoparkdistrict.com.* Chicago's lakefront reflects the vision of architect Daniel Burnham, whose 1909 Plan for Chicago specified that the shoreline remain publicly owned and enjoyed by all. It is also one of the things that make this city sparkle. After all, how many major cities have bathing beaches—31 in total—within the city limits? In addition to beaches, the lakefront sports 18 miles of bicycle, jogging, and in-line skating paths, several golf courses and driving ranges, skating rinks, tennis courts, field houses, theaters, and more, all easily accessible and open to the public. Chicagoans rich and poor flock to the

lakefront year-round to exercise, sunbathe, picnic, and simply enjoy the view. If you have the opportunity and the weather cooperates, rent a bicycle at Navy Pier (see) and spend a few hours following the well-marked path north. Look for the chess players at North Avenue Beach and the skyline views from Montrose Harbor.

Chicago Loop Synagogue. *16 S Clark St (60603). In the Loop. Phone 312/346-7370.* (1957) The eastern wall of this building is a unique example of contemporary stained glass, depicting ancient Hebraic symbols whirling through the cosmos.

Chicago Motor Coach Company. *1 N Water Tower (60609). Phone 773/922-8919.* Double-decker tours depart from the Sears Tower (see) at Jackson and Wacker, the Field Museum of Natural History (see), Michigan and Pearson, and Michigan and Wacker.

Chicago neighborhood tours. *78 E Washington St (60602). Phone 312/742-1190. www.chgocitytours.com.* Tours depart at 10 am from the Chicago Cultural Center and last approximately four hours. Narrated tours visit 11 different neighborhoods via motor coach. Tours are held on Saturday only, spotlighting a different area each week. Reservations are strongly recommended. **$$$$**

Chicago Temple. *77 W Washington St (60602). In the Loop. Phone 312/236-4548.* (First Methodist Episcopal Church, 1923) At 568 feet from street level to the tip of its Gothic tower, this is the highest church spire in the world. Tours (Mon-Sat 2 pm, Sun after 8:30 am and 11 am services; no tours holidays).

Chicago Theatre. *175 N State St (60601). Phone 312/443-1130. www.capa.com/chicago.* The Chicago Theatre may be best known for the flashy sign spelling out CHICAGO vertically above its marquee, but visitors to the theater likely will be more impressed by its magnificent French baroque design. Proceed through the front doors, passing underneath a miniature replica of the Arc de Triomphe, and enter an opulent five-story lobby modeled after the Mansarts Chapel at the Palace of Versailles. The extravagant and ornate interior features bronze light fixtures with Steuben glass shades, crystal chandeliers, polished marble, and soaring murals hand-painted on the auditorium's ceiling. Opened in 1921 as the city's first movie palace, the Chicago Theatre today hosts live performances by internationally renowned musicians, comedians, and actors. The theater's original Wurlitzer pipe organ has been restored and still produces a lush, powerful sound.

Chicago Tribune Tower. *435 N Michigan Ave (60611). Near North Side. Phone 312/222-3994.* (1925) Essentially, this 36-story tower is a moderne building with a Gothic-detailed base and crown. It does exactly what publisher Joseph Medill intended: it "thames" the Chicago River. The tower's once strong foundation has been loosening in recent years, and structural engineers have noted that the edifice has been slowly sinking at the rate of almost a foot a year due to seepage from a sublevel bog just west along the riverbank. Bits and pieces of historic structures from around the world are embedded in the exterior walls of the lower floors.

Chicago Trolley Company. *4400 S Racine Ave (60609). Phone 773/648-5000. www.chicagotrolley.com.* One-fee, all-day ride on a trolley or double-decker bus, with the ability to hop on and off at major sites. The tour goes as far north as the John Hancock Center (see), as far south as the Field Museum of Natural History (see), as far west as the Sears Tower (see) and as far east as Navy Pier (see). **$$$$**

Chicago Water Works. *163 E Pearson (60611). Phone toll-free 866/710-0294 (Chicago Office of Tourism).* The pumping station, opened in 1869, is responsible for pumping water to the central Chicago district. Walk through to see how the station works and visit the other attractions inside. Visitor information booth (7:30 am-7 pm). City of Chicago store (Mon-Sat 9 am-5 pm, Sun 11 am-5 pm). Hot Tix booth (Tues-Sat 10 am-6 pm, Sun noon-5 pm).

Chicago White Sox (MLB). *US Cellular Field, 333 W 35th St (60616). Phone 312/674-1000; toll-free 866/769-4263. www.whitesox.com.* On paper, it might look like the White Sox changed stadiums to begin the 2003 season, but really it was just the moniker of the building that switched from historic Comiskey Park (honoring former owner Charles) to US Cellular Field. **$$$$**

Chinatown. *Starts at the intersection of Cermak Rd and Wentworth Ave (60616). Phone 312/326-5320 (Chinatown Chamber of Commerce). www.chicagochinatown.org.* Though not as large as New York's or San Francisco's Chinatowns, Chicago's Chinatown is a vibrant and lively cultural center that makes for a fascinating visit. Located south of the Loop at Cermak and Wentworth, Chinatown's boundary is marked by a tiled gateway and traditional architecture that is reflected in the smallest details, such as the rooftops, lampposts, and phone booths. Within a ten-block radius are 10,000 community members, more than 40 restaurants, 20 gifts shops, herbal and tea stores, and bakeries. Locals tend to visit on Sunday mornings for dim sum, but it's also fun to be in the neighborhood during any of the traditional festivals, including Chinese New Year, the Dragon Boat Festival, and the mid-autumn Moon Festival. Chinatown is a 10- to 15-minute cab ride from the Loop. During summer weekends, it also is accessible via a free trolley that departs from the Field Museum of Natural History (see) and from the intersection of State Street and Roosevelt Road. **FREE**

Civic Opera Building. *20 N Wacker Dr (60606). In the Loop. Phone 312/332-2244.* (1929) On the lower levels, under 45 floors of commercial office space, is the richly Art Deco, 3,400-seat Civic Opera House, home of the Lyric Opera of Chicago.

Civic Opera House. *Phone 312/419-0033. www.civicoperahouse.com.* Owned and operated by the Lyric Opera of Chicago.

Lyric Opera of Chicago. *Phone 312/419-0033. www.lyricopera.org.* Chicago's Lyric Opera performs some of the biggest names in operatic theater. Each year offers recognizable stories, as well as a few to broaden the horizons of even the most seasoned opera connoisseur. Often, the operas are done in the language in which they were written, but with English subtitles projected above the stage so that all can follow the story. Each season begins with a new 12-person repertory cast chosen in March and given additional professional training to make Chicago's performances among the finest anywhere. **$$$$**

DePaul University. *Loop campus, 1 E Jackson Blvd (60604). Lincoln Park campus, Fullerton and Sheffield aves, Near North Side. Phone 312/362-8300. www.depaul.edu.* (20,500 students) The Lincoln Park campus, with its blend of modern and Gothic architecture, is an integral part of Chicago's historic Lincoln Park neighborhood (see). The Blue Demons, DePaul's basketball team, play home games at the Allstate Arena (see ROSEMONT). Tours (by appointment).

DuSable Museum of African-American History. *740 E 56th Pl (60637). South Side. Phone 773/947-0600. www.dusablemuseum.org.* African and African-American art objects; displays of black history in

Africa and the United States. Extensive collection includes paintings, sculptures, artifacts, textiles, books, and photographs. (Daily; closed Jan 1, Thanksgiving, Dec 25) Free admission Sun. **$$**

Elks National Veterans Memorial. *2750 N Lakeview Ave (60614). Phone 773/755-4876. www.elks.org/ memorial.* The Elks Fraternal Order, founded in 1868, erected this memorial designed by New York architect Egerton Swarthout in 1926 to honor Americans' profound sacrifices in World War I. The memorial has since become a tribute to Americans who lost their lives in World War II, the Korean War, and the Vietnam War. Visitors are welcome to walk inside the domed structure to view the 100-foot rotunda made of marble and adorned with murals, art-glass windows, and bronze sculptures. The rotunda opens into an ornate reception room, also available for public viewing. (Mon-Fri 9 am-5 pm; Apr-Nov, also Sat-Sun 10 am-5 pm)

⭐ **Field Museum of Natural History.** *1400 S Lake Shore Dr (60605). Phone 312/922-9410. www.fmnh .org.* The Field Museum, dedicated to the world's natural history, has made great strides to improve its already vast collection in recent years, with the biggest addition (literally!) being Sue, the largest and most complete tyrannosaurus Rex skeleton ever unearthed. Sue adds to a fine collection of artifacts from bygone civilizations, like those in Egypt and Mesopotamia. Recent exhibits have included a look at how chocolate has influenced the world and "Baseball As America," detailing how America's pastime follows closely the threads of history that surround it. Be sure to look for the museum's collections from China, Japan, and the rest of the Orient. A list of touchables for the visually impaired is available. (Daily 9 am-5 pm; closed Jan 1, Dec 25) Free admission Sept-Feb, Mon-Tues. **$$**

Ford Center for the Performing Arts Oriental Theater. *24 W Randolph St (60602). Phone 312/977-1700.* The Oriental Theater was originally a movie house that doubled as an entertainment venue for musicians like Duke Ellington during the early 20th century. The theater closed its doors to moviegoers in the 1980s but came back with a flourish. Re-opening in 1998, it was converted into a place to see live shows, sharing the Theater District with places like the Chicago and Shubert theaters. Recent productions have included *The Producers, Mamma Mia, Ragtime,* and *Miss Saigon.*

Fourth Presbyterian Church. *126 E Chestnut St (60611). Near North Side. Phone 312/787-4570.* Completed in 1914, this beautiful church is a fine example of Gothic design. One of its architects, Ralph A. Cram, was a leader of the Gothic Revival in the United States. Tours are available by appointment or after Sun services. (Daily)

Garfield Park and Conservatory. *300 N Central Park Ave (60624). West Side. Phone 312/746-5100. www. garfield-conservatory.org.* Outdoor formal gardens. Conservatory has eight houses and propagating houses on more than 5 acres. Permanent exhibits. Four major shows annually at Horticultural Hall and Show House. (Daily 9 am-5 pm) **FREE**

Goodman Theatre. *170 N Dearborn St (60601). Phone 312/443-3800. www.goodman-theatre.org.* The Goodman Theatre can be considered a breeding ground for up-and-coming actors and productions. A good example is its production of Eugene O'Neill's *A Long Day's Journey into Night,* which took star Brian Dennehy with it to Broadway and captured several Tony Awards. Actors of Dennehy's caliber are not uncommon at the Goodman, as other theater dignitaries like Charles S. Dutton regularly perform works by such noted playwrights as August Wilson and Steven Sondheim. Tickets can be pricey, but not as expensive as a Broadway show, and there are discounts for students and groups. Most shows are adult oriented, but the Goodman does make a point of providing family-friendly fare, including its annual production of Charles Dickens's *A Christmas Carol.*

Grant Park. *331 E Randolph St (60601). Stretches from Randolph St to McFetridge Dr. In the Loop. Phone 312/742-7648. www.chicagoparkdistrict.com.* Grant Park was built on a landfill created by debris from the Great Chicago Fire of 1871. Now, it stands as one of the great landmarks of the city, with majestic Buckingham Fountain as its centerpiece. The fountain is one piece of the original design that has survived and looks as though it's right out of Louis XIV's Palace at Versailles. Each year, the Taste of Chicago (see SPECIAL EVENTS) is held here, as are many picnics and smaller festivals. Grant Park borders The Art Institute of Chicago (see) and runs parallel with Michigan Avenue. You can enjoy concerts at the Petrillo Music Shell or relax on the lawn on summer evenings to watch outdoor movies during the yearly Chicago Outdoor Film Festival (see SPECIAL EVENTS). A beautiful green centerpiece to the Windy

City, the park also includes fragrant rose gardens that frame the north and south end of Buckingham Fountain.

Buckingham Fountain. *Columbus Dr and Congress Pkwy. Phone 312/742-7529. www. chicagoparkdistrict.com.* When the World Cup was held in Chicago in 1994, foreign visitors identified the Buckingham Fountain as the "Bundy fountain" because of its prominent place in the opening credits of the TV show *Married with Children.* That notoriety aside, Buckingham Fountain is an integral part of the city and one of the largest fountains in the world. The fountain was given to the city by Kate Buckingham in 1927 in honor of her brother. Every minute, 133 jets spray approximately 14,000 gallons of water as high as 150 feet. Every hour on the hour, there's a 20-minute water display (accompanied, at dusk, by lights and music). For locals, the fountain marks the changing seasons; when it's turned on—to much fanfare—it heralds the beginning of summer, and, when it's turned off, it signals that the dreaded Chicago winter will soon follow. (May-early Oct, daily) **FREE**

Gray Line Bus Tours. *17 E Monroe St (60603). Phone 312/251-3107; toll-free 800/621-4153. www.grayline .com.* Tours range from 1 1/2 to 7 hours. **$$$$**

Green Mill. *4802 N Broadway St (60640). Phone 773/878-5552.* The oldest jazz club in America, the Green Mill is located in the still-dicey Uptown neighborhood. It's more than a great place to hear jazz; it's also a chance to step back in time. With a vintage sign out front and a gorgeous carved bar inside, this former speakeasy of the Capone gang reeks of atmosphere (and cigarettes) of a bygone era. The jazz, however, is strictly contemporary, showcasing some of the most acclaimed musicians working today, from international performers to local luminaries such as Patricia Barber, Kurt Elling, and Von Freeman. On weeknights, you might find swing or a big band; on weekend nights, several acts pack in aficionados until the wee hours; and, on Sundays, you can experience the Poetry Slam (the nation's first, hosted by Marc Smith, the "godfather" of poetry slams), where area poets test their mettle against audience reaction. (Daily) **$$$**

Harborside International Golf Center. *11001 S Doty Ave E (60628). Phone 312/782-7837.* Located just south of downtown Chicago, Harborside was manufactured by architect Dick Nugent out of a converted landfill into one of the most renowned municipal courses in America. The center has two courses, the Starboard and the Port layouts, and features four tee boxes on each hole to accommodate almost every golfer. The center's practice facility is also top-notch, with driving ranges of longer than 400 yards and many opportunities to practice middle irons and short games—even at night, as the 58-acre practice facility is fully lit. **$$$$**

Haymarket Riot Monument. *1300 W Jackson Blvd (60607).* Erected in 1893, the monument commemorates the riot that killed seven policemen when a bomb exploded during a labor strike on May 4, 1886. The statue still stirs passions over labor issues; labor organizations gather at the statue every year on the Sunday closest to May 4, as well as November 11, the anniversary of Black Friday.

Holy Name Cathedral. *735 N State St (60610). Near North Side. Phone 312/787-8040.* The home to the Chicago archdiocese and Francis Cardinal George, Holy Name is a good example of Gothic Revival architecture in Chicago. Thousands of parishoners attend services at Holy Name each week, many of them to hear Cardinal George on Sunday morning. The church is also affiliated with the Francis Xavier Warde School.

Illinois Institute of Technology (IIT). *3300 S Federal St (60616). South Side. Phone 312/567-3000. www.iit.edu.* (1892) (6,000 students) Students from more than 100 countries converge on this campus to engage themselves in IIT's Interprofessional Project, which aims to teach students the skills they'll need to fit in wherever they choose in a job market that is constantly expanding technologically. Ninety-eight percent of the faculty (who teach almost all the classes, rather than teaching assistants) hold doctorate or other terminal degrees. The campus was designed by architect Mies van de Rohe.

International Museum of Surgical Science. *1524 N Lake Shore Dr (60610). Phone 312/642-6502. www. imss.org.* Covering the advancement of surgical medicine across more than four millennia of history, this four-story museum housed in an old mansion organizes its exhibits into categories like radiology, orthopedics, and "A Day in the Life of a Turn-of-the-Century Apothecary." Located on scenic Lake Shore Drive in the heart of the Windy City, the museum offers free admission on Tuesday. There are permanent exhibits, like the optical history exhibit and displays of Victorian-era surgical implements, as well as rotating features covering subjects like art's depiction of anatomy. (Sept-Apr, Tues-Sat; May-Aug, Tues-Sun; 10 am-4 pm) **$$**

Jackson Park Golf Club. *6400 Richards Dr (60645). 63rd St and Lake Shore Dr. Phone 312/245-0909.* On Chicago's near South Side is this short but still tough course. Several par-fours measure less than 300 yards, but they're all deceptively difficult. The course's two par-fives are situated next to one another on the back nine and can easily ruin a good round of golf. The greens fee is always reasonable, with 18 holes and a cart available for just $20 at most times. For twilight golfers, the rate is just $12. **$$$$**

Jane Addams Hull-House Museum. *800 S Halsted St (60607). On the campus of the University of Illinois at Chicago. West Side. Phone 312/413-5353. www.uic .edu/jaddams/hull/hull_house.html.* Two original Hull-House buildings, the restored Hull Mansion (1856) and dining hall (1905), which formed the nucleus of the 13-building settlement complex founded in 1889 by Jane Addams and Ellen Gates Starr, social welfare pioneers. Exhibits and presentations on the history of Hull-House, the surrounding neighborhood, ethnic groups, and women's history. (Tues-Fri 10 am-4 pm, Sun noon-4 pm; closed holidays) **FREE**

John Hancock Center. *875 N Michigan Ave (60611). Near North Side. Phone 312/751-3681; toll-free 888/875-8439 (observatory). www.hancock-observatory .com.* Anchoring North Michigan Avenue is yet another undeniable Chicago landmark, the John Hancock Center, which at 1,127 feet and 100 floors is the world's 13th tallest building. Since completion in 1969, this innovative office/residential building with its distinctive exterior X bracing—which eliminated the need for inner support beams, thus increasing usable space—has won numerous architectural awards. It also claims many notables, including the world's highest residence and the world's highest indoor swimming pool. The 94th floor observatory features an open-air skywalk, a history wall chronicling Chicago's growth, multilingual "sky tours," and a 360-degree view that spans 80 miles and four states (Michigan, Indiana, Wisconsin, and Illinois). The best viewing is from sunset onward, when the sun shimmers on the skyline and lake. Visitors who want to extend the experience can dine at the Signature Room (see), an upscale restaurant located on the building's 95th floor. (Daily) **$$**

Lincoln Park. *2400 N Stockton Dr (60614). Near North Side. Phone 312/742-7529.* The largest in Chicago, Lincoln Park stretches almost the entire length of the north end of the city along the lake. It contains statues of Lincoln, Hans Christian Andersen, Shakespeare, and others; nine-hole golf course, driving range, miniature golf, bike and jogging paths, obstacle course, protected beaches. In the park are

Lincoln Park Conservatory. *2400 N Stockton Dr, Chicago. Near Fullerton Ave. Phone 312/742-7736.* Has four glass buildings, 18 propagating houses, and 3 acres of cold frames; formal and rock gardens; an extensive collection of orchids. Four major flower shows annually at the Show House. (Daily) **FREE**

Lincoln Park Zoo. *2200 Cannon Dr, Chicago. W entrance, Webster Ave and Stockton Dr; E entrance, Cannon Dr off Fullerton Ave. Phone 312/742-2000. www.lpzoo.com.* The Lincoln Park Zoo may be small (just 35 acres), but it has so much going for it—it's free, it's open 365 days a year, and it's a leader in education and conservation—that this gem of a zoo is a big part of the Chicago experience. Not only can visitors enjoy seeing animals from around the world, including gorillas, big cats, polar bears, exotic birds, and reptiles, but they can do so in style among architecturally significant structures, beautiful gardens, and modern visitor facilities, all in a prime location in the heart of Chicago's famed Lincoln Park. Families can double their fun at the Farm in the Zoo, where children can milk cows, churn butter, groom goats, and experience a working farmhouse kitchen. Also available are paddleboat rentals on the adjacent lagoon, a restaurant, and special events like family sleepovers, trick-or-treating on Halloween, and caroling to the animals during Christmas. (Daily) **FREE**

Lori's Designer Shoes. *824 W Armitage Ave (60614). Phone 773/281-5655. www.lorisshoes.com.* Women all over Chicago know that the place to go for shoes is Lori's. Truly a shoe lover's mecca, you can find everything here from summer sandals to knee-high leather boots from such designers as Kenneth Cole, Fruit, and Via Spiga. Owner Lori Andre, a self-proclaimed shoe addict, makes frequent trips abroad so that she can keep her fashion-conscious clientele up-to-date on the latest trends and cutting-edge styles. And if you happen to find that pair of shoes you just can't do without, but—gasp!—your size is nowhere to be found, no need to worry. The helpful salespeople will be glad to call their other stores in north suburban Highland Park (585 Central Ave, phone 847/681-1532) and Northfield (311 Happ Rd, phone 847/446-3818) to check for your size and have them delivered to the store. Because Lori's is so popular, weekends are usually packed, and the 5,000-square-foot space can become tight. Your best bet is to go on weekdays, when crowds are more subdued. This is especially true during end-of-season sales, when shoes (not to mention accessories like handbags, scarves, hats, and hosiery) are reduced by more than 50 percent. (Mon-Thurs 11 am-7 pm, Fri to 6 pm, Sat 10 am-6 pm, Sun noon-5 pm)

Loyola University. *Lake Shore campus, 6525 N Sheridan Rd (60626). Downtown campus, 820 N Michigan Ave. Phone 773/274-3000 (Lake Shore campus).* (1870) (14,300 students) Four campuses in Chicago. One of the biggest Jesuit universities in the United States. Excellent law and nursing programs. Martin d'Arcy Museum of Art (phone 773/508-2679; Tues-Sat; closed holidays, semester breaks). Fine Arts Gallery of the Edward Crown Center; exhibits (Mon-Fri; closed holidays).

⭐ **The Magnificent Mile.** *N Michigan Ave (60611). Between Oak St and the Chicago River. www.themagnificentmile.com.* Although often compared to Rodeo Drive in Beverly Hills and Fifth Avenue in New York because of the quality and quantity of its stores, Chicago's Michigan Avenue has a vibe all its own. Known as the Magnificent Mile, this 1-mile flower-lined stretch between Oak Street and the Chicago River boasts 3.1 million square feet of retail space, 460 stores, 275 restaurants, 51 hotels, numerous art galleries, and two museums, all set among some of Chicago's most architecturally significant buildings. In addition, there are four vertical malls, including the granddaddy of them all, Water Tower Place; high-end department stores like Neiman Marcus, Saks Fifth Avenue, and Marshall Field's; and international retailers like Hermes, Cartier, Armani, Tiffany, and Burberry. (Daily; closed holidays) Also on the Magnificent Mile are

900 North Michigan Shops. *900 N Michigan Ave, Chicago. Phone 312/915-3916. www.shop900.com.* More than 70 shops and restaurants, including Bloomingdale's and Gucci, surround a marble atrium in this mall that's adjacent to the Four Seasons (see). (Mon-Sat 10 am-7 pm, Sun noon-6 pm; closed holidays)

Chicago Place. *700 N Michigan Ave, Chicago. Phone 312/642-4811. www.chicago-place.com.* This eight-story vertical mall has more than 45 stores and several restaurants. (Mon-Fri 10 am-7 pm, Sat 10 am-6 pm, Sun noon-5 pm; closed Jan 1, Easter, Dec 25)

Crate & Barrel. *646 N Michigan Ave, Chicago. Phone 312/787-5900. www.crateandbarrel.com.* This housewares and home furnishings chain got its start in Chicago in 1962 and has since grown to more than 100 stores nationwide. Its large flagship store on Michigan Avenue brings in hordes of visitors drawn in by its clean designs, eye-catching colors, and reasonable prices. (Mon-Sat 10 am-7 pm, Sun 11 am-6 pm)

Niketown. *669 N Michigan Ave, Chicago. Phone 312/642-6363. www.niketown.com.* Since opening in 1993, this five-story sports store has become a major tourist attraction. It includes the Nike Museum, a video theater, a display of athletic gear worn by Michael Jordan, and a basketball court with a 28-foot likeness of "His Airness." (Daily; closed holidays)

Water Tower Place. *835 N Michigan Ave, Chicago. Phone 312/440-3165. www.shopwatertower.com.* This atrium mall connected to the Ritz-Carlton (see) has more than 100 shops, including Chicago favorite Marshall Field's, plus restaurants and a movie theater complex. (Mon-Sat 10 am-7 pm, Sun noon-6 pm; closed holidays)

Marina City. *300 N State St (60610). Near North Side, N of Chicago River.* (1959-1967) Condominium and commercial building complex with marina and boat storage. Includes two 550-foot-tall cylindrical buildings; home of House of Blues club and hotel (see). Designed by Bertrand Goldberg Associates; one of the most unusual downtown living-working complexes in the United States.

Marshall Field's. *111 N State St (60602). In the Loop. Phone 312/781-4483. www.marshallfields.com.* A Chicago landmark for more than a century and one of the most famous stores in the country. A traditional Chicago meeting place is under its clock, which projects over the sidewalk. On one side is an inner court rising 13 stories, on the other is a six-story rotunda topped by a Tiffany dome made of 1.6 million pieces of glass. (Mon-Sat 10 am-8 pm, Sun 11 am-6 pm; closed Thanksgiving, Dec 25)

Maywood Park Race Track. *8600 W North Ave, Maywood. I-290, exit 1st Ave N.* Phone 708/343-4800. *www.maywoodpark.com.* Pari-mutuel harness racing. Nightly Mon, Wed, Fri. Also TV simulcast thoroughbred racing (daily).

McCormick Place Convention Complex. *2301 S Martin Luther King Dr (60616). E 23rd St and S Lake Shore Dr.* Phone 312/791-7000. *www.mccormickplace.com.* McCormick Place, the largest convention and meeting space in the world, underwent an almost complete overhaul in the late 1990s to make it one of the most modern facilities imaginable. With over 2.2 million square feet of exhibition space and more than 110 meeting rooms, McCormick Place can accommodate any gathering. Annual outdoor and auto shows happen every year, and the facility also includes the newly renovated Arie Crown Theatre (see). Shops and restaurants are located inside the campus's four buildings (with a fifth—the west wing—in design), and a Hyatt Regency hotel (see) is attached to the convention center for easy access for presenters and visitors.

Merchandise Mart. *222 Merchandise Mart Plz (60654). On Wells St just N of the Chicago River.* Phone 312/527-7600. *www.merchandisemart.com.* The world's largest commercial building, built in 1930; restaurants, shopping, and special events.

Mercury Skyline Cruiseline. *Wacker Dr and Michigan Ave (60601). S side of Michigan Ave Bridge.* Phone 312/332-1353. Offers 1-hour, 1 1/2-hour, and 2-hour lake and river cruises; also Sun brunch, dinner, and luncheon cruises. (May-Oct) **$$$$**

Mexican Fine Arts Center Museum. *1852 W 19th St (60608).* Phone 312/738-1503. *www.mfacmchicago.org.* Showcase of Mexican art and heritage; museum features revolving exhibits of contemporary and classical works by renowned Mexican artists. (Tues-Sun 10 am-5 pm; closed Mon; also holidays) **FREE**

Michigan Avenue Bridge. *At the Chicago River between Michigan and Wabash aves.* This well-known Chicago landmark offers stunning views of the city as it crosses the Chicago River. The bridge was completed in 1920, designed by Edward Burnnett based on the Alexander III Bridge over the Seine River in Paris. Four 40-foot limestone bridge houses (two on either end) were added in 1928. Each contains a sculptured relief depicting historic Chicago events.

Monadnock Building. *53 W Jackson Blvd (60604). In the Loop.* (1889-1891) Highest wall-bearing building in Chicago was, at the time of its construction, the tallest and largest office building in the world. It is now considered one of the masterworks of the Chicago school of architecture. Designed by Burnham & Root; south addition by Holabird & Roche (1893).

Museum of Contemporary Art. *220 E Chicago Ave (60611). Near North Side.* Phone 312/280-2660. *www.mcachicago.org.* Just a half a block east of Michigan Avenue in the tiny Streeterville neighborhood lies Chicago's Museum of Contemporary Art, one of the nation's largest facilities dedicated to post-1945 works. With a large, rotating permanent collection and a reputation for cutting-edge exhibits, the museum showcases some of the finest artists working today, whether in painting, sculpture, video and film, photography, or performance. The museum—in a new building since 1995—also positions itself as a cultural center, and its 300-seat theater hosts a variety of programming, from lectures and films to experimental theater and music festivals. An annual highlight is the 24-hour summer solstice celebration, which attracts art lovers and partygoers in droves. The museum also has a stellar gift shop and bookstore, a restaurant run by Wolfgang Puck, and a terraced sculpture garden with views of Lake Michigan that serves as a peaceful urban sanctuary just steps from the heart of Chicago. (Tues-Sun; closed Jan 1, Thanksgiving, Dec 25) Free admission Tues. **$$**

Museum of Contemporary Photography. *600 S Michigan Ave (60605).* Phone 312/663-5554. *www.mocp.org.* Museum affiliated with Columbia College Chicago focuses on photography from 1950 to the present. (Mon-Fri 10 am-5 pm, Thurs until 8 pm, Sun noon-5 pm) **FREE**

Museum of Holography. *1134 W Washington Blvd (60607). West Side.* Phone 312/226-1007. Permanent collection of holograms (three-dimensional images made with lasers) featuring pieces from the United States and many European and Asian countries. (Wed-Sun afternoons; closed holidays) **$**

⭐ **Museum of Science and Industry.** *5700 S Lake Shore Dr (60637). South Side.* Phone 773/684-1414; toll-free 800/468-6674. *www.msichicago.org.* Chicago's Museum of Science and Industry is one of the preeminent museums in the entire country. Constantly improving, the museum seems to always have new hands-on exhibits that interests adults and children alike. The museum includes a free tour of a German U-Boat captured during World War II, a recreation of a coal mine that visitors can tour, and a model train layout that encapsulates almost the entire country. The museum also includes an exhibit on genetics and the improvements made to medicine through the Human Genome Project, as well as several rooms dedicated to the telling of time, with more than 500 unique instruments for doing so. An Omnimax theater can be found inside the giant space exploration exhibit, with the theater changing its films frequently, from looks at a tour of the Rolling Stones to a 2003 film about how helicopters are important in many walks of life. If you visit one museum in Chicago, visit this one. (Daily; closed Dec 25) Free admission varies by season; see Web site for details. **$$** Also here is

Henry Crown Space Center. *5700 S Lake Shore Dr, Chicago. Phone 773/684-1414; toll-free 800/ 468-6674. www.msichicago.org/exhibit/apollo.* This 35,000-square-foot space center houses the latest in space exhibitions; 334-seat Omnimax theater in a 76-foot-diameter projection dome. **$$**

Music Box Theatre. *3733 N Southport Ave (60613). Phone 773/871-6604. www.musicboxtheatre.com.* Those raised on multiplex cinemas are in for a treat at the Music Box Theatre, a neighborhood art house that attracts a loyal following—and not just because it's one of the few places in town devoted to independent, foreign, cult, documentary, and classic films. The Music Box is one of the last surviving old-time movie palaces. Built in 1929 and restored in 1983, its style is what one architectural critic called "an eclectic mélange of Italian, Spanish, and Pardon-My-Fantasy put together with passion," including a ceiling replete with "twinkling stars" and moving cloud formations, plus a genuine organ, still played on Saturday nights and at special events. The theater is also home to periodic productions of *The Rocky Horror Picture Show;* sing-alongs to classics (for example, *The Sound of Music*); and screenings for the Chicago International Film Festival (see SPECIAL EVENTS), held for three weeks each October. The theater is located in trendy Lakeview, a neighborhood of small shops and diverse restaurants. (Daily) **$$**

National Vietnam Veterans Art Museum. *1801 S Indiana Ave (60616). South Side. Phone 312/326-0270. www.nvvam.org.* Houses more than 1,000 pieces of fine art created by artists who served in the Vietnam

War. Interactive dioramas, artifacts; museum store, café. (Tues-Sun; closed holidays) **$$**

Navy Pier. *600 E Grand Ave (60611). Near North Side. Phone 312/595-7437. www.navypier.com.* Known as one of the city's top venues for families, Navy Pier—an old naval station renovated during the 1990s and converted into an urban playground—seems to offer something for everyone. Its most visible attraction, the 150-foot-high Ferris wheel, offers spectacular views of the lake and skyline and is modeled after the world's first, built in Chicago in 1893. During the summer, families flock to the pier for boat cruises, free outdoor concerts, and fireworks; during the winter, they can ice skate (free). Year-round, visitors can enjoy an IMAX theater, a Shakespeare theater, a stained-glass museum, a children's museum, shops and kiosks, a food court, and six restaurants catering to tastes from casual "street food" to formal—and pricey—fare (see also RIVA). Many of the pier's attractions are free, but parking can be expensive; instead, take advantage of the city's free trolley service from downtown hotels and other locations. (Daily) **FREE** Also here is

Chicago Children's Museum. *700 E Grand Ave, Chicago. Phone 312/527-1000. www. chichildrensmuseum.org.* Chock full of interesting and interactive activities, the Chicago Children's Museum at Navy Pier strikes a near-perfect balance between fun and learning. Plus, with an ever-changing slate of exhibits and activities, it's the kind of place that children can return to again and again. Overall, the exhibits encourage imagination, exploration, curiosity, and learning through experience; there's a play maze, an inventing lab where kids can perform experiments, and Treehouse Trails for children under 5 to explore the great outdoors. A recent exhibit called "Face to Face" dealt with prejudice and discrimination, and an Afghan children's art exhibit made the realities of life during wartime real for American kids. The programming is stellar, and, in any given week, the museum may have programs such as trilingual storytelling (English, Spanish, and American Sign Language), sing-alongs, art shows, ethnic festivals and celebrations, theater shows, art classes, and even a clown college for kids. (Tues-Sun 10 am-5 pm) **$$**

The Newberry Library. *60 W Walton St (60610). Near North Side. Phone 312/943-9090. www.newberry.org.* (1887) Houses more than 1.4 million volumes and several million manuscripts. Internationally famous collections on the Renaissance, Native Americans, the Chicago Renaissance, the American West, local and family history, music history, the history of printing, calligraphy, cartography, and others. Exhibits open to the public. Admission to reading rooms by registration. (Tues-Sat; closed holidays) Tours (Thurs, Sat). **FREE**

Northwestern University Chicago Campus. *357 E Chicago Ave (60611). At Lake Shore Dr. Near North Side.* Phone 312/503-8649. (1920) (5,400 students) Schools of Medicine, Law, Dentistry, and University College. (See also EVANSTON)

Oak Street. *Michigan Ave and Oak St (60611). Near North Side.* The block between Michigan Avenue and North Rush Street is lined with small shops that specialize in high fashion and the avant-garde from around the world.

Old Chicago Water Tower and Pumping Station. *806 N Michigan Ave (60611). Near North Side. Phone 312/742-0808 (City Gallery).* One of the few buildings to survive the Great Chicago Fire of 1871 that ravaged the city, the old Water Tower and the Chicago Avenue Pumping Station are rare monuments to Chicago's early history. Built in 1869 by W. W. Boyington and granted city landmark status in 1972, these gingerbready, castlelike Gothic Revival buildings house a visitor center and City Gallery, presenting photography exhibits with a Chicago theme. They recently became the new home of the acclaimed Lookingglass Theater Company. For first-time visitors to Chicago, the old Water Tower, located at North Michigan and Chicago avenues in the heart of the Magnificent Mile, makes a good starting point for getting oriented. The visitor center is stocked with information about city attractions and tours and is just steps away from shopping, restaurants, hotels, museums, entertainment, and Lake Michigan beaches. (Mon-Sat 10 am-6:30 pm, Sun 10 am-5 pm; closed Thanksgiving, Dec 25) **FREE**

The Oprah Winfrey Show. *1058 W Washington Blvd (60607). Phone 312/591-9222 (reservations). www. oprah.com.* One of the most coveted tickets in town is for *The Oprah Winfrey Show*, taped at Harpo Studios in the West Loop area. It may be tough to plan a visit to Chicago around the show, because it generally tapes only on Tuesdays, Wednesdays, and Thursdays from September through early December and from January to June. The only way to get tickets is to call the

studio's Audience Department in advance. Note that security for the show is tight and that you must be over 18 to attend (although teens ages 16 and 17 can attend with a parent or legal guardian if they bring a copy of their birth certificate for check-in). If you do get to a taping, allow yourself extra time to explore the surrounding neighborhood. Amid loft condos and meatpacking plants, you'll find some of the hottest restaurants and bars in the city (see BLACKBIRD and REDLIGHT, for example). **FREE**

Osaka Garden. *Jackson Park, 6401 S Stony Island Ave (60637). Phone 312/744-8074. www.osakagarden.org.* This tranquil Japanese strolling garden was established in 1934 as a thank you to Japan for a building given to Chicago for the 1893 World Columbian Exposition. Visitors can tour the garden with its pavilion, moon bridge, Shinto gate, and typical Japanese foliage and participate in assorted Japanese cultural activities.

Our Lady of Sorrows Basilica. *3121 W Jackson Blvd (60612). West Side.* Phone 773/638-0159. (1890-1902) Worth seeing are the Shrine Altar of the Seven Holy Founders of the Servites (main altar of Carrara marble) and the beautiful English baroque steeple, chapels, paintings, and other architectural ornamentations (daily). Tours (by reservation).

Outdoor art.

Batcolumn. *600 W Madison St, Chicago. Outside the Harold Washington Social Security Administration Building plz. In the Loop.* (1977) Designed by artist Claes Oldenburg. This 100-foot-tall, 20-ton welded steel sculpture resembles a baseball bat, set in a concrete base.

Flamingo. *Federal Center Plaza, Adams and Dearborn sts, Chicago. In the Loop.* (1974) Sculptor Alexander Calder's famous red stabile, a Chicago landmark, is 53 feet high and weighs 50 tons.

The Four Seasons. *First National Plaza, Monroe and Dearborn sts, Chicago. In the Loop.* (1974) This 3,000-square-foot mosaic designed by Marc Chagall contains more than 320 different shades and hues of marble, stone, granite, and glass.

Miro's Chicago. *The Brunswick Building, 69 W Washington Blvd, Chicago. In the Loop.* (1981) The structure, made of steel, wire mesh, concrete, bronze, and ceramic tile, is 39 feet tall.

Picasso. *50 W Washington Blvd, Chicago.* No one's really sure what it is—perhaps a horse, a bird, or a woman—but people around the world know that the Picasso sculpture outside Daley Plaza represents Chicago. Since its unveiling in 1967, this 50-foot-tall, 162-ton steel work of art has become an unofficial logo and an unlikely icon for the city. Some consider it a miracle that the city's famously conservative mayor, Richard J. Daley (aka "the Boss"), would commission a work of cubist abstract expressionism from the bad boy of modern art, but with one of Chicago's leading architectural firms as liaison, the project came to fruition. It led the way for other major public art projects, including the Miro statue (69 W Washington Blvd), the Chagall mosaic (First National Plaza), Calder's Flamingo (Federal Center Plaza), and the Dubuffet outside the James R. Thompson Center (100 W Randolph St), that give the Loop its distinctive and accessible feel.

Untitled Sounding Sculpture. *Amoco Building, 200 E Randolph St, Chicago. In the Loop.* (1975) Unique "sounding sculpture" set in a reflecting pool. Designed by Harry Bertoia.

Peace Museum. *Garfield Park Dome, 100 N Central Park Ave (60624). One block E and four blocks N of Independence St exit of Eisenhower Expy. Phone 773/638-6450. www.peacemuseum.org.* Exhibits focusing on the role of the arts, the sciences, labor, women, minorities, and religious institutions on issues of war and peace and on the contributions of individual peacemakers. (Tues-Wed, Sat 11 am-4 pm; closed Jan 1, Dec 24-25, 31) **$$**

Peggy Notebaert Nature Museum. *2430 N Cannon Dr (60614). At Lake Shore Dr and Fullerton Pkwy. Phone 773/755-5100. www.naturemuseum.org.* Hands-on exploration of nature is the mission of the Peggy Notebaert Nature Museum. This newest of Chicago museums—built in 1999 as an offshoot of the Chicago Academy of Sciences, Chicago's first museum—takes its mission seriously. Here, visitors and city dwellers alike can connect with the natural world via indoor exhibits and outdoor adventures. Children can dress up like animals, adults can explore the Midwestern landscape, and urbanites can forget their cares while surrounded by wildflowers. Permanent exhibits include a 28-foot-high butterfly haven, a city science interactive display, a family water lab, a wilderness walk, and a children's gallery designed for kids ages 3 to 8. Special exhibits are real kiddie-pleasers, judging by two recent ones:

"Grossology: The Impolite Science of the Human Body" and "Monster Creepy Crawlies." The museum is beautifully situated in Lincoln Park (see) and is within walking distance of the Lincoln Park Zoo (see), the lagoon, and Fullerton Avenue Beach. Free admission Thurs. (Mon-Fri 9 am-4:30 pm, Sat-Sun 10 am-5 pm) **$$**

Pistachios. *1 E Delaware Pl (60611). Phone 312/988-9433. www.pistachiosonline.com.* This gem of a jewelry store (actually, "gallery" is more appropriate) features contemporary, one-of-a-kind items crafted by artists from the United States and Europe. Selections include silver and platinum rings, earrings, cufflinks, knitted bracelets, hand-blown glass items, and metal items for the home (including oh-so-chic salt and pepper shakers). And, with your purchase, you receive a little gift: a bag of—what else?—pistachios. (Mon-Fri 10:30 am-7 pm, Sat 10:30 am-6 pm, Sun noon-5 pm)

Polish Museum of America. *984 N Milwaukee Ave (60611). Near North Side. Phone 773/384-3352. www.prcua.org.* Exhibits on Polish culture, folklore, and immigration; art gallery, archives, and library; Paderewski and Kosciuszko rooms. The museum has one of the best collections of Polish music and literature outside of Warsaw, catering to Chicago's large Polish population. Founded in 1935, many Polish scholars attend the museum to complete research on projects they produce. (Fri-Wed 11 am-4 pm; closed Thurs; also Jan 1, Good Friday, Dec 25) **DONATION**

Prairie Avenue Historic District. *1800 S Prairie Ave (60616). Between 18th and Cullerton sts. South Side. Phone 312/326-1480.* This is the area where millionaires lived during the 1800s. The Clarke House (circa 1835), the oldest house still standing in the city, has been restored and now stands at a site near its original location. The Glessner House (1886), 1800 South Prairie Avenue, is owned and maintained by the Chicago Architecture Foundation. Designed by architect Henry Hobson Richardson, the house has 35 rooms, many of which are restored with original furnishings; interior courtyard. Two-hour guided tour of both houses (Wed-Sun). Other houses on the cobblestone street are Kimball House (1890), 1801 South Prairie Avenue, replica of a French château; Coleman House (circa 1885), 1811 South Prairie Avenue; and Keith House (circa 1870), 1900 South Prairie Avenue. Architectural tours. Free admission Wed. **$$$**

⭐ **Pullman Historic District Walking Tours.** *614 W 113th St (60628). Phone 773/785-3828.* Built in 1880-1884 to house the workers at George M. Pullman's Palace Car Company, the original town was a complete model community with many civic and recreational facilities (see PULLMAN VILLAGE: AMERICAN'S COMPANY TOWN). Unlike in most historic districts, nine-tenths of the original buildings are still standing. The 1 1/2-hour tour starts at the Historic Pullman Center. Tours (May-Oct, first Sun of the month, two departures). **$$**

Richard J. Daley Center and Plaza. *50 W Washington Blvd (60602). Randolph and Clark sts. In the Loop. Phone 312/603-7980.* This 31-story, 648-foot building houses county and city courts and administrative offices. In the plaza is the Chicago Picasso sculpture (see OUTDOOR ART); across Washington Street is Miro's Chicago sculpture (see OUTDOOR ART).

River North Gallery District. With the highest concentration of art galleries outside Manhattan, Chicago's River North Gallery District, just a short walk from Michigan Avenue and the Loop, offers world-class art in a stylish setting of renovated warehouses and upscale restaurants. Although the district is loosely bordered by the Chicago River, Orleans Street, Chicago Avenue, and State Street, you'll find the majority of galleries on Superior and Franklin streets. If you happen to be in town on the second Friday of the month, wander over to the opening-night receptions (5-7 pm) for a glass of wine and a glimpse of Chicago's black-clad art scenesters. Serious collectors may want to visit Carl Hammer and Judy Saslow for outsider art, Ann Nathan for contemporary art, Douglas Dawson and Primitive Artworks for tribal art, Manifesto for high-end furniture, Aldo Castillo for global art, and Douglas Rosin for 20th-century modern art. (Tues-Sat) **FREE**

The Rookery. *209 S LaSalle St (60604). In the Loop.* (1886) Oldest remaining steel-skeleton skyscraper in the world. Designed by Burnham & Root, the remarkable glass-encased lobby was remodeled in 1905 by Frank Lloyd Wright.

Roosevelt University. *430 S Michigan Ave (60605). In the Loop. Phone 312/341-3500.* (1945) (6,400 students) Campuses in Chicago and northwest suburban Schaumburg. Auditorium Building designed by Louis Sullivan and engineered by Dankmar Adler in 1889.

Royal George Theatre. *1641 N Halsted St (60614). Phone 312/988-9000.* Located in Chicago's Lincoln Park neighborhood (see), this theater features seats that are sparse in number but well spaced, enabling a relaxing theater experience. The stage has hosted such shows as Tony Kushner's acclaimed *Angels in America* and the review *Forever Plaid*.

⭐ **Sears Tower.** *233 S Wacker Dr (60660). In the Loop. Phone 312/875-9696 (skydeck). www.sears-tower.com or www.theskydeck.com.* It seems fitting that the town that gave birth to the skyscraper should lay claim to North America's tallest building (and the world's tallest until 1996). Built in 1974 by Skidmore, Owings & Merrill, the 110-story Sears Tower soars 1/4 mile (1,450 feet) above the city, making it the most prominent building in the skyline. The building, which houses 10,000 office workers and hosts 25,000 visitors daily, was constructed of black anodized aluminum in nine bundled square tubes, an innovation that provides both wind protection and the necessary support for its extraordinary height. The elevators that whisk visitors to the 103rd-floor observatory are among the world's fastest—and well worth the ride. The observatory offers panoramic views of the city; on a clear day, you can easily see 35 miles away. During the height of tourist season—the summer—expect long waits. (May-Sept, daily 10 am-10 pm; Oct-Apr, daily 10 am-8 pm) **$$**

The Second City. *1616 N Wells St (60614). Phone 312/337-3992. www.secondcity.com.* The Second City is known worldwide as the home to smart, cutting-edge comedy. Opened in 1959 by a group of University of Chicago students, The Second City has launched the careers of many successful comics, the likes of which include John Belushi, Bill Murray, Gilda Radner, John Candy, and Mike Myers. Resident troupes perform original comedy revues nightly on two stages: The Second City Mainstage, seating 340, and The Second City e.t.c., which seats 180. The Second City also operates a comedy training center, with student productions held at Donny's Skybox Studio Theatre (1608 N Wells St).

⭐ **Shedd Aquarium.** *1200 S Lake Shore Dr (60605). At Roosevelt Rd. Phone 312/939-2438. www.sheddnet.org.* Not all the best aquariums are on the ocean. Shedd, the world's largest indoor aquarium, features more than 8,000 freshwater and marine animals displayed in 200 naturalistic habitats; divers hand-feed fish, sharks,

Pullman Village: America's Company Town

He dreamed of an American utopia and almost achieved it. If it hadn't been for the struggle of a new American ideal, his story might have had a very different ending.

He climbed toward his utopia via the American dream. He started from humble beginnings as a store clerk and a cabinetmaker. He ran an oil refinery. He supervised the raising and moving of buildings to shore up their foundations. And with the capital he accumulated, George M. Pullman set about developing a luxury railroad car, something that would make the upcoming age of railroad travel—which he correctly saw as the wave of the future—less boring and much more comfortable for the increasingly wealthy professional class. With its gourmet meals, leather seats, beautiful upholstery, electric lighting, chandeliers, first-rate heating and air-conditioning, and other well-appointed touches, the Pullman car suddenly made trains the preferred method of transportation. And when his rail car was included as part of Abraham Lincoln's funeral procession, Pullman achieved worldwide acclaim and established the Pullman Palace Car Company in Chicago.

As his company grew, so, too, did Pullman's labor force, most of whom were immigrants and migrants who flocked to Chicago for the promise of steady work and good wages. In an effort to stave off the unions, which were gaining in popularity and number, Pullman used an approach he believed would discourage strikes and instead encourage loyalty and honesty: to build a city for his workers, with beautiful homes, clean streets, shops with abundant offerings, a library, a post office, and a theater. It would be built around his factories and would provide his employees everything they would need to live happy, safe, culturally enriched lives—the epitome of a company town.

In 1880, Pullman purchased 4,000 acres of land 14 miles south of Chicago. In the center were the factory buildings. To the north and south were brick houses rented to employees of the Pullman Palace Car Company, beautiful houses with such modern conveniences as indoor plumbing, gas, and regular garbage pickup. The company maintained the entire town—lawns, streets, and a beautiful man-made lake. A state-of-the-art sewage system was installed. The town had a bakery, a stable, a school, office buildings, and a church. Visitors, many of whom came simply to see the amazing planned city, stayed at the Hotel Florence, named for Pullman's daughter.

What visitors saw was a beautiful, well-functioning city. What was happening under the surface indicated otherwise.

Because Pullman Village was privately owned, George Pullman made all the decisions, including which plays the theater could show and which meals the restaurants could offer. The town's only tavern served the town's visitors, not its residents; if the residents wanted alcohol, they had to go to the next town. This was the mandate of Pullman, who sought to direct morality as well as action. He chose the library's books, the town's stores, and even the religion of the church. And if a resident wanted to own his own home, he had to move out of Pullman Village. George Pullman only allowed his residents to rent.

For reasons other than the residents' growing dissatisfaction, the winter of 1893-1894 proved to be George Pullman's undoing. At the start of a severe depression, he cut wages by 30 percent—but left rents as they were. A worker's wages suddenly might have been cut to $9.08, while his rent remained at $9, leaving him with just eight cents to feed and clothe his family. Along came Eugene

Debs, founder of the American Railway Union. Pullman wouldn't discuss workers' concerns, Debs led workers on a strike that stopped all trains with Pullman cars, and management fired 90 percent of Pullman's employees.

The strikes turned violent, with President Cleveland sending federal troops to protect the Pullman factory. After the troops left in 1884, the situation in Pullman Village returned to pre-strike status. George Pullman died three years later, and in 1898, the Illinois Supreme Court mandated that the Pullman Company sell the nonindustrial land to the residents, which meant that those renting

their homes could buy them and make changes to the company-dictated sameness. The last vestige of George Pullman's company town had come to an end.

Bus tours of Pullman Village are offered on selected Saturdays in June, July, and September. They depart promptly from the Chicago Cultural Center Visitor Information Center (77 E Randolph St) at 10 am (check-in is at 9:30 am). Tickets are $25 for adults and $20 for students and seniors. Tours are 4 to 4 1/2 hours and include light refreshments. (See also PULLMAN HISTORIC DISTRICT WALKING TOURS.)

eels, and turtles several times daily in the 90,000-gallon Caribbean Reef exhibit. The Oceanarium re-creates a Pacific Northwest ecosystem with whales, dolphins, sea otters, and seals. A colony of penguins inhabits a Falkland Islands exhibit; while the Seahorse Symphony exhibit takes a look at some of the ocean's smaller creatures. In the summer, Chicago's music scene invades the aquarium for "Jazzin' at the Shedd," with live performances weekly. (Daily 9 am-5 pm; closed Jan 1, Dec 25) Free admission Mon-Tues (Sept-Feb only). **$$$$**

Shoreline Marine Company. *474 N Lake Shore Dr (60611). Phone 312/222-9328. www.shorelinesightseeing .com.* Thirty-minute tours of the lakefront. Departures from Shedd Aquarium (see), afternoons, and Buckingham Fountain (see GRANT PARK), evenings. (May-Sept, daily) **$$$**

Shubert Theatre. *22 W Monroe St (60603). Phone 312/977-1710. www.broadwayinchicago.com.* Traveling companies set up shop at the Shubert and stay for a month or two, bringing Broadway action to downtown Chicago. The theater originally opened in 1906, and with the history of the venue and the popularity of the shows that play here comes a fairly standard price tag of $30-$70 for most shows. **$$$$**

Soldier Field. *425 E McFetridge Dr (60605). Phone 847/295-6600. www.soldierfield.net.* Soldier Field opened in 1924 as Municipal Grant Park Stadium, and the first game played there saw Notre Dame down Northwestern 13-6. The Chicago Bears didn't

play home games at the stadium until 1971, when they moved from baseball's Wrigley Field (see). The stadium was part of a recent lakefront improvement project costing more than $500 million, with benefits including the addition of more seats and better amenities to the historic building. Soldier Field also plays host to the Chicago Fire of Major League Soccer, as well as several larger concert events each summer.

Chicago Bears (NFL). *Soldier Field, 425 E McFetridge Dr, Chicago. Phone 847/295-6600. www.chicagobears.com.* After playing the 2002 season at the University of Illinois's Memorial Field, the Bears moved back into Chicago's storied Soldier Field in 2003 following a multimillion-dollar renovation. The stadium now sports a more modern look, but it still retains the feel of an early-20th-century arena. Whatever the team's performance, season-ticket holders are seemingly immune to the lakefront weather and loyal to the orange and blue. Don't miss taking in a game here if you're a true football fan.

Chicago Fire (MLS). *Soldier Field, 425 E McFetridge Dr, Chicago. Phone toll-free 888/657-3473. www. chicago-fire.com.* The Fire won one of the first Major League Soccer Cups and have consistently been a playoff team since the league's inception. The team has replaced the veterans who garnered it early success with a recent youth movement and continues to be one of the better-drawing clubs in the league. Like the Bears, the Fire moved back into Soldier Field after millions of dollars were spent to revive and renovate the old structure.

Spertus Museum. *618 S Michigan Ave (60605). At the Spertus Institute of Jewish Studies. In the Loop. Phone 312/322-1747. www.spertus.edu/museum.html.* Permanent collection of ceremonial objects from many parts of the world; sculptures, graphic arts, and paintings; ethnic materials spanning centuries; changing exhibits in fine arts; documentary films and photographs. Rosenbaum Artifact Center has hands-on exhibits on ancient Near East archaeology. (Mon-Fri, Sun; closed holidays and Jewish holidays) Free admission Fri. **$**

Spirit of Chicago cruises. *Navy Pier, 455 E Illinois St (60611). Phone 312/836-7899; toll-free 866/211-3804.* Take a cruise leaving year-round from Chicago's Navy Pier (see) out onto Lake Michigan for a couple hours away from the hustle and bustle of the mainland. Tickets can be purchased individually, or groups can rent the ship for gatherings and celebrations. **$$$$**

State Street Shopping District. *Between Lake St and Jackson Blvd. In the Loop.* Yes, State Street is "that great street" alluded to in song. Once dubbed the busiest intersection in the world, State Street today is a Loop shopping mecca anchored by Chicago's two most famous department retailers: Marshall Field's (see) and Carson Pirie Scott (see). These flagship stores have been joined by national chains, discount stores, and specialty shops. More interesting than the merchandise available for purchase, however, may be the street's architecture. Check out the graceful Louis Sullivan grillwork at Carson's main entrance, the Tiffany dome inside Field's, and the exterior of the Burnham Hotel (see), a masterful renovation and restoration of the former Reliance Building, once termed "the crown jewel of Chicago architecture." For lunch, try Marshall Field's venerable Walnut Room or the Atwood Café (see) in the Burnham Hotel. And if you need to meet up with someone, do so under the Marshall Field's clock at Washington Boulevard and State Street as Chicagoans have done for generations. (Daily)

Steppenwolf Theater Company. *1650 N Halsted St (60614). At North Ave and Halsted St; accessible by red line trains. Phone 312/335-1650. www.steppenwolf .org.* One of the most acclaimed theater groups in the country, Steppenwolf not only helped put Chicago theater on the map, but also gave many famous actors, including John Malkovich, Joan Allen, Gary Sinise, Laurie Metcalf, and John Mahoney, their start. The dozens of awards its shows and performers have won, including Tonys, Emmys, and Obies, belie its humble founding in a suburban church basement in 1974 by Sinise, Terry Kinney, and Jeff Perry. Steppenwolf quickly became known for its risky choices and edgy performances, an approach critics aptly termed "rock-and-roll theater." Today, the company has its own state-of-the-art building in the Lincoln Park neighborhood (see) (just a short cab or "L" train ride from downtown), which includes a studio space and a school and hosts several specialty series. Steppenwolf performances are almost uniformly excellent, with stunning sets, strong acting, and plenty of original material; theater lovers should try to reserve tickets as far in advance of their Chicago visit as possible.

Sur La Table. *50-54 E Walton St (60611). Phone 312/337-0600. www.surlatable.com.* In the 1970s, Seattle spawned this clearinghouse for hard-to-find kitchen gear, and it soon became known as a source for cookware, small appliances, cutlery, kitchen tools, linens, tableware, gadgets, and specialty foods. Sur La Table has since expanded to include cooking classes (**$$$$**), chef demonstrations, and cookbook author signings, as well as a catalog and online presence. Cooking connoisseurs discover such finds as cool oven mitts, zest graters, copper whisks, onion soup bowls, and inspired TV dinner trays. (Daily)

Swedish-American Museum Center. *5211 N Clark St (60640). Phone 773/728-8111. www.samac.org.* Pays tribute to Swedish heritage and history. Exhibits on Swedish memorabilia. The museum features a children's museum dedicated to immigration, as well as several exhibits detailing how Swedes came to reside in Chicago over the years. Museum also includes periodic performances of traditional Swedish music and dance to enhance the sense of Scandinavian folklore. (Tues-Fri 10 am-4 pm, Sat-Sun 11 am-4 pm) **$**

Symphony Center. *220 S Michigan Ave (60604). In the Loop. Phone 312/294-3000 (tickets). www.cso.org.* (1904) The historic Symphony Center is the home of the Chicago Symphony Orchestra and the stage for the Civic Orchestra of Chicago, chamber music groups, diverse musical attractions, and children's programs. Includes Buntrock Hall, a ballroom, rehearsal space, and restaurant.

Chicago Symphony Orchestra (CSO). *220 S Michigan Ave, Chicago. Phone 312/294-3333. www.cso.org.* Long considered one of the great orchestras of the world, the CSO has been a fixture on the Chicago cultural scene for more than 100 years. It may have reached its highest acclaim under the late, great Sir Georg Solti, when so many of its recordings were virtual shoe-ins for Grammy awards, but today, with three conductors and an award-winning composer in residence, the orchestra continues to produce innovative and inspiring music in a classically beautiful setting at the Symphony Center across from the Art Institute of Chicago (see). While the big-name shows may sell out in advance, it is often possible to get day-of-show or single-seat tickets at the box office—especially for weeknight and Friday afternoon performances—at a reasonable price.

Theatre Building. *1225 W Belmont Ave (60657). Phone 773/327-5252. www.theatrebuildingchicago.org.* The Theatre Building serves as the impromptu home for traveling companies to show their wares. More often than not, these shows are a little more "off the beaten path" and do not include names or plays that may be recognizable, but this does not take away from the enjoyment of the experience. Shows are generally cheaper than at other area theaters, but may not be for the entire family.

United Center. *1901 W Madison St (60612). Phone 312/455-4500; fax 312/455-4511. www.unitedcenter.com.* Affectionately known as "the house that Michael built," the United Center replaced the cavernous Chicago Stadium in the mid-1990s as the home of Chicago Bulls professional basketball team. Even though the Blackhawks professional hockey team skates here and numerous concerts and special events are held here, the giant statue of Michael Jordan in front of the building's north entrance attests to the building's true provenance. Inside is a shrine to the glory years of Chicago sports: hanging from the rafters are banners from the Bulls' six championship seasons, the Blackhawks' Stanley Cup wins, and a variety of retired jerseys, including Jordan's number 23. Although the Bulls aren't packing in the crowds the way they did when "His Airness," as the local sportswriters called him, ruled the courts, a visit to the United Center enables you to see where history took

place. Tours of the arena are available through the Guest Relations office. The United Center is accessible via public transportation, but because the neighborhood is in transition, it's probably safer to take a cab or to drive (there is ample parking close by).

Chicago Blackhawks (NHL). *United Center, 1901 W Madison St, Chicago. Phone 312/455-7000. www.chicagoblackhawks.com.* The Chicago Blackhawks are one of the oldest NHL teams in the league. Although their last Stanley Cup victory was in 1961, the Hawks have a loyal (and raucous) fan base that can contest the game as hotly in their seats as the players do on the ice. And although, like all professional sports contests, Blackhawks games are marketed as family events, you still get a sense that within the plush confines of the United Center lies the same rough-and-tumble crowd that rocked the old Chicago Stadium.

Chicago Bulls (NBA). *United Center, 1901 W Madison St, Chicago. Phone 312/455-4500. www.nba.com/bulls.* Although the team has not enjoyed much success since the second retirement of Michael Jordan, the Bulls continue to rebuild around young players, as well as veterans. Tickets are relatively easy to come by, although still on the expensive side. **$$$$**

United States Post Office. *433 W Harrison (60607). In the Loop. Phone 312/983-7550.* (1933) Largest in the world under one roof. Individuals may join 1 1/2-hour guided group tours (Mon-Fri, three tours daily; no tours holidays and Dec). No cameras, packages, or purses. Reservations required. **FREE**

The University of Chicago. *5801 S Ellis Ave (60637). South Side. Phone 773/702-8374. www.uchicago.edu.* (1892) (12,750 students) On this campus, Enrico Fermi produced the first sustained nuclear reaction. The University of Chicago also has had one of the highest numbers of Nobel Prize winners of any institution. The campus includes the Oriental Institute, Robie House, Rockefeller Memorial Chapel, and David and Alfred Smart Museum of Art (5550 S Greenwood Ave) (Tues-Sun; free; phone 773/702-0200). Guided one-hour campus tours leave from 1212 E 59th St. On campus are

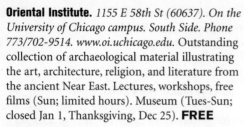

Oriental Institute. *1155 E 58th St (60637). On the University of Chicago campus. South Side. Phone 773/702-9514. www.oi.uchicago.edu.* Outstanding collection of archaeological material illustrating the art, architecture, religion, and literature from the ancient Near East. Lectures, workshops, free films (Sun; limited hours). Museum (Tues-Sun; closed Jan 1, Thanksgiving, Dec 25). **FREE**

Robie House. *5757 S Woodlawn Ave (60637). Near the University of Chicago campus. South Side. Phone 773/834-1847. www.wrightplus.org/robiehouse.* (1909) Designed by Frank Lloyd Wright, this may be the ultimate example of a Prairie house. Designed and built for Excelsior sewing machine magnate Frederick Robie, the house was nearly torn down in the 1960s after having been used as a dormitory by the University of Chicago. However, it was saved and is in the middle of an ambitious ten-year restoration plan to bring it back to the splendor of almost a century ago. Tours. (Daily; closed holidays) **$$**

Rockefeller Memorial Chapel. *5850 S Woodlawn Ave, Chicago. On the University of Chicago campus. South Side. Phone 773/702-2100.* Designed by Bertram Grosvenor Goodhue Associates; noted for its Gothic construction, vaulted ceiling, 8,600-pipe organ, and 72-bell carillon. Guided tours by appointment.

University of Illinois at Chicago. *1200 W Harrison (60607). Near I-94 and I-290. West Side. Phone 312/996-4350. www.uic.edu.* (1965) (25,000 students) Comprehensive urban university. On campus is Jane Addams Hull-House Museum (see). The Flames plays NCAA Division I athletics, and basketball games are usually well attended. Easy access to the campus from Eisenhower Expressway. UIC Medical Center is one of the leading teaching and research hospitals in the city of Chicago.

Untouchable Tours. *610 N Clark St (60610). Phone 773/881-1195.* Guided tour of gangster hotspots of the 1920s and 1930s. Tour with dinner and revue also available. (Daily; reservations strongly recommended) **$$$$**

Victory Gardens Theater. *2257 N Lincoln Ave (60614). Phone 773/549-5788. www.victorygardens.org.* Although it often produces plays by lesser-known authors,

the Victory Gardens did win the Regional Theatre Tony Award in 2001. The year 2003 saw Joel Drake Johnson's *The End of the Tour* and Lonnie Carter's *Concerto Chicago*, among other productions. Some better-known playwrights and plays have been produced here as well, with Neil Simon's *Lost in Yonkers* being one of the more recent examples.

Wabash Avenue. *Wabash Ave and Congress Pkwy (60604). S of the river to Congress Ave. In the Loop.* This unique street, always in the shadow of the elevated train tracks, is known for its many specialty stores—books, music, musical instruments, records, men's clothing, tobacco, etc.—as well as being the center of the wholesale and retail jewelry trade.

Wendella boat tours. *400 N Michigan Ave (60611). At the Wrigley Building (NW side of Michigan Ave Bridge). Phone 312/337-1446. www.wendellaboats.com.* Lake and river cruises (1, 1 1/2, and 2 hours) on the RiverBus, featuring live narration. (Apr-mid-Oct, daily) **$$$$**

Wicker Park/Bucktown neighborhood. *1608 N Milwaukee Ave (60647). Neighborhood starts at the intersection of North, Milwaukee, and Damen aves. Blue Line "L" train-Damen stop. Phone 773/384-8672. www.wickerparkbucktown.com.* Just a short cab or "L" train ride northwest of downtown Chicago is one of the city's liveliest and most diverse areas, the Wicker Park/Bucktown neighborhood. You may recognize it from the film *High Fidelity*, shot on location here. The area is home to artists and musicians, urban pioneers and hipsters, plus a wealth of trendy stores and restaurants. Start at the neighborhood's epicenter, the intersection of North, Milwaukee, and Damen avenues. Within a several block radius, you'll find antique stores and thrift shops, art galleries, boutiques, design studios, day spas, nightclubs, coffeehouses, bars, and nationally recognized restaurants (see MOD). Be sure to walk down Pierce and Hoyne streets, where the beer barons lived, as well as around the park itself for a glimpse of the grand homes from this historic neighborhood's past—a combination of German, Polish, Ukrainian, and, more recently, Latino roots.

Wrigley Building. *410 N Michigan Ave (60611). Near North Side. Phone 312/923-8080. www.wrigley.com.* Perched on the north bank of the Chicago River

Did Somebody Say "Second City"?

In any given week, in any given season, you can walk into the Steppenwolf Theatre (1650 N Halsted St) and probably see the award-winning actor Gary Sinese on stage. He may work all over the world, but he has said that his heart is here in Chicago at the company he helped found.

Over at the Goodman Theatre (170 N Dearborn St), you might see a pre-Broadway tryout on its way to becoming a multiple Tony Award winner, such as the acclaimed revival of Arthur Miller's *Death of a Salesman,* starring Brian Dennehy.

Besides terrific performances with superb performers and solid production values in a city of outstanding theater, what do these companies have in common? Both have received Tony Awards for the best regional theater in America, making Chicago the only city in the country with three theaters that have won that prestigious award.

Chicago is "second city" to none when it comes to theater. A place of multiple companies, it has main-stream stages and storefront theaters, front-page attention-getters and neighborhood gems. And there are names galore. When he graduated from Northwestern University, long before he became a *Friend*, actor David Schwimmer co-founded Lookingglass Theatre (806 N Michigan Ave), a company known for its sometimes acrobatic, always colorful, and highly creative performances. Pegasus Players (1145 W Wilson Ave) has a knack for getting the rights to Stephen Sondheim's works. Sometimes the productions are smaller and less frequently produced, like *Anyone Can Whistle*; sometimes they are coups, like the American premiere of Sondheim's first effort, *Saturday Night*.

Actor John Malkovich got his start here. He began his career at the Steppenwolf alongside Sinese and still comes back to perform from time to time. So do Laurie Metcalf (of television's *Roseanne* fame) and stage actor Jeff Perry. Joan Cusack lives here, as does John Mahoney, formerly of *Frasier*. He, too, appears at the Steppenwolf, as well as at other venues around town.

And there are plenty of venues—enough for both the famous and the becoming-famous. Chicago-style entertainment comes in dozens of styles and sizes. The adventurous Bailiwick Repertory Theatre (1229 W Belmont Ave) frequently puts on performances for the deaf; its production of *Our Town* featured both hearing and hearing-impaired actors. ETA Creative Arts Foundation (7558 S Chicago Ave) puts on original or seldom-seen dramatic works by African-American writers. While presenting full-length plays on its main stage, Noble Fool Theater (16 W Randolph St) uses its studio for *Flanagan's Wake,* its signature "interactive Irish wake." Roadworks (1239 N Ashland Ave) is a young company, a strong ensemble cast that focuses on Midwest and world premieres.

Each week from June through August, a different independent theater company puts on a production at Theatre on the Lake, a screened-in Prairie school-style building in Lincoln Park (see) on the shore of Lake Michigan. The relaxed atmosphere, lake breezes, and smart performances are accentuated by a bonus: walking out of the theater at intermission and gazing south at the city's gorgeous skyline.

---

on Michigan Avenue, the sparkling white Wrigley Building has been one of Chicago's most recognized skyscrapers since its completion in 1924 by prominent architects Graham, Anderson, Probst, and White. The building's triangular shape is patterned after the Seville Cathedral's Giralda Tower in Spain, and its ornamental design is an adaptation of French Renaissance style. Note that the building is actually two towers linked by an open walkway at street level and two enclosed walkways on the third and 14th floors. Today, the building remains the headquarters of the Wrigley family of chewing gum fame, although other firms also rent office space. At night, the exterior, clad with more than 250,000 glazed terra-cotta tiles, is floodlit, making it one of the nation's major commercial lighting displays and one of the most highly visible symbols of the city. Unfortunately, no tours of the building's interior are available.

Wrigley Field. *1060 W Addison St (60613). Phone 773/404-2827. www.cubs.com.* America's second-oldest National League ballpark is also one of its most unique, located within a vibrant city neighborhood where residents often watch games from their roof decks. While the Cubs' perpetual losing streak is a running joke in Chicago, it never keeps people away from the ballpark; during the summer, it's one of the hottest tickets in town, mostly because "the Friendly Confines," as it is known, offers the ultimate old-time baseball experience. The best place to sit is in the box seats just past first or third base, where the players in their bull pens will talk to the fans. If you want to catch a home run, try the left field bleachers, especially during batting practice. Be sure to walk to the upper deck at sunset for spectacular views of the city. After the game, you can continue the party at one of the dozens of bars and restaurants within walking distance of the park.

Chicago Cubs (MLB). *1060 W Addison St, Chicago. Phone 773/404-2827. www.cubs.com.* Although Hall of Fame players like Ernie Banks and Billy Williams have come and gone, the team still remains the favorite among Chicagoans. Fans come from miles around just to watch a baseball game in Wrigley Field, one of the oldest ballparks anywhere.

Special Events

57th Street Art Fair. *57th St between Kenwood and Dorchester, Chicago (60637). Phone 773/493-3247. www.57thstreetartfair.org.* Every year, the 57th Street Art Fair shuts down a city block between Kenwood and Dorchester to vend the wares of more than 300 artists from around the country. Participants are chosen by a panel of professional artists and curators in March for the early June celebration. There is no corporate sponsorship for the fair, which includes painting, sculpture, photography and ceramics, among other media. Early June.

Air and Water Show. *1600 N Lake Shore Dr, Chicago (60614). Phone 312/744-2400 (Chicago Office of Tourism). egov.cityofchicago.org.* The nation's largest two-day air show, attracting more than 2 million people every August, is a free event and a favorite of kids and adults alike. There are daredevil pilots, parachute teams, and jets flying in formation, as well as a water-skiing and boat-jumping component for additional thrills. The great thing about this festival is that it's visible from almost everywhere along the Chicago lakefront (see). Grandstand seats for the water show are located at North Avenue Beach, but some of the best viewing points are farther north, at Montrose Harbor and between Belmont and Addison. Mid-Aug. **FREE**

Around the Coyote Arts Festival. *1579 N Milwaukee Ave, #352, Chicago (60622). At the intersection of Milwaukee, North, and Damen aves (Blue Line "L" train-Damen stop). Phone 773/342-6777. www. aroundthecoyote.org.* With one of the highest concentrations of artists in the country residing in the Wicker Park/Bucktown neighborhood (see), it made sense to find a way to showcase their work. That's exactly what Paris art dealer Jim Happy-Delpesh did when he came back to Chicago in 1989. Although the festival revolves around visual artists, it also encompasses cutting-edge dance, theater, poetry, film and video, fashion, and furniture design. Typically, the timing of the festival—held the second weekend in September—results in glorious early fall weather, and tens of thousands of people walk through the neighborhood visiting galleries, group shows, the Flat Iron Arts Building, and artists' homes and studios. And because the neighborhood is spilling over with hip boutiques and dozens of trendy restaurants and outdoor cafés, many people make a day of it. A smaller winter version of the festival is held in February. Second weekend in Sept, Feb. **FREE**

Art Chicago. *Navy Pier, 600 E Grand Ave, Chicago (60611). Phone 312/587-3300.* In conjunction with Chicago's Museum of Contemporary Art (see), this festival gives collectors and admirers of fine art a chance to see some of the newest and hippest pieces in the art world. Art Chicago takes place at Navy Pier (see) in mid-May each year and attracts hundreds of dealers from around the globe. Before the show opens, serious collectors can attend the Vernissage party for $125 a ticket and preview the art before the general public is admitted the following day. Mid-May.

Chicago Auto Show. *McCormick Place, 2301 S Lake Shore Dr, Chicago (60616). Phone 312/744-3370.* The world's largest auto show takes up all of the south wing of Chicago's enormous McCormick Place (see). It is often here that domestic and international automakers first put their latest models on public display.

Those Darn Cubs

If there's one thing everybody knows about Chicago, it's the curse of the Cubs. William Sianis, owner of the Billy Goat Tavern, bought two tickets to the last game of the 1945 World Series, one for himself and one for his goat. Upon arriving at the park, Sianis was told that his animal would not be admitted because of its smell. Infuriated, he put a curse on the ball club: "Never again will a World Series be played at Wrigley Field!" Never has a curse worked so well.

Beyond curses and goats, other facts about the Cubs are worth noting. For instance, did you know that it was the Chicago Cubs—not the White Sox—who were originally called the White Stockings? Here are some other juicy bits of early Chicago Cubs trivia:

In 1871, the Chicago White Stockings were one of the founding members of the National Association. They played a full season despite the Great Chicago Fire that destroyed their park, their uniforms, and their business records.

In 1876, the White Stockings became one of eight charter members of the National League. Their manager was A. G. Spaulding, who doubled as pitcher and recorded the first National League shutout, a 4-0 win over Louisville. Spaulding later went on to create a sporting goods empire.

There may have been only eight teams, but the Chicago White Stockings won the inaugural National League championship. In fact, they became the first league dynasty, winning six of the first 11 titles. This, of course, was before the famous curse.

Charles Weeghman, an owner from the just-folded Federal League, purchased the Cubs in 1916 and moved them into the park he'd built two years earlier for his defunct ball club. In 1926, Cubs Park was renamed Wrigley Field (see) after chewing gum magnate William Wrigley bought out Weeghman's share of the Cubs. Wrigley Field is the second-oldest ballpark in the major leagues, after Boston's Fenway Park.

The Cubs were poised to become one of the first teams to install lights in their ballpark, but after the bombing of Pearl Harbor in 1941, they donated their recently purchased lighting materials to the War Department. A Cubs first did occur that year, however, when the team became the first to accompany the game with organ music.

The Cubs vs. the Chicago White Sox was the first big-league baseball game broadcast on WGN-TV. It happened at Wrigley field on April 16, 1948. The Sox won, 4-1.

The famous Cubs trio, Tinkers-to-Evers-to-Chance, made famous in a poem by a *New York Times* sportswriter bemoaning the trio's ill effects on the Giants ("These are the saddest of possible words, Tinker to Evers to Chance, A trio of bear Cubs and fleeter than birds, Tinker to Evers to Chance"), recorded the first double play in 1902.

Other names for the Cubs have included the Chicago White Stockings (1876-1889), the Chicago Colts (1890-1897), and the Chicago Orphans (1898-1902).

The show has been an annual Chicago staple since 1901 and has grown right along with the industry itself. It's a good opportunity to see celebrities, as well as the expected concept cars and latest models of old favorites. Feb.

Chicago Blues Fest. *Grant Park, 331 E Randolph St, Chicago (60602). Phone 312/774-6630 (Chicago Office of Tourism). egov.cityofchicago.org.* In a city virtually synonymous with the blues (see SINGIN' THE BLUES), Chicago's annual Blues Fest, held in late May-early June, is the crème de la crème of blues festivals, attracting local stars such as Buddy Guy, Koko Taylor, Otis Rush, Sugar Blue, and Son Seals, as well as national names like Bo Diddley, Ruth Brown, Howlin' Wolf, Muddy Waters, Honeyboy Edwards, and the North Mississippi Allstars. With such a wealth of local talent, even the small stages and daytime shows rival the best blues clubs

Singin' the Blues

It all started in a small, lopsided former automobile parts factory at 2120 S Michigan Ave, an address immortalized by the Rolling Stones in their bluesy instrumental of the same name. The building was purchased by the Chess brothers, and, from 1957 to 1967, it operated as the home of Chess Records, the recording studio that gave the world the sad, edgy sound of the "Chicago blues."

They all recorded here, or wanted to: the great Muddy Waters, Koko Taylor, and Etta James. Willie Dixon, who, with Magic Sam, Otis Rush, and Luther Allison, helped define Chicago's West Side scene. Junior Wells, whose harmonica playing—"harps," as it was called—influenced countless blues greats, including Junior's longtime friend and partner, Chicago legend Buddy Guy. Junior met Buddy at a Battle of the Blues event, which Buddy won. They hit it off and collaborated for years, taking the sound of the Chicago blues a step further.

What exactly were the Chicago blues? When blacks migrating from the Mississippi Delta came through Memphis and settled in Chicago, their soulful music took on a tougher edge, mandated by the rhythms of the city and the noise of the clubs. Chicago blues were the Southern blues gone edgier and amplified.

In the early days, Buddy was a red-hot backup musician. But as the years wore on, he became a showman, a flamboyant stylist who would hit his guitar against a microphone to get an acoustic sound, pluck its strings with his tongue, or hit the strings with a belt or drumstick to get a tone. He could coax any sound he wanted out of that thing,

they said. Buddy made his guitar talk to you, they said. They said other things, too. Eric Clapton called him the greatest blues guitar player in the world and asked Buddy to play with him at Royal Albert Hall. The accolades inspired Guy's ironically titled album, *Damn Right I've Got the Blues*, the first of his four albums to win Grammys. Clapton wasn't the only rock star influenced by Guy, nor was he the first. The Rolling Stones asked Buddy and Junior Wells to open for them on their 1970 tour.

In 1989, Buddy opened a club on Chicago's South Side, Buddy Guy's Legends, so that blues artists would have a home in the Windy City. At Legends, blues fans eat from a Cajun-inspired menu while listening to a jam on Mondays, an acoustic blues artist on Fridays and Saturdays, and a consistently high level of talent the other four nights of the week. You never know when Mick Jagger and Ron Wood will drop in for an impromptu jam of "Little Red Rooster," as they did when the Stones were last in town for a gig. And you know it's January, because that's when Buddy's in town, stunning the crowd, plucking the guitar with his tongue, as great as he ever was—even greater, richer, more soulful. Damn right, he's still got the blues.

Buddy Guy's Legends is open Sunday 6 pm-2 am, Monday-Thursday 5 pm-2 am, Friday 4 pm-2 am, and Saturday 5 pm-3 am. Tickets are available for general admission; you can buy them through Ticketmaster, but plan to arrive at the small, 120-seat club early for a decent seat. For general information, phone 312/427-0333 or visit the Web site www.buddyguys.com.

in the United States. Low-key and racially diverse, this free outdoor festival attracts more than 600,000 visitors over its four-day run. It's a great place to experience a true cross-section of the city while enjoying barbecue, the start of summer, and the best in traditional and contemporary blues music. Late May-early June. **FREE**

Chicago Humanities Festival. *500 N Dearborn St, Suite 1028, Chicago (60610). Phone 312/661-1028.*

www.chfestival.org. For years, this festival was one of the best-kept secrets in Chicago: world-renowned authors, scholars, poets, policymakers, artists, and performers would gather for a weekend in November to celebrate the power of ideas in human culture and the role of the humanities in our daily lives. Dozens of lectures, performances, panels, and seminars, featuring names like Gore Vidal, Mira Nair, V. S. Naipul, Arthur Miller, Germaine Greer, Stephen Sondheim, and Robert Pinsky—were available to the public for just $5. Now, in its 13th year, the festival lasts for two weeks, features hundreds of events, and takes on a particular theme. For example, 2003 was Saving & Spending; other past themes have included Brains & Beauty, Crime & Punishment, Work & Play, Love & Marriage, and He/She. Tickets are still only $5 per event, yet now it's better to purchase them in advance since the secret is out. Two weeks in fall. **$**

Chicago International Film Festival. *32 W Randolph St, Chicago (60601). Phone 312/425-9400. www. chicagofilmfestival.com.* The oldest international film festival in North America. For three weeks each October, Chicagoans are introduced to some of the best cinema from around the world, as well as from those creating great work in the United States. Over the years, the festival has helped introduce innovative filmmakers like Martin Scorsese and John Carpenter. There are categories for feature films, first- and second-time directors, documentaries, and short films (including animation and student productions), all judged by The International Feature Film Jury, which is comprised of professional actors, directors, and critics. Oct.

Chicago Jazz Fest. *Grant Park, 331 E Randolph St, Chicago (60602). Phone 312/774-6630 (Chicago Office of Tourism). egov.cityofchicago.org.* Held each Labor Day weekend for the past 25 years, this event is worth planning a trip to Chicago around. During the four days of this most prestigious of United States jazz festivals, Grant Park (see) becomes a giant outdoor jazz café with more than 300,000 people in attendance. Lesser-known and local artists perform during the day on the small stages near the food concession area, but the main headliners—world-class jazz musicians such as Herbie Hancock, Cassandra Wilson, Betty Carter, Wayne Shorter, and Roy Hargrove—take the main stage at the Petrillo Music Shell after 5 pm. You need to arrive early to get a seat near the stage, but most folks prefer to picnic on the lawn, enjoying the perfect skyline views and listening to the strategically placed speakers. Labor Day weekend. **FREE**

Chicago Outdoor Film Festival. *Grant Park, 331 E Randolph St, Chicago (60602). Phone 312/774-6630 (Chicago Office of Tourism). egov.cityofchicago.org.* What started out as a small twice-a-month event at Grant Park (see) a few years ago has become a real phenomenon—the urban equivalent of an old-fashioned drive-in movie. Once a week in July and August, couples, families, and groups of friends flock

to the park to see free classic movies, from *Casablanca* and *Vertigo* to *West Side Story* and *Singin' in the Rain.* With the city skyline as the backdrop, the lake breeze for air-conditioning, and homemade picnics instead of overpriced movie concessions, it's a near-perfect outing. Movies start at dusk, but go early because it gets crowded. Mid-July-late Aug. **FREE**

Chicago to Mackinac Races. *400 E Monroe St, Chicago (60603). Phone 312/744-3370. www. chicagomackinac.com.* For more than a century, yacht racers have taken on mighty Lake Michigan in a race from the Windy City to Mackinac Island in Michigan's Upper Peninsula. Run by the Chicago Yacht Club, the race attracts around 300 vessels every year to take advantage of brisk northerly winds the third weekend in July. Participation is by invitation only and usually takes between 40 and 60 hours to complete. There are several different levels of competition, depending on the type of boat making the 333-mile trip. It is a great spectacle to watch as the boats leave Chicago. July.

Grant Park July 3 Concert. *Petrillo Music Shell, 235 S Columbus Dr, Chicago (60601). Phone 312/744-3370.* The lakefront blazes with cannon flashes as the Grant Park Symphony welcomes Independence Day with Tchaikovsky's 1812 Overture; fireworks. July 3.

Grant Park Music Festival. *Petrillo Music Shell, 235 S Columbus Dr, Chicago (60601). Phone 312/742-4763.* Concerts Wed, Fri-Sat, late June-Sept. **FREE**

Magnificent Mile Lights Festival. *N Michigan Ave, Chicago (60611). Phone 312/409-5560. www. themagnificentmile.com.* As a kickoff to the holiday season, for the last 13 years the North Michigan Avenue Association has sponsored the Magnificent Lights Festival, during which the avenue's trademark tiny white lights get turned on to much fanfare. Generally held the weekend before Thanksgiving, the festival has grown to become a family day, starting with carolers, gingerbread decorating, ice-carving displays, Disney character stage shows, and a lively procession down Michigan Avenue, culminating in the lighting and fireworks spectacular. Attendance is usually high; of course, all depends on Chicago's unpredictable winter weather. Late Nov. **FREE**

Marshall Field's holiday window displays. *111 N State St, Chicago (60602). Phone 312/781-1000. www. marshallfields.com.* Every holiday season, children and adults alike flock to Marshall Field's State Street store (see) to gaze in wonder at the elaborate and magical window displays. It's a Chicago ritual to line up outside the windows, three, four, and five deep, the day after Thanksgiving for the unveiling of the new season's displays. Although Field's has been delighting Chicagoans for more than a century with its innovative decorations, not until 1946 did its stores feature "stories"—from a reenactment of "'Twas the Night Before Christmas" to recent tales of Harry Potter—that progress from window to window. To avoid the crowds, visit right after Christmas. When you've stood out in the cold long enough, treat yourself to lunch in the store's elegant Walnut Room—another Chicago holiday tradition—where every table offers a view of its famous 40-plus-foot Christmas tree. Mid-Nov-mid-Jan.

Navy Pier Art Fair. *Navy Pier, 331 E Randolph St, Chicago (60601). Phone 312/744-3370.* Month-long exhibit of local artists' work. Jan. **FREE**

Ravinia Festival. *Highland Park (60035). Phone 847/266-5100. www.ravinia.org.* (See HIGHLAND PARK) June-mid-Sept.

Spring Flower Show. *Garfield Park Conservatory, 300 N Central Ave, Chicago (60624). Phone 312/746-5100. www.garfield-conservatory.org.* Apr.

St. Patrick's Day Parade. *Downtown Chicago. Phone 312/744-3370. www.chicagostpatsparade.com.* Chicago's St. Patrick's Day parade is famous around the world, not because of its size (although it is one of the largest) or its spirit (it is one of the rowdiest), but for the fact that on the day of the parade, the city dyes the Chicago River green, a tradition started during the early 1960s. If nothing else, this tells you how seriously Chicago takes the holiday. Held annually on the Saturday closest to St. Patrick's Day, the parade features dozens of bands, thousands of Irish step dancers, a multitude of floats, representatives of unions and local organizations, politicians, dignitaries, and many a surprise guest—often famous people with Chicago roots—all "wearin' the green." Mostly, however, the parade is one big party for hundreds of thousands of Chicagoans and visitors alike, where everyone gets to be Irish, at least for an afternoon. Weekend closest to St. Patrick's Day. **FREE**

Taste of Chicago. *331 E Randolph St, Chicago (60602). Phone 312/774-6630 (Chicago Office of Tourism). egov. cityofchicago.org.* What started out more than 20 years ago as a way to sample cuisines from some of the city's best-known restaurants has become an all-out food fest and Fourth of July celebration that attracts more than 3.5 million visitors a year and features booths from more than 50 area vendors. At this ten-day event, you can stick to Taste favorites—Lou Malnati's pizza, Eli's cheesecake, Robinson's ribs, giant turkey drumsticks, and sautéed goat meat and plantains from Vee-Vee's African restaurant—or indulge in more refined specialties, like coconut lime sorbet, duck with lingonberries, grilled lobster tail, and alligator on a stick. In addition to food, you'll find free live music by big-name headliners, amusement park rides, and even a parent helper tent with free diapers. The crowds can get oppressive, so the earlier in the day you go, the better; don't forget to bring water, sunscreen, patience, and, perhaps, some wetnaps. Also try to buy food tickets in advance to avoid long lines. Late June-early July. **FREE**

Venetian Night. *Monroe Harbor, 100 N Harbor Dr, Chicago (60603). Phone 312/747-2474.* Venetian aquatic parade, fireworks. Late July. **FREE**

Winter Delights. *Mayor's Office of Special Events, 121 N LaSalle St, Room 703, Chicago (60602). Citywide. Phone 312/744-3315. www.winterdelights.com.* Includes snow-carving contests. First two weeks in Feb.

Limited-Service Hotels

★ ★ **COURTYARD BY MARRIOTT.** *30 E Hubbard St, Chicago (60611). Phone 312/329-2500; fax 312/329-0293. www.courtyard.com.* 337 rooms, 15 story. Check-in 4 pm, check-out noon. Restaurant, bar. Fitness room. Indoor pool, whirlpool. **$$**

★ **FAIRFIELD INN.** *216 E Ontario St, Chicago (60611). Phone 312/787-3777; fax 312/787-8714. www.fairfieldsuiteschicago.com.* Just a block off the Magnificent Mile (see) and three blocks from the lake, this new, clean, well-maintained hotel is a great choice for budget-minded travelers who don't want to give up on location to save money. Although the property doesn't have much in the way of extra amenities, it has an attractive and inviting lobby, and the staff is very accommodating. If you'd prefer to spend the bulk of your vacation dollars on shopping and fine dining rather than on accommodations, this is THE choice in downtown Chicago. 185 rooms. Complimentary continental breakfast. Check-in 3 pm, check-out noon. Fitness room. **$**

★ **HAMPTON INN.** *33 W Illinois St, Chicago (60610). Phone 312/832-0330; fax 312/832-0333. www.hamptoninn.com.* This Hampton Inn's convenient location, reasonable rates, and comfortable rooms make it a great choice for visitors to downtown Chicago. With its large number of suites and ample meeting space, the hotel welcomes families and business travelers. Ruth's Chris Steak House is connected to the hotel by a second-floor skywalk, and guests have plenty of other restaurants to choose from in the surrounding area. 230 rooms, all suites. Complimentary continental breakfast. Check-in 3 pm, check-out noon. Fitness room. Indoor pool. Business center. **$**

★ ★ **TREMONT HOTEL.** *100 E Chestnut St, Chicago (60611). Phone 312/751-1900; toll-free 800/621-8133; fax 312/751-8691. www.tremontchicago.com.* This European-style boutique hotel features 5,000 square feet of meeting space. Amenities are limited, but its proximity to Michigan Avenue and its cozy guest rooms make it a fine choice for an overnight stay or a romantic getaway. 130 rooms, 16 story. Pets accepted. Check-in 3 pm, check-out noon. Restaurant. Fitness room. **$$**

Full-Service Hotels

★ ★ ★ **ALLERTON CROWNE PLAZA.** *701 N Michigan Ave, Chicago (60611). Phone 312/440-1500; toll-free 800/621-8311; fax 312/440-1819. www.allertonchi.crowneplaza.com.* The Gold Coast's long-standing Allerton Crowne Plaza boasts both Historic Landmark Hotel status, designated by the city of Chicago, and a $60 million renovation that brought the hotel up to today's standards. Business and leisure travelers are attracted to the ideal location on Chicago's Magnificent Mile (see), as well as to all-day dining at Taps on Two restaurant and a 25th-floor health club where guests gasp for breath over both exercise and a view of the city spread out beneath them. No two guest rooms have the same layout or design. 443 rooms, 25 story. Pets accepted, some restrictions; fee. Check-in 3 pm, check-out noon. High-speed Internet access. Restaurant, bar. Fitness room. Airport transportation available. Business center. **$$**

★ ★ ★ **AMALFI HOTEL CHICAGO.** *20 W Kinzie, Chicago (60610). Phone 312/395-9000; fax 312/395-9001. www.amalfihotelchicago.com.* 215 rooms. Check-in 3 pm, check-out noon. High-speed Internet access. Restaurant, bar. Fitness room. Whirlpool. Airport transportation available. Business center. **$$**

★ ★ ★ **BURNHAM HOTEL.** *1 W Washington Blvd, Chicago (60602). Phone 312/782-1111; toll-free 877/294-9712; fax 312/782-0899. www.burnhamhotel.com.* Reviving the historic Reliance Building (predecessor of the modern skyscraper and early 1900s home of department store Carson Pirie Scott), the Burnham retains the integrity of the landmark architecture, integrating it with a whimsically elegant, clubby ambience. In the Loop near the downtown theater district, major museums, and parks, the hotel is appropriate for business or leisure travel. Rooms and suites offer dramatic views of the Chicago cityscape. The in-house Atwood Café (see) serves upscale American comfort food (including breakfast, lunch, dinner, Sunday brunch, and pre-theater options). The hotel offers 24-hour room service, as well as pampering pet treatments. 122 rooms, 15 story. Pets accepted. Check-in 3 pm, check-out noon. Restaurant, bar. Fitness room. **$$**

★ ★ ★ **CROWNE PLAZA.** *10 S Wabash Ave, Chicago (60603). Phone 312/372-7696; fax 312/372-7320. www.crowneplaza.com.* This historic hotel features unusual characteristics, such as rooms with 12-foot ceilings, 10-foot windows, and oversized bathrooms. Guests are within walking distance of the Art Institute (see) and Symphony Center (see), local theaters, and the heart of the financial district. 206 rooms, 10 story. Check-in 3 pm, check-out noon. Restaurant, bar. Fitness room. Business center. **$$**

★ ★ ★ **DOUBLETREE HOTEL.** *198 E Delaware Pl, Chicago (60611). Phone 312/664-1100; toll-free 800/222-8733; fax 312/664-9881. www.doubletreehotels.com.* In an ideal location one block east of Michigan Avenue, guests won't know where to head first when heading off-site—to the John Hancock Center (see) across the street, to the Magnificent Mile (see) and Oak Street shops (see), to the beach and the park, or to nearby restaurants. All the guest accommodations are two-room suites with a living room and separate bedroom. Sleeper sofas, two televisions, and in-suite refreshment centers make this a good choice for families or extended stays. 345 rooms, 30 story, all suites. Check-in 3 pm, check-out noon. Restaurant, bar. Fitness room. Indoor pool, whirlpool. Business center. **$$**

★ ★ ★ **THE DRAKE HOTEL.** *140 E Walton Pl, Chicago (60611). Phone 312/787-2200; toll-free 800/553-7253; fax 312/787-1431. www. thedrakehotel.com.* A favorite landmark in the Michigan Avenue skyline, The Drake is a luxury lakefront hotel offering both spectacular views and a prime Gold Coast location. Built in 1920 as a summer resort, extensive renovations have preserved the ornate, elegant charm of this venerable classic. Amenities include executive floors, luxurious bathrooms, an exercise facility, a shopping arcade, and multiple dining options. The clubby Cape Cod Room (see) is famous for its oyster bar and seafood, the Oak Terrace for its lakefront views, and the Coq d'Or for its piano bar. Afternoon tea in the lobby's Palm Court and 24-hour room service are also offered. 537 rooms, 10 story. Check-in 3 pm, check-out noon. Restaurants, bar. Fitness room. Business center. **$$**

★ ★ ★ **EMBASSY SUITES.** *600 N State St, Chicago (60610). Phone 312/943-3800; toll-free 800/362-2779; fax 312/943-7629. www. embassysuiteschicago.com.* Both business- and family-friendly, this all-suite hotel boasts a prime River North location, just a short walk to a multitude of galleries and dining and entertainment venues, as well as to Michigan Avenue shopping. Beautifully appointed two-room suites are modern and spacious and include kitchen appliances and sleeper sofas. Lush with greenery and fountains, the inviting lobby leads to an 11-story atrium. Immediately adjacent are both a Starbucks and the quaint Papagus Greek Taverna (see). Other amenities include VIP rooms; complimentary breakfast; on-site car rental; business, meeting, and conference facilities; and fitness facilities with sauna and pool. 358 rooms, 11 story, all suites. Complimentary full breakfast. Check-out noon. Restaurant, bar. Fitness room. Indoor pool, whirlpool. **$$**

★ ★ ★ **EMBASSY SUITES CHICAGO LAKEFRONT.** *511 N Columbus Dr, Chicago (60611). Phone 312/836-5900; fax 312/836-5901. www. embassysuites.com.* 455 rooms, all suites. Check-in 4 pm, check-out noon. Restaurant, bar. Fitness room. Indoor pool, whirlpool. Airport transportation available. Business center. **$**

★ ★ ★ **THE FAIRMONT CHICAGO.** *200 N Columbus Dr, Chicago (60601). Phone 312/ 565-8000; toll-free 800/866-5577; fax 312/856-1032. www.fairmont.com.* The Fairmont hotel is at once traditional and contemporary. Just a short distance from the lake and near the renowned shopping of the Magnificent Mile (see), its sleek tower rests on the edge of leafy Grant Park (see). The interiors are refined, with rich colors and antique reproductions, and spectacular lakefront views define many of the elegant accommodations. Diners and critics alike are singing the praises of the American dishes at Aria restaurant (see), and afternoon tea is a special event at the Lobby Lounge. The comprehensive business center keeps travelers in touch with the office, while fitness-minded visitors appreciate the guest privileges at the adjoining Lakeshore Athletic Club and Waves day spa. Noteworthy for its indoor rock-climbing wall, this establishment is often considered the city's top exercise facility. 692 rooms, 41 story. Pets accepted, some restrictions; fee. Check-in 3 pm, check-out noon. Restaurant, bar. Fitness room, spa. Indoor pool, outdoor pool, whirlpool. Business center. **$$**

★ ★ ★ ★ **FOUR SEASONS HOTEL CHICAGO.** *120 E Delaware Pl, Chicago (60611). Phone 312/280-8800; fax 312/280-9184. www. fourseasons.com/chicagofs.* Located in a 66-story building atop the world-renowned shops of 900 North Michigan (see), the Four Seasons Hotel Chicago is a well-heeled shopper's paradise. More than 100 world-class stores, including Gucci and Bloomingdale's, await only steps from your door. This palatial skytop hotel exudes glamour, from its gleaming marble lobby with grand staircase to its regal accommodations. Even exercise is refined here, with a marvelous Roman-columned indoor pool. Occupying the 30th through 46th floors of the tower, the guest rooms afford jaw-dropping views of the magnificent skyline and Lake Michigan. From this vantage point, guests truly feel on top of the world. The accommodations have an opulent character enhanced by jewel tones, rich fabrics, and timeless furnishings. Body and mind are calmed at the spa (see), where a whimsical element inspires the decadent champagne cocktail and caviar facials. Edible indulgences include French dishes at Seasons restaurant (see) and continental favorites at The Café. 343 rooms, 66 story. Pets accepted, some restrictions; fee. Check-in 3 pm, check-out noon. Restaurant, bar. Fitness room, spa. Indoor pool, whirlpool. Business center. **$$$$**

★ ★ ★ **HARD ROCK HOTEL CHICAGO.**
230 N Michigan Ave, Chicago (60601). Phone 312/ 345-1000; fax 312/345-1012. www.hardrock.com. 381 rooms. Check-in 3 pm, check-out noon. High-speed Internet access. Restaurant, bar. Fitness room. Airport transportation available. Business center. **$$$**

★ ★ ★ **HILTON CHICAGO.** *720 S Michigan Ave, Chicago (60605). Phone 312/922-4400; fax 312/ 332-7301. www.chicagohilton.com.* Built in 1927 as the world's largest hotel, this grande dame of Michigan Avenue overlooks Grant Park (see) and Lake Michigan. Its central location and rich history make it a popular stop, even with those who elect to stay elsewhere. Pay a visit to the lobby's Great Hall and take in the ceiling mural 40 feet overhead, framed by imposing Italian marble columns. Even more spectacular, the Versailles-inspired Grand Ballroom, with its gold leaf molding, mirrors, and crystal chandeliers, has played host to kings and queens, presidents, diginitaries, and celebrities. Tower rooms on the top floors offer slightly more luxurious accommodations. Amenities include three restaurants and a 28,000-square-foot athletic club with a 20-yard swimming pool and sun deck. 1,544 rooms, 25 story. Check-out 11 am. Restaurants, bar. Fitness room. Indoor pool, whirlpools. Business center. **$$**

★ ★ ★ **HOTEL INTERCONTINENTAL CHICAGO.** *505 N Michigan Ave, Chicago (60611). Phone 312/944-4100; fax 312/944-1320. www.chicago. intercontinental.com.* Built in 1929 as a luxury men's club (the original swimming pool remains in the fitness center), the InterContinental has undergone extensive renovations in recent years. Uniting the modern main tower and the historic north tower, the dramatic lobby is open and airy, with mosaic tile flooring, a four-story rotunda, and a grand staircase. The Magnificent Mile location, luxuriously appointed rooms with Michigan Avenue or Lake Michigan views, numerous ballrooms, and unique meeting spaces are among the draws. Room service is available 24 hours, and the hotel's restaurant, Zest, serves contemporary Mediterranean fare. High tea is also offered in the Salon. 807 rooms, 42 story. Check-in 3 pm, check-out noon. High-speed Internet access. Restaurant, two bars. Fitness room (fee). Indoor pool. Airport transportation available. Business center. **$$**

★ ★ ★ **HOTEL MONACO CHICAGO.** *225 N Wabash Ave, Chicago (60601). Phone 312/960-8500; fax 312/960-1883. www.monaco-chicago.com.* In the heart of downtown, between the Loop and the Magnificent Mile (see), the Monaco's stylishly eclectic, Euro aesthetic is equally suited to business or pleasure travel. The front desk recalls a vintage steamer trunk; the lobby has the feel of a posh living room, with a grand limestone fireplace. Colorful rooms are retreats of creature comfort, with plush furnishings, distinctive bath products (and Fuji tubs in the suites), and even a companion goldfish on request. Enjoy round-the-clock room service or visit the South Water Kitchen, the hotel's restaurant, for breakfast, lunch, or dinner. Pets also are accommodated with aplomb. 192 rooms, 14 story. Pets accepted. Check-in 3 pm, check-out noon. Restaurant. Fitness room. Business center. **$$**

★ ★ ★ **HOUSE OF BLUES HOTEL, A LOEWS HOTEL.** *333 N Dearborn, Chicago (60610). Phone 312/245-0333; fax 312/245-0504. www. loewshotels.com.* With its exotic Gothic-Moroccan-East Indian décor, eye-popping art collection, and adjacent live concert venue, the hip House of Blues Hotel appeals to a new generation of travelers. Guest rooms are spacious and well appointed; vast meeting space and related services cater to business travelers. The namesake restaurant serves Southern American fare and hosts a popular Sunday gospel brunch. In the same complex are the chic, wine-themed bistro Bin 36 (see) and Smith & Wollensky Steak House. The location puts guests in the heart of the River North gallery, dining, and entertainment district (see) and close to the Loop and Michigan Avenue. 367 rooms, 15 story. Pets accepted. Check-in 3 pm, check-out noon. Restaurant, bar. Fitness room, spa. Business center. **$$**

★ ★ ★ HYATT AT UNIVERSITY VILLAGE.

625 S Ashland Ave, Chicago (60607). Phone 312/491-1234; fax 312/529-6095. www.hyatt.com. This hotel is conveniently located to downtown Chicago and 20 minutes from O'Hare International Airport. Amenities include a fitness center and access to the Chicago Health Club, which is just five blocks from the hotel. Enjoy a fireside dinner at Jaxx Restaurant and then a night cap at Jaxx Lounge, both located on-site. 114 rooms, 4 story. Check-out noon. Restaurant, bar. Fitness room. Business center. Near the University of Illinois Chicago campus. **$$**

★ ★ ★ HYATT ON PRINTERS ROW. *500*

S Dearborn St, Chicago (60605). Phone 312/986-1234; fax 312/939-2468. www.hyatt.com. The guest rooms in this national historic landmark feature 12-foot vaulted ceilings. Another key attraction, Prairie restaurant, serves up cuisine from America's heartland in a setting inspired by Frank Lloyd Wright's Prairie school of architecture. 161 rooms, 12 story. Check-in 3 pm, check-out noon. Restaurant, bar. Fitness room. Airport transportation available. **$$$**

★ ★ ★ HYATT REGENCY MCCORMICK

PLACE. *2233 S Martin Luther King Dr, Chicago (60616). Phone 312/567-1234; fax 312/528-4000. www.mccormickplace.hyatt.com.* Conveniently connected by the enclosed Grand Concourse walkway to three exposition buildings, this hotel offers a splendid stay for the busy executive or the guest who just needs to unwind. Providing guests with spacious and well-furnished accommodations and just steps from downtown Chicago, State Street shopping (see), and Michigan Avenue, this hotel has something for every-one and guarantees return visits by even the most discriminating traveler. 800 rooms, 33 story. Check-in 3 pm, check-out noon. Restaurant, bar. Fitness room. Indoor pool. Business center. **$$**

★ ★ ★ LE MERIDIEN CHICAGO. *521 N Rush*

St, Chicago (60611). Phone 312/645-1500; fax 312/645-1550. www.lemeridien.com. Perched atop The Shops at North Bridge and Nordstrom, with a main entrance on Rush Street and an entrance on Michigan Avenue, this hotel has an ideal location—close to the Loop, the Merchandise Mart (see), and Navy Pier (see). Cerise restaurant (see) offers exceptional cuisine in a casual setting, while Le Rendez Vous bar provides an intimate place to mingle and sample the signature chocolate martini. Work off the indulgence in the 24-hour fitness center. Rooms offer high-tech accoutrements such as CD player/clock radios, cordless phones, and electronic safes with charging capabilities. 311 rooms, 12 story. Pets accepted, some restrictions. Check-in 3 pm, check-out noon. High-speed Internet access. Restaurant, bar. Fitness room. Business center. **$$$**

★ ★ ★ MARRIOTT CHICAGO DOWNTOWN.

540 N Michigan Ave, Chicago (60611). Phone 312/836-0100; fax 312/836-6139. www.marriott.com. Business travelers appreciate this hotel's convenient location along the Magnificent Mile (see) and near many Loop corporate offices. Leisure travelers walk steps from the lobby to area attractions and a wealth of shops, including the nearby Shops at North Bridge containing Nordstrom. Guest rooms are designed for working travelers, with data ports, voice mail, lamp-lit work areas, and high-speed Internet access. 1,192 rooms, 46 story. Check-in 4 pm, check-out noon. Two restaurants, bars. Fitness room, spa. Indoor pool, whirlpool. Business center. **$$$**

★ ★ ★ OMNI AMBASSADOR EAST. *1301*

N State Pkwy, Chicago (60610). Phone 312/787-7200; toll-free 800/843-6664; fax 312/787-4760. www.omnihotels.com. A prime Gold Coast location and the world-famous Pump Room restaurant (see) are two reasons to stay at this grand hotel, designated a Historic Hotel of America. The 14 Celebrity Suites honor some of the many notable guests who have stayed or eaten on-site. Enjoy French-inspired American cuisine and live jazz music in the Pump Room, which has served a steady stream of patrons since 1926. 285 rooms, 17 story. Pets accepted, some restrictions; fee. Check-in 3 pm, check-out noon. High-speed Internet access. Wireless Internet access. Restaurant, bar. Fitness room. Airport transportation available. Business center. **$$**

★ ★ ★ **OMNI CHICAGO HOTEL.** *676 N Michigan Ave, Chicago (60611). Phone 312/944-6664; toll-free 800/788-6664; fax 312/266-3015. www. omnihotels.com.* In the center of Michigan Avenue within a mixed-use building sits this 347-suite property, host to many famous guests of *The Oprah Winfrey Show* (see). All accommodations offer spacious sitting rooms with bedrooms hidden behind French doors, great for corporate clientele needing their room to double as an office. The fourth floor Cielo restaurant provides fantastic views of the street excitement below. 347 rooms, 25 story. Pets accepted, some restrictions; fee. Check-in 3 pm, check-out noon. Restaurant, bar. Children's activity center. Fitness room. Indoor pool, whirlpool. Business center. **$$**

★ ★ ★ **THE PALMER HOUSE HILTON.** *17 E Monroe St, Chicago (60603). Phone 312/726-7500; fax 312/917-1707. www.hilton.com.* Grand and gilded, the Palmer House Hilton has harbored visitors to the Windy City for 130 years, making it America's longest-operating hotel. This Loop landmark has undergone a full renovation to restore designer-builder Potter Palmer's original French Empire opulence, including the breathtaking Beaux Arts ceiling in the palatial lobby. Amenities include an 11-room penthouse suite, executive levels with private elevator, an entire floor of "deluxe-tech" conference and meeting facilities, a fitness club, and a shopping arcade. Four restaurants and bars include the 1940s-themed Big Downtown restaurant and bar and the retro Polynesian favorite, Trader Vic's. 1,639 rooms, 25 story. Pets accepted. Check-in 3 pm, check-out 11 am. Restaurants, bar. Fitness room. Indoor pool, whirlpool. Airport transportation available. Business center. **$$**

★ ★ ★ **PARK HYATT CHICAGO.** *800 N Michigan Ave, Chicago (60611). Phone 312/335-1234; toll-free 800/778-7477; fax 312/239-4000. www. parkhyattchicago.com.* From its stylish interiors to its historic Water Tower Square location, the Park Hyatt is intrinsically tied to the history of Chicago. Occupying a landmark building in the heart of the Magnificent Mile (see) shopping area, the hotel has a sleek, modern attitude. The public and private spaces celebrate the city's long-lasting love affair with architecture and its artists. Mies van der Rohe, Eames, and Noguchi furnishings are showcased throughout the guest rooms, while photography commissioned by The Art Institute of Chicago (see) graces the walls. A health club, spa, and salon are the perfect antidotes to stress, and the flawless service always ensures a carefree visit. The nouvelle cuisine at NoMI (see) is a standout, although the dramatic seventh-floor views from the floor-to-ceiling windows are not for the faint of heart. To escape the urban pace, visitors head to the NoMI Garden for American barbecue favorites. 202 rooms, 18 story. Pets accepted, some restrictions; fee. Check-in 3 pm, check-out noon. Restaurant, bar. Fitness room, spa. Indoor pool, whirlpool. Business center. **$$$$**

★ ★ ★ ★ ★ **THE PENINSULA CHICAGO.** *108 E Superior St, Chicago (60611). Phone 312/337-2888; fax 312/932-9529. www.peninsula.com.* Reigning over Chicago's famed Magnificent Mile, the Peninsula Chicago hotel basks in a golden aura. From the sun-filled lobby to the gleaming, gilded details, this hotel simply sparkles. With Tiffany and Ralph Lauren downstairs and Saks and Neiman Marcus across the street, the gracious bellmen outfitted in crisp white uniforms are a shopper's savior. Asian sensibilities are expertly blended with details highlighting the city's Art Deco heritage in the public spaces. Soft lighting, polished woods, and golden hues create glorious shelters in the guest rooms. Proving the point that modern amenities are a hallmark of this property, all rooms are fitted with bedside electronic control panels and flat-screen televisions. Guests escape the pressures of the everyday at the state-of-the-art exercise facility and spa, complete with an outdoor sundeck. Whether taking tea, nibbling flammekuchen, sampling Asian specialties, or savoring seafood, guests traverse the world at five distinctive dining venues. *Secret Inspector's Notes: The Peninsula Chicago is one of the most perfect hotel experiences a traveler can expect in this country. The staff attends to every detail with such attention and care that it is impossible to conceive of the luxury offered at this high-tech hotel until you have experienced it. Nothing can compare to luxuriating in your deep bathtub, watching television while enjoying room service at a culinary level of some of the best restaurants in the city. The bar is a fantastic spot to enjoy a drink and perhaps an appetizer, and the adjacent Pierrot Gourmet serves delightful European fare in a bright setting. Eating breakfast in the palatial lobby restaurant is as impressive an experience as you can find while watching the sun rise over the skyline. Find a way to stay here, whether for a night or a week. Your expectations of hotels will be changed forever.* 339 rooms, 20 story. Pets accepted, some restrictions. Check-in

3 pm, check-out noon. Restaurants, bar. Fitness room, spa. Indoor pool, children's pool, whirlpool. Business center. **$$$$**

★ ★ ★ RENAISSANCE CHICAGO
HOTEL. *1 W Wacker Dr, Chicago (60601). Phone 312/372-7200; fax 312/372-0093. www. renaissancehotels.com.* This Marriott-owned Loop high-rise features stone and glass exterior towers that rise above the intersection of State and Wacker. The Renaissance is a welcome haven to its audience of business travelers and vacationers looking for a central location accessible to theaters and museums. The handsome lobby sets a posh, executive tone; comfortable rooms boast spectacular views (especially on the higher floors). The Great Street Restaurant in the hotel's atrium serves American breakfast, lunch, and dinner (and has a bargain theater menu) with a view of the river. Additional amenities include 24-hour room service, expanded club-level rooms, a fitness club and pool, a lobby bar, and a 24-hour Kinko's business center. 553 rooms, 27 story. Pets accepted, some restrictions; fee. Check-in 3 pm, check-out 1 pm. Restaurants, bar. Fitness room. Indoor pool, whirlpool. Business center. **$$$**

★ ★ ★ ★ ★ THE RITZ-CARLTON, A FOUR
SEASONS HOTEL. *160 E Pearson St, Chicago (60611). Phone 312/266-1000; toll-free 800/621-6906; fax 312/266-1194. www.fourseasons.com.* Guests of the esteemed Ritz-Carlton Chicago often wonder if heaven could get any better than this. The unparalleled levels of service, commitment to excellence, and meticulous attention to detail make this one of the country's finest hotels. Gracing the upper levels of prestigious Water Tower Place on the Magnificent Mile (see), the hotel's guest rooms afford picture-perfect views through large windows. Rich tones and dignified furnishings define the accommodations. Managed by the Four Seasons, The Ritz-Carlton offers guests a taste of the luxe life, from the resplendent décor and seamless service to the superlative cuisine at the four restaurants and lounges. The sublime contemporary French menu and sensational ambience at The Dining Room (see) make it one of the most coveted tables in town. Human guests, however, are not the only ones to be spoiled—furry visitors feast in-room on filet mignon and salmon! *Secret Inspector's Notes: The Ritz-Carlton Chicago is elegance*

taken to the highest possible level and then translated into giddy grandeur and opulence. The staff at The Ritz-Carlton exudes such cheerfulness and genialness that you wish they would sell it in a bottle. The concierges at this home to the fortunate could not be better; they are capable of handling any request with such a personal touch that it remains in your mind for many months to follow. Breakfast at The Ritz-Carlton is an exercise in being taken care of, where the sweet waitstaff makes sure that you leave feeling both satiated and nourished. 435 rooms, 31 story. Pets accepted, some restrictions. Check-in 3 pm, check-out noon. High-speed Internet access. Three restaurants, bars. Fitness room, fitness classes available, spa (see). Indoor pool, whirlpool. Business center. **$$$$**

★ ★ ★ SHERATON CHICAGO HOTEL &
TOWERS. *301 E North Water St, Chicago (60611). Phone 312/464-1000; toll-free 800/233-4100; fax 312/464-9140. www.sheratonchicago.com.* Contemporary yet comfortable, every room of the handsomely appointed Sheraton Chicago Hotel & Towers promises a sweeping view of the cityscape, the Chicago River, or Lake Michigan. The central location is just minutes from the Magnificent Mile (see), the Loop, Navy Pier (see), and McCormick Place (see). The spacious lobby is appointed in imported marble and rich woods, and luxurious fitness facilities feature a pool and sauna. Close to numerous fine restaurants, the Sheraton's five in-house dining options include Shula's Steak House and an indoor-outdoor café overlooking the river. Extensive and elegant meeting facilities, a full-service business center, and club-level rooms cater to business travelers. 1,200 rooms, 34 story. Pets accepted, some restrictions; fee. Check-in 3 pm, check-out noon. Restaurants, bar. Fitness room. Indoor pool. Business center. **$$**

★ ★ ★ SOFITEL. *20 E Chestnut St, Chicago
(60611). Phone 312/324-4000; fax 312/324-4026. www. sofitel.com.* A stunning design created by French architect Jean-Paul Viguier gives this hotel an unmistakable presence on the Gold Coast, just off the Magnificent Mile (see). Le Bar is a popular after-work place to meet and mingle, while Café des Architectes serves up French cuisine in a contemporary setting. 415 rooms, 32 story. Pets accepted, some restrictions. Check-in 3 pm, check-out noon. Restaurant, bar. Fitness room. **$$**

★ ★ ★ **THE SUTTON PLACE HOTEL.** *21 E Bellevue Pl, Chicago (60611). Phone 312/266-2100; toll-free 800/810-6888; fax 312/266-2103. www. suttonplace.com.* Stylish understatement is the mantra of this luxurious 23-story hotel, an Art Deco-inspired building housing a handsome, modern interior. The prime Gold Coast location offers immediate access to such attractions as Magnificent Mile shopping, Rush Street nightlife, and some of the city's finest restaurants. Soundproofed rooms feature deep-soaking tubs, separate glass-enclosed showers, plush robes, and lavish bath accessories. Room service is 24/7, and destination dining and people-watching are available at the Whiskey Bar & Grill. Popular with corporate travelers, Sutton Place is equally suited to private getaways—even with your pet (with some restrictions). 246 rooms, 23 story. Pets accepted, some restrictions; fee. Check-in 3 pm, check-out noon. Restaurant, bar. Fitness room. Airport transportation available. Business center. **$$**

★ ★ ★ **SWISSÔTEL CHICAGO.** *323 E Wacker Dr, Chicago (60601). Phone 312/565-0565; fax 312/565-0540. www.swissotel-chicago.com.* High ceilings, dark woods, and a well-lit lobby dominate the first glimpse into the tastefully decorated and operated Swissôtel Chicago. Stunning views of Lake Michigan and Grant Park (see) lend a tranquil feel and help guests forget the hustle and bustle outside, despite the central location near Navy Pier (see) and Michigan Avenue. With oversized rooms and cheerful service, this hotel is a solid choice for even the most discerning traveler. 632 rooms, 43 story. Check-in 3 pm, check-out noon. Two restaurants. Fitness room. Indoor pool, whirlpool. Business center. **$$**

★ ★ ★ **W CHICAGO–CITY CENTER.** *172 W Adams St, Chicago (60603). Phone 312/332-1200; fax 312/917-5771. www.whotels.com.* Blending in perfectly in a decidedly urban setting in the city's financial district, this hotel provides a much-needed, hip hotspot for locals and tourists alike. Old architecture of the former Midland Hotel mixes with modern accents in the W Living Room, where an after-work crowd mingles with drinks beneath the vaulted ceiling while listening to tunes spun by the DJ from a balcony above. Guest rooms are modern but comfortable, providing a respite from the commotion below. Grab a light bite at the W Café or dine on more substantial Italian fare at Wë. Rande Gerber's adjacent Whiskey Blue bar gives guests a choice Chicago nightspot just steps from the hotel elevators. 390 rooms, 20 story. Pets accepted, some restrictions; fee. Check-in 3 pm, check-out noon. High-speed Internet access. Restaurant, bar. Fitness room. **$$$**

★ ★ ★ **THE WESTIN CHICAGO RIVER NORTH.** *320 Dearborn St, Chicago (60610). Phone 312/744-1900; fax 312/527-2650. www. westinrivernorth.com.* The Westin Chicago River North enjoys a wonderful location overlooking the Chicago River in the heart of the city's financial and theater districts. This luxury hotel is an impressive sight and offers a welcoming home for business or leisure travelers visiting the Windy City. Attractive and comfortable, the rooms use a blend of brass, black, and caramel tones to create a soothing atmosphere, the furnishings a contemporary interpretation of classic design. Westin's signature Heavenly Beds make for luxurious slumber, and the Heavenly Baths ensure aquatic therapy. Athletic-minded guests reap the rewards of the full-service fitness center. The Kamehachi Sushi Bar delights fish lovers; the Celebrity Café features all-day dining with a focus on American dishes; and the Hana Lounge entertains nightly with hors d'oeuvres and live music. 424 rooms, 20 story. Pets accepted, some restrictions. Check-in 3 pm, check-out noon. Restaurants, bar. Fitness room, spa. Business center. **$$**

★ ★ ★ **THE WHITEHALL HOTEL.** *105 E Delaware Pl, Chicago (60611). Phone 312/944-6300; toll-free 800/948-4255; fax 312/944-8552. www. thewhitehallhotel.com.* A historic Gold Coast landmark, this venerable hotel is just off the Magnificent Mile and steps from Water Tower Place (see). Built in 1927 and extensively renovated in recent years, the independent Whitehall retains its stature as a small sanctuary with personal service and sedate, old-world charm. Rooms combine traditional décor (including some four-poster beds) and modern technology. The California-Mediterranean restaurant, Molive, offers an excellent wine program, a bar, and outdoor dining. Additional highlights include club floors and complimentary sedan service (within 2 miles). 221 rooms, 21 story. Pets accepted, some restrictions. Check-in 3 pm, check-out noon. Restaurant, bar. Fitness room. **$$**

★ ★ ★ **WYNDHAM CHICAGO DOWNTOWN.**
*633 N St. Clair St, Chicago (60611). Phone 312/
573-0300; toll-free 800/996-3426; fax 312/346-0974.
www.wyndhamchicago.com.* Escape the stresses of city
life without venturing too far from the hub of activity
at this hotel, just blocks from Chicago's Magnificent
Mile. Attractions, restaurants, and shops are an easy
walk or a quick cab ride away, including the Museum
of Contemporary Art (see) and the John Hancock
Building (see). Caliterra Bar & Grill (see) offers a
convenient dining option, serving Californian and
Italian cuisine, with live jazz in the evenings. The
comfortable guest rooms feature pillowtop mattresses,
Herman Miller work chairs, and Golden Door bath
products. 417 rooms, 17 story. Check-in 3 pm, check-
out noon. High-speed Internet access. Restaurant, bar.
Fitness room. Indoor pool, whirlpool. Business center.
$$

⊡ ⊡ ⊡ ⊡

Specialty Lodgings

The following lodging establishments are approved
by Mobil Travel Guide but, due to their unique and
individualized nature have not been given a traditional
Mobil Star rating. Included in this listing you may find
bed-and-breakfasts, limited-service inns, guest ranches,
and other unique hotel properties.

GOLD COAST GUEST HOUSE. *113 W Elm St,
Chicago (60610). Phone 312/337-0361; fax 312/
337-0362. www.bbchicago.com.* Tucked into the heart
of the lively Gold Coast neighborhood, this bed-and-
breakfast provides an unlikely oasis of calm for guests
staying in one of the four cozily furnished rooms, all
individually air-conditioned and with private baths.
This 1873 brick townhome features a 20-foot glass
window off the living room, overlooking a small two-
level garden out back. Guests can enjoy the view while
having breakfast. 4 rooms, 3 story. Children over 12
years only. Complimentary continental breakfast.
Check-in by arrangement, check-out 11 am. **$**

⊡

OLD TOWN BED & BREAKFAST. *1442 N North
Park Ave, Chicago (60610). Phone 312/440-9268. www.
oldtownchicago.com.* Guests staying in this modern,
four-suite bed-and-breakfast (an Art Deco mansion)
are afforded amenities such as a private bathroom,
walk-in closet with a wall safe, television, VCR, and
private-line telephone. Situated on a residential, tree-
lined street, accommodations are close to restaurants,

theaters, and an eclectic array of shops. 4 rooms, 4
story. Complimentary continental breakfast. Check-
out 11 am. Fitness room. **$$**

⊡ ⊡

THE WHEELER MANSION. *2020 S Calumet
Ave, Chicago (60616). Phone 312/945-2020; fax
312/945-2021. www.wheelermansion.com.* 11 rooms.
Complimentary full breakfast. Check-in 3 pm, check-
out noon. **$$$**

Spas

★ ★ ★ **THE SPA AT THE CARLTON CLUB,
THE RITZ-CARLTON CHICAGO.** *160 E Pearson
St, Chicago (60611). Phone 312/266-1000; toll-free
800/621-6906. www.fourseasons.com.* Escape from the
rat race at The Spa at The Carlton Club. The state-
of-the-art fitness center is a boon for those who want
to keep in shape while on the road. Treadmills, stair
climbers, elliptical trainers, and stationary bicycles
are equipped with televisions and VCRs to entertain
you while you work up a sweat. The center also offers
terrific group fitness classes, including Pilates, yoga,
cardio boxing, aerobics, water aerobics, and even
salsa dancing. After an intense workout, relax in the
whirlpool or unwind in the sauna or steam room. The
lap pool provides a refreshing fitness alternative, and
with dazzling views of the city and lake, the sundeck is
a perfect spot to unwind before or after you exercise.

At the spa, relish your quiet time away from the hustle
and bustle of the city. If you prefer to enjoy the spa
life in the privacy of your own room, many facials,
massages, and nail care services can be booked as
in-room treatments. Deep tissue, Swedish, healing
stone, and aromatherapy massages are wonderful ways
to reward yourself, and The Carlton Club signature
massage blends components of deep tissue and aro-
matherapy for total relaxation. The herbal body wrap
is a spa signature, while the seaweed mud body wrap
envelops you in seaweed, minerals, botanical extracts,
fruit enzymes, and customized aromatherapy oils to
soften and soothe your skin.

From The Carlton Club signature facial that includes
hand and foot reflexology massages as well as a hand
paraffin treatment to the deep-cleansing facial aux
champagne that concludes with a glass of Louis
Roederer champagne in the lounge, the spa's skin care
services are decadent. Even the manicures and pedi-
cures—with tea tree paraffin treatments that heal dry

skin, citrus C treatments that revitalize your hands and feet, and aromatherapy or reflexology therapies that calm sore muscles—pamper in style.

★ ★ ★ ★ THE SPA AT FOUR SEASONS HOTEL CHICAGO. *120 E Delaware Pl, Chicago (60611). Phone 312/280-8800; toll-free 800/819-5053. www.fourseasons.com/chicagofs.* The Four Seasons Hotel Chicago redefines luxury from its perch above the city's Magnificent Mile. Stressed-out urbanites can work off anxiety in the fitness center, where the elliptical trainers, stationary bicycles, and treadmills come complete with views of the Magnificent Mile. Individual fitness consultations are available, and for those who prefer to exercise outside, jogging routes are mapped out based on personal preferences. Swimming laps takes on a grander element at this Four Seasons, where the indoor pool is capped off by a glass-domed ceiling with Roman columns.

Once you are safely ensconced inside The Spa, the hectic pace and noise of city living become distant memories. Five soundproofed treatment rooms are available to coax the tension from your muscles and let your body unwind. Decadent and luxurious, this spa wants you to spoil yourself. Drink a toast to your skin with the champagne cocktail facial or savor the splendid benefits of the perle de caviar facial. Melt away with a Swedish, hot stone, sports conditioning, or scalp rejuvenator massage. The elixir paraffin wrap combines olive stones, lavender, juniper berries, and grapefruit to produce baby-soft skin. Your body will thank you after receiving a crushed pearls and lavender body polish, a citrus refresher body scrub, or a green tea and ginger mud body mask. Enjoy an aroma blend massage, which uses different scents and types of massage to celebrate the season of your choice, or take a journey through all four with the Four Seasons In One treatment. A variety of therapies, including manicures and pedicures, pamper and primp hands and feet.

Restaurants

★ ★ 312 CHICAGO. *136 N LaSalle St, Chicago (60602). Phone 312/696-2420; fax 312/236-0153.* Named for Chicago's urban area code, 312 Chicago is adjacent to the Hotel Allegro in the heart of the Loop's business, shopping, and theater district. The tempting menu marries fresh, contemporary Italian fare with more rustic options. The bilevel setting is clubby yet airy, with a bustling open kitchen and an aromatic rotisserie. The restaurant also serves upscale breakfast and lunch, and the chic bar is a great spot for cocktails. American menu. Breakfast, lunch, dinner. Closed Jan 1, Thanksgiving, Dec 25. Bar. Casual attire. **$$**

★ A LA TURKA. *3134 N Lincoln Ave, Chicago (60657). Phone 773/935-6101; fax 773/935-8894. www.turkishkitchen.us.* Belly dancing shows and sunken tables surrounded by pillow seats lend exotic allure to this North Side Turkish eatery. Sharable starters are ideally suited to grazing. For a complete culinary journey, progress from bread spreads and salads to grilled meats, concluding with muddy Turkish coffee. Make like the Turks who frequent A La Turka and bring the late-night gang to its weekend dances. Turkish menu. Dinner, late-night. Closed holidays. Bar. Casual attire. Outdoor seating. **$**

★ ABU NAWAS. *2411 N Clark St, Chicago (60614). Phone 773/529-1705.* For good, cheap, and plentiful portions of savory Middle Eastern fare, it's hard to beat Abu Nawas. This cheerful, smoke-free Lincoln Parker serves heaping plates of hummus and the eggplant spread baba ghanoush with pita bread, falafel with mango sauce, and grilled lamb kebab skewers. Wash it down with juice, tea, a yogurt drink, or Turkish coffee (alcohol is BYOB). Its prime location near Clark and Fullerton streets makes Abu Nawas a great lunchtime shopping stop. Middle Eastern menu. Lunch, dinner. Casual attire. **$**

★ ★ ADOBO GRILL. *1610 N Wells St, Chicago (60614). Phone 312/266-7999; fax 312/266-9299. www.adobogrill.com.* Fans of beyond-the-taco Mexican food will appreciate this upscale, up-tempo Old Towner known for its extensive tequila list, tableside guacamole preparation, and intriguing (and extensive) menu offerings—with some equally intriguing cocktails. The scene at night can be raucous; brunch-time is quieter. Mexican menu. Dinner, brunch. Closed holidays. Two vintage bars. Children's menu. Casual attire. Outdoor seating. **$$**

★ AMARIND'S. *6822 W North Ave, Chicago (60607). Phone 773/889-9999.* Amarind's creative and inexpensive fare may well warrant a drive out to the western edge of the city (Amarind's is closer to suburban River Forest than to downtown). The chef/owner hails from Arun's (see), the North Side gourmet eatery consistently ranked as one of the country's best Thai restaurants. His experience shows in offerings such as spicy curry pork, ginger scallop salad, and spinach noodles with shrimp and crab. With the exception of

a couple of "market price" items, nothing tops $11 here. Thai menu. Lunch, dinner. Closed Mon. Casual attire. Reservations recommended. **$**

★ ★ ★ ★ **AMBRIA.** *2300 N Lincoln Park W, Chicago (60614). Phone 773/472-5959. www.leye.com.* Ambria is located at the base of Lincoln Park (see) in The Belden-Stratford, a 1922 architectural landmark turned residential hotel on Chicago's romantic lakefront. With dark mahogany walls and luxuriously appointed tabletops set with tiny shaded votive lamps, this beautiful, graceful space is filled with radiant women and striking men, who glow in the room's creamy amber light. Ambria is a civilized spot, ideal for business or pleasure. The menu is as elegant as the room, with Mediterranean accents from Italy, Spain, and beyond (saffron, piquillo peppers, olives, and polenta) turning up the flavor on the kitchen's top-quality selection of fish, game, lamb, and beef. In addition to the enticing á la carte menu, the kitchen offers the Ambria Classic menu, a decadent five-course prix fixe option that should be ordered if a big enough appetite presents itself. The service is helpful, efficient, and warm, making dining here a delight on every level. *Secret Inspector's Notes: The staff at Ambria is enjoyably warm and enthusiastic, making each decision throughout your meal an exercise in pleasure. Nervous about wine? The wine steward makes every diner feel comfortable during that decision-making process.* French menu. Dinner. Closed Sun; holidays. Bar. Jacket required. Reservations recommended. Valet parking. **$$$$**

★ **ANN SATHER.** *929 W Belmont Ave, Chicago (60657). Phone 773/348-2378; fax 773/348-1731. www.annsather.com.* Open since 1945, this Swedish family of comfy, come-as-you-are restaurants may be best known for its sinful cinnamon rolls, but fans of all ages also appreciate the hearty Swedish and American classics (for example, Swedish pancakes with lingon-berries or roast turkey dinner), the no-nonsense service, and the reasonable prices. The breakfast menu is available all day. Four additional locations can be found on the city's North Side: 5207 N Clark, 1448 N Milwaukee, 3416 N Southport, and 3411 N Broadway. Swedish, American menu. Breakfast, lunch, dinner. Bar. **$$**

★ ★ **ARCO DE CUCHILLEROS.** *3445 N Halsted St, Chicago (60657). Phone 773/296-6046.* Located in a storefront in the bustling Lakeview neighborhood, this charming eatery features more than 40 different selections of soups, hot and cold tapas, and larger entrées, as well as what has been said to be the best sangria in the city. Enjoy the authentic Spanish cuisine at one of the cozy tables tucked away in the dining room or, in warmer months, dine on the outdoor backyard patio, aglow with torches and candles. Spanish, tapas menu. Dinner, Sun brunch. Closed Mon; holidays. Bar. Casual attire. Outdoor seating. **$**

◉ ★ ★ ★ **ARIA.** *200 N Columbus Dr, Chicago (60601). Phone 312/444-9494. www.ariachicago.com.* Globe-trotting food in a trendy setting make Aria one of the city's more fashionable eateries. Though lodged in the Fairmont Chicago (see), Aria distances itself from the bland stereotype of hotel restaurants by maintaining a street entrance to encourage local patrons to visit. Aria's Asian-inspired décor features Tibetan artwork, orchids, and plush upholstery, underscoring the menu's Eastern orientation. Chef James Wierzelewski formerly worked in Thailand and Malaysia, influences that show up in steamed black bass and crispy duck leg confit, although Indian, Italian, and French notes also flavor the fare. The bar serves a small-bites menu to the cocktail crowd. International/Fusion menu. Breakfast, lunch, dinner. **$$**

◉ ★ ★ ★ **ARUN'S.** *4156 N Kedzie Ave, Chicago (60618). Phone 773/539-1909; fax 773/539-2125. www.arunsthai.com.* Arun's version of Thai food is as similar to neighborhood take-out as caviar is to peanut butter. Regarded as the best Thai interpreter in the city, if not the country, Arun's takes a fine-dining turn with the complex cooking of Thailand, but without the attendant snobbery of many serious restaurants. A phalanx of eager, well-informed servers cheerfully work the alcove-lodged tables in the tranquil, Asian-art-filled rooms. Chef Arun Sampanthavivat prepares an original prix fixe menu nightly, proffering 12 courses, half of them small appetizers, served family style. You won't know what's on until you arrive, but the kitchen easily adapts to food and spice sensitivities. Thai menu. Dinner. Closed Mon; holidays. Bar. Reservations recommended. **$$$$**

★ ★ ★ **ATLANTIQUE.** *5101 N Clark St, Chicago (60640). Phone 773/275-9191; fax 773/275-9199.* An Andersonville neighborhood joint with cooking worthy of a downtown address, Atlantique specializes in seafood. From the huge marlin over the bar to the starfish-shaped sconces, the décor plays up the menu motif. Chef/owner Jack Jones borrows from the culinary cultures of Asia, Italy, and France in dishes like panko-dusted crab cakes, warm lobster salad with truffle oil, and seared tuna au poivre. Oysters often turn up among specials, and landlubbers get interesting choices, too, such as venison and duck confit. American, seafood menu. Dinner. Closed Mon. Bar. Casual attire. Reservations recommended. Outdoor seating. **$$$**

★ ★ ★ **ATWOOD CAFÉ.** *1 W Washington Blvd, Chicago (60602). Phone 312/368-1900; fax 312/357-2875. www.atwoodcafe.com.* The whimsical ground-floor occupant of the Burnham Hotel (see), Atwood draws a cross-section of travelers, desk jockeys, theatergoers, and shoppers in for chef Heather Terhune's café menu. Modern dishes like grilled calamari and tuna carpaccio balance comfort food classics like grilled pork chops with spaetzle. Soak up the Loop scene through floor-to-ceiling windows framing the downtown bustle at lunch and romantic, marquee-lit streetscapes at dinner. Cozy velvet banquettes and settees encourage lingering. American menu. Breakfast, lunch, dinner, brunch. Closed holidays. Bar. Children's menu. Casual attire. Outdoor seating. **$$**

★ ★ **AVEC.** *615 W Randolph St, Chicago (60661). Phone 312/377-2002.* Thinking man's Mediterranean comfort food is served in a chic sliver of space next to parent restaurant Blackbird (see). An ultra-hip power crowd mingles with restaurant industry insiders; the wood walls, floor, and long communal seating area blend together to create the illusion of an upscale mess hall-cum-sauna. The wine bar concept is fulfilled by a daring list of lesser-known and small-production bottles (40 by the mini carafe). Mediterranean menu. Dinner, late-night. Bar. Casual attire. Outdoor seating. **$$**

★ ★ ★ **AVENUES.** *108 E Superior, Chicago (60611). Phone 312/573-6754. www.chicago.peninsula.com.* Set in an elegant space on the fifth floor of the Peninsula hotel (see), Avenues offers creative contemporary fare with an emphasis on seafood, served by polished professionals in a refined ambience. The wine list is expertly chosen to harmonize with the food. Hushed tones and a discreet, old-world service attitude bespeak this modern restaurant's spot in the upper echelon of fine urban hotel dining. American, Asian menu. Breakfast, lunch, dinner. Bar. Casual attire. **$$$$**

★ ★ **AZURÉ.** *832 W Randolph St, Chicago (60607). Phone 312/455-1400.* Azuré brings California-Italian to Randolph Street's sophisticated restaurant row.

Foods native to California, including fish, shellfish, and plenty of fresh produce, get the Italian treatment here. Sample dishes include grilled calamari, the Italian seafood stew cioppino, and chicken Pisa, a dish piled playfully high to resemble the landmark Leaning Tower. Seating options cover two floors. For great views of the city skyline from this West Loop corner locale, opt for a table on the second floor. Italian menu. Dinner. Closed Sun. Bar. Casual attire. Reservations recommended. Outdoor seating. **$$**

★ ★ **BANDERA.** *535 N Michigan Ave, Chicago (60611). Phone 312/644-3524. www. banderarestaurants.com.* A shopper's delight one story above Michigan Avenue, Bandera boosts its Mag Mile views with a crowd-pleasing American menu. The emphasis is on Western (think baby-back ribs) and rotisserie fare (spit-roasted chicken), but the restaurant offers enough variety to please most tastes. Vintage photographs of Chicago localize this link in the Houston's restaurant chain. American menu. Lunch, dinner. Closed Sun; Thanksgiving, Dec 25. Bar. Children's menu. Casual attire. **$$**

★ **BASTA PASTA.** *6733 Olmstead St, Chicago (60631). Phone 773/763-0667; fax 773/763-1114. www. bastapastachicago.com.* Homemade Italian food like "mama" used to make is the order of the day at this restaurant, located in a former bank in the Edison Park neighborhood (the rest rooms are the former vaults). Favorites like spaghetti, linguini, and rigatoni are served in gargantuan portions that, when you're done eating, may feel as if they were the size of the giant bowl of pasta perched on the building outside. But despite its name, pasta isn't the only reason to visit—the menu also offers a good selection of home-style seafood and chicken dishes, pizzas, and salads. Italian menu. Lunch, dinner. Closed Mon. Bar. Children's menu. Casual attire. Outdoor seating. **$$**

★ **BELLA DOMANI.** *4603 N Lincoln Ave, Chicago (60625). Phone 773/561-9177.* Bella Domani specializes in traditional Italian meals in Lincoln Square, an area with a growing reputation for dining. The Lincoln Avenue storefront covers its bases with steak, fish, and pasta dishes, including classic Sicilian rice balls. Although the menu prices aren't cheap, most entrées come with soup, salad, and side that prove amply filling. Both area families and couples appreciate the restaurant's casual tone. Italian menu. Dinner. Closed Mon. Bar. Casual attire. **$$**

★ **THE BERGHOFF.** *17 W Adams St, Chicago (60603). Phone 312/427-3170; fax 312/427-6549. www.berghoff.com.* The Loop's beloved Berghoff, a landmark of 100-plus years, mingles tourists and locals alike. Out-of-towners line up for the German restaurant's lavishly trimmed dining room, where warm potato salad accompanies oversized weiner schnitzel and smoky sausages. Office workers pack the long, wood-paneled barroom slugging mugs of the house beer and munching carved roast beef sandwiches. The bar proudly displays the city's first post-Prohibition liquor license. German menu. Lunch, dinner. Closed Sun; holidays. Bar. Children's menu. Casual attire. **$$**

★ ★ **BICE.** *158 E Ontario St, Chicago (60611). Phone 312/664-1474; fax 312/664-9008. www. biceristorante.com.* A chain that grew out of Milan, Bice stays true to its northern Italian roots at its Chicago link. The Art Deco inspired design provides a glamorous backdrop in sync with the chic Streeterville neighborhood in which it resides. While the menu changes monthly, expect hits including veal Milanese and beef carpaccio. For a cheaper, more casual version of Bice food, try its sibling next door, Bice Café, a lunchtime favorite of Michigan Avenue shoppers. Italian menu. Lunch, dinner. Closed Jan 1, Dec 25. Bar. Children's menu. Casual attire. Valet parking. Outdoor seating. **$$**

★ ★ **BIN 36.** *339 N Dearborn St, Chicago (60610). Phone 312/755-9463; fax 312/755-9410. www. bin36.com.* This wine-centric River North restaurant and bar pairs 50 wines with moderately priced, creative American food. There's an environment for every occasion, from an after-work cocktail at the bar to a light bite in the lounge to a full meal in the dining room. A retail section sells wine and related goodies. American menu. Breakfast, lunch, dinner. Bar. Casual attire. **$$**

★ ★ ★ **BLACKBIRD.** *619 W Randolph St, Chicago (60606). Phone 312/715-0708; fax 312/715-0774. www.blackbirdrestaurant.com.* The minimalist chic Blackbird girds style with substance. Aluminum chairs and pale mohair banquettes seat guests at tables within easy eavesdropping distance of one another. But instead of the boring details of someone's career, what you're likely to hear are raves for chef Paul Kahan's French-influenced cooking. Like the décor, his style is spare, hitting just the right contemporary notes without drowning in too many flavors. The market-driven menu changes frequently, with seasonal favorites such as homemade charcuterie, quail with foie gras, and braised veal cheeks. Noise levels are high but the elegantly attired fans who flock here consider it simply good buzz. American menu. Lunch, dinner. Closed Sun; Jan 1, Thanksgiving, Dec 25. Bar. Casual attire. Valet parking. Outdoor seating. **$$$**

★ ★ **BLUE FIN.** *1952 W North Ave, Chicago (60622). Phone 773/394-7373.* A good choice for sushi in the Wicker Park/Bucktown area (see), Blue Fin manages to engender romance in a neighborhood that parties hardy. But its modern sensibility—lots of candlelight and low-key techno music—make it at home in the 'hood. In addition to a good range of raw-based sushi, sashimi, and maki rolls, Blue Fin entertains fans of cooked food with tempura and fish choices on the nicely priced menu. Expect crowds on weekends. Japanese, sushi menu. Dinner. Closed Sun. Casual attire. Outdoor seating. **$$**

★ ★ **BLUEPOINT OYSTER BAR.** *741 W Randolph St, Chicago (60661). Phone 312/207-1222. www.rdgchicago.com.* A clubby setting for seafood in the Randolph Market District, upscale Bluepoint is known for its extensive selection of fresh fish and shellfish. The wine list includes a generous array of wines by the glass and the half-bottle. Budget-minded diners might want to consider a lunchtime visit. Seafood menu. Lunch, dinner. Closed holidays. Bar. Children's menu. Casual attire. Outdoor seating. **$$**

★ ★ ★ **BOB SAN.** *1805-1807 W Division, Chicago (60622). Phone 773/235-8888. www. bob-san.com.* Sushi-savvy urban diners will appreciate this comfortably hip Wicker Park Japanese entry with a long list of fresh fish offerings that includes a multitude of maki—and entrées are no afterthought. A sequel to Sushi Naniwa, Bob San maintains the pace with a contemporary, loftlike space; centralized sushi bar; fashionable servers; and a generous sake selection (plus specialty martinis). Sushi chefs will go off the menu for you if they're not too busy. Japanese, sushi menu. Dinner. Bar. Casual attire. Outdoor seating. **$$$**

★ ★ **BONGO ROOM.** *1470 N Milwaukee Ave, Chicago (60622). Phone 773/489-0690.* Sleepyheads, mother-daughter duos, and Wicker Park (see) locals of all ages crowd into this funky favorite for bohemian breakfast, Bongo style. Known for long weekend waits, decadent pancakes, and other inventive, seasonal brunch-lunch fare, this is an eclectically decorated, come-as-you-are destination for daytime dining only (no dinner service). American menu. Breakfast, lunch. Bar. Casual attire. **$$**

★ ★ ★ **BRASSERIE JO.** *59 W Hubbard St, Chicago (60610). Phone 312/595-0800; fax 312/ 595-0808. www.leye.com.* In the brasserie tradition, Jean Joho's spacious, lively River North spot welcomes café society for a quick bite with a glass of moderately priced French wine or handcrafted beer, iced fruits de mer at the zinc bar, or a leisurely meal of robust, reasonably priced Alsatian-French fare. Menu classics include salad Niçoise, choucroute, coq au vin, and bouillabaisse. Light floods in from the street-level windows; vast murals, woven café chairs, and tile floors create a chic, vintage Parisian atmosphere. To finish your meal, request a visit from the "cheese chariot." French bistro menu. Lunch, dinner. Closed Thanksgiving, Dec 24-25. Bar. Valet parking. Outdoor seating. **$$**

★ ★ **BRETT'S.** *2011 W Roscoe St, Chicago (60618). Phone 773/248-0999.* Although Brett's is a popular spot for weekend brunch, the dim lighting, understated décor, and soft background music make it an ideal destination for a romantic dinner as well. But don't be afraid to bring the whole family—a children's menu offers the little ones a variety of pastas and sandwiches, and, although the dining experience is relatively upscale, the atmosphere remains casual. You can even bring along the family dog in good weather, when man's best friend is allowed at outdoor tables. American menu. Dinner, brunch. Closed Mon-Tues; holidays. Bar. Casual attire. Outdoor seating. **$$**

★ ★ **BRICKS.** *1909 N Lincoln Ave, Chicago (60614). Phone 312/255-0851.* If you're craving gourmet pizza (and maybe a nice cold beer to accompany it), head to this restaurant and pub, a favorite with locals. Build your own pizza from a list of toppings that includes Maytag blue, gouda, and goat cheeses; banana peppers; and BBQ sauce; or enjoy one of Bricks' own creations, like the Ditka, a pizza tribute to the former Chicago Bears coach. An impressive selection of craft brews and imports is on hand, as are a number of wines by the glass, half-bottle, and bottle. Pizza. Dinner. Closed holidays. Bar. **$$**

★ ★ **BUTTERFIELD 8.** *711 N Wells St, Chicago (60610). Phone 312/327-0940.* A see-and-be-seen River North hotspot, Butterfield 8 mingles the business of food with the pleasures of society. An underlit floor, high-backed booths, and bright colors set the stage for Butterfield's good-looking patrons. Despite its fashion-forwardness, the restaurant dares to revive culinary classics like steak tartare, oysters Rockefeller, shrimp de Jonghe, and veal schnitzel. Great people-watching and a long list of creative martinis serve to root you to your chair long after dessert. American menu. Dinner. Closed Sun. Bar. Casual attire. Reservations recommended. Outdoor seating. **$$**

★ ★ **CAFE ABSINTHE.** *1954 W North Ave, Chicago (60622). Phone 773/278-4488; fax 773/ 278-5291.* You'd never know what lies behind the walls of this Wicker Park restaurant from the looks of the unassuming façade (and the entrance off an alley behind the building): an intimate and elegant bistro with some of most innovative cuisine in the city. Take note, however, that it is definitely an "urban" experience—the restaurant can become crowded and, at times, very noisy. American menu. Dinner. Closed holidays. **$$$**

★ ★ **CAFE BA-BA-REEBA!** *2024 N Halsted St, Chicago (60614). Phone 773/935-5000; fax 773/ 935-0660. www.cafebabareeba.com.* The granddaddy of Chicago tapas spots, Cafe Ba-Ba-Reeba! was serving up those small plates long before "tapas" and "sangria" became household words. The colorful Mediterranean décor is the perfect complement to the lively Spanish cuisine. The authentic atmosphere is noisy and fun, and seating in the outdoor dining area is highly coveted in warm weather. You may find yourself waiting for a table, especially on weekends. Too hungry to wait? Take a seat at the front or back bar, where the full menu is available. Spanish, tapas menu. Lunch, dinner. Bar. Casual attire. Reservations recommended. Valet parking. Outdoor seating. **$$**

★ ★ **CAFÉ BERNARD.** *2100 N Halsted St, Chicago (60614). Phone 773/871-2100. www.cafebernard.com.* If you're looking for a no-frills country French meal, you'll find it here. This intimate little café is sometimes overlooked for its flashier competition, but Café Bernard has been serving moderately priced fare in a cozy setting for more than 30 years. The kitchen offers dishes such as mussels, escargots, and steak au poivre that are simply yet elegantly presented. The menu is somewhat limited, but daily specials on the blackboard keep regulars returning. The low-lit, homey dining room, decorated with French posters, etchings, and dried flowers, serves as the perfect backdrop to the restaurant's cuisine and is a great spot for an intimate dinner for two. French menu. Dinner. Closed Dec 25. Bar. Casual attire. Outdoor seating. **$$**

★ ★ **CAFE IBERICO.** *739 N LaSalle Dr, Chicago (60610). Phone 312/573-1510; fax 312/751-0098. www.cafe-iberico.com.* Elbow your way into this River North tapas hotspot for small plates of hot and cold Spanish fare, refreshing sangria, and casual camaraderie. The food is great for sharing—whether in a group or on a date—and the atmosphere, while boisterous during prime time, creates a festive mood. Spanish, tapas menu. Lunch, dinner. Closed July 4, Thanksgiving, Dec 24-25. Bar. Casual attire. Outdoor seating. **$$**

★ ★ ★ **CALITERRA.** *633 N St. Clair St, Chicago (60611). Phone 312/274-4444; fax 312/274-0164. www.wyndham.com.* Aptly named considering its Cal-Ital culinary concept (Tuscany meets northern California), this handsome—and somewhat hidden—oasis in the Wyndham Chicago hotel (see) draws a well-heeled Gold Coast business and shopping crowd. Innovative seasonal fare emphasizes organic produce and non-hormone-treated meats; additional monthly specialty menus showcase a particular ingredient in various preparations. The dining room is dressed in wood and textiles, with a display kitchen and a glass mural of a grape arbor as focal points. The gracious cocktail lounge, noteworthy cheese cart, and Italian-American wine list are additional highlights. California, Italian menu. Dinner. Children's menu. **$$$**

★ ★ **CALLIOPE CAFE.** *2826 N Lincoln Ave, Chicago (60657). Phone 773/528-8055.* Lakeview's Calliope Cafe, popular with the neighborhood lunch crowd, distinguishes itself from the average deli with upscale sandwiches, splashes of colorful paint, and funky mismatched tables and chairs. Popular options include the salmon club, steak and avocado wrap, and pesto chicken sandwich, plus addictive homemade potato chips. You're unlikely to walk by this stretch of Lincoln Avenue, but the café offers an adjacent parking lot to encourage mealtime commuters. Deli menu. Lunch, dinner. Children's menu. Casual attire. Outdoor seating. **$**

★ ★ **CANTARE.** *200 E Chestnut, Chicago (60611). Phone 312/266-4500.* This upscale, sedate spot offers traditional Italian fare in a stylized Italianate setting. A few secluded booths line one wall, providing a romantic dining experience for a lucky few. This is white-tablecloth, Gold Coast dining—nothing too inventive, simply a hearty selection of steaks, veal, seafood, and pasta dishes, plus an enticing dessert cart. The bar is a nice place to take a shopping break or wait for your date. Italian menu. Dinner. Bar. Casual attire. **$$**

★ **CAPE COD ROOM.** *140 E Walton Pl, Chicago (60611). Phone 312/440-8486; toll-free 800/553-7253; fax 312/787-0256. www.thedrakehotel.com.* Escape to a New England fishing town without leaving the city at this nautically themed seafood restaurant in the Drake Hotel (see). Decorated with dark wood walls, low-beamed ceilings, and red-and-white-checked tablecloths, the Cape Cod Room offers a comfortable place to dine, along with an extensive selection of seafood. From Dover sole and tuna to oysters and clams, seafood lovers will find everything their hearts desire here. Seafood menu. Lunch, dinner. Closed Dec 25. Bar. Casual attire. Valet parking. Outdoor seating. **$$$**

★ ★ ★ **THE CAPITAL GRILLE.** *633 N St. Clair St, Chicago (60611). Phone 312/337-9400; fax 312/337-1259. www.thecapitalgrille.com.* This Washington, DC-based chain deliberately cultivates the old boys' network vibe. The clubby, masculine décor features dark woods and original oil paintings of fox hunts, cattle drives, and the like. But even if cigars and cell phones aren't your thing, you'll find it hard to resist the top-notch steakhouse fare served up here. Sizable à la carte entrées like porterhouse steak, filet mignon, and broiled fresh lobster, along with traditional sides that serve three, tempt the taste buds and ensure that you'll leave feeling quite full. Beef is dry-aged on the premises for 14 days and hand-cut daily. The restaurant sits just off the Magnificent Mile in the same building that houses the Wyndham Chicago hotel (see). Steak menu. Lunch, dinner. Closed July 4, Thanksgiving, Dec 25. Bar. Valet parking. **$$$**

★ ★ **CARMINE'S.** *1043 N Rush St, Chicago (60611). Phone 312/988-7676; fax 312/988-7957. www.rosebudrestaurants.com.* This Italian steak and seafood house, located in the ritzy Gold Coast area, has been a Chicago favorite since opening in 1995. Generously sized chops and steaks and hearty portions of seafood and pasta are served in the dim—and usually packed—dining room, where politicians, sports personalities, and celebrities have been known to turn up. Italian menu. Lunch, dinner, brunch. **$$**

★ ★ **CERISE.** *520 N Michigan Ave, Chicago (60611). Phone 312/327-0564.* The fine-dining room of the French-owned Le Meridien Chicago (see), Cerise hews to the hotel's nationality with a French menu. There are plenty of haut classics like foie gras and duck consommé, but the greatest applause here comes for the fish dishes and French comfort foods like chicken "gran mere." Finish with the chocolate and cherry crepes before heading next door to the convivial Le Rendezvous lounge for a digestif. French menu. Breakfast, lunch, dinner. Bar. Children's menu. Casual attire. Outdoor seating. **$$**

★ ★ ★ ★ ★ **CHARLIE TROTTER'S.** *816 W Armitage Ave, Chicago (60614). Phone 773/248-6228; fax 773/248-6088. www.charlietrotters.com.* Charlie Trotter's is a place for people who equate food with the highest form of art. It is also a restaurant for those who value a chef's masterful ability to transform sustenance into culinary wonder. But even those who doubt these two tenets will leave Charlie Trotter's understanding that food is not just for eating. It is for savoring, honoring, marveling at, and, most of all, thoroughly enjoying. Set inside a two-story brick brownstone, Charlie Trotter's is an intimate, peaceful temple of cuisine of the most refined and innovative variety. Trotter is the Nobel laureate of the kitchen—a mad maestro of gastronomy, if you will—and you must experience his talent for yourself to understand the hype. Charlie Trotter's offers several magnificent menus, including The Grand Tasting, The Vegetable Menu, and The Kitchen Table Degustation. Each combines pristine seasonal products (Trotter has a network of more than 90 purveyors, many of them local small farms) with impeccable French techniques and slight Asian influences. Trotter prefers saucing with vegetable juice-based vinaigrettes, light emulsified stocks, and purees, as well as delicate broths and herb-infused meat and fish essences. The result is that flavors are remarkably intense, yet dishes stay light. Dining at Charlie Trotter's is an astonishing and extraordinary dining journey. *Secret Inspector's Notes: Don't worry if one of the menus doesn't appeal to your tastes; the staff will gladly take your preferences into consideration and customize your meal for you. The service couldn't be more gracious, warm, and inviting. Surprisingly, there is very little pretension here.*

American menu with French and Asian influences. Dinner. Closed Sun-Mon; holidays. Jacket required. Reservations recommended. Valet parking. **$$$$**

★ ★ ★ **CHEZ JOEL.** *1119 W Taylor St, Chicago (60607). Phone 312/226-6479; fax 312/226-6589.* Just a few minutes from the Loop, tiny Chez Joel dares to be French within the friendly confines of Little Italy. Classic bistro fare (paté, escargots, coquilles St. Jacques, coq au vin, steak frites) is seasoned with more adventurous specials and an appealing sandwich selection at lunch. The cozy room invites with a buttery glow, courtesy of soft yellow walls accented with French prints and posters; in warm weather, the outdoor garden is a charming oasis. The wine list is moderately priced, and a limited reserve list is offered. Make reservations; the secret is out. French bistro menu. Lunch, dinner. Bar. Casual attire. Outdoor seating. **$$$**

★ ★ **CHICAGO CHOP HOUSE.** *60 W Ontario St, Chicago (60610). Phone 312/787-7100; toll-free 800/229-2356; fax 312/787-3219. www. chicagochophouse.com.* Choosing a steakhouse among the many in Chicago is no easy task, but independently owned Chicago Chop House stands out for its affinity for the metropolis. Papered in 1,400 photos of the city, its meat packers, and mayors, most taken before 1930, the Chop House provides a history lesson as a side dish to meals centered on steaks and chops. Steak menu. Lunch, dinner. Closed holidays. Bar. Casual attire. Valet parking. Outdoor seating. **$$$**

★ **CHICAGO DINER.** *3411 N Halsted St, Chicago (60657). Phone 773/935-6696. www. veggiediner.com.* If you think that vegetarian cuisine is nothing but lettuce leaves and sprouts, think again. Since 1983, this Lakeview diner has been serving hearty meatless fare that has won over the taste buds of vegetarians and meat lovers alike. Craving a hot dog? Try the "No Dog." How about Mexican food? They offer a "No Meata Fajita." Using products like seitan (wheat gluten), tofu (soybean curd), and tempeh (fermented soybean cake) along with grains, beans, and fresh vegetables, the Chicago Diner creates healthy alternatives to traditional meat dishes. A second location has opened in Highland Park at 581 Elm Place. Vegetarian menu. Lunch, dinner. Closed Jan 1, Dec 25. Bar. Casual attire. **$**

★ ★ ★ **CHILPANCINGO.** *358 W Ontario St, Chicago (60610). Phone 312/266-9525; fax 312/ 266-6428.* Chef Geno Bahena cooked at Frontera Grill before breaking out on his own with Ixcapuzalco (see) in Logan Square and the follow-up Chilpancingo downtown. Festooned in colorful folk art and murals, Chilpancingo creates a lively setting where authentic Mexican market fare, including quail and rabbit, merge with more familiar standards, such as enchiladas and ceviche, on the menu. Mexican menu. Lunch, dinner. Closed Jan 1, Dec 25. Bar. Casual attire. **$$**

★ ★ **CLUB LUCKY.** *1824 W Wabansia Ave, Chicago (60622). Phone 773/227-2300; fax 773/227-2236. www. clubluckychicago.com.* In the 1920s, it was a hardware store. In the 1930s, it was a banquet hall. Throughout the 1980s, it was a bar. Today, the building tucked away on the corner of Honore and Wabansia—smack-dab in the middle of one of the city's hottest neighborhoods, Wicker Park/Bucktown (see)—is Club Lucky, a 1940s-style restaurant and lounge. It's a place to bring a group of friends and enjoy heaping portions of traditional Italian favorites, as well as a martini or two. Italian menu. Dinner. Closed holidays. Children's menu. **$$**

★ ★ ★ **COCO PAZZO.** *300 W Hubbard St, Chicago (60610). Phone 312/836-0900; fax 312/ 836-0257.* A renovated loft with velvet swagged curtains and rustic wood floors sets an aptly dramatic stage for the robust Italian cooking on offer at Coco Pazzo. Chef Tony Priolo mans the stoves, turning out recipes that range from the sophisticated but uncomplicated beef carpaccio with black truffle oil to the crowd-pleasing rigatoni with sausage and cream. Pastas come in appetizer portions, allowing you to save room for the traditional Italian "second plate" of Florentine steak or wood-fired salmon. A longtime River North resident, Coco Pazzo draws dealmakers among the ad and art world types working nearby. Italian menu. Lunch, dinner. Closed Thanksgiving, Dec 25. Bar. Casual attire. Valet parking. Outdoor seating. **$$**

★ **COMO.** *695 N Milwaukee Ave, Chicago (60622). Phone 312/733-7400.* Longtime Chicago restaurateurs the Marchetti brothers cashed in on the beloved and enormous Como Inn in River West to make room for residential development. They resurfaced with the downscaled Como nearby, trading in their Italian murals and rambling rooms for a contemporary space with soaring headroom. The menu sticks to Italian classics in chicken Vesuvio and pasta Bolognese, the very thing that keeps old Como Inn fans coming around to Como. Italian menu. Dinner. Closed Mon. Bar. Casual attire. Outdoor seating. **$$**

★ ★ ★ **COOBAH.** *3423 N Southport Ave, Chicago (60657). Phone 773/528-2220.* Latin eats and lots of drinks make hip Coobah a restaurant that crosses over into a late-night hangout. The kitchen puts in long hours, beginning with a creative weekend brunch that includes a Spanish-style granola and chorizo gravy with biscuits, plus sandwiches such as the Cuban reuben. Dinner is the main event; you can get it until 1 am nightly, 2 am on Saturday. Tamales, lamb adobo, and fish with Spanish olives testify to the range of dishes offered here. Freely flowing mojitos, sangria, and "Coobah libres" encourage diners to stick around this swinging Southport stop. Latin American menu. Breakfast, lunch, dinner, late-night. Bar. Casual attire. Outdoor seating. **$$**

★ ★ ★ ★ **CROFTON ON WELLS.** *535 N Wells St, Chicago (60610). Phone 312/755-1790; fax 312/755-1890. www.croftononwells.com.* Suzy Crofton's acclaimed American cuisine is served in simply stylish, neutral-chic surroundings in this River North storefront. Expect a gracious, grown-up dining experience; the quiet, understated room and absence of "scene" diminish distractions from what's on your plate. Seasonal ingredients star on classically trained Crofton's limited menu of sophisticated regional cuisine, which features bold and earthy undertones. The carefully selected, reasonably priced wine list offers perfect pairings for the menu's attractions. American menu. Dinner. Closed Sun; holidays. Bar. Valet parking. **$$$**

★ ★ **CYRANO'S BISTROT AND WINE BAR.** *546 N Wells St, Chicago (60610). Phone 312/467-0546; fax 312/467-1850. www.cyranosbistrot.com.* Cozy and unpretentious, Cyrano's is a country French getaway in Chicago's frenzied River North area. The rustic, un-Americanized menu encompasses bistro classics (including game and offal dishes), with a specialty in rotisserie meats. The décor is all sunny yellow walls, gilded mirrors, and provincial French accoutrements. The regional French wine list and bargain four-course lunch are added attractions, and an outdoor café makes diners part of the neighborhood scene in warm weather. Live cabaret and jazz entertainment is featured Fridays and Saturdays. French menu. Lunch, dinner. Closed Sun-Mon; July 4, Thanksgiving. Bar. Casual attire. Outdoor seating. **$$**

★ ★ ★ ★ **THE DINING ROOM.** *160 E Pearson St, Chicago (60611). Phone 312/266-1000; fax 312/266-1194. www.fourseasons.com.* Innovative contemporary French cuisine is served in quiet luxury at The Dining Room, the opulent restaurant of The Ritz-Carlton (see). The décor of this striking, clubby room is rich and luxurious, from the fabrics to the breathtaking fresh flowers updated weekly. In addition to the superb à la carte choices—a signature dish is a succulent Maine lobster served with wild mushrooms over a crisp golden lobster cake—the chef offers an adventurous, personalized eight-course tasting menu, a five-course degustation menu, and a five-course vegetarian menu. To complement the fantastic fare, the award-winning wine list emphasizes boutique wines from Bordeaux, Burgundy, and California. The service at The Dining Room is in keeping with the décor. Waiters are tuxedoed and formal, and each presentation detail matches the classic atmosphere that The Dining Room strives to represent. *Secret Inspector's Notes: The Dining Room is an excuse for decadence. For a true culinary splurge, enjoy the Sunday brunch, a spread like no other. At dinner, the twice-baked potato with truffles is a starch lover's fantasy, and desserts created by award-winning pastry chefs surprise the sweet tooth in everyone.* French menu. Dinner, Sun brunch. Closed Mon. Children's menu. Reservations recommended. Valet parking. **$$$**

★ ★ **DINOTTO RISTORANTE.** *215 W North Ave, Chicago (60610). Phone 312/202-0302.* With caring service, a warm atmosphere, and substantial, rustic Italian fare, Dinotto endears itself to Old Town residents and tourists passing through. Chili-spiced grilled calamari and goat cheese ravioli rank among the standouts on the menu, which offers plenty of chicken and veal options to succeed its pastas. In addition to the bustling dining room, in season, seating spills onto a charming brick-walled outdoor patio. Italian menu. Lunch, dinner. Bar. Casual attire. Outdoor seating. **$$**

★ **ED DEBEVIC'S.** *640 N Wells St, Chicago (60610). Phone 312/664-1707; fax 312/664-7444. www.eddebevics.com.* Treat your tweens and teens to Ed Debevic's, a retro 1950s diner where sassy,

gum-snapping servers in period uniforms delight in giving diners a hard time. It's all in good fun, as is the lighthearted menu of burgers, hot dogs, and shakes, plus hearty Middle American staples like meat loaf and pot roast. American menu. Lunch, dinner. Closed Thanksgiving, Dec 24-25. Bar. Children's menu. Casual attire. Valet parking. **$**

★ ★ **ELI'S THE PLACE FOR STEAK.** *215 E Chicago Ave, Chicago (60611). Phone 312/642-1393; fax 312/642-4089. www.eliplaceforsteak.com.* When Chicagoans hear the name Eli's, one thing comes to mind: cheesecake. But Eli's The Place for Steak was around long before the now-famous dessert was; the late Eli Schulman opened his restaurant in 1966, and his cheesecake made its debut in 1980. Over the years, the restaurant has attracted many famous faces, from Frank Sinatra and Sean Connery to Chicago politicians and sports figures, and has also expanded its menu. No longer just "the place for steak," it's also the place for chops, seafood, and "Liver Eli." Steak menu. Lunch, dinner. Closed holidays. Bar. Children's menu. Casual attire. Valet parking. **$$**

★ ★ ★ **ERAWAN.** *729 N Clark St, Chicago (60611). Phone 312/642-6888.* Far above the run-of-the-mill corner Thai spot, this fine-dining upstart follows the example of the famed Arun's (see) in upping the Thai ante with its menu, presentations, and prices. Contemporary, sometimes Westernized versions of classic dishes are elaborately plated with carved vegetables and other decorative flourishes; there's even a seasonal degustation menu. The stylish setting, luxury table appointments, and soft-spoken service remind you that you're on a different sort of Thai dining adventure. The well-chosen wine list complements the food nicely. Thai menu. Lunch, dinner. Bar. Casual attire. Reservations recommended. **$$$$**

★ ★ **ERWIN.** *2925 N Halsted St, Chicago (60657). Phone 773/528-7200; fax 773/528-1931. www.erwincafe.com.* Low on contrivance, high on flavor, chef/owner Erwin Dreschler's "urban heartland" cuisine is right at home in his comfy and convivial North Side restaurant. This is the thinking man's American comfort food, served amid a nature-inspired scheme of warm woods, forest green walls, and white tablecloths. The well-chosen wines, including extensive by-the-glass options, are central to the concept of the ever-changing seasonal menu (Dreschler is a champion of local foodstuffs and leads tours of area farmers' markets). With choices like banana-cinnamon French toast, eggs Benedict, and rainbow trout, Erwin is also a popular brunch destination. American menu. Dinner, Sun brunch. Closed Mon; holidays. Bar. Valet parking. **$$**

★ ★ ★ ★ **EVEREST.** *440 S LaSalle St, Chicago (60605). Phone 312/663-8920; fax 312/663-8802. www. leye.com.* Perched high atop the city on the 40th floor of the Chicago Stock Exchange building, chef/owner Jean Joho's restaurant, Everest, affords spectacular views and equally fabulous contemporary French cuisine. Joho blends European influences with local, seasonal American ingredients; he is not afraid to pair noble ingredients like caviar and foie gras with humbler fruits of American soil such as potatoes and turnips. The à la carte menu offers several signature dishes, including the Fantasy of Chocolate—five different riffs on the decadent cocoa theme artfully piled onto one glorious plate. Everest's dining room is luxuriously decorated with polished gold railings, vaulted draped ceilings, mirrored walls, and, of course, floor-to-ceiling windows for fabulous unobstructed views. *Secret Inspector's Notes: The view at Everest draws mostly heavy hitters looking to impress clients or other important business contacts. Although everything about the restaurant is ideal for an important business meal, it may not be an appropriate destination for a romantic evening or a special occasion. With the high floor and high guest expectations, the prices may cause altitude sickness upon presentation of the check.* French menu. Dinner. Closed Sun-Mon; Jan 1, Dec 25. Bar. Reservations recommended. Valet parking. **$$$$**

★ ★ **FINESTRA DI CALO.** *5341 N Clark St, Chicago (60640). Phone 773/334-4525.* An upscale spin-off of the long-standing Italian restaurant Calo next door, Finestra takes aim at Andersonville's more youthful residents with contemporary décor, including floor-to-ceiling front windows that open completely onto Clark Street in summer. Although Finestra has experimented with modernized Italian food, it relies on Calo staples, including pizzas, ribs, and red-sauced pastas. Italian menu. Dinner. Closed Mon. Bar. Casual attire. **$$**

★ ★ **FLO.** *1434 W Chicago Ave, Chicago (60622). Phone 312/243-0477.* A storefront hidden away on a strip of Chicago Avenue teeming with secondhand shops and dollar stores, Flo is a diamond in the rough. A friendly staff serves fresh and flavorful dishes from the mostly Southwestern-inspired menu in two bright and cozy dining rooms, which are decorated with vibrant pieces of art. Weekend brunch packs in crowds who wait in line for hearty egg dishes like huevos rancheros and chilaquiles, as well as for the blueberry and strawberry pancakes with homemade syrup. Southern Mexican menu. Breakfast, lunch, dinner, Sat-Sun brunch. Closed Mon. Casual attire. Reservations recommended. **$$**

★ ★ **FOGO DE CHÃO.** *661 N LaSalle St, Chicago (60610). Phone 312/932-9330. www.fogodechao.com.* If you're in a carnivorous mood, this upscale, aromatic Brazilian churrascaria is the place to indulge. Fifteen all-you-can-eat grilled and roasted meats waft through the room on spits, borne by efficient "gauchos" who descend upon you at your whim. The massive salad bar and side dishes represent the other food groups—but at this price, save room for plenty of meat. Brazilian, steak menu. Lunch, dinner. Bar. Casual attire. **$$$**

★ ★ ★ **FRONTERA GRILL.** *445 N Clark St, Chicago (60610). Phone 312/661-1434; fax 312/661-1830. www.fronterakitchens.com.* Born of chef/owner Rick Bayless's genius for, and scholarly pursuit of, regional Mexican cuisine, this River North superstar's brand has become a name to reckon with. The casual, more accessible of Bayless's side-by-side duo (see also TOPOLOBAMPO), Frontera introduces a wealth of deceptively simple Mexican dishes—and a world of flavors—that you won't find at your neighborhood taco stand. An exhaustive tequila list for sipping or for shaken-to-order margaritas and a fine wine list stand up to the food. A seat here is a coveted one, as reservations are for parties of five to ten only. Mexican menu. Lunch, dinner, Sat brunch. Closed Sun-Mon; holidays. Bar. Children's menu. Casual attire. Valet parking. Outdoor seating. **$$$**

★ ★ **GEJA'S CAFE.** *340 W Armitage Ave, Chicago (60614). Phone 773/281-9101; fax 773/281-0849. www. gejascafe.com.* The fondue craze never ended at this venerable Lincoln Park classic, always at or near the top of all those "most romantic" lists. It's dark and cozy inside, and, after all, there is something flirtatious about swirling your food around in a pot and occasionally crossing forks with your tablemate(s) to the stylings of live flamenco guitar music. A variety of wines are sold by the glass. Fondue menu. Dinner. Closed holidays. Bar. Casual attire. **$$$**

★ ★ **GENE & GEORGETTI.** *500 N Franklin St, Chicago (60610). Phone 312/527-3718; fax 312/527-2039. www.geneandgeorgetti.com.* A veteran steakhouse with a masculine, insider's ambience and a past (it opened in 1941, long before River North was a hip 'hood), Gene & Georgetti is an old-school Chicago carnivore's haunt. Prime steaks, gigantic "garbage salad," and gruff service are among the draws. Italian, American menu. Lunch, dinner. Closed Sun; holidays; also the first week in July. Bar. Casual attire. Valet parking. **$$$**

★ ★ ★ **GIBSON'S STEAKHOUSE.** *1028 N Rush St, Chicago (60611). Phone 312/266-8999; fax 312/787-5649. www.gibsonssteakhouse.com.* The theme at Gibson's is outsized, from the massive steaks on the plate to the stogie-puffing personalities—a blend of politicians, sports figures, celebrities, and conventioneers—who energize the room. Carnivores crave the generous porterhouses here, but the kitchen also manages to issue some of the sea's biggest lobster tails and desserts that easily feed a four-top. Do call for a reservation, but don't be surprised if you still have to wait. In that case, squeeze into the smoky, convivial bar, order a martini, and prepare to make new friends. Steak, seafood menu. Lunch, dinner. Closed Easter, Thanksgiving, Dec 24-25. Bar. Casual attire. Valet parking. Outdoor seating. **$$$**

★ ★ **GIOCO.** *1312 S Wabash Ave, Chicago (60605). Phone 312/939-3870; fax 312/939-3858. www.gioco-chicago.com.* A riot of earthy flavors is in store at this chic former speakeasy in the South Loop. The simply sophisticated Italian food is offered up in a comfortable setting that's simultaneously rustic and clubby—and the seasonal outdoor patio is a rare treat in this up-and-coming neighborhood. Italian menu. Lunch, dinner. Closed holidays. Bar. Casual attire. **$$$**

★ ★ **GLORY.** *1952 N Damen Ave, Chicago (60647). Phone 773/235-7400.* Occupying a classically sunken Bucktown bungalow, Glory looks very Chicago, but its menu has a strong New England accent. Glory dares to go East Coastal with seafood, carving a unique niche for itself on the competitive culinary scene. Start with Ipswich clams and Johnny cakes, but save room for the lobster pot pie and substantial clam bake, which includes shrimp, lobster, and sausage as well as clams. Casual digs and affordable pricing make this neighborhood gem worthy of repeat visits. American, seafood menu. Breakfast, lunch, dinner. Bar. Children's menu. Casual attire. Outdoor seating. **$$**

★ ★ **HARRY CARAY'S.** *33 W Kinzie St, Chicago (60610). Phone 312/828-0966; fax 312/828-0962. www.hcrestaurantgroup.com.* Although the legendary Cubs announcer died in 1998, his boisterous spirit thrives at this restaurant in River North, a vintage brick building emblazoned with Caray's signature expression, "Holy cow!" Inside, choose from the casual saloon with numerous sports-tuned TVs or the white-tablecloth dining room specializing in Harry's favorite food, Italian. Wherever you sit, you'll find a casual vibe and walls plastered with baseball memorabilia. Steak menu. Lunch, dinner. Closed Jan 1, Thanksgiving, Dec 25. Bar. Children's menu. Casual attire. Valet parking. **$$**

★ ★ **HATSUHANA.** *160 E Ontario St, Chicago (60611). Phone 312/280-8808; fax 312/280-4545. www.hatsuhana.com.* Located just off the busy Magnificent Mile (see), Hatsuhana attracts not only a number of tourists and travelers, but also locals who are hardcore sushi lovers. Serving fresh, high-quality sushi and sashimi is priority #1 at this elegant restaurant, where tuna, salmon, crab, octopus, clam, and other delicacies are offered both for lunch and dinner along with other items such as miso soup, tempura, and edamame. Sushi menu. Lunch, dinner. Closed Sun; holidays. Casual attire. Outdoor seating. **$$**
🄳

★ ★ ★ **HEAT.** *1507 N Sedgwick, Chicago (60610). Phone 312/397-9818; toll-free 866/230-6387. www.heatsushi.com.* Top-tier, ultra-fresh sushi—some of which is still swimming in tanks under the bar—is the draw at this upscale spot in an up-and-coming stretch of Old Town. The menu changes daily, with occasional esoteric offerings that have earned Heat a loyal following of sushi purists. The multicourse, prix fixe omakase and kaiseki menus are beautifully presented culinary adventures. The minimal modern décor, gracious service, and fine selections of sake and wine complete the elevated experience. Japanese, sushi menu. Lunch, dinner. Closed Sun. Bar. Casual attire. **$$$$**

★ ★ **HEAVEN ON SEVEN ON RUSH.** *600 N Michigan Ave, Chicago (60611). Enter at the corner of Rush and Ohio sts. Phone 312/280-7774. www.heavenonseven.com.* Chef Jimmy Bannos is Chicago's answer to New Orleans, cooking up Cajun and Creole dishes in this just-off-Michigan Avenue outpost. Cop a spot under the shelved hot sauce collection known as the Wall of Fire and order up red beans and rice, gumbo, and po' boy sandwiches. In addition to such standards, the dinner menu elaborates on the theme with gussied-up entrées like grilled salmon on andouille sausage and a multicourse tasting menu. Cajun/Creole menu. Lunch, dinner. Bar. Casual attire. **$$**

★ **HEMA'S KITCHEN.** *6406 N Oakley Ave, Chicago (60645). Phone 773/338-1627.* A small, intimate room with about ten tables is what makes up Hema's Kitchen. Chef Hema Potla runs this no-frills restaurant off the main Devon Avenue drag, where diners can choose from plenty of delicious and inexpensive traditional Indian dishes. You'll probably see Hema herself circling the room as she makes menu suggestions to her customers. But be forwarned— because of the restaurant's small size and its growing popularity, you may have to wait a while for a table. Indian menu. Lunch, dinner. Casual attire. **$**

★ ★ **INDIAN GARDEN.** *2546 W Devon Ave, Chicago (60659). Phone 773/338-2929; fax 773/338-3930.* A trip to the strip of Devon Street's Little India is worth the ride for lovers of Indian food. This classic is more upscale than some, with a bright interior and the requisite aromatic ambience. The generous buffet is a great deal, and there are plenty of vegetarian offerings. Indian menu. Lunch, dinner. Bar. Casual attire. Reservations recommended. **$$**

★ ★ **IXCAPUZALCO.** *2919 N Milwaukee Ave, Chicago (60618). Phone 773/486-7340; fax 773/486-7348.* Authentic, regional Mexican fare is the draw at this unpretentious neighborhood storefront. While a few dishes are recognizable renditions, Ixcapuzalco presents an opportunity to savor more intriguing, less familiar preparations for lunch, dinner, or Sunday brunch. There's also a traditional mole of the day, paired with a variety of meats. Dozens of premium tequilas may be sipped or shaken into margaritas. Candlelight and white tablecloths, rustic hand-carved wood chairs, and brilliant-hued artwork warm the small, smoke-free main dining room (which can be noisy due to the presence of the small, open kitchen; the back room is quieter). Mexican menu. Lunch, dinner, Sun brunch. Closed Tues. Bar. Casual attire. **$$$**

★ ★ **JANE'S.** *1655 W Cortland St, Chicago (60622). Phone 773/862-5263. www.janesresaurant.com.* Befitting the Bucktown location, this eclectic American girl is something of a funky flower child. The quaint setting and creative menu offerings (including some vegetarian choices) make it a favorite of neighborhood denizens and dating couples. American menu. Dinner, brunch. Closed holidays. Bar. Casual attire. Outdoor seating. **$$**

★ ★ ★ **JAPONAIS.** *600 W Chicago Ave, Chicago (60610). Phone 312/822-9600. www.japonaischicago .com.* This spacious River North restaurant is a sensuous, hip setting for contemporary Japanese fare that includes, but goes far beyond, traditional sushi. The creative menu inspires sharing and ordering in phases while enjoying the exotic cocktails or selections from the extensive sake and wine lists. Four dazzling environments set different moods; in warm weather, the subterranean riverfront terrace is an exotic escape. Japanese, sushi menu. Lunch, dinner. Bar. Casual attire. Reservations recommended. Outdoor seating. **$$$**

★ ★ **JIN JU.** *5203 N Clark St, Chicago (60640). Phone 773/334-6377.* Korean food gets the hipster treatment at Jin Ju. What emerges is a polished neighborhood ethnic with enough flair to entice newcomers to the exotic fare. By juicing the scene with techno beats and sleek décor, the Andersonville restaurant boosts the atmosphere missing at most Korean barbecue eateries. Despite the Western trappings, the food remains fairly traditional, including bi bim bop, kimchee soup, and barbecued short ribs. Don't miss the martinis made with the Korean liquor soju. Korean menu. Dinner. Closed Mon. Bar. Casual attire. **$$**

★ **JOE'S BE-BOP CAFE.** *700 E Grand Ave, Chicago (60611). Phone 312/595-5299; fax 312/832-6986. www.joesbebop.com.* On tourist-centric Navy Pier, Joe's unites two Chicago favorites, ribs and jazz. Cajun jambalaya and lighter salads supplement the tangy, slow-cooked ribs on the menu. Entertainment runs the jazz gamut from swing to Latin, with acts performing atop a raised stage that ensures good sightlines from around the expansive restaurant. Sunday brunch serves up a Bloody Mary bar and a big band. Barbecue menu. Lunch, dinner, Sun brunch. Closed Thanksgiving, Dec 25. Bar. Children's menu. Casual attire. Valet parking. Outdoor seating. **$$**

★ **JOHN'S PLACE.** *1202 W Webster Ave, Chicago (60614). Phone 773/525-6670.* A solid neighborhood café in an unlikely residential locale—at the corner of Racine and Webster in the DePaul University area—guarantees John's a steady clientele. The food is comforting but conscientious. John's touts organic produce and line-caught fish in a menu that includes roast chicken, baked whitefish, and several vegetarian options. Families in particular crowd John's; expect to climb over strollers at lunch and the popular weekend brunch. American menu. Lunch, dinner, brunch. Closed Mon. Children's menu. **$$$**

★ ★ ★ **KEEFER'S.** *20 W Kinzie, Chicago (60610). Phone 312/467-9525. www.keefersrestaurant.com.* In bustling River North, stylish Keefer's offers prime steaks, chops, seafood, and some bistro dishes served up in a handsome round dining room with a contemporary Arts and Crafts feel. Soups, salads, and sides are predominantly steakhouse classics (lobster bisque, Caesar salad, creamed spinach), along with some updated but not fussy alternatives. They also serve a somewhat pared-down lunch menu, plus there's the adjacent "Keefer's Kaffe" with a menu of soups, salads, and simple sandwiches, great for quick take-out. Steak menu. Lunch, dinner. Closed Sun. Bar. Casual attire. Outdoor seating. **$$$**

★ ★ ★ **KEVIN.** *9 W Hubbard, Chicago (60610). Phone 312/595-0055. www.kevinrestaurant.com.* Chicago fans of chef Kevin Shikami chased him from kitchen to kitchen around town for years. But in Kevin, his eponymous restaurant, they finally know where to find the talented chef each night. From delicate fish to juicy meats, Shikami brings an Asian flair to contemporary dishes that include tuna tartare, sesame-crusted opakapaka (a Hawaiian fish), and sautéed buffalo strip steak. The smart but warm River North room and polished servers make Kevin a good choice for shoppers and business lunches. American, French, Asian menu. Lunch, dinner. Closed Sun. Bar. Outdoor seating. **$$$**

★ ★ ★ **KIKI'S BISTRO.** *900 N Franklin St, Chicago (60610). Phone 312/335-5454; fax 312/335-0614.* Long before bistros were blossoming all over town, this little charmer on an out-of-the-way corner in River North was pleasing patrons with its traditional bistro fare and regional specials. The softly lit dining rooms are appointed in wood, rose-pink draping and upholstery, and lace curtains. A somewhat older crowd frequents cozy, casual Kiki's for its romantic, country inn ambience, reliable kitchen, and free valet parking (a real boon in this bustling neighborhood). It's also fun to dine at the bar here. French bistro menu. Lunch, dinner. Closed Sun; holidays. Bar. Casual attire. **$$**

★ ★ **KLAY OVEN.** *414 N Orleans St, Chicago (60610). Phone 312/527-3999; fax 312/527-1563. www.klayoven.com.* White tablecloths, exotic textiles, and tasteful serving carts set the tone for fine Indian dining at Klay Oven. Offerings include several tandoori options, plenty of vegetarian choices, and eight varieties of fresh-baked bread. Wine and beer options exceed expectations, and the lunch buffet is a great deal for the quality. Indian menu. Lunch, dinner. Closed holidays. Bar. Casual attire. Outdoor seating. **$$**

★ ★ **LA BOCCA DELLA VERITA.** *4618 N Lincoln Ave, Chicago (60618). Phone 773/784-6222; fax 773/784-6272. www.laboccachicago.com.* Lincoln Square's long-standing Italian storefront La Bocca Della Verita was here and popular before the neighborhood took off (witness the restaurant's wall of fame featuring old headshots of past stars who have dined here). Ample portions of well-priced northern Italian dishes cooked with the flair of a downtown café bring guests back for more. Raves go to the duck breast ravioli and sea bass baked in salt. Neighboring the Davis Theatre, Bocca makes a great pre- or post-movie dinner date. Italian menu. Lunch, dinner. Closed Mon; holidays. Casual attire. Outdoor seating. **$$**

★ **LA CREPERIE.** *2845 N Clark St, Chicago (60657). Phone 773/528-9050.* A Clark Street staple since 1971, La Creperie is Chicago's sole source for eat-out French crepes. Everything from coq au vin to curry gets wrapped in thin, pastry-style pancakes. That goes for dessert, too: the options here include the classic flaming crepes Suzette. French posters and candlelight create café romance in the storefront locale. French bistro menu. Breakfast, lunch, dinner. Closed Mon. Bar. Casual attire. Outdoor seating. **$$**

Ⓝ ★ ★ ★ **LA SARDINE.** *111 N Carpenter St, Chicago (60607). Phone 312/421-2800; fax 312/421-2318. www.lasardine.com.* Perhaps a bit large for a bistro, La Sardine nevertheless delivers the requisite aromas, creature comforts, and menu classics. Warm and bustling (and sometimes noisy) despite a fairly industrial location, La Sardine draws both hip and mature urbanites for the likes of escargots, brandade, bouillabaisse, roast chicken, and profiteroles. Servers wear butcher aprons; the walls are buttery yellow; and those scents waft from an open kitchen and rotisserie. The impressive wine list includes some hard-to-find French selections. French menu. Lunch, dinner. Closed Sun; holidays. Bar. Casual attire. **$$**

★ ★ **LA STRADA.** *155 N Michigan Ave, Chicago (60601). Phone 312/565-2200; fax 312/565-2216. www. lastradaristorante.com.* If you're looking for La Strada at the corner of Michigan Avenue and Randolph Street in the Loop, look down: this elegant Italian restaurant sits below street level. But an atrium of windows allows light to flood in, revealing warm, wood-trimmed rooms and linen-topped tables with handsome appointments. Veal is the house specialty at La Strada, supplemented by beef, chicken, and fish main courses. Get friendly with the crowd over after-dinner drinks in the piano bar. Italian menu. Lunch, dinner. Closed Sun; holidays. Bar. Valet parking. **$$$**

★ ★ **LA TACHE.** *1475 W Balmoral Ave, Chicago (60640). Phone 773/334-7168.* La Tache—French for "the spot"—looks and eats like a downtown restaurant. But to the good fortune of North Siders, it's located in Andersonville and priced accordingly. The smart French bistro offers comforting classics like sautéed escargot, duck à l'orange, and steak frites with enough creative spin to pique your palate. The service is far more professional than you'd expect in a neighborhood joint, and the owners invested La Tache with warm good looks courtesy of wood paneling and ceiling-suspended lamp shades. The busy bar traffics in wine and appetizers. French menu. Lunch, dinner, late-night. Bar. Casual attire. Outdoor seating. **$$**

★ ★ **LAWRY'S THE PRIME RIB.** *100 E Ontario St, Chicago (60611). Phone 312/787-5000; fax 312/ 787-1264. www.lawrysonline.com.* As the name suggests, prime rib is the star at Lawry's The Prime Rib. At this unpretentious dining spot, it is offered in a variety of cuts for different tastes and appetites, from the smaller California cut to the extra-thick "Diamond Jim Brady" cut. Housed in the 1896 English manor-style McCormick Mansion, the restaurant exudes a stately feel, with hardwood furnishings, opulent chandeliers, a grand staircase, and a pair of brass lions outside the main dining area. Steak menu. Lunch, dinner. Closed Dec 25. Bar. Casual attire. Valet parking. **$$$**

★ ★ **LE BOUCHON.** *1958 N Damen Ave, Chicago (60647). Phone 773/862-6600; fax 773/524-1208. www. lebouchonofchicago.com.* Tiny Le Bouchon is known almost as much for its cozy, oh-so-Parisian space with crowded tables, lace curtains, and a pressed-tin ceiling as it is for its authentic French bistro cuisine at reasonable prices. A regular following of Bucktown locals and foodies is willing to wait for a table here (reservations are strongly recommended). French menu. Dinner. Closed Sun; holidays. Bar. Casual attire. Reservations recommended. **$$**

★ ★ **LE COLONIAL.** *937 N Rush St, Chicago (60611). Phone 312/255-0088. www.lecolonialchicago.com.* While other, more daring Asian fusion concepts have come along, this Gold Coast link in an upscale chain holds its own with refined Vietnamese cuisine and elegant, escapist décor circa French-colonial Vietnam. This is a great place for a date or a Magnificent Mile shopping break, and the second-floor terrace tables are coveted seats in warm weather. Vietnamese menu. Lunch, dinner. Bar. Outdoor seating. **$$**

★ ★ ★ ★ **LES NOMADES.** *222 E Ontario St, Chicago (60611). Phone 312/649-9010; fax 312/ 649-0608. www.lesnomades.net.* Les Nomades is a serene little spot tucked away from the bustle of Michigan Avenue in an elegant turn-of-the-century townhouse. Romantic and intimate, with a fireplace; hardwood floors; deep, cozy banquettes; and gorgeous flower arrangements, Les Nomades was originally opened as a private club. It is now open to the public, and what a lucky public we are. While many of Chicago's hottest dining rooms are filled with as much noise as they are with wonderful food, Les Nomades is a peaceful, reserved restaurant that offers perfect service and a magnificent menu of French fare flecked with Asian accents. Excessive noise is not present to distract you from the task at hand. Any spontaneous exclamations of love directed toward the delicious dishes you are consuming (game, foie gras, scallops, lamb, and fish among them) should be kept to a quiet roar, as the tables are closely spaced and exclamations of wonder are often shared. Dining here is a wonderful gastronomic experience, thus this is not a place for a casual dinner. Men are required to dine in jackets and ties, and women are comparably fitted for the occasion. Even children who are rightfully pampered by the attentive staff dress in their holiday best for a memorable evening. *Secret Inspector's Notes: This is a truly special place. After dining, you feel like you've been let in on a magnificently kept secret. It's a wonder to find such artful charm and atmosphere under one small roof.* French menu. Dinner. Closed Sun-Mon; holidays. Bar. Jacket required. Valet parking. **$$$$**

★ **MAGGIANO'S LITTLE ITALY.** *516 N Clark St, Chicago (60610). Phone 312/644-7700; fax 312/644-1077. www.maggianos.com.* From this River North location, Maggiano's ode to classic Italian-American neighborhoods has spawned spin-offs around the country. Fans love it for its big-hearted spirit as expressed in huge portions of familiar red-sauced pastas and the genuine warmth of servers and staff. But be forewarned: it's loud and crowded, better suited to convivial groups than to intimacy-seeking couples. Italian menu. Lunch, dinner. Closed Dec 25. Bar. Casual attire. Valet parking. Outdoor seating. **$$**

★ ★ **MARCHÉ.** *833 W Randolph St, Chicago (60607). Phone 312/226-8399; fax 312/226-4169. www.marche-chicago.com.* Located along restaurant row in the West Loop, Marche serves imaginative versions of classic French bistro fare in a nightclub-like setting. Vibrant paintings and ultra-modern furnishings give the restaurant an eclectic feel and may make you feel as if you have stepped onto the set of *Moulin Rouge.* Sit back with a glass of Veuve and enjoy the theatrical surroundings of this grand French brasserie. French bistro menu. Lunch, dinner. Closed holidays. Bar. Casual attire. Valet parking. Outdoor seating. **$$$**

★ ★ **MAS.** *1670 W Division St, Chicago (60622). Phone 773/276-8700.* This Wicker Park favorite is a good place for a Nuevo Latino feast, a wonderful alternative to more familiar cuisines. The fresh, spicy, and creative fare is best paired with a caipirinha, batida, or mojito to get, literally, in the spirit. Exposed brick and tile and an open kitchen set a hip yet earthy mood. Nuevo Latino menu. Dinner. Bar. Casual attire. Outdoor seating. **$$$**

★ ★ **MAZA.** *2748 N Lincoln Ave, Chicago (60657). Phone 773/929-9600.* Chicago's not strong on Middle Eastern eats, but it hardly needs to be with a standout like Maza. This unassuming Lincoln Park spot specializes in small-plate appetizers that could constitute a grazer's meal. When you're ready to commit to something more substantial, try the shawirma or the rack of lamb. Complete your thematic meal with a bottle of Lebanese red wine. Lebanese menu. Dinner. Casual attire. **$$**

★ ★ ★ **MENAGERIE.** *1232 W Belmont, Chicago (60657). Phone 773/404-8333.* Across the street from the Theatre Building (see) in Lakeview, Menagerie aims to please audiences with creative modern American meals. The co-chefs—whose resumes include past stints at such high-profile restaurants as Bistro 110, Spring (see), and Green Dolphin Street—do best when they dare the most. Fish-and-chips are reinvented here in an Asian style, and duck confit is paired with macaroni and cheese. For-sale works of local artists decorate the walls. Expect a sizable bar crowd for drinks and nibbles post-curtain. International/Fusion menu. Lunch, dinner. Closed Tues. Bar. Casual attire. Outdoor seating. **$$**

★ ★ ★ **MERITAGE.** *2118 N Damen Ave, Chicago (60647). Phone 773/235-6434. www.meritagecafe.com.* For a storefront Bucktown restaurant, Meritage aims high, dishing seafood-focused fare inspired by the cuisine and wines of the Pacific Northwest. Pacific Rim influences edge into seared salmon with taro pancake and Japanese spiced roast scallops. Meat lovers and red wine drinkers are ably served with seared lamb and duck confit. Though the spacious outdoor patio is enclosed and heated in winter, only a canopy cloisters the space in summer, making Meritage one of the city's best open-air eateries. American menu. Dinner, Sun brunch. Closed holidays. Bar. Casual attire. Outdoor seating. **$$$**

★

★ ★ **MIA FRANCESCA.** *3311 N Clark St, Chicago (60657). Phone 773/281-3310; fax 773/281-6671. www.miafrancesca.com.* The original of an ever-expanding family of restaurants, still-trendy (and loud) Mia Francesca packs 'em in for the earthy, ever-changing, moderately priced northern Italian fare. The casually stylish, colorful crowd is comprised of all ages and persuasions; the décor manages to be simultaneously sleek and warm. The second floor is a bit calmer; the outdoor tables are a lucky score for summer dining. Long waits at the vintage bar or in the coach house are often part of the dining experience here, as Mia takes no reservations. Italian menu. Dinner. Closed Thanksgiving, Dec 25. Bar. Children's menu. Valet parking. Outdoor seating. **$$**

★ ★ **MIKE DITKA'S.** *100 E Chestnut St, Chicago (60611). Phone 312/587-8989. www.mikeditkaschicago.com.* Former Chicago Bears coach Mike Ditka's namesake restaurant is manly, naturally, yet surprisingly civilized. While a museum installation-quality sports memorabilia display decorates the clubby restaurant, the patrons exhibit more steakhouse than stadium behavior. Conveniently located near the Magnificent Mile (see) and its many hotels and shopping destinations, Ditka's dishes up generous portions of quality meats (including a massive signature pork chop and "training table" pot roast), as well as seafood, pastas, and salads. The cigar-friendly bar is a louder, more casual destination for snacks and televised sports; upstairs, the cigar lounge features live piano music. American menu. Lunch, dinner, brunch. Closed Dec 25. Bar. Children's menu. Casual attire. Outdoor seating. **$$$**

★ ★ ★ **MIRAI SUSHI.** *2020 W Division St, Chicago (60622). Phone 773/862-8500; fax 773/ 862-8510. www.miraisushi.com.* Wicker Park's funky, hip sushi hotspot is serious about sushi. Offering more than just your everyday maki and nigiri, Mirai ups the ante on sushi (fish is flown in daily, and some selections are still swimming), sake (a generous list), and Japanese culinary creativity (with an intriguing menu items and specials). The bilevel restaurant boasts a bright, smoke-free main-floor dining area and sushi bar, your best bet for experiencing the sushi chef's specials; the upstairs sake bar is dark and seductive, with a choice of barstools, tables, or sleek lounge furniture, with DJ music on weekends. Sushi menu. Dinner. Closed holidays. Bar. Casual attire. Outdoor seating. **$$$**

★ ★ ★ **MK.** *868 N Franklin St, Chicago (60610). Phone 312/482-9179; fax 312/482-9171. www. mkchicago.com.* Style meets substance at Michael Kornick's mk, where refined yet real contemporary cuisine is offered in a perfectly compatible setting. The seasonal American food is clean and uncontrived, the multitiered architectural space linear and neutral without severity. Mergers (stylish couples) and acquisitions (salt-and-pepper-haired types in fashionable eyewear) are all a part of the mk dining experience—as are knowledgeable service, a fine wine list (including private-label selections), and excellent desserts. Degustation menus are available, and the chic lounge area is perfect for a before-or-after glass of bubbly. American menu. Dinner. Closed holidays; week of July 4. Bar. **$$$**

★ ★ ★ **MOD.** *1520 N Damen Ave, Chicago (60622). Phone 773/252-1500.* Don't let the trippy, geometric-acrylic décor fool you; the food here is serious enough,

as evidenced by the commitment to seasonal ingredients and composed plate presentations. The American fare, wine list, and background music could all be described as intelligently eclectic, making MOD a hit with both the hipster Wicker Park crowd and more seasoned, suited-up diners with a sense of adventure. A happening bar scene, Sunday brunch, and seasonal outdoor dining add to the restaurant's appeal. American menu. Dinner, Sun brunch. Bar. Outdoor seating. **$$**

★ ★ ★ **MON AMI GABI.** *2300 N Lincoln Park W, Chicago (60614). Phone 773/348-8886. www.leye.com.* This charming (and aromatic) setting in Lincoln Park's Belden Stratford is so French, you may start speaking with an accent. Solid bistro fare, including a juicy selection of steak preparations and fresh fruits de mer, is a big draw, as are the cozy ambience and rolling wine cart. French bistro menu. Dinner. Closed holidays. Bar. Children's menu. Casual attire. Outdoor seating. **$$**

★ ★ **MONSOON.** *2813 N Broadway, Chicago (60657). Phone 773/665-9463.* A fascinating menu of contemporary Indian-Asian fusion is presented in an exotic, erotic setting. It's easy to give yourself over to your senses in this upscale opium den dining room; between courses of intriguing food and creative cocktails, you can catch the action in the open kitchen (with tandoor oven) or study the Kama Sutra artwork in the rest rooms. Pan-Asian, Indian menu. Dinner. Closed Mon. Bar. Casual attire. Outdoor seating. **$$$**

★ ★ ★ **MORTON'S OF CHICAGO.** *1050 N State St, Chicago (60610). Phone 312/266-4820; fax 312/ 266-4852. www.mortons.com.* This steakhouse chain, which originated in Chicago in 1978, appeals to serious meat lovers. With a selection of belt-busting carnivorous delights (like the house specialty, a 24-ounce porterhouse), as well as fresh fish, lobster, and chicken entrées, Morton's rarely disappoints. If you just aren't sure what you're in the mood for, the tableside menu presentation may help you decide. Here, main course selections are placed on a cart that's rolled to your table, where servers describe each item in detail. Steak menu. Dinner. Closed holidays. Bar. Casual attire. Valet parking. **$$$**

★ ★ ★ **NACIONAL 27.** *325 W Huron, Chicago (60610). Phone 312/664-2727. www.leye.com.* The name hints at the 27 Latin countries informing the menu at this stylish, even sexy, River North restaurant.

Exotic ingredients and creative preparations (including some refreshingly different desserts) lend an escapist feel to a meal here; an array of tapas is one dining option. The ambience is upscale, contemporary supper club, with a posh lounge that's a popular gathering place for after-work or date drinks. Things really heat up on weekends with late-night DJ dancing (with a cover charge for nondiners). Latin American menu. Dinner, late-night (Fri-Sat). Closed Sun. Bar. Casual attire. Outdoor seating. **$$$**

★ ★ ★ **NAHA.** *500 N Clark St, Chicago (60610). Phone 312/321-6242; fax 312/321-7561. www.naha-chicago.com.* Chef Carrie Nahabadian cooked at the Four Seasons Beverly Hills before opening her own River North spot, Naha, where she merges her Armenian background with her California training. The result is a luscious Mediterranean-like blend of flavors in creative dishes such as sea scallops with grapefruit, bass with olive oil-poached tomatoes, and roast pheasant with grilled asparagus. The sleek, sophisticated décor and attentive service vault Naha above area competitors. American menu. Lunch, dinner. Closed Sun; holidays. Bar. Casual attire. Outdoor seating. **$$$**

★ ★ **NANIWA.** *607 N Wells, Chicago (60610). Phone 312/255-8555. www.sushinaniwa.com.* You don't expect an overlooked gem of a restaurant to be housed on busy Wells Street in River North. But Naniwa is hidden in plain sight. Distinct from the many trendy sushi joints that double as lounges, Naniwa plays it straight with good, fresh fish and deluxe maki rolls. Indoor tables are close together, but in season the patio offers prime viewing of the passing parades on Wells. Open for lunch, Naniwa does a big to-go business with area office workers. Japanese menu. Lunch, dinner. Bar. Children's menu. Casual attire. Reservations recommended. Outdoor seating. **$$**

★ ★ **NICK'S FISHMARKET.** *51 S Clark St, Chicago (60603). Phone 312/621-0200; fax 312/ 621-1118. www.nicksfishmarketchicago.com.* Although Nick's specializes in seafood, it acts in every other way like a steakhouse. Consider the dark, subterranean room with low ceilings and attentive tuxedoed waiters. Traditional preparations like lobster bisque and lobster thermador encourage the simile. But in the kitchen, Nick is all about fish. An operation born in Hawaii in the mid-1960s, Nick's reveals its roots in Hawaiian fish specials and the "Maui Wowie" salad. Appetizers feature shellfish, sashimi, and caviar, followed by sole, salmon, and lobster entrées. The

street-level bar serves casual versions. American menu. Lunch, dinner. Closed Sun; holidays. Bar. Children's menu. Valet parking. **$$$**

★ ★ ★ **NINE.** *440 W Randolph St, Chicago (60606). Phone 312/575-9900. www.n9ne.com.* A scene-setter in the West Loop, this Vegas-worthy spot blends sophistication and sizzle and backs it up with serious American steakhouse fare, a central champagne and caviar bar, and great people-watching. Equally suited to business and social dining, Nine is a one-stop evening out, with a large bar/lounge area and another late-night upstairs lounge, the Ghost Bar. American menu. Lunch, dinner. Closed Sun; holidays. Bar. Casual attire. **$$$**

★ ★ **NIX.** *163 E Walton Pl, Chicago (60611). Phone 312/867-7575; toll-free 866/866-8086; fax 312/751-9205. www.millenium-hotels.com.* This stylishly modern, eclectic offering in the Loop's Millennium Knickerbocker Hotel serves a breakfast buffet, lunch, and dinner, with selections running the gamut from upscale comfort food to global fusion. The crowd is a mix of business types, Loop denizens, and traveling families. Don't miss the 44-strong martini list. American menu. Breakfast, lunch, dinner, Sun brunch. Bar. Children's menu. Casual attire. Valet parking. Outdoor seating. **$$$**

★ ★ ★ **NOMI.** *800 N Michigan Ave, Chicago (60611). Phone 312/239-4030; fax 312/239-4029. www.nomirestaurant.com.* A posh perch over Chicago's famed Magnificent Mile, NoMI (an acronym for North Michigan) is the Park Hyatt's (see) stylish, civilized destination for critically acclaimed contemporary French cuisine. Asian influences are evident in sushi and sashimi selections on the sophisticated menu. Luxurious materials combine in the streamlined décor, highlighted by an eye-catching art collection, glittering open kitchen, and scintillating view from floor-to-ceiling windows. The wine list is both impressive and extensive, with 3,000 or so bottles. NoMI also serves breakfast and lunch and offers outdoor terrace dining in fair weather. French menu. Breakfast, lunch, dinner. Bar. Reservations recommended. Outdoor seating. **$$$**

★ ★ ★ **NORTH POND.** *2610 N Cannon Dr, Chicago (60614). Phone 773/477-5845; fax 773/ 477-3234. www.northpondrestaurant.com.* North Pond delivers a dining experience like no other. Seasonal, contemporary American food emphasizing regional ingredients is paired with an all-American wine list and served in a one-of-a-kind location on the Lincoln Park lagoon. The handsome Arts and Crafts décor gives the feeling that Frank Lloyd Wright had a hand in the proceedings. No roads lead here; cab it or look for parking along Cannon Drive and then follow the garden path to the restaurant. Sunday brunch is a refined indulgence, and outdoor dining is a special treat in seasonable weather. American menu. Dinner, Sun brunch. Closed Mon; holidays. Outdoor seating. **$$$**

★ **NORTHSIDE CAFE.** *1635 N Damen Ave, Chicago (60647). Phone 773/384-3555; fax 773/ 384-6337.* The perfect place for people-watching in the hip Bucktown neighborhood (see WICKER PARK/BUCKTOWN NEIGHBORHOOD) or for a late-night snack (the kitchen is open until 2 am), Northside Cafe is a local favorite for standard—but tasty—bar food, such as burgers, salads, and sandwiches. Summer is especially popular here, when the patio opens up and patrons can enjoy the great weather while sipping on one of Northside's famous frozen margaritas. American menu. Lunch, dinner, late-night. Closed Thanksgiving, Dec 24-25. Bar. Casual attire. Outdoor seating. **$$**

★ **OAK TREE.** *900 N Michigan Ave, Chicago (60611). Phone 312/751-1988.* With its location on the sixth floor of the busy indoor mall at 900 North Michigan (known to locals as the Bloomingdale's Building), Oak Tree is a popular spot with shoppers and tourists who need a break from the hustle and bustle of the Magnificent Mile. The varied menu features everything from Americanized versions of Asian, Mexican, and Italian dishes to dressed-up breakfast items (served all day) such as pancakes, omelets, and eggs Benedict. If you can't snag a window seat to enjoy the views of Michigan Avenue, don't worry— the bright, nature-inspired dining room makes for a pleasurable experience nonetheless. American menu. Breakfast, lunch, dinner. Closed holidays. Children's menu. Casual attire. **$**

★ ★ **OHBA.** *2049 W Division St, Chicago (60622). Phone 773/772-2727; fax 773/862-8500. www. ohbalounge.com.* A spin-off of nearby sushi hotspot Mirai (see), this minimalist, chic hipster haunt on the Division Street restaurant row puts out lovely presentations of contemporary "world cuisine" with an Asian accent. Expect luxury ingredients and unusual preparations, plus an extensive sake list, including flights and sake-based cocktails. Fusion, Japanese

menu. Lunch, dinner. Closed Mon; holidays. Bar. Casual attire. Outdoor seating. **$$**

★ ★ ★ **ONE SIXTYBLUE.** *160 N Loomis, Chicago (60607). Phone 312/850-0303; fax 312/ 829-3046. www.onesixtyblue.com.* Award-winning, haute contemporary cuisine and sleek, high-styled décor by famed designer Adam Tihany define this adult, urban dining experience in the West Loop. Bold American fare with French roots is at home in the contemporary yet comfortable dining room, done in dark wood and citrus hues with discreet lighting and great sightlines. The open kitchen and dramatic wine storage are focal points. A cocoa bar offers sinful chocolate creations; the chic lounge is a hot cocktail spot. The buzz over former Chicago Bull Michael Jordan's partnership is a mere whisper now that his limelight has dimmed. American menu. Dinner. Closed Sun; holidays. Bar. Casual attire. **$$$**

★ ★ ★ **OPERA.** *1301 S Wabash Ave, Chicago (60605). Phone 312/461-0161.* Helping to position the gentrifying South Loop as a foodie destination, Opera updates Chinese fare by banning gummy sauces and upping the presentation appeal. Top picks include five-spice squid and slow-roasted pork shoulder. The lively, art-filled interior—don't miss the Asian girlie collages—encourages lingering over cocktails. Romantics are served by tables set within a series of narrow vaults in this former film storage warehouse. Chinese menu. Dinner. Closed holidays. Bar. Casual attire. **$$$**

★ **ORANGE.** *3231 N Clark St, Chicago (60657). Phone 773/549-4400.* This Wrigleyville breakfast and lunch spot made its mark in the restaurant-mad neighborhood with inventive fare like "green eggs and ham" (pesto eggs and pancetta), jelly donut pancakes, and steak sandwiches with Spanish blue cheese. The juice bar will squeeze anything garden-grown, from oranges to cucumbers to beets. The colorful interior, family-friendly vibe, and budget-minded menu spread good cheer here. American menu. Brunch. Children's menu. Casual attire. Outdoor seating. **$**

★ ★ **THE PALM.** *323 E Wacker Dr, Chicago (60601). Phone 312/616-1000; fax 312/616-3717. www. thepalm.com.* While some people feel that this classic concept has become watered down, The Palm in the Swissôtel (see) still delivers on its promise of giant steaks and lobsters in a business-casual steakhouse atmosphere, complete with a caricature wall of fame and platinum-card prices. Seasonal outdoor seating offers great views. Steak menu. Lunch, dinner. Bar. Casual attire. Valet parking. Outdoor seating. **$$$**

★ ★ ★ **PANE CALDO.** *72 E Walton St, Chicago (60611). Phone 312/649-0055; fax 312/274-0540. www. pane-caldo.com.* This little gem off the Magnificent Mile is home to some of the best Italian food this side of Piedmont. It's easy to miss this tiny restaurant— look for the ultra-posh shoppers enjoying a midday respite and the suit-coated businessmen having power lunches over risotto Milanese. An extensive wine list complements the kitchen's lovely creations, made with organic meats and locally grown organic produce. Italian menu. Lunch, dinner. Closed Mon. Bar. Business casual attire. Reservations recommended. **$$$**

★ **PAPAGUS GREEK TAVERNA.** *620 N State St, Chicago (60610). Phone 312/642-8450; toll-free 888/538-8823; fax 312/642-8132. www.leye.com.* Chicago hit-making restaurant group Lettuce Entertain You runs Papagus, a crowd-pleaser for rustic Greek tavern-style food. In addition to Grecian staples like flaming cheese, eggplant spread, and roast lamb, Papagus serves a variety of authentic small plates that encourage experimentation. Pair them affably with a bottle from the list of imported Greek wines. Greek menu. Lunch, dinner. Bar. Children's menu. Casual attire. Valet parking. Outdoor seating. **$$**

★ **PARTHENON.** *314 S Halsted St, Chicago (60661). Phone 312/726-2407; fax 312/726-3203. www.theparthenon.com.* A Greektown landmark, this long-standing, family-run favorite is known for its convivial taverna atmosphere and solid renditions of moderately priced, classic Greek fare (flaming cheese and lamb dishes are standouts)—and the free valet parking is a bonus. Greek menu. Lunch, dinner. Closed Thanksgiving, Dec 25. Bar. Children's menu. Casual attire. Valet parking. **$$**

★ **PENNY'S NOODLE SHOP.** *3400 N Sheffield Ave, Chicago (60657). Phone 773/281-8222.* Hungry bargain-hunters have been slurping up Penny's namesake noodles by the carload ever since this convenient (and expanding) concept opened its doors a few years ago. Draws include the healthful fare, low prices, and low-key atmosphere. Thai menu. Lunch, dinner. Closed Mon; holidays. Casual attire. Outdoor seating. **$**

★ **PIECE.** *1927 W North Ave, Chicago (60622). Phone 773/772-4422.* Chicago may be the home of deep-dish pizza, but you'll never find it on the menu at this Wicker Park pizzeria. The only pizza served here is the East Coast-style thin-crust variety (one of the co-owners hails from Connecticut). Diners can order one of Piece's specialty pizzas or create their own using one of the bases—red, white, or plain—and a variety of ingredients ranging from the traditional tomatoes and mushrooms to the more adventurous clams and bacon. And what's pizza without beer? Ten regional microbrews and seven house-brewed beers are on hand to wash it all down. Pizza. Lunch, dinner, late-night. Bar. Casual attire. **$**

★ ★ ★ **PILI PILI.** *230 W Kinzie St, Chicago (60610). Phone toll-free 877/878-0553. www.pilipilirestaurant.com.* A contemporary take on the earthy fare of Provence and neighboring Mediterranean regions is offered in a tastefully rustic setting. Expect pure flavors that come from fresh seasonal ingredients, with many dishes emanating from the aromatic wood-burning rotisserie or brick oven. The well-chosen, French-focused wine list includes some flights. Grand aioli and charcuterie presentations draw the eye to the center of the dining room; a smaller café area is open all day. The unusual name comes from a North African hot pepper used in a regional infused oil. Mediterranean menu. Lunch, dinner. Bar. Casual attire. Outdoor seating. **$$$**

★ **PIZZA D. O. C.** *2251 W Lawrence, Chicago (60625). Phone 773/784-8777.* Italian menu. Dinner. Entertainment. Closed Tues; holidays. **$**

★ **PIZZERIA UNO.** *29 E Ohio St, Chicago (60611). Phone 312/321-1000. www.unos.com.* Surely you've heard about Chicago-style pizza: the kind made of a flaky, pielike crust and stuffed with generous amounts of meats, cheeses, vegetables, and spices. This legendary deep-dish pizza originated at Pizzeria Uno, a casual eatery decorated with hardwood booths and pictures of famous Chicagoans. Because these pizzas take up to 45 minutes to prepare, your order is taken while you wait for your table. Not willing to wait for a seat? Head across the street to Pizzeria Due, which was opened to handle the overflow of crowds at Pizzeria Uno. Pizza. Lunch, dinner. Closed Thanksgiving, Dec 25. Bar. Children's menu. Casual attire. Outdoor seating. **$**

Pizza—A Chicago Original

Chicagoans have never been satisfied with the ordinary. From the world's largest airport to the world's tallest building (until 1998—now is North America's tallest), Chicago does things in a big way. No wonder the city that turned a regular brownstone into the world's first skyscraper also transformed the familiar pizza pie into what we now know as the Chicago-style pizza.

It must be noted that Chicago-style pizza has about as much in common with a normal thin-crust pizza as a bicycle does with a tank. Both have some type of tomato sauce and cheese, but all similarities end there. Contrary to popular belief, the crust on a classic Chicago pizza isn't thick at all. It's actually a normal pizza crust that is put into a special pizza pan with deep sides. This crust is then built up the sides of the pan to form the familiar "deep dish" shape.

The first thing laid onto the crust, however, isn't the sauce; it's the cheese, which is pressed down to make a nice bed for all of the other ingredients. At this point, it's up to the pizza maker to decide what goes in next. Remember, it's bad form for the crust around the edge to perch over the pizza, so this space must be filled with three to four times the quantity of ingredients on a normal pizza. Sausage is a must, and is cited as the most frequently requested ingredient on pizzas in the city. Peppers, onions, pepperoni, olives, and all of the best-loved standbys of the classic pizza are piled high to fill that waiting crust.

After the ingredients are selected and placed, the last item—a thick, chunky tomato sauce—is added. It is poured liberally over the ingredients and then sprinkled with a light dusting of cheese before baking. Good things come to those who wait, and Chicago-style pizza is no exception; average baking times hover around the 45-minute mark at Chicago's most famous pizzerias.

When it finally comes out of the oven, one piece is a meal unto itself. Two will prevent the need for breakfast. And three slices will make you famous in this city of "big shoulders." The original home of Chicago-style pizza can be found at **Pizzeria Uno** (29 E Ohio St; phone 312/321-1000); its sister restaurant, **Pizzeria Due** (619 N Wabash Ave; phone 312/943-2400), is just down the street. **Lou Malnati's** (439 N Wells St; phone 312/828-9800), started by a former Pizzeria Uno chef, is another windy city original, while **Gino's East** (633 N Wells; phone 312/943-1124) rounds out the listings for great Chicago-style pizza. Regardless of where you stop, though, you're sure to find great pizza in Chicago.

★ **POT PAN.** *1750 W North Ave, Chicago (60622). Phone 773/862-6990; fax 773/862-6993.* This simple noodle house is a favorite with Wicker Park/Bucktown locals, who enjoy the homey décor and inexpensive Thai food. Pot Pan is known for its outstanding pan-ang curry as well as its great spring rolls. Thai menu. Lunch, dinner. **$**

★ **PREGO RISTORANTE.** *2901 N Ashland Ave, Chicago (60657). Phone 773/472-9190.* A modest storefront Italian eatery, Prego is a welcome addition to busy Ashland Avenue in Lakeview. Candles and paper-topped tables provide warmth, as does a caring owner who frequently patrols the floor to inquire after the food. Although the menu changes often to reflect the season, hits include risotto, squash ravioli, and fish specials, offered regularly. The fare is no match for downtown challengers, but in the neighborhood, Prego is a charmer. Italian menu. Lunch, dinner. Closed Sun-Mon. Bar. Casual attire. Outdoor seating. **$$**

★ ★ ★ **PUMP ROOM.** *1301 N State Pkwy, Chicago (60610). Phone 312/266-0360; fax 312/266-1798. www.pumproom.com.* This revered Chicago classic combines the grand, gracious hotel dining of yesteryear with contemporary French-American fare. Having undergone several chef changes in recent years (and a major renovation a few years ago), the Pump Room remains popular with tourists and special-occasion celebrants. Booth One lives on, complete with vintage telephone; the bar could have been transported from a *Thin Man* set. The photo wall is a sentimental journey down the memory lane of film, music, and politics. Highlights include live music with a small dance floor and Sunday champagne brunch; the "upscale casual" dress code attests to the times. American menu. Breakfast, lunch, dinner, Sun brunch. Bar. Children's menu. Jacket required. Valet parking. **$$$**

★ ★ **RAS DASHEN.** *5846 N Broadway, Chicago (60660). Phone 773/506-9601; fax 773/506-9685.* Feel free to eat with your hands at Ras Dashen, an Ethiopian eatery that provides an authentic taste of the North African nation. In native style, diners tear hunks of the spongy inerja bread that forms a plate for chicken and lamb dishes and use it to scoop up tasty bites. Ethiopian art and artifacts, including imported straw tables and chairs, fill the tidy Uptown storefront. Ethiopian menu. Lunch, dinner. Closed Tues. Bar. Children's menu. Casual attire. Reservations recommended. **$$**

★ **REDFISH.** *400 N State St, Chicago (60610). Phone 312/467-1600; fax 312/467-0325. www. redfishamerica.com.* This thematic Cajun spot goes all out with N'awlins décor, a catch-all of voodoo dolls, Mardis Gras masks, and hot sauces. The namesake redfish leads the menu (have it blackened) along with crab-stuffed salmon and pastas. In keeping with its Big Easy affinity, drinking is a sport here. To encourage late-night guzzling, the restaurant brings in zydeco and R & B bands on the weekends. Cajun menu. Lunch, dinner, late-night. Closed Easter, Thanksgiving, Dec 25. Bar. Children's menu. Casual attire. Valet parking. Outdoor seating. **$$**

★ ★ **REDLIGHT.** *820 W Randolph St, Chicago (60607). Phone 312/733-8880. www.redlight-chicago .com.* Asian fusion in an avant garde, fantasy atmosphere defines this Randolph restaurant row favorite. Renowned chef Jackie Shen has taken over the kitchen, which produces fresh, creative combinations of Chinese, Thai, Japanese, and American ingredients and preparations. This hotspot can be very noisy during prime time. Chinese, Thai menu. Lunch, dinner. Closed Jan 1, Thanksgiving, Dec 25. Bar. Casual attire. Valet parking. Outdoor seating. **$**

★ ★ **RIVA.** *700 E Grand Ave, Chicago (60611). Phone 312/644-7482; fax 312/206-7035. www. stefanirestaurants.com.* Bustling with Navy Pier tourists and locals alike, this elegant restaurant is popular for its fresh seafood, as well as its spectacular views of the Chicago skyline. Along with a 40-foot-long open kitchen, the dining room features nautical décor that re-creates the atmosphere of the Italian Riviera. On Wednesdays (9:30 pm) and Saturdays (10:15 pm) from Memorial Day to Labor Day, enjoy Navy Pier's dazzling evening fireworks displays while you dine. Seafood menu. Lunch, dinner. Closed Thanksgiving, Dec 24-25. Bar. Children's menu. Casual attire. Valet parking. Outdoor seating. **$$**

★ ★ ★ **RODAN.** *1530 N Milwaukee Ave, Chicago (60622). Phone 773/276-7036.* A funky, globe-trotting Wicker Parker, Rodan unites the foods of South America and Asia on its menu. Graze from gingered swordfish and shrimp rolls back West to adobo Cornish hen and fish tacos with mango salsa. Somewhere in between lie the tasty wasabi tempura fries. Go casual to Rodan, and go late-night if you're looking for a hip lounge. As the night progresses, the lights come down, the music comes up, and the bar fills with revelers. South American, Southeast Asian menu. Dinner, late-night. Bar. Casual attire. **$$**

★ ★ **ROSEBUD.** *1500 W Taylor St, Chicago (60607). Phone 312/942-1117. www.rosebudrestaurants.com.* The Taylor Street original of this expanding family of old-school Italian restaurants is a Little Italy tradition, revered for its boisterous, Sinatra-swagger ambience; clubby, carved wood décor; and giant portions with inevitable doggie bags. There's a large bar area for waiting during peak periods. Italian menu. Lunch, dinner. Bar. Casual attire. Outdoor seating. **$$**

★ ★ ★ **ROY'S.** *720 N State St, Chicago (60610). Phone 312/787-7599. roysrestaurant.com.* Don't expect luau fare—and don't wear your Hawaiian shirt—at this sleek, contemporary Hawaiian chain member. Lots of creative seafood dishes populate the menu, with several unusual fish varieties offered; French and Asian fusion elements are evident throughout. There are also several meat dishes for the seafood squeamish. Menu selections are listed with suggested wine pairings (the restaurant has its own wine label produced by various houses—plus its own range of sake, which partners nicely with much of the food). Hawaiian menu. Dinner. Closed Thanksgiving, Dec 25. Bar. Children's menu. Casual attire. Outdoor seating. **$$$**

★ ★ **RUSHMORE.** *1023 W Lake St, Chicago (60607). Phone 312/421-8845; toll-free 888/874-8719. www.rushmore-chicago.com.* American regional food shines at Rushmore in the trendy West Loop. The kitchen plucks comfort food classics from around the country to include smoked cheddar macaroni and cheese, cornmeal-crusted fried chicken, and fish-and-chips fancied up to include trout and matchstick potatoes. In contrast to the homey food, the atmosphere leans toward the contemporary, providing a window to the front line cooks. American menu. Lunch, dinner. Closed Sun. Bar. Casual attire. **$$**

★ ★ **RUSSIAN TEA TIME.** *77 E Adams St, Chicago (60603). Phone 312/360-0000; fax 312/360-0575. www.russianteatime.com.* Despite the name, the emphasis here is on Russian food rather than tea. Classics like borscht, salmon blinis, and stuffed cabbage wave the old-world torch, as does the time-warp look of red booths, brass chandeliers, and waiters in tuxedos. Neighboring both The Art Institute of Chicago and Symphony Center, Russian Tea Time draws a cultured crowd. Russian menu. Traditional caviar service. Lunch, dinner. Closed holidays. Bar. Casual attire. Outdoor seating. **$$**

★ ★ **SAI CAFÉ.** *2010 N Sheffield Ave, Chicago (60614). Phone 773/472-8080. www.saicafe.com.* This old-guard Lincoln Park neighborhood standby for sushi and classic Japanese cuisine was crowded long before the wave of hip sushi spots hit town. It's a comfortable, low-attitude place for reliable fare and friendly service—and the selection of both sushi and maki rolls is extensive. Sushi menu. Dinner. Bar. Casual attire. Reservations recommended. Outdoor seating. **$$**

🄳

★ ★ **THE SALOON.** *200 E Chestnut St, Chicago (60611). Phone 312/280-5454; fax 312/280-6986. www.saloonsteakhouse.com.* If you're looking for a light bite, The Saloon is not the place to go. This classic steakhouse offers mega-sized portions of meat-heavy fare, like the 2-pound porterhouse and the 14-ounce strip loin. Located on a somewhat secluded strip just off of busy Michigan Avenue, The Saloon is the perfect place for escaping the crowds of power shoppers on the Magnificent Mile. Steak menu. Lunch, dinner. Closed holidays. Bar. Casual attire. **$$$**

★ ★ **SALPICON.** *1252 N Wells St, Chicago (60610). Phone 312/988-7811; fax 312/988-7715. www.salpicon .com.* In a town where chef Rick Bayless and his Frontera Grill (see) rule the gourmet Mexican roost, Salpicon remains an in-the-know treasure. Chef Priscilla Satkoff grew up in Mexico City and honors her native cuisine here with rich moles, tender-roasted meats, and upscale twists on both, such as ancho chile quail. The extensive wine list, managed by the chef's husband, has won numerous awards. But it's hard to get past the 50-some tequilas on offer to mix in margaritas (knowing servers ably steer agave gringos). Salpicon's boldly colored interiors generate a spirit of fiesta. Mexican menu. Dinner, Sun brunch. Closed Thanksgiving, Dec 25. Bar. Valet parking. Outdoor seating. **$$**

★ ★ **SANTORINI.** *800 W Adams St, Chicago (60607). Phone 312/829-8820; fax 312/829-6263. www. santoriniseafood.com.* This Greektown seafood specialist represents an oasis of calm amid its more boisterous companions on the neighborhood's busy strip. Authentic, fresh fish (especially the whole grilled offerings) and the airy, Mediterranean seaside atmosphere with whitewashed walls transport patrons to the island of the same name. Greek menu. Lunch, dinner. Closed Thanksgiving, Dec 25. Bar. Children's menu. Casual attire. Valet parking. Outdoor seating. **$$**

★ **SAUCE.** *1750 N Clark St, Chicago (60614). Phone 312/932-1750; fax 312/932-0056. www.saucechicago .com.* Opposite Lincoln Park on the fringe of Old Town, Sauce intends to be a restaurant. But a pack of young, martini-swilling regulars have claimed it as a hangout. The menu ranges far and wide to include bar fare (artichoke dip, quesadillas, pizza), comfort food (lasagna), and trendy options (seared tuna). If you're only after the food, come early. But if it's eye candy you crave, drop by late. American menu. Lunch, dinner, late-night. Closed Sun; Jan 1, Dec 25. Bar. Casual attire. Outdoor seating. **$$**

★ **SAYAT NOVA.** *157 E Ohio St, Chicago (60611). Phone 312/644-9159; fax 312/644-6234.* For something completely different, try this family-run Armenian spot for a touch of foreign intrigue and bargain-priced kebabs, lamb dishes, stuffed grape leaves, and other traditional Middle Eastern fare. Opened in 1969, Sayat Nova is now a pleasant anachronism in its chichi off-Mag Mile location. Middle Eastern menu. Lunch, dinner. Closed holidays. Bar. **$$**

★ ★ **SCOOZI.** *410 W Huron, Chicago (60610). Phone 312/943-5900; fax 312/943-8969. www.leye.com.* An early pioneer of now-booming River North, this Lettuce Entertain You Italian concept—once hip, now comfortable—is a convivial place to gather for cocktails in the large bar area, cracker-crust pizzas, goodies from the generous antipasto bar, or full-blown Italian dining. The cavernous space gets warmth and gravitas from the faux-antiqued décor. Italian menu. Lunch, dinner. Closed Thanksgiving, Dec 25. Bar. Valet parking. Outdoor seating. **$$**

★ ★ ★ **SEASONS.** *120 E Delaware Pl, Chicago (60611). Phone 312/649-2349; fax 312/649-2372. www.fourseasons.com/chicagofs.* Dining at Seasons, the upscale and elegant restaurant of the Four Seasons Hotel Chicago (see), is the sort of experience that may cause whiplash. Your head will whip back and forth as you watch stunning plates pass by in the rich and refined dining room. Each dish looks better than the next. On a nightly basis, the dining room is filled with food envy. Perhaps this is because the kitchen prepares every plate with a deep respect for ingredients, making every inventive dish on the menu of New American fare a delight to admire from afar and devour from up close. The chef offers five-course and eight-course tasting menus. What's more, while a restaurant of this stature could easily feel pretentious, the staff's warmth and charm makes dining here easy and comfortable—a pleasure from start to finish. American, French menu. Lunch, dinner, Sun brunch. Bar. Children's menu. Valet parking. Casual attire. **$$$$**

★ ★ ★ **SHANGHAI TERRACE.** *108 E Superior, Chicago (60610). Phone 312/573-6744. www.chicago.peninsula.com.* Fittingly, the Asian-run Peninsula hotel (see) gives Chicago its best Chinese restaurant. Intimate and trimmed in rich hues of ruby red and lacquer black, Shanghai Terrace is the best looking of its category, too. Start with the eatery's refined three-bite dim sum dishes. Save room for flavorful entrées like spicy Sichuan beef and wok-fried lobster. You'll find Shanghai Terrace one level below the ornate hotel lobby. The restaurant adjoins an expansive terrace offering alfresco dining in the summer six stories above Michigan Avenue. Asian menu. Lunch, dinner. Closed Sun-Mon. Bar. Children's menu. Casual attire. Outdoor seating. **$$$**

★ ★ **SHAW'S CRAB HOUSE.** *21 E Hubbard St, Chicago (60611). Phone 312/527-2722; fax 312/527-4740. www.shawscrabhouse.com.* A longtime seafood standard-bearer in River North, popular Shaw's goes the extra mile to fly in an extensive variety of fresh seafood, served in a choice of environments—upscale clubby dining room or East Coast-style oyster bar ambience in the Blue Crab Lounge. Seafood menu. Lunch, dinner. Closed Thanksgiving, Dec 25. Bar. Casual attire. Valet parking. Outdoor seating. **$$$**

★ ★ **SHE SHE.** *4539 N Lincoln Ave, Chicago (60625). Phone 773/293-3690.* Fine dining-caliber food in funky digs endears She She to residents of the Lincoln Square neighborhood. Although the menu changes seasonally, expect chef Nicole Parthemore's signature coconut-crusted shrimp, salmon maki rolls, and contemporized entrées like duck confit linguine. While the food is serious, the scene—from the leopard print seats to the RuPaul martini—is anything but. American menu. Dinner. Closed Mon; Thanksgiving, Dec 25. Bar. Children's menu. Casual attire. Outdoor seating. **$$**

★ ★ **SIGNATURE ROOM AT THE 95TH.** *875 N Michigan Ave, Chicago (60611). Phone 312/787-9596; fax 630/968-7779. www.signatureroom.com.* Situated atop one of the world's tallest buildings, the John Hancock Center, and towering 1,000 feet above the Magnificent Mile, the Signature Room is deservedly famous for its breathtaking vistas. It affords spectacular views from every part of its dining room. Sumptuous Art Deco surroundings complement picture-perfect scenes of the city and Lake Michigan, visible through the floor-to-ceiling windows that circle the room. The food is contemporary American (consider the reasonably priced lunch buffet or Sunday brunch). Convenient to downtown hotels and shopping, the Signature Lounge is also a popular spot for a romantic rendezvous or business cocktails. American menu. Lunch, dinner, Sun brunch. Closed Jan 1, Dec 25. Bar. Casual attire. **$$**

★ ★ **SOUK.** *1552 N Milwaukee Ave, Chicago (60622). Phone 773/227-1818; fax 773/278-1408. www.soukrestaurant.com.* Stepping into the exotic surroundings of Souk (Arabic for "marketplace") is like entering another world—tile artwork, beads, candles, leather-topped tables, and long, plush banquettes decorate the cozy dining room. It is the perfect atmosphere in which to dine on a menu that reflects all cultures of the Mediterranean, including Turkey, Greece, Morocco, and Egypt. Familiar dishes like hummus and baba ghanoush are among the selections, as are some not-so-familiar dishes like toshka and keba. Entertainment, which includes jazz and belly dancing, is offered weekly and is perfect to watch while enjoying a postdinner shisha (water pipe) filled with fruit tobacco. Mediterranean menu. Dinner. Bar. Casual attire. Reservations recommended. **$$**

★ ★ ★ **SPIAGGIA.** *980 N Michigan Ave, Chicago (60611). Phone 312/280-2750; fax 312/943-8560. www. spiaggiarestaurant.com.* Next to Spiaggia, you'd have to fly to Milan to get a dose of the sort of contemporary, sophisticated Italian cuisine served here. Chef Tony Mantuano has a light, refined touch, working with artisanal and exotic ingredients like Piemontese beef and seasonal white truffles. Expect frequent menu changes, but typical dishes include wood-roasted scallops with porcini mushrooms and Parmesan shavings, pumpkin risotto with seared foie gras, and lamb chops with slow-cooked lamb shoulder. Favored by both expense accounts and special-occasion affairs, the opulent trilevel room completes the seduction, offering each table a view over Lake Michigan. Italian menu. Dinner. Closed holidays. Bar. Jacket required (dinner). Reservations recommended. Valet parking. **$$$$**

★ ★ ★ ★ **SPRING.** *2039 W North Ave, Chicago (60647). Phone 773/395-7100. www.springrestaurant. net.* You don't expect it of the bohemian Wicker Park surroundings, but Spring is one of the city's most sophisticated foodies. Chef Shawn McClain has a deft touch with seafood, the specialty here prepared with Asian touches. Artistic yet unfussy dishes change seasonally but might include tuna tartare with quail egg or cod in crab and sweet pea sauce. Lodged in a former bathhouse with the white ceramic wall tiles to prove it, Spring faces east for inspiration, greeting diners in the foyer with a Zen-inspired rock garden. American menu. Dinner. Closed holidays; also early Jan. Bar. Casual attire. **$$$**

★ **STANLEY'S.** *1970 N Lincoln Ave, Chicago (60614). Phone 312/642-0007.* As you enter through the front door, Stanley's looks like a typical Lincoln Park bar. But walk a little farther into the dining area and you'll feel like you've entered someone's home; this family-friendly space is decorated with photos, children's drawings, and knickknacks. And the food will make you feel at home, too. Large portions of American comfort food like mac and cheese, meatloaf, and mashed potatoes and gravy are sure to bring back memories of the way Mom used to cook. American menu. Lunch, dinner. Bar. Casual attire. Outdoor seating. **$$**

★ **SU CASA.** *49 E Ontario St, Chicago (60611). Phone 312/943-4041; fax 312/943-6480.* A River North staple for Tex-Mex, Su Casa has been dishing its brand of south-of-the-border hospitality since 1963. Founded by the same golden-touch restaurateur who established Pizzeria Uno (see), Su Casa sticks to crowd-pleasing favorites like fajitas, chimichangas, and burritos. Colorful Mexican piñatas and murals help generate a fiesta feel. Mexican menu. Lunch, dinner. Closed Thanksgiving, Dec 25. Bar. Valet parking. Outdoor seating. **$$**

★ ★ **SUSHI SAMBA RIO.** *504 N Wells St, Chicago (60610). Phone 312/595-2300. www.sushisamba.com.* Flashy and splashy, this New York/Miami import serves up a wild fusion menu of sushi with Japanese and Brazilian dishes—and cocktails to match. The high-concept contemporary décor offers multiple environments (including a crowded bar area), plenty of people-watching, and a nightclub-like ambience when busy. The all-weather rooftop dining area is exposed in summer, enclosed in winter. Japanese, Brazilian menu. Lunch, dinner. Bar. Casual attire. Reservations recommended. Outdoor seating. **$$$**

★ ★ **SUSHI WABI.** *842 W Randolph St, Chicago (60607). Phone 312/563-1224; fax 312/563-9579. www. sushiwabi.com.* Chicago's first in a wave of hipster sushi bars draws a fashionable crowd to the West Loop market district for the fresh fish, industrial-chic atmosphere, and late-night DJ music. The clubby (noisy) scene is secondary to the seafood, and savvy sushi lovers know that reservations are a must. Japanese, sushi menu. Lunch, dinner, late-night. Closed holidays. Bar. Casual attire. Reservations recommended. **$$**

★ ★ **SWK.** *710 N Wells St, Chicago (60610). Phone 312/274-9500; fax 312/274-0711. www. swankchicago.com.* The former nightclub-with-food Swank has morphed into SWK, a restaurant with nightclub sensibilities, meaning that patrons can still enjoy the lounge vibe while indulging in playfully exotic fare like ostrich satay, corn-fried oysters, and "duck, duck, goose" duck breast, foie gras, and goose ravioli. You can dine late in the loftlike spot, but after 11 pm, the music gets louder and the tables are moved back, as SWK becomes a swanky lounge anew.

American menu. Dinner, late-night. Closed Sun-Mon. Bar. Casual attire. Outdoor seating. **$$**

★ ★ **SZECHWAN EAST.** *340 E Ohio St, Chicago (60611). Phone 312/255-9200; fax 312/642-3907. www. szechwaneast.com.* The refined atmosphere at Szechwan East makes it a fitting resident of the tony Streeterville area. The Chinese restaurant rounds up an appreciative lunch crowd of office workers eager to sample its value-priced lunch buffet. Off-the-menu favorites include hot and sour soup and sesame chicken. Szechwan fare tends to be spicy, but the kitchen will tone it down upon request. Dine after 9 pm on weekends to catch live pop music acts along with your meal. Chinese menu. Dinner, Sun brunch. Closed Thanksgiving. Bar. Valet parking. Outdoor seating. **$$**

★ ★ **TIZI MELLOUL.** *531 N Wells St, Chicago (60610). Phone 312/670-4338; fax 312/670-4254. www.tizimelloul.com.* A hipster version of Morocco is as close as a cab ride to River North's Tizi Melloul. Filtered through a modern design sensibility, Tizi references North Africa in its spice market color palette and circular communal dining room lit by lanterns. Grilled octopus, tabbouleh salad, and coriander-roasted duck complete the culinary tour. Come on a Sunday for cocktail hour belly dancing. Mediterranean menu. Dinner. Closed holidays. Bar. Children's menu. Casual attire. Outdoor seating. **$$**

★ **TOAST.** *2046 N Damen Ave, Chicago (60647). Phone 773/772-5600.* This popular breakfast and lunch spot gives classic favorites a trendy twist: eggs Benedict are served with a decadent white truffle hollandaise, and a mountain of French toast is stuffed with strawberries and mascarpone cheese. Prices are reasonable, and the atmosphere is fun, with vintage toasters decorating the small, colorful dining room. American menu. Breakfast, lunch. Closed holidays. Casual attire. **$**

★ ★ **TOPO GIGIO RISTORANTE.** *1516 N Wells St, Chicago (60610). Phone 312/266-9355.* Old Town favorite Topo Gigio draws diners from near and far for crowd-pleasing Italian dishes in a bustling café setting featuring exposed-brick walls and paper-topped tables. The friendly owner also does the cooking and draws up a slate of daily specials to supplement his menu of salads, pastas, and meats. Table waits can be lengthy. For best results, come in summer—early—and snag a table on the outdoor patio or have a drink

at the outdoor bar. Italian menu. Lunch, dinner. Bar. Casual attire. Outdoor seating. **$$**

★ ★ **TOPOLOBAMPO.** *445 N Clark St, Chicago (60610). Phone 312/661-1434; fax 312/661-1830. www. fronterakitchens.com.* Pioneering chef/owner Rick Bayless is a cookbook author, television personality, and perennial culinary award winner with a devoted following. His celebration of the regional cuisines of Mexico is realized at Topolobampo, the upscale counterpart to his famed Frontera Grill (see)—and the shrine where the faithful gather to revel in the bright, earthy flavors of his fine-dining Mexican fare. The seasonal menu is paired with a tome of premium tequilas and an excellent wine list. White tablecloths and colorful folk art help set the tone for a memorable Mexican meal. Mexican menu. Lunch, dinner. Closed Sun-Mon; holidays. Bar. Children's menu. Casual attire. Valet parking. Outdoor seating. **$$$**

★ ★ **TRATTORIA NO. 10.** *10 N Dearborn St, Chicago (60602). Phone 312/984-1718; fax 312/ 984-1525. www.trattoriaten.com.* A rustic yet elegant respite from the hectic rush of the Loop business district, Trattoria No. 10 welcomes diners with arched ceilings, murals, and ceramic tile floors. House-made ravioli is a specialty, as are pastas, risottos, and fresh seafood selections on the menu of updated Italian classics. A popular lunch and dinner spot for downtown denizens, Trattoria No. 10 is perhaps best known for its bountiful, bargain-priced cocktail hour buffet—a great pre-theater option or a pick-me-up after museums and shopping. Italian menu. Lunch, dinner. Closed Sun; holidays. Bar. Casual attire. Valet parking. **$$**

★ **TRE KRONOR.** *3258 W Foster Ave, Chicago (60625). Phone 773/267-9888; fax 773/478-3058.* Although it's out of the way, Tre Kronor warrants a trip to the North Park neighborhood for its sincere welcome and delicious Scandinavian comfort food. The family-run storefront serves meals all day, from muesli and Danish blue cheese omelets at breakfast to Swedish meatball sandwiches at lunch and roast pork with figs at dinner. The servers are cheerful, as is the folk-art décor. Scandanavian menu. Breakfast, lunch, dinner. Closed holidays. Casual attire. **$$**

★ ★ ★ ★ **TRU.** *676 N St. Clair St, Chicago (60611). Phone 312/202-0001; fax 312/202-0003. www.trurestaurant.com.* Awash in white and set in a chic, lofty space, TRU's modern, airy dining room is a stunning stage for chef and co-owner Rick Tramonto's savory, progressive French creations and co-owner pastry chef Gale Gand's incredible, one-of-a-kind sweet and savory endings. Tramonto offers plates filled with flawless ingredients that are treated to his unmatched creativity and artistic flair. The result is food that is precious and, some say, overdone. Indeed, many of the plates are so beautiful and complicated that you may not want to dig in and ruin the presentation, or you may be unable to decipher the appropriate way to consume the dish. TRU offers three- to eight-course "Collections" (prix fixe menus) and a unique and extraordinary four-course dessert and champagne dessert tasting. Like the savory side of the menu, the desserts have a distinctive sense of ingredient choice, style, and humor. *Secret Inspector's Notes: The details at TRU are adorable, from the small velvet ottomans provided for ladies' purses to the replacement of napkins each time a guest visits the rest room. The service, however, can be spotty and often is snooty, which could turn some guests off.* French menu. Dinner. Closed Sun. Bar. Jacket required. Reservations recommended. Valet parking. **$$$$**

★ **TUCCI BENUCCH.** *900 N Michigan Ave, Chicago (60611). Phone 312/266-2500; fax 312/266-7702. www. leye.com.* This is a spot for weary shoppers in the 900 North Michigan mall (see) to come and relax after they've spent more money than they should have. Tucci Benucch offers reasonably priced (and generously sized) salads, pizzas, and Italian dishes, along with a homey atmosphere. The dining area is modeled after rooms in an Italian country house, with different sections decorated as a sunroom, patio, living room, and barn. Italian menu. Lunch, dinner. Closed Thanksgiving, Dec 25. Bar. Children's menu. Casual attire. **$$**

★ ★ **TUSCANY.** *1014 W Taylor St, Chicago (60612). Phone 312/829-1990; fax 312/829-8023. www.stefanirestaurants.com.* With its cozy dining area, wood-burning ovens, and rustic atmosphere, this upscale Little Italy eatery is reminiscent of an Italian trattoria. The northern Italian menu features homemade pastas and gourmet pizzas, as well as a selection of grilled items like pork, chicken, duck, veal, and steak. And who can forget dessert? Classic Italian sweets like gelato, tiramisu, and cannoli are among the ways to end your meal. Italian menu. Lunch, dinner. Closed Jan 1, Dec 25. Bar. Valet parking. **$$**

★ **TWIN ANCHORS RESTAURANT AND TAVERN.** *1655 N Sedgwick St, Chicago (60614).*

Phone 312/266-1616. www.twinanchorsribs.com. Make no bones about it: Chicago is a meat-and-potatoes kind of town, and there are few things that native Chicagoans like more than a great slab of ribs. Choices abound, but a local favorite is Twin Anchors Restaurant and Tavern in the Old Town neighborhood just north of downtown (and a fairly short cab ride away). Although this former speakeasy was reincarnated as a restaurant in 1932, it maintains its hole-in-the-wall appeal, complete with diner-style booths, linoleum tabletops, a jukebox stocked with an eclectic mix of tunes, and an extensive collection of beers. The real attraction, however, is the ribs; rumor has it that they were Frank Sinatra's favorites. Order them zesty, like a local, and then let the feast begin. The menu may be limited, but the portions are generous. If ribs aren't your style, the hamburgers and filet mignon are also excellent. Be prepared for a long wait, though; this 60-seat restaurant fills up fast. Barbecue menu. Lunch, dinner. Bar. Casual attire. Outdoor seating. **$$**

★ ★ **VIVERE.** *71 W Monroe St, Chicago (60603). Phone 312/332-4040; fax 312/332-2656. www. italianvillage-chicago.com.* The high end of a trio of restaurants that comprises the Loop's long-standing Italian Village, Vivere plays it cool with showy décor and luxurious meals. The warmly lit dining room with decorative scrolls and swirls aims to distract, but the food stands its ground with riffs on the familiar, such as squid ink tortellini stuffed with bass. The Italian wine list rates among the country's best, making this a solid special-occasion choice. Italian menu. Lunch, dinner. Closed Sun; holidays. Bar. Casual attire. Reservations recommended. Valet parking. **$$**

★ ★ **VIVO.** *838 W Randolph St, Chicago (60607). Phone 312/733-3379; fax 312/733-4436. www. vivo-chicago.com.* With the distinction of having pioneered the now-booming Randolph Street restaurant row, Vivo continues to draw a hip crowd for its groovy, contemporary grotto atmosphere (exposed brick, candlelight, and piles of wine bottles) and straightforward Italian fare. The antipasti spread near the entrance is a welcoming, authentic touch. Italian menu. Lunch, dinner. Closed Jan 1, Dec 25. Bar. Casual attire. Valet parking. Outdoor seating. **$$$**

⊙ ★ ★ ★ **VONG'S THAI KITCHEN.** *6 W Hubbard, Chicago (60610). Phone 312/644-8664. www.vongsthaikitchen.com.* This toned-down version of renowned chef Jean-Georges Vongerichten's original, pricier Vong remains a stylish destination for well-crafted Thai-French fusion cuisine. The posh ambience is a bit more casual now, with hip background music—but retains a refined air thanks to rich appointments and polished service. Exotic cocktails enhance the escapist mood; booths in the lounge are a plush place to stop for a sip and a snack. Thai menu. Lunch, dinner. Bar. Children's menu (lunch). Casual attire. Outdoor seating. **$$**

★ ★ **WAVE.** *644 N Lake Shore Dr, Chicago (60611). Phone 312/255-4460. www.whotels.com.* Located in the W hotel across from Lake Michigan, Wave delivers ultra-stylish dining in a chic, modern space. The creative, contemporary seafood menu is laced with exotic spices; "tasting plates" are great for grazing with drinks. The loungy bar also offers elaborate cold seafood concoctions from the "ice bar" paired with high-concept cocktails. Mediterranean menu. Breakfast, lunch, dinner. Bar. Casual attire. Outdoor seating. **$$**

★ ★ ★ **WEST TOWN TAVERN.** *1329 W Chicago Ave, Chicago (60622). Phone 312/666-6175. www. westtowntavern.com.* Beloved Chicago chef Susan Goss and her wine-knowing husband Drew Goss run West Town Tavern, an upscale comfort foodie in a handsome brick-walled storefront that encourages repeats with genuine warmth. If it's on the menu, start with the beer cheese ball, the kind of spreadable Cheddar last seen on New Year's Eve in the late 1960s. Entrées include maple-cured pork chops, steak in zinfandel sauce, and duck confit. Desserts finish charmingly via the classed-up s'mores with homemade marshmallows. West Town's wine selection roams far and wide on the interesting and largely affordable list. American menu. Dinner. Closed Sun. Bar. Casual attire. Outdoor seating. **$$**

★ **WISHBONE.** *1001 W Washington Blvd, Chicago (60607). Phone 312/850-2663; fax 312/850-4332. www.wishbonechicago.com.* Casual Southern dishes at reasonable prices in colorful settings filled with faux-outdoor art comprise the winning combination at Wishbone, which draws throngs to locations in both the West Loop and Lakeview. Lunches and dinners serve up bean-based hoppin' John, blackened catfish, and shrimp and grits. Breakfast offers plenty of unusual choices, such as crab cakes, to round out the egg offerings. Be an early bird at any meal to expect to dine here on a weekend. Southern/Soul menu. Lunch, dinner, brunch. Closed holidays. Children's menu. **$$**

★ ★ **XIPPO.** *3759 N Damen, Chicago (60618). Phone 773/529-9135. www.xippo.com.* Velvet chairs, swagged curtains, exposed-brick walls, and a DJ booth transformed a former North Center corner bar into the lounge eatery Xippo. The menu outclasses the average neighborhood saloon in Chicago, with ambitious dishes like pretzel-crusted pork chops and pan-seared duck breast. On weekends, don't be surprised if the young crowd is more likely to have a cake shot than a slice of cake for dessert. American menu. Dinner. Bar. Casual attire. **$$**

★ ★ ★ **YOSHI'S CAFÉ.** *3257 N Halsted St, Chicago (60657). Phone 773/248-6160.* Namesake chef Yoshi Katsumura comes from a fine-dining background, which accounts for the quality and sophistication of his French-Japanese fusion cuisine. But the long-standing Lakeview café stays dear to its neighbors by keeping the atmosphere relaxed, with good service and even a children's menu—the kind of casual shop that invites repeat dining. Although the menu changes frequently, it maintains the chef's high standards as it meanders from shrimp cappuccino soup all the way to sirloin steak. Eurasian, American menu. Lunch, dinner. Closed Mon. Bar. Casual attire. Outdoor seating. **$$**

★ ★ ★ **ZEALOUS.** *419 W Superior St, Chicago (60610). Phone 312/475-9112; fax 312/475-0165. www.zealousrestaurant.com.* Charlie Trotter protégé Michael Taus runs Zealous with a Trotter-like attention to detail and innovation. Menus change constantly, but you can expect the daring, like veal sweetbread-topped beignets, taro root and mushroom ravioli with sea-urchin sauce, and star-anise braised veal cheeks. Put yourself in the chef's hands with a five- or seven-course degustation menu. This is event dining, amplified by the thoughtful Asian-influenced décor. Bamboo planters, skylit 18-foot ceilings, and a glass-clad wine room make Zealous a fitting resident of the River North gallery district (see). American menu. Lunch, dinner. Closed Sun-Mon; holidays. Bar. Casual attire. Reservations recommended. Outdoor seating. **$$$**

Chicago O'Hare Airport Area

See also Arlington Heights, Chicago, Elmhurst, Itasca, Rosemont, Schaumburg

Information Des Plaines Chamber of Commerce, 1401 Oakton St, 60018; phone 847/824-4200
Web site www.ohare.com/ohare

Known as the world's busiest airport, O'Hare is surrounded by an array of hotels, restaurants, and entertainment facilities—a city unto itself, crossing municipal boundaries.

Airport Information

Information Phone 773/686-2200 or toll-free 800/832-6352
Lost and Found Phone 773/686-2201

Airlines Aer Lingus, AeroMexico, Air Canada, Air France, Air India, Air Jamaica, Alaska Airlines, Alitalia, America West, American Airlines, American Eagle Airlines, Aviacsa, BMI British Midland, British Airways, Continental Airlines, Delta Air Lines, EL AL, Iberia Airlines, Japan Airlines (JAL), KLM Royal Dutch, Korean Air, Kuwait Airways, LOT Polish Airlines, Lufthansa, Mexicana, Northwest Airlines, Pakistan International, Royal Jordanian, Ryan Air, Scandinavian Airlines (SAS), Spirit Airlines, SWISS, TACA Airlines, Turkish Airlines, United Airlines, United Express, US Airways, USA 3000 Airlines

What to See and Do

Cernan Earth and Space Center. *2000 N 5th Ave, River Grove. 4 miles S via River Rd. On the campus of Triton College. Phone 708/583-3100.* Unique domed theater providing "wraparound" multimedia programs on astronomy, geography, and other topics; free exhibits on space exploration; gift shop. Show (Thurs-Sat evenings, matinee Sat; no shows holidays). **$$$**

Donald E. Stevens Convention Center. *5555 N River Rd, Rosemont (60018). Phone 847/692-2220; fax 847/696-9700. www.rosemont.com.*

Limited-Service Hotel

★ ★ **MARRIOTT SUITES CHICAGO O'HARE.** *6155 N River Rd, Rosemont (60018). Phone 847/696-4400; fax 847/696-2122. www.marriott.com.* This hotel was designed with the business traveler in mind—near most major highways for easy access. It also features 3,475 square feet of meeting space. After a long day of meetings, guests can work out at the health club and then relax in the pool, sauna, or whirlpool. 256 rooms, 11 story, all suites. Check-in 2 pm, check-out noon. Restaurant. Fitness room. Indoor pool, whirlpool. Airport transportation available. **$$**

⊠ ⊼ ⊵

Full-Service Hotels

★ ★ ★ **HYATT ROSEMONT.** *6350 N River Rd, Rosemont (60018). Phone 847/518-1234. www.hyatt.com.* 206 rooms, 8 story. Check-in 3 pm, check-out noon. High-speed Internet access. Restaurant. Fitness room. Airport transportation available. **$$**

⊠ ⊼ Ⓓ

★ ★ ★ **SOFITEL.** *5550 N River Rd, Rosemont (60018). Phone 847/678-4488; toll-free 800/233-5959; fax 847/678-9756. www.sofitel.com.* Conveniently located near O'Hare International Airport, this traditional European-style hotel provides free airport shuttle service. The hotel also offers guests such amenities as a swimming pool, fitness center, and three restaurants. 300 rooms, 10 story. Pets accepted; fee. Check-out noon. Restaurants, bar. Fitness room. Indoor pool. Airport transportation available. Business center. **$$**

⊠ ⊼ ⊼ 🐾 ⊵

★ ★ ★ **THE WESTIN O'HARE.** *6100 N River Rd, Rosemont (60018). Phone 847/698-6000; fax 847/698-3993. www.westin.com.* This hotel is conveniently located near O'Hare International Airport and provides free shuttle transportation. Amenities include a fitness center, an indoor swimming pool, and golf courses nearby. 525 rooms, 12 story. Check-in 3 pm, check-out 1 pm. High-speed Internet access. Restaurant, bar. Fitness room. Indoor pool, whirlpool. Business center. **$$**

⊠ ⊼ ⊼ ⊵

Cicero (A-5)

See also Brookfield, Chicago, La Grange, Oak Park

Founded 1867
Population 85,616
Elevation 606 ft
Area Code 708
Zip 60650
Information Chamber of Commerce, 4937 W 25th St, Room 209; phone 708/863-6000

Cicero, named after the Roman orator, is second only to Chicago as a manufacturing center; nearly 200 industrial plants are located here. Many fine ethnic bakeries and restaurants can be found along Cermak Road.

What to See and Do

Hawthorne Race Course. *3501 S Laramie Ave (60804). Phone 708/780-3700; fax 708/780-3677. www. hawthorneracecourse.com.* Thoroughbred racing (Oct-Dec) and harness racing (Jan-Feb) on a 1-mile track. (Daily) **$$**

Collinsville (E-3)

See also Alton, Belleville, Cahokia, Edwardsville

Population 24,707
Elevation 550 ft
Area Code 618
Zip 62234
Information Chamber of Commerce, 221 W Main St, phone 618/344-2884; or the Convention and Tourism Bureau, 1 Gateway Dr, phone 618/345-4999

What to See and Do

Fairmount Park. *9301 Collinsville Rd. 2 miles W on Hwy 40 at jct I-255. Phone 618/345-4300; fax 618/344-8218. www.fairmountpark.com.* Thoroughbred racing (mid-Apr-Oct, Sun-Tues 1 pm, Fri-Sat 7:30 pm). **$**

Special Event

Italian Fest. *Main St, Collinsville (62234). Downtown. Phone 618/345-5598.* Entertainment, food, bocce ball tournament, 10K run. Usually mid-late Sept.

Limited-Service Hotels

★ **BEST WESTERN HERITAGE INN.** *2003 Mall Rd, Collinsville (62234). Phone 618/345-5660; toll-free 800/780-7234; fax 618/345-8135. www.bestwestern.com.* 80 rooms, 2 story. Complimentary continental breakfast. Check-out noon. Fitness room. Indoor pool, whirlpool. **$**

★ ★ **HOLIDAY INN.** *1000 Eastport Plaza Dr, Collinsville (62234). Phone 618/345-2800; toll-free 800/551-5133; fax 618/345-9804. www.holiday-inn.com.* 229 rooms, 5 story. Pets accepted; fee. Complimentary full breakfast. Check-out noon. Restaurant, bar. Fitness room. Indoor pool, whirlpool. Airport transportation available. **$**

Danville (C-5)

See also Champaign/Urbana

Founded 1827
Population 33,904
Elevation 597 ft
Area Code 217
Zip 61832
Information Danville Area Convention and Visitors Bureau, 100 W Main St, Room 146, PO Box 992, 61834; phone 217/442-2096 or toll-free 800/383-4386
Web site www.danvillecvb.com

The site of Danville is mentioned in old French records as Piankeshaw, "center of more Native American trails than any spot within a six-day journey." Named for Dan Beckwith, its first settler, it has been under the flags of France, Great Britain, and the United States and was the scene of a battle between Spanish forces and the Kickapoo. It has approximately 150 industries and is the center of a wide trade area.

What to See and Do

Forest Glen Preserve. *20301 E 900 North Rd, Westville. 10 miles SE. Phone 217/662-2142.* Nature preserve, wildlife refuge. Observation tower overlooks Vermilion River. Picnicking, camping (fee). Pioneer homestead, trails, arboretum. (Daily) **FREE**

Kickapoo State Park. *10906 Kickapoo Park Rd. 4 miles W on I-74, exit 210. Phone 217/442-4915.* Several lakes on 2,843 acres. Fishing, boating (ramp, electric motors), rentals. Hunting, hiking, horseback riding (rentals), picnicking, concession, camping. (Daily) **FREE**

Vermilion County Museum. *116 N Gilbert St. Phone 217/442-2922.* House built in 1855 by William Fithian, physician and statesman; Abraham Lincoln stayed here September 21, 1858; period furnishings, natural history room, art gallery; carriage house, herb garden. (Tues-Sun; closed holidays) **$$**

Special Event

Hoopeston Sweet Corn Festival. *McFerron Park, Hoopeston. 15 miles N. Phone 217/283-7873.* Twenty-nine tons of corn-on-the-cob, tractor pulls, antique auto show, horse show, National Sweetheart Pageant. Labor Day weekend.

Limited-Service Hotel

★ **FAIRFIELD INN.** *389 Lynch Rd, Danville (61834). Phone 217/443-3388; toll-free 800/228-2800; fax 217/443-3388. www.fairfield.com.* 55 rooms, 3 story. Complimentary continental breakfast. Check-out noon. Indoor pool, whirlpool. **$**
🏊

Decatur (C-4)

See also Arcola, Lincoln, Springfield

Founded 1829
Population 81,860
Elevation 670 ft
Area Code 217
Information Decatur Area Convention and Visitors Bureau, 202 E North St, 62523; phone 217/423-7000 or toll-free 800/331-4479
Web site www.decaturcvb.com

In 1830, 21-year-old Abraham Lincoln drove through what would later become Decatur with his family to settle on the Sangamon River, a few miles west. He worked as a farmer and rail-splitter and made his first political speech in what is now Decatur's Lincoln

Square. Today, agri-business, manufacturing, Richland Community College, and Millikin University provide a varied economy.

What to See and Do

Birks Museum. *1184 W Main St. In Gorin Hall on the campus of Millikin University. Phone 217/424-6337.* Decorative arts museum with more than 1,000 pieces of china, crystal, and pottery; some from 15th and 16th centuries. (Sept-June, daily; June-Aug by appointment only) **FREE**

Fairview Park. *Jct Hwy 36, 48. Phone 217/422-5911.* Approximately 180 acres. Swimming pool (fee). Tennis, biking trail, picnicking, playground, baseball diamonds, horseshoe pits. (Daily) For further details on recreational facilities in the city's 1,967 acres of municipal parks, contact the Decatur Park District, 620 E Riverside, 62521. **FREE**

Friends Creek Regional Park. *3939 Nearing Ln. 16 miles NE via I-72, Argenta exit. Phone 217/423-7708.* Nature trails, picnicking, playground, camping (showers, dump station; fee).

Lake Decatur. *2203 E Lake Shore Dr (62521). SE edge of town, on the Sangamon River. Phone 217/424-2837.* Shoreline drive; boating, fishing.

Macon County Historical Society Museum. *5580 N Fork Rd. Phone 217/422-4919.* Exhibit center with displays of local artifacts; 1890s Victorian farmhouse exhibit; also Prairie Village with 1860s schoolhouse, 1850s printing shop, 1880s log cabin, blacksmith shop, 1890s train depot, and Macon County's first court-house, where Lincoln once practiced law. (Tues-Sun afternoons; closed holidays) **DONATION**

Millikin Place. *Entrance adjacent to 125 N Pine St.* This housing development (1909) was laid out and landscaped by Walter Burley Griffin, who designed Australia's capital, Canberra, in an international competition. The street features a Prairie school entrance, naturalized landscaping, and houses by Marion Mahony, Griffin's wife, and Frank Lloyd Wright, for whom both Griffin and Mahony worked at the famous Oak Park Studio. Numbers 1 and 3 Millikin Place are by Mahony; 2 Millikin Place is attributed to Wright. (Houses private)

Rock Springs Center for Environmental Discovery. *3939 Nearing Ln. S on Hwy 48, W 2 miles on Rock Spring Rd. Phone 217/423-7708.* Approximately 1,320 acres with hiking and self-guided interpretive trails; picnic area, shelter, asphalt bike trail. Ecocenter hands-on educational exhibits. Visitor center holds scheduled events and programs throughout year. (Daily; closed Easter, Thanksgiving, Dec 25) **DONATION**

Scovill Family Park Complex. *Country Club and Lost Bridge rds. E shore of Lake Decatur, S of Hwy 36, on S Country Club Rd. Phone 217/422-5911.* Complex includes

Children's Museum. *55 S Country Club Dr, Decatur. Phone 217/423-5437.* Features hands-on exhibits of arts, science, and technology. (Tues-Sat, Sun afternoons; closed holidays) **$$**

Hieronymus Mueller Museum. *61 S Country Club Rd, Decatur. Phone 217/423-6161.* Exhibits include inventions of "Decatur's unsung genius," whose work revolutionized everyday lives. (Apr-Sept, Thurs-Sun afternoons; rest of year, Fri-Sun afternoons) **$**

Oriental Garden. *620 E Riverside Ave, Decatur. Phone 217/422-5911.* Greenery, rocks, sand, and water ornamented with sculpture. Chinese Fu dog guards entrance. (Daily) **FREE**

Scovill Park and Zoo. *71 S Country Club Rd, Decatur. Phone 217/421-7435.* Zoo has more than 500 animals. ZO & O Express train takes visitors around zoo. Picnicking, playground. (Apr-Oct, daily) **$**

Limited-Service Hotels

★ **BAYMONT INN.** *5100 Hickory Point Frontage Rd, Decatur (62526). Phone 217/875-5800; fax 217/875-7537. www.baymontinns.com.* 102 rooms, 2 story. Pets accepted, some restrictions; fee. Complimentary continental breakfast. Check-out noon. **$**

★ ★ **HOLIDAY INN.** *4191 Hwy 36 and Wyckles Rd, Decatur (62522). Phone 217/422-8800; toll-free 800/465-4329; fax 217/422-9690. www. holiday-inn.com.* 370 rooms, 4 story. Check-out noon. Restaurant, bar. Fitness room. Indoor pool, children's pool, whirlpool. Tennis. Airport transportation available. Business center. **$**

✈ 🏃 👤 🌊 🏊

DeKalb (A-4)

See also Aurora, Geneva, Oregon, Rockford, St. Charles

Population 39,018
Elevation 880 ft
Area Code 815
Zip 60115
Information Nehring Cultural and Tourism Center, 164 E Lincoln Hwy; phone 815/756-6306
Web site www.dekalb.org

What to See and Do

Ellwood House Museum. *509 N 1st St. Entrance at rear, off Augusta Ave. Phone 815/756-4609.* Victorian mansion built by Isaac Ellwood, early manufacturer of barbed wire; restored interiors 1880-1915; horse-drawn vehicles, barbed wire, and farm implements; 1890s playhouse; extensive grounds and gardens. Visitor center with historical gallery and special exhibits. Guided tours. (Mar-early Dec, Tues-Sun afternoons; closed holidays) **$$**

Northern Illinois University. *W Lincoln Hwy (Rte 38). Phone 815/753-0446. www.niu.edu.* (1895) (22,000 students) Anthropology museum in Stevens Building has Native American and Southeast Asian displays (free). Art galleries in several locations; displays change frequently. One-hour guided tour of campus leaves Office of Admissions, Williston Hall, once a day (Mon-Sat; no tours holidays). Also self-guided walking tour booklets.

Special Events

Corn Fest. *DeKalb downtown business district. Phone 815/748-2676.* Three-day street festival. Last full weekend in Aug.

Stage Coach Theater. *DeKalb. 2 miles N, then 1/2 mile E on Barber Greene Rd. Phone 815/758-1940.* Summer community theater. Reservations suggested. Mid-June-mid-Sept.

Limited-Service Hotel

★ **HOWARD JOHNSON.** *1321 W Lincoln Hwy, DeKalb (60115). Phone 815/756-1451; fax 815/756-7260. www.hojo.com.* 60 rooms, 2 story. Complimentary continental breakfast. Check-out noon. **$**

Restaurant

★ ★ **THE HILLSIDE RESTAURANT.** *121 N 2nd St, DeKalb (60115). Phone 815/756-4749. www.hillsiderestaurant.com.* The oldest restaurant in DeKalb, The Hillside Restaurant has hosted politicians and traveling celebrities since 1955. American menu. Lunch, dinner. Closed Tues. **$**

Dixon (A-3)

See also Oregon

Settled 1830
Population 15,941
Elevation 659 ft
Area Code 815
Zip 61021
Information Dixon Area Chamber of Commerce, 101 W Second St; phone 815/284-3361
Web site www.dixonil.com

At the southernmost point of the Black Hawk Trail, Dixon sits on the banks of the Rock River. Established as a trading post and tavern by John Dixon, it now is a center for light industry. The 40th president of the United States, Ronald Reagan, was born in nearby Tampico and grew up in Dixon.

What to See and Do

John Deere Historic Site. *8393 S Main, Grand Detour. 6 miles NE on Hwy 2. Phone 815/652-4551.* Site where the first self-scouring steel plow was made in 1837; reconstructed blacksmith shop (demonstrations Wed-Sun); restored house and gardens; 2-acre natural prairie. (Apr-Oct, daily) **$$**

Lincoln Statue Park. *100 Lincoln Statue Dr. Along the N bank of river between Galena and Peoria aves. Phone 815/288-3404.* Park includes the site of Fort Dixon, around which the town was built, and a statue of Lincoln as a young captain in the Black Hawk War of 1832. A plaque summarizes Lincoln's military career; at the statue's base is a bas-relief of John Dixon. **FREE** Also in the park is

   Old Settlers' Memorial Log Cabin. *113 Madison Ave, Dixon. Phone 815/284-1134.* Built in 1894 and dedicated to the area's early settlers; period furnishings. (Memorial Day-Labor Day, Sat-Sun; rest of year, by appointment) **FREE**

Ronald Reagan's boyhood home. *816 S Hennepin. Phone 815/288-3404.* Two-story, three-bedroom house with 1920s furnishings; memorabilia connected with the former president's childhood and acting and political careers. Visitor center adjacent. (Mar-Nov, daily; rest of year, Sat-Sun) **FREE**

Special Event

Petunia Festival. *Downtown Dixon (61021). Phone 815/284-3361.* Carnival, parade, arts and crafts, bicycle race, tennis tournament, festival garden, fireworks. July 4 week.

Limited-Service Hotel

★ ★ **BEST WESTERN REAGAN HOTEL.** *443 Rte 2, Dixon (61021). Phone 815/284-1890; toll-free 800/780-7234; fax 815/284-1174. www.bestwestern.com.* 91 rooms, 2 story. Pets accepted; fee. Complimentary continental breakfast (Mon-Fri). Check-out noon. Restaurant, bar. Fitness room. Outdoor pool, whirlpool. **$**

Downers Grove

See also Hinsdale, Naperville, Oak Brook

Settled 1832
Population 48,724
Elevation 725 ft
Area Code 630
Zip 60515, 60516
Information Visitors Bureau, 5202 Washington St, Suite 2; phone toll-free 800/934-0615
Web site www.vil.downers-grove.il.us

What to See and Do

Historical Museum. *831 Maple Ave (60515). Phone 630/963-1309.* Victorian house (1892) contains eight rooms of period furnishings, antiques, and artifacts; changing exhibits. (Sun-Fri 1-3 pm) **FREE**

Morton Arboretum. *4100 Rte 53, Lisle (60532). Just W of I-355 and N of I-88. Phone 630/968-0074. www.mortonarb.org.* If you need a break from the urban Chicago experience, head out to the Morton Arboretum, located just 25 miles west of the city in Lisle. Founded in 1923 by Joy Morton, scion of the Morton salt family (whose father was Secretary of

Agriculture under Cleveland and founder of Arbor Day), this 1,700-acre facility is renowned for its lush collection of trees and plants from around the world. The extensive pathways make this a prime hiking spot; visitors are free to wander on their own or participate in guided walks, tours, or special events. Calling itself an "outdoor classroom," the arboretum has a reputation as a leader in research and education and attracts those interested in learning more about the environment, gardening, science, and ecosystems around the world. Open 365 days a year, the arboretum offers Chicagoans and visitors to the area a peaceful retreat no matter what the season. (Daily) **$$**

Full-Service Hotel

★ ★ **DOUBLETREE GUEST SUITES AND CONFERENCE CENTER.** *2111 Butterfield Rd, Downers Grove (60515). Phone 630/971-2000; toll-free 800/222-8733; fax 630/971-1021. www. doubletreedownersgrove.com.* Whether guests are traveling on business or leisure, this hotel offers a wide range of activities and dining choices. Work out in the Esplanade Fitness Center, which includes a fitness room, basketball court, racquetball court, and indoor lap pool. Afterwards, relax in the Jacuzzi and sauna. 247 rooms, 7 story, all suites. Pets accepted, some restrictions. Check-in 3 pm, check-out noon. High-speed Internet access. Restaurant, bar. Fitness room, fitness classes available. Indoor pool, whirlpool. Business center. **$**

Du Quoin (E-3)

See also Benton, Carbondale, Marion, Mount Vernon

Population 6,448
Elevation 468 ft
Area Code 618
Zip 62832

Du Quoin, in the fertile agricultural and mining region southeast of St. Louis, Missouri, is a shipping point for coal, grain, livestock, and fruit.

Special Event

Du Quoin State Fair. *655 Executive Dr, Du Quoin. Phone 618/542-1515.* Farm, house, art, and livestock shows; concerts; auto, harness racing; demolition derby, tractor pulls; World Trotting Derby.

Restaurant

★ ★ **TO PERFECTION.** *1664 S Washington, Du Quoin (62832). Phone 618/542-2002.* Seafood, steak menu. Lunch, dinner. Closed Sun. Bar. **$$**

Dundee

See also Elgin

Settled 1835
Population 3,550
Elevation 750 ft
Area Code 847
Zip 60118

Two Potawatomi villages were nearby when settlers first arrived in 1835. A Scotsman won a lottery and was permitted to name the settlement after his hometown in Scotland, Dundee.

What to See and Do

Haeger Factory Outlet. *7 Maiden Ln. Van Buren St, 2 blocks S of Rte 72. Phone 847/783-5420.* Ceramic museum. Pottery, artware factory outlet store (Mon, Thurs-Sun; closed holidays). **FREE**

Racing Rapids Action Park. *880 E Main St. Rtes 25, 72. Phone 847/426-5525.* Features water slides, tube slide, go-carts, bumper boats, lazy river, and children's pool area. (June-Aug, daily; also Labor Day weekend) Free parking. **$$$$**

Santa's Village Theme Park. *601 Dundee Ave. At jct Rtes 25, 72. Phone 847/426-6751; fax 847/426-8163. www.santasvillageil.com.* More than 30 rides; live shows, petting zoo. Picnic areas. Polar Dome Ice Arena for skating (late Sept-Mar, Sat-Sun; also holidays). (June-Aug, daily; Mother's Day-Memorial Day, Sept, weekends only) Free parking. **$$$$**

Specialty Lodging

The following lodging establishment is approved by Mobil Travel Guide but, due to its unique and individualized nature has not been given a traditional Mobil Star rating. Included in this listing you may find bed-and-breakfasts, limited-service inns, guest ranches, and other unique hotel properties.

VICTORIAN ROSE GARDEN BED & BREAKFAST. *314 Washington St, Algonquin (60102). Phone 847/854-9667; toll-free 888/854-9667; fax 847/854-3236. www.sleepandeat.com.* Built in 1886. 4 rooms, 2 story. Children over 8 years only. Complimentary full breakfast. Check-in 4 pm, check-out 11 am. High-speed Internet access. **$**

Restaurants

★ **CHA CHA CHA.** *16 E Main St (Rte 72), Dundee (60118). Phone 847/428-4774; fax 847/428-4784. www. chachachamexicanrestaurant.com.* Mexican menu. Lunch, dinner. Closed Thanksgiving, Dec 25. Bar. **$$**

★ ★ **DURAN'S BY BRIAN.** *8 S River St, East Dundee (60118). Phone 847/428-0033; fax 847/428-0065.* Dining in a restored house. Lunch, dinner. Closed Mon; holidays. Children's menu. **$$**

★ ★ **MILK PAIL.** *14N630 Rte 25 (Milk Pail Village), Dundee (60118). Phone 847/742-5040. www.themilkpail .com.* American menu. Lunch, dinner, Sun brunch. Closed Dec 25. Bar. Children's menu. Seasonal theatre productions. **$$**

★ ★ **PORT EDWARD.** *20 W Algonquin Rd, Algonquin (60102). Phone 847/658-5441; fax 847/658-5690. www.portedward.com.* Seafood menu. Lunch, dinner, Sun brunch. Closed July 4, Thanksgiving, Dec 25. Bar. Children's menu. **$$**

East Dubuque

Restaurant

★ ★ **BITTERSWEET ON THE BLUFF.** *7010 Donna's Dr, East Dubuque (61025). Phone 815/747-2360. www.bittersweetonthebluff.com.* Family-owned and -operated business, overlooking the Mississippi River, with 20-year history. American menu. Dinner. **$$**

Edwardsville (D-3)

See also Alton, Belleville, Cahokia, Centralia, Collinsville

Population 21,491
Elevation 552 ft
Area Code 618
Zip 62025
Information Edwardsville/Glen Carbon Chamber of Commerce, 200 University Park Dr, Suite 260; phone 618/656-7600
Web site www.ci.edwardsville.il.us

What to See and Do

Madison County Historical Museum. *715 N Main St. Phone 618/656-7562.* Ten-room house (1836) contains period rooms, history and genealogy reference library, pioneer and Native American artifacts; seasonal exhibits. (Wed-Fri, Sun; closed holidays) **FREE**

Southern Illinois University Edwardsville. *6 Hairpin Dr (62026). Phone 618/650-2000. www.siue.edu.* (1957) (11,800 students) Louis Sullivan Architectural Ornament collection on second floor of Lovejoy Library (daily). Campus tours (Mon-Fri by appointment).

Limited-Service Hotel

★ **COMFORT INN.** *3080 S SR 157, Edwardsville (62025). Phone 618/656-4900; toll-free 800/228-5150; fax 618/656-0998. www.comfortinn.com.* 68 rooms, 3 story. Complimentary continental breakfast. Check-out noon. Fitness room. **$**
🕊

Restaurant

★ ★ **RUSTY'S.** *1201 N Main St, Edwardsville (62025). Phone 618/656-1113; fax 618/656-3051.* Former trading post built in 1819. Italian, American menu. Lunch, dinner, Sun brunch. Closed holidays. Bar. Children's menu. **$$**

Effingham (D-4)

See also Altamont, Mattoon

Settled 1853
Population 12,384
Elevation 592 ft
Area Code 217
Zip 62401
Information Convention and Visitors Bureau, 201 E Jefferson Ave, PO Box 648; phone 217/342-5305 or toll-free 800/772-0750
Web site www.effinghamil.com

This town is a regional center and the seat of Effingham County. Industry includes housing and furniture components, graphic arts, and refrigeration. Outdoor recreation is popular here, with Lake Sara offering fishing, boating, and golfing opportunities.

Limited-Service Hotels

★ ★ **BEST WESTERN RAINTREE INN.**
1809 W Fayette Ave, Effingham (62401). Phone 217/342-4121; fax 217/342-4121. www.bestwestern.com. 65 rooms, 2 story. Pets accepted, some restrictions. Complimentary continental breakfast. Check-out 11 am. Restaurant, bar. Pool. **$**

★ **COMFORT INN.** *1310 W Fayette Rd, Effingham (62401). Phone 217/342-3151; toll-free 800/228-5150; fax 217/342-3555. www.comfortsuites.com.* 65 rooms, 3 story. Pets accepted, some restrictions. Complimentary continental breakfast. Check-out 11 am. Restaurant. Indoor pool. **$**

★ **HOLIDAY INN EXPRESS.** *1103 Avenue of Mid-America, Effingham (62401). Phone 217/540-1111; toll-free 888/232-2525; fax 217/347-7341. www.holiday-inn.com.* 122 rooms, 4 story. Complimentary continental breakfast. Check-out noon. Indoor pool. **$**

Restaurant

★ **NIEMERG'S STEAK HOUSE.** *1410 W Fayette Ave, Effingham (62401). Phone 217/342-3921; fax 217/342-4210.* American menu. Breakfast, lunch, dinner. Closed Dec 25. Bar. Children's menu. **$$**

Elgin (A-4)

See also Dundee, St. Charles, Union

Founded 1835
Population 94,487
Elevation 752 ft
Area Code 847
Information Elgin Area Convention and Visitors Bureau, 77 Riverside Dr, 60120; phone 847/695-7540 or toll-free 800/217-5362
Web site www.enjoyelgin.com

It was here that the famous Elgin watch was produced. It also was here that the process of packing milk for long transport, or "condensing" it, was invented right after the Civil War by a young man named Gail Borden. Located in the heart of the Fox River Valley, Elgin has many interesting turn-of-the-century houses. The scenic Fox River divides the town and is used primarily for canoeing, fishing, and cycling along the Fox River Bicycle Trail.

What to See and Do

Blackhawk Forest Preserve. *35W003 Rte 31, South Elgin. S on Rte 31, at the Fox River. Phone 847/741-7883.* On 186 acres. Historic burial mound. Fishing, boating (ramp), canoeing; hiking, bicycle, and bridle trails; picnicking (shelter). **FREE**

Burnidge. *38W235 Big Timber Rd. Coombs Rd. Phone 847/695-8410 (camping reservations).* On 484 acres. Hiking, cross-country skiing, picnicking.

Elgin Area Historical Society Museum. *360 Park St. Between College St and Academy Pl. Phone 847/742-4248. www.elginhistory.org.* In Old Main, a mid-19th-century school building once known as Elgin Academy; contains artifacts of area history. (Mar-Jan, Wed-Sat) **$**

Fox River Trolley Museum. *365 S LaFox St, South Elgin (60177). S on Rte 31. Phone 847/697-4676.* Historic and antique railway equipment displays; oldest interurban railcar in America. Optional 3-mile ride along the scenic Fox River on interurban railcars and trolleys of the early 1900s. (See SPECIAL EVENTS) (July-Aug, Sat-Sun; mid-May-June, Sept-Oct, Sun; also Memorial Day, July 4, Labor Day) **$$**

Grand Victoria **Casino Elgin.** *250 S Grove Ave (60120).* *Phone 847/888-1000; toll-free 888/508-1900. www. grandvictoria-elgin.com.* Located on the Fox River 41 miles northwest of Chicago, this paddlewheeler gaming boat can hold up to 1,200 passengers and hosts as many as 11,000 visitors daily. Games include 1,000 slot and video machines and 45 gaming tables for blackjack, roulette, craps, Caribbean stud poker, and baccarat. The connecting pavilion offers a number of restaurants, a sports bar, and a three-screen cinema with four shows daily. Note that the gambling age in Illinois is 21. (Daily) **FREE**

Lords Park. *325 Hiawatha Dr. Phone 847/931-6120.* On 120 acres; includes zoo, tennis courts, pool, lagoons, playgrounds, and picnic areas. Also here is

Elgin Public Museum. *225 Grand Blvd, Elgin. Phone 847/741-6655.* Displays include stuffed birds, fish, animals; local and regional history, anthropology, and natural history; discovery room. (Apr-Oct, daily; rest of year, Sat-Mon) **$**

Tyler Creek. *401 Davis Rd. Rte 31. Phone 847/741-5082.* On 50 acres. Hiking trails, picnicking.

Villa Olivia. *Rte 20 and Naperville Rd, Bartlett (60103). Phone 630/289-1000. www.villaolivia.com.* Twelve runs; 40 percent beginner, 40 percent intermediate, 10 percent advanced, 10 percent expert. Longest run 1/4 mile; vertical drop 180 feet. Quad chair lift, six rope tows; school, rentals, snowmaking; restaurant. Night skiing, snowboarding, cross-country skiing, snow tubing. (Mon-Thurs 1-10 pm, Fri-Sat 9 am-11 pm, Sun 9 am-10 pm) **$$$$**

Voyageurs Landing. *50 Airport Rd. Frontage Rd via Rte 31. Phone 847/741-0106.* On 16 acres. Boat ramp; picnic shelter.

Special Events

Elgin Symphony Orchestra. *20 DuPage Court, Elgin (60120). Phone 847/888-4000. www.elginsymphony.org.* Classical and pop concerts. Oct-May.

Historic Cemetery Walk. *40 Hill Ave, Elgin. Phone 847/742-4248.* Historical society conducts tours of Bluff City Cemetery. Actors in period costumes stand at gravesites and tell stories of past lives. Late Sept.

Touching on Traditions. *Lords Park pavilion, 225 Grand Blvd, Elgin (60120). Phone 847/741-6655.* Display honors over 50 countries whose people who have made their homes in Elgin. Costumes, decorations, objects of traditional importance. Sat after Thanksgiving-first Sat in Jan.

Trolley Fest. *Fox River Trolley Museum, Rte 31, South Elgin. Phone 847/697-4676.* Features once-a-year operation of historic and antique rail equipment; also model trolley displays. Aug.

Elmhurst

See also Chicago, Chicago O'Hare Airport Area, Itasca, La Grange, Oak Brook

Settled 1843
Population 42,762
Elevation 680 ft
Area Code 630
Zip 60126
Information Chamber of Commerce and Industry, 113 Adell Pl; phone 630/834-6060
Web site www.elmhurst.org

What to See and Do

Elmhurst Historical Museum. *120 E Park Ave. Phone 630/833-1457.* Housed in a 1892 building; changing exhibits on suburbanization and local history. Research and genealogy collections. Self-guided architectural walking tours. (Tues-Sun afternoons; also by appointment; closed holidays) **FREE**

Lizzadro Museum of Lapidary Art. *Wilder Park, 220 Cottage Hill Ave. Phone 630/833-1616. www. lizzadromuseum.org.* Large collection of jade and other hard-stone carvings, including displays of minerals, animal dioramas, fossils, and gemstones. (Tues-Sat, Sun afternoons; closed holidays) **$$**

Restaurant

★ **LAS BELLAS ARTES.** *112 W Park Ave, Elmhurst (60126). Phone 630/530-7725; fax 630/530-7753. www.lasbellasartes.com.* Mexican menu. Dinner, Sun brunch. Closed Mon; holidays; also two weeks in summer. Bar. **$$$**

Evanston (A-5)

See also Chicago, Skokie, Wilmette

Settled 1853
Population 74,239
Elevation 600 ft
Area Code 847
Information Convention and Visitors Bureau, One Rotary Center, 1560 Sherman Ave, Suite 860, 60201; phone 847/328-1500
Web site www.cityofevanston.org

Evanston sits immediately north of Chicago, occupying an enviable expanse of land along Lake Michigan. The city hosts the Fountain Square Art Festival early each summer, a well-attended gathering of artists who line up on the downtown streets to market their works, ranging from paintings and photographs to jewelry and hand blown glass. The home to Northwestern University, Evanston boasts a multitude of art galleries, theaters, shops, and restaurants. The community is serviced by the Purple Line of Chicago's famed "L" mass-transit system.

What to See and Do

Charles Gates Dawes House. *225 Greenwood St (60201). Off Sheridan Rd. Phone 847/475-3410. www. evanstonhistoricalsociety.org.* (1895) The 28-room house of General Charles G. Dawes, Nobel Peace Prize winner (1926) and vice president under Calvin Coolidge. National landmark with original furnishings and artifacts in restored rooms; local history exhibits; large research collection. Gift shop. Tours. (Tues-Sat afternoons; closed holidays) **$**

Frances E. Willard Home/National Woman's Christian Temperance Union (WCTU). *1730 Chicago Ave (60201). Phone 847/328-7500.* House where Frances E. Willard, founder of the worldwide WCTU, lived with her family; authentically preserved house contains many souvenirs of her career. Administration building on grounds houses Willard Memorial Alcohol Research Library. (Mon-Fri by appointment; closed holidays; also one week in July-Aug) **DONATION**

Gross Point Lighthouse. *Sheridan Rd and Central St (60201). Phone 847/328-6961.* (1873) Constructed after a Lake Michigan wreck near Evanston cost 300

lives. Guided tours of keeper's quarters, museum, and tower are available 2-4 pm on a first-come, first-served basis (June-Sept, Sat-Sun; closed holiday weekends). Call for details. No children under age 8 permitted. **$**

Ladd Arboretum. *2024 McCormick Blvd (60201). Between Golf and Green Bay rds. Phone 847/ 864-5181. www.laddarboretum.org.* Jogging and biking trails; canoeing, fishing; bird-watching; camping. International Friendship Garden. (Daily) **FREE**
Also here is

Evanston Ecology Center. *2024 McCormick Blvd, Evanston. Phone 847/864-5181.* Home of Evanston Environmental Association. Nature education and activities. Environmental educational programs; greenhouse; library. (Mon-Sat) **FREE**

Merrick Rose Garden. *Lake and Oak sts (60203).* Seasonal displays; All-American Test Garden; 1,200 rose bushes, 65 varieties. **FREE**

Mitchell Museum of the American Indian. *2600 Central Park (60201). At Kendall College. Phone 847/475-1030. www.mitchellmuseum.org.* Collection of more than 3,000 items of Native American art and artifacts; baskets, pottery, jewelry, Navajo rugs, beadwork, clothing, weapons, tools, stoneware. (Tues-Fri 10 am-5 pm, Sat until 8 pm; Sun noon-4 pm; closed holidays) **$**

Northwestern University. *633 Clark St (60208). Clark St at Sheridan Rd. Phone 847/491-3741. www. northwestern.edu.* (Founded in 1851, opened in 1855) (11,700 students) Undergraduate and graduate schools in Evanston, professional schools in Chicago; John Evans Center, 1800 Sheridan Road, has information (Mon-Fri). Dearborn Observatory (1888), 2131 Sheridan Road, has free public viewings (Fri, two viewings; by reservation only, phone 847/491-7650). Other places of interest are the Shakespeare Garden, University Library, Norris University Center, Alice Millar Religious Center, Theatre and Interpretation Center, Mary and Leigh Block Museum of Art (Tues-Sun), Pick-Staiger Concert Hall (many free performances), Ryan Field (football), and Welsh-Ryan Arena (basketball). Guided walking tours of the lakefront campus leave 1801 Hinman Avenue (academic year, one departure Mon-Sat; July-Aug, two departures Mon-Fri; reservations, phone 847/491-7271).

Special Event

Custer's Last Stand Festival of Arts. *600 Main St, Evanston (60201). Jct of Main St and Chicago Ave. Phone 847/328-2204.* Festival featuring over 400 artists and crafters. Weekend in mid-June.

Limited-Service Hotel

★ ★ **HOTEL ORRINGTON.** *1710 Orrington Ave, Evanston (60201). Phone 847/866-8700; fax 847/866-8724. www.hotelorrington.com.* Located across from Northwestern University (see), this elegant nine-story hotel features such amenities as an on-site fitness center and access to the Evanston Athletic Club and Henry Crown Sports Pavilion/Norris Aquatics Center. 280 rooms, 9 story. Pets accepted, some restriction; fee. Check-in 3 pm, check-out noon. Restaurant, bar. Fitness room. Business center. **$**

Restaurants

★ ★ ★ **CAMPAGNOLA.** *815 Chicago Ave, Evanston (60202). Phone 847/475-6100.* Evanston proves that sophisticated dining does venture outside Chicago's city limits, and Campagnola is a fine example of this trend. Chef/owner Michael Altenberg's rustic but elegant menu features many seasonal organic ingredients. A knowledgeable waitstaff serves diners in two dining areas: a formal dining room upstairs and a more casual (and less pricey) trattoria downstairs. Italian menu. Dinner. Closed Mon; holidays. Reservations recommended. Valet parking. **$$$**

★ **CARMEN'S.** *1012 Church St, Evanston (60201). Phone 847/328-0031.* In a college town, you can't go wrong opening a pizza restaurant. Carmen's, a long-standing Evanston hit, assured its success by offering a range of pizzas, including classic stuffed versions, deep-dish pies, and more daring renditions such as pesto pizza. Extending its appeal to families and business folk in addition to campus types, Carmen's keeps shop in a modest but cozy, two-story den warmed by wood beams and a fireplace. Salads and substantial pastas round out the offerings. Dinner. Closed holidays. Bar. **$**

★ ★ **THE DINING ROOM AT KENDALL COLLEGE.** *2408 Orrington Ave, Evanston (60201). Phone 847/866-1399. www.kendall.edu.* Students at Evanston's Kendall College, which emphasizes culinary arts and hotel management, staff both the front and back of the house in the campus' intimate Dining Room. Menus change frequently, but the cooking remains remarkably accomplished in dishes like ostrich filet with dried cherry risotto, braised lamb shank with rapini, and lobster risotto. Spy the kitchen staff at work from behind plate-glass windows while you dine. Expect amiable but not polished service; those who work the floor are in training at the stoves too. The price is right, with most entrées under $20. Dinner. Closed Sun; holidays. Reservations recommended. **$$**

★ **JILLY'S CAFE.** *2614 Green Bay Rd, Evanston (60201). Phone 847/869-7636. www.jillyscafe.com.* Romance is on the menu at this small café. Rising above its storefront confines, Jilly's manages to affect a French country inn where bonhomie reigns among close-set tables. The kitchen produces classic but substantial meals, with raves for escargot, roast pork tenderloin, and seared veal medallions. Service is accomplished, courses paced. Try the prix fixe Sunday brunch for a leisurely indulgence. French menu. Dinner, Sun brunch. Closed Mon; holidays. **$$$**

★ **LAS PALMAS.** *817 University Pl, Evanston (60201). Phone 847/328-2555.* The Evanston outpost of Las Palmas—there are several others in and around Chicago—proffers authentic and familiar Mexican fare at moderate, crowd-pleasing prices. More traditional dishes, including grilled shrimp, skirt steak tacos (tacos al carbon), chiles rellenos, and mole enchiladas, are supplemented by the popular fajitas. Rustic wooden tables under beamed ceilings provide fiesta-ready and family-friendly seating. Mexican menu. Lunch, dinner. Closed Thanksgiving, Dec 25. Bar. **$$**

★ **LUCKY PLATTER.** *514 Main St, Evanston (60202). Phone 847/869-4064.* Lucky Platter's kitschy flea-market décor—you can't miss the paint-by-numbers artwork on the walls, retro lamps, and mounted deer head—creates a lighthearted atmosphere for border-busting fare. The menu ranges from all-American pot roast to Jamaican jerk chicken, with forays into India and Thailand. At peak meal times (read: weekends), you may be lucky to get a table at the popular Platter, so plan accordingly. Service is often amateurish but usually well-meaning. Continental menu. Breakfast, lunch, dinner. **$$**

★ **MERLE'S #1 BARBECUE.** *1727 Benson St, Evanston (60201). Phone 847/475-7766.* Merle's takes a Southern tour through St. Louis, Memphis, and Texas, serving up slow-cooked barbecue in down-home digs. The regional menu offers both wet (with sauce) and dry-spice-rubbed ribs, pulled beef sandwiches, and sides, including Texas fries, baked beans, and North Carolina red rice. With a crowd in tow, try the generous "barnyard" sampler platter. Country music memorabilia and Elvis photos contribute to the roadhouse aura. Barbecue menu. Dinner. Closed Thanksgiving, Dec 25. Bar. Children's menu. **$$**

★ ★ **NEW JAPAN.** *1322 Chicago Ave, Evanston (60201). Phone 847/475-5980.* Both sushi lovers and sushi snubbers find common ground in New Japan, a neighborhood favorite with a large following of regulars. Aficionados tout its reasonable prices and high quality in both its raw fish selections as well as its often-French-accented cooked dishes, including steak teriyaki, stir-fried vegetables, curry rice, and whole salmon. Genuine warmth distinguishes the staffers here. Japanese, French menu. Lunch, dinner. Closed Mon; holidays. **$$**

★ ★ **OCEANIQUE.** *505 Main St, Evanston (60202). Phone 847/864-3435. www.oceanique.com.* As the name suggests, this softly lit restaurant serves mainly seafood, all intelligently prepared, including a stellar bouillabaisse of squid, salmon, and shrimp in a saffron-scented broth. The room, relaxed and social, is filled with residents and academics of the Northwestern University (see) town. In a historic building (1929). French, American menu. Dinner. Closed Sun; holidays. **$$$**

★ ★ **PETE MILLER'S STEAKHOUSE.** *1557 Sherman Ave, Evanston (60201). Phone 847/328-0399.* Evanstonians acclaim the longstanding Pete Miller's for both excellent food and 1940s-vintage décor. Dim lighting, wood and brass accents, and old black-and-white street photography conjure another era. Bask in it over steakhouse classics such as bone-in ribeye, double baked potatoes, lobster tail, and, to finish, bananas Foster. Superior hamburgers satisfy simpler tastes. Stick around after 8:30 pm, when the live jazz band strikes up. Steak menu. Lunch, dinner. Closed July 4, Thanksgiving, Dec 25. Bar. Valet parking. Separate billiard room. **$$**

★ **PRAIRIE MOON.** *1502 Sherman Ave, Evanston (60201). Phone 847/864-8328; fax 847/864-3302. www. prairiemoonrestaurant.com.* This uncluttered, modern dining room in central Evanston (conveniently located across from a parking garage) celebrates American diversity. Regional festival posters adorn the walls, and a different festival is featured each month, with food and drink specials from the region to match. The menu, which offers both small and big plates, is stocked with regional specialties like Cheapeake blue crab cakes, Colorado brook trout, and Texas sheet cake. American menu. Lunch, dinner, late-night, Sun brunch. Closed Thanksgiving, Dec 25. Bar. Children's menu. Casual attire. Outdoor seating. **$$**

★ ★ ★ ★ **TRIO.** *1625 Hinman Ave, Evanston (60201). Phone 847/733-8746; fax 847/733-8748. www. trio-restaurant.com.* Located in a quiet little inn just north of Chicago in the suburb of Evanston, Trio offers guests the opportunity to dine on a unique menu of progressive American fare. The kitchen honors fresh, seasonal ingredients with sauces, vinaigrettes, and purees that support and accent each ingredient's texture and flavor. Hearty meat dishes are packed with bold flavors, while simpler plates of shimmering seafood shine as well. The kitchen works hard at being responsibly creative—you'll taste a dish and be struck with wonder and delight rather than fear. The four- and eight-course tasting menus are both excellent options for experiencing Trio's innovative repertoire. The dining room strikes a perfect balance of rustic charm and urban style with a brick fireplace, warm weathered walls, and finely appointed tabletops, making it a perfect spot for dinner with friends, family, or your significant other. Avant-garde American menu with French and Asian influences. Dinner. Closed Mon-Tues; holidays. Reservations recommended. **$$$$**

★ ★ **VA PENSIERO.** *1566 Oak Ave, Evanston (60201). Phone 847/475-7779; fax 847/475-7825.* One of best Italian restaurants on the North Shore, Va Pensiero warrants special-occasion dining. The airy room posted by Roman columns creates an elegant setting for sophisticated preparations such as olive oil-braised tuna, pesto tiger prawns, and lobster ravioli, as well as classics including carpaccio, risotto, and lamb chops. Despite the upscale trappings, Va Pensiero, inside the Margarita European Inn, is family friendly. Servers are adept at guiding you through the mostly Italian wine list. Italian menu. Dinner. Closed holidays. Bar. Outdoor seating. **$$**

Fort Kaskaskia State Historic Site (E-3)

See also Carbondale

6 miles NW of Chester, near Ellis Grove, off Rte 3.

This 275-acre park includes the earthworks of the old fort, built in 1733, rebuilt in 1736 by the French, and finally destroyed to prevent British occupation after the Treaty of Paris. As a result of post-Revolutionary War anarchy (1784), the ruins of the fort, while in the hands of Connecticut renegade John Dodge, were the scene of murders and revelry. Nearby is Garrison Hill Cemetery, where 3,800 old settlers' remains rest, removed from the original graveyard when floodwaters threatened to wash them away. The Pierre Menard Mansion, at the base of bluffs along the Mississippi, was built in 1802 in the style of a French colonial house. The home has been called the "Mount Vernon of the West." Some original furnishings have been reclaimed and reinstalled by the state; tours (daily). The park provides hiking, picnicking, tent and trailer camping (dump station, hookups; standard fees). For information, contact Site Manager, 4372 Park Rd, Ellis Grove 62241, phone 618/859-3741 or 618/859-3031 (Menard Mansion).

Freeport (A-3)

See also Rockford

Settled 1838
Population 26,443
Elevation 780 ft
Area Code 815
Zip 61032
Information Stephenson County Convention and Visitors Bureau, 2047 AYP Rd; phone 815/233-1357 or toll-free 800/369-2955
Web site www.stephenson-county-il.org

According to legend, Freeport is named for the generosity of its pioneer settler, William Baker, who was chided by his wife for running a "free port" for everyone coming along the trail. It was the scene of the second Lincoln-Douglas debate; the site is marked by a memorial boulder and a life-size statue of Lincoln and Douglas in debate. Freeport, an agricultural and industrial center, is the seat of Stephenson County.

What to See and Do

Freeport Arts Center. *121 N Harlem Ave. Phone 815/235-9755.* Collection includes Asian and Native American art; European paintings and sculptures; Egyptian, Greek, and Roman antiquities; contemporary exhibits. (Tues-Sun afternoons; closed holidays) **$**

Krape Park. *1200 Park Lane Dr (60132). Phone 815/235-6114.* Merry-go-round (mid-May-mid-Sept), garden, waterfall, duck pond. Boat rentals, tennis courts, miniature golf, picnicking, playground, concession (mid-May-mid-Sept). (Daily) **FREE**

Silvercreek and Stephenson Railroad. *5478 S Clover Rd. Phone 815/232-2306.* Trips on a 1912, 36-ton steam locomotive with three antique cabooses and a flat car. Also historical museum. (Memorial Day-Labor Day, periodic weekends) **$$**

Stephenson County Historical Museum. *1440 S Carroll Ave. Phone 815/232-8419.* In the 1857 Oscar Taylor house, museum features 19th-century furnishings and changing exhibits. On grounds with arboretum are 1840 log cabin, turn-of-the-century schoolhouse, blacksmith shop, and farm museum. (May-Oct, Wed-Sun; rest of year, Fri-Sun afternoons; closed holidays) **$**

Special Event

Stephenson County Fair. *2250 S Walnut, Freeport (61032). Phone 815/235-2918.* Seven days in mid-Aug.

Limited-Service Hotel

★ **RAMADA INN.** *1300 E South St, Freeport (61032). Phone 815/297-9700; toll-free 800/272-6232; fax 815/297-2729.* 90 rooms, 2 story. Pets accepted; fee. Check-out noon. Restaurant, bar. Fitness room. Pool. **$**

Restaurant

★ **BELTLINE CAFE.** *325 W South St, Freeport (61032). Phone 815/232-5512; fax 815/232-5512.* Built in 1890. American menu. Breakfast, lunch. Closed Easter, Thanksgiving, Dec 25. **$**

Galena (A-2)

Founded 1826
Population 3,460
Elevation 609 ft
Area Code 815
Zip 61036
Information Galena/Jo Daviess County Convention & Visitors Bureau, 720 Park Ave; phone toll-free 800/747-9377
Web site www.galena.org

A quiet town of historical and architectural interest set on terraces cut by the old Fever River, Galena was once a major crossroads for French exploration of the New World and the commercial and cultural capital of the Northwest Territory. Deposits of lead were discovered in the region by the mid-18th century; when the town was laid out, it was named for the ore. By 1845, the area was producing nearly all the nation's lead, and Galena was the richest and most important city in the state. With wealth came opulence; the grand mansions standing today were built on fortunes acquired from the lead and steamboat businesses. However, the mining of lead peaked just before the outbreak of the Civil War. After the war, the city's importance declined rapidly. Although Galena's sympathies were divided at the outbreak of the Civil War, two companies were formed to support the Union. Ulysses S. Grant, who had recently come to Galena from St. Louis, Missouri, accompanied local troops to Springfield as drillmaster.

The town has changed little since the middle of the last century. To walk the streets of Galena today is to take a step back in time. The 19th-century architecture varies from Federal to Greek Revival and from Italianate to Queen Anne. Ninety percent of the town's buildings are listed on the National Register of Historic Places. A favorite destination of weekend travelers from surrounding areas, especially Chicago, Galena is also a mecca for antique hunters and specialty shoppers.

What to See and Do

Belvedere Mansion. *1008 Park Ave (61036). Phone 815/777-0747.* (1857) Italianate/Steamboat Gothic mansion (22 rooms) restored and furnished with antiques, including pieces used on set of *Gone With the Wind.* (Memorial Day-Oct, daily) Combination ticket with Dowling House (see). **$$**

Chestnut Mountain Resort. *8700 W Chestnut Rd (61036). 8 miles SE. Phone 815/777-1320; toll-free 800/397-1320. www.chestnutmtn.com.* Two quad, three triple chairlifts; three surface lifts; patrol, school, rentals, snowmaking; restaurants, cafeteria, bars, lodge, nursery. Longest run 3,500 feet; vertical drop 475 feet. (Mid-Nov-mid-Mar, daily) **$$$$**

Dowling House. *220 N Diagonal St (61036). Phone 815/777-1250.* (circa 1826) Restored stone house, oldest in Galena, is authentically furnished as a trading post with primitive living quarters. Guided tours. (May-Dec, daily; rest of year, limited hours) Combination ticket with Belvedere Mansion (see). **$$**

Eagle Ridge. *444 Eagle Ridge Dr (61036). Phone 815/777-5200; toll-free 800/892-2269. www.eagleridge.com.* Eagle Ridge has three 18-hole courses and one nine-hole layout to tempt all golfers, from the most casual to the most diehard. The signature course is The General, built in 1997 and co-designed by former US Open winner Andy North. Though not overwhelmingly long, the course forces players to forego some distance in favor of accuracy. If you want to score low, play carefully and think a shot or two ahead. The facility also has a 10,000-square-foot clubhouse, as well as many other amenities of the inn and resort at players' fingertips following a round. **$$$$**

Galena/Jo Daviess County History Museum. *211 S Bench St (61036). Phone 815/777-9129. www.galenahistorymuseum.org.* Located in an 1858 Italianate house, museum displays Civil War artifacts, decorative arts; "A Ripple in Time," an audiovisual presentation on the way of life of the town's earliest settlers; original Peace in Union, Thomas Nast's version of the surrender at Appomattox. (Daily; closed holidays) **$$**

Galena Post Office and Customs House. *110 Green St (61036). Phone 815/777-0225.* Named a "Great American Post Office" by the Smithsonian Institution, the first post office to receive the honor; built in 1859, it is the second-oldest post office in the United States still in use. (Mon-Sat)

Grace Episcopal Church. *309 Hill St (61036). Phone 815/777-2590.* (1848) Gothic Revival church was later remodeled by William LeBaron Jenney, father of the skyscraper. Contains Belgian stained-glass windows; eagle lecturn carved by early Galena crafter; one-manual organ in use since 1838, brought from New York City to New Orleans and then by steamboat to Galena. (Sun; also by appointment) **DONATION**

Old Market House State Historic 1846 Site. *123 N Commerce St (61036). Phone 815/777-2570.* Restored building once housed a vast marketplace on the ground floor, the city council upstairs, and a jail in the basement. Permanent exhibit on the building's history; seasonal exhibitions. (Thurs-Sun) **DONATION**

Sightseeing. *11367 W Industrial Park Ave (61036).* Several trolley tours are available. Contact the Convention and Visitors Bureau.

Ulysses S. Grant Home State Historic Site. *500 Bouthillier St (61036). Phone 815/777-3310. www.granthome.com.* This Italianate house was given to General Grant upon his return from the Civil War in 1865. It features original furnishings and Grant family items. Interpretive tours and picnicking are available. (Wed-Sun 9 am-5 pm; closed holidays) **DONATION**

Vinegar Hill Lead Mine & Museum. *8885 N Three Pines Rd (61036). 6 miles N on Hwy 84, then E on Furlong Rd. Phone 815/777-0855.* Guided tour of an old mine showing early mining techniques. (June-Aug, daily; May, appointment only; Sept-Oct, weekends) **$$**

Special Events

Antique Town Rods Car Show. *E bank of Galena River, Galena (61036). Phone 815/777-2088.* Pre-1949 vehicles. July.

Fall Tour of Homes. *Galena. Phone 815/777-0229.* Last full weekend in Sept.

Galena Arts Festival. *N of Hwy 20 on E bank of Galena River, Galena (61036). Phone 815/777-9341.* Third weekend in July.

Galena Country Fair. *Grant City Park, Park and Basilia aves, Galena (61036). Phone 815/777-1048.* Exhibits, entertainment, country food. Columbus Day weekend.

June Tour of Historic Homes. *Galena. Phone 815/777-9129.* Five houses open to the public. Second weekend in June.

Ladies' Getaway. *Galena. Phone 815/777-9050.* Entertainment and demonstrations especially for women. Mid-Sept.

Stagecoach Trail Festival. *609 N Schuyler St, Lena (61048). Phone 815/369-2786.* A celebration of pioneer and Native American history. Fourth weekend in June.

Limited-Service Hotels

★ **ALLEN'S VICTORIAN PINES LODGING.** *11383 Hwy 20 W, Galena (61036). Phone 815/777-2043; toll-free 866/847-4637; fax 815/777-2625. www.victorianpineslodging.com.* Complex consists of a motel; Ryan House (1876), a 24-room Italianate/Victorian mansion with antiques; and Bedford House (1850), an Italianate structure with original chandeliers, leaded glass, and walnut staircase. 96 rooms, 2 story. Complimentary continental breakfast. Check-in 3 pm, check-out 11 am. Fitness room. Indoor pool, whirlpool. **$**

★ **BEST WESTERN QUIET HOUSE & SUITES.** *9923 Hwy 20 E, Galena (61036). Phone 815/777-2577; toll-free 800/780-7234; fax 815/777-0584. www.bestwestern.com.* 42 rooms, 3 story. Pets accepted, some restrictions; fee. Check-in 2 pm, check-out 11 am. Fitness room. Indoor pool, outdoor pool, whirlpool. **$**

★ ★ **DESOTO HOUSE HOTEL.** *230 S Main St, Galena (61036). Phone 815/777-0090; toll-free 800/343-6562; fax 815/777-9529. www.desotohouse.com.* Renovated historic hotel built in 1855. 55 rooms, 4 story. Check-in 3 pm, check-out 11 am. Two restaurants, bar. **$**

★ **LONGHOLLOW POINT RESORT.** *5129 Longhollow Rd, Galena (61036). Phone 815/777-6010; toll-free 800/551-5129; fax 815/777-2348. www.longhollowpoint.com.* 67 rooms, 3 story. Check-in 3 pm, check-out 11 am. Fitness room. Indoor pool, whirlpool. **$**

Full-Service Resort

★ ★ ★ **EAGLE RIDGE INN & RESORT.** *444 Eagle Ridge Dr, Galena (61036). Phone 815/777-2444;*

toll-free 800/892-2269; fax 815/777-4502. *www. eagleridge.com.* A 6,800-acre resort located just a few miles from the historic town of Galena, the Eagle Ridge features 63 holes of some of the best championship golf in the nation, as well as a complete line of spa amenities. 80 rooms, 2 story. Check-in 4 pm, check-out noon. Three restaurants, bar. Children's activity center. Fitness room, spa. Indoor pool, whirlpool. Golf, 63 holes. Tennis. Airport transportation available. Business center. **$$**

Specialty Lodgings

The following lodging establishments are approved by Mobil Travel Guide but, due to their unique and individualized nature have not been given a traditional Mobil Star rating. Included in this listing you may find bed-and-breakfasts, limited-service inns, guest ranches, and other unique hotel properties.

ALDRICH GUEST HOUSE. *900 3rd St, Galena (61036). Phone 815/777-3323; fax 815/777-3323. www. aldrichguesthouse.com.* Built in 1845. 5 rooms, 2 story. Children over 12 years only. Complimentary full breakfast. Check-in 4-6 pm, check-out 11 am. **$**

HELLMAN GUEST HOUSE. *318 Hill St, Galena (61036). Phone 815/777-3638. hellmanguesthouse.com.* Queen Anne–style house (1895). 4 rooms, 3 story. Children over 12 only; package plans. Complimentary full breakfast. Check-in 2 pm, check-out 11 am. **$**

PARK AVENUE GUEST HOUSE. *208 Park Ave, Galena (61036). Phone 815/777-1075; toll-free 800/359-0743; fax 815/771-1097. www.galena.com/par-kave.* Built in 1893. 4 rooms, 3 story. Children over 12 years only. Complimentary full breakfast. Check-in 4 pm, check-out 11 am. **$**

PINE HOLLOW INN BED & BREAKFAST. *4700 N Council Hill Rd, Galena (61036). Phone 815/777-1071. www.pinehollowinn.com.* On a 120-acre evergreen tree farm. 5 rooms, 2 story. Children over 12 years only. Complimentary full breakfast. Check-in 3 pm, check-out 11 am. **$**

Restaurants

★ **BACKSTREET STEAK & CHOPHOUSE.** *216 S Commerce St, Galena (61036). Phone 815/777-4800. www.backstreetgalena.com.* Offers a traditional steakhouse experience in beautiful downtown Galena. Steak menu. Dinner. **$$$**

★ ★ **BERNADINE'S TEA ROOM.** *513 Bouthiller St, Galena (61036). Phone 815/777-0557. www. stillmaninn.com.* Located in historic downtown Galena in a restored bed-and-breakfast. American menu. Dinner. Closed Sun-Thurs. **$$**

★ ★ **CAFE ITALIA/TWISTED TACO CAFE.** *301 N Main St, Galena (61036). Phone 815/777-0033.* Built in 1855. American, Italian menu. Dinner. Bar. Children's menu. **$$**

★ ★ **FRIED GREEN TOMATOES.** *1301 Irish Hollow Rd, Galena (61036). Phone 815/777-3938. www.friedgreen.com.* Three dining levels in a historic (1851) rural setting. American, Italian menu. Dinner. Closed Thanksgiving, Dec 25. Bar. **$$**

★ **LOG CABIN.** *201 N Main St, Galena (61036). Phone 815/777-0393.* Seafood, steak menu. Lunch, dinner. Closed Mon; Thanksgiving, Dec 24-25. Bar. Children's menu. **$$**

★ ★ **WOODLANDS RESTAURANT.** *444 Eagle Ridge Dr, Galena (61036). Phone 815/777-5050; toll-free 800/998-6338. www.eagleridge.com.* Serving Midwest regional cuisine in a refined setting with beautiful lake views. American menu. Breakfast, lunch, dinner. **$$**

Galesburg (B-3)

See also Bishop Hill, Macomb, Moline, Monmouth

Settled 1837
Population 33,706
Elevation 773 ft
Area Code 309
Zip 61401
Information Convention and Visitors Bureau, 2163 E Main St; phone 309/343-2585
Web site www.visitgalesburg.com

Eastern pioneers came to this area on the prairie to establish a community centering around a school for the training of ministers, Knox College (see). The town was named for their leader, G. W. Gale. Galesburg was an important station on the Underground Railroad. It is also the birth and burial place of poet Carl Sandburg.

What to See and Do

Carl Sandburg State Historic Site. *331 E 3rd St. Phone 309/342-2361.* (1860) Restored birthplace cottage; antique furnishings, some from the Sandburg family; adjacent museum contains memorabilia. Remembrance Rock, named for Sandburg's historical novel, is a granite boulder under which his ashes were placed. (Daily; closed Jan 1, Thanksgiving, Dec 25) **$**

Knox College. *2 E South St Building #1 (61401). Phone 309/341-7313. www.knox.edu.* (1837) (1,100 students) Old Main (1856), original college building and site of Lincoln-Douglas debate. Fine Arts Center houses exhibits by students and faculty. Tours (when school is in session).

Lake Storey Recreational Area. *1033 S Lake Storey Rd. 1/4 mile N on Hwy 150, then 1/2 mile W on S Lake Storey Rd. Phone 309/345-3683.* Water park (Memorial Day-Labor Day), boat rentals, 18-hole golf course (late Mar-Nov; fee), tennis, picnicking (Apr-Oct), playground, gardens, concessions, camping (mid-Apr-mid-Oct; hookups, dump station, two-week maximum; fee). Pets on leash only. (Daily)

Special Events

Railroad Days. *Downtown Galesburg (61402). Phone 309/343-2485.* Tour of trains, yards, depot; memorabilia displays, carnival, fun runs, street fair. Fourth weekend in June.

Sandburg Days Festival. *Downtown Galesburg (61402). Phone 309/343-2485.* Three-day festival includes literary, history, sporting, and children's events. Late Apr.

Stearman Fly-In Days. *Galesburg Municipal Airport. Galesburg (61401). Phone 309/343-2485.* Air shows, exhibits, Stearman contests. First weekend after Labor Day.

Limited-Service Hotels

★ ★ **BEST WESTERN PRAIRIE INN.** *300 S Soangetaha Rd, Galesburg (61401). Phone*

309/343-7151; toll-free 866/343-7151; fax 309/343-7168. www.bestwestern.com. This 109-room hotel combines old European elegance and the comfort of amenities such as an indoor pool, an award-winning restaurant, and in-house entertainment. 109 rooms, 2 story. Pets accepted, some restrictions; fee. Check-in 3 pm, check-out noon. High-speed Internet access. Restaurant, bar. Fitness room. Indoor pool, whirlpool. Airport transportation available. **$**

★ ★ **RAMADA INN.** *29 Public Sq, Galesburg (61401). Phone 309/343-9161; toll-free 888/298-2054; fax 309/343-0157. www.ramada.com.* Near Knox College (see) campus. 96 rooms, 7 story. Pets accepted; fee. Check-out noon. Restaurant, bar. Indoor pool, whirlpool. **$**

Restaurants

★ **LANDMARK CAFE & CREPERIE.** *62 S Seminary St, Galesburg (61401). Phone 309/343-5376; fax 309/342-7594. www.seminarystreet.com.* American, French menu. Breakfast, lunch, dinner. Closed Sun; holidays. Outdoor seating. **$$**

★ **PACKINGHOUSE.** *441 Mulberry, Galesburg (61401). Phone 309/342-6868; fax 309/342-7594. www. seminarystreet.com.* In a former meatpacking plant (1912). Steak, seafood menu. Lunch, dinner. Closed holidays. Children's menu. **$$**

★ ★ **THE STEAK HOUSE.** *951 N Henderson (Hwy 150), Galesburg (61401). Phone 309/343-9994.* Steak menu. Dinner. Closed Sun; holidays. Bar. **$$**

Geneva (A-4)

See also Aurora, DeKalb, St. Charles, Wheaton

Settled 1833
Population 19,515
Elevation 720 ft
Area Code 630
Zip 60134
Information Chamber of Commerce, 8 S 3rd St, PO Box 481; phone 630/232-6060
Web site www.genevachamber.com

Lured by the stories of soldiers returning from the Black Hawk War, Easterners settled here on both sides of the Fox River. Geneva became a rallying place and supply point for pioneers continuing farther west. The first retail establishment was a hardware and general store; the second sold satin and lace, which began Geneva's unique tradition as a place hospitable to highly specialized retailing. Today, the town has more than 100 specialty stores. Geneva's greatest asset, however, is its historic district, which has more than 200 buildings listed on the National Register of Historic Places. Cyclists and hikers enjoy the trails that wind through the parks adjacent to the Fox River.

What to See and Do

Garfield Farm Museum. *3N016 Garfield Rd (60147). 5 miles W on Rte 38 to Garfield Rd, near La Fox. Phone 630/584-8485. www.garfieldfarm.org.* This 281-acre living history farm includes an 1846 brick tavern, an 1842 haybarn, and an 1849 horse barn; poultry, oxen, sheep; gardens and prairie. Special events throughout the year. Grounds (June-Sept, Wed, Sun 1-4 pm; other times by appointment). **$$**

Wheeler Park. *710 Western Ave (60134). Off Rte 31, N of Rte 38. Phone 630/232-4542 (park).* This 57-acre park features flower and nature gardens, hiking, tennis, ball fields, access to riverside bicycle trail, picnicking, miniature golf (late May-early Sept, daily; rest of May, Sept, Fri-Sun; fee). Park (daily). **FREE** In the park is

> **Geneva Historical Society Museum.** *400 Wheeler Dr, Geneva. Phone 630/232-4951.* (Daily) **FREE**

Special Events

Christmas Walk. *Rtes 31, 38, Geneva (60134). Phone 630/232-6060.* First Fri-Sat in Dec.

Festival of the Vine. *Rtes 31, 38, Geneva (60134). Phone 630/232-6060.* Autumn harvest celebration. Food, wine tasting. Music, craft show, antique carriage rides. Second weekend in Sept.

Swedish Days. *Rtes 31, 38, Geneva (60134). Phone 630/232-6060.* Six-day festival with parade, entertainment, arts and crafts, music, food. Begins Tues after Father's Day.

Full-Service Inn

★ ★ ★ **THE HERRINGTON INN.** *15 S River Ln, Geneva (60134). Phone 630/208-7433; toll-free 800/216-2466; fax 630/208-8930. www.herringtoninn.com.* Built in the late 1800s. 63 rooms, 3 story. Complimentary continental breakfast. Check-in 4 pm, check-out noon. Restaurant. Fitness room. Airport transportation available. Business center. On river. **$$**

Restaurants

★ ★ **ATWATER'S.** *15 S River Ln, Geneva (60134). Phone 630/208-8920. www.herringtoninn.com.* International menu. Breakfast, lunch, dinner, Sun brunch. Bar. Casual attire. Outdoor seating. **$$**

★ ★ **MILL RACE INN.** *4 E State St, Geneva (60134). Phone 630/232-2030; fax 630/232-2069. www.themillraceinn.com.* Gazebo dining. On Fox River. American menu. Lunch, dinner, Sun brunch. Closed Dec 25. Bar. Children's menu. Casual attire. Valet parking. **$$**

Glen Ellyn

See also Wheaton

Population 26,999
Elevation 750 ft
Area Code 630
Zip 60137
Information Chamber of Commerce, 490 Pennsylvania Ave; phone 630/469-0907
Web site www.glen-ellyn.com

Glen Ellyn contains over 24 houses that are more than 100 years old and are listed as historic sites. Although not open to the public, these houses are identified by plaques and make for a pleasant walking tour. Most can be found between the 300 and 800 blocks on Main Street, as well as on Forest and Park streets north of the railroad. Glen Ellyn's many antique shops make the town popular with collectors and weekend browsers.

What to See and Do

Stacy's Tavern Museum. *557 Geneva Rd. At Main St. Phone 630/858-8696.* (1846) Old country inn was once a popular stagecoach stop for travelers going from

Chicago to the Fox River Valley. Restored with period furnishings. (Mar-Dec, Wed and Sun afternoons; closed holidays) **FREE**

Special Event

Taste of Glen Ellyn. *557 Geneva Rd, Glen Ellyn. Phone 630/469-0907.* Mid-May.

Glenview

See also Northbrook, Skokie, Wheeling, Wilmette

Population 41,847
Elevation 635 ft
Area Code 847
Zip 60025
Information Chamber of Commerce, 2320 Glenview Rd; phone 847/724-0900
Web site www.glenviewchamber.com

Glenview is located 20 miles north of downtown Chicago, squeezed between Interstates 94 and 294. Following the Great Fire in 1871, the Chicago and Milwaukee Railroad was constructed to facilitate the rapid rebuilding of Chicago. The railroad passed through Glenview, then a sparsely populated agrarian community known as South Northfield. The introduction of the railroad spurred the community's growth, and today Glenview boasts numerous shops and restaurants, desirable residential neighborhoods, and exceptional public schools.

What to See and Do

The Grove National Historic Landmark. *1421 N Milwaukee Ave. Just S of Lake Ave. Phone 847/299-6096.* This 124-acre nature preserve includes miles of hiking trails and three structures: the restored 1856 Kennicott House (tours Sun, Feb-Sept); the Interpretative Center (daily), a nature center museum; and the Redfield Center (now a banquet facility that is not open to the public), a house designed by George G. Elmslie, who studied under and worked with Louis Sullivan. During the 1930s, author Donald Culross Peattie, who wrote *A Prairie Grove* about his experiences at the Grove, lived in this stone house. (See SPECIAL EVENTS) (Park open daily; closed Jan 1, Dec 25) **FREE**

Hartung's Automotive Museum. *3623 W Lake St. Phone 847/724-4354.* Display of more than 100 antique autos, trucks, tractors, and motorcycles; many unrestored. License plate collection; 75 antique bicycles; promotional model cars; antique auto hub caps, radiator emblems, and auto mascots. Also includes some Model T Fords (1909-1926), a 1926 Hertz touring car, a 1932 Essex Terraplane, and other rare, classic automobiles. (Daily, hours vary) **$$**

Special Events

Civil War Living History Days. *The Grove National Historic Landmark, 2320 Glenview Rd, Glenview (60025). Phone 847/299-6096.* Features realistic battle reenactment with hospital tent and camps of the period; participants in authentic clothing and uniforms. Exhibits, lectures, house tours. Last weekend in July.

Grovefest. *The Grove National Historic Landmark, 2320 Glenview Rd, Glenview (60025). Phone 847/299-6096.* Crafts, music, activities, and food; costumed volunteers gather to re-create a typical afternoon of the mid-1800s. First Sun in Oct.

Summer Festival. *Glenview Rd, between Waukegan Rd and the Milwaukee train, Glenview. Phone 847/724-0900.* Entertainment, vendors, and food. Last Sat in June.

Restaurants

★ ★ ★ **MK NORTH.** *305 Happ Rd, Northfield (60093). Phone 847/716-6500.* Style meets substance at this North Shore outpost of Michael Kornick's mk, where refined yet real contemporary cuisine is offered in a perfectly compatible setting. The seasonal American food is clean and uncontrived, featuring such specialties as lobster bisque and salmon with Chinese mustard glaze. Knowledgeable service, a fine wine list (including private-label selections), and excellent desserts are all a part of the mk dining experience. Degustation menus are available, and the chic lounge area is perfect for a before-or-after glass of bubbly. American menu. Lunch, dinner. Closed Sun. Bar. Children's menu. Casual attire. Reservations recommended. Outdoor seating. **$$$**

★ **MYKONOS.** *8660 Golf Rd, Niles (60714). Phone 847/296-6777; fax 847/296-7339. www.mykonosgreekrestaurant.com.* Greek menu. Lunch, dinner. Closed Thanksgiving, Dec 25. Bar. Casual attire. Valet parking. Outdoor seating. **$$**

★ **PERIYALI GREEK TAVERNA.** *9860 Milwaukee Ave, Glenview (60016). Phone 847/296-2232; fax 847/296-3250.* The large outdoor seating area is the big draw at this authentic Greek restaurant at the south end of town, which used to be a Red Lobster. The equally sizable dining room is great for families and groups. Greek menu. Lunch, dinner. Closed Thanksgiving, Dec 25. Bar. Casual attire. Outdoor seating. **$$**

Grayslake

See also Gurnee, Libertyville, Waukegan

Population 18,506
Elevation 790 ft
Area Code 847
Zip 60030
Information Chamber of Commerce, 10 Seymour Ave; phone 847/223-6888

Special Event

Lake County Fair. *Fairgrounds, 50 S Rte 45, Grayslake. Phone 847/223-2204.* Rodeo, exhibits, contests, midway; horse show, tractor and horse pulls. Late July.

Restaurant

★ ★ **COUNTRY SQUIRE.** *19133 W Rte 120, Grayslake (60030). Phone 847/223-0121. www. csquire.com.* Restored Georgian mansion (1938), once owned by Wesley Sears; extensive gardens, fountain. American menu. Lunch, dinner, Sun brunch. Closed Mon. Bar. Children's menu. **$$**

Greenville (D-3)

See also Vandalia

Settled 1815
Population 6,955
Elevation 619 ft
Area Code 618
Zip 62246
Information Chamber of Commerce, 405 S Third St; phone 618/664-9272
Web site www.greenvilleillinois.com

This rural community, nestled in the center of Bond County, is within easy commuting distance of downtown St. Louis, Missouri. The community is host to a number of manufacturing companies and the home of Greenville College.

What to See and Do

Richard W. Bock Museum. *315 E College Ave. Greenville College. Phone 618/664-2800. www. greenville.edu/campus/bock.* Inside the original Almira College house (1855) is a collection of works by sculptor Richard W. Bock (1865-1949), who, between 1895 and 1915, executed a number of works for Frank Lloyd Wright-designed buildings. Also on display are Wright-designed prototypes of leaded-glass windows and lamps for Wright's Dana House in Springfield (see SPRINGFIELD). (Wed, Fri-Sat; closed during summer, call for appointment) **FREE**

Gurnee

See also Antioch, Grayslake, Illinois Beach State Park, Libertyville, McHenry, Waukegan, Woodstock

Population 28,834
Elevation 700 ft
Area Code 847
Zip 60031
Information Lake County Chamber of Commerce, 5221 W Grand Ave, 60031-1818; phone 847/249-3800
Web site www.lakecounty-il.org

What to See and Do

Gurnee Mills. *6170 Grand Ave (60031). At the intersection of I-94 and Grand Ave (Rte 132). Phone 847/263-7500; toll-free 800/937-7467. www. gurneemills.com.* For outlet mavens and bargain hunters, Gurnee Mills is a must-visit, attracting groups from around the United States and from as far as Europe and Japan. Located about 45 minutes north of Chicago's city limits, this mega-mall features more than 200 outlet stores and restaurants, including Polo, Banana Republic, OFF 5TH-Saks Fifth Avenue, Liz Claiborne, Levi's, Tommy Hilfiger Jeans, Guess, and Nine West, as well as Rainforest Cafe and a 20-screen cinema. (Daily; closed Easter, Thanksgiving, Dec 25)

Six Flags Great America. *On Grand Ave, off I-94, exit Rte 132. Phone 847/249-1776. www.sixflags.com.* This 200-acre entertainment center features rides, shows, shops, and restaurants. Among the rides and attractions are Deja Vu, the world's tallest and fastest suspending, looping boomerang coaster; The Giant

Drop, a seated, vertical, high-speed drop; Batman, The Ride, a suspended, looping thrill ride; Iron Wolf, a stand-up, looping steel roller coaster; ShockWave, a steel roller coaster; American Eagle, two racing wooden roller coasters; Condor, a spinning thrill ride; water rides; and a children's area. Theaters feature live stage shows daily. (Fourth week in May-last week in Aug, daily; late Apr-fourth week in May, Sept-mid-Oct, weekends) Admission includes all rides and shows. **$$$$**

Limited-Service Hotels

★ **BAYMONT INN.** *5688 N Ridge Rd, Gurnee (60031). Phone 847/662-7600; fax 847/662-5300. www. baymontinns.com.* 102 rooms, 4 story. Pets accepted, some restrictions. Complimentary continental breakfast. Check-in 3 pm, check-out noon. Indoor pool, whirlpool. **$**

★ **HAMPTON INN.** *5550 Grand Ave, Gurnee (60031). Phone 847/662-1100; toll-free 800/426-7866; fax 847/662-2556. www.hamptoninn.com.* Six Flags Great America is two blocks away. 134 rooms, 5 story. Complimentary full breakfast. Check-in 3 pm, check-out noon. High-speed Internet access. Outdoor pool. **$**

Havana (C-3)

See also Petersburg

Settled 1824
Population 3,577
Elevation 470 ft
Area Code 309
Zip 62644
Information Chamber of Commerce, PO Box 116; phone 309/543-3528

Once a bustling steamboat and fishing port at the confluence of the Spoon and Illinois rivers, Havana is now a quiet river town, important as a grain center with a few light industries. One of the famous Lincoln-Douglas debates took place in what is now Rockwell Park.

What to See and Do

⭐ **Dickson Mounds Museum.** *10956 N Dickson Mounds Rd. 5 miles NW via Hwy 78/97, on hill above Spoon and Illinois rivers. Phone 309/547-3721. www. museum.state.il.us.* Exhibits include multimedia programs relating to Native American inhabitants over 12,000-year time span. Also agricultural plot and remains of excavated houses. Picnic area. (Daily; closed holidays) **FREE**

Illinois River National Wildlife and Fish Refuges. *19031 E County Rd 2110 N. 9 miles NE on Manito Rd. Phone 309/535-2290. midwest.fws.gov/illinoisriver.* These 4,488 acres are used as a resting, breeding, and feeding area for waterfowl. Concentrations of shorebirds (Aug-Sept). Eagles are seen here (Nov-Feb). Sportfishing (daily) and waterfowl hunting (fall) permitted in specified areas. Designated public-use areas open all year. Interpretive nature trail; wheelchair access. Contact Refuge Manager, US Fish and Wildlife Service, Illinois River National Wildlife and Fish Refuges, RR 2, PO Box 61B. **FREE**

Special Event

Spoon River Scenic Drive Fall Festival. *2000 N Main St, Havana. 5 miles NW on Hwy 78/97 to Dickson Mounds, then marked, circular route through Fulton County. Phone 309/647-8980.* Autumn drive through small towns and rolling, wooded countryside noted for fall color (complete drive 140 miles); 19th- and early-20th-century crafts, exhibits, demonstrations; antiques, collectibles; produce, food. First and second weekend in Oct.

Highland Park (A-5)

See also Chicago, Highwood, Northbrook

Settled 1834
Population 31,365
Elevation 690 ft
Area Code 847
Zip 60035
Information Chamber of Commerce, 508 Central Ave, Suite 206; phone 847/432-0284
Web site www.highland-park.com

What to See and Do

Francis Stupey Log Cabin. *326 Central Ave. Phone 847/432-7090.* (1847) Oldest structure in town; restored with period furnishings. (May-Oct, Sat-Sun; also by appointment) **FREE**

Highland Park Historical Society. *Headquarters in Jean Butz James Museum, 326 Central Ave. Phone 847/432-7090.* Restored Victorian house (1871) has several period rooms; changing exhibits of local artifacts. On grounds is the Walt Durbahn Tool Museum with household items and primitive implements used in lumbering and local trades. (Daily; closed Mon; holidays) **FREE**

Special Event

Ravinia Festival. *418 Sheridan Rd, Highland Park (60035). On Green Bay Rd at Lake Cook Rd. Phone 847/266-5100. www.ravinia.org.* Located on the North Shore, this summer playground for thousands of Chicago's music lovers also is the summer home of the Chicago Symphony Orchestra (see SYMPHONY CENTER under CHICAGO). This former amusement park—turned classy outdoor classical music venue—features programming that spans the musical and artistic spectrum, from Bonnie Raitt and Los Lobos to Tony Bennett, Herbie Hancock, and Itzhak Perlman. Special programs include Jazz in June, the Young Artists series, and Kids Concerts. While there is a 3,200-seat, open-air pavilion and two indoor venues for chamber music and smaller concerts, the majority of festivalgoers prefer the lawn, where you can relax with a picnic and listen via the excellent sound system. Plus, it's fun to watch the one-upmanship of the surrounding picnickers; china, crystal, and candelabras are not uncommon. Out-of-towners can still enjoy the lawn and not bring a thing; the park offers five restaurants, a picnic catering facility, chair rentals, and wine kiosks. June-mid-Sept.

Restaurants

★ **CAFE CENTRAL.** *455 Central Ave, Highland Park (60035). Phone 847/266-7878; fax 847/266-7373.* This suburban eatery, located in the heart of downtown Highland Park, is within easy walking distance of area shops. The restaurant serves up French cuisine in a casual setting. Sample locally acclaimed dishes such as risotto or poached chicken salad, as well as selections ranging from quiche and salads to sandwiches and pasta. French menu. Lunch, dinner. Closed Mon; Jan 1, July 4, Dec 25. Bar. Children's menu. Casual attire. Outdoor seating. **$$**

★ ★ ★ **CARLOS'.** *429 Temple Ave, Highland Park (60035). Phone 847/432-0770. www. carlos-restaurant.com.* Owned by husband-and-wife hosts Carlos and Debbie Nieto, Carlos' is a uniquely elegant and intimate restaurant, with mismatched vintage china, fresh flowers, and deep, fabric-covered banquettes. For more than 20 years, the Nietos have been graciously welcoming guests celebrating anniversaries, birthdays, weddings, and just about every other excuse they can make up for dining here. While the Nietos are generous hosts, it is not only their welcome that makes this homey dining room so popular. In all fairness, the gifted chefs also deserve some credit. Carlos' is known for its stellar haute cuisine served in classic French style: entrées arrive topped with silver domes, which the restaurant's charming staff lift in unison on the count of "One, two, three, voilà!" The wine list is as impressive as the cuisine, with more than 3,500 international selections to choose from. *Secret Inspector's Notes: If you are seeking "fusion cuisine" or innovative, unrecognizable entrées, Carlos' is not the place for you. But if you desire a classic destination for elegant dining and proper service, away from the noise and traffic of downtown Chicago, this is the perfect match.* French menu. Dinner. Closed Tues; holidays. Jacket required. Reservations recommended. Valet parking. **$$$**

★ **MICHAEL'S RESTAURANT.** *1879 Second St, Highland Park (60035). Phone 847/432-3338. www. michaelshotdogs.com.* Savor some of Chicago's finest hot dogs at this longstanding institution in central Highland Park. Diners travel from Chicago and the surrounding suburbs to enjoy high-end fast food served in a colorful, casual setting that's perfect for families. Lunch and dinner entrées include potatoes with every manner of fixing; a wide variety of wraps; a create-your-own salad bar; pita pockets; grilled items; and sundaes and other sweet confections. A children's menu downsizes several options to suit smaller appetites. Don't miss a char dog, burger, or chicken breast sandwich, and save room for an order of cheddar fries. American menu. Lunch, dinner. No credit cards accepted. **$**

★ ★ **TIMBERS CHARHOUSE.** *295 Skokie Valley Rd, Highland Park (60035). Phone 847/831-1400; fax 847/831-0552.* Steak menu. Lunch, dinner. Closed holidays. Bar. Children's menu. **$$**

Highwood

See also Highland Park

Population 4,143
Elevation 685 ft
Area Code 847
Zip 60040

Sandwiched between Highland Park and Lake Forest, this suburban community along Chicago's North Shore is known both for its numerous restaurants and its close association to Fort Sheridan, a former army base. Local attractions include Everts Park, the Robert McClory Bicycle Path, and the 18-hole Lake County Forest Preserve golf course at the Fort Sheridan Club. All are open to the public.

Restaurants

★ ★ **DEL RIO.** *228 Green Bay Rd, Highwood (60040). Phone 847/432-4608.* A genuine bite of Highwood's past as an Italian immigrant enclave, the family-run Del Rio has been dishing heaping portions of Italian classics since the 1930s. The menu breaks no new ground, but that's just the way fans like it, pouring in for generous helpings of lasagna, sausage and peppers, veal parmigiana, chicken cacciatore, and homemade pastas. Italian maps and menus decorate the walls of the homey and usually crowded eatery. Italian menu. Dinner. Closed holidays. Bar. **$$$**
🅳

★ ★ ★ **FROGGY'S.** *306 Green Bay Rd, Highwood (60040). Phone 847/433-7080; fax 847/433-6852. www.froggyscatering.com.* This cheery bistro offers country French cuisine at reasonable prices (try the bargain prix fixe menu), with regional specialties like onion soup, coq au vin, and rabbit casserole rounding out the menu. The nice-sized wine list features a number of red and white Burgundies, Bordeaux, and champagnes, and decadent cakes and carry-out items can be purchased from the adjacent bakery. French menu. Lunch, dinner. Closed Sun; holidays. Bar. **$$$**
🅳

★ ★ ★ **GABRIEL'S.** *310 Green Bay Rd, Highwood (60040). Phone 847/433-0031. www.egabriels.com.* Chef/owner Gabriel Viti, formerly of Carlos' in Highland Park (see), turns out complex French-Italian dishes from his open kitchen in his namesake restaurant. Entrées range from grilled veal porterhouse to roasted Maine lobster with baby bok choy and ginger butter sauce, with seasonal specials and a degustation menu available. Attentive service characterizes this upscale-casual restaurant, whose décor features hand-painted tiles and linen-topped tables. French, Italian menu. Dinner. Closed Sun-Mon; holidays. Bar. Reservations recommended. Valet parking. Outdoor seating. **$$$$**

Hinsdale

See also Brookfield, Downers Grove, La Grange, Oak Brook

Population 16,029
Elevation 725 ft
Area Code 630
Zip 60521
Information Chamber of Commerce, 22 E First St; phone 630/323-3952

Named for a pioneer railroad director, Hinsdale includes what was once the town of Fullersburg. It is a quiet and secluded commuter community with a quaint shopping district.

What to See and Do

Robert Crown Center for Health Education. *21 Salt Creek Ln. Phone 630/325-1900.* Programs teach about the body's physical and emotional health. Displays include Valeda, a talking Plexiglas model. Reservations required. (Sept-June, Mon-Fri; closed holidays) **$$**

Homewood

Population 19,543
Elevation 650 ft
Area Code 708
Zip 60430

Located 24 miles south of Chicago's Loop, Homewood boasts two city blocks of fascinating art; New York muralist Richard Haas refurbished older business buildings with trompe l'oeil artwork on the backs of the structures.

What to See and Do

Midwest Carvers Museum. *16236 Vincennes Ave, South Holland. NE via Thornton/Blue Island Rd. Phone 708/331-6011.* Housed in historic farmhouses, this museum features hundreds of examples of carvers' art, including an ornate doll carriage and a realistically carved bald eagle. Wood-carving classes; gift shop. (Mon-Sat; closed holidays) **DONATION**

Restaurants

★ **AURELIO'S PIZZA.** *18162 Harwood Ave, Homewood (60430). Phone 708/798-8050. www.*

aureliospizza.com. In former shipping warehouse. Italian menu. Lunch, dinner. Closed holidays. Bar. Children's menu. Outdoor seating. **$$**

★ ★ **DRAGON INN.** *18431 S Halsted St, Glenwood (60425). Phone 708/756-3344.* American, Chinese menu. Dinner. Closed Mon; Thanksgiving. Bar. **$$**
🄳

Illinois Beach State Park

See also Gurnee, Waukegan

1 Lakefront Dr, Zion (60099). 3 miles N of Waukegan, E of Rte 131; off Sheridan Rd. Phone 847/662-4811.

This 6 1/2-mile sand beach on Lake Michigan is a summer playground for more than 2 1/2 million visitors annually. The 4,160-acre park has facilities for beach swimming (no lifeguard) and beach houses available. Other activities include fishing and hiking. There is a boat marina in the park and a boat launch. Cross-country skiing is popular in winter. The park has picnic shelters, a playground, a concession area, and a lodge. Camping is permitted (standard fees). There is an interpretive center on the grounds. **FREE**

Limited-Service Hotel

★ ★ **ILLINOIS BEACH RESORT AND CONFERENCE CENTER.** *1 Lakefront Dr, Zion (60099). Phone 847/625-7300; toll-free 866/452-3224; fax 847/625-0665. www.ilresorts.com.* 92 rooms, 3 story. Check-in 3 pm, check-out noon. Restaurant, bar. Fitness room. Indoor pool, children's pool, whirlpool. Airport transportation available. On beach. **$**
🄳 ≊

Itasca

See also Chicago, Chicago O'Hare Airport Area, Elmhurst, Schaumburg

Population 8,302
Elevation 686 ft
Area Code 630
Zip 60143

Full-Service Resorts

★ ★ ★ **DORAL EAGLEWOOD RESORT.** *1401 Nordic Rd, Itasca (60143). Phone 630/773-1400; toll-free 800/487-1969; fax 630/773-1709. www. doraleaglewood.com.* 295 rooms, 9 story. Check-in 3 pm, check-out noon. Restaurant, bar. Fitness room, spa. Indoor pool, whirlpool. Golf. **$**
🄳 🄳 ≊

★ ★ ★ **INDIAN LAKES GOLF RESORT AND CONFERENCE CENTER.** *250 W Schick Rd, Bloomingdale (60108). Phone 630/529-0200; toll-free 888/757-2437; fax 630/529-9271. www. indianlakesresort.com.* As its slogan goes, the Indian Lakes Resort is "a getaway that's not too far away." And with conference and banquet facilities, two 18-hole golf courses, swimming pools, a spa, and tennis courts, any occasion can be an occasion to visit. 308 rooms, 6 story. Check-in 4 pm, check-out noon. High-speed Internet access. Three restaurants, three bars. Fitness room, spa. Indoor pool, outdoor pool, whirlpool. Golf, 36 holes. Tennis. Business center. **$**
🄳 🄳 🄳 ≊ 🄳

Jacksonville (D-3)

See also Springfield

Founded 1825
Population 18,940
Elevation 613 ft
Area Code 217
Zip 62650
Information Jacksonville Area Visitor & Convention Bureau, 155 W Morton; phone toll-free 800/593-5678
Web site www.jacksonvilleil.org

Although settled by Southerners, the town was largely developed by New Englanders and became an important station on the Underground Railroad. A center of education, culture, and statesmanship, Jacksonville was named in honor of Andrew Jackson and nurtured the careers of Stephen A. Douglas and William Jennings Bryan. Abraham Lincoln often spoke here in the 1850s. Illinois College (1829), the oldest college west of the Alleghenies, and MacMurray College (1846) have played an important part in the city's history. This also is the home of the Illinois School for the Visually Impaired (1849), the Illinois School for the Deaf (1839), and Jacksonville Developmental Center (1846). Several national manufacturing companies are located here.

What to See and Do

Lake Jacksonville. *RR 5. 4 1/2 miles SE off Hwy 67. Phone 217/479-4646.* Swimming (fee), fishing, boating (dock); camping (mid-Apr-mid-Oct; fee).

Restaurant

★ ★ **LONZEROTTI'S.** *600 E State St, Jacksonville (62650). Phone 217/243-7151.* In the restored Chicago and Alton Railroad depot (1909). Italian, American menu. Lunch, dinner. Closed Sun; holidays. Bar. Children's menu. Outdoor seating. **$$**

Joliet (B-4)

See also Aurora, Lockport, Morris

Settled 1831
Population 106,221
Elevation 564 ft
Area Code 815
Information Heritage Corridor Convention and Visitors Bureau, 81 N Chicago St, 60432; phone 815/727-2323 or toll-free 800/926-2262
Web site www.heritagecorridorcvb.com

The Des Plaines River, the Chicago Sanitary and Ship Canal, and railroad freight lines triggered Joliet's growth as a center of commerce and industry. The canal's Brandon Road Locks, to the south of Joliet, are among the largest in the world, and the canal continues to carry many millions of tons of barge traffic annually through the city. Joliet once supplied limestone (Joliet/Lemont) to much of the nation and was once a major center for steel production. Although Joliet was named in honor of Louis Jolliet, the French-Canadian explorer who visited the area in 1673, it was incorporated in 1837 as Juliet, companion to the nearby town of Romeo (now renamed Romeoville).

What to See and Do

Bicentennial Park Theater/Band Shell Complex. *201 W Jefferson St. Phone 815/724-3760; fax 815/740-2399. www.bicentennialpark.org.* Joliet Drama Guild and other productions (fee). Also outdoor concerts in band shell (June-Aug, Thurs evenings). Historic walks. (See SPECIAL EVENTS) **FREE**

Empress Casino Joliet. *I-55, exit 248, left 3 miles to Empress Ln. Phone toll-free 888/436-7737.* (Daily)

Harrah's Joliet Casino. *150 N Joliet St (60432). Downtown. Phone 815/740-7800; toll-free 800/427-7247. www.harrahs.com.* Located in Joliet, about 40 miles southwest of Chicago on the Des Plaines River, Harrah's features two riverboats—one a 210-foot "mega-yacht" and the other a re-creation of a Mississippi paddle wheeler. Illinois gaming boats are no longer required to cruise, so there is open boarding between 8:30 am and 6:15 am daily. Games include more than 900 slots (from 5-cent to $100 machines), blackjack, Caribbean stud poker, mini-baccarat, craps, roulette, video poker, and video keno. Adjacent to the boats' berths is a pavilion featuring daily live entertainment and a variety of restaurants, bars, and lounges. (Daily) **FREE**

Pilcher Park. *Gougar Rd and Rte 6. Off Hwy 30. Phone 815/741-7277.* Walking, driving, and bicycle trails; nature center (daily), greenhouse, picnicking, playground.

Rialto Square Theatre. *102 N Chicago St. Phone 815/726-6600; fax 815/726-0352. www.rialtosquare.com.* (1926) Performing arts center, designed by the Rapp brothers, is considered one of the most elaborate and beautiful of old 1920s movie palaces. Tours (Tues and by appointment). **$$**

Special Events

Festival of the Gnomes. *Bicentennial Park, 201 W Jefferson, Joliet (60435). Phone 815/740-2216.* Celebration includes stage performances of gnome legends, gnome-related arts and crafts, refreshments. Costumed gnomes. Sat in early Dec.

Route 66 Raceway. *3200 S Chicago St, Joliet. Phone 815/722-5500.* Facility includes a 2-mile road course and an off-road and motorcross track. Late May-Sept.

Waterway Daze. *Bicentennial Park, 201 W Jefferson, Joliet (60435). Along the waterway wall. Phone 815/724-3760.* Features parade of decorated, lighted watercraft; food, entertainment. Three days in early Aug.

Restaurants

★ ★ **BAROLO RISTORANTE.** *158 N Chicago St, Joliet (60432). Phone 815/722-1744.* Located in historic downtown Joliet with a convivial European atmosphere. Italian menu. Lunch, dinner. Closed Sun. **$$**

★ ★ **TRUTH RESTAURANT.** *808 W Jefferson St, Joliet (60435). Phone 815/744-5901.* Serving American regional cuisine in an inviting neighborhood atmosphere. American menu. Dinner. Closed Sun-Mon. **$$**

Kankakee (B-5)

Founded 1855
Population 27,491
Elevation 663 ft
Area Code 815
Zip 60901
Information Kankakee River Valley Chamber of Commerce, PO Box 905; phone 815/933-7721
Web site www.visitkankakee.com

Kankakee was originally part of the old French settlement of Bourbonnais but was incorporated as a separate community around the Illinois Central rail lines and the river in the 1850s. The region retains early French characteristics in its old buildings and in its culture. Limestone quarried from the riverbed was used to erect many area walls.

What to See and Do

Antique shopping. *145 S Schuyler Ave. Phone 815/937-4957.* There are over 600 antique dealers in the area, including the Kankakee Antique Mall at 147 South Schuyler Avenue, the largest in Illinois with over 50,000 square feet and 225 dealers. Contact the Convention and Visitors Bureau for a complete list of shops. (Daily; closed holidays)

Gladiolus fields. *Momence. E on Rte 17 to Momence.* More than 150,000 flowers are harvested here, from early summer to the first frost.

Kankakee County Historical Society Museum. *Small Memorial Park, 801 S 8th Ave. Phone 815/932-5279.* History of Kankakee County. George Gray Barnard sculptures; also Native American artifacts, Civil War relics, toys, costumes, dishes; historical library.

Adjacent is the 1855 house in which Governor Len Small was born; many original furnishings, temporary exhibits. Also on property is restored, one-room Taylor School (1904-1954). Gift shop. (Mon-Thurs, Sat-Sun afternoons; closed holidays) **DONATION**

Kankakee River State Park. *5314 W Rte 102. 8 miles NW. Phone 815/933-1383.* Approximately 4,000 acres. Woodlands on both banks of the Kankakee River and canyon of Rock Creek. Fishing, boating (canoe rentals, ramp). Hunting, hiking, cross-country skiing, snowmobiling, picnicking, game and playground facilities, concession, camping. Interpretive program. **FREE**

Olivet Nazarene University. *240 E Marsile St, Bourbonnais. 3 miles N on Hwy 45/52 at Rte 102. Phone 815/939-5011. www.olivet.edu.* (1907) (3,400 students) On 200-acre campus are 29 major buildings, including the Strickler Planetarium and Science Museum, Benner Library, and Larsen Fine Arts Center; Snowbarger Athletic Park; Parrott Convocation/Athletic Center; and Weber Center. Tours.

River excursions. *Reed's Canoe Trips, 907 N Indiana Ave. Phone 815/932-2663.* Canoe trips on the Kankakee River ranging from two hours to a full day. Canoes, kayaks, paddles, life jackets, and transportation provided. (Apr-mid-Oct, daily) Reservations suggested. **$$$$**

Special Events

Gladiolus Festival. *Momence High School and Island Park, Momence. Phone 815/472-6353.* Gladiolus fields in Momence. Thousands of visitors gather for celebration that includes parades, flower shows, antique car show. Second weekend in Aug.

Kankakee County Fair. *Kankakee County Fairgrounds, Rtes 45/52, Kankakee. Phone 815/932-6714.* First week in Aug.

Kankakee River Fishing Derby. *Kankakee River, Kankakee.* Ten days in late June.

Kankakee River Valley Bicycle Classic. *125 N Chestnut St, Kankakee. Phone 309/852-2141.* Late June.

Kankakee River Valley Regatta. *1600 Cobb Blvd, Kankakee (60901). Phone toll-free 800/747-4837.* Features the American Power Boat Association's

Outboard Performance Category (OPC) National Championships; raft races, carnival, entertainment. Labor Day weekend.

Kewanee (B-3)

See also Bishop Hill

Population 12,944
Elevation 820 ft
Area Code 309
Zip 61443
Information Chamber of Commerce, 113 E 2nd St; phone 309/852-2175
Web site www.kewanee-il.com

What to See and Do

Historic Francis Park. *RR 3. 4 miles E on Hwy 34. Phone 309/852-0511.* Within this 40-acre park is Woodland Palace, a unique house built by Fred Francis, inventor, mechanical engineer, artist, and poet. Francis began the house in 1889, incorporating many early forms of modern conveniences, including an air-cooling system, a water-purification system, automatically opening and closing doors, and circulating air. Also here is miniature log cabin built by Francis as a memorial to his parents. Hiking, picnicking, playground, camping. (See SPECIAL EVENTS) (Mid-Apr-Oct, daily) **$**

Johnson Sauk Trail State Park. *27500 N 1200 Ave. 5 miles N on Hwy 78. Phone 309/853-5589.* A focal point of this 1,361-acre park is Ryan's Round Barn, a massive cattle barn that contains interpretive exhibits; also 58-acre artificial lake. Fishing, boating (rentals). Hiking, ice skating, snowmobiling, cross-country skiing, picnicking, camping (electric hookups, dump station). (See SPECIAL EVENTS) (Daily) **FREE**

Special Events

Hog Capital of the World Festival. *Kewanee. Phone 309/852-2175.* Midway, entertainment, arts and crafts, variety of pork dishes. Labor Day weekend.

Sauk Trail Heritage Days. *27500 N 1200 Ave, Kewanee (61443). Francis Park and Johnson Sauk Trail State Park. Phone 309/853-8307.* Four-day celebration including powwow, Native American crafts, and storytelling. Railroad display and demonstrations. Tours. Food. Children's activities. Fireworks. Weekend of July 4.

Limited-Service Hotel

★ **SUPER 8.** *901 S Tenney St, Kewanee (61443). Phone 309/853-8800; fax 309/853-8800. www. super8.com.* 41 rooms. Check-in 1 pm, check-out 11 am. **$**

Restaurants

★ **ANDRIS WAUNEE FARM.** *2314 Hwy 34, Kewanee (61443). Phone 309/852-2481.* Polynesian, American menu. Dinner. Closed Sun-Tues. Bar. Children's menu. **$$**

★ ★ **CELLAR.** *137 S State St, Geneseo (61254). Phone 309/944-2177.* Casual dining in the basement of a downtown commercial building; original artwork. Steak menu. Dinner. Closed Mon; Dec 24-25. Bar. Children's menu. **$$$**

La Grange

See also Brookfield, Cicero, Elmhurst, Hinsdale, Oak Brook

Population 15,608
Elevation 650 ft
Area Code 708
Zip 60525
Information West Suburban Chamber of Commerce, 47 S 6th Ave; phone 708/352-0494
Web site www.westsuburbanchamber.org

What to See and Do

Historic District. *47th St and Brainard Ave.* Bordered by 47th Street on the south, Brainard Avenue on the west, and 8th Avenue on the east, the area is split by the Burlington Northern Railroad tracks; an area north of the tracks, roughly bordered by Stone and Madison avenues, is also part of the Historic District. Here are a number of historically and culturally significant homes dating from the late 19th and early 20th centuries; included are houses designed by such prominent architects as Frank Lloyd Wright, J. C. Llewelyn, E. H. Turnock, and John S. Van Bergen.

Special Event

Pet Parade. *La Grange. Phone 708/352-0494.* First begun in 1946, this parade attracts thousands of visitors each year. First Sat in June.

Restaurant

★ ★ **CAFE 36.** *22 Calendar Court, La Grange (60525). Phone 708/354-5722.* French menu. Lunch, dinner. Closed Mon. Bar. Children's menu. Casual attire. **$$**

Lake Forest

See also Highland Park, Highwood

Lake Forest has long been regarded as an enclave of affluence and prestige. Here, sprawling estates spread out upon bluffs overlooking Lake Michigan. Thirty miles north of Chicago, Lake Forest is the home to Lake Forest College, as well as Halas Hall, the headquarters for the legendary Chicago Bears. Lake Forest's central business district, Market Square, was listed on the National Register of Historic Places in 1979.

Full-Service Inn

★ ★ ★ **DEER PATH INN.** *255 E Illinois Rd, Lake Forest (60045). Phone 847/234-2280; toll-free 800/788-9480; fax 847/234-3352. www.dpihotel.com.* Built in 1929. 54 rooms, 3 story. Pets accepted, some restrictions. Complimentary full breakfast. Check-in 3 pm, check-out noon. Restaurant, bar. Airport transportation available. Business center. **$$**

Restaurants

★ ★ **BANK LANE BISTRO.** *670 Bank Ln, Lake Forest (60045). Phone 847/234-8802.* Posters of Paris and large picture windows framing Lake Forest's historic downtown entertain diners at Bank Lane Bistro. Although the menu changes frequently, you can count on such French bistro classics as escargot, braised lamb shank, and roast pork, as well as crispy pizzas from the wood-burning oven. Service is assured, but with prices on the high side, fans recommend Bank Lane on occasion rather than regularly. French menu. Lunch, dinner. Closed Sun. Bar. Casual attire. Outdoor seating. **$$$**

★ ★ ★ **ENGLISH ROOM.** *255 E Illinois St, Lake Forest (60045). Phone 847/234-2280.* Set inside the historic Deer Path Inn (see), which opened in 1929 and has been a destination for weekend getaways and fine dining ever since, The English Room is an elegant, traditional dining room. The conservative dinner menu includes options like lobster bisque, roasted rack of lamb, and Dover sole; lunch options are a bit more varied and adventurous. The Sunday Champagne brunch is especially treasured here, with is carving stations, ample seafood selections, and sinful desserts. American menu. Lunch, dinner, Sun brunch. Bar. Children's menu. Jacket required. Outdoor seating. **$$$**

★ ★ **SOUTH GATE CAFE.** *655 Forest Ave, Lake Forest (60045). Phone 847/234-8800. www. southgatecafe.com.* Peering over namesake South Gate Square, this upscale café serves American food with a passport to the country's food-centric regions as well as more exotic cultures. Options range from Asian pork satay to Norwegian salmon, beef tenderloin with mushrooms, and, as a last act, bread pudding made with Kentucky bourbon. The environs are somewhat austere, but servers lend warmth. The leafy outdoor patio generates North Shore destination traffic, so arrive early or expect to wait. American menu. Lunch, dinner. Closed holidays. Bar. Outdoor seating. **$**

Lemont

What to See and Do

Cog Hill Golf Club. *12294 Archer Ave (60439). Phone 630/264-4455. www.coghillgolf.com.* Easily the best course in Chicagoland and home to the PGA Tour's Western Open each year, the Dubsdread Course features so many bunkers that average players might think they're playing on a beach. Still, the course is beautifully manicured and is open to the public. It is pricey to play, with the average round costing between $125 and $135, but the cost is well worth the experience of playing on a course where Jack Nicklaus, Tiger Woods, and Arnold Palmer have dazzled. If you're not in the mood for quite such a challenge, there are three other courses to choose from at this magnificent facility. **$$$$**

Ruffled Feathers Golf Club. *1 Pete Dye Dr (60439). Phone 630/257-1000.* Home to the Illinois Professional Golf Association, Ruffled Feathers has been open since

1991 and is yet another gem from course designer Pete Dye. Like Lemont neighbor Cog Hill (see), the course has more than 100 sand bunkers but has wide fairways to compensate. Sixteen of the holes have water, so if your shots hook or slice unexpectedly, you might spend almost as much on lost balls as you do on the greens fee. **$$$$**

Restaurant

★ **WHITE FENCE FARM.** *Joliet Rd, Romeoville (60439). Phone 630/739-1720; fax 630/739-4466. www.whitefencefarm.com/chicago.* This charming country farmhouse proclaims that it serves the world's greatest chicken. Whether that statement is true or not is up to you, but White Fence Farm has won praises for its fried chicken, which is coated with a secret breading recipe, baked, and then flash fried. Aged steaks and a few fish selections round out the menu of home-style favorites, which are served in ten quaint dining rooms. But more than just a restaurant famous for fried chicken, White Fence Farm is a place to spend the day with the family. On its sprawling grounds are an antique car museum, kiddie rides, and a petting zoo with llamas, sheep, and goats. American menu. Lunch, dinner. Closed Mon; Thanksgiving, Dec 24-25; also Jan. Children's menu. Casual attire. **$$**

Libertyville

See also Grayslake, Gurnee

Founded 1836
Population 20,742
Elevation 700 ft
Area Code 847
Zip 60048
Information Chamber of Commerce, 731 N Milwaukee Ave; phone 847/680-0750

Marlon Brando, Helen Hayes, and Adlai Stevenson are a few of the famous personalities who have lived in Libertyville. The St. Mary of the Lake Theological Seminary (Roman Catholic) borders the town; there are four lakes near the village limits.

What to See and Do

Cuneo Museum and Gardens. *1350 N Milwaukee Ave, Vernon Hills. N on Rte 21, then W on Rte 60. Phone 847/362-3042. www.lake-online.com/cuneo.* Opulent Venetian-style mansion featuring Great Hall with arcade balconies, chapel with stained glass and fresco ceiling, and ship's room with hidden bookshelves. Collection of master paintings, 17th-century tapestries, Oriental rugs, Capo di Monte porcelain. Grounds (75 acres) include fountains, gardens, sculptures, and a conservatory. (Tues-Sun) **$$$**

David Adler Cultural Center. *1700 N Milwaukee Ave. Phone 847/367-0707.* The summer residence of the distinguished neoclassical architect David Adler. Folk concerts and children's events (fee for all). Exhibits and tours. **FREE**

Lambs Farm. *14245 W Rockland Rd. Jct I-94 and Rte 176 exit. Phone 847/362-0098.* Includes children's farmyard, small animal nursery, miniature golf (fees), thrift shop, country store, bakery, restaurant. Hayrides, bounce house, discovery center, pet shop, miniature-train rides (fee). Gift shops. Nonprofit residential and vocational community benefitting mentally retarded adults. (Daily; closed holidays) **FREE**

Restaurants

★ ★ **GALE STREET INN.** *906 Diamond Lake Rd, Mundelein (60060). Phone 847/566-1090.* American menu. Lunch, dinner. Closed Mon; Thanksgiving, Dec 25. Bar. Outdoor seating. **$$**

★ **THE LAMBS FARM COUNTRY INN.** *At jct I-94 and Rte 176, Libertyville (60048). Phone 847/362-5050.* Libertyville's down-on-the-farm breakfast and lunch specialist serves up a dose of country setting as a side to filling American fare made from scratch. Snag a table amid the antiques and dig into skillets and omelets at breakfast or homemade soups and comfort food specials, including barbecue ribs, fried chicken, and country ham, at lunch. House-baked breads come from the on-site bakery. American menu. Breakfast, lunch, Sun brunch. Closed Mon; holidays. Children's menu. Reservations recommended. **$$**

★ ★ ★ **TAVERN IN THE TOWN.** *519 N Milwaukee Ave, Libertyville (60048). Phone 847/367-5755.* Along a stretch of near-wasteland suburbia sits this surprising bastion of Victorian charm. Guests dine in a romantic room of flowing curtains and brick and brass accents. American menu. Lunch, dinner. Closed Sun; holidays. Bar. **$$$**

Lincoln (C-3)

See also Bloomington, Decatur, Springfield

Founded 1853
Population 15,369
Elevation 591 ft
Area Code 217
Zip 62656
Information Abraham Lincoln Tourism Bureau of Logan County, 303 S Kickapoo St; phone 217/732-8687
Web site www.logancountytourism.org

Of all the cities named for Abraham Lincoln, this is the only one named with his knowledge and consent and before he was elected president. Lincoln participated in the legal work involved in the organization of the town site and its incorporation as the seat of Logan County. Later, he acquired a lot here as compensation for a note he had endorsed.

What to See and Do

Mount Pulaski Courthouse State Historic Site. *12 miles SE on Hwy 121. Phone 217/792-3919.* (1848) This restored Greek Revival building served as the county courthouse until 1855. It is one of two surviving Eighth Circuit courthouses in Illinois visited by Lincoln. Interpretive program. (Tues-Sat afternoons; closed holidays) **DONATION**

Postville Courthouse State Historic Site. *914 5th St. I-55 Business, on the W side of town. Phone 217/732-8930.* Replica on the site of the original courthouse that Henry Ford acquired and restored for his Greenfield Village museum in Dearborn, Michigan. Lincoln practiced law in the original courthouse twice a year while Postville was the county seat (1840-1848). Interpretive program. (See SPECIAL EVENTS) (Fri-Sat afternoons; closed holidays) **DONATION**

Special Events

1800s Craft Fair. *Postville Courthouse, 914 5th St, Lincoln. Phone 217/732-8930.* Artisans demonstrate skills from the 1800s, including blacksmithing, quilting, wood carving, and broom making. Traditional music. Late Aug.

Abraham Lincoln National Railsplitting Contest & Crafts Festival. *Logan County Fairgrounds, 47 Gavin St, Lincoln. Phone 217/732-7146.* Contests, entertainment, flea market. Mid-Sept.

Logan County Fair. *Logan County Fairgrounds, 11th and Jefferson sts, Lincoln (62656). Phone 217/732-3311.* Tractor pulls, agricultural and farm machinery exhibits; horse races; livestock shows. Early Aug.

Limited-Service Hotel

★ **COMFORT INN.** *2811 Woodlawn Rd, Lincoln (62656). Phone 217/735-3960; toll-free 800/221-2222; fax 217/735-3960. www.comfortinn.com.* 52 rooms, 2 story. Pets accepted; fee. Complimentary continental breakfast. Check-out 11 am. Indoor pool, whirlpool. **$**
🐾 🏊

Lincoln's New Salem State Historic Site (C-3)

What to See and Do

Kelso Hollow Outdoor Theatre. *Rte 1, Box 244 A, Petersburg (62675). Phone 217/632-5440; toll-free 800/710-9290.* Performances nightly (early June-late Aug, Thurs-Sun). **$$$**

⭐ **Lincoln's New Salem State Historic Site.** *Petersburg. 2 miles S on Hwy 97. Phone 217/632-4000.* The wooded, 700-acre park incorporates a complete reconstruction, based on original maps and family archives, of New Salem as the village appeared when Lincoln lived there (1831-1837). Authentic reconstruction began in the early 1930s, with much of the work carried out by the New Deal's Civilian Conservation Corps (CCC). Today, New Salem consists of 12 timber houses; a school; and ten shops, stores, and industries, including the Denton Offutt store (where Lincoln first worked), the Lincoln-Berry store, the Rutledge tavern, and the saw and gristmill. The only original building is the Onstot cooper shop, which was discovered in Petersburg and returned to its original foundation in 1922. Interior furnishings are, for the most part, authentic to the 1830s period of Lincoln's residency. A variety of programs are offered throughout the year; self-guided tours; historical demonstrations; interpreters in period clothing; scheduled special events (see SPECIAL EVENTS under PETERSBURG); rides in a horse-drawn wagon. Visitor center offers 180-minute orientation film; exhibits. Picnicking, concession. Gift shop. Camping, tent and trailer sites (standard fees). (Daily; closed holidays) **DONATION**

Talisman Riverboat. *Petersburg. Dock near gristmill, across Hwy 97 from park (62675).* Phone 217/632-7681. Replica of *Talisman*, a small riverboat that went up the Sangamon River in Lincoln's day, offers hourly trips in season. (May-Labor Day, Tues-Sun; after Labor Day-Oct, Sat-Sun) **$$**

Lincolnshire

What to See and Do

Crane's Landing Golf Course. *10 Marriott Dr (60069). Phone 847/634-5935. www.marriott.com.* Originally designed by George Fazio and opened in 1975, this 6,290-yard, 18-hole course on 170 acres of parkland features views of the Des Plaines River and the surrounding woodlands. Standout features include 14 water holes; bent grass greens, tees, and fairways; and highly bunkered greens. **$$$$**

Marriott Lincolnshire Resort Theater. *10 Marriott Dr, Lincolnshire (60069). Phone 847/634-0200; fax 847/634-7022. www.marriotttheatre.com.*

Limited-Service Hotel

★ **HAMPTON INN AND SUITES.** *1400 N Milwaukee Ave, Lincolnshire (60069). Phone 847/478-1400; fax 847/478-1451. www.hamptoninn.com.* 117 rooms. Complimentary continental breakfast. Check-in 3 pm, check-out noon. High-speed Internet access. Fitness room. Indoor pool, whirlpool. Business center. **$**

Lockport

See also Joliet

Founded 1836
Population 15,191
Elevation 604 ft
Area Code 815
Zip 60441
Information Chamber of Commerce, 132 E 9th; phone 815/838-3357
Web site www.lockport.org

Lockport was founded as headquarters of the Illinois and Michigan Canal. In its heyday, the town boasted five different locks (four remain). Shipbuilding was once an important industry. The Old Canal Town National Historic District preserves several buildings from this bygone era.

What to See and Do

Illinois and Michigan Canal Museum. *803 S State St.* Phone 815/838-5080. (1837) Building originally used as Canal Commissioner's Office. Museum includes artifacts, pictures, and documents relating to the construction and operation of the canal. Guided tours by costumed docents. (Daily, afternoons; closed holidays; also weeks of Thanksgiving, Dec 25) **FREE** Also here are

Gaylord Building. *200 W 8th St, Lockport.* Phone 815/838-7400. (1838) Includes the Lockport Gallery, a branch site of the Illinois State Museum, which features art of various media by the state's past and present artists (Tues-Sun). Also in the building is the Illinois and Michigan Canal visitor center with interpreters and theater productions that highlight the area (Wed-Sun) and a restaurant with views of the canal (Tues-Sun).

Old Stone Annex Building. *803 S State St, Lockport.* Depicts early banking history and other exhibits. (Mid-Apr-Oct, daily) **FREE**

Pioneer Settlement. *Lockport.* Log cabins, village jail, root cellar, tinsmith and blacksmith shops, workshop, one-room schoolhouse, mid-19th-century farmhouse, smokehouse, privy, and railroad station. (Mid-Apr-Oct, afternoons) **FREE**

Special Events

Old Canal Days. *222 E 9th St, Lockport. Phone 815/838-4744.* Pioneer craft demonstrations, horse-drawn wagon tours, Illinois and Michigan Canal walking tours, Lockport prairie tours, museum open house, races, games, carnival, entertainment, food. Third weekend in June.

Western Open Golf Tournament. *12294 S Archer Ave, Lemont (60439). Phone 630/257-5872.* Approximately 8 miles N via Archer Ave, at Cog Hill Golf Club in Lemont (see). Early July.

Restaurants

★ ★ **PUBLIC LANDING.** *200 W 8th St, Lockport (60441). Phone 815/838-6500; fax 815/838-8917.* Built in 1838; an Illinois Historic Landmark. American menu. Lunch, dinner. Closed Mon. Bar. Children's menu. **$$**

★ ★ ★ **TALLGRASS.** *1006 S State, Lockport (60441). Phone 815/838-5566.* Master chef Robert Burcenski and executive chef Laura White (as well as their extraordinarily gracious servers) offer a well-balanced, contemporary menu. Diners can choose from three to five courses (including appetizer and dessert). French menu. Dinner. Closed Mon-Tues; holidays. Bar. Reservations recommended. **$$$**

Lombard

Restaurants

★ ★ ★ **BISTRO BANLIEUE.** *44 Yorktown Convenience Center, Lombard (60148). Phone 630/629-6560; fax 630/629-6562. www.bistrob.com.* Don't let the strip mall location fool you. French menu. Dinner. Closed holidays. **$$**

★ ★ **GREEK ISLANDS WEST.** *300 E 22nd St, Lombard (60148). Phone 630/932-4545; fax 630/932-4547.* Greek menu. Lunch, dinner. Bar. Children's menu. **$$**

Macomb (C-2)

See also Galesburg, Monmouth, Nauvoo

Founded 1830
Population 18,558
Elevation 700 ft
Area Code 309
Zip 61455
Information Macomb Area Convention and Visitors Bureau, 201 S Lafayette St; phone 309/833-1315
Web site www.macomb.com

Originally known as Washington, the town was renamed to honor General Alexander Macomb, an officer in the War of 1812. Macomb is best known as the home of Western Illinois University (see).

What to See and Do

Argyle Lake State Park. *640 Argyle Park Rd. 7 miles W on Hwy 136, then 1 1/2 miles N. Phone 309/776-3422.* The park has 1,700 acres with a 95-acre lake. Fishing, boating (ramp, rentals; motors, 10-hp limit). Hunting, hiking, cross-country skiing, snowmobiling, picnicking, playground, concession, shelter house, camping (showers). (Daily) **FREE**

Spring Lake Park. *595 Spring Lake Park Rd. 3 miles N on Hwy 67, then 2 miles W, then 1 mile N. Phone 309/833-2052.* On 300 acres. Fishing; picnicking; camping (fee). **FREE**

Western Illinois University. *1 University Cir. NW edge of city. Phone 309/298-1993. www.wiu.edu.* (1899) (12,000 students) The 1,050-acre campus includes an art gallery (Mon-Fri; free); 600,000-volume library; Illinois/National Business Hall of Fame in Stipes Hall; agricultural experiment station at the north edge of campus; Geology Museum, first floor of Tillman Hall; and a nine-hole public golf course, Tower Road (Apr-Oct, daily; fee). Also on campus are

Biological Sciences Greenhouse. *1 University, Macomb. S of Waggoner Hall. Phone 309/298-1004.* Gardens and nature area. Includes tropical and temperate plants; native aquatic, prairie, and woodland plants and herbs. (Mon-Fri) **FREE**

Limited-Service Hotel

★ ★ **DAYS INN.** *1400 N Lafayette St, Macomb (61455). Phone 309/833-5511; fax 309/836-2926. www. daysinn.com.* 144 rooms, 2 story. Check-out 11 am. Restaurant, bar. Pool. **$**

🅿 ⛔

Marion (F-4)

See also Benton, Carbondale, Du Quoin

Founded 1839
Population 16,035
Elevation 448 ft
Area Code 618
Zip 62959
Information Greater Marion Area Chamber of Commerce, 2305 W Main St, PO Box 307; phone 618/997-6311
Web site www.cc.marion.il.us

A regional trade center serving 90,000 people, Marion is the seat of Williamson County.

What to See and Do

⭐ **Crab Orchard National Wildlife Refuge.** *RR 2, Box J. Headquarters, 5 miles W on Hwy 13, then 2 1/2 miles S on Hwy 148. Phone 618/997-3344.* Refuge for wintering Canada geese includes 7,000-acre Crab Orchard Lake, west of headquarters; Little Grassy Lake, 8 miles south; and Devil's Kitchen Lake, just east of Little Grassy. Swimming, fishing, boat ramps and rentals. Hunting, trapping, nature trails, picnicking; camping at Crab Orchard, Little Grassy, and Devil's Kitchen (rest rooms, showers at all campgrounds; fees). Pets on leash only. Headquarters (Mon-Fri; closed holidays). Area (all year, daily). **$$**

Lake of Egypt. *Pyramid Acres Campground and Marina, 75 Egyptian Pkwy. 8 miles S via I-57, Hwy 37. Phone 618/964-1184.* Activities on 2,300-acre stocked lake include water-skiing, fishing, boating (rentals, launching); camping. (Daily)

⭐ **Shawnee National Forest.** *50 Hwy 145 S (62946). Via I-57, I-24. Phone 618/253-7114.* Approximately 278,000 acres, bordered on east by Ohio River, on west by Mississippi River; unusual rock formations, varied wildlife. Swimming, fishing, boating. Hunting, hiking and bridle trails, picnicking, camping on a

first-come, first-served basis. Fees may be charged at recreation sites. Contact Forest Supervisor, 901 S Commercial St, Harrisburg 62946. **$$**

Special Event

Williamson County Fair. *Marion. Phone 618/997-6311.* June.

Limited-Service Hotel

★ **COMFORT INN.** *2600 W Main St, Marion (62959). Phone 618/993-6221; fax 618/993-8964. www.comfortinn.com.* 122 rooms, 2 story. Complimentary continental breakfast. Check-out noon. Fitness room. Pool. Airport transportation available. **$**

🏃 ⛔

Restaurant

★ ★ **TONY'S STEAK HOUSE.** *105 S Market St, Marion (62959). Phone 618/993-2220; fax 618/997-6031.* Steak menu. Dinner. Closed Sun; holidays. Bar. **$$**

Marshall (D-5)

Founded 1835
Population 3,771
Elevation 641 ft
Area Code 217
Zip 62441
Information Chamber of Commerce, 708 Archer Ave, PO Box 263; phone 217/826-2034

The site on which Marshall is now located was purchased from the federal government in 1833 by Colonel William Archer and Joseph Duncan, sixth governor of Illinois. They named the town after John Marshall, fourth Chief Justice of the United States Supreme Court. Seat of Clark County, Marshall serves as a business center for the surrounding agricultural community.

What to See and Do

Lincoln Trail State Park. *16985 E 1350th Rd. Phone 217/826-2222.* The Lincoln family passed through here en route from Indiana in 1830. This 1,022-acre park has fishing in an artificial lake, boating (ramp, rentals; motors, 10-hp limit). Hiking, picnicking, concession, camping. (Daily) **FREE**

Mill Creek Park. *20482 N Park Entrance Rd. 7 miles NW on Lincoln Heritage Trail.* Swimming, fishing, boating; camping, cabins; bridle and ATV trails (weather permitting). (Daily, late Mar-Oct) **FREE**

Special Event

Autumn Fest. *Town Square, Marshall (62441). Phone 217/826-5645.* Third weekend in Sept.

Mattoon (D-4)

See also Arcola, Charleston, Effingham

Founded 1854
Population 18,291
Elevation 726 ft
Area Code 217
Zip 61938
Information Mattoon Chamber of Commerce, 1701 Wabash Ave; phone 217/235-5661 or -5666
Web site www.mattoonchamber.com

Named for a railroad official who built the Big Four Railroad from St. Louis, Missouri, to Indianapolis, Indiana, Mattoon is an industrial town and a retail and market center for the surrounding farm area. Products vary from heavy road machinery to bagels and magazines. In 1861, General Ulysses S. Grant mustered the 25th Illinois Infantry into service in Mattoon.

What to See and Do

Lake Mattoon. *6 miles S on Hwy 45, I-57, then 3 miles W.* Fishing, boating, launching facilities; picnicking; camping.

Special Event

Bagelfest. *1701 Wabash Ave, Mattoon. Phone 217/235-5661.* World's biggest bagel breakfast. Bagelfest Queen Pageant, Beautiful Bagel Baby Contest. Parade, talent show, music. Last Sat in July.

Limited-Service Hotel

★ ★ **RAMADA INN.** *300 Broadway Ave E, Mattoon (61938). Phone 217/235-0313; fax 217/235-6005. www.ramada.com.* 124 rooms, 2 story. Pets accepted, some restrictions. Check-out noon. Restaurant, bar. Indoor pool, outdoor pool, whirlpool. **$**

McHenry (A-4)

See also Gurnee, Woodstock

Population 21,501
Elevation 761 ft
Area Code 815
Zip 60050
Information Chamber of Commerce, 1257 N Green St; phone 815/385-4300

What to See and Do

Moraine Hills State Park. *914 S River Rd. Phone 815/385-1624.* Three small lakes on 1,690 acres. Fishing, boating (rentals); bike and hiking trails (11 miles); cross-country skiing (rentals); picnicking, concession. Nature center. (Daily; closed Dec 25) **FREE**

Volo Auto Museum and Village. *27582 Volo Village Rd, Volo. 1/2 mile W of Rte 12 on Rte 120. Phone 815/385-3644. www.volocars.com.* Display of more than 300 antique and collector cars. Largest display of TV and movie cars including the "Batmobile" and the "General Lee" from *The Dukes of Hazard*. Collection also includes "K.I.T.T" from *Knight Rider*, "Christine" from the movie based on Stephen King's book, and cars driven in *The Fast and the Furious* and *Gone in 60 Seconds*. Easily accessible by Metra commuter train, there also are gift, antique, and craft shops. Autos displayed and sold. Restaurant. (Daily; closed holidays) **$$**

Limited-Service Hotel

★ ★ **HOLIDAY INN.** *Rte 31 and Three Oaks Rd, Crystal Lake (60014). Phone 815/477-7000; toll-free 800/465-4329; fax 815/477-7027. www.holidayinncrystallake.com.* 197 rooms, 6 story. Check-in 3 pm, check-out noon. High-speed Internet access. Restaurant, two bars. Fitness room. Indoor pool, whirlpool. Airport transportation available. **$**

Restaurants

★ **JENNY'S.** *2500 N Chapel Hill Rd, McHenry (60050). Phone 815/385-0333; fax 815/385-0153. www.chapelhillgolf.com.* American menu. Dinner, Sun brunch. Closed Mon-Tues; Dec 25. Bar. Children's menu. **$$**

★ ★ ★ **LE VICHYSSOIS.** *220 W Hwy 120, Lakemoor (60050). Phone 815/385-8221. www. levichyssois.com.* Situated across from a lake in northwest suburban Lakemoor, this bucolic inn is a civilized retreat for classic French cuisine (chef/owner Bernard Cretier trained under Paul Bocuse). The prices are quaint, too, including the wine list (and the four-course "bistro menu" is the best bargain of all). It's romantic and cozy here, with classical background music, a central fireplace, painted plates, and prints of country scenes lining the walls. French bistro menu. Dinner. Closed Mon-Tues; holidays. Reservations recommended. **$$$**

Metropolis (F-4)

Specialty Lodging

The following lodging establishment is approved by Mobil Travel Guide but, due to its unique and individualized nature has not been given a traditional Mobil Star rating. Included in this listing you may find bed-and-breakfasts, limited-service inns, guest ranches, and other unique hotel properties.

ISLE OF VIEW BED & BREAKFAST. *205 Metropolis St, Metropolis (62960). Phone 618/524-5838; toll-free 800/566-7491. www.isle-of-view.net.* Built in 1889 and renowned as one of the area's finest bed-and-breakfasts, this Victorian inn lies one block from the Ohio River. 5 rooms, 3 story. **$**

Moline (B-2)

See also Galesburg, Rock Island

Founded 1848
Population 43,768
Elevation 580 ft
Area Code 309
Zip 61265
Information Quad Cities Convention & Visitors Bureau, 2021 River Dr; phone 309/788-7800 or toll-free 800/747-7800
Web site www.visitquadcities.com

Settled by a significant number of Belgians, Moline takes its name from the French moulin (mill), in reference to the many mills that were built along the Mississippi River to take advantage of the limitless supply of water power. Today, the city produces goods varying from farm implements to elevators. Moline and Rock Island, along with Bettendorf and Davenport, Iowa (across the Mississippi River), constitute the Quad Cities metropolitan area.

What to See and Do

Center for Belgian Culture. *712 18th Ave. Phone 309/762-0167.* Houses Belgian memorabilia. (Wed, Sat afternoons) **FREE**

✪ **Deere & Company World Headquarters.** *1 John Deere Pl. Phone 309/765-8000. www.deere.com.* World headquarters for manufacturers of farm, industrial, lawn, and garden equipment. Administrative Center (1964), designed by Eero Saarinen, who also designed the arch in St. Louis, Missouri, is considered a masterpiece of modern architecture. On 1,000 acres overlooking Rock River Valley, the center consists of a main office building with display floor, 400-seat auditorium, and the newer west office building. Main office building was constructed of corrosion-resistant unpainted steel and is set across the floor of a wooded ravine; display floor includes three-dimensional mural, designed by Alexander Girard, composed of more than 2,000 items dating from 1837 to 1918 that relate to agriculture and life in mid-America during that period. West office building (1978), designed by Roche and Dinkeloo with a skylighted interior garden court, has been cited for its harmonious relation to the original buildings. Grounds include two large pools with many fountains and an island with a Henry Moore sculpture. Tours of Administrative Center (Mon-Fri; closed holidays). Factory tours (children over 11 years only). Main building (daily). **FREE**

John Deere Commons. *1400 River Dr. Phone 309/765-1001. www.johndeerecommons.com.* On the banks of the Mississippi River, this complex is home to the John Deere Pavilion, a visitor center with interactive displays about agriculture and vintage and modern John Deere equipment. Also here are a John Deere Store; a restaurant; a hotel; The MARK of the Quad Cities, a 12,000-seat arena hosting high-profile events; and Centre Station, the transportation hub and information center for the Quad Cities. (Daily) **FREE**

Niabi Zoo. *13010 Niabi Zoo Rd, Coal Valley (61240). 10 miles SE on Hwy 6. Phone 309/799-5107. www. niabizoo.com.* Miniature railroad (fee); children's zoo;

picnicking, snack bar. (Daily; closed Jan 1, Dec 25) Free admission Tues. **$$**

Limited-Service Hotel

★ **HAMPTON INN.** *6920 27th St, Moline (61265). Phone 309/762-1711; fax 309/762-1788. www. hamptoninn.com.* 138 rooms, 2 story. Pets accepted; fee. Complimentary continental breakfast. Check-out noon. Airport transportation available. **$**

Monmouth (B-2)

See also Galesburg, Macomb

Founded 1831
Population 9,489
Elevation 770 ft
Area Code 309
Zip 61462
Information Monmouth Area Chamber of Commerce, 68 Public Sq; phone 309/734-3181

Monmouth was named to commemorate the Revolutionary War Battle of Monmouth, New Jersey, and was the birthplace of Wyatt Earp. There is a memorial to Earp in Monmouth Park. The town is located on the prairie in a region famous for the production of corn, soybeans, hogs, and cattle.

What to See and Do

Buchanan Center for the Arts. *64 Public Sq. Phone 309/734-3033.* Art and cultural exhibits in a modern gallery. (Mon-Sat) **FREE**

Pioneer Cemetery. *200 N 6th St (61462). E Archer Ave near 5th St. Phone 309/734-3181.* Relatives of Wyatt Earp are buried here.

Wyatt Earp Birthplace. *406 S 3rd St. Phone 309/734-3181.* The US Deputy Marshal's first family home from his birth in 1848 until 1850, when the family left for the California gold rush. (Memorial Day-Labor Day, Sun afternoons; also by appointment) **DONATION**

Special Events

Maple City Summerfest. *Downtown Monmouth (61462). Phone 309/734-3181.* Flea market, games, entertainment, bike run. Mid-July.

Warren County Prime Beef Festival. *N 11th St, Monmouth (61462). Phone 309/734-3181.* Beef and hog shows and auctions. Displays, events, entertainment, carnival, parade. Four days beginning Wed after Labor Day.

Limited-Service Hotel

★ **HAWTHORN INN & SUITES.** *1200 W Broadway, Monmouth (61462). Phone 309/734-0909; toll-free 877/777-3099; fax 309/734-0910. www. hawthorn.com.* 62 rooms. Check-in 3 pm, check-out noon. Indoor pool, whirlpool. **$**

Morris (B-4)

See also Joliet, Ottawa

Founded 1842
Population 11,928
Elevation 519 ft
Area Code 815
Zip 60450
Information Grundy County Chamber of Commerce and Industry, 112 E Washington St; phone 815/942-0113

What to See and Do

Gebhard Woods State Park. *401 Ottawa St. W edge of town. Phone 815/942-0796.* The Illinois and Michigan Canal flows along the southern edge of this 30-acre park, which offers fishing and canoeing in small ponds, Nettle Creek, and the canal; hiking, biking, snowmobiling, picnicking, primitive camping. (Daily) **FREE**

Illinois and Michigan Canal State Trail. *401 Ottawa St. Phone 815/942-0796.* The Illinois and Michigan Canal, completed in 1848 at a cost of $6.5 million, stretched 61 miles, linking Lake Michigan and Chicago with the Illinois River at La Salle. Four state parks have been established on the 60-mile trail, among them Buffalo Rock (see OTTAWA). (Daily)

Special Event

Grundy County Corn Festival. *Morris. Phone 815/942-0113.* Music, horse show, parade. Last week in Sept.

Limited-Service Hotel

★ ★ **HOLIDAY INN.** *200 Gore Rd, Morris (60450). Phone 815/942-6006; toll-free 800/465-4329; fax 815/942-8255. www.holiday-inn.com.* 120 rooms, 2 story. Pets accepted, some restrictions. Check-out noon. Restaurant, bar. Indoor pool, whirlpool. **$**

Restaurants

★ **R-PLACE FAMILY EATERY.** *21 Romines Dr, Morris (60450). Phone 815/942-3690; fax 815/942-3698.* Truck stop with Victorian-era décor; chandeliers, Tiffany-style lamps; extensive collection of Americana, antique toys, mechanical puppets, gas station memorabilia. American menu. Breakfast, lunch, dinner, late-night. Children's menu. **$**

★ **ROCKWELL INN.** *2400 W Hwy 6, Morris (60450). Phone 815/942-6224; fax 815/942-6266. www. rockwellinn.50megs.com.* Norman Rockwell prints; bar from 1893 Columbian Exposition. American menu. Lunch, dinner, Sun brunch. Closed Dec 25. Bar. Children's menu. **$$**

Mount Vernon (E-4)

See also Benton, Centralia, Du Quoin, Salem

Population 16,269
Elevation 500 ft
Area Code 618
Zip 62864
Information Convention and Visitors Bureau, 200 Potomac Blvd; phone 618/242-3151 or toll-free 800/252-5464
Web site www.southernillinois.com

What to See and Do

Cedarhurst. *Richview Rd. Phone 618/242-1236 (museum).* An 85-acre estate that includes Mitchell Museum, a nature walk, and bird sanctuary; Sculpture Park, an outdoor art center with visual and performing arts programs; Art Center provides year-round classes and workshops (fee); Chamber Music offers a series of concerts. (Tues-Sat, Sun afternoons; closed holidays) **FREE**

Special Events

Cedarhurst Craft Fair. *1800 Richview Rd, Mount Vernon (62864). Phone 618/242-1236.* Entertainment, food, juried art and craft show. Sat-Sun after Labor Day.

Sweet Corn-Watermelon Festival. *Downtown, Mount Vernon (62864). Phone 618/242-3151.* Entertainment, flea market, parade. Free sweet corn and watermelon. Third week in Aug.

Limited-Service Hotel

★ ★ **HOLIDAY INN.** *222 Potomac Blvd, Mount Vernon (62864). Phone 618/244-7100; toll-free 800/243-7171; fax 618/242-8876. www. holiday-inn.com.* 223 rooms, 5 story. Pets accepted, some restrictions; fee. Check-out 1 pm. Restaurant, bar. Indoor pool, whirlpool. Airport transportation available. **$**

Naperville (A-4)

See also Aurora, Downers Grove, Wheaton

Settled 1831
Population 128,358
Elevation 700 ft
Area Code 630
Information Visitors Bureau, 131 W Jefferson Ave, 60540; phone 630/355-4141
Web site www.napervilleil.com

Naperville, the oldest town in DuPage County, was settled by Captain Joseph Naper. Soon after, in the late 1830s, settlers of German ancestry came from Pennsylvania to transform the prairie into farmland. Although today's city is at the center of a "research and high-technology corridor" and has been cited as one of the fastest-growing suburbs in the nation, Naperville retains something of the atmosphere of a small town with its core of large Victorian houses and a beautiful historic district. The downtown shopping district features more than 100 shops and restaurants in historic buildings; it adjoins the Riverwalk, a 3 1/2-mile winding brick pathway along the DuPage River.

What to See and Do

Naper Settlement. *523 S Webster St (60540). Phone 630/420-6010.* A 13-acre living history museum of

25 buildings in a village setting depicts a 19th-century northern Illinois town (circa 1830-1900). Tour by costumed guides includes four residences of the period; Martin-Mitchell Mansion, with period furnishings; several public buildings and working businesses, such as a printshop, smithy, and stonecutter's shop. Also Les Schrader Art Gallery, with a 42-painting exhibit depicting the growth and development of a Midwest town, and a museum shop. Special events throughout year (fee). (Apr-Oct, Tues-Sun; rest of year, Tues-Fri) (See SPECIAL EVENT) **$$**

Special Event

Christmas in the Village. *Naper Settlement, 212 S Webster St, Naperville (60540). Phone 630/305-7701.* Nineteenth-century festivities, period decorations. Dec.

Limited-Service Hotels

★ **COURTYARD BY MARRIOTT.** *1155 E Diehl Rd, Naperville (60563). Phone 630/505-0550; toll-free 800/228-9290; fax 630/505-8337. www.courtyard.com.* 147 rooms. Check-in 3 pm, check-out 1 pm. Fitness room. Indoor pool, whirlpool. **$**

★ **HAMPTON INN.** *1087 E Diehl Rd, Naperville (60563). Phone 630/505-1400; fax 630/505-1416. www.hamptoninn.com.* 128 rooms, 4 story. Complimentary continental breakfast. Check-in 3 pm, check-out noon. Fitness room. Outdoor pool. Business center. **$**

Full-Service Hotels

★ ★ ★ **HYATT LISLE.** *1400 Corporetum Dr, Lisle (60532). Phone 630/852-1234; fax 630/852-1260. www.lisle.hyatt.com.* Guests may want to venture out for a round of golf at one of three courses that are within an 8-mile radius of this hotel. 312 rooms, 14 story. Check-in 3 pm, check-out noon. Restaurant, bar. Fitness room. Indoor pool, whirlpool. **$$**

★ ★ ★ **WYNDHAM LISLE HOTEL.** *3000 Warrenville Rd, Lisle (60532). Phone 630/505-1000; toll-free 800/996-3426; fax 630/505-1165. www.wyndham.com.* 242 rooms, 8 story. Check-in 3 pm,

check-out noon. High-speed Internet access. Restaurant, bar. Fitness room. Indoor pool, whirlpool. **$**

Restaurants

★ ★ **ELAINE.** *10 W Jackson St, Naperville (60540). Phone 630/548-3100.* International/Fusion menu. Dinner. Closed Sun. Bar. Casual attire. Outdoor seating. **$$$**

★ ★ ★ **MESON SABIKA.** *1025 Aurora Ave, Naperville (60540). Phone 630/983-3000; fax 630/983-0715. www.mesonsabika.com.* There's no chance of boredom at this colorful Spanish tapas restaurant, with eight different, ornately decorated dining rooms; an extensive menu of small, shareable dishes; and plenty of sangria. This beautiful Victorian mansion (circa 1847) is surrounded by gardens and has a pleasant outdoor terrace. Spanish, tapas menu. Lunch, dinner, Sun brunch. Closed holidays. Bar. Children's menu. Casual attire. Outdoor seating. **$$**

★ ★ **RAFFI'S ON 5TH.** *200 E 5th Ave, Naperville (60563). Phone 630/961-8203.* Exposed-brick walls and soaring ceilings create an urban loft setting, fitting for the cosmopolitan Raffi's. Middle Eastern rugs and artwork should tip you off that Raffi's best dishes, despite a pan-Mediterranean menu, hail from that region. Raves go the grilled lamb chops, chicken kebobs, couscous, tabbouleh, and stuffed grape leaves. The sophisticated setting makes this a favored choice for daters. Mediterranean menu. Lunch, dinner. Bar. Casual attire. **$$**

★ ★ **SAMBA ROOM.** *22 E Chicago Ave, Naperville (60540). Phone 630/753-0985; fax 630/753-0992.* Loud, brash, and spicy, Samba Room conjures the sexy, free-spirited aura of pre-Castro Cuba. Bossa nova in the air and the potent mojitos freely flowing from the bar make party-hardy patrons feel at home. But foodies will be satisfied too with the cumin-rubbed pork tenderloin, whole fried snapper, and rum-glazed mahi mahi. The serpentine bar and colorful interiors distract diners waiting for tables on weekends. You'll find several sibling Samba Rooms, a small Dallas-based chain, around the country. Latin American menu. Lunch, dinner. Closed Dec 25. Bar. Casual attire. Outdoor seating. **$$**

Nauvoo (C-2)

See also Macomb

Settled 1839
Population 1,063
Elevation 659 ft
Area Code 217
Zip 62354
Information Tourist Center, 1295 Mulholland (Hwy 96), PO Box 41; phone 217/453-6648

Once the largest city in Illinois, Nauvoo has a colorful history. When the Mormon prophet Joseph Smith was driven out of Missouri, he came with his Latter-day Saints to a tiny village called Commerce on a promontory overlooking the Mississippi River and established what was virtually an autonomous state. A city of 8,000 houses was created, and, in 1841, construction began on a great temple. A schism in the church and the threat of Mormon political power led to riots and persecution of the Mormons. Joseph Smith and his brother were arrested and murdered by a mob while in the Carthage jail. Brigham Young became leader of the Nauvoo Mormons. When the city charter was repealed and armed clashes broke out anew, Young led much of the population westward in 1846 to its final settlement in Utah. Nauvoo became a ghost city, and the almost-completed temple was set on fire by an arsonist. In 1849, the Icarians, a band of French communalists, migrated to Nauvoo from Texas and established their short-lived experiment in communal living. They attempted to rebuild the temple, but a storm swept the building back into ruin. The Icarians failed to prosper and in 1856 moved on. The city was gradually resettled by a more conventional group of Germans, who developed the wine culture begun by the French group.

What to See and Do

Baxter's Vineyards. *2010 E Parley St. Phone 217/453-2528.* Established in 1857. Tours, wine tasting. (Daily; closed Jan 1, Thanksgiving, Dec 25) **FREE**

Joseph Smith Historic Center. *149 Water St. One block W of Hwy 96. Phone 217/453-2246.* A 50-minute tour begins in the visitor center and includes an 18-minute video. Book/gift shop. (Daily; closed Jan 1, Thanksgiving, Dec 25; also Dec 24, 31) **FREE** Tour includes

Grave of Joseph Smith. *149 Water St, Nauvoo. Phone 217/453-2246.* Also burial place of Smith's wife, Emma, and his brother Hyrum; the location of these graves, originally kept secret, was eventually lost; they were found in 1928 after an extensive search.

Joseph Smith Homestead. *149 Water St, Nauvoo. Phone 217/453-2246.* (1803) Log cabin the prophet occupied upon coming to Nauvoo in 1839 and town's oldest structure; period furnishings.

Smith's Mansion. *149 Water St, Nauvoo. Phone 217/453-2246.* (1843) Refined, Federal-style frame house occupied by Smith from 1843 to 1844; period furnishings.

Smith's Red Brick Store. *149 Water St, Nauvoo. Phone 217/453-2246.* (1842) Reconstructed building. Gift shops. Merchandise on shelves reflects items sold in 1842-1844.

⭐ **Nauvoo Restoration, Inc, Visitor Center.** *Young and N Main sts. Phone 217/453-2237.* Center has a 20-minute movie on Nauvoo history; exhibits; pamphlet with suggested tour and information on points of interest (daily). Also here are Seventy Hall; an 1840s meetinghouse; Lyon Drug Store; the Nauvoo Temple site; Montrose Crossing Monument; Sarah Kimball Home, William Weeks Home, and Noble-Smith Home; Pendleton log house; Webb blacksmith and wagon shop; Stoddard tin shop; Riser Cobbler shop; an 1840 theater; brick kiln; Clark store; Old Post Office and Merryweather Mercantile; Family Living Center with barrel-, candle-, and pottery-making; Jonathan Browning Home and Gun Shop; Scovil Bakery; and other significant structures. **FREE** Guide service in the following buildings:

Brigham Young Home. *Kimball and Granger sts, Nauvoo. Phone 217/453-6413.* Restored house of Joseph Smith's successor. **FREE**

Heber C. Kimball Home. *Munson and Partridge sts, Nauvoo.* Restored house of one of Joseph Smith's 12 apostles. **FREE**

Print Shop. *Main and Kimball sts, Nauvoo.* Restored offices of Mormon newspaper and post office.

Wilford Woodruff Home. *Durphy and Hotchkiss sts, Nauvoo.* Restored house of apostle and missionary. **FREE**

Nauvoo State Park. *980 S Bluff St. S on Hwy 96. Phone 217/453-2512.* On 148 acres. Restored house with wine cellar and century-old adjoining vineyard; museum (May-Sept). Fishing, boating (ramp, electric motors only). Hiking, picnic area (shelter), playgrounds, camping. (See SPECIAL EVENTS) (Daily) **FREE**

Old Carthage jail. *307 Walnut St, Carthage. 12 miles S on Hwy 96, then 14 miles E on Hwy 136. Phone 217/357-2989.* (1839-1841) Restored jail where Joseph Smith and his brother were killed; ten-minute tour; visitor center has 18-minute film presentation, pamphlets, exhibits. (Daily) **FREE**

Special Events

City of Joseph Pageant. *Main and Young sts, Nauvoo. Phone 217/453-2237.* Weekends in late July.

Grape Festival. *Nauvoo State Park, 980 S Bluff St, Nauvoo (62354). Phone 217/453-2512.* Includes classic French ceremony Wedding of the Wine and Cheese. Labor Day weekend.

Full-Service Inn

★ ★ ★ **HOTEL NAUVOO.** *1290 Mulholland St, Nauvoo (62354). Phone 217/453-2211; fax 217/453-6100. www.hotelnauvoo.com.* Restored historic inn (1840), originally a private residence. 8 rooms. Check-in 4 pm, check-out 11 am. Restaurant, bar. **$**
🄳

Restaurants

★ **GRANDPA JOHN'S.** *1255 Mulholland St, Nauvoo (62354). Phone 217/453-2310; fax 217/453-6100.* Established in 1912. American menu. Breakfast, lunch. Closed Jan-Feb. Children's menu. **$**

★ ★ ★ **HOTEL NAUVOO.** *1290 Mulholland St (Hwy 96), Nauvoo (62354). Phone 217/453-2211. www.hotelnauvoo.com.* Built in 1840 for Mormon founder Joseph Smith, this restored eight-room inn and restaurant reside in west-central Illinois along the Mississippi River. From mid-April to mid-November, visitors can sample the all-American prix fixe buffet that includes such favorites as fried chicken and apple pie. American menu. Dinner, Sun brunch. Closed Mon; mid-Nov-mid-Mar. Bar. **$$**

Northbrook

See also Glenview, Highland Park, Wheeling

Population 33,435
Elevation 650 ft
Area Code 847
Zip 60062
Information Chamber of Commerce, 2002 Walters Ave; phone 847/498-5555

The earliest European settlers in the Northbrook area were German immigrants who arrived after the construction of the Erie Canal in 1825. In 1901, the town was incorporated as Shermerville, in honor of one of the founding families. Brickyards played a major role in the prosperity and growth of the community. After the Great Chicago Fire of 1871, brick manufacturing surpassed farming as a leading industry; 300,000 bricks per day were produced between 1915-1920. In 1923, Shermerville was renamed Northbrook in reference to the middle forks of the north branches of the Chicago River, which run through the town. Today, Northbrook, located in the heart of Chicago's North Shore, is the headquarters of a number of major corporations.

What to See and Do

⭐ **Chicago Botanic Garden.** *1000 Lake Cook Rd, Glencoe. 1/2 mile E of I-94 (Hwy 41), Lake Cook Rd exit. Phone 847/835-5440.* Managed by the Chicago Horticultural Society, this garden includes 300 acres of formal plantings, lakes, lagoons, and wooded naturalistic areas. Specialty gardens include bulb, aquatic, perennial, and herb landscaped demonstration gardens; Japanese garden; English walled garden; prairie and nature trail; fruit and vegetable garden; heritage garden; rose garden; waterfall garden; sensory garden for the visually impaired; and learning garden for the disabled. The Education Center consists of an auditorium, floral arts museum, exhibit hall, shop, greenhouses, concession. Narrated tram ride. (Daily; closed Dec 25) **$$**

River Trail Nature Center. *3120 N Milwaukee Ave. 1/2 mile S of Willow Rd. Phone 847/824-8360.* A 300-acre nature preserve within the Forest Preserve District of Cook County. Nature trails; interpretive museum (Mon-Thurs, Sat-Sun); special activities (see SPECIAL EVENT); naturalist. (Daily; closed Jan 1, Thanksgiving, Dec 25) **FREE**

Special Event

Maple Sugar Festival. *River Trail Nature Center, 3120 N Milwaukee Ave, Northbrook (60062). Phone 847/824-8360.* Native American, pioneer, and modern methods of maple sugaring demonstrated by staff naturalist. Last Sun in Mar.

Limited-Service Hotel

★ ★ **COURTYARD BY MARRIOTT.** *800 Lake Cook Rd, Deerfield (60015). Phone 847/940-8222; toll-free 800/321-2211; fax 847/940-7741.* 131 rooms, 2 story. Check-in 3 pm, check-out noon. Restaurant. Fitness room. Indoor pool, whirlpool. **$**

Full-Service Hotels

★ ★ ★ **HYATT DEERFIELD.** *1750 Lake Cook Rd, Deerfield (60015). Phone 847/945-3400; fax 847/945-3563. www.hyatt.com.* 301 rooms, 6 story. Check-in 3 pm, check-out noon. Restaurant, bar. Fitness room. Indoor pool, whirlpool. **$**

★ ★ ★ **RENAISSANCE CHICAGO NORTH SHORE HOTEL.** *933 Skokie Blvd, Northbrook (60062). Phone 847/498-6500; fax 847/498-9558. www.renaissancehotels.com.* This property features 22,000 square feet of meeting space that can accommodate up to 700 people. The hotel is 17 miles from O'Hare International Airport and just minutes from such area locations as Chicago Botanic Garden, Ravinia (see HIGHLAND PARK), Six Flags Great America (see GURNEE), and Northbrook Court mall. The dining facilities include Ruth's Chris Steak House and Eden Street Cafe. 385 rooms, 10 story. Check-in 3 pm, check-out noon. Restaurant, bar. Fitness room. Indoor pool. Business center. **$**

Restaurants

★ ★ **CEILING ZERO.** *500 Anthony Trail, Northbrook (60062). Phone 847/272-8111.* Housed in a former airplane hangar once a part of Northbrook's airport, Ceiling Zero is well grounded in continental cuisine. The menu sticks to classics like lobster bisque, white fish almandine, peppercorn filet mignon and thick-cut pork chops. The reverent atmosphere and assured but formal service combine to make Ceiling Zero a special occasion eatery in old school style. American menu. Lunch, dinner. Closed holidays. Bar. Casual attire. **$$**

★ **FRANCESCO'S HOLE IN THE WALL.** *254 Skokie Blvd, Northbrook (60062). Phone 847/272-0155; fax 847/482-0267.* Tiny, thronged, and beloved, Francesco's trades in old-country neighborhood Italian fare, crowd-pleasing and well-priced dishes like chicken Vesuvio, veal chops, homemade pastas, and daily fish specials. Impatient and urgently hungry diners will be challenged by Francesco's inevitable waits for one of its mere 17 tables. But those in Francesco's fan camp rave for the cozy confines and friendly service. Bring cash, as credit cards are not accepted. Italian menu. Lunch, dinner. Closed Tues; holidays; also Jan. Casual attire. No credit cards accepted. **$$**

★ **TONELLI'S.** *1038 Waukegan Rd, Northbrook (60062). Phone 847/272-4730; fax 847/272-9370.* Northbrook Italian Tonelli's serves up immigrant Italian-American food that takes you back to the old neighborhood. Go hungry for generous portions of lasagna, spaghetti with meatballs, baked mostaccioli, and, for the "dolce" course, tiramisu. Fans consider the pizza among the North Shore's best. Portions are huge and prices reasonable, making Tonelli's a good value choice for families. Italian menu. Lunch, dinner. Closed Easter, Thanksgiving, Dec 25. Bar. Children's menu. Casual attire. Outdoor seating. **$$**

Oak Brook

See also Brookfield, Downers Grove, Elmhurst, Hinsdale, La Grange

Population 2,300
Elevation 675 ft
Information Village of Oak Brook, 1200 Oak Brook Rd; phone 630/990-3000

Known as Fullersburg in the mid-1800s, Oak Brook is the home of Butler National Golf Club. Sports and recreation have long been important in this carefully planned village; it has established and maintains 12 miles of biking and hiking paths and over 450 acres of parks and recreation land. Today, Oak Brook is identified as both a mecca for international polo players and the headquarters of many major corporations.

What to See and Do

Fullersburg Woods Environmental Center. *3609 Spring Rd (60523). Phone 630/850-8110.* Observation of wildlife in natural setting (all year); environmental center and theater, native marsh ecology exhibit; four nature trails. (Daily) **FREE**

Graue Mill and Museum. *York and Spring rds (60523). Phone 630/655-2090.* Restored mill built in 1852; the only operating water-powered gristmill in the state; station of the Underground Railroad. Mill demonstrates grinding of corn on buhrstones. Exhibits include farm and home implements of the period; rooms in Victorian and earlier periods; demonstrations of spinning and weaving. (Mid-Apr-mid-Nov, daily) **$$**

Special Event

Sunday Polo. *700 Oak Brook Rd, Oak Brook (60523). Phone 630/990-2394.* Mid-June-mid-Sept.

Limited-Service Hotels

★ **HAMPTON INN.** *222 E 22nd St, Lombard (60148). Phone 630/916-9000; toll-free 800/426-7866; fax 630/916-8016. www.hamptoninn.com.* 128 rooms, 4 story. Complimentary continental breakfast. Check-in 3 pm, check-out noon. High-speed Internet access. Fitness room. **$**

★ ★ **HILTON SUITES OAKBROOK TERRACE.** *10 Drury Ln, Oakbrook Terrace (60181). Phone 630/941-0100; toll-free 800/445-8667; fax 630/941-0299. www.oakbrookterracesuites.hilton.com.* 211 rooms, 10 story, all suites. Check-in 3 pm, check-out noon. Restaurant. Fitness room. Indoor pool, whirlpool. Business center. Drury Lane Theater adjacent. **$**

Full-Service Resort

★ ★ ★ **OAK BROOK HILLS RESORT.** *3500 Midwest Rd, Oak Brook (60523). Phone 630/850-5555; toll-free 800/445-3315; fax 630/850-5569. www.oakbrookhills-chicagohotel.com.* The Oak Brook Hills Resort is a superior conference destination. This 150-acre resort is truly a world of its own, yet it is only a short distance from Chicago's city limits. Recreational pursuits are endless here, with indoor and outdoor pools, a comprehensive fitness center, spa and salon services, volleyball and basketball courts, and even seasonal cross-country skiing. This resort is a golfer's delight, with the 18-hole Willow Crest Golf Club, considered one of the Midwest's finest courses, awaiting play just outside the door. The lush fairways wind their way along the resort's property and serve as a scenic backdrop for the three restaurants. From the informal ease of the Grille and Lobby Bar to the casual elegance of Windows Restaurant, the dining here always hits the mark. 384 rooms, 11 story. Check-in 4 pm, check-out noon. Three restaurants, bar. Fitness room, spa. Indoor pool, outdoor pool, whirlpool. Golf, 18 holes. Tennis. Business center. **$**

Restaurants

★ ★ **BRAXTON SEAFOOD GRILL.** *3 Oak Brook Center Mall, Oak Brook (60523). Phone 630/574-2155; fax 630/574-2256. www.braxtonseafood.com.* A mini-chain with several locations nationwide, Braxton Seafood Grill makes regionally sourced fresh seafood its theme. Lodged in the Oakbrook Center Mall, Braxton serves shoppers and area office workers a vast menu sure to please most fish lovers. Look for signature dishes including almond-crusted tilapia, Maryland crabcakes, grilled swordfish, cioppino seafood stew, and shrimp scampi, as well as live Maine lobster. Line cooks plating dishes behind the glass-enclosed kitchen provide entertainment. Seafood menu. Lunch, dinner. Closed holidays. Bar. Children's menu. **$$**

★ ★ **FOND DE LA TOUR.** *40 N Tower Rd, Oak Brook (60521). Phone 630/620-1500; fax 630/620-1858.* Oak Brook's tony French restaurant Fond de la Tour serves up classic fare in a formal setting to largely special-occasion celebrants. Nothing on the menu breaks new ground, but the cooking is practiced, from the overture sweetbreads and oysters Rockefeller to the encore cherries jubilee. Accomplished tableside service by tuxedoed waiters warrants ordering Caesar salad, steak tartare, and Dover sole. French menu.

Lunch, dinner. Closed Sun-Mon; holidays. Bar. Casual attire. Valet parking. **$$$**

★ **MELTING POT.** *17W633 Roosevelt Rd, Oakbrook Terrace (60181). Phone 630/495-5778. www.meltingpot .com.* Fondue menu. Dinner. Closed holidays. Bar. **$$**

★ ★ **MORTON'S OF CHICAGO.** *1 Westbrook Corporate Center, Westchester (60153). 22nd and Wolf rds. Phone 708/562-7000; fax 708/562-7073. www. mortons.com.* Steak menu. Dinner. Closed holidays. Bar. Valet parking. **$$$**

Oak Lawn (A-5)

Population 55,245
Elevation 615 ft
Area Code 708
Information Chamber of Commerce, 5314 W 95th St, 60453; phone 708/424-8300

In 1856, Oak Lawn was a settlement known as Black Oaks Grove. When the Wabash Railroad began to lay tracks through the community in 1879, an agreement was made with the railroad builder to create a permanent village. As a result of this agreement, the new town of Oak Lawn was officially established in 1882.

Full-Service Hotel

★ ★ ★ **HILTON.** *9333 S Cicero Ave, Oak Lawn (60453). Phone 708/425-7800; toll-free 800/445-9993; fax 708/425-1665. www.oaklawn.hilton.com.* Conveniently located near Midway Airport, this hotel provides free shuttle service for its guests. Area attractions include Balmoral Park (see CHICAGO), Chicago Motor Speedway, and riverboat casinos. The property amenities include a swimming pool and a fitness center. 184 rooms, 12 story. Check-in 3 pm, check-out noon. High-speed Internet access. Restaurant, bar. Fitness room. Indoor pool, whirlpool. Airport transportation available. Business center. **$**

✈ ⚚ ⛹ ⌑

Restaurants

★ ★ **OLD BARN.** *8100 S Central Ave, Burbank (60459). Phone 708/422-5400; fax 708/422-0295. www. theoldbarn.biz.* First opened in 1921, the Old Barn has been the watering hole for everyone from Charles Lindbergh Jr., to W. C. Fields. But the fact that they— and a host of other well-known personalities—were

once regulars here is not what draws customers. Mouthwatering American classics like filet mignon, T-bone steak, and prime rib so good it has been voted "#1 prime rib" by a local newspaper, are what keep them coming back. The original building (1933) was a speakeasy during Prohibition; original door buzzer. American menu. Lunch, dinner. Closed holidays. Bar. Children's menu. Valet parking. **$$**

★ ★ **PALERMO'S.** *4849 W 95th St, Oak Lawn (60453). Phone 708/425-6262.* This family-run restaurant just southwest of the city has been a local favorite for over 30 years. The dimly lit dining room is reminiscent of old-world Italy and is the perfect atmosphere for either a romantic dinner or a casual night out with the family. The menu of Italian-American fare is sizable and features standards like chicken Vesuvio and veal Parmigiana, as well as a variety of pastas and seasonal specials. And if it's pizza you're craving, look no further. Palermo's pizza—regular or thin crust, traditional or Chicago-style deep dish—is renowned throughout the area and is available for carry-out along with a selection of items from the dining room menu. Italian menu. Lunch, dinner. Closed Tues. Bar. Children's menu. Casual attire. **$$**

★ **WHITNEY'S GRILLE.** *9333 S Cicero Ave, Crestwood (60453). Phone 708/229-8888. www. oaklawn.hilton.com.* American menu. Breakfast, lunch, dinner, Sun brunch. Bar. Children's menu. **$$**

Oak Park

See also Cicero

Settled 1837
Population 52,524
Elevation 620 ft
Area Code 708
Information Oak Park-River Forest Chamber of Commerce, Oak Park Village Hall, 123 Madison St, 60302; phone 708/383-6400
Web site www.vil.oak-park.il.us

Oak Park, one of Chicago's oldest suburbs, is a village of well-kept houses and magnificent trees. The town is internationally famous as the birthplace of Ernest Hemingway and for its concentration of Prairie school houses by Frank Lloyd Wright and other modern architects of the early 20th century. Wright both lived in the town and practiced architecture from his Oak Park studio between 1889 and 1909.

What to See and Do

Ernest Hemingway Museum. *Arts Center, 200 N Oak Park Ave (60302). Phone 708/848-2222. www. hemingway.org.* Restored 1890s Victorian home. Exhibits include rare photos, artifacts, and letters. Four video presentations. Walking tours of Hemingway sites, including his birthplace. (Sun-Fri 1-5 pm, Sat 10 am-5 pm; closed holidays) **$$**

⭐ **Frank Lloyd Wright Home and Studio.** *951 Chicago Ave (60302). Phone 708/848-1976. www.wrightplus.org.* Wright built this house in 1889, when he was 22 years old. He remodeled the inside on an average of every 18 months, testing his new design ideas while creating the Prairie school of architecture in the process. Guided tours (daily, inquire for schedule; closed Jan 1, Thanksgiving, Dec 25). National Trust for Historic Preservation property. **$$**

Oak Park Visitors Center. *158 N Forest Ave (60301). Forest Ave at Lake St. Phone 708/848-1976. www. oprf.com/opvc.* Information guidebooks; orientation program on the Frank Lloyd Wright Prairie School of Architecture National Historic District; recorded walking tour (fee); admission tickets for tours of Wright's home and studio; other walking tours. (Daily)

Pleasant Home (John Farson House). *217 S Home Ave (60302). Phone 708/383-2654. www.oprf.com/phf.* Opulent 30-room mansion designed by prominent Prairie school architect George W. Maher in 1897. Second floor is home to the Oak Park/River Forest Historical Society and Museum. (Thurs-Sun afternoons, guided tours on the hour) **$$**

Unity Temple. *875 Lake St (60301). Phone 708/ 848-6225.* (Unitarian Universalist Church) National landmark was designed by Frank Lloyd Wright in 1906. The church is noted as his first monolithic concrete structure and his first public building. Self-guided tour (Mon-Fri afternoons; weekend tours available). **$$**

Restaurant

⭐ ⭐ **CAFÉ LE COQ.** *734 Lake St, Oak Park (60301). Phone 708/848-2233.* Affordable bistro classics endear Oak Parkers to Café Le Coq. Chef Steven Chiapetti worked at Rhapsody in downtown Chicago before resurfacing with this suburbanite. His lusty cooking distinguishes bistro standards like Lyonnais salad, onion soup, mussels in white wine, and steak frites. Daily changing specials, known as "plat du jour," may include coq au vin. The pleasant storefront is trimmed in French fleur de lis symbols and images of the restaurant's namesake rooster. The wine list, like the food, is reasonably priced. French bistro menu. Dinner. Closed Mon. Bar. Casual attire. Outdoor seating. **$$**

Olney (E-4)

Population 8,631
Elevation 482 ft
Area Code 618
Zip 62450
Information Chamber of Commerce, 309 E Main St, PO Box 575; phone 618/392-2241

Olney is locally famous as the "home of the white squirrels." Local legend has it that the white squirrels first appeared here in 1902 when a hunter captured a male and female albino and put them on display. An outraged citizen, learning of their capture, ordered their release into the woods. Although the male was killed shortly thereafter, baby white squirrels were seen in the woods weeks later. The population has since increased to approximately 800 of these unusual albino squirrels. Olney is serious about its albino colony and has passed laws for their protection, including right-of-way for the white squirrels on any street in town.

What to See and Do

Bird Haven-Robert Ridgway Memorial. *East St. N on East St to Miller's Grove.* Arboretum and bird sanctuary on 18 acres. Established on land purchased in 1906 by Robert Ridgway, noted naturalist, scientist, artist, and author. The sanctuary contains dozens of varieties of trees, shrubs, and vines, many of which are still being identified; nature trails; replica of the original porch of the Ridgway cottage; Ridgway's grave. (Daily) **FREE**

Special Events

Fall Festival of Arts & Crafts. *4903 N Watergate Rd, Olney. Phone 618/395-4444.* Juried fine arts and crafts show. Last Sat in Sept.

Richland County Fair. *Fairgrounds, 2699 N Hwy 130, Olney. Phone 618/392-2241.* Livestock shows and exhibits, car races, horse show, entertainment, food. Week in mid-July.

Oregon (A-3)

See also DeKalb, Dixon, Rockford

Settled 1833
Population 4,060
Elevation 702 ft
Area Code 815
Zip 61061
Information Chamber of Commerce, 201 N 3rd St, Suite 14; phone 815/732-2100

Generations of artists have found inspiration in the scenic beauty of the region surrounding Oregon. In 1898, sculptor Lorado Taft and others founded a colony for artists and writers. Located on Rock River, Oregon is the home of Lorado Taft Field Campus, Northern Illinois University (see DEKALB).

What to See and Do

Castle Rock State Park. *900 W Castle Rd. Approximately 3 miles SW on Hwy 2. Phone 815/ 732-7329.* On 2,000 acres. Fishing, boating (motors, launching ramp). Hiking and ski trails, tobogganing, picnicking. Nature preserve. Canoe camping only (May-Oct; fee). **FREE**

Ogle County Historical Society Museum. *111 N 6th St. Phone 815/732-6876.* (1878) Restored frame house was home of Chester Nash, inventor of the cultivator. Displays local historical exhibits. (May-Oct, Thurs, Sun, limited hours; also by appointment) **FREE**

Oregon Public Library Art Gallery. *300 Jefferson St. Phone 815/732-2724.* Displays work of the original Lorado Taft Eagle's Nest art group. (Mon-Sat; closed holidays) **FREE**

Pride of Oregon. *1469 Illinois St (Hwy 2 N). Departs from Maxson Manor. Phone 815/732-6761.* Lunch and dinner excursions aboard turn-of-the-century paddle-wheeler along the Rock River (2 1/2 hours). (Apr-Nov, daily) **$$$$**

Scenic drive. *N on Hwy 2, along the Rock River.* Two miles north of town is

    The Eternal Indian. *Oregon.* Rising 48 feet above brush-covered bluffs, this monumental work by

Lorado Taft was constructed in 1911 of poured Portland cement. The statue is usually referred to as Black Hawk and is regarded as a monument to him.

Lowden Memorial State Park. *1411 N River Rd, Oregon. Phone 815/732-6828.* Park established on 207 acres in memory of former Illinois Governor Frank O. Lowden, who lived nearby. Fishing, boating (ramp). Hiking, picnicking, concession, camping. (Mid-May-mid-Oct) **FREE**

The Soldier's Memorial. *Galena Ave and Stephenson St, Oregon.* On courthouse sq, downtown. *Phone toll-free 800/369-2955.* War memorial by Beaux Arts sculptor Lorado Taft, completed in 1916, consists of two life-size soliders on either side of an allegorical figure symbolizing peace.

Stronghold Castle. *1922 Hwy 2 N, Oregon. Phone 815/732-6111.* Replica of Old English castle built in 1929 by newspaper publisher Walter Strong; now owned by the Presbytery of Blackhawk, Presbyterian Church. Grounds (daily). Tours available; group of 15 minimum, by appointment only (Mon-Fri). (See SPECIAL EVENT) **$**

White Pines Forest State Park. *8 miles W on Pines Rd, near Mt Morris. Phone 815/946-3717.* On 385 acres. Contains the northernmost large stand of virgin white pine in Illinois. Fishing, hiking, cross-country skiing, picnicking, concession, lodge, dining facilities, camping. **FREE**

Special Event

Autumn on Parade. *Oregon. Phone 815/732-2100.* Farmers' market, entertainment, parade, demonstrations; tours of Stronghold Castle (see). First weekend in Oct.

Specialty Lodging

The following lodging establishment is approved by Mobil Travel Guide, but due to its unique and individualized nature has not been given a traditional Mobil Star rating. Included in this listing you may find bed-and-breakfasts, limited-service inns, guest ranches, and other unique hotel properties.

PINEHILL INN BED & BREAKFAST. *400 Mix St, Oregon (61061). Phone 815/732-2067; toll-free 800/851-0131. www.pinehillbb.com.* This Italianate country estate was built in 1874 and is listed on the National Historic Register. 4 rooms, 3 story. **$$**

Ottawa (B-4)

See also Morris, Peru, Starved Rock State Park

Founded 1829
Population 18,307
Elevation 480 ft
Area Code 815
Zip 61350
Information Ottawa Area Chamber of Commerce & Industry, 100 W Lafayette St, PO Box 888; phone 815/433-0084
Web site www.ottawa.il.us

Founded by the commissioners of the Illinois and Michigan Canal, Ottawa took root only after the Black Hawk War of 1832. The first of the Lincoln-Douglas debates took place in the town's public square; a monument in Washington Park marks the site. Located at the confluence of the Fox and Illinois rivers, many industries are now located in this "Town of Two Rivers."

What to See and Do

Buffalo Rock State Park. *Buffalo Rock Rd. 5 miles W off Hwy 6 on Dee Bennett Rd. Phone 815/433-2220.* Part of the Illinois and Michigan Canal State Trail on 243 acres. Live buffalo. Hiking, picnicking (shelters), playground. **FREE** Adjacent is

Effigy Tumuli Sculpture. *1100 Canal St, Ottawa. Phone 815/433-2220.* The largest earth sculptures since Mount Rushmore were formed as part of a reclamation project on the site of a former strip mine. Fashioned with the use of earthmoving equipment, the five enormous figures—a snake, turtle, catfish, frog, and water strider—were deliberately designed and formed to recall similar earth sculptures done by pre-Columbian Native Americans as ceremonial or burial mounds called tumuli. (Daily) **FREE**

Skydive Chicago, Inc. *Ottawa Airport, off I-80. Phone 815/433-0000.* Largest skydiving center in the Midwest. (Daily) **$$$$**

William Reddick Mansion. *100 W Lafayette St. Phone 815/434-2737 (visitor center).* Italianate, antebellum mansion (built 1856-1857) has 22 rooms, ornate walnut woodwork, and ornamental plasterwork; period room contains many original furnishings. House served as public library from 1889 to early 1970s. Mansion (Mon-Fri); guided tours (by appointment).

Special Event

Ottawa's Riverfest Celebration. *301 W Madison St, Ottawa. Phone 815/433-0161.* Parade, fireworks, carnival, family activities, Gospel concert, and Polkafest. Ten days in late July-early Aug.

Limited-Service Hotel

★ **HOLIDAY INN EXPRESS.** *120 W Stevenson Rd, Ottawa (61350). Phone 815/433-0029; fax 815/433-0382. www.hiexpress.com.* 70 rooms. Check-in 2 pm, check-out noon. Indoor pool, whirlpool. **$**

Restaurants

★ **CAPTAIN'S COVE BAR AND GRILL.** *Starved Rock Marina, Ottawa (61350). Phone 815/434-0881.* Steak, seafood menu. Lunch, dinner. Closed Mon; Jan-Feb. Bar. Outdoor seating. **$$**

★ **MONTE'S RIVERSIDE INN.** *903 E Norris Dr, Ottawa (61350). Phone 815/434-5000.* Adjacent boat docking at Fox River. American menu. Lunch, dinner. Closed Dec 25. **$$**

Park Ridge

See Chicago O'Hare Airport Area

Peoria (C-3)

See also Bloomington

Settled 1691
Population 112,936
Elevation 510 ft
Area Code 309
Information Peoria Area Convention & Visitors Bureau, 456 Fulton St, Suite 300, 61602; phone 309/676-0303 or toll-free 800/747-0302
Web site www.peoria.org

In the heart of a rich agricultural basin on the Illinois River, Peoria is the oldest settlement in the state. Louis Jolliet and Père Marquette, along with a French party, discovered the area in 1673. Rene Robert Cavalier, Sieur de la Salle established Fort Créve Coeur on the eastern shore of Peoria Lake (a wide stretch in the Illinois River) in 1680. Between 1691 and 1692, Henri Tonti and Francois Dauphin, Sieur de LaForest established Fort St. Louis II on a site within the city. The settlement that grew around the fort has, except for a brief period during the Fox Wars, been continuously occupied. The British flag flew over Peoria from 1763 to 1778, and, for a short time in 1781, the Spanish held Peoria. The city is named for the Native Americans who occupied the area when the French arrived.

Peoria is the international headquarters of Caterpillar, Inc., makers of earthmoving equipment used worldwide. The city also is known for steel; information/high-tech firms; and agricultural-based companies, including stockyards and a commodity market. Peoria is the home of Bradley University (1897) and the University of Illinois College of Medicine at Peoria.

What to See and Do

Corn Stock Theater. *1700 N Park Rd. Bradley Park. Phone 309/676-2196; fax 309/676-9036. www.cornstocktheatre.com.* Theater-in-the-round summer stock under circus-type big top; dramas, comedies, musicals. (June-Aug) Call for schedule and pricing.

Eureka College. *300 E College Ave, Eureka (61530). 18 miles E on Hwy 24. Phone 309/467-6318.* (1855) (500 students) Liberal arts and sciences. One of the first coeducational colleges in the country. The school's most famous graduate is Ronald Reagan. The ground's Peace Garden honors Ronald Reagan's famous 1982 speech regarding the end of the Cold War. There is a bronze bust of the president and a piece of the Berlin Wall. Also of interest are the historic Burrus Dickinson Hall (1857) and the chapel (1869). Also here is

Forest Park Nature Center. *5809 Forest Park Dr. 1/2 mile off Hwy 29. Phone 309/686-3360.* More than 800 acres of hardwood forest with reconstructed prairie (1 1/2 acres); nature trails (5 miles); natural science museum. (Daily) **FREE**

Glen Oak Park and Zoo. *7716 N Radnor Rd, Ottawa. Prospect Rd and McClure Ave. Phone 309/686-3365 (zoo).* Park on heavily wooded bluffs includes zoo with more than 250 species; amphitheater (concerts in summer); Queen Anne/Victorian pavilion, tennis courts, playground, fishing lagoon, concession. Free on Tues. (Daily) **$$** Also here is

George L. Luthy Memorial Botanical Garden. *2218 N Prospect Rd, Peoria. Phone 309/686-3362.* All-season gardens, rose garden, herb garden, perennial garden on 4 1/2 acres. Conservatory includes floral display areas, tropical plants; orchid, Easter lily display; also mum display (Nov), poinsettia display (Dec). Conservatory (daily; closed Jan 1, Dec 25; special schedule for displays). Gardens (daily). **DONATION**

Jubilee College State Historic Site. *11817 W Jubilee College Rd, Brimfield. 15 miles NW on Hwy 150. Phone 309/243-9489.* Historic site on 90 acres, preserved Jubilee College campus, one of the first educational institutions in Illinois (1840-1862). Original Gothic Revival building and chapel have been restored. Hiking, picnicking. (Daily; closed Jan 1, Thanksgiving, Dec 25) 3 miles northwest on Highway 150 is

Jubilee College State Park. *13921 W Hwy 150, Peoria. Phone 309/446-3758.* More than 3,000-acre park with hiking, bridle, cross-country, and snowmobile trails; picnicking; camping. **FREE**

Lakeview Museum of Arts and Sciences. *1125 W Lake Ave. At University St N. Phone 309/686-7000.* Contains permanent and changing exhibits in the arts and sciences; 300-seat auditorium for concerts, lectures, movies; natural science history area; Children's Discovery Center; special exhibits. Gift shop. Sculpture garden and picnic area. (Tues-Sun; closed holidays) **$$** Also here is

Planetarium. *1125 W Lake Ave, Peoria. Phone 309/686-6682.* Multimedia shows and constellation programs (schedule varies). Large scale model of our solar system. **$$**

Metamora Courthouse State Historic Site. *113 E Partridge, Metamora. 10 miles NE on Hwy 116. Phone 309/367-4470.* One of two remaining courthouse structures on the old Eighth Judicial Circuit, in which Abraham Lincoln practiced law for 12 years. The building (1845), constructed of native materials, is a fine example of Classical Revival architecture. On the first floor is a museum containing a collection of pioneer artifacts and an exhibit pertaining to the old Eighth Judicial Circuit; on the second floor is the restored courtroom. Guide service. (Tues-Sat; closed Jan 1, Thanksgiving, Dec 25) **FREE**

Peoria Historical Society Buildings.

Flanagan House. *942 NE Glen Oak Ave, Peoria. Phone 309/674-0322.* Oldest standing house in Peoria (circa 1837), Federal style, contains pre-Civil War furniture, primitive kitchen, children's room with antique toys, carpenter's shop with large collection of antique tools. Location on bluffs above Illinois River affords beautiful view of entire river valley. (Wed-Sun or by appointment) **$$**

Pettengill-Morron House. *1212 W Moss Ave, Peoria. Phone 309/674-4745.* (1868) Italianate/Second Empire mansion, built by Moses Pettengill, was purchased by Jean Morron in 1953 to replace her ancestral house, which was being destroyed to make way for a freeway. She moved a two-century accumulation of household furnishings and family heirlooms, as well as such architectural pieces as the old house's cast-iron fence, chandeliers, marble mantles, and brass rails from the porch. (By appointment) (See SPECIAL EVENTS) **$$**

Peoria Players. *4300 N University St. Phone 309/688-4473; fax 309/688-4483. www.peoriaplayers.org.* Dramas, comedies, musicals. (Early Sept-early May, Thurs-Sun; closed holidays) Call for schedule and pricing.

Spirit of Peoria. *401 N Main St, Peoria. Departs from The Landing at foot of Main St. Phone 309/636-6169; toll-free 800/676-8988.* Replica of turn-of-the-century stern-wheeler offers cruises along Illinois River. Ninety-minute sight-seeing cruise; Starved Rock State Park cruise, with overnight stay; Peoria to Père Marquette State Park cruise, with two-night stay.

Wheels O' Time Museum. *11923 N Knoxville Ave, PO Box 9636. 8 miles N on Hwy 40. Phone 309/243-9020.* Many antique autos, tractors, and farm implements; fire engines; antique clocks; musical instruments; tools; model railroads and railroad memorabilia; kitchen equipment; early radios. Hands-on exhibits;

outdoor display of steam-era train; changing exhibits; many items relating to Peoria history. (May-Oct, Wed-Sun, also Memorial Day, July 4, Labor Day) **$$**

★ **Wildlife Prairie Park.** *3826 N Taylor Rd. 10 miles W via I-74, Edwards exit 82, then 3 miles S on Taylor Rd. Phone 309/676-0998.* Wildlife and nature preserve with animals native to Illinois—bears, cougars, bobcats, wolves, red foxes, and more—in natural habitats along wood-chipped trails. Pioneer homestead has working farm from late 1800s with authentic log cabin and one-room schoolhouse. Walking trails, playground, picnicking, food service; informational slide show (free); lectures and special events throughout summer; 24-inch scale railroad runs along park perimeter. Gift shop, country store. Park (daily); buildings, train, activities (Mar-mid-Dec, daily). No pets permitted. **$$**

Special Events

Candlelight Christmas. *1212 W Moss Ave, Peoria. Phone 309/674-4745.* Victorian Christmas setting at Pettengill-Morron House (see). Carolers and costumed volunteers. Early-mid-Dec.

Spoon River Scenic Drive. *Peoria. 19 miles W on Hwy 116 at Farmington, then marked, circular route through Fulton County. Phone 309/547-3234.* Autumn drive through small towns and rolling, wooded countryside noted for fall color (complete drive 140 miles); 19th- and early-20th-century crafts, exhibits, demonstrations; antiques, collectibles; produce, food. Fall festival usually the first two full weekends in Oct.

Steamboat Festival. *Riverfront Festival Park, Main St, Peoria (61603). Phone 309/681-0696.* Riverboat races, boat parade; band concerts, carnival, entertainment, pageant. Three days at Father's Day weekend.

Limited-Service Hotels

★ ★ **BEST WESTERN SIGNATURE INN PEORIA.** *4112 N Brandywine Dr, Peoria (61614). Phone 309/685-2556; fax 309/685-2556. www.bestwestern.com.* 123 rooms, 3 story. Pets accepted; fee. Complimentary continental breakfast. Check-in 3 pm, check-out 11 am. Fitness room. Outdoor pool. Airport transportation available. Business center. **$**

★ **COMFORT INN.** *4021 N War Memorial Dr, Peoria (61614). Phone 309/688-3800; toll-free 800/ 424-6423; fax 309/688-3800. www.comfortsuites.com.* 66 rooms, 2 story. Pets accepted; fee. Complimentary continental breakfast. Check-in 3 pm, check-out 11 am. High-speed Internet access. Indoor pool, whirlpool. **$**

★ ★ **HOTEL PÈRE MARQUETTE.** *501 Main St, Peoria (61602). Phone 309/637-6500; toll-free 800/ 447-1676; fax 309/671-9445. www.hotelperemarquette .com.* Restored 1920s hotel. 288 rooms, 12 story. Pets accepted; fee. Check-in 4 pm, check-out noon. High-speed Internet access. Two restaurants, bar. Fitness room. Airport transportation available. **$**

★ ★ **MARK TWAIN HOTEL DOWNTOWN PEORIA.** *225 NE Adams St, Peoria (61602). Phone 309/676-3600; toll-free 800/556-4638; fax 309/ 676-3159. www.marktwainhotels.com.* 110 rooms. Pets accepted; fee. Complimentary full breakfast. Check-in 3 pm, check-out 11 am. High-speed Internet access. Fitness room. Airport transportation available. **$**

★ **STONEY CREEK INN.** *101 Mariners Way, East Peoria (61611). Phone 309/694-1300; fax 309/659-2220. www.stoneycreekinn.com.* 165 rooms. Complimentary continental breakfast. Check-in 3 pm, check-out 11 am. High-speed Internet access. Bar. Children's activity center. Fitness room. Indoor pool, outdoor pool, whirlpool. Airport transportation available. Business center. **$**

Restaurant

★ ★ ★ **PEORIA CASTLE LODGE.** *117 N Western Ave, Peoria (61604). Phone 309/673-8040. www.jumers.com.* Minutes from the riverfront, this restaurant is housed in a 175-room, Bavarian-style lodge and offers classic German specialties such as sauerbraten and wiener schnitzel along with steak, prime rib, and seafood. The ornate room is filled with carved wood, chandeliers, and burgundy velvet. German, American menu. Breakfast, lunch, dinner. Bar. Children's menu. **$$**

Père Marquette State Park

See also Alton, Cahokia

5 miles W of Grafton on Hwy 100.

This is Illinois's largest state park, with 8,000 acres at the confluence of the Illinois and Mississippi rivers. It is named after Père Jacques Marquette, who passed the site with Louis Jolliet in 1673. They were the first white men to enter the present state of Illinois. Fishing, boating (ramp, motors). Hiking and bridle paths (horses may be rented), hunting, picnic areas, playground, concession, lodge, restaurant, campgrounds (standard fees). Interpretive center. Schedule of free guided trips is posted in the visitor center. For information, contact the Park Superintendent, PO Box 158, Grafton 62037, phone 618/786-3323 or 618/786-2331 (lodge).

Peru (B-4)

See also Ottawa, Starved Rock State Park

Settled 1830
Population 9,835
Elevation 500 ft
Information Illinois Valley Area Chamber of Commerce and Economic Development, 300 Bucklin St, PO Box 446, La Salle 61301; phone 815/223-0227
Web site www.ivaced.org

What to See and Do

Illinois Waterway Visitor Center. *950 N 27th Rd. E on Dee Bennett Rd, S of Utica. Phone 815/667-4054.* Located at the Starved Rock Lock and Dam; site offers excellent view across river to Starved Rock (see STARVED ROCK STATE PARK). The history of the Illinois River from the time of the Native Americans, the French explorers, and the construction of canals to the modern Illinois Waterway is portrayed in a series of exhibits. The role of river transport in the nation's economy is also highlighted, with an actual riverboat pilot house on display. Featured is a three-screen, 12-minute slide presentation, "The Connecting Link," tracing humans' use of the Illinois River for more than 6,000 years. (Daily) **FREE**

La Salle County Historical Museum. *Canal and Mill sts, Utica. 5 miles E on I-80, 1 1/2 miles S on Rte 178. Phone 815/667-4861.* (1848) Exhibits include pioneer furnishings, Native American artifacts, and agricultural displays; Lincoln carriage; historical library, local memorabilia. Prairie grass area; blacksmith shop, turn-of-the-century barn, and one-room schoolhouse. (Wed-Sun; closed holidays) **$**

Lake de Pue. *6 miles W on Hwy 29.* Water-skiing, fishing, boating (ramp); picnicking.

Matthiessen State Park. *9 miles SE via I-80 E, Rte 178 S in Utica (61373). Phone 815/667-4868.* This 1,938-acre park is particularly interesting for its geological formations, which can be explored via 7 miles of hiking trails. Hikers should remain on marked trails because of steep cliffs and the depth of the canyon. The upper area and blufftops are generally dry and easily hiked, but trails into the interiors of the two dells can be difficult, especially in spring and early summer. The dells feature scenic waterfalls. Also here is a replica of a small fort stockade of the type built by the French in the Midwest during the late 1600s and early 1700s. Model airplane field; archery range with sight-in area and eight separate fields; cross-country skiing, horseback riding (weekends), bridle trails, picnicking, playground, vending area, park office (in dells area). Observation platform. (Daily) **FREE**

Special Events

Cross-Country Ski Weekend. *Rtes 71 and 178, Utica (61373). Phone 815/667-4868.* Guided ski hikes to Matthiessen State Park (see); ski rentals, instruction. Feb.

Mendota Sweet Corn Festival. *Rte 34 and Illinois Ave, Mendota (61342). Downtown. Phone 815/539-6507. www.sweetcornfestival.com.* If you're looking for tradition and a bargain, head to Mendota, Illinois. Each year, the town serves free sweet corn on the Sunday of its festival to all who attend. There is also a beer garden, a queen pageant, and a flea market with more than 200 dealers represented. You also can purchase sweet corn to take home from one of the nation's largest corn-producing areas. Few things are better on a summer evening than sweet corn, with salt and pepper, from the Midwest. Second weekend in Aug.

Montreal Canoe Weekends. *Rtes 71 and 178, Peru (61373). Phone 815/667-4906.* Begins at Point Shelter at east end of Starved Rock (see STARVED ROCK STATE PARK). Ride a replica of the 34-foot "voyageur canoe" that the French used to explore North America. June.

National Championship Boat Races. *Lake de Pue, Peru. Phone 217/632-7681.* Seventeen classes of power-boats compete for national title; beer gardens and live entertainment. Late July.

Wildflower Pilgrimage. *Rtes 71 and 178, Utica (61373). Phone 815/667-4906.* Departs from Starved Rock visitor center. Guided hikes of Starved Rock (see STARVED ROCK STATE PARK). May.

Winter Wilderness Weekend. *Rtes 71 and 178, Utica (61373). Phone 815/667-4906.* Departs from Starved Rock visitor center. Guided hikes to see the spectacular ice falls of Starved Rock (see STARVED ROCK STATE PARK). Cross-country skiing (rentals, instruction). Jan.

Limited-Service Hotel

★ **COMFORT INN.** *5240 Trompeter Rd, Peru (61354). Phone 815/223-8585; fax 815/223-9292. www.comfortinn.com.* 50 rooms, 3 story. Complimentary continental breakfast. Check-out 11 am. Pool. **$**

Restaurants

★ **THE MAPLES.** *1401 Shooting Park Rd, Peru (61354). Phone 815/223-1938.* Lunch, dinner. Closed July 4. Bar. Children's menu. **$$**

★ ★ **UPTOWN GRILL.** *601 1st St, La Salle (61301). Phone 815/224-4545. www.uptowngrill.com.* Lunch, dinner. Closed Thanksgiving, Dec 25. Bar. Children's menu. Casual attire. Outdoor seating. **$$**

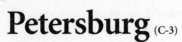

Petersburg (C-3)

See also Havana, Springfield

Founded 1833
Population 2,299
Elevation 524 ft
Area Code 217
Zip 62675
Information Chamber of Commerce, 125 S 7th St, PO Box 452; phone 217/632-7363
Web site www.petersburgil.com

Surveyed by Abraham Lincoln in 1836, Petersburg was made the seat of Menard County in 1839. Most of the residents of nearby New Salem then moved to Petersburg, and the village where Lincoln spent six years and began his political career eventually sank into ruin. Ironically, a later generation of Petersburg residents was responsible for the rebirth of New Salem.

What to See and Do

Edgar Lee Masters Memorial Home. *125 S 7th St. Jackson and 8th sts. Phone 217/632-7363.* Boyhood residence of the poet. Living room restored to 1870-1875 period. Rest of house is museum of family history. (Memorial Day-Labor Day, Tues, Thurs-Sat, limited hours) Contact the Chamber of Commerce. **FREE**

Oakland Cemetery. *Oakland Ave. Phone 217/632-7363.* Graves of Ann Rutledge, who some believe to have been Lincoln's first love, and poet Edgar Lee Masters, Petersburg native who wrote *Spoon River Anthology*.

Special Events

Candlelight Tour of New Salem. *Lincoln's New Salem State Historic Site, Rte 97, Petersburg (62675). Phone 217/632-4000.* Early Oct.

Prairie Tales at New Salem. *Lincoln's New Salem State Historic Site, Rte 97, Petersburg (62675). Phone 217/632-4000.* Two-day festival of nationally acclaimed storytellers. Early Aug.

Summer Festival at New Salem. *Lincoln's New Salem State Historic Site, Rte 97, Petersburg (62675). Phone 217/632-4000.* Reenactment of a summer day in early 1830s New Salem; crafts; interpretive activities. Weekend in mid-July.

Traditional Music Festival. *Lincoln's New Salem State Historic Site, Rte 97, Petersburg (62675). Phone 217/632-4000.* Early-Sept.

Quincy (C-2)

Settled 1822
Population 40,366
Elevation 601 ft
Area Code 217
Zip 62301
Information Quincy Area Chamber of Commerce, 300 Civic Center Plz, Suite 245, 62301-4169; phone 217/222-7980
Web site www.quincychamber.org

Quincy, the seat of Adams County, was named for President John Quincy Adams. Located on the east bank of the Mississippi River, the town was the site of the sixth Lincoln-Douglas debate on October 13, 1858; a bronze bas-relief in Washington Park marks the spot. Quincy was, in the mid-19th century, the second-largest city in Illinois and an industrial, agricultural, and river transportation center. Today, Quincy, which remains a center of industry, is known for its historical business district and fine Victorian residences.

What to See and Do

John Wood Mansion. *425 S 12th St. Phone 217/222-1835.* (1835) This two-story, Greek Revival mansion was the residence of the founder of Quincy and a former governor of Illinois. Moved to its present location in about 1864, the house was cut in half and moved across a special bridge. Restored; original furnishings of the period include the first piano in Quincy, three-story Victorian doll house; artifacts of the area; traveling exhibits; museum. (June-Aug, daily; Apr-May, Sept-Oct, Sat-Sun; also by appointment) **$**

Quincy Museum. *1601 Maine St. Phone 217/224-7669.* Located in the Newcomb-Stillwell mansion, a Richardson Romanesque-style building. Rotating exhibits and a children's discovery room. (Tues-Sun afternoons) **$**

Limited-Service Hotel

★ ★ **HOLIDAY INN.** *201 S 3rd St, Quincy (62301). Phone 217/222-2666; fax 217/222-3238. www.holiday-inn.com.* 152 rooms. Complimentary continental breakfast. Check-in 2 pm, check-out noon. Restaurant, bar. Indoor pool, whirlpool. Airport transportation available. **$**

Rock Island (B-2)

See also Moline

Settled 1828
Population 39,684
Elevation 560 ft
Zip 61201
Information Quad Cities Convention & Visitors Bureau, 2021 River Dr, 61265; phone 309/788-7800 or toll-free 800/747-7800
Web site www.rigov.org

One of the cities of the Quad City metropolitan area (along with Moline, Illinois, and Bettendorf and Davenport, Iowa), Rock Island is rich in Native American, steamboat, and Civil War lore. Here, Lincoln was sworn into the Illinois Militia under Zachary Taylor, and Black Hawk and his warriors were defeated. The great steamboat era brought nearly 2,000 ships annually to Rock Island, and the first railway bridge across the Mississippi River was opened here in 1855. One of the most important and notorious Union military prisons of the Civil War was on the 1,000-acre island in the river. Rock Island Arsenal (see), one of the largest manufacturing arsenals in the world, was established in 1862. Augustana College (1860), which has an art gallery, geology museum, and planetarium, is located here.

What to See and Do

Black Hawk State Historic Site. *1510 46th Ave. On the S edge of town. Phone 309/788-0177 (park).* These wooded, steeply rolling hills provided the site on which the westernmost battle of the Revolutionary War was fought. The area was occupied for nearly a century by the capital villages of the Sauk and Fox nations. The Watch Tower, on a promontory 150 feet above the Rock River, provides views of the river valley and surrounding countryside. The Hauberg Indian Museum contains an outstanding collection of Native American artifacts, paintings, and relics, plus dioramas of Sauk and Fox daily life and changing displays. Fishing; hiking; picnicking. (Daily) **DONATION**

Quad City Botanical Center. *2525 4th Ave. Phone 309/794-0991.* Sun garden conservatory features over 100 tropical plants and trees, 14-foot waterfall over reflecting pools; horticulture resource center; gift shop. (Daily) **$$**

Rock Island Arsenal and US Army Armament, Munitions, and Chemical Command. *17th St. Phone 309/782-6001.* On Arsenal Island, between Rock Island, Illinois, and Davenport, Iowa, is the Rock Island Arsenal Museum, which contains an extensive firearms collection and Court of Patriots memorial (daily; closed holidays; free; phone 309/782-5021); a replica of Fort Armstrong blockhouse; Colonel Davenport house (Sat-Sun; free; phone 309/786-7336); Confederate soldiers' cemetery; the Rock Island National Cemetery, at the center of the island, which has approximately 1,300 interments. Site of the first railroad bridge to span the Mississippi River, lock, and dam. Visitor center (daily; phone before visiting for site restrictions). Bicycle trail (7 miles) around island.

Special Event

Genesius Guild. *Lincoln Park, 40th St and 11th Ave, Rock Island (61201). Phone 309/788-7113.* Free open-air presentations of opera, Shakespeare, and Greek classics. Sat-Sun evenings. Mid-June-mid-Aug.

Rockford (A-4)

See also DeKalb, Freeport, Oregon

Founded 1834
Population 150,115
Elevation 721 ft
Area Code 815
Information Rockford Area Convention & Visitors Bureau, Memorial Hall, 211 N Main St, 61101; phone 815/963-8111 or toll-free 800/521-0849
Web site www.gorockford.com

The state's second-largest city grew up on both sides of the Rock River and took its name from the ford that was used by the Galena-Chicago Stagecoach Line. The early settlers of Rockford were primarily from New England. Today, much of its population is of Swedish and Italian descent. A commercial center for a vast area, it is the largest manufacturer of screw products and fasteners in the United States and one of the most important machine tool producers in the world.

What to See and Do

Anderson Japanese Gardens. *Spring Creek and Parkview. Phone 815/229-9390.* Formal 9-acre gardens with waterfall, ponds, bridges, tea house, guest house, and footpaths. (May-Oct, daily) **$$**

Burpee Museum of Natural History. *737 N Main St. Phone 815/965-3433. www.burpee.com.* New 40,000-square-foot addition. New exhibits, including full-size skeletal cast of a T-Rex; 85-foot-long, two-story-high handpainted mural of prehistoric life; Olson viewing lab; Native American exhibit "First People," state-of-the-art "Geo-Science" exhibit. (Daily) **$$**

Discovery Center Museum. *Riverfront Museum Park, 711 N Main St. Phone 815/963-6769.* Hands-on learning museum with more than 120 exhibits illustrating scientific and perceptual principles; visitors can leave their shadow hanging on a wall, create a bubble window, see a planetarium show, learn how a house is built, star in a TV show, or visit a carboniserous coal forest. Adjacent Rock River Discovery Park features weather station, earth, and water exhibits. (Tues-Sun, some Mon holidays) **$$**

Erlander Home Museum. *404 S 3rd St. Phone 815/963-5559.* (1871) Rockford's Swedish heritage is reflected in this two-story brick house built for John Erlander, an early Swedish settler. Restored Victorian interior; display of numerous pioneer artifacts. (Wed-Fri afternoons, Sun limited hours; also by appointment; closed holidays) **$$**

Forest City Queen. *324 N Medicine St. Phone 815/987-8894.* Narrated tours; dinner cruises. (June-early Sept, Tues-Sun; closed July 4) **$$**

Magic Waters. *7820 N Cherryvale Blvd, Cherry Valley. Hwy 20 and Hwy 51. Phone 815/332-3260; toll-free 800/373-1679. www.magicwaterswaterpark.com.* This 35-acre water theme park includes five five-story water slides, a wave pool, a children's wading pool, an island tree house, a sand beach, a tubing river, a playground, concession, picnicking. (Memorial Day-Labor Day, daily) **$$$$**

Midway Village & Museum Center. *6799 Guilford Rd. Phone 815/397-9112. www.midwayvillage.com.* Museum contains permanent and changing exhibits of area history; aviation gallery. Village features blacksmith shop, general store, bank, schoolhouse, church, police station, town hall, law office, residences, hospital, plumbing shop, and hotel. (Memorial Day-Labor Day, daily; Apr-May, Sept-Oct, Thurs-Sun) **$$**

Rock Cut State Park. *7318 Harlem Rd. NE via Hwy 251, W on Hwy 173. Phone 815/885-3311.* A 3,092-acre park with two artificial lakes. Swimming beach (Memorial Day-Labor Day), fishing, ice fishing, boating (ramp, rentals; motors, 10-hp limit), ice boating. Horseback trail, cross-country skiing, snowmobiling, picnicking, concession, camping (fee). (Daily) **FREE**

Rockford Art Museum. *711 N Main St. Phone 815/968-2787.* Permanent collection of 19th- and 20th-century American and European paintings. Also sculptures, graphics, photographs, decorative arts; changing exhibits. (Tues-Sun; closed holidays) (See SPECIAL EVENTS) **FREE**

Rockford Trolley. *Phone 815/987-8894.* Scenic ride along the Rock River and Sinnissippi Park aboard replica of a turn-of-the-century trolley car; narrated. (June-early Sept, Tues, Thurs, Sat-Sun) **$$**

Sinnissippi Gardens. *1300-1900 N 2nd St. Phone 815/987-8858.* Sunken gardens, 30-foot-wide floral clock, greenhouse with aviary, lagoon; recreational trail. (Daily; closed Dec 25) **FREE**

Tinker Swiss Cottage Museum. *411 Kent St. Phone 815/964-2424.* Built in 1865 by a local industrialist to duplicate a Swiss chalet. The 20-room house contains Victorian furniture, art, textiles, porcelain, and handcrafted treasures from the Tinker family. The house features elaborate parquet floors, fine woodwork, and intricately painted ceiling and wall murals; walnut spiral staircase. Tours. (Tues-Sun; closed holidays) **$$**

Trailside Equestrian Center at Lockwood Park. *Lockwood Park, 5209 Safford Rd. Phone 815/987-8809.* Pony- and horse-drawn wagon rides; petting corral, riding stable, horsemanship classes; special events. (Apr-Nov, daily) Fee for activities.

Special Events

Greenwich Village Art Fair. *Rockford Art Museum, 711 N Main St #3, Rockford (61103). Phone 815/968-2787.* Weekend in mid-Sept.

Illinois Snow Sculpting Competition. *1401 N 2nd St, Rockford. Phone 815/987-8800.* Teams from throughout Illinois compete to represent the state at national and international competitions. Jan.

New American Theater. *118 N Main St, Rockford (61101). Phone 815/964-6282.* Professional theater; six main-stage shows each season. Sept-June.

Rockford Speedway. *9572 Forest Hills Rd, Rockford. Phone 815/633-1500.* Stock car racing; special auto events. Apr-Oct.

Winnebago County Fair. *500 W First St, Pecatonica (61063). Phone 815/239-1641.* Aug.

Limited-Service Hotels

★ ★ **BEST WESTERN CLOCK TOWER RESORT & CONFERENCE CENTER.** *7801 E State St, Rockford (61125). Phone 815/398-6000; toll-free 800/358-7666; fax 815/398-8062. www.clocktowerresort.com.* 247 rooms, 2 story. Check-in 4 pm, check-out noon. Three restaurants, two bars. Children's activity center. Fitness room, fitness classes available, spa. Indoor pool, two outdoor pools, children's pool, whirlpools. Tennis. Airport transportation available. Business center. **$**

★ ★ **COURTYARD BY MARRIOTT.** *7676 E State St, Rockford (61108). Phone 815/397-6222; fax 815/397-6254. www.courtyard.com.* 147 rooms, 3 story. Check-in 3 pm, check-out noon. High-speed Internet access. Fitness room. Indoor pool, whirlpool. Business center. **$**

★ **HAMPTON INN.** *615 Clark Dr, Rockford (61107). Phone 815/229-0404; fax 815/229-0175. www.hampton-inn.com.* 122 rooms, 4 story. Complimentary full breakfast. Check-in 2 pm, check-out noon. Fitness room. Indoor pool, whirlpool. **$**

Restaurants

★ **CAFE PATOU.** *3929 Broadway, Rockford (61108). Phone 815/227-4100; fax 815/227-0778. www.cafepatou.com.* French menu. Lunch, dinner. Closed Sun; holidays. Bar. Children's menu. Casual attire. **$$**

★ ★ ★ **GIOVANNI'S.** *610 N Bell School Rd, Rockford (61107). Phone 815/398-6411. www.giodine.com.* The restaurant is nominally Italian, but the startlingly endless menu offers so much we're surprised it doesn't include the kitchen sink. Dishes include Chesapeake Bay crab cakes, tagliatelle carbonara, poppy-seed swordfish, Hunan stir-fry, and on and on and on. Extensive cognac list. Lunch, dinner. Closed Sun; holidays. Bar. Children's menu. **$$**

Rosemont

Rosemont sits to the immediate east of O'Hare International Airport, a 17-mile drive from downtown Chicago on the Kennedy Expressway (I-90/94). The community annually welcomes millions of visitors to the Donald E. Stephen's Convention Center, the nation's tenth largest meeting and convention center. The 18,500-seat Allstate Arena hosts professional sports and big-name musical acts, while the plush Rosemont Theatre offers live entertainment in a more intimate environment. As would be expected given its location near O'Hare, Rosemont has a wide variety of hotels, adding up to more than 5,600 rooms available to visitors of the community.

What to See and Do

Allstate Arena. *6920 Mannheim Rd (60018). Off Northwest Tollway (I-90), Lee St exit. Phone 847/768-1285.* Auditorium with 18,500 seating capacity hosts concerts, sports, and other events. Box office (Mon-Sat).

Limited-Service Hotel

★ ★ **DOUBLETREE O'HARE.** *5460 N River Rd, Rosemont (60018). Phone 847/292-9100; fax 847/292-9295. www.doubletree.com.* 369 rooms. Check-in 3 pm, check-out noon. Restaurant, bar. Fitness room. Indoor pool, whirlpool. Airport transportation available. Business center. **$**

Restaurants

★ ★ **CAFE LA CAVE.** *2777 Mannheim Rd, Des Plaines (60018). Phone 847/827-7818; fax 847/ 827-3390. www.cafelacaverestaurant.com.* O'Hare Airport neighbor Cafe La Cave divides patrons between a simulated grotto, favored by romance-seeking couples, and the elegant main dining room peopled by business diners on expense accounts. Both constituencies come for La Cave's classic continental menu starring steak Diane flamed tableside, delicate Dover sole, and rich bananas Foster, again flamed at your table. Prices reflect the high level of service practiced here. French, continental menu. Dinner. Closed holidays. Bar. Casual attire. Valet parking. **$$**

★ ★ **CARLUCCI.** *6111 N River Rd, Rosemont (60018). Phone 847/518-0990; fax 847/518-0999. www. carluccirestaurant.com.* Tucked inside an office building complex, Carlucci can be tough to find—look for the sign on River Road. The restaurant prides itself on its robust and simple Tuscan fare, with a variety of antipasti, hearty pasta dishes, and grilled meats rounding out the menu. More than 75 wines from Italy and California are available as well. Italian menu. Lunch, dinner. Closed holidays. Bar. Casual attire. Valet parking. Outdoor seating. **$$**

★ ★ ★ **MORTON'S OF CHICAGO.** *9525 W Bryn Mawr Ave, Rosemont (60018). Phone 847/678-5155. www.mortons.com.* This steakhouse chain, which originated in Chicago in 1978, appeals to serious meat lovers. With a selection of belt-busting carnivorous delights (like the house specialty, a 24-ounce porterhouse), as well as fresh fish, lobster, and chicken entrées, Morton's rarely disappoints. If you just aren't sure what you're in the mood for, the tableside menu presentation may help you decide. Here, main course selections are placed on a cart that's rolled to your table, where servers describe each item in detail. Steak menu. Dinner. Closed holidays. Bar. Valet parking. **$$**
🄳

★ ★ ★ **NICK'S FISHMARKET.** *10275 W Higgins Rd, Rosemont (60018). Phone 847/298-8200; fax 847/298-3755. www.nicksfishmarketchicago.com.* An operation born in Hawaii in the mid-1960s, Nick's reveals its roots in Hawaiian fish specials and the "Maui Wowie" salad. Appetizers feature shellfish, sashimi, and caviar, followed by sole, salmon, and lobster entrées. This location, one of three in the metro

area, features three enormous aquariums. The fish to pay attention to, however, are on the menu. Seafood menu. Dinner. Closed holidays. Bar. Children's menu. Casual attire. Valet parking. **$$$**

Salem (E-4)

See also Centralia, Mount Vernon

Population 7,909
Elevation 544 ft
Area Code 618
Zip 62881
Information Greater Salem Chamber of Commerce, 615 W Main St; phone 618/548-3010
Web site www.ci.salem.il.us

Salem is located 75 miles east of St. Louis, Missouri. It is the birthplace of William Jennings Bryan, whose statue by Gutzon Borglum stands in Bryan Memorial Park.

What to See and Do

Halfway Tavern. *7 miles E on Hwy 50.* Tavern received its name for being halfway between St. Louis, Missouri, and Vincennes, Indiana. Present structure is reconstructed; original was built in 1818 and served as a stagecoach stop until 1861. Located on a trail used by George Rogers Clark when he crossed Illinois in 1799, the tavern was frequently used by Abraham Lincoln as a stopover. Interior not open to public.

Ingram's Log Cabin Village. *138A-234B RR 2, Kinmundy. 12 miles N via Rte 37. Phone 618/547-7123.* On 74 acres with 17 authentic log buildings dating from 1818 to 1860; 13 authentically furnished and open to the public. Picnicking. (Mid-Apr–mid-Nov, daily) **$**

One-room schoolhouse. *1200 N Broadway. N on Rte 37, located on campus of Salem Community High School. Phone 618/548-2499.* Restored schoolhouse contains artifacts, old photos; traces the history of every one-room school district in Marion County. (Apr-Aug, Sat limited hours; other times by appointment) **FREE**

Stephen A. Forbes State Park. *6924 Omega Rd, Kinmundy. 8 miles E on Hwy 50, then 7 miles N on Omega Rd. Phone 618/547-3381.* Approximately 3,100 acres. Swimming, water-skiing, fishing, boating (ramp, rentals, motors). Hunting, hiking, bridle trails, picnicking, concession, camping, horse campground.

William Jennings Bryan Birthplace/Museum. *408 S Broadway. Phone 618/548-7791.* (1852) Restored house contains personal artifacts and memorabilia of the famous orator, who was born here in 1860. (Mon-Wed, Fri-Sun afternoons; closed holidays) **FREE**

Special Events

Bluegrass and Chowder Festival. *Bryan Memorial Park, 101 S Broadway, Salem (62881). Phone 618/548-2222.* Second weekend in Sept.

Days Fest. *215 E Main St, Salem. Phone 618/548-6400.* Main Street celebration of the television show *Days of Our Lives.* Souvenirs, celebrities, contests, and crafts. Late Apr.

Marion County Fair. *Fairgrounds, Salem. Phone 618/548-3010.* Late July-Aug.

Schaumburg

See also Arlington Heights, Chicago O'Hare Airport Area, Itasca

Population 75,386
Elevation 799 ft
Area Code 847
Information Greater Woodfield Convention and Visitors Bureau, 1430 Meacham Rd, 60173; phone 847/490-1010
Web site www.ci.schaumburg.il.us

What to See and Do

The Chicago Athenaeum at Schaumburg. *190 S Roselle Rd (60193). Phone 847/895-3950. www.chi-athenaeum.org.* This museum honors the history of design in all apsects of civilization, from fashion to urban development. (Wed-Sun) **$**

IKEA. *1800 E McConnor Pkwy (60173). Phone 847/969-9700. www.ikea-usa.com.* People travel from hundreds of miles away to visit this mecca of minimalist Scandinavian design offered at affordable prices. Although it's set in a large suburban retail area and sits off the main road, you can't miss its blue-and-yellow signage and theme park-sized

parking lot. Your best bet is to go during the week to avoid the substantial weekend crowds. Make sure to rest up beforehand, too—the place is enormous and can be overwhelming. The store features everything you could want for the home, from sofas to office furnishings to kitchen cabinetry and dishware. In the Marketplace area, you can sift through rugs, clocks, picture frames, and much more. If you need a break, recharge at the third-floor restaurant, which offers Swedish and American fare.

Schaumburg Golf Club. *401 N Roselle Rd (60194). Phone 847/885-9000. www.parkfun.com.* Easily accessible courses are at the Schaumburg Golf Club, which features 27 holes that can be played in different combinations, whether on the Tournament Course or the Players Course. With wide fairways, the courses are forgiving, but bunkers exist to catch errant shots near the greens. Fees are reasonable for nonresidents and a steal for those who live in Schaumburg. This is a very well-maintained park district course. **$$$$**

Woodfield Shopping Center. *5 Woodfield Dr (60173). Golf Rd at Rte 53. Phone 847/330-1537. www.shopwoodfield.com.* With more than 250 specialty shops and department stores, Woodfield is a shopper's paradise. Whether browsing the aisles of Chicago's own Marshall Field's is your thing or trying on the latest gear at Hot Topic is more your style, this mall has a store to outfit everyone. It is anchored by some of the biggest names in retail, including Nordstrom and Lord & Taylor. If the big names don't tickle your fancy, it also offers a plethora of specialty shops, such as ar.Abesque, Steve Madden, Z Gallerie, Sephora, Harry & David, and Coach. After a marathon shopping spree, you can fuel up at one of the many restaurants: indulge your sweet tooth at the Cheesecake Factory, sip coffee and munch on baguettes at Vie de France Bakery, or sit down to a hearty hamburger at John's Garage. Make sure to note where you parked! (Daily)

Full-Service Hotel

★ ★ ★ **HYATT REGENCY WOODFIELD.** *1800 E Golf Rd, Schaumburg (60173). Phone 847/605-1234; fax 847/605-8641. www.hyatt.com.* This beautiful hotel, with spacious guest suites, is packed with amenities for any visitor. Two pools, a health club, several restaurants, and the hottest nightclub in town connected to the hotel provide visitors with everything under one roof. 470 rooms, 5 story. Check-in 4 pm, check-out noon. Restaurant, bar. Fitness room. Indoor pool, outdoor pool, whirlpool. **$$**

Restaurant

★ ★ **SAL & CARVÃO.** *801 E Algonquin Rd, Schaumburg (60173). Phone 847/925-0061; fax 847/925-1663. www.salecarvao.com.* Brazilian menu. Lunch, dinner. Closed Thanksgiving. Bar. Children's menu. Casual attire. **$$$**

Skokie

See also Evanston, Glenview, Wilmette

Population 63,348
Elevation 623 ft
Area Code 847
Information Chamber of Commerce, 5002 Oakton St, PO Box 53; phone 847/673-0240
Web site www.skokiechamber.org

Originally called Niles Center, it was not until 1940 that the village changed its name to Skokie. In its early history, farmers of the area produced food for the growing city of Chicago; market trails carved by farm wagons later became paved roads, which accounts for the odd curves of Lincoln Avenue. Today, Skokie is the location of many major corporate headquarters.

What to See and Do

North Shore Center for the Performing Arts. *9501 Skokie Blvd. Phone 847/679-9501; fax 847/679-1879. www.northshorecenter.org.* Houses two individual theaters that offer many types of performances.

Restaurant

★ ★ **DON'S FISHMARKET.** *9335 Skokie Blvd, Skokie (60077). Phone 847/677-3424; fax 847/679-5849. www.donsfishmarket.com.* More than 25 years old, this subtly nautical-themed restaurant and tavern boasts a friendly staff and reasonably priced fare. The stars of the menu are—you guessed it—a variety of fresh seafood selections, from Chilean sea bass to whitefish from the Great Lakes to Alaskan king crab legs. Steaks and chops are available for those who prefer to dine off the land. Seafood menu. Lunch, dinner. Closed Jan 1, Thanksgiving, Dec 25. Bar. Children's menu. Casual attire. **$$**

Spring Grove

What to See and Do

Chain O'Lakes State Park. *8916 Wilmot Rd (60081). 6 miles W on Hwy 173. Phone 815/585-5512. www.dnr .state.il.us.* One of the most popular—and sometimes congested, especially in summer—recreation areas in Chicagoland is the Chain O'Lakes State Park near the Illinois-Wisconsin border. The park's 2,793 acres adjoin a 3,230-acre conservation area and border three lakes and a river, which makes it ideal for boating, canoeing, rafting, fishing, and wildlife watching (including white-tailed deer, mink, foxes, beavers, coyotes, and eagles). However, this is truly a year-round playground; there are plenty of opportunities to camp, bike, ski, sled, ride horses, toboggan, snowmobile, and take advantage of extensive running trails. (Daily) **FREE**

Springfield (C-3)

See also Decatur, Jacksonville, Lincoln, Petersburg

Settled 1819
Population 111,454
Elevation 600 ft
Area Code 217
Information Convention and Visitors Bureau, 109 N 7th, 62701; phone 217/789-2360 or toll-free 800/545-7300
Web site www.visit-springfieldillinois.com

Near the geographical center of the state, Springfield, the capital of Illinois, is surrounded by rich farmland underlaid with veins of coal, which were, at one time, intensively mined. The city has the grace of a Southern capital; the economic stability of an educational, professional, and service-oriented center; and the fame of having been Abraham Lincoln's home for a quarter of a century.

Illinois had already become a state when Elisha Kelly came to the area from North Carolina. Impressed by fertile land and plentiful game, he later returned and settled here with his father and four brothers. A small community formed around the Kelly cabin. When Sangamon County was created in 1821, Springfield was selected as the seat and named for a nearby spring located on Kelly land. On February 25, 1837, as a result of a campaign led by Lincoln, Springfield—then a town of 1,500—was proclaimed the state capital. In April of that year, Lincoln moved to Springfield from New Salem. He practiced law, married, and raised his family in the new capital. On February 11, 1861, Lincoln made his famous farewell address when he left to become president. In May of 1865, Lincoln's body was returned to Springfield to be buried in the city's Oak Ridge Cemetery.

What to See and Do

Dana-Thomas House State Historic Site. *301 E Lawrence Ave (62703). At 4th St, two blocks S of Governor's Mansion (see EXECUTIVE MANSION). Phone 217/782-6776.* (1902-1904) Designed by Frank Lloyd Wright for Springfield socialite Susan Lawrence Dana, this house is the best preserved and most complete of the architect's Prairie period. The fully restored, highly unified interior boasts terra-cotta sculptures, more than 100 pieces of original furniture, 35 rooms and doors, 250 art-glass windows, and 200 art-glass light fixtures and light panels. The house was one of the largest and most elaborate of Wright's career. (Wed-Sun; closed holidays) **DONATION**

Daughters of Union Veterans of the Civil War Museum. *503 S Walnut St (62704). Phone 217/544-0616.* Civil War relics, documents. (Mon-Fri; also by appointment) **FREE**

Edwards Place. *700 N 4th St (62702). Phone 217/523-2631.* (1833) Built by Benjamin Edwards (brother of Ninian Edwards, early Illinois governor married to Mary Todd Lincoln's older sister), this Italianate mansion was Springfield's social and political center in the years before the Civil War; Lincoln addressed the public from the front gallery. Well-preserved house is furnished with original pieces and period antiques. (By appointment only) **DONATION** Adjacent is

    Springfield Art Association. *700 N 4th St, Springfield. Phone 217/523-2631.* Working studios, library, exhibition galleries. (Mon-Sat; closed holidays) **DONATION**

Executive Mansion. *410 Jackson Pkwy (62701). Phone 217/782-6450.* Red brick Italianate mansion has been the residence of Illinois governors since 1855 (although the current governor has chosen not to live here); Georgian detailing dates from 1970s remodeling. Half hour tours through 14 rooms. (Tues, Thurs, Sat mornings; closed holidays) **FREE**

Henson Robinson Zoo. *1100 E Lake Dr (62707). 4 miles SE on Lake Springfield. Phone 217/753-6217.* A 14-acre zoo with exotic and domestic animals, penguin exhibit; contact area; picnic area. (Daily) **$$**

Illinois State Museum. *Spring and Edwards sts (62701). Phone 217/782-7386. www.museum.state.il.us.* Contains natural history, geology, anthropology, and art exhibits with life-size dioramas of wildlife and early inhabitants of Illinois; displays depict the state's botanical, zoological, ecological, and Native American heritage; art galleries of photography, fine and decorative arts with works by 19th- and 20th-century Illinois artists. Special hands-on discovery room for children. Audio tours (fee); special programs, films, lectures, tours. (Mon-Sat, also Sun afternoons; closed holidays) **FREE**

⭐ **Lincoln Depot.** *10th and Monroe sts (62703). Phone 217/544-8695.* Restored depot where Lincoln delivered his farewell address before departing for Washington on February 11, 1861. Exhibits; DVD presentation. (Apr-Aug, daily) **FREE**

Lincoln-Herndon Law Office Building. *6th and Adams sts (62701). Opposite the Old State Capitol (see). Phone 217/785-7289.* Restored building from which Lincoln practiced law. (Daily; closed holidays) **DONATION**

Lincoln Home National Historic Site. *Visitor center, 426 S 7th St (62701). Approximately five blocks S and E of Old State Capitol (see). Phone 217/492-4241. www.nps.gov/liho.* Site features the only home Abraham Lincoln ever owned. In 1844, Abraham and Mary Lincoln purchased their 1 1/2-story cottage and enlarged it several times to a full two-story house. The Lincoln family lived there until their February 1861 departure for Washington, DC. The home has been restored with Lincoln family furnishings, period artifacts, reproduced wallpapers, and window hangings. The Lincoln Home stands in the midst of a four-block historic neighborhood, which the National Park Service is restoring, so that the neighborhood, like the house, will appear much as Lincoln would have remembered it. Exhibits are available for viewing in the neighboring Dean and Arnold Houses. The visitor center includes exhibits, film, and museum shop. Tickets required to tour house (obtain at visitor center; free). (Daily; closed Jan 1, Thanksgiving, Dec 25) **FREE**

Lincoln Memorial Garden and Nature Center. *2301 E Lake Dr (62707). 8 miles S, on E bank of Lake Springfield. Phone 217/529-1111. www.imgnc.com.* An 80-acre garden of trees, shrubs, and flowers native to Illinois designed in naturalistic style by landscape architect Jens Jensen. Extensive display of spring wildflowers (late Apr-early May); fall foliage (mid-Oct). Nature trails (5 miles). Cross-country skiing in winter. Nature Center contains exhibits and shop (Tues-Sun; closed Dec 24-Jan 1). Garden (daily). (See SPECIAL EVENTS) **FREE**

Lincoln Tomb State Historic Site. *Oak Ridge Cemetery, 1441 Monument Ave (62702). Approximately 16 blocks N of the Old State Capitol (see), via 2nd St to N Grand, then W to Monument Ave. Phone 217/782-2717.* Under a 117-foot granite obelisk, a belvedere, accessible via exterior staircases, offers views of 10-foot statue of Lincoln and four heroic groupings representing Civil War armed forces. The tomb interior follows a circular route lined with statues commemorating periods of Lincoln's life. In the center of the domed burial chamber is a monumental sarcophagus. However, Lincoln is actually buried 10 feet below (grave robbers made attempts upon the remains). Mary Todd Lincoln and three of four Lincoln sons are interred within the wall opposite. Self-guided tours; interpretive program. (Daily; closed holidays) (See SPECIAL EVENTS) **FREE**

Old State Capitol State Historic Site. *Adams and 5th sts (62701). Downtown mall, between Adams, Washington, 5th, and 6th sts. Phone 217/785-7961.* Restored Greek Revival sandstone structure was first state house in Springfield (state's fifth). Although first occupied in 1839, it was not fully completed until 1853; it became the Sangamon County courthouse after being vacated by the state in 1876. Called the most historic structure west of the Alleghenies, it was here that Lincoln made his famous "House Divided" speech. Restored between 1966 and 1969, interior features intersecting double staircases; reconstructed house, senate, and supreme court chambers; state offices. Living history program (Fri-Sat; no programs May). (Daily; closed holidays) **DONATION**

Oliver P. Parks Telephone Museum. *529 S 7th St (62703). Phone 217/789-5303.* Contains more than 100 antique telephones dating from 1882; film, exhibits, and displays relating to the telephone. (Mon-Fri; closed holidays) **FREE**

Springfield Children's Museum. *619 E Washington St (62701). Phone 217/789-0679.* Exhibits and programs featuring art, architecture, health, nature, and science. Children can discover weather phenomena, dig for a fossil, or put on a puppet show. (Mon, Wed-Sun; closed holidays) **$$**

State Capitol. *301 S 2nd St (62701). Phone 217/782-2099.* One of the tallest buildings in central Illinois, the capitol dome, 405 feet high, can be seen for miles across the prairie. Built between 1868 and 1888, the state house is a Victorian combination of Renaissance Revival and Second Empire. Marble, granite, bronze, black walnut, encaustic tiles, stained and etched glass, and stencil work were employed throughout the structure; heroically scaled murals depict state history. Free guide service, first floor information desk (every 30 minutes, daily; closed holidays). **FREE** Nearby is

Capitol Complex Visitors Center. *Capitol Ave and Edwards St, Springfield. Phone 217/524-6620.* Displays, brochures, information. Picnic shelters. (Mon-Sat; closed holidays)

Thomas Rees Memorial Carillon. *Washington Park, W Fayette Ave and Chattam Rd (62703). Phone 217/753-6219.* A 132-foot tower with three observation decks and 66-bell carillon. Bell museum. Concerts (June-Aug, Tues-Sun; Apr-May, Sept-Nov, weekends only). Ten-minute film. **$**

Special Events

114th Infantry Flag Retreat Ceremony. *Oak Ridge Cemetery, Lincoln Tomb State Historic Site (see), 1441 Monument Ave, Springfield (62702). Phone 217/782-2717.* Illinois Volunteer Infantry, in authentic period uniforms, demonstrates drill movements and musket firings as part of a retreat ceremony. June-Aug, Tues evenings.

Ethnic Festival. *State Fairgrounds, Springfield (62794). Phone 217/529-8189.* Ethnic foods, cultural exhibits; entertainment. Labor Day weekend.

Illinois State Fair. *State Fairgrounds, Springfield (62794). Phone 217/782-6661.* Contact PO Box 19427, 62794. Mid-Aug.

International Carillon Festival. *Thomas Rees Memorial Carillon (see), Washington Park, 2500 S 11th St, Springfield (62701). Phone 217/753-6219.* Evening concerts by visiting international carillonneurs. Entertainment. Early July.

LPGA State Farm Classic. *Rail Golf Club, 427 E Monroe St, Springfield (62701). Phone 217/528-5742.* Women's professional 54-hole golf tournament. Late Aug.

Maple Syrup Time. *Lincoln Memorial Garden and Nature Center (see), 2301 E Lake Dr, Springfield (62707). Phone 217/529-1111.* Watch maple syrup being made, from tapping trees to boiling the sap. Mid-Feb-early Mar, Sat-Sun afternoons.

Municipal Band Concerts. *Douglas Park, Springfield. Phone 217/525-8586.* A 50-piece concert band performs a wide variety of music. June-July, Tues, Thurs evenings.

Springfield Air Rendezvous. *Capital Airport, 1200 Capital Airport Dr, Springfield (62707). Phone 217/789-4400.* Mid-Oct.

Springfield Muni Opera. *815 E Lake Dr, Springfield (62701). Phone 217/793-6864.* Broadway musicals presented in an outdoor theater. June-Aug.

Summer Festival. *New Salem Village, Rte 97, Petersburg (62675). Phone 217/632-4000.* July.

Limited-Service Hotels

★ **COMFORT INN.** *3442 Freedom Dr, Springfield (62704). Phone 217/787-2250; toll-free 800/228-5150; fax 217/787-2250. www.comfortinn.com.* 67 rooms, 2 story. Pets accepted, some restrictions; fee. Complimentary continental breakfast. Check-out 11 am. Indoor pool, whirlpool. **$**

★ ★ **COURTYARD BY MARRIOTT.** *3462 Freedom Dr, Springfield (62704). Phone 217/793-5300; toll-free 800/321-2211; fax 217/793-5300. www. courtyard.com.* 78 rooms, 3 story. Check-out noon. Bar. Fitness room. Indoor pool, whirlpool. **$**

★ **HAMPTON INN.** *3185 S Dirksen Pkwy, Springfield (62703). Phone 217/529-1100; toll-free 800/426-7866; fax 217/529-1105. www. hamptoninn.com.* 124 rooms, 4 story. Complimentary continental breakfast. Check-out noon. Fitness room. Indoor pool, whirlpool. **$**

Full-Service Hotels

★ ★ ★ **HILTON SPRINGFIELD.** *700 E Adams St, Springfield (62701). Phone 217/789-1530; fax 217/789-0709. www.hilton.com.* This being the only skyscraper in Springfield, guests can enjoy amazing views of the city. The hotel also has spacious guest rooms with options for both short- and long-term needs. 367 rooms, 30 story. Pets accepted, some restrictions; fee. Check-out noon. Restaurant, bar. Fitness room. Indoor pool. Airport transportation available. Business center. **$**

★ ★ ★ **RENAISSANCE SPRINGFIELD HOTEL.** *701 E Adams St, Springfield (62701). Phone 217/544-8800; toll-free 800/228-9898; fax 217/544-9607. www.renaissancehotels.com.* This hotel"s design reflects the era of Abraham Lincoln, a native of Springfield. With a concourse leading to the convention center and 13,000 square feet of meeting space, it's popular with corporate travelers. Try Lindsay's Gallery Restaurant for Sunday brunch. 316 rooms, 12 story. Check-in 3 pm, check-out noon. Restaurant, bar. Fitness room. Indoor pool, whirlpool. Airport transportation available. Business center. **$**

Restaurants

★ ★ **CHESAPEAKE SEAFOOD HOUSE.** *3045 Clear Lake Ave, Springfield (62702). Phone 217/522-5220; fax 217/522-5993.* Barbecue, seafood menu. Dinner. Closed Sun; Dec 25. Bar. Children's menu. **$$**

★ **HERITAGE HOUSE.** *3851 S 6th St, Springfield (62703). Phone 217/529-5571.* Dinner. Closed Dec 25. **$**

★ ★ **MALDANER'S.** *222 S 6th St, Springfield (62701). Phone 217/522-4313; fax 217/522-1720.* Restored 19th-century bar. American menu. Dinner. Closed Sun; Jan 1, July 4, Dec 25. Bar. **$$**

St. Charles (A-4)

See also Aurora, DeKalb, Elgin, Geneva

Settled 1838
Population 27,896
Elevation 697 ft
Area Code 630
Information Greater St. Charles Convention and Visitors Bureau, 311 N 2nd St, 60174; phone 630/ 377-6161 or toll-free 800/777-4373
Web site www.visitstcharles.com

Located on the Fox River just one hour west of Chicago, St. Charles is a residential and light industry town. The downtown areas on both sides of the river contain antique and specialty shops housed in historic buildings.

What to See and Do

Fox River Valley Trail. *Phone 630/897-0516 (Fox Valley Park District). www.trailsfromrails.com/fox_river_trail .htm.* Those who love the outdoors will find more than enough activities to fill a day in the Fox River Valley. Located among rolling hills and historic old towns, the Fox River winds a lazy path, making it ideal for recreational canoeing. Several outfitters offer canoe rentals, and there are at least four entry points, depending on what part of the river you want to travel. The river is a favorite for fishing; one of the more popular spots is at Pickerel Point on Riverside Drive and Nellie Avenue in South Elgin. If you have a bike, the well-maintained Fox River Trail runs parallel to the river extending as far north as Crystal Lake and as far south as Aurora. The area also sports several parks and rest areas ideal for picnicking. (Daily) **FREE**

Pheasant Run Dinner Theatre. *4051 E Main St, St. Charles (60174). W on Rte 64. Phone 630/584-6300; toll-free 800/474-3272; fax 630/584-9831. www. pheasantrun.com.*

Pheasant Run Resort & Spa. *4051 E Main St, St. Charles (60174). Phone toll-free 800/474-3272; fax 630/584-9831. www.pheasantrun.com.* In terms of bang for your buck, Pheasant Run in west suburban St. Charles offers great golf for prices lower than at most courses in the area. The course also plays only a little more than 6,300 yards, so great scores are definitely within reach. Great especially during the summer when the evenings are long, golfers can play 18 holes for just $23, cart included, from 5:30 pm until dark. If the day of golf doesn't go as planned, the resort has high-quality dining, big-name shows, and even a spa to take the stress away. **$$$$**

Pottwatomie Park. *On 2nd Ave, 1/2 mile N of Main St (Rte 64) (60174). Phone 630/584-1028.* A mile of frontage on the Fox River with swimming pools (first weekend June-Labor Day; fee), nine-hole golf (Mar-Oct; fee), tennis, 18-hole miniature golf (fee), playgrounds, ball fields. Also access to the Fox River Valley Trail (see), used for biking, jogging, and cross-country skiing. Picnic area, snack bars. (Daily) **$$** Also here are

St. Charles Belle II and Fox River Queen. *St. Charles. Phone 630/584-2334.* These 132-passenger paddle-wheel boats offer afternoon sightseeing trips (45 minutes) along the Fox River. Boats depart from the park and follow the river trail of the Pottawatomie. (June-Aug, daily; May, Sept-mid-Oct, Sat-Sun)

St. Charles History Museum. *215 E Main St, St. Charles (60174). Phone 630/584-6967.* Museum of local history, built in a unique Tudor-style filling station from the 1920s. (Tues-Sun) Call for pricing.

Special Events

Kane County Flea Market. *Kane County Fairgrounds, St. Charles (60174). On Randall Rd S of Rte 64. Phone 630/377-2252. www.kanecountyfleamarket.com.* One of the nation's largest flea and antique markets. (First Sat-Sun of the month) **$$**

Pride of the Fox RiverFest. *Main St (Rte 64) and 2nd St (Rte 31), St. Charles (60174). Phone 630/ 377-6161.* Four-day event features river events, food, entertainment, craft show. Second weekend in June.

Scarecrow Festival. *Lincoln Park, 4th and Main sts, St. Charles (60174). Phone 630/377-6161; toll-free 800/777-4373. www.scarecrowfest.com.* Display of up to 100 scarecrows; entertainment, food, crafts. Second full weekend in Oct.

Restaurant

★ **FILLING STATION ANTIQUE EATERY.** *300 W Main St, St.Charles (60174). Phone 630/584-4414. www.filling-station.com.* In a renovated 1930s filling station; antiques. American menu. Lunch, dinner. Closed holidays. Bar. Children's menu. Casual attire. Outdoor seating. **$**

Starved Rock State Park (B-4)

See also Ottawa, Peru

Utica. From Chicago, take I-294 or I-355 S to I-55. Take I-55 S to I-80. Go W on I-80 45 miles to exit 81 (Rte 178, Utica). Go S (left) 3 miles on Rte 178 and follow signs to the park. Phone 815/667-4726. dn.rstate.il.us.

A local favorite for recreation and outdoor sports, Starved Rock State Park, located about an hour and a half southwest of Chicago, provides ample opportunities for adventure amid a dramatic backdrop of glacial canyons, sandstone bluffs, unusual rock formations, and colorful forests. The park offers 13 miles of well-marked hiking trails, fishing and boating along the Illinois River, equestrian trails, picnicking, camping, and winter sports, including cross-country skiing, tobogganing, sledding, and ice skating. In addition, the park has a refurbished lodge with a hotel wing with 72 luxury rooms, an indoor pool with spa and sauna, and a restaurant; 22 cabins also are available. Though it's open year-round, a prime time to visit is early spring, when waterfalls form at the heads of the more than 18 canyons and create a glittering natural spectacle. (Daily) **FREE**

Full-Service Resort

★ ★ **STARVED ROCK LODGE AND CONFERENCE CENTER.** *Rtes 71 and 178, Utica (61373). Phone 815/667-4211; toll-free 800/868-7625; fax 815/667-4455.* 93 rooms, 3 story. Check-in 3 pm, check-out 11 am. Restaurant, bar. Indoor pool, children's pool, whirlpool. Rolling, wooded country. **$**

Union

See also Elgin

Population 576
Elevation 842 ft
Area Code 815
Zip 60180

What to See and Do

Donley's Wild West Town. *8512 S Union Rd. Hwy 20 and S Union Rd. Phone 815/923-2214; fax 815/923-2253. www.wildwesttown.com.* Large displays, including antique phonographs, movies, music boxes, toys, telephones; general store. Outdoor Western village features Wild West gunfights, pony rides, train rides, panning for gold pyrite; gift shops. (Memorial Day-Labor Day, daily; Apr-May, Sept-Oct, weekends) **$$$**

Illinois Railway Museum. *7000 Olson Rd. Phone 815/923-4000.* Outdoor displays, on 56 acres, of historic and antique railroad cars, steam engines, coaches, and trolleys; rides (3 1/2 miles). Picnicking. (Memorial Day-Labor Day, daily; May, Sept, Sat-Sun; Apr, Oct, Sun) Special events throughout the year. Admission includes unlimited rides. **$$$**

McHenry County Historical Museum. *6422 Main St. Phone 815/923-2267. www.mchsonline.org.* Contains artifacts dating from first settlement in the 1830s-present; also local history research library (by appointment). On the grounds are rural schoolhouse (1895) and original log cabin (1847), authentically furnished and used for pioneer demonstrations. (May-Oct, Tues-Fri afternoons, Sun afternoons) **$$**

Vandalia (D-4)

See also Altamont, Greenville

Founded 1819
Population 6,975
Elevation 515 ft
Area Code 618
Zip 62471
Information Tourism Committee, Chamber of Commerce, 1408 N 5th St, PO Box 238; phone 618/283-2728
Web site www.vandalia.net

The Illinois State Legislature chose the wilderness in the Kaskaskia River Valley as the site for the state's second capital, laid out the city, and sold lots. Vandalia housed the state legislature from 1819 to 1839, when Abraham Lincoln led a successful campaign to transfer the capital to Springfield.

What to See and Do

Little Brick House Museum. *621 St. Clair St (62471). Phone 618/283-0667.* Simple Italianate architecture with six restored rooms furnished primarily in the 1820-1839 period; antique wallpapers, china, wooden utensils, dolls, doll carriages, pipes, parasols, powder horn, oil portraits, and engravings. The Berry-Hall Room contains memorabilia of artist James Berry and writer James Hall. Pays tribute to members of the Tenth General Assembly of Illinois. Outbuildings and period garden with original brick pathways around the house. (Tours by appointment) **$$**

Ramsey Lake State Park. *2850 N and Intersection 700 E, Ramsey (62080). 13 miles N on Hwy 51, then W on 2900 N. Phone 618/423-2215. dnr.state.il.us.* Approximately 1,960 acres with 47-acre lake stocked with bass, bluegill, and red ear sunfish. Fishing, boating (ramp, rentals; electric motors only). Hunting, hiking, horseback riding, picnicking (shelters), concession, camping (standard fees). **FREE**

⭐ **Vandalia Statehouse State Historic Site.** *315 W Gallatin St. Phone 618/283-1161.* Abraham Lincoln and Stephen Douglas served in the House of Representatives in this two-story, Classical Revival building built by townspeople in 1836 in an effort to keep the capital in Vandalia. Many antiques and period furnishings. Guide service. (Daily) (See SPECIAL EVENT) **FREE**

Special Event

Grande Levée. *Vandalia Statehouse State Historic Site (see), Vandalia. Phone 618/283-1161.* Capitol Days (1820-1839) are celebrated with period crafts, music, and food. Candlelight tour of the building. Father's Day weekend.

Limited-Service Hotel

⭐ **RAMADA LIMITED.** *2707 Veterans Ave, Vandalia (62471). Phone 618/283-1400; fax 618/283-3465. www.ramada.com.* 61 rooms, 2 story. Pets accepted, some restrictions; fee. Complimentary continental breakfast. Check-out noon. Fitness room. Pool. **$**

🏃 🐾 🏊

Waukegan (A-5)

See also Antioch, Grayslake, Gurnee, Illinois Beach State Park

Settled 1835
Population 87,901
Elevation 644 ft
Area Code 847
Information Lake County Chamber of Commerce, 5221 W Grand Ave, Gurnee, 60031; phone 847/249-3800
Web site www.lakecounty-il.org

On the site of what was once a Native American village and a French trading post, Waukegan was first incorporated as Little Fort because of a French stockade there. For many years, it was barred to settlement by treaty, but after the establishment of a general store by a Chicago merchant, it became a United States port of entry and thrived. On April 2, 1860, Abraham Lincoln delivered his "unfinished speech" here—he was interrupted by a fire. Waukegan is the most industrialized of all lakeshore communities north of Chicago. Waukegan Port, on Lake Michigan, provides dockage for lake-going vessels that serve local industry. Waukegan was the birthplace of comedian Jack Benny and author Ray Bradbury, who used the town as a background in many of his works.

Limited-Service Hotel

⭐ ⭐ **COURTYARD BY MARRIOTT.** *800 Lakehurst Rd, Waukegan (60085). Phone 847/689-8000; toll-free 800/321-2211; fax 847/689-0135. www.courtyard.com.* 149 rooms, 3 story. Check-in 3 pm, check-out 1 pm. Restaurant. Fitness room. Indoor pool, whirlpool. Six Flags Great America (see GURNEE) nearby. **$**

🏃 🏊

West Chicago (A-5)

What to See and Do

Prairie Landing Golf Club. *2325 Longest Dr (60185). Phone 630/208-7600. www.prairielanding.com.* In West Chicago is a gem of a links-style course designed by the master himself, Robert Trent Jones, Jr. Along with the water-lined course, the facility offers three practice holes that can be played along with use of the driving range for just $30 for three hours. These holes are great for play-testing new clubs or working out sore spots in your game. The course is easily accessible by car from a number of different routes and is worth the drive every time. **$$$$**

Saint Andrews Golf and Country Club. *3 N 441 Rte 59. Phone 630/231-3100.* Saint Andrews evokes the feel of its Scottish namesake with its two 18-hole championship courses. It's a public facility with a private atmosphere nestled among some of Chicagoland's fastest growing suburbs. The fees go down drastically as twilight sets in, but even playing during the day won't break the bank. **$$$$**

Wheaton (A-4)

See also Geneva, Glen Ellyn, Naperville

Population 55,416
Elevation 753 ft
Area Code 630
Zip 60187
Information Wheaton Chamber of Commerce, 108 E Wesley St, 60187; phone 630/668-6464
Web site www.wheatonchamber.org

Wheaton, the seat of DuPage County, is primarily a residential community with 39 churches and the headquarters of approximately two dozen religious publishers and organizations. The town's most famous citizens are football great Red Grange, Elbert Gary, who created the Indiana steel city that bears his name, and evangelist Billy Graham.

What to See and Do

Cantigny. *1S151 Winfield Rd. Phone 630/668-5161.* This is the 500-acre estate of the late Robert R. McCormick, editor and publisher of the *Chicago Tribune.* Picnic area, woodland trails; 10 acres of formal gardens. (Daily) **$$** On the grounds are

Cantigny Golf and Tennis. *27 W 270 Mack Rd (60187). Phone 630/668-3323.* In suburban Wheaton at Cantigny, golfers can find one of the more interesting layouts in the area. Cantigny has 27 holes, which can be played in any combination of 18 the golfer likes. The area is full of tall deciduous trees, and there also is water with which to contend. The area also is well suited for picnics and has top-quality tennis facilities. Only 6,709 yards in length, Cantigny can be enjoyed as much for the accessible golf as for its surroundings. **$$$$**

First Division Museum. *1S151 Winfield Rd, Wheaton. Phone 630/668-5185.* Narrated displays dramatize story of First Infantry Division in action in World War I, World War II, and Vietnam. (Mar-Dec, Tues-Sun; Feb, Fri-Sun; closed Thanksgiving, Dec 25; also Jan) **$$**

Robert R. McCormick Museum. *1S151 Winfield Rd, Wheaton. Phone 630/668-5161.* Georgian residence begun by Joseph Medill (1896), enlarged by his grandson, Robert McCormick, in the 1930s. Original furnishings; unique Chinese mural in dining room; personal artifacts, photographs, paintings. Chamber music presentation (summer, Sun limited hours; rest of year, first Sun of month); reservations required. Guided tours (Mar-Dec, Tues-Sun; Feb, Fri-Sun; closed Thanksgiving, Dec 25; also Jan). **$$**

Cosley Animal Farm and Museum. *1356 N Gary Ave. Phone 630/665-5534.* Children's petting zoo; antique farm equipment display; railroad caboose and equipment; aviary; herb garden; outdoor education center. (Daily; closed Jan 1, Thanksgiving, Dec 25) **FREE**

DuPage County Historical Museum. *102 E Wesley St. Phone 630/682-7343.* Historic Romanesque limestone building (1891) houses changing exhibitions on county history; costume gallery; period rooms. Extensive HO-scale model railroad display. Research library. (Mon, Wed, Fri-Sun; closed holidays) **FREE**

Wheaton College. *501 College Ave. Phone 630/752-5000. www.wheaton.edu.* (1860) (2,400 students) Liberal arts, conservatory of music, graduate school. Tours. On campus are art exhibits, the Perry Mastodon exhibit, and

Billy Graham Center Museum. *501 College Ave, Wheaton. Phone 630/752-5909.* Museum features exhibits on the history of evangelism in America and the ministries of the Billy Graham Evangelistic Association; also Rotunda of Witnesses, Gospel theme area. (Mon-Sat, Sun afternoons; call for holiday hours)

Marion E. Wade Center. *351 E Lincoln, Wheaton. Phone 630/752-5908.* Collection of books and papers of seven British authors: Owen Barfield, G. K. Chesterton, C. S. Lewis, George MacDonald, Dorothy L. Sayers, J. R. R. Tolkien, and Charles Williams. (Mon-Sat; closed holidays)

Special Events

Autumn Fest. *Memorial Park, Union and Hale sts, Wheaton (60187). Phone 630/668-6464.* Second weekend after Labor Day.

Cream of Wheaton. *501 College Ave, Wheaton (60187). Downtown. Phone 630/668-6464.* First weekend after Memorial Day.

DuPage County Fair. *Fairgrounds, 2015 W Manchester Rd, Wheaton. Phone 630/668-6636. www.dupagecountyfair .org.* Late July.

Wheeling

See also Arlington Heights, Glenview, Northbrook

Population 34,496
Elevation 650 ft
Area Code 847
Zip 60090
Information Wheeling/Prospect Heights Area Chamber of Commerce and Industry, 395 E Dundee Rd; phone 847/541-0170
Web site www.wheeling.com

The Wheeling area was first occupied by the Potawatomi. Settlers arrived in 1833 and began farming the fertile prairie soil. In 1836, a stagecoach route was established along Milwaukee Avenue, which was the main northbound route out of Chicago. The first commercial enterprise was a tavern-hotel (1837), followed by the establishment of a brewery (1850) on the Des Plaines River.

Limited-Service Hotel

★ **HAWTHORN SUITES.** *10 Westminster Way Rd, Lincolnshire (60069). Phone 847/945-9300; toll-free 800/527-1133; fax 847/945-0013. www. hawthorn.com.* 125 rooms, 3 story, all suites. Pets accepted, some restrictions; fee. Complimentary full breakfast. Check-in 4 pm, check-out noon. High-speed Internet access. Fitness room. Indoor pool, whirlpool. Business center. **$**

Full-Service Hotel

★ **MARRIOTT SPRINGHILL SUITES LINCOLNSHIRE.** *300 Marriott Dr, Lincolnshire (60069). Phone 847/793-7500; toll-free 888/287-9400; fax 847/793-0322. www.springhillsuites.com.* 161 rooms, all suites. Complimentary continental breakfast. Check-in 3 pm, check-out noon. High-speed Internet access. Fitness room. Indoor pool, whirlpool. Business center. **$**

Full-Service Resort

★ ★ ★ **MARRIOTT LINCOLNSHIRE RESORT.** *10 Marriott Dr, Lincolnshire (60069). Phone 847/634-0100; toll-free 800/228-9290; fax 847/634-1278. www.marriott.com.* With an 18-hole championship golf course, theater-in-the-round (900 seats) featuring live musical comedies, two pools, and two restaurants, no wonder guests keep coming back time and time again. This resort also has 60,000 square feet of meeting space, tennis, and much more. 390 rooms, 3 story. Pets accepted. Check-in 3 pm, check-out noon. High-speed Internet access. Two restaurants, four bars. Fitness room. Indoor pool, outdoor pool, whirlpool. Golf, 18 holes. Tennis. Airport transportation available. Business center. **$**

Restaurants

★ ★ **94TH AERO SQUADRON.** *1070 S Milwaukee Ave (Rte 21), Wheeling (60090). Phone 847/459-3700.* A thematic neighbor to the Palwaukee Airport next door, 94th Aero Squadron boosts its World War II fighter theme with a faux bombed-out interior and images of vintage planes. The something-for-everyone menu includes prime rib, steak, shrimp, and fish. Repeat customers say the food is nothing special, but it's group-friendly, and the Sunday brunch is worth the trek. American menu. Dinner, Sun brunch. Bar. Children's menu. Outdoor seating. **$$**

★ ★ **BOB CHINN'S CRAB HOUSE.** *393 S Milwaukee Ave (Rte 21), Wheeling (60090). Phone 847/520-3633; fax 847/520-3944. www.bobchinns.com.* Wheeling's high-volume draw Bob Chinn's draws diners from around Chicagoland—ranging from business groups to casually dressed clans—on the strength of its fresh seafood cooked in umpteen ways. The best dishes are the simplest: cold or steamed crab legs, sautéed Hawaiian-caught fish, and raw bar oysters. House mai tais elevate spirits among those waiting for tables in the barny roadhouse decked in coastal décor. Seafood menu. Lunch, dinner. Closed Thanksgiving, Dec 25. Bar. Children's menu (dinner). **$$**

★ ★ **DON ROTH'S.** *61 N Milwaukee Ave (Rte 21), Wheeling (60090). Phone 847/537-5800. www. donroths.com.* Period music and memorabilia from the original downtown Blackhawk restaurant in its 1920s-, 30s-, and 40s-prime lend Chicago swagger to this Wheeling institution. Steaks, prime rib, and seafood center the menu, although many fans make the trip specifically for the famous "spinning salad bowl" rite in which waiters whip up salads tableside. The food is old-fashioned, but the genuine welcome is perennially fresh. Steak menu. Dinner. Closed Dec 25. Bar. Outdoor seating. **$$**

★ ★ **GILARDI'S.** *23397 Rte 45 N, Vernon Hills (60061). Phone 847/634-1811.* In a turn-of-the-century mansion; Art Deco décor. Italian, American menu. Lunch, dinner. Closed holidays. Bar. Valet parking. **$$**

Wilmette

See also Evanston, Glenview, Skokie

Settled 1829
Population 27,651
Elevation 610 ft
Area Code 847
Zip 60091
Information Chamber of Commerce, 1150 Wilmette Ave; phone 847/251-3800
Web site www.wilmettechamber.org

Immediately north of Evanston and 15 miles from downtown Chicago, Wilmette possesses an idyllic location on Lake Michigan's shoreline. Visually, this community has changed little over the years, with old-fashioned lampposts standing alongside tree-lined brick streets. The Wilmette Park District manages 19 public parks, including the popular Gillson Beach. Wilmette is home to the Baha'i House of Worship, a domed architectural marvel that was placed on the National Register of Historic Places in 1978.

What to See and Do

Baha'i House of Worship. *100 Linden Ave (60091). At Sheridan Rd. Phone 847/853-2300.* Spiritual center of the Baha'i faith in the United States, a remarkable nine-sided structure given lightness and grace by the use of glass and tracery. It is 191 feet high and overlooks Lake Michigan. Surrounded by nine gardens and fountains. Exhibits and slide programs in visitor center on lower level. (Daily) **FREE**

Gillson Park. *Washington and Michigan aves (60091). Phone 847/256-9656.* Contains Wilmette Beach with 1,000 feet of sandy shoreline, lifeguards, and beach house (June-Labor Day, daily; fee), sailing (lessons), fishing pier. Tennis, cross-country skiing, ice skating, picnic facilities, playground, concession. Sunfish and Hobie 16 catamaran rentals. Park (daily). **$$**

Kohl Children's Museum. *165 Green Bay Rd (60091). Phone 847/512-1300. www.kohlchildrensmuseum.org.* Science, interactive music, construction, and arts participatory exhibits designed for children up to 8; miniature food store; makeup area; special activities. (Daily; closed holidays) **$$**

Wilmette Historical Museum. *609 Ridge Rd (60091). Phone 847/853-7666.* Local history; costumes; rotating exhibits; archives, reference library. (Sept-June, Tues-Thurs, Sat-Sun afternoons; closed holidays; also the week of Dec 25) **FREE**

Restaurants

★ ★ **BETISE.** *1515 N Sheridan Rd, Wilmette (60091). Phone 847/853-1711.* Great food, a convivial setting, and a casual vibe make Wilmette's Betise a popular North Shore stop. Classic bistro fare, including grilled fish and roasted meats, is supplemented by more daring specials. Although the restaurant is large, it's divided into smaller dining nooks, all posted with sketch art on the walls, carving out intimacy within the high-spirited setting. French bistro menu. Lunch, dinner, Sun brunch. Closed holidays. **$$**

★ **CONVITO ITALIANO.** *1515 N Sheridan Rd, Wilmette (60091). Phone 847/251-3654; fax 847/ 251-0123. www.convitoitaliano.com.* Half gourmet import store, half casual trattoria, North Shore mainstay Convito Italiano earns applause for its light, seasonal Italian fare available both eat-in and take-out. Diners after the former are seated at marble tables in a skylit room for plates of homemade pasta, veal, and fish. Hit the deli side of the shop for frozen pastas and sauces, fresh salads, breads, desserts, and wine. Seasonal dining on the terrace offers glimpses of Lake Michigan. Italian menu. Dinner. Closed holidays. **$$**

★ ★ **TANGLEWOOD.** *566 Chestnut St, Winnetka (60093). Phone 847/441-4600.* American menu. Lunch, dinner. Closed Sun; holidays. Children's menu. Outdoor seating. **$$**

★ **WALKER BROTHERS ORIGINAL PANCAKE HOUSE.** *153 Green Bay Rd, Wilmette (60091). Phone 847/251-6000; fax 847/251-6191.* If you love breakfast food, this north suburban eatery is the place for you. Fresh, hot pancakes (chocolate chip, apple, banana, . . .), hearty French toast, sweet and savory crepes, and a variety of omelet creations are a treat any time of the day or night. The quaint dining room, with mahogany tables and booths, Tiffany-style stained glass accents, and antique touches, attracts a considerable crowd for weekend breakfast and brunch. Other locations in Arlington Heights (825 Dundee Rd), Glenview (1615 Waukegan Rd), Highland Park (620 Central Ave), Lake Zurich (767 S Rand Rd), and Lincolnshire (200 Marriott Dr) are just as popular with scads of weekend brunchers. American menu. Breakfast, lunch, dinner, brunch. Closed Thanksgiving, Dec 25. Children's menu. **$**

Woodstock (A-4)

See also Gurnee, McHenry

Population 20,151
Elevation 942 ft
Area Code 815
Zip 60098
Information Chamber of Commerce, 136 Cass St; phone 815/338-2436
Web site www.woodstockil.com

Orson Welles, who went to school and performed his first Shakespearean role here, once described Woodstock as the "grand capital of mid-Victorianism in the Midwest." The Victorian charm has been carefully retained, especially in the town square with its ornate gazebo, wooded park, cobblestone streets, and many historic houses and buildings that now contain antique shops.

What to See and Do

Chester Gould-Dick Tracy Museum. *101 N Johnson St. In Old Courthouse Arts Center on Woodstock Sq. Phone 815/338-8281.* Exhibits include permanent collection of original art of Tracy; Gould family memorabilia, Chester Gould's original drawing board, and various changing exhibits. Gift shop. (Thurs-Sat, Sun afternoons) **FREE**

Woodstock Opera House. *121 Van Buren St. Phone 815/338-5300.* (1889) Restored; built in a style described as "steamboat Gothic" in reference to the exterior's resemblance to a cathedral and the interior's similarity to the salon of a Mississippi River steamboat. Especially worth noting is the stencilled auditorium ceiling. (Daily) (See SPECIAL EVENT) **FREE**

Special Event

Mozart Festival. *Woodstock Opera House, 121 Van Buren St, Woodstock (60098). Phone 815/338-5300.* Performances by Woodstock Festival Orchestra and renowned soloists. Late July-early Aug.

The St. Louis metropolitan area extends from Missouri into southwestern Illinois, so this barely qualifies as a side trip. But, if you're in southern Illinois and you're yearning for a little urban culture, St. Louis should fit the bill. The city has a wonderful zoo, professional sports teams, and a growing theater scene.

St. Louis, MO (E-2)

10 minutes, 5 miles from Cakolia, IL

Settled 1764
Population 396,685
Elevation 470 ft
Area Code 314
Information Convention and Visitors Commission, 1 Metropolitan Sq, Suite 1100, 63102; phone 314/421-1023 or toll-free 800/ 325-7962
Web site www.explorestlouis.com
Suburbs Clayton, St. Charles, Wentzville

One of the oldest settlements in the Mississippi Valley, St. Louis was founded by Pierre Laclede as a fur trading post and was named for Louis IX of France. Early French settlers, a large German immigration in the mid-1800s, and a happy mix of other national strains contribute to the city's cosmopolitan flavor.

A flourishing French community by the time of the Revolutionary War, St. Louis was attacked by a band of British-led Native Americans, but was successfully defended by its citizens and a French garrison. In 1804, it was the scene of the transfer of Louisiana to the United States, which opened the way to the westward expansion that overran the peaceful town with immigrants and adventurers. The first Mississippi steamboat docked at St. Louis in 1817. Missouri's first constitutional convention was held here in 1820. During the Civil War, though divided in sympathy, the city was a baseof Union operations. In 1904, the Louisiana Purchase Exposition, known as the St. Louis World's Fair, brought international fame to the city and added to its cultural resources; its first art museum was established in connection with the fair.

For more than 200 years, St. Louis has been the dominant city in the state. It is the home of St. Louis University (1818) (see), the University of Missouri-St. Louis (1963), and Washington University (1853), which lies at the border of St. Louis and Clayton. Distinguished by wealth, grace, and culture, St. Louis also is a city of solid and diversified industry. It is one of the world's largest markets for wool, lumber, and pharmaceuticals and a principal grain and hog center. It also is the center for the only industrial area in the country producing six basic metals: iron, lead, zinc, copper, aluminum, and magnesium. St. Louis is an important producer of beer, chemicals, and transportation equipment. Strategically located near the confluence of the Missouri and Mississippi rivers, the city is one of the country's major railroad terminals and trucking centers. Seven bridges span the Mississippi here.

After the steamboat era, St. Louis grew westward, away from the riverfront, which deteriorated into slums. This original center of the city now has been developed as the Jefferson National Expansion Memorial (see). Municipal and private redevelopment of downtown and riverfront St. Louis also has been outstanding: America's Center, St. Louis's convention complex, is the hub of the 16-square-block Convention Plaza; Busch Stadium brings St. Louis Cardinals (see) fans into the downtown area; and the rehabilitated Union Station (see ST. LOUIS UNION STATION) offers visitors a unique shopping experience within a restored turn-of-the-century railroad station.

Additional Visitor Information

The St. Louis Convention and Visitors Commission, 1 Metropolitan Sq, Suite 1100, 63102, has brochures on things to see in St. Louis; phone 314/421-1023 or toll-free 800/325-7962. Also obtain brochures at the St. Louis Visitors Center, 7th and Washington. *St. Louis Magazine*, at newsstands, has up-to-date information on cultural events and articles of interest to visitors. For 24-hour tourist information, phone 314/421-2100.

Public Transportation

Bi-State Transit System Phone 314/231-2345

Airport For additional accommodations, see ST. LOUIS LAMBERT AIRPORT area, which follows ST. LOUIS.

What to See and Do

Aloe Plaza. *Market St, between 18th and 20th sts. Across from Union Station* (see ST. LOUIS UNION STATION). Contains an extensive fountain by Carl Milles symbolizing the meeting of the Mississippi and Missouri rivers.

Anheuser-Busch, Inc. *1127 Pestalozzi St, St. Louis (63118). 12th and Lynch sts. Phone 314/577-2626. www.budweisertours.com.* Guided brewery tours. (Mon-Sat; closed holidays) **FREE**

Butterfly House and Education Center. *Faust Park, 15193 Olive Blvd, Chesterfield (63017). 20 miles W via Hwy 40. Phone 314/361-3365. www.butterflyhouse.org.* Three-story crystal palace conservatory with over 2,000 butterflies in free flight. Educational programs, films, miracle of metamorphosis display. (Tues-Sun) **$$**

Campbell House Museum. *1508 Locust St, St. Louis. Phone 314/421-0325.* Mansion with original 1840-1880 furnishings. (Mar-Dec, Wed-Sun; closed holidays) **$$**

Cathedral of St. Louis. *4431 Lindell Blvd. At Newstead Ave. Phone 314/533-0544.* (1907) The city's cathedral is a fine example of Romanesque architecture with Byzantine details; the interior mosaic work is among the most extensive in the world. Mosaic museum (fee). Tours (by appointment; fee).

Christ Church Cathedral. *1210 Locust St, St. Louis. Phone 314/231-3454.* (1859-1867). The first Episcopal parish west of the Mississippi River; founded in 1819. English Gothic sandstone building; altar carved in England from stone taken from a quarry in Caen, France; Tiffany windows on north wall. Occasional concerts. (Sun-Fri) Tours (by appointment).

⭐ ***Delta Queen*** and ***Mississippi Queen****. Phone toll-free 800/543-1949. www.deltaqueen.com.* Paddle wheelers offer three- to eight-night cruises on the Ohio, Cumberland, Mississippi, and Tennessee rivers.

Contact Delta Queen Steamboat Co, 30 Robin St Wharf, New Orleans, LA 70130-1890.

DeMenil Mansion and Museum. *3352 DeMenil Pl, St. Louis. Phone 314/771-5828.* Antebellum, Greek Revival house with period furnishings; restaurant (lunch) in carriage house. Mansion on old Arsenal Hill in the colorful brewery district. Gift shop. (Tues-Sat) **$$**

The Dog Museum. *Edgar M. Queeny Park* (see), *1721 Mason Road, St. Louis. W via I-64 (Hwy 40). Phone 314/821-3647.* Museum with exhibits of dog-related art; reference library, videotapes. (Tues-Sat, Sun afternoons; closed holidays) **$**

Dr. Edmund A. Babler Memorial. *800 Guy Park Dr, St. Louis (63005). 25 miles W on Hwy 100, then N on Hwy 109. Phone 314/458-3813.* Approximately 2,500 acres. Swimming pool. Hiking trail, picnicking, playground, improved camping (dump station). Interpretive center, naturalist. (Daily) **FREE**

Eads Bridge. *Riverfront area.* (1874) Designed by engineer James B. Eads, the Eads was the first bridge to span the wide southern section of the Mississippi River and the first bridge in which steel and the cantilever were used extensively; approach ramps are carried on enormous Romanesque stone arches.

Edgar M. Queeny Park. *19 miles W via I-64 (Hwy 40) or Clayton Rd, S on Mason Rd. Phone 636/391-0922.* A 569-acre park. Swimming pool. Hiking trail, tennis, ice rink (fee), picnicking, hayrides, horseback riding trails, playground. (Daily)

Eugene Field House and Toy Museum. *634 S Broadway, St. Louis. Phone 314/421-4689.* (1845) Birthplace of famous children's poet; mementos, manuscripts, and many original furnishings; antique toys and dolls. (Wed-Sat, Sun afternoons; closed holidays) **$$**

⭐ **Forest Park.** *Skinker Blvd, Kingshighway Blvd, and Oakland Ave, St. Louis (63110). W via I-64 (Hwy 40). Phone 314/289-5300.* This 1,200-acre park was the site of most of the 1904 Louisiana Purchase Exposition. Many of the city's major attractions are here. (See SPECIAL EVENTS)

Gateway Riverboat Cruises. *50 N Leonor K Sullivan Blvd, St. Louis (63102). Dock is below Gateway Arch. Phone 314/621-4040; toll-free 800/878-7411. www.*

gatewaycruises.com. One-hour narrated cruise of the Mississippi River aboard the *Huck Finn, Tom Sawyer,* and *Becky Thatcher* riverboats, replicas of 19th-century stern-wheelers. (Memorial Day-Labor Day, daily) **$$$**

Grant's Farm. *10501 Gravois Rd, St. Louis. SW via I-55. Phone 314/843-1700. www.grantsfarm.com.* This 281-acre wooded tract contains a log cabin (1856) and land once owned by Ulysses S. Grant. Anheuser-Busch Clydesdale barn; carriage house with horse-drawn vehicles, trophy room; deer park where deer, buffalo, longhorn steer, and other animals roam freely in their natural habitat; bird and elephant show, small-animal feeding area. Tours by miniature train. (Early May-Aug, Tues-Sun; mid-Apr-early May, Sept-Oct, Wed-Sun) **FREE**

Gray Line bus tours. *312 W Morris, St. Louis (62232). Phone 314/421-4753; toll-free 800/542-4287.*

Hidden Valley Ski Area. *Eureka. 28 miles W on I-44, then 3 miles S on Hwy F to Hidden Valley Dr. Phone 636/938-5373. www.hiddenavalleyski.com.* Two triple chair lifts, four rope tows; patrol, school, rentals, snowmaking; cafeteria, restaurant, concession, bar. Longest run 1,760 feet; vertical drop 282 feet. Night skiing. (Dec-Mar, daily; closed Dec 24-25) **$$$$**

International Bowling Museum & Hall of Fame and Museum. *111 Stadium Plz, St. Louis (63102). Across from Busch Stadium. Phone 314/231-6340. www.bowlingmuseum.com.* Exhibits and displays trace the history of bowling from an Egyptian child's game to the present. Computerized and old-time alleys where visitors may bowl. Gift shop. (Daily; closed holidays) **$$$**

Jefferson Barracks Historical Park. *533 Grant Rd, St. Louis (63125). S Broadway at Kingston, 10 miles S on I-55, S Broadway exit. Phone 314/544-5714.* Army post established in 1826, used through 1946. St. Louis County now maintains 424 acres of the original tract. Restored buildings include stable (1851), laborer's house (1851), two powder magazines (1851, 1857), ordnance room, and visitor center. Picnicking. Buildings (Tues-Sun; closed holidays). **FREE**

Jefferson National Expansion Memorial. *11 N 4th St, St. Louis. Phone 314/982-1410. www.stlouisarch.com.* Eero Saarinen's Gateway Arch is a 630-foot stainless steel arch that symbolizes the starting point of the westward expansion of the United States. Visitor center (fee) includes capsule transporter to observation deck (fee). Museum of Westward Expansion offers exhibits on people and events of 19th-century western America; special exhibits and films (fee) on St. Louis, construction of the arch, and the westward movement (daily; closed Jan 1, Thanksgiving, Dec 25). Videotapes for the hearing impaired, tours for the visually impaired. Observation deck inaccessible to wheelchairs. *Note:* there is often a wait for observation deck capsules, which are small and confining. **$**

Jewel Box Floral Conservatory. *Wells and McKinley drs, St. Louis.* Seventeen-and-a-half acre site with formal lily pools; floral displays; special holiday shows. Free admission Mon-Tues mornings. (Daily) **$**

Laclede's Landing. *720 N 2nd St, St. Louis. N edge of riverfront, between Eads and King bridges. Phone 314/241-1155.* Early St. Louis commercial district (mid-1800s) includes nine-block area of renovated pre-Civil War and Victorian buildings that house specialty shops, restaurants, and nightclubs.

Laumeier Sculpture Park. *12580 Rott Rd (63127). Geyer and Rott rds. Phone 314/821-1209.* Sculptures by contemporary artists on grounds of the Laumeier mansion; art gallery (Wed-Sun). Nature trails, picnic area. (Daily) **FREE**

Lone Elk Park. *Hwy 141 and N Outer Rd, 23 miles SW on I-44, adjacent to Castlewood State Park. Phone 314/615-7275.* Approximately 400-acre preserve for bison, elk, deer, and Barbados sheep. Picnicking. (Daily) **FREE**

The Magic House, St. Louis Children's Museum. *516 S Kirkwood Rd, Kirkwood. 8 miles W via I-44, Lindbergh Blvd exit. Phone 314/822-8900. www.magichouse.com.* Hands-on exhibits include electrostatic generator and a three-story circular slide. (Tues-Sun; closed holidays) **$$$**

Mastodon State Historic Site. *1050 Museum Dr, St. Louis (62052). 20 miles S off Hwy 55, near Hwy 67 Imperial exit. Phone 636/464-2976.* Excavation of mastodon remains and Native American artifacts; museum (fee). Hiking, picnicking. (Daily) **FREE**

Missouri Botanical Garden. *4344 Shaw Blvd, St. Louis. Phone 314/577-5141; toll-free 800/642-8842. www.mobot.org.* This 79-acre park includes rose, woodland,

and herb gardens; scented garden for the blind. Electric tram rides (fee). Restaurant; floral display hall. Sections of the botanical garden are well over a century old. (Daily; closed Dec 25) **$$** Included in admission are

Climatron. *St. Louis.* Seventy-foot-high, prize-winning geodesic dome—first of its kind to be used as a conservatory—houses a two-level, half-acre tropical rain forest with canopies, rocky outcrops, waterfalls, and mature tree collection; exhibits explain the many facets of a rain forest. Entrance to Climatron through series of sacred lotus and lily pools.

Japanese Garden. *Missouri Botanical Garden, St. Louis. Phone toll-free 800/642-8842.* Largest traditional Japanese garden in North America, with lake landscaped with many varieties of water iris, waterfalls, bridges, and teahouse.

Tower Grove House. *4344 Shaw Ridgeway Center, St. Louis. Phone 314/577-5150.* (Circa 1859) Restored country residence of garden founder, Henry Shaw; Victorian furnishings. In grove of trees before house is Shaw's Gothic Revival tomb. (Feb-Dec, daily; closed Dec 25)

Missouri History Museum—Missouri Historical Society. *Jefferson Memorial Building, 225 S Skinker Blvd, St. Louis (63105). Lindell Blvd and DeBaliviere. Phone 314/746-4599. www.mohistory.org.* Exhibits on St. Louis and the American West; artwork, costumes, and decorative arts; toys; firearms; 19th-century fire-fighting equipment; St. Louis history slide show; ragtime-rock 'n' roll music exhibit; 1904 World's Fair and Charles A. Lindbergh collections. (Daily; closed holidays) **FREE**

Museum of Transportation. *3015 Barrett Station Rd, Kirkwood. 16 miles SW via I-44, N on I-270 to Big Bend and Dougherty Ferry rds exits. Phone 314/965-7998. www.museumoftransport.org.* One of the more interesting collections anywhere in the country can be found near St. Louis. The Museum of Transportation houses an extensive collection of passenger and freight train equipment (ranging from elevated "L" cars from Chicago to the last steam locomotive to operate in Missouri), as well as the riverboats and airplanes that local history has helped support. Visitors can ride on some of the railroad equipment or take a more leisurely trip on more primitive modes of transport (like horse-drawn carts). (Tues-Sun, holiday Mon; closed Jan 1, Thanksgiving, Dec 25) **$$**

Old Cathedral. *209 Walnut St, St. Louis. At Memorial Dr, under Gateway Arch. Phone 314/231-3250.* (1831) Basilica of St. Louis, King of France, on the site of the first church built in St. Louis in 1770; museum on the west side contains the original church bell and other religious artifacts. (Daily) **$**

Old Courthouse. *11 N 4th St, St. Louis (63102). At Market St. Phone 314/655-1600.* Begun in 1837 and completed in 1862, this building houses five museum galleries on St. Louis history, including various displays, dioramas, and films; two restored courtrooms. First two trials of the Dred Scott case were held in this building. Guided tour. (Daily; closed Jan 1, Thanksgiving, Dec 25) **FREE**

Powell Symphony Hall. *718 N Grand Blvd, St. Louis. Phone 314/534-1700 (box office).* (1925) Decorated in ivory and 24-karat gold leaf, the hall, built as a movie and vaudeville house, is now home of the St. Louis Symphony Orchestra (see) (mid-Sept-mid-May). After-concert tours available by appointment.

President Casino on the *Admiral*. *St. Louis. Docked at Laclede's Landing (see). Phone 314/622-3000.* (Daily)

Purina Farms. *200 Checkerboard Dr, Gray Summit (63039). 35 miles W via I-44, Gray Summit exit, then two blocks N on Hwy 100 and 1 mile W on County MM. Phone 314/982-3232.* Domestic animals, educational graphic displays, videos, hands-on activities. Grain bin theater. Petting areas, animal demonstrations, play area with maze, ponds. Snack bar, gift shop. Self-guided tours. (Mid-Mar-Nov, Wed-Sun) Reservations required. **FREE**

Six Flags St. Louis. *30 miles SW via I-44, exit 261, Eureka. Phone 636/938-4800. www.sixflags.com.* A 200-acre entertainment park with more than 100 rides, shows, and attractions, including wooden and looping steel roller coasters and white-water raft rides. (Late May-late Aug, daily; Mar-late May, late Aug-late Oct, weekends) **$$$$**

Soldiers' Memorial Military Museum. *1315 Chestnut St, St. Louis. Phone 314/622-4550.* Honoring St. Louis's war dead; memorabilia from pre-Civil War, World War I, World War II, Korea, and Vietnam. (Daily; closed Jan 1, Thanksgiving, Dec 25) **FREE**

The St. Louis Art Museum. *1 Fine Arts Dr. Phone 314/721-0072.* Built for 1904 World's Fair as Palace of Fine Arts. Collections of American and European paintings, prints, drawings, and decorative arts. Also African, Asian, and pre-Columbian art; 47-foot statue in front depicts St. Louis the Crusader astride his horse. Lectures, films, workshops. Restaurant, museum shop. (Wed-Sun, Tues afternoons; closed Jan 1, Thanksgiving, Dec 25)

St. Louis Blues (NHL). *Savvis Center, 1401 Clark Ave, St. Louis. Phone 314/241-1888.*

St. Louis Cardinals (MLB). *Busch Stadium, 250 Stadium Plz, St. Louis. Phone 314/421-3060.*

St. Louis Cardinals Hall of Fame Museum. *Busch Stadium, 100 Stadium Plz, between gates 5 and 6. Phone 314/421-3263.* St. Louis baseball from 1860-present; Stan Musial memorabilia. Gift shop. Also stadium tours (Apr-Dec, daily; rest of year, limited hours). Building (daily). **$$$**

St. Louis Centre. *Locust and 6th sts, downtown.* One of the largest urban shopping malls in the country; features 130 shops and Taste of St. Louis food court with 28 restaurants. (Daily)

St. Louis Rams (NFL). *Edward Jones Dome, 901 N Broadway, St. Louis. Phone 314/425-8830. www.stlouisrams.com.* Professional football team.

St. Louis Science Center. *5050 Oakland Ave. Phone 314/289-4444; toll-free 800/456-7572. www.slsc.org.* Features three buildings with more than 700 exhibits. Also Omnimax theater, planetarium, children's discovery room (various fees). Outdoor science park. Gift shops. Restaurant. (Daily; closed Thanksgiving, Dec 25)

St. Louis Union Station. *Market St, between 18th and 20th sts. Phone 314/421-6655.* This block-long stone châteauesque railroad station (1894) was the world's busiest passenger terminal from 1905 to the late 1940s. After the last train pulled out—on October 31, 1978—the station and train shed were restored and redeveloped as a marketplace with more than 100 specialty shops, restaurants, nightclubs, and a hotel, as well as entertainment areas, plazas, and a 1 1/2-acre lake. The station was designed by a local architect to be modeled after a walled medieval city in southern France; its interior features high Romanesque and Sullivanesque design. "Memories,"

a collection of photographs, letters, memorabilia, and films, brings the station's history to life.

St. Louis University. *221 N Grand. Phone 314/977-8886. www.slu.edu.* (1818) (10,000 students) Oldest university west of the Mississippi River; includes Pius XII Memorial Library with Vatican Microfilm Library—the only depository for copies of Vatican documents in the Western Hemisphere (academic year, daily; closed holidays). On campus is

> **Cupples House and Art Gallery.** *St. Louis University campus, 3673 W Pine Mall, St. Louis. On John E Connelly Mall (formerly W Pine Blvd), W of Pius XII Memorial Library. Phone 314/977-3025.* Historic Romanesque building (1889) with 42 rooms, 22 fireplaces, original furnishings, period pieces; houses 20th-century graphics collection. (Tues-Sat, hours vary) **$$**

St. Louis Zoological Park. *S side of park. Phone 314/781-0900. www.stlzoo.org.* More than 6,000 animals in natural settings on 90 acres; apes and monkeys; walk-through aviary: big cat exhibit, cheetah survival exhibit; herpetarium. Living World education and visitor center features interactive computers, video displays, animatronic robot of Charles Darwin, and live animals. Sea lion show (summer; fee); children's zoo with contact area (fee); miniature railroad (mid-Mar-Nov, daily; fee). Zoo (daily; closed Jan 1, Dec 25). **FREE**

Steinberg Memorial Skating Rink. Roller skating (June-Sept), ice skating (Nov-Mar); rentals. **$$**

Ulysses S. Grant National Historic Site. *7400 Grant Rd, St. Louis. Off Gravois Rd. Phone 314/842-3298.* Site consists of five historic structures: two-story residence known as White Haven, stone outbuilding, barn, ice house, and chicken house. The White Haven property was a focal point in Ulysses's and wife Julia's lives for four decades. Grounds feature more than 50 species of trees and are a haven for a variety of wildlife. Visitors center includes exhibits and information on the Grants and White Haven. Guided tours. (Daily; closed Jan 1, Thanksgiving, Dec 25)

West Port Plaza. *Page and I-270, Maryland Heights. Approximately 15 miles W via I-64 (Hwy 40), N on I-270, E on Page Blvd to W Port Plaza Dr. Phone 314/576-7100.* Alpine-like setting with approximately 30 European-style shops and 20 restaurants. (Daily)

Special Events

Fair St. Louis. *St. Louis. On riverfront. Phone 314/434-3434.* Three-day festival with parade, food, air and water shows, entertainment. July 4 weekend.

Great Forest Park Balloon Race. *5600 Clayton Ave, Forest Park, St. Louis (63110). Phone 314/289-5300.* Food, entertainment, parachute jumps, and other contests. Mid-Sept.

Gypsy Caravan. *8001 Natural Bridge, St. Louis. Phone 314/286-4452.* One of the largest flea markets in the Midwest, with more than 600 vendors; arts and crafts, entertainment, concessions. Memorial Day.

Muny Opera. *5600 Clayton Ave, Forest Park, St. Louis (63110). Phone 314/361-1900.* Outdoor theater (12,000 seats). Light opera and musical comedy. Mid-June-Aug.

Repertory Theatre of St. Louis. *130 Edgar Rd, St. Louis. Phone 314/968-4925. Off I-44 Elm St exit in Webster Groves.* Nine-play season includes classics and new works. Sept-Apr.

St. Louis Symphony Orchestra. *Powell Symphony Hall, St. Louis. Phone 314/534-1700.* Mid-Sept-mid-May.

Limited-Service Hotels

★ ★ **CHESHIRE LODGE.** *6300 Clayton Rd, St. Louis (63117). Phone 314/647-7300; toll-free 800/325-7378; fax 314/647-0442. www.cheshirelodge.com.* Elegant Tudor décor. 106 rooms, 4 story. Check-out 2 pm. Restaurant, bar. Indoor pool, outdoor pool. **$**

★ ★ **COURTYARD BY MARRIOTT.** *2340 Market St, St. Louis (63103). Phone 314/241-9111; fax 314/241-8113. www.courtyard.com.* 151 rooms, 4 story. Check-out noon. Bar. Fitness room. Indoor pool, whirlpool. **$**

★ ★ **DOUBLETREE HOTEL.** *16625 Swingley Ridge Rd, Chesterfield (63017). Phone 636/532-5000; fax 636/532-9984. www.doubletree.com.* Located in the wooded suburb of Chesterfield, this hotel is convenient to the St. Louis International Airport. It offers large guest rooms, state-of-the-art meeting facilities, a complimentary morning paper and breakfast, and

much more. 223 rooms, 12 story. Check-out noon. Restaurant, bar. Children's activity center. Fitness room. Indoor pool, outdoor pool, children's pool, whirlpool. Tennis. Airport transportation available. Business center. **$$**

★ ★ **DRURY INN.** *201 S 20th St, St. Louis (63103). Phone 314/231-3900; fax 314/231-3900. www.drury-inn.com.* Restored 1907 railroad hotel. 176 rooms, 7 story. Pets accepted, some restrictions. Complimentary continental breakfast. Check-out noon. Restaurant, bar. Fitness room. Indoor pool, whirlpool. **$**

★ **HAMPTON INN.** *2211 Market St, St. Louis (63103). Phone 314/241-3200; toll-free 800/426-7866; fax 314/241-9351. www.hamptoninn.com.* 239 rooms, 11 story. Pets accepted, some restrictions. Complimentary continental breakfast. Check-out noon. Bar. Fitness room. Indoor pool, whirlpool. **$**

★ ★ **HOLIDAY INN.** *811 N 9th St, St. Louis (63101). Phone 314/421-4000; toll-free 800/289-8338; fax 314/421-5974. www.holiday-inn.com.* 295 rooms, 4 story. Check-out noon. Restaurant, bar. Fitness room. Indoor pool, whirlpool. Business center. **$**

★ ★ **RADISSON HOTEL & SUITES ST. LOUIS DOWNTOWN.** *200 N 4th St, St. Louis (36102). Phone 314/621-8200; toll-free 800/333-3333; fax 314/621-8073. www.radisson.com.* This hotel offers a lobby lounge, a restaurant on the second floor, and a rooftop pool. It is located in the downtown area of St. Louis and is near many shops, restaurants, and entertainment establishments. 454 rooms, 29 story. Check-out noon. Restaurant, bar. Pool. **$$**

★ **STAYBRIDGE SUITES.** *1855 Craigshire Rd, St. Louis (63121). Phone 314/878-1555; toll-free 800/833-4353; fax 314/878-9203. www.wyndham.com.* This all-suite property offers a choice between one- and two-room suites. Each room features a kitchen and a living area with a TV and VCR along with a pull-out sofa bed. A buffet breakfast is included. 106 rooms, 2 story, all suites. Pets accepted; fee. Check-out noon. Fitness room. Pool, whirlpool. Airport transportation available. **$**

Full-Service Hotels

★ ★ ★ **HILTON ST. LOUIS FRONTENAC.** *1335 S Lindbergh Blvd, St. Louis (63131). Phone 314/993-1100; toll-free 800/325-7800; fax 314/993-8546. www.hilton.com.* Located between downtown St. Louis and Lambert International Airport, this hotel offers spacious guest rooms and suites with European charm. It is near the St. Louis Zoo, the St. Louis Science Center, Six Flags amusement park (see all), and more. 264 rooms, 3 story. Check-out noon. Restaurant, bar. Fitness room. Pool. Airport transportation available. Business center. **$**

★ ★ ★ **HYATT REGENCY ST. LOUIS.** *1 St. Louis Union Station, St. Louis (63103). Phone 314/231-1234; fax 314/923-3970. www.hyatt.com.* With facilities like an outdoor pool, a health club, saunas, a pizzeria, and a fine-dining restaurant, this hotel is a perfect place for both business and leisure travelers. It is located above a mall where visitors will find many stores. In renovated Union Station (see ST. LOUIS UNION STATION) railroad terminal (1894); main lobby and lounge occupy Grand Hall. 538 rooms, 6 story. Check-out noon. Restaurant, bar. Fitness room. Pool. **$$**

★ ★ ★ **MARRIOTT ST. LOUIS PAVILION.** *1 S Broadway, St. Louis (63102). Phone 314/421-1776; fax 314/331-9029. www.marriott.com.* With a central location across from Busch Stadium and only two blocks from the Gateway Arch, this hotel is easily acessable from the airport via the city's Metrolink transit system. 672 rooms, 25 story. Check-out noon. Restaurant, bar. Fitness room. Indoor pool, whirlpool. Business center. **$$**

★ ★ ★ **OMNI MAJESTIC HOTEL.** *1019 Pine St, St. Louis (63101). Phone 314/436-2355; toll-free 800/843-6664; fax 314/436-0223. www.omnihotels.com.* This European-style hotel (1913) is located in downtown St. Louis and is listed on the National Register of Historic Buildings. It offers 91 guest rooms and many modern amenities, including a full-service fitness center. 91 rooms, 9 story. Check-in 3 pm, check-out noon. Restaurant, bar. Fitness room. Airport transportation available. **$$**

★ ★ ★ **RENAISSANCE ST. LOUIS SUITES.** *800 Washington Ave, St. Louis (63101). Phone 314/621-9700; fax 314/621-9702. www.renaissancehotels.com.* 165 rooms, 24 story. Check-out noon. Restaurant. Fitness room. Whirlpool. Business center. **$**

★ ★ ★ **SHERATON CLAYTON PLAZA HOTEL ST. LOUIS.** *7730 Bonhomme Ave, St. Louis (63105). Phone 314/863-0400; toll-free 888/625-5144; fax 314/863-8513. www.sheraton.com.* 257 rooms, 15 story. Pets accepted. Check-out noon. Restaurant. Fitness room. Indoor pool. Business center. **$$**

★ ★ ★ **SHERATON ST. LOUIS CITY CENTER HOTEL AND SUITES.** *400 S 14th St, St. Louis (63103). Phone 314/231-5007; toll-free 888/625-5144; fax 314/231-5008. www.sheraton.com.* 288 rooms, 13 story. Check-out noon. Restaurant. Fitness room. Indoor pool. Business center. **$$**

★ ★ ★ **THE WESTIN ST. LOUIS.** *811 Spruce St, St. Louis (63102). Phone 314/621-2000; fax 314/552-5700. www.westin.com.* 221 rooms, 9 story. Check-out noon. Restaurant. Fitness room. Business center. **$$**

★ ★ ★ **WYNDHAM MAYFAIR HOTEL.** *806 St. Charles St, St. Louis (63101). Phone 314/421-2500; toll-free 800/757-8483; fax 314/421-6254. www.wyndham.com.* 132 rooms, 18 story. Pets accepted, some restrictions; fee. Check-out noon. Restaurant, bar. Fitness room. Business center. **$**

Restaurants

★ **BAR ITALIA.** *13 Maryland Pl, St. Louis (63108). Phone 314/361-7010.* Italian menu. Lunch, dinner. Closed Mon; Jan 1, Thanksgiving, Dec 25. Bar. Children's menu. Outdoor seating. **$$**

★ **BLUEBERRY HILL.** *6504 Delmar Blvd, St. Louis (63130). Phone 314/727-0880. www.blueberryhill.com.* Lunch, dinner. Closed Superbowl Sun. Bar. **$**

★ **BROADWAY OYSTER BAR.** *736 S Broadway, St. Louis (63102). Phone 314/621-8811. www.broadwayoysterbar.com.* Cajun/Creole menu. Lunch, dinner. Closed Easter, Dec 25. Bar. Outdoor seating. **$$**

★ ★ **CAFE BALABAN.** *405 N Euclid Ave, St. Louis (63108). Phone 314/361-8085. www.cafebalaban.com.* Mediterranean menu. Lunch, dinner. Closed holidays. Bar. **$$**

★ ★ **CANDICCI'S.** *12513 Olive Street Rd, St. Louis (63141). Phone 314/878-5858; fax 314/878-8702. www.candiccis.com.* Italian menu. Lunch, dinner. Closed holidays. Bar. Children's menu. Outdoor seating. **$$**

★ ★ **CARDWELL'S AT THE PLAZA.** *94 Plaza Frontenac, St. Louis (63131). Phone 314/997-8885; fax 314/872-8835. www.saucecafe.com/cardwellsattheplaza.* International/Fusion menu. Lunch, dinner. Closed Easter, Thanksgiving, Dec 25. Bar. Children's menu. **$$$**

★ **CHARCOAL HOUSE.** *9855 Manchester Rd, St. Louis (63119). Phone 314/968-4842; fax 314/968-2405.* Seafood, steak menu. Lunch, dinner. Closed Sun; holidays. Bar. Children's menu. **$$$**

★ ★ **CHARLIE GITTO'S.** *207 N 6th St, St. Louis (63101). Phone 314/436-2828; fax 314/436-3024. www.charliegittos.com.* Italian, American menu. Lunch, dinner. Closed Sun; holidays. Bar. Children's menu. **$$**

★ ★ **CHESHIRE INN.** *6300 Clayton Rd, St. Louis (63117). Phone 314/647-7300; fax 314/647-0186.* Seafood, steak menu. Dinner, Sat brunch. Bar. Children's menu. Valet parking. **$$**

★ **CROWN CANDY KITCHEN.** *1401 St. Louis Ave, St. Louis (63106). Phone 314/621-9650.* Breakfast, lunch, dinner. Closed holidays. Homemade candy. **$**

★ ★ **CUNETTO HOUSE OF PASTA.** *5453 Magnolia Ave, St. Louis (63139). Phone 314/781-1135; fax 314/781-5674. www.cunetto.com.* In an old Italian neighborhood. Italian menu. Lunch, dinner. Closed Sun; holidays. Bar. **$$**

★ ★ **DIERDORF & HART'S STEAK HOUSE.** *323 West Port Plz, St. Louis (63146). Phone 314/878-1801; fax 314/878-8989. www.dierdorfhartstl.com.* Steak menu. Lunch, dinner. Closed July 4, Thanksgiving. Bar. **$$$**

★ ★ ★ **DOMINIC'S RESTAURANT.** *5101 Wilson Ave, St. Louis (63110). Phone 314/771-1632. www.dominicsrestaurant.com.* Italian menu. Dinner. Closed Sun; holidays. Bar. Jacket required. Valet parking. **$$$**

★ **FRAZER'S TRAVELING BROWN BAG.** *1811 Pestalozzi, St. Louis (63118). Phone 314/773-8646. www.frazergoodeats.com.* Eclectic menu. Dinner. Closed Sun; holidays. Bar. Outdoor seating. **$$**

★ **GINO'S.** *4502 Hampton Ave, St. Louis (63109). Phone 314/351-4187.* Italian menu. Lunch, dinner. Closed Mon; holidays. Bar. Children's menu. **$$**

★ ★ ★ **GIOVANNI'S.** *5201 Shaw Ave, St. Louis (63110). Phone 314/772-5958; fax 314/772-0343.* This restaurant is best described as timeless Italian. The highlight is its focus on fresh seafood, which is flown in daily. The veal and beef dishes also are exceptional. Italian menu. Closed Sun; holidays. Valet parking. **$$$**

★ ★ **GIUSEPPE'S.** *4141 S Grand Blvd, St. Louis (63118). Phone 314/832-3779.* Italian menu. Lunch, dinner. Closed Mon; holidays; also July 1. Bar. **$$**

★ ★ ★ **THE GRILL.** *100 Carondelet Plz, St. Louis (63105). Phone 314/863-6300. www.ritzcarlton.com.* Located at the elegant Ritz-Carlton hotel near downtown St. Louis, this upscale dining room serves grilled beef, seafood, and fresh pasta and has a seafood buffet on Wednesdays. Dinner. Closed Feb 14. Bar. Children's menu. Valet parking. **$$$**

★ ★ **HACIENDA.** *9748 Manchester Rd, Rockhill (63119). Phone 314/962-7100. www.hacienda-stl.com.* Built as a residence for local steamboat captain (1861). Mexican menu. Lunch, dinner. Closed holidays. Bar. Outdoor seating. **$$**

★ **HAMMERSTONE'S.** *2028 S 9th, St. Louis (63104). Phone 314/773-5565; fax 314/773-6818.* Breakfast, lunch, dinner. Closed Easter, Memorial Day, Dec 25. Bar. Children's menu. Outdoor seating. **$$**

★ **HANNEGAN'S.** *719 N 2nd St, St. Louis (63102). Phone 314/241-8877. www.hannegansrestaurant.com.* Replica of United States Senate dining room; political memorabilia. Lunch, dinner. Closed Thanksgiving, Dec 25. Bar. Children's menu. **$$**

★ ★ **HARRY'S.** *2144 Market St, St. Louis (63103). Phone 314/421-6969; fax 314/421-5114.* Lunch, dinner. Closed Sun; holidays. Bar. Valet parking. **$$$**

★ ★ **HARVEST.** *1059 S Big Bend, St. Louis (63117). Phone 314/645-3522. www.harveststlouis.com.* Dinner. Closed Mon; July 4, Thanksgiving, Dec 25. Bar. Children's menu. **$$$**

★ ★ **J. F. SANFILIPPO'S.** *705 N Broadway, St. Louis (63102). Phone 314/621-7213. www.sanfilippos.com.* Lunch, dinner. Closed Sun (except football season); holidays. Bar. Children's menu. **$$**

⊙ ★ **JOHN D. MCGURK'S.** *1200 Russell Blvd, St. Louis (63104). Phone 314/776-8309. www.mcgurks.com.* Housed in an 1861 building. Irish, American menu. Lunch, dinner. Closed holidays. Bar. Children's menu. **$$**

★ ★ **JOSEPH'S ITALIAN CAFE.** *107 N 6th St, St. Louis (63101). Phone 314/421-6366; fax 314/421-1664.* Italian menu. Lunch, dinner. Closed Sun. Outdoor seating. **$$**

★ ★ **K. C. MASTERPIECE.** *611 N Lindbergh, St. Louis (63141). Phone 314/991-5811; fax 314/991-4781.* Barbecue menu. Lunch, dinner. Closed Jan 1, Thanksgiving, Dec 25. Bar. Children's menu. **$$**

⊡

★ ★ ★ **KEMOLL'S.** *1 Metropolitan Sq, St. Louis (63102). Phone 314/421-0555. www.kemolls.com.* Since 1927, this downtown-landmark restaurant has served upscale, classic specialties in an elegant atmosphere. The name was originally shortened from the Sicilian name Camuglia, and the restaurant is still run by fourth-generation family members. Five dining rooms. Italian menu. Dinner. Closed holidays. **$$$**

★ **KING & I.** *3157 S Grand Blvd, St. Louis (63118). Phone 314/771-1777.* Thai menu. Lunch, dinner. Closed Mon; holidays. Bar. **$$**

★ **LE PETIT BISTRO.** *172 W County Center, Des Peres (63131). Phone 314/965-1777; fax 314/965-1760.* French, Italian menu. Lunch, dinner. Closed holidays. Casual attire. Outdoor seating. **$**

★ ★ **LEONARDO'S LITTLE ITALY.** *5901 Southwest Ave, St. Louis (63139). Phone 314/781-5988. www.leonardoslittleitaly.com.* Located in an old Italian neighborhood. Italian menu. Dinner. Closed Mon; holidays. Bar. **$$**

★ ★ ★ **LOMBARDO'S TRATTORIA.** *201 S 20th St, St. Louis (63103). Phone 314/621-0666; fax 314/231-3900.* Family-owned and -operated for three generations, this restaurant has several diving areas on the lower level of a converted historic hotel. The menu boasts coveted family classics, as well as creative seasonal entrées. Italian menu. Lunch, dinner. Closed Sun; holidays. Bar. Children's menu. **$$$**

★ ★ **LORUSSO'S CUCINA.** *3121 Watson Rd, St. Louis (63139). Phone 314/647-6222; fax 314/647-2821. www.lorussos.com.* Italian menu. Lunch, dinner. Closed Mon; holidays. Bar. Children's menu. **$$**

★ ★ **LYNCH STREET BISTRO.** *1031 Lynch St, St. Louis (63118). Phone 314/772-5777. www.lynchstreetbistro.com.* International/Fusion menu. Lunch, dinner. Closed Sun; holidays. Bar. Children's menu. **$$**

★ **MAGGIE O'BRIEN'S.** *2000 Market St, St. Louis (63103). Phone 314/421-1388; fax 314/421-6712.* Irish, American menu. Own potato chips. Breakfast, lunch, dinner. Closed holidays. Children's menu. Valet parking. Outdoor seating. **$$**

★ ★ ★ **MALMAISON AT ST. ALBANS.** *3519 St. Albans Rd, St. Albans (63073). Phone 636/458-0131. www.fivestarfrench.com.* A rustic replica of a French inn tucked away in the countryside outside of St. Louis, this restaurant offers a small yet fresh seasonal menu that promises to entice guests' senses. French menu. Dinner, Sun brunch. Closed Mon-Tues. Bar. Jacket required. Reservations recommended. Outdoor seating. **$$$**

★ ★ **MAMA CAMPISI'S.** *2132 Edwards St, St. Louis (63110). Phone 314/771-1797.* Italian menu. Lunch, dinner. Closed Mon; holidays. Bar. **$$**

★ **MARCIANO'S.** *333 Westport Plz, St. Louis (63146). Phone 314/878-8180; fax 314/878-2108.* Italian menu. Lunch, dinner. Closed Easter, Thanksgiving, Dec 25. Bar. Children's menu. Outdoor seating. **$$**

★ ★ **MIKE SHANNON'S.** *100 N 7th St, St. Louis (63101). Phone 314/421-1540. www.shannonsteak.com.* Dinner. Closed Easter, Thanksgiving, Dec 25. Bar. Sports memorabilia. **$$$**

★ **MUSEUM CAFE.** *1 Fine Arts Dr, St. Louis (63110). Phone 314/721-5325. www.slam.org.* Menu items reflect current museum exhibits. American menu. Lunch, dinner, Sun brunch. Closed Mon; Thanksgiving, Dec 25. Children's menu. **$$**

★ **ONCE UPON A VINE.** *3559 Arsenal St, St. Louis (63118). Phone 314/776-2828.* Lunch, dinner. Closed Sun; holidays. Bar. Children's menu. Outdoor seating. **$$**

★ ★ **PATRICK'S.** *342 Westport Plz, St. Louis (63146). Phone 314/878-6767.* Lunch, dinner, Sun brunch. Closed holidays. Bar. Children's menu. **$$**

★ **RED SEA.** *6511 Delmar Blvd, St. Louis (63130). Phone 314/863-0099.* Ethiopian menu. Lunch, dinner, Sun brunch. Closed Dec 25. Bar. **$$**

★ **ROBATA OF JAPAN.** *111 Westport Plz, St. Louis (63146). Phone 314/434-1007.* Japanese menu. Lunch, dinner. Closed Thanksgiving. Bar. Children's menu. **$$**

★ **SALEEM'S LEBANESE CUISINE.** *6501 Delmar Blvd, St. Louis (63130). Phone 314/721-7947; fax 314/721-2295.* Middle Eastern menu. Dinner. Closed Sun; Thanksgiving, Dec 25. **$**

★ ★ **SIDNEY STREET CAFE.** *2000 Sidney St, St. Louis (63104). Phone 314/771-5777.* In a restored building (circa 1885); antiques. American menu. Dinner. Closed Sun-Mon; holidays. Bar. **$$**

★ **SPIRO'S.** *3122 Watson Rd, St. Louis (63139). Phone 314/645-8383.* Greek menu. Lunch, dinner. Closed Sun; holidays. Children's menu. Reservations recommended. **$$**

★ ★ **ST. LOUIS BREWERY AND TAP ROOM.** *2100 Locust St, St. Louis (63103). Phone 314/241-2337; fax 314/241-8101. www.schlafly.com.* Lunch, dinner. Closed Jan 1, Easter, Dec 25. Bar. **$$**

★ **SUNFLOWER CAFE.** *5513 Pershing Ave, St. Louis (63112). Phone 314/367-6800.* Italian, American menu. Lunch, dinner. Closed Sun; holidays. Bar. Children's menu. Outdoor seating. **$$**

★ **THAI CAFE.** *6170 Delmar Blvd, St. Louis (63112). Phone 314/862-6868.* Thai menu. Lunch, dinner. Closed Sun; Dec 25. Valet parking. **$$**

★ ★ ★ ★ **TONY'S.** *410 Market St, St. Louis (63102). Phone 314/231-7007; fax 314/231-4740. www.tonysstlouis .com.* Italian food may bring to mind images of red sauce and mozzarella cheese, but at Tony's, a consistent favorite for the rustic dishes of this Mediterranean country, you'll find a menu of luscious Italian fare prepared with a measured and sophisticated hand. Expect appetizers like smoked salmon with mascarpone cheese and asparagus and Belgian endive, pastas like penne with lobster and shrimp, and entrées like tenderloin of beef with foie gras in a port wine demi-glaze and truffle-sauced veal loin chop. In terms of ambience, Tony's is one of those stylish eateries that works just as well for entertaining a business colleague as for sharing dinner with a more intimate acquaintance. The room has an urban, postmodern style, with sleek low lighting, widely spaced linen-topped tables, and glossy, butter-toned wood-paneled walls. The chef's tasting menu is a nice choice for gourmands with healthy appetites. Italian menu. Dinner. Closed Sun; holidays; also the first week of Jan, first week of July. Bar. Jacket required. Valet parking. **$$$$**

★ ★ **TRATTORIA MARCELLA.** *3600 Watson Rd, St. Louis (63109). Phone 314/352-7706; fax 314/352-0848.* Italian menu. Dinner. Closed Sun-Mon; holidays. Bar. Outdoor seating. **$$**

★ ★ **YEMANJA BRASIL.** *2900 Missouri Ave, St. Louis (63118). Phone 314/771-7457; fax 314/771-7457.* Lunch, dinner. Closed Mon; holidays. Bar. Outdoor seating. **$$**

★ **ZIA'S.** *5256 Wilson Ave, St. Louis (63110). Phone 314/776-0020; fax 314/776-5778. www.zias.com.* Informal, modern corner restaurant. Italian menu. Lunch, dinner. Closed Sun; holidays. Bar. Outdoor seating. **$$**

Indiana

At the crossroads of the nation, Indiana is one of the most typically American states in the country. Against a still visible background of Native American history and determined pioneer struggle for survival, it stands out today as a region that has come of age. It is a manufacturing state with widely distributed industrial centers surrounded by fertile farmlands and magnificent forests.

In the wooded hill country north of the Ohio River are pioneer villages where time seems to have stood still. Central Indiana is one of the richest agricultural regions in the United States. The Calumet District in the northwest has a large industrial area. Miles of sand dunes and beaches have made Lake Michigan's south shore the state's summer playground. In the northeastern section are hundreds of secluded lakes, an angler's paradise. Trails at state parks and recreation areas are marked for hiking and horseback riding. In the winter, skiing, ice skating, and tobogganing are popular sports.

Indiana's highways and roads are lined with reminders of its colorful history. A pre-Columbian race of mound builders developed a highly ceremonial culture here. Their earth structures still can be seen in many parts of the state. In 1673, two Frenchmen, Père Marquette and Louis Jolliet, wandered across northern Indiana and preached to the Native Americans. Between 1679 and 1685, Indiana was thoroughly explored by Robert de La Salle and became a part of the French provinces of Canada and Louisiana. After the French and Indian War, most of Indiana came under British control (1763), which was violently opposed by a Native American confederation led by Chief Pontiac. In 1779, General George Rogers Clark occupied southern Indiana with French assistance and claimed it for the state of Virginia. But Virginia was as unable to control the region as the British. Indiana became

Population:	6,080,485
Area:	35,936 square miles
Elevation:	320-1,257 feet
Peak:	Near Bethel (Wayne County)
Entered Union:	December 11, 1816 (19th state)
Capital:	Indianapolis
Motto:	The Crossroads of America
Nickname:	The Hoosier State
Flower:	Peony
Bird:	Cardinal
Tree:	Tulip
Fair:	Mid-August in Indianapolis
Time Zone:	Eastern and Central
Web site:	www.enjoyindiana.com

public domain in 1784 and remained chiefly Native American territory during the next 15 years.

Continuing pressure by the federal government in Washington and by white settlers on Native American land led the great Shawnee chief Tecumseh to form an unsuccessful confederation of Indian Nations, extending from the Great Lakes to the Gulf of Mexico. The Battle of Tippecanoe in 1811, brought about by General William Henry Harrison while Tecumseh was in the South, dealt a fatal blow to the Native American organization. In 1812, Native Americans, their towns and granaries burned by federal troops and militia, made a last furious attempt to defend their land. But Tecumseh's death in the Battle of the Thames in 1813 marked the end of the Native American era. In 1816, Indiana became the 19th state of the Union. Abraham Lincoln was 7 years old when his family moved to southern Indiana in 1816. He lived here for 14 years.

Today, Indiana's industries manufacture transportation equipment, electrical supplies, heavy industrial machinery, and food products. More

Calendar Highlights

APRIL

Little 500 Bicycle Race *(Bloomington). Indiana University campus. Phone 812/855-9152.* Bicycle and tricycle races, golf jamboree, entertainment.

MAY

500 Festival *(Indianapolis). Phone 317/ 636-4556 or toll-free 800/638-4296.* Month-long celebration precedes the Indianapolis 500, held Memorial Day weekend. Numerous events include the 500 Ball, Mechanic's Recognition Party, Delco Electronics 500 festival parade, mini-marathon, memorial service.

Indianapolis 500 *(Indianapolis). Phone 317/ 484-6780.* A full schedule of activities, including mini-marathon, mayor's breakfast, and hot air balloon race, lead up to the big race.

Little 500 *(Anderson). Anderson Speedway. Phone 765/642-0206.* Auto races.

JULY

Three Rivers Festival *(Fort Wayne). Phone 260/426-5556. www.trfonline.org.* More than 280 events, including parades, balloon races, arts and crafts, music, ethnic dancing, sports, and fireworks, at various locations in Fort Wayne.

AUGUST

Amish Acres Arts & Crafts Festival *(Nappanee). Amish Acres. Phone Amish Acres visitor center, 219/773-4188 or toll-free 800/800-4942. www. amishacres.com.* Entries from many states; paintings, ceramics, jewelry; entertainment, dancing, feasts.

Indiana State Fair *(Indianapolis). Fairgrounds. Phone 317/927-7500 or 317/923-3431 (evenings).* Grand circuit horse racing, livestock exhibitions, entertainment, and special agricultural exhibits.

SEPTEMBER

Fairmount Museum Days/Remembering James Dean *(Fairmount/Marion). James Dean/ Fairmount Historical Museum. Phone 765/ 948-4555.* Large car show, including 2,500 classic and custom autos; James Dean look-alike contest; 1950s dance contest; parade; downtown street fair.

OCTOBER

Parke County Covered Bridge Festival *(Rockville). Phone 765/569-5226.* Celebration of Parke County's 32 historic covered bridges. Five self-guided tours are available. Arts and crafts, craft demonstrations, food, animals, rides at living museum.

---

than 60 percent of the building limestone used in the United States is supplied by quarries in the Hoosier State. Soft coal deposits, mainly found in southwest Indiana, are the most abundant natural resource. Indiana's principal farm products are soybeans, tomatoes, corn, spearmint, peppermint, livestock, poultry, and wheat and dairy products.

Several explanations have been offered as to why Indianans are called "Hoosiers." The most logical is that in 1826, a contractor on the Ohio Falls Canal at Louisville, Samuel Hoosier, gave employment preference to men living on the Indiana side of the river. The men in his work gangs were called "Hoosier's men," then "Hoosiers."

When to Go/Climate

Hot, humid summers and cold, snowy winters are the norm in Indiana. The flat terrain provides no buffer against wind and storms, and tornadoes are not uncommon in spring and summer.

AVERAGE HIGH/LOW TEMPERATURES (° F)

Fort Wayne

Jan 30/15	**May** 71/49	**Sept** 76/54
Feb 34/18	**June** 81/59	**Oct** 63/43
Mar 46/29	**July** 85/63	**Nov** 49/34
Apr 60/39	**Aug** 82/61	**Dec** 36/22

Indianapolis

Jan 34/17	**May** 74/52	**Sept** 78/56
Feb 38/21	**June** 83/61	**Oct** 66/44
Mar 51/32	**July** 86/65	**Nov** 52/34
Apr 63/42	**Aug** 84/63	**Dec** 39/23

Parks and Recreation

Water-related activities, hiking, biking, various other sports, picnicking, and visitor centers, as well as camping, are available in many of these areas. Standard admission fees to state parks are $4/carload (out-of-state, $5/carload); $22/year permit; use of horses, fee varies. Camping, limited to two weeks, is on a first-come, first-served basis at most parks: $8-$21/night/site/family; winter, half price. Camping permitted all year, except at Bass Lake. Campsite reservations are accepted for all parks, except at Harmonie, Huntington Lake, Shades, Summit Lake, and Tippecanoe. Several parks have housekeeping cabins. Six parks have inns, open all year. Pools and beaches are open from Memorial Day-late August (varies at each park); swimming permitted only when lifeguards are on duty. Pets on leash only. For detailed information, contact the Indiana Department of Natural Resources, Division of State Parks and Reservoirs, 402 W Washington St, Room W-298, Indianapolis 46204, phone 317/232-4124.

FISHING AND HUNTING

Nonresident licenses are available for hunting, five-day hunting, deer hunting, fishing (one-, three-, and seven-day; annual), and trapping; trout/salmon, game bird, and waterfowl stamps. Resident licenses are available for hunting, deer hunting, fishing, one-day fishing, trapping, and turkey hunting. Youth hunting license allows children under 18 to hunt all game. Residents ages 17-65 and all non-residents must obtain fishing license. For additional information, including exceptions, bag limits, and license fees, contact the Indiana Department of Natural Resources, Division of Fish and Wildlife, 402 W Washington St, Room W-273, Indianapolis 46204, phone 317/232-4080. A free quarterly newsletter, *Focus*, is available to keep sportspersons up to date on division activities. Write to *Focus* at the same address.

Driving Information

Safety belts are mandatory for all persons in the front seat of a vehicle. Children under 5 years—anywhere in a vehicle—must be in approved passenger restraints; ages 3 and 4 may use regulation safety belts; age 2 and under must use approved safety seats. Phone 317/232-1295.

INTERSTATE HIGHWAY SYSTEM

The following alphabetical listing of Indiana towns in this book shows that these cities are within 10 miles of the indicated interstate highways. Check a highway map for the nearest exit.

Highway Number	Cities/Towns within 10 Miles
Interstate 64	Corydon, Jeffersonville, New Albany, Wyandotte.
Interstate 65	Columbus, Indianapolis, Jeffersonville, Lafayette, New Albany, Remington.
Interstate 69	Anderson, Angola, Fort Wayne, Huntington, Indianapolis, Marion, Muncie, Noblesville.
Interstate 70	Brazil, Greencastle, Greenfield, Indianapolis, New Castle, Richmond, Terre Haute.
Interstate 74	Batesville, Crawfordsville, Indianapolis.
Interstate 94	Hammond, Michigan City.

Additional Visitor Information

Six-issue subscriptions to *Outdoor Indiana* may be obtained by contacting the Department of Natural Resources, 402 W Washington St, Room W-160, Indianapolis 46204, phone 317/232-4200. This official publication of the Department of Natural Resources is $10 for one year or $18 for two years.

Brochures on attractions, calendars of events, and information about historic sites and other subjects are available from the Indiana Department of Commerce, Tourism and Film Development Division, 1 N Capitol St, Suite 700, Indianapolis 46204, phone toll-free 800/289-6646.

There are welcome centers on highways entering southern Indiana, as well as travel information centers located at highway rest areas throughout Indiana. Those who stop will find information and brochures most helpful in planning visits to points of interest. All are open daily, 24 hours.

DUNE COUNTRY

Just as Californians head for the sand and surf of Malibu and Easterners flock to sandy expanses of the Jersey shore, Midwesterners journey to the rolling sand dunes and hidden beaches of northwestern Indiana. A popular way to "do the dunes" is to travel along Highway 12, known colloquially as "the Dunes Highway." Roughly paralleling the lakefront between Gary and Michigan City, the route passes through vast protected areas of lakeshore, tunneling through shady avenues of trees. Large expanses of "dune country" are protected by the 2,182-acre Indiana Dunes State Park (see) and Indiana Dunes National Lakeshore (see), a federally administered preserve containing about 15,000 acres. Together, these areas contain some of the most diverse flora and fauna in the Midwest. They also provide a wide range of highly popular interpretive programs.

Begin at West Beach, part of the National Lakeshore north of Highway 12 and east of Country Line Road. It offers 4 miles of open beach, a modern bathhouse, nature-study activities, picnic areas, duneland grass prairie, a lake, and 3 miles of hiking trails. A boardwalk provides panoramic views from elevations of up to 110 feet. Continue east on Highway 12 and take Highway 49 north to Indiana Dunes State Park. Diverse park interpretive programs range from naturalist hikes to explore the semiarid, desertlike dune environment to a video presentation about edible wild foods. Other kid-friendly, fun programs include beach-blanket bingo and scavenger hunts that teach participants about the unique habitats found in and around the dunes. The park offers 3 miles of beach, flanked by one of the nation's finest examples of a preserved natural dune ecosystem. More than 16 miles of trails offer a variety of challenges, including the opportunity to scale Mount Tom, the tallest dune at 192 feet.

Heading north on Highway 49 to Interstate 94, find excellent lodgings and a pampering health-and-beauty spa at Indian Oak Resort & Spa (see VALPARAISO) that offers lakeside rooms with fireplaces and whirl-pool tubs and a variety of body treatments and massages. It's a tranquil spot, nestled around a private lake on 100 acres of wooded trails that thread through towering oaks. Nearby on Highway 49 is the Yellow Brick Road Gift Shop and Fantasy Museum, full of memorabilia related to the classic movie *The Wizard of Oz* and the work of its creator, L. Frank Baum. Return to the Dunes Highway and continue east to Kemil Road. **(Approximately 26 miles)**

Anderson (C-3)

See also Indianapolis, Muncie

Founded 1823
Population 59,734
Elevation 883 ft
Area Code 765
Information Anderson/Madison County Visitors and Convention Bureau, 6335 S Scatterfield Rd, 46013; phone 765/643-5633 or toll-free 800/533-6569
Web site www.madtourism.com

Originally, this was the site of a Delaware village in the hills south of the White River. The city was named for Kikthawenund, also called Captain Anderson, a well-known chief of the Delawares. The discovery of natural gas pockets underneath the city in 1886 sparked a ten-year boom, which gave the city the title "Queen of the Gas Belt." One hundred Newport-style gaslights have been added to what is now known as Historic West 8th Street (see). Restored Victorian homes reflect the area's fashionable past.

Anderson is the seat of grain and livestock production in Madison County and is an important manufacturing center. Two subsidiaries of General Motors, Delco-Remy America and Delphi Interior Lighting Systems, manufacture automotive equipment. Other industrial products include castings, glass, cabinets, corrugated boxes, recreation equipment, and packaging machinery. The international headquarters of the nonsectarian Church of God is in Anderson.

What to See and Do

Anderson University. *E 5th St and College Dr (46012). Phone 765/649-9071; toll-free 800/428-6414. www. anderson.edu.* (1917) (2,000 students) School of Theology (Sept-June) has collection of Holy Land artifacts. Also on campus are the Jessie Wilson Art Galleries, Boehm Bird Collection, and 2,250-seat Reardon Auditorium. The Indianapolis Colts hold summer training camp here (mid-July-mid-Aug). Tours (by appointment). **FREE**

Gruenewald Historic House. *626 Main St. Phone 765/648-6875.* (1873) Twelve-room, Second Empire town house of successful German saloonkeeper, decorated in style of 1890s. (Apr-mid-Dec) Living history tours (by appointment). One-hour house tours (Tues-Fri). **$$**

Historic West 8th Street. *6335 Scatterfield Rd (46013). Phone 765/643-5633.* Eleven blocks of restored Victorian homes lined with Newport-style gaslights re-create the 1890s. **FREE**

Historical Military Armor Museum. *2330 Crystal St. I-69, exit 26. Phone 765/649-8265.* Large collection of lightweight tanks from World War I to the present; completely restored and operational. (Tues, Thurs, Sat; closed holidays) **$$**

Mounds State Park. *4306 Mounds Rd (46017). 2 miles E on Hwy 232. Phone 765/642-6627.* Within this 290-acre park of rolling woodlands are several well-preserved earth formations constructed many centuries ago by a prehistoric race of Adena-Hopewell mound builders. On bluffs overlooking the White River are earth structures that were once an important center of an ancient civilization of which very little is known. The largest earth structure is 9 feet high and nearly 1/4 mile in circumference. Smaller structures nearby include conical mounds and a fiddle-shaped earthwork. **$$**

Paramount Theatre and Centre Ballroom. *1124 Meridian Plz. Phone 765/642-1234.* Restored 1929 atmospheric theatre designed to appear as a Spanish courtyard. Tours (by appointment; closed holidays) **$$**

Special Event

Little 500. *Anderson Speedway, 1311 Pendleton Ave, Anderson (46013). Phone 765/642-0206.* Auto races. Reservations necessary. Weekend of Indianapolis 500 (Memorial Day weekend). (See SPECIAL EVENTS under INDIANAPOLIS)

Limited-Service Hotels

★ **BEST INN.** *5706 S Scatterfield Rd, Anderson (46013). Phone 765/644-2000; toll-free 800/237-8466; fax 765/683-1747. www.bestinn.com.* 93 rooms, 2 story. Pets accepted; fee. Complimentary continental breakfast. Check-out 1 pm. **$**

★ ★ **HOLIDAY INN.** *5920 Scatterfield Rd, Anderson (46013). Phone 765/644-2581; toll-free 800/465-4329; fax 765/642-8545. www.holiday-inn.com.* 158 rooms, 2 story. Check-out 11 am. Restaurant, bar. Indoor pool, outdoor pool, whirlpool. Airport transportation available. **$**

Angola (A-4)

See also Auburn

Population 7,344
Elevation 1,055 ft
Area Code 219
Zip 46703
Information Steuben County Tourism Bureau, 207 S Wayne St; phone toll-free 800/525-3101
Web site www.lakes101.org

This tranquil town lies in the northeastern corner of Indiana's resort area. The wooded hills surrounding Angola provide more than 100 lakes for swimming, boating, and fishing in the summer and ice skating in the winter.

What to See and Do

Pokagon State Park. *450 Ln 100 Lake James (46703). Hwy 80/90 and I-69, exit 154. Phone 219/833-2012.* A 1,203-acre park on the shores of Lake James and Snow Lake in the heart of the northern Indiana lake country. Swimming beach, bathhouse, water-skiing, fishing, boating (rentals). Hiking trails, saddle barn, skiing, ice skating, tobogganing, ice fishing, picnicking, concession, camping. Nature center, wildlife exhibit, naturalist service. (Daily)

Limited-Service Hotel

★ ★ **POTAWATOMI INN.** *6 Ln 100A Lake James, Angola (46703). Phone 260/833-1077; toll-free 877/768-2928; fax 260/833-4087.* Located in the beautiful Pokagon State Park (see), visitors will be adorned with nature, recreation, and adventure here. This inn is a perfect place for visitors to unwind after a long, adventurous day horseback riding, boating, or hiking. Built in 1926; land acquired from the Potawatomi Indians. 142 rooms, 2 story. Check-in 4 pm, check-out noon. Restaurant. Fitness room. Private beach. Indoor pool, whirlpool. On Lake James. **$**

🏃 🖼️

Auburn (A-4)

See also Angola, Fort Wayne

Population 12,074
Elevation 870 ft
Area Code 219
Zip 46706
Information Chamber of Commerce, 208 S Jackson St; phone 219/925-2100 or DeKalb County Visitors Bureau, 204 N Jackson; phone 219/927-1499 or toll-free 877/833-3282
Web site www.dekalbcvb.org

What to See and Do

Auburn-Cord-Duesenberg Museum. *1600 S Wayne St. Phone 219/925-1444.* More than 140 examples of these and other well-known antique, classic, and special-interest cars are displayed in the original showroom of the Auburn Automobile Company; collections of automotive literature. (Daily; closed Jan 1, Thanksgiving, Dec 25) (See SPECIAL EVENT) **$$$**

Gene Stratton Porter Historic Site. *1205 Pleasant Pt, Rome City. 25 miles NW on I-69, Hwy 6, or Hwy 9, near Rome City. Phone 219/854-3790.* Home of well-known Indiana author, naturalist, and photographer. Built on Sylvan Lake in a forested area with a great variety of wildflowers and wildlife; designed by Mrs. Porter and completed in 1914. Two-story log cabin is furnished with many original pieces, photographs, and memorabilia. Special events. Tours of the cabin. (Apr-mid-Dec, Tues-Sun; closed Easter, Thanksgiving, Dec 25) **DONATION**

National Automotive and Truck Museum. *1000 Gordon M. Buerig Pl. Phone 219/925-9100.* More than 100 cars and trucks on display with a focus on post-World War I automobiles; auto-related exhibits. (Daily; closed Jan 1, Thanksgiving, Dec 25) **$$$**

Special Event

Auburn-Cord-Duesenberg Festival. *1600 S Wayne St, Auburn (46706). Phone 219/925-3600.* Auto auction, classic car show, parades, many events. Late Aug.

Limited-Service Hotel

★ **COUNTRY HEARTH INN-AUBURN.** *1115 W 7th St, Auburn (46706). Phone 260/925-1316; toll-free 800/280-0229; fax 260/927-8012. www.countryhearth .com.* 78 rooms, 2 story. Complimentary continental breakfast. Check-out noon. Pool. **$**

Aurora (D-4)

Founded 1819
Population 3,965
Elevation 501 ft
Area Code 812
Zip 47001
Information Office of the Mayor, PO Box 158; phone 812/926-1777

What to See and Do

Hillforest. *213 5th St. Phone 812/926-0087.* (circa 1855) Fully restored Italian Renaissance villa on 10 acres. Architecture and period furnishings incorporate characteristics of steamboat era. (Apr-mid-Dec, Tues-Sun; closed holidays) (See SPECIAL EVENTS) **$$**

Special Events

Aurora Farmers' Fair. *228 2nd St, Aurora (47001). Phone 812/926-2176.* Three-day fair featuring rides, games, parade, entertainment. First weekend in Oct.

Victorian Christmas. *213 5th St, Aurora (47001). Hillforest. Phone 812/926-0087.* Re-creation of a Victorian Christmas. First two weekends in Dec.

Limited-Service Hotel

★ ★ **GRAND VICTORIA CASINO & RESORT BY HYATT.** *600 Grand Victoria Dr, Rising Sun (47040). Phone 812/438-1234; toll-free 800/472-6311; fax 812/438-5151. www.hyatt.com.* 201 rooms, 3 story. Check-out 11 am. Restaurant. Fitness room. Indoor pool, whirlpool. Business center. **$**

Batesville (D-4)

See also Connersville

Population 6,033
Elevation 983 ft
Area Code 812
Zip 47006
Information Chamber of Commerce, 132 S Main; phone 812/934-3101

What to See and Do

Whitewater Canal State Historic Site. *19083 Clayborn St, Metamora. 14 miles N on Hwy 52. Phone 812/647-6512.* Includes part of a restored 14-mile section of the Whitewater Canal, which provided transportation between Hagerstown and the Ohio River at Lawrenceburg from 1836 to 1860. The *Ben Franklin III* canal boat offers 25-minute horse-drawn boat cruises through the Duck Creek aqueduct (1848) to the canal's only remaining operating lock (May-Oct, Tues-Sun; other times by appointment). Working gristmill in Metamora (Tues-Sun; free). Fishing, canoeing; hiking; picnicking permitted along the canal. **$**

Specialty Lodging

The following lodging establishment is approved by Mobil Travel Guide but, due to its unique and individualized nature has not been given a traditional Mobil Star rating. Included in this listing you may find bed-and-breakfasts, limited-service inns, guest ranches, and other unique hotel properties.

SHERMAN HOUSE. *35 S Main St (Hwy 229), Batesville (47006). Phone 812/934-1000; toll-free 800/ 445-4939; fax 812/934-1230. www.sherman-house.com.* Inn since 1852. 23 rooms, 2 story. Check-in 1 pm, check-out 11 am. Restaurant (see). Fitness room. **$**

Restaurant

★ ★ **SHERMAN HOUSE.** *35 S Main St (Hwy 229), Batesville (47006). Phone 812/934-2407. www. sherman-house.com.* Established in 1852. German, American menu. Breakfast, lunch, dinner. Closed Jan 1, Dec 25. Bar. Children's menu. Lobster tank. **$$$**

Bedford (E-3)

See also Bloomington, French Lick, Spring Mill State Park

Founded 1825
Population 13,768
Elevation 699 ft
Area Code 812
Zip 47421
Information Lawrence County Tourism Commission, 1116 16th St, PO Box 1193; phone 812/275-4493 or toll-free 800/798-0769
Web site www.kiva.net/bedford

Bedford is the center of Indiana limestone quarrying, one of the state's foremost industries. Limestone quarried here was used in the construction of the World War Memorial in Indianapolis (see), the Empire State Building in New York, and the Federal Triangle in Washington, DC.

This agricultural area produces livestock, grain, and fruit. The headquarters of the Hoosier National Forest (see) and Wayne National Forest (see IRONTON, OHIO) are here. Williams Dam, 11 miles southwest on Highway 450, offers fishing on the White River.

What to See and Do

Bluespring Caverns. *Stumphole Bridge Rd. 6 miles SW via Hwy 50. Phone 812/279-9471. www.bluespringcaverns .com.* One of the world's largest cavern systems; more than 20 miles of explored passageways and 15 miles of underground streams join to form the large river upon which tour boats travel. Electric lighting reveals many unusual sights, including eyeless blindfish and blind crawfish. Picnicking. Gift shop. (Apr-Oct) **$$$**

Hoosier National Forest. *811 Constitution Ave (47421). Both N and S of Bedford: to reach the N portion, NE on Hwy 58 (or E on Hwy 50 then N on Hwy 446); to reach the S portion, SW on Hwy 50 (or S on Hwy 37 and W on Hwy 60). Phone 812/275-5987.* Approximately 189,000 acres spread through nine counties. Swimming, boating, fishing; picnicking, hiking, horseback trails, hunting, nature study; historic sites. Campsites at Hardin Ridge (Monroe County), German Ridge, Celina Lake, Tipson Lake, Indian Lake (Perry County), and Springs Valley (Orange County) recreation areas. Campsites on first-come, first-served basis. Fees are charged at recreation sites for camping; entrance fee at Hardin Ridge. In the portion of the forest south of Bedford is

Pioneer Mothers Memorial Forest. *Paoli. From Paoli, S on Hwy 37, in Orange County.* An 88-acre forest of virgin timber that includes white oak and black walnut trees of giant dimensions.

Lawrence County Historical Museum. *12 Courthouse (47421). Phone 812/275-4141.* Display of Indiana limestone, Native American artifacts, Civil War items, pioneer relics, World War I and World War II items; genealogical library. (Mon-Fri; closed holidays) **FREE**

Osborne Spring Park. *17 miles NW via Hwy 58 to Owensburg, then 3 miles NW on Osborne Spring Rd.* Approximately 30 acres. Restored log cabin (1817). Picnicking, camping (fee). (Daily) **$$**

Limited-Service Hotel

★ ★ **STONEHENGE LODGE.** *911 Constitution Ave, Bedford (47421). Phone 812/279-8111; toll-free 800/274-2974; fax 812/279-0172. www.stonehengelodge .com.* 97 rooms, 3 story. Check-out noon. Restaurant, bar. Pool. **$**

Bloomington (D-2)

See also Bedford, Columbus, Nashville, Spring Mill State Park

Settled 1818
Population 69,291
Elevation 745 ft
Area Code 812
Information Bloomington/Monroe County Convention and Visitors Bureau, 2855 N Walnut St, 47404; phone 812/334-8900 or toll-free 800/800-0037
Web site www.visitbloomington.com

The home to Indiana University (IU) (see), Bloomington is widely regarded as one of America's best college towns, a reputation founded on the community's relaxed atmosphere, eclectic shops and restaurants, vast cultural offerings, and scenic setting.

Bloomington's official population falls just short of 70,000, a figure that includes few of the 39,000 students at IU.

The university's campus—graced by subtle hills, dense woods, and narrow streams—was rated as one of America's five most beautiful campuses by author/ architect Thomas Gaines, who wrote *The Campus as a Work of Art.* Many campus buildings were constructed in the Gothic style using limestone from nearby quarries. One such structure, the Indiana Memorial Union, houses 500,000 square feet of space, making it the largest student union in the United States.

Bloomington's downtown area, situated a couple of blocks west of the university, is anchored by the Monroe County Courthouse, its eloquent stained-glass dome rising above the town square. The square is a wondrous sight during the holidays, with a 360-degree canopy of lights draping from the court-house to the buildings across the street. Downtown Bloomington offers restaurants to satisfy any palate, ranging from the popular pizzeria Mother Bear's to gourmet fare at the elegant Scholars Inn to ethnic offerings such as Afghan, Indian, Moroccan, and Tibetan. Shoppers flock to the boutiques and galleries in the enclosed Fountain Square Mall, just south of the courthouse. Bars and pubs abound on nearby Kirkwood Avenue, where Nick's English Hut, with its walls adorned by photos of IU athletic heroes, is a must-stop for Hoosier fans.

Bloomington possesses a vibrant arts scene, thanks in part to the university's high-ranking drama and music schools. The Indiana University Art Museum, designed by renowned architect I. M. Pei, boasts a collection of more than 35,000 pieces, including paintings by Monet and Picasso. Each fall, Bloomington hosts the Lotus World Music and Arts Festival (see SPECIAL EVENTS), a celebration of the world's diverse cultures.

Spring brings the annual Little 500 Bicycle Race (see SPECIAL EVENTS), made famous by the 1979 film *Breaking Away.* Many avid cyclists live in Bloomington, and they can be seen pedaling on the streets and numerous riding trails in and around town. Basketball is immensely popular throughout Indiana, and locals take pride in the fact that IU's men's program has won five national championships.

Hoosier National Forest (see BEDFORD), Lake Monroe (see), and Brown County State Park (see) are all within 20 miles of Bloomington, providing the opportunity to fish, hike, canoe, or simply sit under a tree and relax.

What to See and Do

Bloomington Antique Mall. *311 W 7th St. Phone 812/332-2290.* Largest antique mall in southern Indiana. Over 120 dealers under one roof. (Daily)

Butler Winery. *1022 N College Ave. Phone 812/ 339-7233. www.butlerwinery.com.* Wines made in vineyard; cheeses and preserves; tastings. (Daily; closed Jan 1, Dec 25) **FREE**

Indiana University. *107 S Indiana Ave (47405). 5 blocks E of public square. Phone 812/855-4848. www.indiana.edu.* (1820) (39,000 students) One of the outstanding state universities in the country. Notable are the Lilly Library of Rare Books (Mon-Sat); Dailey Family Collection of Hoosier Art and Thomas Hart Benton murals in auditorium (Mon-Sat; special tours; phone 812/855-9528); Art Museum (Tues-Sun); Glenn Black Laboratory of Archaeology (daily); Hoagy Carmichael Room (by appointment); William H. Mathers Museum (Tues-Sun; summer hours vary); Musical Arts Center (tours by appointment, phone 812/855-9055). All buildings closed university holidays. Campus includes

Jordan Hall and Greenhouse. *1001 E 3rd St, Bloomington. Phone 812/855-7717.* Displays re-creations of flora from different environments, including desert and rain forest. (Daily) **FREE**

Lake Monroe. *4850 S State Rd 446 (47401). 7 miles SE via Hwy 46 to Hwy 446. Phone 812/837-9546.* Joint project of Indiana Department of Natural Resources and the US Army Corps of Engineers. A 10,000-acre lake with approximately 150 miles of shoreline. Water-skiing, swimming at Hardin Ridge, Fairfax, and Paynetown areas (Memorial Day-Labor Day); fishing (all year), boating (ramps); picnicking; tent and trailer sites (standard fees; no camping at Fairfax). Paynetown State Recreation Area (standard fees). Hardin Ridge Federal Recreation Area in Hoosier National Forest (see BEDFORD). Contact Monroe Reservoir, Department of Natural Resources, 4850 S State Rd 446, 47401. **$$**

McCormick's Creek State Park. *Hwy 46, Spencer. 12 miles NW on Hwy 46. Phone 812/829-2235.* The creek plunges headlong through a limestone canyon in this 1,833-acre park to join the White River at its border. Trails, bridle paths, and roads lead through beech and pine forests, ravines, and gullies. Wolf Cave and the stone bridge over McCormick's Creek are unusual features. Swimming pool, creek fishing. Tennis, picnicking, playground, camping, cabins, inn. Nature center, nature trails, naturalist service. **$**

Monroe County Historical Society Museum. *202 E 6th St (47408). Phone 812/332-2517.* Displays depicting history of county and limestone industry. (Tues-Sat, Sun afternoons; closed holidays) **FREE**

Oliver Winery. *8024 N Hwy 37 (47404). 7 miles N on Hwy 37. Phone 812/876-5800; toll-free 800/258-2783.* Tastings, food and gift items. Tours (weekends). (Mon-Sat, Sun afternoons; closed holidays) **FREE**

Special Events

Fourth Street Art Fair. *4th and Grant sts, Bloomington (47406). Downtown. Phone 812/334-8900.* Pottery, jewelry, paintings, glass art. Labor Day weekend.

Indiana Heritage Quilt Show. *Monroe County Convention Center, 302 S College Ave, Bloomington. Phone toll-free 800/800-0037.* Quilts from all over the country. Classes, quilt style show. Early Mar.

Little 500 Bicycle Race. *Indiana University* (see) *campus, 1606 N Fee Ln, Bloomington (47405). Phone 812/855-9152.* Bicycle and tricycle races, golf jamboree, entertainment. Apr.

Lotus World Music and Arts Festival. *Downtown Bloomington. Phone 812/336-6599.* Musicians from around the globe perform in five venues. Late Sept.

Madrigal Feasts. *Indiana University* (see) *campus, 900 E 7th St, Bloomington (47405). Phone 812/855-0463.* Dec.

Monroe County Fair. *Monroe County Fairgrounds, 5454 W Airport Rd, Bloomington (47403). Phone 812/825-7439.* Rodeo; midway; exhibits. Late July-early Aug.

Limited-Service Hotels

★ ★ **COURTYARD BY MARRIOTT.** *310 S College Ave, Bloomington (47403). Phone 812/335-8000; fax 812/336-9997. www.courtyard.com.* 117 rooms, 5 story. Check-out noon. Fitness room. Indoor pool, whirlpool. **$**

★ **HAMPTON INN.** *2100 N Walnut, Bloomington (47404). Phone 812/334-2100; fax 812/334-8433. www.hamptoninn.com.* 131 rooms, 4 story. Pets accepted. Check-out noon. Pool. **$**

★ ★ **HOLIDAY INN.** *1710 N Kinser Pike, Bloomington (47404). Phone 812/334-3252; fax 812/333-1702. www.holiday-inn.com.* 189 rooms, 4 story. Check-out noon. Restaurant, bar. Indoor pool, whirlpool. Airport transportation available. University stadium two blocks. **$**

Limited-Service Hotel

★ ★ **FOURWINDS RESORT.** *9301 Fairfax Rd, Bloomington (47401). Phone 812/824-9904; fax 812/824-9816.* 126 rooms, 3 story. Check-in 4 pm, check-out noon. Restaurant, bar. Children's activity center. Public beach. Indoor pool, outdoor pool, whirlpool. Airport transportation available. Overlooks Lake Monroe Reservoir. **$**

Restaurants

★ ★ **COLORADO STEAKHOUSE.** *1800 N College Ave, Bloomington (47404). Phone 812/339-9979; fax 812/335-1642. www.colorado-steakhouse.com.* Atrium dining area. Steak menu. Lunch, dinner. Closed Dec 25. Bar. Children's menu. **$$**

★ **GRISANTI'S.** *850 Auto Mall Rd, Bloomington (47401). Phone 812/339-9391; fax 812/339-6842.* Italian menu. Lunch, dinner. Closed Thanksgiving, Dec 25. Bar. **$$**

★ **LE PETIT CAFE.** *308 W 6th St, Bloomington (47404). Phone 812/334-9747.* American menu. Lunch, dinner. Closed Mon; holidays. **$$**

Brazil (D-2)

See also Greencastle, Terre Haute

Population 8,188
Elevation 659 ft
Area Code 812
Zip 47834
Information Clay County Chamber of Commerce, PO Box 23; phone 812/448-8457

A former mining center, Brazil (named for the South American country) was also widely known for its manufacture of building brick, tile, and block coal. Bituminous coal is taken extensively from huge open strip mines. Farmers in surrounding Clay County grow corn, wheat, and soybeans and raise livestock.

What to See and Do

Clay County Historical Museum. *100 E National Ave. Phone 812/446-4036.* Post office is now museum offering exhibits of past and present. (Mar-Dec; closed holidays) **FREE**

Forest Park. *1018 S John Steele Dr. S on Hwy 59. Phone 812/442-5681 (golf).* Outdoor auditorium and stadium; 18-hole golf adjacent (fee); swimming pool, wading pool (Memorial Day-Labor Day; fee); playground, ball fields, picnic areas (shelters); Sunday evening band concerts in summer. Log cabins preserved from pioneer days, with a display of relics. The Chafariz dos Contas, a granite fountain presented to the city by the Republic of Brazil, is located here. **FREE**

Special Event

Christmas in the Park. *Forest Park, Brazil. Phone 812/448-8457.* Includes parade, holiday fireworks display, musical events, and decorated homes and businesses. Day after Thanksgiving-Dec 26.

Brown County State Park (D-3)

See also Columbus, Nashville

S and E of Nashville on Hwy 46. Phone 812/988-6406.

There are 15,800 acres of hilly woodland here, with two lakes, streams, a covered bridge, and miles of drives and trails. Among the wildlife commonly seen here are white-tailed deer, raccoon, gray squirrel, and various birds, including robin, white-breasted nuthatch, blue jay, cardinal, and junco.

This is the largest of Indiana's parks. Swimming (Memorial Day-Labor Day), fishing; hiking, bridle trails, saddle barn (Apr-Nov); picnicking, concession (Apr-Nov); camping. Nature center, naturalist service; 80-foot observation tower with view on Weed Patch Hill. (Daily) Contact the Superintendent, PO Box 608, Nashville 47448, phone 812/988-6406.

Carmel (C-3)

See also Indianapolis

Restaurant

★ ★ **GLASS CHIMNEY.** *12901 Old Meridian St, Carmel (46032). Phone 317/844-0921; fax 317/574-1360.* French, American menu. Dinner. Closed Sun; Thanksgiving, Dec 25. Bar. Outdoor seating. **$$$**

Columbus (D-3)

See also Bloomington, Brown County State Park, Nashville

Settled 1820
Population 39,059
Elevation 656 ft
Area Code 812
Information Visitors Center, 506 5th St, 47201; phone 812/378-2622 or toll-free 800/468-6564
Web site www.columbus.in.us

The architectural designs of many modern buildings in Columbus have attracted international attention. In the heart of the prairie, the project was launched in the late 1930s with the commissioning of Eliel Saarinen to design a church. Since then, more than 50 public and private buildings have been designed by architects such as Saarinen, John Carl Warnecke, Harry Weese, I. M. Pei, Kevin Roche, Eliot Noyes, and J. M. Johansen.

What to See and Do

Columbus Area Visitors Center. *Phone toll-free 800/468-6564.* Video presentation. Architectural tours of the town are given; reservations advised. (Daily)

The Commons. *4th and Washington sts. Phone 812/372-4541.* Downtown common area; features shopping mall, recreational facilities, museums, and Chaos I, a sculpture by noted artist Jean Tinguely.

Indianapolis Museum of Art-Columbus. *390 The Commons. Phone 812/376-2597.* Displays changing exhibits from the Indianapolis Museum of Art (see INDIANAPOLIS) collection. Special exhibitions. (Tues-Sun; closed holidays) **FREE**

Otter Creek Golf Course. *11522 E 50 N (47203). 4 miles E on 25th. Phone 812/579-5227. www.ocgc.com.* Bent grass tees; 90 sand bunkers; rolling hills; Robert Trent Jones design. Golf packages. (Mar-Nov) **$$$$**

Special Event

Columbus Bluegrass & Craft Show. *Columbus. Downtown. Phone 812/376-2535.* Free festival features bluegrass performances. Food and crafts. Second weekend in Mar.

Limited-Service Hotel

★ ★ **HOLIDAY INN.** *2480 W Jonathan Moore Pike, Columbus (47201). Phone 812/372-1541; toll-free 800/ 465-4329; fax 812/378-9049. www.holiday-inn.com.* Turn-of-the-century atmosphere. 253 rooms, 7 story. Pets accepted, some restrictions; fee. Check-out 11 am. Restaurant, bar. Fitness room. Indoor pool, whirlpool. **$**

Connersville (D-4)

See also Batesville

Founded 1813
Population 15,411
Elevation 835 ft
Area Code 765
Zip 47331
Information Chamber of Commerce, 504 Central Ave; phone 765/825-2561
Web site www.connersvillein.com/chamber

John Connor, who established a fur trading post here in 1808, later founded the town. Connor was kidnapped from his parents as a child and raised by Native Americans. He served as a Native American guide for General William H. Harrison in 1812, took a Native American wife, and became a wealthy landowner and businessman.

Auburn, Cord, McFarlan, and Lexington automobiles were once manufactured here. Today, the most important industrial products are dishwashers, automobile components, and building supplies.

What to See and Do

Brookville Lake State Reservoir. *14108 Hwy 101, Brookville. 12 miles E on Hwy 44 to Liberty, then 5 miles S on Hwy 101. Phone 765/647-2657.* United States government flood control project, now a state recreation area. Approximately 16,500 acres. Swimming, water-skiing, fishing, boating (ramps, rentals). Hiking, hunting, picnicking, camping. (Summer, daily; winter, Mon-Fri) **$$**

Mary Gray Bird Sanctuary of the Indiana Audubon Society. *3499 S Bird Sanctuary Rd (47331). 3 1/2 miles S on Hwy 121, then 3 1/2 miles W on County Rd 350 S. Phone 765/827-0908.* Has 686 wooded acres with marked trails and picnicking facilities. Museum and library (by appointment). (Daily) **DONATION**

Whitewater Memorial State Park. *1418 S Hwy 101 (47353). 12 miles E on Hwy 44 to Liberty, then 1 mile S on Hwy 101. Phone 765/458-5565.* More than 1,700 acres, with lake. Swimming beach, bathhouse, fishing, boating (electric motors only; ramps, dock, rentals). Hiking and bridle trails, picnicking (shelters), concession, campground, family cabins. Visitor center. Park (daily). **$**

Whitewater Valley Railroad. *300 S Eastern Ave. 1 mile S on Hwy 121. Phone 765/825-2054.* Round-trip excursions on vintage railroad cars. (May-Sept, Sat-Sun, holidays; Oct, Thurs-Fri) Contact PO Box 406. **$$$$**

Special Events

Fall Festival, Car Show, and 5K Pumpkin Run/Walk. *Connersville. Phone 765/825-2561.* Fourth weekend in Sept.

Fayette County Free Fair. *Park Rd. Connersville. Phone 765/825-1351.* Agricultural and industrial displays; midway; entertainment; horse racing. Last weekend in July-early Aug.

Veterans Armed Forces Celebration. *827 Earl Dr, Connersville (47331). Phone 765/825-7538.* Vintage and modern military aircraft exhibits; marching bands with military flyovers. Second Sat in May.

Corydon (F-3)

See also New Albany, Wyandotte

Founded 1808
Population 2,715
Elevation 549 ft
Area Code 812
Zip 47112
Information Chamber of Commerce of Harrison County, 310 N Elm St; phone 812/738-2137 or toll-free 888/738-2137

Corydon was the scene of the only battle fought on Indiana soil during the Civil War. A Confederate raiding party under General John Hunt Morgan occupied the town briefly on July 9, 1863, holding the home guard captive.

What to See and Do

Battle of Corydon Memorial Park. *124 S Mulberry St (47112). S on Hwy 135 Business. Phone 812/738-8236.* Approximately 5 1/3 acres, with period cabin, authentic Civil War cannon, and nature trail. Park marks the site of one of the few Civil War battles (July 9, 1863) fought on Northern soil. (Daily) **FREE**

Buffalo Trace Park. *Palmyra. Approximately 10 miles N on Hwy 135, then 1/2 mile E on Hwy 150. Phone 812/364-6112.* Approximately 150 acres with sports facilities, camping (fee), picnicking. Thirty-acre lake with swimming, fishing, boating; petting zoo; bumper boats. (May-Oct, daily) Some fees. **$**

Corydon Capitol State Historic Site. *200 N Capitol Ave (47112). Phone 812/738-4890.* Corydon was the seat of the Indiana Territorial government (1813-1816) when the first constitutional convention assembled here. Following Indiana's admission to the Union in 1816, this building was the state capitol, housing the first sessions of the state legislature and supreme court, until 1825. Construction of the blue limestone building started in 1814 and was completed in 1816. Nearby is Governor Hendricks's headquarters (see), home of Indiana's second governor; restored. (Tues-Sun; closed Jan 1, Thanksgiving, Dec 25) **DONATION** Nearby are

Constitution Elm Monument. *High St, Corydon.* Indiana's first constitution was drawn up here in June 1816, in the shade of this large elm tree.

Governor Hendricks's headquarters. *202 E Walnut St, Corydon. Phone 812/738-4890.* (1817) Governor's headquarters from 1822 to 1824. A restoration project by the state of Indiana portrays Indiana home life in three distinct time periods between 1820 and 1880. (Early Apr-early Dec; Tues-Sun; closed Jan 1, Thanksgiving, Dec 25) **DONATION**

Marengo Cave Park. *360 E Hwy 64, Marengo (47140). Approximately 10 miles N of I-64 via Hwy 66 exit 92. Phone 812/365-2705.* Dripstone Trail tour (1 mile) of underground cave features huge corridors with colorful formations. Crystal Palace tour (1/3 mile) features underground palace. (Daily; closed Thanksgiving, Dec 25) Also picnic area (shelters), nature trail, camping (Apr-Oct). **$$$**

Squire Boone Caverns and Village. *100 Squire Boone Rd SW, Mauckport. 10 miles S on Hwy 135. Phone 812/732-4381.* Caverns discovered in 1790 by Daniel Boone's brother, Squire, while hiding from Native Americans. Travertine formations, stalactites, stalagmites, underground streams, and waterfalls. Above-ground village includes restored working gristmill, craft shops, demonstrations. Hayrides; 110 acres of forest with nature trails and picnic areas. One-hour cavern tours. (Memorial Day weekend-Labor Day weekend, daily) Admission includes all activities and facilities. **$$$**

Zimmerman Art Glass. *395 Valley Rd. Phone 812/738-2206.* Glass sculpturing, paperweights, and hand-blown objects. (Tues-Sat) **FREE**

Special Events

Christmas on the Square. *202 E Walnut St, Corydon (47112). Phone 812/738-4890.* Sat after Thanksgiving.

Harrison County Fair. *Old Hwy 135 S, Corydon (47112). Phone 812/738-2137.* Livestock, poultry, farm, and 4-H Club exhibits; harness racing. Held annually since 1860. Late July-early Aug.

Old Capitol Day. *202 E Walnut St, Corydon (47112). Phone 812/738-4890.* Early July.

Specialty Lodging

The following lodging establishment is approved by Mobil Travel Guide but, due to its unique and individualized nature has not been given a traditional Mobil Star rating. Included in this listing you may find bed-and-breakfasts, limited-service inns, guest ranches, and other unique hotel properties.

KINTNER HOUSE INN. *101 S Capitol Ave, Corydon (47112). Phone 812/738-2020; fax 812/738-7181.* Brick Victorian house (1873); antique furnishings. 15 rooms, 3 story. Complimentary full breakfast. Check-in 1 pm, check-out 11 am. **$**

Restaurant

★ **MAGDALENA'S.** *103 E Chestnut St, Corydon (47112). Phone 812/738-8075; fax 812/738-6249.* Lunch, dinner. Closed holidays. Casual attire. **$$**

Crawfordsville (C-2)

Settled 1822
Population 15,243
Elevation 769 ft
Area Code 765
Zip 47933
Information Montgomery County Visitors & Convention Bureau, 218 E Pike St; phone 765/362-5200 or toll-free 800/866-3973
Web site www.crawfordsville.org

Crawfordsville, "the Athens of the Hoosier State," has long been a literary center. It has been the home of nearly a dozen authors and playwrights, among them General Lew Wallace, who wrote *Ben Hur* here; Maurice Thompson, author of *Alice of Old Vincennes;* and Meredith Nicholson, author of *House of a Thousand Candles.* The all-male Wabash College is located here.

Printing, steel, and the production of travel trailers, fencing, nails, and plastics are some of the local industries. Montgomery County, of which Crawfordsville is the seat, is a rich corn and hog region.

What to See and Do

Ben Hur Museum. *E Pike St and Wallace Ave. (47933). Phone 765/362-5769.* The study of General Lew Wallace, author of *Ben Hur;* he also was a soldier, diplomat, and painter. Memorabilia from the movie *Ben Hur* along with war relics, art objects, and personal items. (June-Aug, Tues-Sun; early Apr-May, Sept-Oct, Tues-Sun afternoons) **$$**

Clements Canoes. *613 Old Lafayette Rd. Phone 765/362-2781.* Canoe livery with more than 500 units available. Canoe on Sugar Creek, designated by the Department of Natural Resources as the state's most scenic waterway. Various length trips available; also guided or self-guided rafting available. (Apr-Oct, daily) **$$$$**

Lake Waveland. *Hwy 47 W, Waveland. 13 miles S via Hwy 47. Phone 765/435-2073.* A 360-acre lake with canoeing, boating (rentals; fee), swimming, water slide, fishing; tennis courts. Also 248-acre park with camping (fee), tent and trailer sites (fee), showers, picnic area. (Apr-Oct) **$$$$**

Lane Place. *212 S Water St. Phone 765/362-3416.* Greek Revival residence of Henry S. Lane (1811-1881), Indiana governor and United States senator. Collection of colonial, Federal, and Victorian furnishings, dolls, and china; Civil War memorabilia; furnished log cabin (by appointment). (Apr-Oct, Tues-Fri, Sun; closed holidays (See SPECIAL EVENTS) **$$**

Old Jail Museum. *225 N Washington St. Phone 765/362-5222.* Completed in 1882, the building's unique feature is a two-story cylindrical cellblock; the cells rotate while the bars remain stationary. Sheriff's residence has changing exhibits. (June-Aug, daily; Apr-May, Sept-Oct, Wed-Sun afternoons) (See SPECIAL EVENTS) **FREE**

Shades State Park. *Rtes 1, 234, Waveland (47989). 9 miles SW on Hwy 47, then 5 miles W on Hwy 234. Phone 765/435-2810.* Approximately 3,000 acres of woods. Deep ravines, high sandstone cliffs, overlooks. Fishing in Sugar Creek; hiking trails, picnicking, playground, campsites (no electric hookups). Backpack and canoe camps. Naturalist service (May-Aug). (Daily) **$$**

Special Events

Old Jail Museum Breakout. *Old Jail Museum (see), 225 N Washington St, Crawfordsville (47933). Phone 765/362-5222.* Craft booths, refreshments, entertainment. Labor Day.

Strawberry Festival. *Lane Place (see), Crawfordsville. Phone toll-free 800/866-3973.* Sport tournaments, parade, arts and crafts, food, entertainment. Second weekend in June.

Sugar Creek Canoe Race. *Elston Park South, 613 LaFayette Ave, Crawfordsville (47933). Phone 765/362-3875.* Late Apr.

Limited-Service Hotel

★ ★ **HOLIDAY INN.** *2500 N Lafayette Rd, Crawfordsville (47933). Phone 765/362-8700; toll-free 800/465-4329; fax 765/362-8700. www.holiday-inn.com.* 150 rooms, 2 story. Pets accepted, some restrictions; fee. Check-out noon. Restaurant, bar. Fitness room. Pool. **$**

Restaurant

★ **BUNGALOW.** *210 E Pike St, Crawfordsville (47933). Phone 765/362-2596.* Italian, American menu. Lunch, dinner. Closed Sun; holidays. Bar. **$$**

Elkhart (A-3)

See also Goshen, Mishawaka, Nappanee, South Bend

Founded 1832
Population 51,874
Elevation 748 ft
Area Code 574
Information Elkhart County Convention and Visitor Bureau, 219 Caravan Dr, 46514; phone toll-free 800/262-8161
Web site www.elkhart.org

Located at the confluence of the St. Joseph and Elkhart rivers and on Christiana Creek, Elkhart is a community of bridges. Originally a crossroads of Native American trails, the town was named for a small island in the St. Joseph River that Native Americans said was shaped like an elk's heart.

A 19th-century grocer (cornetist in the town band) suffered an injured upper lip in a brawl and devised a soft rubber mouthpiece for cornets. He received so many requests for mouthpieces that in 1875 he rented a one-room building and started the manufacture of brass cornets. This led to Elkhart's becoming the band instrument center of the country. Approximately 50 percent of the nation's band instruments are manufactured here by 15 firms.

Elkhart also has many industrial plants, producing diverse items such as pharmaceuticals, mobile homes, recreational vehicles, electronic components, construction machinery, and plastic machinery.

What to See and Do

Elkhart County Historical Museum. *304 W Vistula St, Bristol. 8 miles E via Hwy 120 (Vistula St). Phone 574/848-4322.* Furnished cottage; Victorian home, country store, schoolroom, barn; room depicting a 1930s house; uniforms from Civil War through Vietnam; research library; Native American artifacts; railroad room; special programs. (Tues-Fri, Sun; closed holidays; also mid-Dec-Feb) **DONATION**

Midwest Museum of American Art. *429 S Main St. Phone 574/293-6660.* Permanent collection of 19th- and 20th-century artists, including Rockwell, Wood, Avery, and Grandma Moses; traveling exhibits; lectures; tours. (Tues-Sun; closed holidays) **$$**

National New York Central Railroad Museum. *721 S Main St. Phone 574/294-3001. www.nycrrmuseum.org.* Large collection of memorabilia from New York Central railroad stations and rail cars, along with videos of New York Central trains in action. Housed in a late-1880s freight house, the museum also boasts three restored locomotives: a 3001 L-3A "Mohawk" steam locomotive (the only one of its kind in existence), the E-8 diesel locomotive, and the GG-1 electric locomotive. (Tues-Sun limited hours; closed holidays) **$$**

Ruthmere. *302 E Beardsley Ave. Phone 574/264-0330.* (Circa 1910) Restored mansion features elaborate handcrafted ceilings, walls, and woodwork; murals, silk wall coverings; period furnishings; landscaped grounds. Guided tours (Apr-mid-Jan, Tues-Sun; closed holidays). **$$$**

S. Ray Miller Antique Auto Museum. *2130 Middlebury St. Phone 574/522-0539.* More than 35 antique and classic cars on display; dozens restored to showroom quality. Includes 1930 Duesenberg "J" Murphy convertible, 1928 Rolls-Royce Phantom I Town Car, 1931 Stutz, and 1954 Corvette. Also extensive collection of radiator auto emblems; artifacts of early auto industry; vintage clothing. (Daily; closed holidays) **$$**

Woodlawn Nature Center. *604 Woodlawn Ave. Phone 574/264-0525.* A 10-acre trail system provides a forest in its natural state for exploring and a center with displays and a nature library. In the center, a working beehive, a Native American artifacts room, and a rare collection of bird eggs gathered in 1896 can be found. (Tues-Sat; closed holidays) **$**

Limited-Service Hotel

★ **SIGNATURE INN.** *3010 Brittany Court, Elkhart (46514). Phone 574/264-7222; toll-free 800/822-5252. www.signatureinn.com.* 125 rooms, 2 story. Pets accepted; fee. Complimentary continental breakfast. Check-in 3 pm, check-out 11 am. Outdoor pool. **$**

Evansville (F-1)

See also New Harmony

Founded 1819
Population 121,582
Elevation 394 ft
Area Code 812
Information Evansville Convention & Visitors Bureau, 401 SE Riverside Dr, 47713; phone toll-free 800/433-3025
Web site www.evansvillecvb.org

Separated from Kentucky by the Ohio River, Evansville has retained some of the atmosphere of the busy river town of the days when steamboats plied the waters of the Ohio and Mississippi rivers. The largest city in southern Indiana, Evansville combines the pleasant and leisurely ways of the South with the industrious activity of the North.

Evansville is the principal transportation, trade, and industrial center of southwestern Indiana. A modern river/rail/highway terminal facilitates simultaneous exchange of cargo between trucks, freight trains, and riverboats. Local industry manufactures refrigerators, agricultural equipment, aluminum ingots and sheets, furniture, textiles, nutritional and pharmaceutical products, and plastics.

The Ohio River offers many recreational opportunities for boating, swimming, water-skiing, and fishing.

What to See and Do

⭐ **Angel Mounds State Historic Site.** *8215 Pollack Ave. 7 miles E on Hwy 662. Phone 812/853-3956.* Largest and best-preserved group of prehistoric mounds (1100-1450) in Indiana. Approximately 100 acres. Interpretive center has film, exhibits, and artifacts; reconstructed dwellings on grounds. (Mid-Mar-Dec, Tues-Sun; closed holidays) **DONATION**

Burdette Park. *5301 Nurrenbern Rd. Phone 812/435-5602.* County park, approximately 160 acres. Fishing, pool, water slides (summer); picnicking (shelters), cabins; miniature golf (Apr-Oct), tennis courts. Some fees.

Evansville Museum of Arts, History, and Science. *411 SE Riverside Dr. On the Ohio River. Phone 812/425-2406.* Permanent art, history, and science exhibits; sculpture garden, Koch Planetarium (fee). Rivertown USA, re-creation of turn-of-the-century village. Tours. (Tues-Sun; closed holidays) **DONATION**

Mesker Park Zoo. *2421 Bement Ave. NW edge of town in Mesker Park. Phone 812/428-0715.* Zoo has more than 700 animals; bird collection; children's petting zoo. Also the Discovery Center Education Building. Tour train and paddleboats (Apr-Oct). (Daily) **$$**

Reitz Home Museum. *224 SE 1st St. In Historic Riverfront District. Phone 812/426-1871.* (1871) French Second Empire mansion of pioneer lumber baron John Augustus Reitz; gold leaf cornices, family furniture. (Tues-Sun; closed holidays; also first two weeks in Jan) **$$**

University of Southern Indiana. *8600 University Blvd (47712). 5 miles W on Hwy 62 (Lloyd Expy). Phone 812/464-8600. www.usi.edu.* (1965) (9,362 students) On 300-acre campus is the Bent Twig Outdoor Education Center, 25 acres with foot trails, log lodges, and a lake (daily).

Wesselman Park. *N Boeke Rd and Iowa St (47771). Phone 812/424-6921.* Approximately 400 acres; picnicking, tennis, handball, softball, basketball, bike trails, jogging trail, playground, 18-hole golf course (fee). Half of park is devoted to nature preserve (free; phone 812/479-0771). Hartkey swimming pool and Swonder ice rink (fees) adjacent (phone 812/479-0989). **FREE** Also here is

Roberts Municipal Stadium. *2600 Division St, Evansville. Lloyd Expy, exit Vann St. Phone 812/476-1383.* Ice shows, circuses, rodeos, musicals, concerts, basketball tournaments.

Special Events

Evansville Freedom Festival. *Citywide. Phone 812/433-4069.* Parade, fireworks, food. Hydroplane racing. June.

Evansville Philharmonic Orchestra. *530 Main St, Evansville (47708). Phone 812/425-5050.* May-Sept.

Germania Maennerchor Volkfest. *916 N Fulton Ave, Evansville (47710). Phone 812/422-1915.* German food, beer, and music. Aug.

Limited-Service Hotels

★ **HAMPTON INN.** *8000 Eagle Crest Blvd, Evansville (47715). Phone 812/473-5000; fax 812/479-1664. www.hampton-inn.com.* 143 rooms, 5 story. Complimentary continental breakfast. Check-out noon. Fitness room. Indoor pool. **$**

★ ★ **HOLIDAY INN.** *4101 Hwy 41 N, Evansville (47711). Phone 812/424-6400; fax 812/424-6409. www.holiday-inn.com.* 198 rooms, 2 story. Check-out 11 am. Restaurant, bar. Fitness room. Indoor pool, children's pool, whirlpool. Airport transportation available. Business center. **$**

★ **SIGNATURE INN.** *1101 N Green River Rd, Evansville (47715). Phone 812/476-9626; toll-free 800/822-5252; fax 812/476-9626. www.signatureinn.com.* 125 rooms, 2 story. Complimentary continental breakfast. Check-out noon. Pool. **$**

Full-Service Hotel

★ ★ ★ **MARRIOTT EVANSVILLE AIRPORT.** *7101 Hwy 41 N, Evansville (47725). Phone 812/867-7999; fax 812/867-0241. www.marriott.com.* A beautiful tropical, glass-enclosed atrium lobby is the setting for guests as they enter this hotel conveniently located at the airport. Whether traveling for business or pleasure, guests can count on comfortable amenities and affordable prices. 199 rooms, 5 story. Check-out 11 am. Restaurant, bar. Fitness room. Indoor pool, whirlpool. Airport transportation available. **$**

Restaurant

 ★ **THE OLD MILL RESTAURANT.** *5031 New Harmony Rd, Evansville (47720). Phone 812/963-6000.* A local favorite that hosts the annual Germanfest. American menu. Lunch, dinner. **$**

Fort Wayne (B-4)

See also Auburn, Geneva, Huntington

Settled circa 1690
Population 205,727
Elevation 767 ft
Area Code 260
Information Fort Wayne/Allen County Convention and Visitors Bureau, 1021 S Calhoun St, 46802; phone 260/424-3700 or toll-free 800/767-7752
Web site www.fwcvb.org

The Fort Wayne area is one of the most historically significant in Indiana. The point where the St. Joseph and St. Mary's rivers meet to form the Maumee was, for many years before and after the first European explorers ventured into eastern Indiana, the head-quarters of the Miami Native Americans. Among the first settlers were French fur traders; a French fort was established about 1690. The settlement became known as Miami Town and Frenchtown. In 1760, English troops occupied the French fort, but were driven out three years later by warriors led by Chief Pontiac. During the next 30 years, Miami Town became one of the most important trading centers in the West. President Washington sent out two armies in 1790-1791 to establish a fort for the United States at the river junction, but both armies were defeated by the Miami under the leadership of the famous Miami chief, Little Turtle. A third American army, under General "Mad Anthony" Wayne, succeeded in defeating Little Turtle and set up a post, Fort Wayne, across the river from Miami Town. From this humble beginning, Fort Wayne has grown steadily. Today, it is the second-largest city in Indiana and a commercial center.

Establishment of the first railroad connections with Chicago and Pittsburgh in the 1850s laid the foundation for the city's development. Today, its widely diversified companies include General Electric, Phelps Dodge, ITT, Lincoln National Corporation, North American Van Lines, Central Soya, Essex Group, General Motors, Magnavox, Uniroyal, Goodrich Tire Company, and many others. Most of the world's wire die tools come from here.

Fort Wayne is home to Indiana University-Purdue University Fort Wayne (1964), St. Francis College (1890), and the Indiana Institute of Technology (1930).

Fort Wayne Fun Fact

• The first professional baseball game was played in Fort Wayne on May 4, 1871.

What to See and Do

Allen County-Fort Wayne Historical Society Museum. *302 E Berry St. In Old City Hall. Phone 260/426-2882.* Exhibits on six themes: earliest times to the Civil War, 19th-century industrialization (1860s-1894), culture and society (1894-1920), 20th-century technology and industry (1920-present), old city jail and law enforcement (1820-1970), ethnic heritage. Special temporary exhibits. (Tues-Sun; closed holidays) **$$**

Cathedral of the Immaculate Conception and Museum. *1100 S Calhoun St. Phone 260/424-1485 (museum).* Bavarian stained-glass windows. Features Gothic wood carvings at the main altar; statues and furnishings; wood-carved reredos in the sanctuary. Museum at southwest corner of Cathedral Square (Wed-Fri, second and fourth Sun of month; also by appointment). Cathedral (daily; closed holidays). **FREE**

Embassy Theatre. *125 W Jefferson St. Phone 260/424-5665.* Entertainment and cultural center hosts musicals, concerts, ballet companies; distinctive architecture; Grand Page pipe organ. Tours (Mon-Fri by appointment). **$**

Foellinger-Freimann Botanical Conservatory. *1100 S Calhoun St. Phone 260/427-6440.* Showcase House with seasonally changing displays of colorful flowers; Tropical House with exotic plants; Arid House with cacti and other desert flora native to Sonoran Desert. Cascading waterfall. (Daily; closed Dec 25) **$$**

Fort Wayne Children's Zoo. *3411 Sherman Blvd. In Franke Park. Phone 260/427-6800.* Especially designed for children. Exotic animals, pony rides, train ride, contact area; 22-acre African Veldt area allows animals to roam free while visitors travel by miniature safari cars; tropical rain forest; also 5-acre Australian Outback area with dugout canoe ride, kangaroos, Tasmanian devils. (Late Apr-mid-Oct, daily) **$$$**

Fort Wayne Museum of Art. *311 E Main St. Phone 260/422-6467.* A 1,300-piece permanent collection; changing exhibitions. Art classes, interactive programs, and lectures. (Tues-Sun; closed holidays) **$$**

Lakeside Rose Garden. *1401 Lake Ave. Phone 260/ 427-6000.* Approximately 2,000 plants of about 225 varieties; display rose garden (June-mid-Oct). Garden (all year, daily). **FREE**

The New Lincoln Museum. *200 E Berry St. Phone 260/455-3864.* Museum dedicated to Abraham Lincoln. Facility (30,000 square foot); interactive exhibits; 11 galleries; theaters; gift shop. (Tues-Sun) **$$**

Special Events

Foellinger Theatre. *705 E State Blvd, Fort Wayne (46805). Phone 260/427-6715.* Covered open-air theater. Concerts and special attractions. Programs vary. June-Sept.

Germanfest. *Fort Wayne. Phone 260/436-4064.* Celebration of city's German heritage; ethnic food, music, exhibits. Eight days in mid-June.

Johnny Appleseed Festival. *Johnny Appleseed Park, 1500 E Coliseum Blvd, Fort Wayne (46805). Phone 260/420-2020.* Pioneer village, period crafts; contests, entertainment; Living History Hill; farmers' market. Third weekend in Sept.

Three Rivers Festival. *102 Three Rivers N, Fort Wayne (46802). Phone 260/426-5556. www.trfonline.org.* More than 280 events, including parades, balloon races, arts and crafts, music, ethnic dancing, sports, and fireworks, at various locations in Fort Wayne. Ten days in mid-July.

Limited-Service Hotels

★★ **COURTYARD BY MARRIOTT.** *1619 W Washington Center Rd, Fort Wayne (46818). Phone 260/ 489-1500; toll-free 800/321-2211; fax 260/489-3273. www.courtyard.com.* 142 rooms, 2 story. Check-out noon. Fitness room. Indoor pool, outdoor pool, whirlpool. **$**

★★ **HOLIDAY INN.** *300 E Washington Blvd, Fort Wayne (46802). Phone 260/422-5511; fax 260/424-1511. www.holiday-inn.com.* 208 rooms, 14 story. Check-out noon. Restaurant, bar. Fitness room. Indoor pool, whirlpool. Airport transportation available. **$**

★ **SIGNATURE INN.** *1734 W Washington Center, Fort Wayne (46818). Phone 260/489-5554; toll-free 800/822-5252; fax 260/489-5554. www.signatureinn.com.* 102 rooms, 2 story. Complimentary continental breakfast. Check-out noon. Pool. **$**

Full-Service Hotels

★★★ **HILTON FORT WAYNE CONVENTION CENTER.** *1020 S Calhoun St, Fort Wayne (46802). Phone 260/420-1100; toll-free 800/744-1500; fax 260/ 424-7775. www.hilton.com.* Located in the heart of downtown Fort Wayne, this hotel and convention center prides itself on great service with a smile. Among the amenities are three restaurants and lounges, a Jacuzzi, a fitness area, and an indoor pool. 250 rooms, 9 story. Check-out 11 am. Three restaurants, three bars. Fitness room. Indoor pool, whirlpool. Airport transportation available. **$**

★★★ **MARRIOTT FORT WAYNE.** *305 E Washington Center Rd, Fort Wayne (46825). Phone 260/484-0411; fax 260/483-2892. www.marriott.com.* Guests can rely on good service and a friendly staff at this hotel. With a fitness facility, pool, and oversized guest suites, travelers will have a memorable stay. Try Red River Steaks and BBQ Restaurant for a pleasurable dining experience. 222 rooms, 6 story. Pets accepted, some restrictions; fee. Check-out noon. Restaurant, bar. Fitness room. Indoor pool, outdoor pool, whirlpool. Airport transportation available. **$$**

Restaurants

★ **DON HALL'S FACTORY.** *5811 Coldwater Rd, Fort Wayne (46825). Phone 260/484-8693. www. donhalls.com.* Lunch, dinner. Closed holidays. Bar. Children's menu. **$$**

★★ **FLANAGAN'S.** *6525 Covington Rd, Fort Wayne (46804). Phone 260/432-6666.* Victorian décor; garden gazebo, carousel. Lunch, dinner. Closed Thanksgiving, Dec 25. Bar. Children's menu. **$$**

French Lick (E-2)

See also Bedford

Founded 1811
Population 1,941
Elevation 511 ft
Area Code 812
Zip 47432
Information French Lick-West Baden Chamber of Commerce, PO Box 347; phone 812/936-2405

In the early 18th century, this was the site of a French trading post. The post, plus the existence of a nearby salt lick, influenced the pioneer founders of the later settlement to name it French Lick.

Today, this small community is a well-known health and vacation resort centered around the French Lick springs, situated on 1,600 acres of woodland. Near it is an artesian spring, Pluto, covered by an edifice of marble and tile. The water contains a high concentration of minerals.

What to See and Do

Diesel Locomotive Excursion. *1 Monon St. On Hwy 56. Phone 812/936-2405.* French Lick, West Baden, and Southern Railway operate a diesel locomotive that makes 20-mile round-trips through wooded limestone country and a 2,200-foot tunnel. Train departs from the Monon Railroad station in French Lick (Apr-Nov, Sat-Sun, holidays). Museum (Mon-Fri; free). Contact Indiana Railway Museum, Inc, PO Box 150. **$$$**

Paoli Peaks Ski Area. *2798 W County Rd 25 S, Paoli. N via Hwy 56, then E on Hwy 150; 1 1/2 miles W of Paoli off Hwy 150. Phone 812/723-4696.* Quad, one double, three triple chair lifts, three surface tows; snowmaking, rentals, school, patrol; cafeteria. Longest run 3,300 feet; vertical drop 300 feet. (Dec-Mar, daily; open 24 hours on weekends) **$$$$**

Special Event

Orange County Pumpkin Festival. *1 Monon St, French Lick (47432). Phone 812/936-2405.* Parades, arts and crafts displays, entertainment. First week in Oct.

Full-Service Resort

★ ★ ★ **FRENCH LICK SPRINGS RESORT & SPA.** *8670 W Hwy 56, French Lick (47432). Phone 812/936-9300; toll-free 800/457-4042; fax 812/936-2986. www.frenchlick.com.* This breathtaking, historical resort is set among a beautiful array of plush gardens, mineral springs, and blooming flowers. With gorgeous guest suites, golf, tennis, a spa, several restaurants, and much more, guests will find grand style at its best. Country estate setting on 2,600 acres; landscaped grounds, woodland trails. 500 rooms, 6 story. Check-in 4 pm, check-out noon. Restaurants, bar. Children's activity center. Fitness room, spa. Indoor pool, outdoor pool, whirlpool. Golf. Tennis. **$**
🏂 🎿 🏊 ⛷

Gary (A-2)

What to See and Do

Trump Casino. *1 Buffington Harbor Dr (46406). Phone toll-free 888/218-7867. www.trumpindiana.com.* Though probably one of the least scenic cities in the country, Gary offers Chicagoans a major reason to visit: casinos less than a half hour drive from downtown. One of the newest, Trump Casino and Hotel, offers 1,400 slots and more than 50 gaming tables featuring Big Six, Caribbean Stud, craps, roulette, mini-baccarat, traditional baccarat, Spanish 21, and 21 Madness. The nearby 300-room hotel offers free valet parking and a shuttle to the casinos. The Trump Casino shares a pavilion with the 3,500-passenger *Majestic Star* riverboat, where you will find a steakhouse, a sushi bar, and even a retail store. (Daily) **FREE**

Restaurant

★ ★ ★ **MILLER BAKERY CAFÉ.** *555 S Lake St, Gary (46403). Phone 219/938-2229.* Located in the Miller Beach area, this charming restaurant's name comes from its setting in a renovated bakery building. The kitchen serves up mostly modern American fare, with specialties including pasta and seafood dishes. Fusion menu. Lunch, dinner. Closed Mon. Casual attire. Reservations recommended. **$$**

Geneva (B-4)

See also Fort Wayne

Population 1,280
Elevation 846 ft
Area Code 219
Zip 46740

This town in eastern Indiana, near the Ohio border, is surrounded by the "Limberlost Country," which Gene Stratton Porter used as background for her romantic stories of life in the swamplands. Geneva is near the headwaters of the Wabash River and includes a large settlement of Old Order Amish families.

What to See and Do

Amishville. *844 E 900 S, Geneva (Adams County) (46704). 3 miles E via local road. Phone 219/589-3536.* Amish house (tour); farm, barn, animals; working gristmill; buggy rides. Swimming, fishing; picnicking, camping (Apr-Oct); activities; restaurant. (Apr-mid-Dec, daily; closed Thanksgiving) **$$**

Bearcreek Farms. *8339 N 400 E, Geneva (Adams County) (47326). 4 miles SE near Bryant. Phone 219/997-6822.* Entertainment complex: restaurants, theater, shops, miniature golf course, general store. Fishing. Some fees. Lodging available (reservations required, phone toll-free 800/288-7630).

Limberlost State Historic Site. *200 E 6th St. E of Hwy 27 at S edge of town. Phone 219/368-7428.* A 14-room cedar log cabin, for 18 years the residence of author/naturalist/photographer Gene Stratton Porter and her family. Furniture, books, and photographs. (Apr-mid-Dec, Wed-Sat, Sun afternoons; closed holidays) **FREE**

Goshen (A-3)

See also Elkhart, Mishawaka, Nappanee

Settled 1830
Population 29,383
Elevation 799 ft
Area Code 219
Zip 46526
Information Chamber of Commerce, 232 S Main St; phone 219/533-2102 or toll-free 800/307-4204
Web site www.goshen.org

What to See and Do

Mennonite Historical Library. *Goshen College campus, 304 W Vistula St, Bristol. Phone 219/535-7418.* Anabaptist, Mennonite, and Amish research collection; genealogical resources. (Mon-Fri; closed holidays) **FREE**

The Old Bag Factory. *1100 Chicago Ave. Phone 219/534-2502.* Restored factory (1890) houses various types of crafters as well as 18 shops. (Mon-Sat; closed holidays) **FREE**

Bonneyville Mill. *Goshen. 9 miles N on Hwy 15 to Bristol, then 2 1/2 miles E on Hwy 120, 1/2 mile S on County 131. Phone 219/825-1324.* Restored gristmill (May-Oct, daily). Park (daily). **FREE**

Ox Bow. *Goshen. 5 miles NE off Hwy 33.* Canoeing; sports fields, archery. Per vehicle (Apr-Oct). (Daily) **$**

Limited-Service Hotel

★ ★ **COURTYARD BY MARRIOTT.** *1930 Lincolnway E (Hwy 33), Goshen (46526). Phone 574/534-3133; toll-free 800/321-2211; fax 574/534-6929. www.courtyard.com.* 98 rooms, 2 story. Complimentary full breakfast. Check-in 3 pm, check-out noon. High-speed Internet access. Restaurant. Fitness room. Indoor pool, outdoor pool. **$**

Full-Service Inn

★ ★ ★ **ESSENHAUS COUNTRY INN.** *240 Hwy 20, Middlebury (46540). Phone 219/825-9471; toll-free 800/455-9471; fax 219/825-0455. www.essenhaus.com.* 40 rooms, 2 story. Check-in 3 pm, check-out 11 am. Restaurant. **$$**

Greencastle (D-2)

See also Brazil, Terre Haute

Founded 1823
Population 9,880
Elevation 849 ft
Area Code 765
Zip 46135
Information Chamber of Commerce, 2 S Jackson St; phone 765/653-4517
Web site www.greencastle.com

Greencastle is within 15 miles of two man-made lakes—Raccoon Lake Reservoir and Cataract Lake—with boating and camping facilities. It is also the home of DePauw University (see), a small liberal arts school.

What to See and Do

DePauw University. *313 S Locust (46135). Phone 765/658-4800. www.depauw.edu.* (1837) (2,300 students) Liberal arts; School of Music; founded by the Methodist Church. The state's oldest Methodist church is on campus, as is the nation's first Greek letter sorority, Kappa Alpha Theta. More than 20 total Greek houses are on campus. Restored 19th-century classroom building (East College). Tours (by appointment).

Lieber State Recreation Area. *1317 W Lieber Rd (46120). 8 miles S via Hwy 231, then 4 miles SW on Hwy 42. Phone 765/795-4576.* Approximately 775 acres on Cataract Lake (1,500 acres). Swimming, lifeguard, bathhouse, water-skiing, fishing, boating (dock, rentals); picnicking, concession, camping. Activity center (Memorial Day-Labor Day). Adjacent are 342 acres of state forest and 7,300 acres of federal land, part of Cagles Mill Flood Control Reservoir Project. **$$**

Full-Service Inn

★ ★ ★ **WALDEN INN.** *2 W Seminary St, Greencastle (46135). Phone 765/653-2761; toll-free 800/225-8655; fax 765/653-4833. www.waldeninn.com.* Located in central Indiana, this beautiful country inn has warmth and charm. Just minutes from DePauw University (see), guests can stroll through town and check out the area's covered bridges. Innkeepers also have created their own cookbook filled with tempting recipes. 55 rooms, 2 story. Check-in 4 pm, check-out 1 pm. Restaurant (see DIFFERENT DRUMMER). **$**

Restaurant

★ ★ ★ **DIFFERENT DRUMMER.** *2 W Seminary St, Greencastle (46135). Phone 765/653-2761. www.waldeninn.com.* Inside the Walden Inn (see), diners will find conservative fare such as chicken cordon bleu, roasted eggplant with spinach, lamb chops, and veal medallions. Appetizers include warm pate of duck breast, as well as a "degustazionne" of salmon, shrimp, and clam. Breakfast, lunch, dinner. Closed Dec 25. Bar. **$$**

Greenfield (C-3)

See also Indianapolis

Population 14,600
Elevation 888 ft
Area Code 317
Zip 46140
Information Greater Greenfield Chamber of Commerce, 1 Courthouse Plz; phone 317/477-4188
Web site www.greenfieldcc.org

This town is the birthplace of poet James Whitcomb Riley.

What to See and Do

James Whitcomb Riley Home. *250 W Main St. Phone 317/462-8539.* (1850) Boyhood home of the poet from 1850 to 1869. Riley wrote "When the Frost is on the Punkin" and many other verses in Hoosier dialect. Tours. Museum adjacent. (Apr-late Dec, Mon-Sat, Sun afternoons) **$**

Old Log Jail and Chapel-in-the-Park Museums. *28 N Apple. Phone 317/462-7780.* Historical displays include arrowheads, clothing, china; local memorabilia. (Apr-Nov, Sat-Sun) **$**

Special Event

James Whitcomb Riley Festival. *312 W Main St, Greenfield (46140). Phone 317/462-2141.* Parade, carnival, entertainment, arts and crafts. Held weekend closest to Riley's birthday, Oct 7.

Limited-Service Hotel

★ **LEES INN.** *2270 N State St, Greenfield (46140). Phone 317/462-7112; toll-free 800/733-5337; fax 317/462-9801. www.leesinn.com.* 100 rooms, 2 story. Pets accepted, some restrictions. Complimentary continental breakfast. Check-out noon. **$**

Hammond (A-1)

See also Indiana Dunes National Lakeshore, Indiana Dunes State Park, Valparaiso; Chicago, IL

Population 83,048
Elevation 591 ft
Area Code 219
Information Chamber of Commerce, 7034 Indianapolis Blvd, 46324; phone 219/931-1000
Web site www.hammondchamber.org

Hammond is one of the highly industrialized cities of the Calumet area on the southwest shore of Lake Michigan. The Indiana-Illinois state line is two blocks from Hammond's business district and separates it from its neighbor community, Calumet City, Illinois. Hammond also is adjacent to Chicago. Industrial products manufactured here include railway supplies and equipment, cold-drawn steel, car wheels, forgings, printing, and hospital and surgical supplies.

What to See and Do

Little red schoolhouse. *7205 Kennedy Ave. Phone 219/844-5666.* (1869) Oldest one-room schoolhouse in Lake County. Used as presidential campaign head-quarters by William Jennings Bryan. Original desks, tower bell, books, desk, and tools. (See SPECIAL EVENT) (By appointment) **FREE**

Wicker Memorial Park. *Hwy 41 and Hwy 6, Highland. Phone 219/838-3420.* Eighteen-hole golf, driving range, pro shop. Tennis; cross-country skiing; picnicking, restaurant; playground. Some fees. (Daily) **FREE**

Special Event

Hammond Fest. *5825 Sohl Ave, Hammond (46320). Phone 219/853-6378.* Carnival, food, entertainment. Weekend in July or Aug.

Limited-Service Hotel

★ ★ **BEST WESTERN NORTHWEST INDIANA INN.** *3830 179th St, Hammond (46323). Phone 219/844-2140; toll-free 800/937-8376; fax 219/845-7760. www.bestwestern.com.* 101 rooms, 4 story. Complimentary continental breakfast. Check-in 4 pm, check-out noon. Restaurant, bar. Fitness room. Outdoor pool. **$**

Restaurants

★ ★ **CAFÉ ELISE.** *435 Ridge Rd, Munster (46321). Phone 219/836-2233.* American, French, Italian menu. Lunch, dinner. Closed Mon. Bar. Children's menu. Casual attire. **$$**

★ ★ **PHIL SMIDT'S.** *1205 N Calumet Ave, Hammond (46320). Phone 219/659-0025; toll-free 800/376-4534; fax 219/659-6955. www.philsmidts.com.* Seafood menu. Lunch, dinner. Closed Mon; holidays. Bar. Children's menu. Casual attire. **$$**

Huntington (B-4)

See also Fort Wayne, Wabash

Founded 1831
Population 17,450
Elevation 739 ft
Area Code 260
Zip 46750
Information Huntington County Visitor & Convention Bureau, 407 N Jefferson, PO Box 212; phone 260/359-8687 or toll-free 800/848-4282
Web site www.visithuntington.org

Originally called Wepecheange, the town was later named for Samuel Huntington, a member of the first Continental Congress. Huntington lies in a farming and industrial area and is home to Huntington College (1897).

What to See and Do

The Dan Quayle Center, Home of the United States Vice-Presidential Museum. *815 Warren St. Phone 260/356-6356. www.quaylemuseum.org.* This is the only vice-presidential museum in the country that has exhibits and educational programs about our nation's past vice presidents. Special focus on the five Indiana natives who have held the position. (Tues-Sat, Sun afternoons; closed holidays) **DONATION**

Forks of the Wabash. *3011 W Park Dr (46750). 2 miles W on Hwy 24. Phone 260/356-1903; toll-free 800/848-4282. www.historicforks.org.* (See SPECIAL EVENTS) Treaty grounds of Miami Native Americans. Tours of Miami Chief Richardville home and log house. Hiking trails, picnic area.

Huntington Reservoir. *517 N Warren Rd (46750). 2 miles S on Hwy 5.* Phone 260/468-2165. A 900-acre lake. Swimming at Little Turtle Area (Memorial Day-Labor Day, daily); primitive campsites (all year; fee). Fishing, boating (launch); hunting; archery range, shooting range; picnicking; hiking trails; interpretive programs. Office (May-Labor Day, daily; rest of year, Mon-Fri; closed holidays, except Memorial Day, July 4, Labor Day). **$$**

Special Events

Forks of the Wabash Pioneer Festival. *3011 W Park Dr, Huntington (46750).* Phone 260/356-1903; toll-free 800/848-4282. Pioneer food, pioneer arts and crafts demonstrations, Civil War encampment, antique show, banjo and fiddle contest. Last weekend in Sept. **$$**

Huntington County Heritage Days. *305 Warren St, Huntington (46750).* Phone 260/356-5300. Parade, bed race, ducky run, arts and crafts, food, entertainment. Three days in mid-June.

Indiana Dunes National Lakeshore (A-2)

See also Hammond, Michigan City

1100 N Mineral Springs Rd, Porter (46304). Along S shore of Lake Michigan, between Gary and Michigan City. Phone 219/926-7561.

In 1966, 8,000 acres surrounding Indiana Dunes State Park (see) were established as Indiana Dunes National Lakeshore. Another 7,139 acres have since been acquired, and development continues.

The lakeshore contains a number of distinct environments—clean, sandy beaches; huge sand dunes, many covered with trees and shrubs; and several bogs and marshes—and the various plants and animals peculiar to each. To preserve these environments, dune buggies and off-road vehicles are prohibited.

The visitor center is located at the junction of Kemil Road and Highway 12, 3 miles east of Highway 49 (daily; closed Jan 1, Thanksgiving, Dec 25). Facilities include a hard-surfaced nature trail for the disabled. Day-use facilities include West Beach, north of Highway 12 between Gary and Ogden Dunes, which has swimming (lifeguard), a bathhouse, visitor information center, picnic area, and marked nature trails; and the Bailly Homestead and Chellberg Farm area, between Highways 12 and 20, which features restored homestead, turn-of-the-century Swedish farm, hiking trails, cultural events, and a visitor information center. Other lifeguarded beaches are located on State Park/Kemil Road, off Highway 12. The Horse Trail, north of Highway 20, has a picnic area, parking facilities, and marked hiking, cross-country skiing, and riding trails. On Highway 12, near Michigan City, is Mount Baldy, largest dune in the lakeshore, with hiking trails and a beach. Camping is available just off the intersection of Highway 12 and Broadway, near Beverly Shores (tent and trailer sites, rest rooms). Contact Superintendent, 1100 N Mineral Springs Rd, Porter 46304, phone 219/926-7561.

Indiana Dunes State Park

See also Hammond, Michigan City

Approximately 15 miles E of Gary via Hwy 12; 4 miles N of Chesterton on Hwy 49. Phone 219/926-4520.

This beautiful and unique 2,182-acre state park extends 3 miles along Lake Michigan's south shore, with white sand dunes and beaches that can accommodate thousands of bathers. Approximately 1,800 acres are densely forested hills with a wide variety of rare flowers and ferns, creating an almost tropical appearance in summer. Many of the sand dunes continue to shift, creating hills such as 192-foot Mount Tom. There are 17 miles of marked hiking trails through forest and dune country. Swimming. Cross-country skiing in winter. Picnic facilities, snack bar, store. Campgrounds. Nature center, naturalist service. Entrance fees. Phone 219/926-4520 or 219/926-1952.

Indianapolis (C-3)

See also Anderson, Greenfield

Founded 1820
Population 791,926
Elevation 717 ft
Area Code 317
Information Convention and Visitors Association,
1 RCA Dome, Suite 100, 46225; phone 317/639-4282
or toll-free 800/323-4639
Web site www.indy.org

The present site of Indianapolis was an area of rolling woodland when it was selected by a group of ten commissioners as the location of the new Indiana state capital on June 7, 1820. It was chosen because it was close to the geographical center of the state. Only scattered Native American villages and two white settler families were located in the region at the time. The city was laid out in the wheel pattern of Washington, DC. In January 1825, the capital of Indiana was moved here from Corydon.

In its early days, the city grew mainly because of its importance as the seat of the state government. By the turn of the century, Indianapolis had emerged as an important manufacturing center in the Midwest and the commercial center of the rich agricultural region surrounding it.

It is the largest city in Indiana, one of the leading United States distribution hubs, and an important business and financial center. The annual 500-mile Formula One automobile race at the Indianapolis Motor Speedway (see), an outstanding race course, has brought international fame to the city. Indianapolis also is referred to as the nation's amateur sports capital. Indianapolis has hosted more than 400 national and international amateur sporting events. Among the city's industrial products are pharmaceuticals, airplane and automobile parts, television sets, electronic equipment, and medical diagnostic equipment.

In the middle of Indianapolis is Circle Centre Mall, which is home not only to the largest mall in the area, but also to the Indianapolis Artsgarden, which houses concerts, botanical displays, and other cultural events. Also downtown are the RCA Dome, home to the Indianapolis Colts of the National Football League; Conseco Fieldhouse, home of the NBA's Indiana Pacers, the WNBA's Indiana Fever, and Arena Football's Indiana Firebirds; and Victory Field, where the Indianapolis Indians, the Triple-A affiliate of baseball's Milwaukee Brewers, play. Victory Field is consistently voted one of the top ballparks in minor league baseball.

Additional Visitor Information

Indianapolis Monthly magazine, available locally, has up-to-date information about events and articles of interest to visitors. *NUVO* is a free weekly newspaper that features a calendar of events, lists of dining establishments, and other information that tourists may find useful.

The Indianapolis City Center, 201 S Capitol Ave, Pan Am Plaza, Suite 200, 46225, phone toll-free 800/323-4639, has general information brochures, maps, and tourist guidebooks. Information also is available through the Convention and Visitors Association, 1 RCA Dome, Suite 100, 46225, phone 317/639-4282.

Public Transportation

Buses (Indy Go). Phone 317/635-3344. Information, phone 317/487-7243

Airport **Indianapolis International Airport**. Cash machines, adjacent to Delta and US Airways ticket offices.; weather phone 317/635-5959

Information Phone 317/487-9594

Lost and found Phone 317/487-5084

Airlines Air Canada, America Trans Air, America West, American Airlines, Continental Airlines, Delta Air Lines, Frontier Airlines, Midwest Airlines, Northwest Airlines, Southwest Airlines, United Airlines, US Airways

What to See and Do

Brickyard Crossing Golf Course. *4400 W 16th St (46222). Phone 317/484-6572. my.brickyard.com/ crossing.* This 18-hole course, redesigned by Pete Dye, lies at the east end of the Indianapolis Motor Speedway's (see) grounds. Views of the speedway allow golfers and racing fans to indulge two passions at once. (Mar-Oct) **$$$$**

Butler University. *4600 Sunset Ave. Phone 317/ 940-8000. www.butler.edu.* (1855) (4,264 students) The 290-acre campus is located 7 miles north of downtown Indianapolis. On campus are

Wandering Around White River State Park

Indiana's first urban state park, 250-acre White River State Park is within easy walking distance of Indianapolis's downtown core. In this parklike setting, visitors can watch professional baseball, enjoy a dolphin show, ride a restored carousel, visit a number of unique museums, or simply stroll alongside a restored canal (or glide a pedal boat on it).

Begin at Pumphouse visitor center. Built in 1870, just five years after the Civil War ended, this is where the first water for drinking and fire protection was pumped throughout Indianapolis. Walk west (or left) to the bridge over the White River. In 1831, the *Robert Hanna* journeyed to Indianapolis in an effort to win a prize offered to the first steamboat able to travel from the Ohio River up the White River. However, the steamboat ran aground on the return trip, discounting the river as a major trade route.

At the far end of the bridge, to the right, is the Indianapolis Zoo. This 64-acre complex is a cageless zoo emphasizing global ecosystems. It is arranged in "biomes," or collections of habitats: Waters, Deserts, Plains, and Forests, plus Encounters (domestic animals from around the world). The zoo has nearly 3,000 animals and 1,700 species of plants and is the only facility in the country accredited as a zoological park, botanical garden, and aquarium. Adjacent to the zoo, 3.3-acre White River Gardens is a year-round botanical showcase. It provides a secluded haven for more than 1,000 varieties of plants and has a towering conservatory that stages many special floral shows. River Promenade, a 1/2-mile walkway lined with flowering trees and evergreens, is

constructed of more than 1,200 blocks of Indiana limestone. Fourteen of the stones feature carved renderings of famous buildings constructed of Indiana limestone.

Walk left off the bridge toward the NCAA Hall of Champions. From track and field, football, and basketball to water polo and field hockey, the hall covers all 22 sports and 81 national championships administered by the NCAA. Interactive displays recapture great moments in collegiate sports and draw visitors into the action. From here, stroll alongside a new version of historic Central Canal, originally built in 1836 to boost trade. Cross the footbridge and follow the canal to the Congressional Medal of Honor Memorial, the nation's first memorial dedicated to recipients of its highest award for military valor. The 1-acre memorial has 27 curved walls of glass, each between 7 and 10 feet high, representing specific conflicts in which medals were awarded. The glass walls feature the names of 3,410 medal recipients. The memorial includes recorded stories of honorees and the conflicts in which they fought. Continuing on, the Eiteljorg Museum is one of only two museums east of the Mississippi River with both Native American objects and Western paintings and bronzes. Built of honey-colored stone, it has a distinctive Southwestern look. The museum houses the work of such icons as Remington, Russell, and Georgia O'Keeffe. If time allows, take in a ball game at the 15,500-seat Victory Field, named the best minor league ballpark in America by *Baseball America* magazine. Try to sit behind home plate for stunning skyline views. The park is home to the Triple-A Indianapolis Indians, top farm team of the Milwaukee Brewers.

Clowes Memorial Hall. *4600 Sunset Ave, Indianapolis. Phone 317/940-6444; toll-free 800/732-0804. www. cloweshall.org.* Performing arts center. Programs (all year).

Hinkle Fieldhouse. *5144 Boulevard Pl, Indianapolis. Phone 317/940-9375. www.butler.edu.* Historic Hinkle Fieldhouse, home of the Butler Bulldogs basketball team, seats 11,000. Built in 1928, it was one of the first

universtity fieldhouses in the country and was the largest basketball arena in the United States for the first 20 years. The final scenes of the movie *Hoosiers* were filmed here, where the state championship games depicted in the movie were actually played.

Holcomb Observatory & Planetarium. *4600 Sunset Ave, Indianapolis. Phone 317/940-9333.* Features the largest telescope in Indiana, a 38-inch Cassegrain reflector. Planetarium shows (call for schedule). **$$**

Children's Museum. *3000 N Meridian St (46208). Phone 317/334-3322. www.childrensmuseum.org.* The largest of its kind, this outstanding children's museum has ten major galleries. Exhibits cover science, culture, space, history, and exploration. Among the highlights are the SpaceQuest Planetarium (additional fee), the 30-foot-high Water Clock, the Playscape gallery for preschoolers, and the Computer Discovery Center, along with hands-on science exhibits, a simulated limestone cave, and an old-fashioned carousel (additional fee for rides). The largest gallery, the Center for Exploration, is designed for ages 12 and up. (Mar-Labor Day, daily 10 am-5 pm; rest of year, Tues-Sun 10 am-5 pm; closed Easter, Thanksgiving, Dec 25) **$$**

Circle Centre Mall. *49 W Maryland St (46204). Phone 317/681-8000. www.circle-centre.com.* Indianapolis's newest mall in the heart of downtown offers more than 100 shopping, dining, and entertainment options. Anchor stores, Nordstrom and Parisian, are flanked by national chains such as Gymboree, Banana Republic, and Williams-Sonoma in this four-story structure that spans two city blocks. (Mon-Sat 10 am-9 pm, Sun noon-6 pm; closed Thanksgiving, Dec 25)

City Market. *222 E Market St (46204). Phone 317/634-9266.* Renovated marketplace was constructed in 1886. This building and two adjacent areas feature smoked meats, dairy, specialty bakery and fruit stands, and ethnic foods. (Mon-Sat; closed holidays) **FREE**

Colonel Eli Lilly Civil War Museum. *1 Monument Cir. Phone 317/233-2124.* Exhibits present Hoosier involvement and perspective of the Civil War. Includes photos, letters, and diaries of Indiana soldiers. (Wed-Sun; closed holidays) **FREE**

Conner Prairie. *13400 Allisonville Rd (46038). Phone 317/776-6000; toll-free 800/966-1836.* A 1,400-acre nationally acclaimed living history museum. Costumed interpreters depict the life and times of early settlement in this 1836 village; contains 39 buildings, including Federal-style brick mansion (1823) built by fur trader William Conner (self-guided tours). Working blacksmith, weaving, and pottery shops; woodworkers complex; self-guided tours. Visitor center with changing exhibits. Hands-on activities at Pioneer Adventure Area; games, toys. Picnic area, restaurant, gift shop. (Tues-Sun; closed holidays) Special events throughout year. **$$$**

Crispus Attucks Museum. *1140 Dr. Martin Luther King Jr. St. Phone 317/226-4613.* Four galleries established to recognize, honor, and celebrate the contributions made by African Americans. (Mon-Fri; closed holidays) **FREE**

Crown Hill Cemetery. *700 W 38th St. Phone 317/925-8231.* This is the third-largest cemetery in the nation. President Benjamin Harrison, poet James Whitcomb Riley, novelist Booth Tarkington, and gangster John Dillinger are among the notables buried here.

Eagle Creek Park. *7840 W 56th St. Just W of I-465. Phone 317/327-7110.* Approximately 3,900 acres of wooded terrain with 1,400-acre reservoir. Fishing, boat ramps, rentals, swimming beach (Memorial Day-Labor Day), bathhouse, water sports center. Shelters, golf course, cross-country skiing, hiking trails, playgrounds, picnicking. (Daily; some facilities closed in winter) **$**

Easley's Winery. *205 N College Ave. Phone 317/636-4516.* Sales room; wine tasting (21 years and over). Tours by appointment. (Daily; closed holidays) **FREE**

Eiteljorg Museum of American Indian and Western Art. *500 W Washington St (46204). Phone 317/636-9378. www.eiteljorg.org.* One of the finest collections of Native American artifacts in the country, the Eiteljorg is reminiscent of the culture of the American West even in its distinctive exterior architecture. Located in White River State Park (see) in downtown Indianapolis, the Eiteljorg brings contemporary Western artists of Native American descent to the forefront of Midwestern culture. The museum also displays artwork and artifacts from cultures of the Pacific Northwest and Alaska. (Memorial Day-Labor Day, Mon-Sat 10 am-5 pm, Sun noon-5 pm; rest of year, Tues-Sat 10 am-5 pm, Sun noon-5 pm; closed Easter, Thanksgiving, Dec 25) **$$**

The Fashion Mall. *8702 Keystone Crossing Blvd (46240). Phone 317/574-4000. www.fashionmallkeystone.com.* This upscale mall features some 95 stores, including Brooks Brothers, Coach, MAC Cosmetics, and a new Saks Fifth Avenue, as well as a few fine restaurants. (Mon-Sat 10 am-9 pm, Sun noon-6 pm)

Garfield Park and Conservatory. *2505 Conservatory Dr. Phone 317/327-7184 (conservatory).* This 128-acre park features a restored pagoda, conservatory (daily; closed holidays; fee), sunken gardens, and illuminated fountains. Conservatory shows (fee): bulb (spring); chrysanthemum (late Nov); poinsettia (Dec). Picnic area; swimming pool (late May-Labor Day, daily; fee); tennis and horseshoe courts, other sports facilities. (Daily; facilities closed holidays) Musical programs in amphitheater (early June-late Aug, Thurs-Sun; free). **FREE**

⭐ **Historic Lockerbie Square.** *New York and College sts.* Late-19th-century private houses have been restored in this six-block area. Cobblestone streets, brick sidewalks, and fine architecture make this an interesting area for sight-seeing. Walking tour **$$**. Here is

> **James Whitcomb Riley Home.** *528 Lockerbie St, Indianapolis. Phone 317/631-5885.* Maintained in same condition as when the "Hoosier Poet" lived here (1893-1916). Tours (Tues-Sun; closed holidays). **$**

Hook's American Drug Store Museum. *201 E Meridian St. Phone 317/924-1503.* Celebrates the 400-year history of drugstores in America. Includes ornate 1852 furnishings, drugstore and medical antiques; operating soda fountain. (Daily; closed holidays; also Mon in winter) **FREE**

Indiana Convention Center & RCA Dome. *100 S Capitol (46225). Phone 317/262-3410 (center). www.iccrd.com.* Features seven exhibition halls, four ballrooms, 48 meeting rooms, and various offices. The 60,500-seat RCA Dome is one of only a few air-supported domed stadiums in the United States. The dome is the home of the Indianapolis Colts (see) football team, conventions, auto shows, trade shows, and more.

Indiana Fever (WNBA). *Conseco Fieldhouse, 125 S Pennsylvania St (46204). Phone 317/917-2500. www.wnba.com/fever.* Women's professional basketball team.

Indiana Firebirds. *Conseco Fieldhouse, 125 S Pennsylvania St (46204). Phone 317/917-2500. www.firebirds.com.* Arena Football League team.

Indiana Historical Society. *450 W Ohio St (46202). Phone 317/232-1882. www.indianahistory.org.* Changing exhibits chronicle the state's history. Films and lectures are held periodically, and a 30,000-square-foot library holds a large collection of letters, photos, and other research material. (Tues-Sat 10 am-5 pm, Sun noon-5 pm; closed Mon; holidays) **FREE**

Indiana Pacers (NBA). *Conseco Fieldhouse, 125 S Pennsylvania St (46204). Phone 317/917-2500. www.nba.com/pacers.* Professional basketball team plays at Conseco Fieldhouse, a retro-style arena in the heart of downtown.

Indiana State Museum. *650 W Washington St (46204). Phone 317/232-1637.* Depicts Indiana's history, art, science, and popular culture with five floors of displays. Exhibits include the Indiana Museum of Sports, Indiana radio, forests of 200 years ago, a small-town community at the turn of the century, paintings by Indiana artists. Changing exhibits. (Daily; closed holidays) **$$**

Indiana University-Purdue University Indianapolis. *425 University Blvd (46202). Main site on W Michigan St, 1 mile W of downtown. Phone 317/274-5555. www.iupui.edu.* (Organized in 1969) (27,000 students) More than 200 areas of study are offered in 19 schools. Home of Indiana University Medical Center, one of the foremost research and treatment centers in the world and a primary international center for sports medicine, fitness, heart research, cancer treatment, and kidney transplants. Includes five teaching hospitals and 90 clinics. IUPUI hosts many national and international athletic competitions, including tennis's RCA Championships (see SPECIAL EVENTS).

Indiana World War Memorial Plaza. *Bounded by New York, St. Clair, Meridian, and Pennsylvania sts. Phone 317/232-7615.* A five-block area dedicated to Indiana citizens who gave their lives in the two World Wars and the Korean and Vietnam wars. The World War Memorial in the middle of the plaza is a massive edifice of Indiana limestone and granite. The Shrine Room (upper level) is dedicated to the American flag; Military Museum (lower level). (Wed-Sun; closed holidays) Outside in the center of the south stairway stands a bronze statue, Pro Patria. The four-story building in the northeast corner of the plaza is national headquarters of the American Legion. Landscaped parks are located north and south of the building; Veterans Memorial Plaza has flags of 50 states. (Wed-Sun) **FREE**

Indianapolis Colts (NFL). *RCA Dome, 100 S Capitol Ave (46225). Phone 317/297-2658. www.colts.com.* Professional football team features star quarterback Peyton Manning and standout wide receiver Marvin Harrison.

⭐ **Indianapolis Motor Speedway and Hall of Fame Museum.** *4790 W 16th St. 7 miles NW. Phone 317/484-6747.* Site of the famous 500-mile automobile classic held each year the Sunday before Memorial Day (see SPECIAL EVENTS). Many innovations in modern cars have been tested at races here. The oval track is 2 1/2 miles long, lined by grandstands, paddocks, and bleachers. Hall of Fame Museum (fee) has exhibit of antique and classic passenger cars, many built in Indiana; more than 30 Indianapolis-winning race cars. (Daily; closed Dec 25) **$**

⭐ **Indianapolis Museum of Art.** *1200 W 38th St. Phone 317/923-1331. www.ima-art.org.* Extensive collections with many special exhibits (fee). Tours. (Tues-Sun; closed Jan 1, Thanksgiving, Dec 25) **DONATION** Includes

Clowes Pavilion. *1200 W 38th St, Indianapolis. Phone 317/940-6444.* Medieval and Renaissance art; J. M. W. Turner watercolors; lecture hall with special programs; courtyard garden.

Krannert Pavilion. *1200 W 38th St, Indianapolis. Phone 317/920-2660.* Collection features American, Asian, and pre-Columbian art; 20th-century art and textiles. Outdoor concert terrace, sculpture court.

Lilly Pavilion of Decorative Arts. *1200 W 38th St, Indianapolis. Phone 317/920-2660.* French château showcases two centuries of English, continental, and American furniture, silver, and ceramics. Also examples of 18th-century German porcelain. Tours.

Mary Fendrich Hulman Pavilion. *1200 W 38th St, Indianapolis. Phone 317/920-2660.* Collection features Baroque through Neo-Impressionist works and the Eiteljorg Gallery of African and South Pacific Art. Allen Whitehill Clowes Special Exhibition Gallery.

Indianapolis Sight-Seeing. *9075 N Meridian St. Phone 317/573-0404.* Contact Indianapolis Sight-Seeing, Inc, 9075 N Meridian, 46260.

Indianapolis Zoo. *1200 W Washington St (Hwy 40). Downtown. Phone 317/630-2010.* This 64-acre facility includes the state's largest aquarium, enclosed whale and dolphin pavilion, and more than 3,000 animals from around the world. Sea lions, penguins, sharks, polar bears; daily whale and dolphin shows; camels and reptiles of the deserts; lions, giraffes, and elephants in the Plains; tigers, bears, and snow monkeys in the Forests. Encounters features domesticated animals from around the world, and a 600-seat outside arena offers daily programs and demonstrations. Living Deserts of the World is a conservatory covered by an 80-foot diameter transparent dome. New White River Gardens is a conservatory and gardens. Commons Plaza includes restaurant and snack bar; additional animal exhibits; amphitheater for shows and concerts. Horse-drawn streetcar, elephant, camel, carousel, and miniature train rides. Stroller and locker rentals. (Daily) **$$$**

Madame Walker Theatre Center. *617 Indiana Ave (46202). Phone 317/236-2099. www.walkertheatre.org.* The Walker Theatre, erected and embellished in an African and Egyptian motif, was built in 1927 as a tribute to Madame C. J. Walker, America's first self-made female millionaire. The renovated theater now features theatrical productions, concerts, and other cultural events. The center serves as an educational and cultural center for the city's African-American community. Tours (Mon-Fri). **$**

Morris-Butler House. *1204 N Park Ave (46202). Phone 317/636-5409.* (1865) A museum of Victorian lifestyles from 1850 to 1886. Belter and Meeks furniture, paintings, silver, and other decorative arts. Special events. (Wed-Sun; closed holidays) **$**

⭐ **NCAA Hall of Champions.** *700 W Washington St. In White River State Park. Phone toll-free 800/735-6222.* This center celebrates intercollegiate athletics through photographs, video presentations, and displays covering 22 men's and women's sports and all NCAA championships. The 25,000-square-foot area contains two levels of interactive displays and multimedia presentations. Three theaters present videos about the Final Four and coaching, for example, while the Hall of Honor contains a salute to individuals who have been honored with an NCAA award. (Memorial Day-Labor Day, Mon; rest of year, Tues-Sun; closed Jan 1, Thanksgiving, Dec 25) **$$**

President Benjamin Harrison Home. *1230 N Delaware St. Phone 317/631-1898. www.presidentbenjaminharrison.org.* (1874) Residence of the 23rd president of the United States. Guided tours depart ever 30 minutes and take visitors through 16 rooms with original furniture, paintings, and the family's personal effects. Herb garden. (Mon-Sat 10 am-3:30 pm; July-Sept also Sun; closed holidays; also first three weeks in Jan, 500 Race Day) **$$**

Scottish Rite Cathedral. *650 N Meridian St. Phone 317/262-3100.* Structure of Tudor/Gothic design, built in 1929. The 212-foot tower has a carillon of 54 bells; auditorium has a 7,500-pipe organ. Interior is elaborately decorated. Tours. (Mon-Fri; closed weekends, holidays) **FREE**

State Capitol. *200 W Washington St. Between Washington and Ohio sts and Capitol and Senate aves. Phone 317/233-5293.* (1878-1888) Structure of Indiana limestone with copper dome. (Daily; closed holidays) Tours by appointment. **FREE**

Special Events

500 Festival. *201 S Capitol, Indianapolis (46225). Phone 317/636-4556; toll-free 800/638-4296.* Month-long celebration precedes the Indianapolis 500 (see), held Memorial Day weekend. Numerous events include the 500 Ball, Mechanic's Recognition Party, Delco Electronics 500 festival parade, mini-marathon, memorial service. May.

Entertainment. *1200 W 38th St, Indianapolis (46208). Phone 317/924-6770.* Indianapolis Civic Theater, 1200 W 38th St, 46208, phone 317/924-6770; Hilbert Circle Theatre (Indianapolis Symphony Orchestra and a variety of other shows), 45 Monument Cir, 46204, phone 317/262-1100; Dance Kaleidoscope (Oct-Nov, Mar, June), 4600 Sunset Ave, phone 317/940-6555; Indiana Repertory Theater (Sept-May), 140 W Washington St, 46204, phone 317/635-5277; Ballet Internationale (July-Apr), 502 N Capitol, Suite B, 46204, phone 317/637-8979; Butler University (see), Edyvean Repertory Theatre, 100 W 42nd St, phone 317/783-4000; Beef & Boards Dinner Theatre, 9301 N Michigan Ave, phone 317/876-0504; Madame Walker Theatre Center (see), 617 Indiana Ave, phone 317/236-2099; and Marian College offer a variety of productions throughout the year. Contact the individual venues for details.

Indiana Black Expo. *3145 N Meridian St, Indianapolis (46208). Phone 317/262-3452.* Consumer exhibits, health fair. July.

Indiana Flower & Patio Show. *State Fairgrounds, 1202 E 38th St, Indianapolis (46205). Phone 317/927-7500.* More than 25 full-size gardens display fine flowers and landscaping techniques. Second weekend in Mar.

Indiana State Fair. *State Fairgrounds, 1202 E 38th St (46205). E 38th St between College Ave and Fall Creek Pkwy. Phone 317/927-7500 or 317/923-3431 (evenings).* Grand circuit horse racing, livestock exhibitions, entertainment, and special agricultural exhibits. Mid-Aug.

Indianapolis 500. *Indianapolis Motor Speedway, 4790 W 16th St. Phone 317/484-6780.* For ticket information, contact the Indianapolis Motor Speedway (see). Sun before Memorial Day.

Penrod Arts Fair. *Indianapolis Museum of Art, 1200 W 38th St, Indianapolis (46208). Phone 317/252-9895.* State's largest art fair. Sept.

RCA Championships (tennis). *Indianapolis Tennis Center, 815 W New York St, Indianapolis. Phone 317/632-4100; toll-free 800/622-5683. www.rcatennis.com.* Stadium (10,000 seats). World-class players compete in this week-long event. Mid-Aug.

Limited-Service Hotels

★ **COURTYARD INDIANAPOLIS AT THE CAPITOL.** *320 N Senate Ave, Indianapolis (46204). Phone 317/684-7733; toll-free 800/228-9290; fax 317/684-7734. www.courtyard.com.* 124 rooms. Check-in 3 pm, check-out noon. Indoor pool, whirlpool. Business center. **$**

★ ★ **COURTYARD BY MARRIOTT DOWNTOWN.** *501 W Washington St, Indianapolis (46204). Phone 317/635-4443; toll-free 800/228-9290; fax 317/687-0029. www.courtyard.com.* 235 rooms. Complimentary continental breakfast. Check-in 3 pm, check-out noon. Restaurant, bar. Outdoor pool. Business center. **$**

★ **HAMPTON INN.** *105 S Meridian St, Indianapolis (46225). Phone 317/261-1200; toll-free 800/426-7866; fax 317/261-1030. www.hampton-inn.com/hi/indpolis-downtown.* 180 rooms, 9 story. Complimentary continental breakfast. Check-in 3 pm, check-out 11 am. Fitness room. **$**

★★ **HILTON GARDEN INN INDIANAPOLIS DOWNTOWN.** *10 E Market St, Indianapolis (46204). Phone 317/955-9700; fax 317/955-9701. www. hiltongardeninn.com.* 180 rooms. Check-in 2 pm, check-out noon. Restaurant, bar. Fitness room. Indoor pool. **$**

★★ **RAMADA INN.** *505 S State Rd 39, Lebanon (46052). Phone 765/482-0500; toll-free 800/272-6232; fax 765/483-8345. www.ramada.com.* 205 rooms, 2 story. Check-in 3 pm, check-out 11 am. Restaurant, bar. Fitness room. Indoor pool, whirlpool. Business center. **$**

Full-Service Hotels

★★★ **CANTERBURY HOTEL.** *123 S Illinois St, Indianapolis (46225). Phone 317/634-3000; toll-free 800/538-8186; fax 317/685-2519. www. canterburyhotel.com.* The Canterbury Hotel transplants the charm and elegance of England to downtown Indianapolis. Since the 1850s, it has enjoyed a proud history as the city's leading hotel. This intimate hotel provides visitors with a convenient city location and private access to the adjacent shopping mall, filled with upscale stores and restaurants. Mahogany furniture and traditional artwork complete the classic décor in the guest rooms. Spacious and inviting, the accommodations are well suited for modern travelers. The lovely restaurant dishes up American and continental favorites for breakfast, lunch, and dinner, while the traditional afternoon tea is a local institution. 99 rooms, 12 story. Complimentary continental breakfast. Check-in 3 pm, check-out noon. Restaurant. Fitness room. **$$**

★★★ **CROWNE PLAZA HOTEL UNION STATION.** *123 W Louisiana, Indianapolis (46225). Phone 317/631-2221; fax 317/236-7474. www. crowneplaza.com/ind-downtown.* Nowhere else can you sleep in one of 26 authentic Pullman sleeper train cars, each one named for and decorated to recall a famous personality from the early 1900s. The hotel is noted also for the life-size "ghosts" (fiberglass figures in period dress) who inhabit the hotel reflecting travelers from a bygone era. Full of old-world charm and modern convenience, this hotel boasts charming stained-glass windows and soaring archways, connects to the modern,

functioning train station, and is within walking distance of downtown sports and arts venues and eateries. 275 rooms, 3 story. Check-in 4 pm, check-out noon. Restaurant. Fitness room. Indoor pool, whirlpool. **$**

★★ **DOUBLETREE HOTEL.** *11355 N Meridian St, Carmel (46032). Phone 317/844-7994; fax 317/ 844-2118. www.doubletree.com.* The oversized guest suites here provide visitors with comfortable amenities such as pullout sleeper sofas and mini-refrigerators. Guests also are in close proximity to nearby museums, the Indianapolis Motor Speedway (see), and many other area attractions. 137 rooms, 3 story. Check-out noon. Restaurant, bar. Fitness room. Indoor pool, outdoor pool, whirlpool. **$**

★★★ **HYATT REGENCY INDIANAPOLIS.** *1 S Capitol Ave, Indianapolis (46204). Phone 317/632-1234; fax 317/616-6299. www.hyatt.com.* This hotel has a great location. It is connected to the Indiana Convention Center & RCA Dome (see) and Circle Centre Mall (see) by a skywalk. It is near many other attractions and only 8 miles from the Indianapolis International Airport. 497 rooms, 21 story. Check-in 3 pm, check-out noon. Restaurant, bar. Fitness room. Indoor pool, whirlpool. Business center. **$$**

★★★ **MARRIOTT INDIANAPOLIS DOWNTOWN.** *350 W Maryland St, Indianapolis (46225). Phone 317/822-3500; toll-free 877/640-7666; fax 317/822-1002. www.marriott.com.* 615 rooms, 19 story. Pets accepted. Check-in 4 pm, check-out 11 am. Restaurant, bar. Fitness room. Indoor pool, whirlpool. Business center. **$**

★★★ **OMNI SEVERIN HOTEL.** *40 W Jackson Pl, Indianapolis (46225). Phone 317/634-6664; fax 317/687-3612. www.omnihotels.com.* With the Circle Centre Mall (see) connected, guests will find shopping among the many activities surrounding this beautiful historic hotel. Spacious guest rooms, a heated indoor pool, and a health club are just a few of the inviting amenities here. Built in 1913. Across from Union Station. 424 rooms, 13 story. Check-in 3 pm, check-out noon. Restaurant, bar. Fitness room. Indoor pool. Business center. **$$**

★ ★ ★ **SHERATON HOTEL AND SUITES.**
8787 Keystone Crossing, Indianapolis (46240). Phone 317/846-2700; fax 317/574-6780. 506 rooms, 15 story. Check-in 3 pm, check-out noon. Restaurant, bar. Indoor pool, whirlpool. Business center. **$**

★ ★ ★ **THE WESTIN INDIANAPOLIS.** *50 S Capitol Ave, Indianapolis (46204). Phone 317/262-8100; fax 317/231-3997. www.westin.com.* Located near the IMAX theater and connected to the RCA Dome and a shopping center, this hotel is convenient for travelers and has a great view of the city. 573 rooms, 15 story. Check-in 3 pm, check-out noon. Restaurant, bar. Fitness room. Indoor pool, whirlpool. Business center. **$**

Specialty Lodgings

The following lodging establishments are approved by Mobil Travel Guide, but due to their unique and individualized nature have not been given a traditional Mobil Star rating. Included in this listing you may find bed-and-breakfasts, limited-service inns, guest ranches, and other unique hotel properties.

THE LOOKING GLASS INN. *1319 N New Jersey, Indianapolis (46202). Phone 317/639-9550; fax 317/684-9536. www.lookingglassinn.com.* 6 rooms. Complimentary full breakfast. Check-in 4 pm, check-out 11 am. **$**

NESTLE INN. *637 N East St, Indianapolis (46202). Phone 317/610-5200; fax 317/610-5210. www.nestleindy.com.* 5 rooms. Complimentary full breakfast. Check-in 4 pm-6 pm, check-out 11 am. **$**

OLD NORTHSIDE INN. *1340 N Alabama St, Indianapolis (46202). Phone 317/635-9132; toll-free 800/635-9127. www.oldnorthsideinn.com.* 7 rooms. Complimentary full breakfast. Check-in 4 pm, check-out 11 am. **$$**

STONE SOUP INN. *1304 N Central Ave, Indianapolis (46202). Phone 317/639-9550; toll-free 866/639-9550. www.stonesoupinn.com.* 9 rooms. Complimentary full breakfast. Check-in 4 pm-6 pm, check-out 11 am. **$**

YELLOW ROSE INN. *1441 N Delaware St, Indianapolis (46202). Phone 317/636-7673; fax 317/635-3522. www.yellowroseinn.com.* 4 rooms, all suites. Complimentary full breakfast. Check-in 3 pm, check-out noon. **$$**

Restaurants

★ **ARISTOCRAT PUB.** *5212 N College Ave, Indianapolis (46220). Phone 317/283-7388; fax 317/283-8410.* Dark wood and art-glass windows make the Aristocrat feel like a classic pub. The good-sized menu, complimented by a nice selection of drinks, runs the gamut from salads to sandwiches to steaks and pasta dishes. Despite its location on a busy street, the outdoor tables out front are popular on balmy evenings. American menu. Lunch, dinner, Sun brunch. Closed Jan 1, Thanksgiving, Dec 25. Bar. Children's menu. Casual attire. Outdoor seating. **$$**

★ **CAFE PATACHOU.** *4911 N Pennsylvania Ave, Indianapolis (46205). Phone 317/925-2823.* Locals flock to this tiny, no-nonsense neighborhood spot for specialty omelettes, cinnamon toast made from thick homemade bread, and heaping bowls of stick-to-your-ribs oatmeal and granola. Lunch items are served as well. Expect a wait on weekends. American menu. Breakfast, lunch, brunch. Casual attire. **$**

★ ★ **DADDY JACK'S.** *9419 N Meridian St, Indianapolis (46260). Phone 317/843-1609; fax 317/571-6987. www.konajacksindy.com.* American menu. Lunch, dinner. Closed Sun; holidays. Bar. Casual attire. Outdoor seating. **$$**

★ ★ **HOLLYHOCK HILL.** *8110 N College Ave, Indianapolis (46240). Phone 317/251-2294; fax 317/251-2295.* Hollyhock Hill is easy to miss; it inhabits what looks like a private residence. Inside it feels a bit like somebody's house, too. The kitchen serves up homey dishes like fried chicken and mashed potatoes, family style—you may just feel like you've landed at Grandma's for dinner. The place fills up with large groups, so calling ahead for a reservation is wise, especially on weekends. American menu. Lunch (Sun only), dinner. Closed Mon; Jan 1, July 4, Dec 24-25. Bar. Children's menu. Casual attire. **$$**

★ **MOUNTAIN JACK'S.** *6901 W 38th St, Indianapolis (46254). Phone 317/329-6929; fax 317/329-6924.* If you get fed up by steakhouses whose sky-high prices include only a slab of naked beef, Mountain Jack's may be more your style. This casual lodgelike spot, part of a small chain, serves up sizzling steaks, sides included. You'll also find a tableside salad bar. Steak menu. Lunch, dinner. Closed Dec 25. Bar. Children's menu. Casual attire. **$$**

★ ★ ★ **RESTAURANT AT THE CANTERBURY.** *123 S Illinois St, Indianapolis (46225). Phone 317/634-3000; toll-free 800/538-8186; fax 317/685-2519. www.canterburyhotel.com.* Decorated more like an English club than a restaurant, this elegant, tranquil hotel dining room serves American continental cuisine, focusing on game dishes. Lunch can be very reasonable, and don't miss the afternoon tea service with live piano music. International/Fusion menu. Breakfast, lunch, dinner, Sun brunch. Bar. Jacket required. Valet parking. **$$$**

★ ★ **ST. ELMO STEAK HOUSE.** *127 S Illinois St, Indianapolis (46225). Phone 317/637-1811; fax 317/635-0636. www.stelmos.com.* Many Hoosiers consider St. Elmo's to be Indianapolis's best steakhouse. It's certainly one of its oldest, having been in its downtown storefront since 1902 (which makes it the oldest Indiana restaurant still in its original location). Inside the turn-of-the-century-style space, tuxedoed waiters bring sizable steaks and chops to a crowd of businessmen on expense accounts, with a starter of either tomato juice or navy bean soup and a side of potato, mashed, baked, or fried. Regulars love the classic shrimp cocktail as well. Steak menu. Dinner. Closed holidays. Bar. Casual attire. Reservations recommended. **$$$**

Jasper (E-2)

Population 12,100
Elevation 472 ft
Area Code 812
Zip 47546
Information Dubois County Tourism Commission, 610 Main St, 2nd floor; phone 812/482-9115 or toll-free 800/968-4578
Web site www.duboiscounty.org

What to See and Do

Monastery of the Immaculate Conception. *802 E 10th St, Ferdinand. S on Hwy 162. Phone 812/367-1411.* (1867) Historic monastery, home to the Sisters of St. Benedict, is located on 190 acres. The church, one of the most famous examples of Romanesque architecture in the country, features brilliant stained-glass windows, handsome wood panels and pews hand-carved in Oberammergau, and an interior dome rising 87 feet from the marble floor. An information office at the main entrance has a historical display, a scale model of the entire complex, and a video about the monastery. Guided tours (by appointment). Monastery (daily).

Limited-Service Hotel

★ ★ **HOLIDAY INN.** *951 Wernsing Rd, Jasper (47547). Phone 812/482-5555; toll-free 800/872-3176; fax 812/482-7908. www.holiday-inn.com.* 200 rooms, 2 story. Check-out noon. Restaurant, bar. Fitness room. Indoor pool, children's pool, whirlpool. **$**

Restaurant

★ ★ **SCHNITZELBANK.** *393 3rd Ave, Jasper (47546). Phone 812/482-2640; fax 812/482-7687.* German, American menu. Breakfast, lunch, dinner. Closed Sun; holidays. Bar. **$$**

Jeffersonville (F-3)

See also New Albany

Founded 1802
Population 27,362
Elevation 448 ft
Area Code 812
Zip 47130
Information Southern Indiana Convention and Tourism Bureau, 315 Southern Indiana Ave; phone 812/282-6654 or toll-free 800/552-3842
Web site www.sunnysideoflouisville.org

Jeffersonville, on the north bank of the Ohio River and opposite Louisville, Kentucky, has a proud history as a shipbuilding center. One of the oldest towns in Indiana, it was built according to plans drawn up by

Thomas Jefferson. The city is an industrial manufacturing center and a terminal for the American Commercial Line, Inc, a large river transportation company. Grain, tobacco, strawberries, and dairy goods are the main farm products in surrounding Clark County.

What to See and Do

Colgate Clock. *Atop the Clarksville Colgate-Palmolive plant.* Said to be the second-largest clock in the world (40 feet in diameter).

Howard Steamboat Museum. *1101 E Market St. Phone 812/283-3728. www.steamboatmuseum.org.* Housed in 22-room mansion featuring stained- and leaded-glass windows, hand-carved panels, brass chandeliers, a grand stairway, Victorian furniture (1893); steamboat models, shipyard artifacts and tools, pictures, and other memorabilia (1834-1941). Tours (Tues-Sun; closed holidays). **$$**

Special Events

Steamboat Days Festival. *1406 Frederick Ave, Jeffersonville (47130). On the riverfront, downtown. Phone 812/282-6654.* Parade, entertainment, 5K run. Early or mid-Sept.

Victorian Chautauqua. *Howard Steamboat Museum, 1101 E Market St, Jeffersonville (47130). Phone 812/283-3728; toll-free 888/472-0606. www. steamboatmuseum.org.* Victorian-style café, speakers, arts and crafts, antiques, plant sale, children's activities. Mid-May.

Limited-Service Hotels

★ **BEST WESTERN GREEN TREE INN.** *1425 Broadway, Clarksville (47129). Phone 812/288-9281; toll-free 800/950-9281; fax 812/288-9281. www. bestwestern.com.* 107 rooms. Pets accepted, some restrictions. Check-out noon. Pool. **$**

★ ★ **RAMADA INN.** *700 W Riverside Dr, Jeffersonville (47130). Phone 812/284-6711; toll-free 888/298-2054; fax 812/283-3686. www.ramada.com.* 187 rooms, 10 story. Pets accepted; fee. Check-out noon. Restaurant, bar. Pool. Airport transportation available. On Ohio River. **$**

Kokomo (B-3)

See also Logansport, Peru

Founded 1842
Population 46,113
Elevation 810 ft
Area Code 765
Information Kokomo Indiana Visitors Bureau, 1504 N Reed Rd, 46901; phone 765/457-6802 or toll-free 800/837-0971
Web site www.kokomo-in.org

This lively manufacturing center is where the first clutch-driven automobile with electric ignition was invented by Elwood Haynes. Since then, Kokomo manufacturers have invented several more useful items, from the first pneumatic rubber tire to canned tomato juice. The automobile industry is represented by Delphi-Delco Electronics and Chrysler plants, which manufacture automotive entertainment systems, semiconductor devices, transmissions, and aluminum die castings. Indiana University has a branch here, and Grissom Air Reserve Base is located 14 miles north of town.

What to See and Do

Elwood Haynes Museum. *1915 S Webster St. Phone 765/456-7500.* Home of Elwood Haynes; memorabilia, items relating to early development of the automobile; 1905 and 1924 Haynes cars on display; industrial exhibits; also Haynes Stellite (alloy used in spaceships). (Tues-Sun; closed holidays) **FREE**

Haynes Memorial. *1915 S Webster St. 3 miles E, off Hwy 31 Bypass. Phone 765/456-7500.* Pumpkinvine Pike is site of the first successful road test of Haynes's car.

Highland Park. *1402 W Defenbaugh St. Phone 765/456-7275.* County's last covered bridge was moved here from Vermont. Recreational facilities. (Daily) **FREE** Also in park are

Old Ben. *1402 W Defenbaugh St, Kokomo.* An enormous, stuffed Hereford steer that weighed 4,720 pounds, was 16 feet, 8 inches long, and was 6 feet, 4 inches high. His life ended in 1910, at the height of his fame, when he slipped and fell on ice.

Sycamore stump. *900 W Defenbaugh St, Kokomo. Phone 765/456-7275.* The original tree died in the early 1900s, leaving a stump that measures 51 feet in circumference. The interior of the stump has held 24 people and once served as a telephone booth.

Seiberling Mansion. *1200 W Sycamore St. Phone 765/452-4314.* (1891) This late Victorian mansion houses exhibits of historical and educational interest, county history, manufacturing artifacts. (Tues-Sun afternoons; closed holidays; also Jan) **$**

Special Events

Greentown Glass Festival. *112 N Meridian, Greentown (46936). E on I-35, downtown. Phone 765/628-6206.* Commemorates the production of Greentown glass. Carnival, beauty pageant, antique show, many events. Second weekend in June.

Haynes Apperson Festival. *519 N Main, Kokomo (46901). Phone toll-free 800/456-1106.* Entertainment, crafts, parade, carnival. July 4 weekend.

Howard County Fair. *Greentown fairgrounds, 610 E Payton St, Greentown (46936). Phone 765/628-3247.* Last week in July.

Limited-Service Hotels

★ **BEST WESTERN SIGNATURE INN.** *4021 S LaFountain St, Kokomo (46902). Phone 765/455-1000; toll-free 800/822-5252; fax 765/455-1000. www.bestwestern.com.* 101 rooms, 2 story. Complimentary continental breakfast. Check-out noon. Fitness room. Indoor pool, whirlpool. **$**

★★ **CLARION HOTEL.** *1709 E Lincoln Rd, Kokomo (46902). Phone 765/459-8001; fax 765/457-6636. www.choicehotels.com.* 132 rooms, 3 story. Check-out noon. Restaurant, bar. Fitness room. Indoor pool. Airport transportation available. **$**

★ **HAMPTON INN.** *2920 S Reed Rd, Kokomo (46902). Phone 765/455-2900; toll-free 800/426-7866; fax 765/455-2800. www.hampton-inn.com.* 105 rooms, 5 story. Pets accepted, some restrictions. Complimentary continental breakfast. Fitness room. Indoor pool. **$**

Restaurant

★★ **SYCAMORE GRILLE.** *115 W Sycamore, Kokomo (46901). Phone 765/457-2220; fax 765/457-3367.* Turn-of-the-century décor. Lunch, dinner. Closed Sun; holidays. Bar. Children's menu. **$$**

La Porte (A-2)

See also Michigan City, South Bend, Valparaiso

Founded 1832
Population 21,621
Elevation 807 ft
Area Code 219
Zip 46350
Information Greater La Porte Chamber of Commerce, 414 Lincolnway, PO Box 486; phone 219/362-3178
Web site www.lpchamber.com

This busy manufacturing center is a popular resort area in both winter and summer. City lakes offer fishing, ice fishing, snowmobiling, and other recreational activities. Seven lakes with fishing and boating facilities border the town on the north and west. The area's chief industrial products are industrial fans, coil coating, corrugated and plastic containers, rubber products, and iron and metal castings.

What to See and Do

Door Prairie Museum. *2405 Indiana Ave. 1 mile S on Hwy 35. Phone 219/326-1337.* Collection covers over 100 years of automobiles, including models by Citroen, Ford, Mercedes Benz, Rolls Royce, and Tucker. (Apr-Dec, Tues-Sun) **$$**

Kingsbury Fish and Wildlife Area. *5344 S Hupp Rd (46350). 5 miles SE via Hwy 35, exit County 500 S. Phone 219/393-3612.* Approximately 8,000 acres of state hunting and fishing areas with access to Kankakee River and Tamarack Lake. Area includes boating, canoeing; nature trails; archery range, shooting range; hunting; picnicking; bird-watching. Mixsawbah State Fish Hatchery adjacent. (Daily)

La Porte County Historical Society Museum. *County Complex, 809 State St. Phone 219/326-6808.* Period rooms, archives, antique gun collection. (Tues-Sat; closed holidays) **FREE**

Special Event

La Porte County Fair. *Fairgrounds, 2581 W State Rd 2, La Porte (46350). Phone 219/362-2647.* Exhibits, livestock judging, harness races, shows, food, rides. July.

Limited-Service Hotel

★ **BEST VALUE.** *444 Pine Lake Ave, La Porte (46350). Phone 219/362-4585; toll-free 888/298-2054; fax 219/324-6993. www.bestvalueinn.com.* 146 rooms, 4 story. Pets accepted; fee. Complimentary continental breakfast. Check-out noon. Restaurant, bar. Fitness room. Indoor pool, outdoor pool, whirlpool. **$**

Full-Service Inn

★ ★ ★ **ARBOR HILL.** *263 W Johnson Rd, La Porte (46350). Phone 219/362-9200; fax 219/326-1778. www.arborhillinn.com.* Built in 1910, this historic Greek Revival inn welcomes guests with its fusion of old-world, turn-of-the-century charm and luxurious modern amenities. Nearby attractions include the Prime Outlet Mall, Notre Dame (see SOUTH BEND), and Lake Michigan. 12 rooms, 3 story. Complimentary full breakfast. Check-in 4 pm, check-out 11 am. **$**

Restaurant

★ **REED'S STATE STREET PUB.** *502 State St, La Porte (46350). Phone 219/326-8339.* Historic art prints, stained-glass church windows. Lunch, dinner. Closed Sun; Jan 1, Dec 25. Bar. Children's menu. **$$**

Lafayette (C-2)

Founded 1825
Population 56,397
Elevation 560 ft
Area Code 765
Information Convention and Visitors Bureau, 301 Frontage Rd, 47905-4564; phone 765/447-9999 or toll-free 800/872-6648
Web site www.lafayette-in.com

Lafayette, on the east bank of the Wabash River, was named for the Marquis de Lafayette, who served as a general under George Washington in the Revolutionary War. The city is surrounded by an extensive farm area, including cattle and dairy farms. A large number of diversified industries in the area manufacture automotive gears and supplies, electrical equipment, and pharmaceuticals. On the west bank of the river in West Lafayette (population 28,778) is Purdue University (see). Established as an agricultural college in 1869, today Purdue is noted for many programs, especially engineering.

What to See and Do

Clegg Botanical Garden. *1782 N 400 E. E on Hwy 25 to County Rd 300 N, then 1 mile E to County Rd 400 E, then 1 1/4 miles S. Phone 765/423-1325.* Approximately 15 acres of rugged terrain with glacier-made ridges, native trees and wildflowers, ravines; nature trails, lookout point. (Daily) **FREE**

Columbian Park. *1915 Scott St. 5 miles SW via I-65 to Hwy 26 Lafayette exit. Phone 765/771-2220.* Zoo (daily; closed Thanksgiving, Dec 25). Amusement park; outdoor theater; water slide, swimming pool; tennis courts; concession, picnicking. Facilities (Memorial Day-Labor Day, Tues-Sun). Park (daily). Some fees. **FREE**

Fort Ouiatenon. *3129 S River Rd, West Lafayette. 4 miles SW of West Lafayette on S River Rd. Phone 765/743-3921.* (1717) A 30-acre park; replica blockhouse with 18th-century French trading post. Museum depicts history of French, Native American, British, and American struggles to control Wabash Valley. (Seasonal) (See SPECIAL EVENTS) Picnicking, boating. Park (daily). **FREE**

Greater Lafayette Museum of Art. *101 S 9th St. Phone 765/742-1128.* Maintains permanent collection of 19th- and 20th-century American art; East and Weil galleries present contemporary and historical exhibits. Rental gallery, library, gift shop, children's activity area. Art classes, lectures, and workshops. (Tues-Sun afternoons; closed holidays; also Aug) **FREE**

Purdue University. *1030 Hovde Hall (47907). In West Lafayette via I-65, Hwy 26. Phone 765/494-4636. www.purdue.edu.* (1869) (38,208 students) More than 140 major buildings on 1,579 acres with private airport.

Tippecanoe Battlefield Museum and Park. *200 Battleground Ave, Battle Ground. I-65 at Hwy 43 exit. Phone 765/567-2147.* Site of 1811 battle in which soldiers and local militia led by General William H.

Harrison, territorial governor of Indiana, defeated a confederation of Native Americans headed by The Prophet, brother of Tecumseh. Wabash Heritage Trail begins here. (See SPECIAL EVENTS) (Daily) **$**

Tippecanoe County Historical Museum. *909 South St.* Phone 765/476-8411. Collection of Americana, period rooms, topic exhibits, housed in an English Gothic-style mansion (1852). (Tues-Sun; closed holidays; also Jan) **$$**

Wolf Park. *4008 E 800 N, Battle Ground (47920). 10 miles NE via I-65, exit 178 or Hwy 43.* Phone 765/567-2265. Education/research facility; home to several packs of wolves, a small herd of bison, some coyotes, and foxes. See wolves close at hand as they eat and socialize. (May-Nov, Tue-Sun afternoons; closed holidays) Also "wolf howl" (all year, Sat evenings; inquire for hours). **$$**

Special Events

Feast of the Hunters' Moon. *Fort Ouiatenon (see), 3129 S River Rd, West Lafayette (47906).* Phone 765/476-8402. Reenactment of life 250 years ago. Features French, English, and Native American lifestyles. Early Oct.

Fiddlers' Gathering. *Tippecanoe Battlefield (see), 200 Battleground Rd, Lafayette.* Phone 765/742-1419. Old-time folk and country musicians from across the country. Late June.

Limited-Service Hotels

★ **FAIRFIELD INN.** *4000 Hwy 26 E, Lafayette (47905).* Phone 317/449-0083; toll-free 888/236-2427; fax 317/449-0083. www.fairfieldinn.com. 79 rooms, 3 story. Complimentary continental breakfast. Check-out noon. Indoor pool, whirlpool. **$**

★ ★ **RADISSON INN.** *4343 Hwy 26 E, Lafayette (47905).* Phone 765/447-0575; fax 765/447-0901. www.radisson.com. This hotel offers all the expected amenities, including an indoor pool, whirlpool, sauna, sundeck, lobby restaurant, lounge, and more. Its location puts it near golf, shopping, and other attractions. 124 rooms, 6 story. Pets accepted, some restrictions; fee. Check-out noon. Restaurant, bar. Indoor pool, whirlpool. **$**

★ **SIGNATURE INN.** *4320 Hwy 26 E, Lafayette (47905).* Phone 765/447-4142; toll-free 800/822; fax 765/447-4142. www.signatureinn.com. 150 rooms, 2 story. Complimentary continental breakfast. Check-out noon. Pool. **$**

★ ★ **UNIVERSITY INN CONFERENCE CENTER AND SUITES.** *3001 Northwestern Ave, West Lafayette (47906).* Phone 765/463-5511; toll-free 800/777-9808; fax 765/497-3850. www.uiccwl .com. With an indoor and outdoor pool, exercise facilities, and more, this hotel is the perfect stop for those traveling for business or pleasure. It is located near a shopping mall, restaurants, and Purdue University (see). 171 rooms, 3 story. Check-out 11 am. Restaurant, bar. Fitness room. Indoor pool, outdoor pool, whirlpool. Airport transportation available. **$**

Specialty Lodging

The following lodging establishment is approved by Mobil Travel Guide but, due to its unique and individualized nature has not been given a traditional Mobil Star rating. Included in this listing you may find bed-and-breakfasts, limited-service inns, guest ranches, and other unique hotel properties.

LOEB HOUSE B & B. *708 Cincinnati St, Lafayette (47901).* Phone 765/420-7737; fax 765/420-7805. www. loebhouseinn.com. Built in 1882; antiques. 5 rooms, 3 story. Pets accepted, some restrictions. Complimentary full breakfast. Check-in 4 pm, check-out 11 am. **$**

Lawrenceburg (D-4)

Population 4,685
Information Dearborn County Chamber of Commerce, 555 Eads Pkwy E, 47025; phone 812/537-0814 or toll-free 800/322-8198

Restaurant

★ **WHISKY'S.** *334 Front St, Lawrenceburg (47025).* Phone 812/537-4239. Dining in two restored buildings (circa 1835 and 1850) joined together. Lunch, dinner. Closed Sun; Easter, July 4, Dec 25. Bar. Children's menu. **$$**

Lincoln Boyhood National Memorial & Lincoln State Park (F-2)

See also Santa Claus

4 miles W of Santa Claus on Hwy 162. Phone 812/937-4541; toll-free 800/264-4223.

Lincoln spent his boyhood years (1816-1830) in this area, reading books, clerking at James Gentry's store, and helping his father with farm work. When Lincoln was 21, his family moved to Illinois, where his political career began. The 200-acre wooded and landscaped park includes the grave of Nancy Hanks Lincoln, mother of Abraham Lincoln. She was 35 years old, and Abraham was 9, when she died on October 5, 1818.

The memorial visitor center has information available on the park, including the cabin site memorial, the park's 2 miles of walking trails, and the gravesite. A film is shown at the visitor center every hour depicting Lincoln's Indiana years. Nearby, on the original Thomas Lincoln tract, is the Lincoln Living Historical Farm, with a furnished log cabin similar to the one the Lincolns lived in, log buildings, animals, and crops of a pioneer farm. Costumed pioneers carry out family living and farming activities typical of an early-19th-century farm. Farm (May-Sept). (Daily; closed Jan 1, Thanksgiving, Dec 25)

The park includes approximately 1,700 acres with a 58-acre lake. Swimming, bathhouse, fishing, boating (no motors; rentals); hiking trails; picnic areas, concessions; primitive and improved camping, cabins, group camp. Naturalist service (June-Aug). Phone 812/937-4710 or 812/937-4541.

The Lincoln Amphitheatre has an outdoor musical/theatrical production about the life of Lincoln when he lived in Indiana between the ages of 7 and 21. Drama is in a covered amphitheater near the site of Lincoln's home. (Mid-June-mid-Aug, Tues-Sun) **$$**

Logansport (B-3)

See also Kokomo, Peru

Founded 1828
Population 19,684
Elevation 620 ft
Area Code 574
Zip 46947
Information Logansport/Cass County Chamber of Commerce, 300 E Broadway, Suite 103; phone 574/753-6388
Web site www.logan-casschamber.com

Located at the confluence of the Wabash and Eel rivers, Logansport is situated in the agricultural heartland. An active trading center for more than a century, batteries, auto-related components, and cement are among the commodities produced here. The rivers and many nearby lakes offer fishing and hunting.

The town was named in honor of James Logan, nephew of the famous Shawnee chief, Tecumseh. Captain Logan was fatally wounded by British-led Native Americans after having served with distinction as leader of a company of Native American scouts fighting for the United States in the War of 1812.

What to See and Do

Cass County Historical Museum (Jerolaman-Long House). *1004 E Market St. Phone 574/753-3866.* Antique china collection, Native American artifacts, paintings, local memorabilia. (Tues-Sat, first Sun of month; closed holidays) **FREE**

France Park. *4505 W Hwy 24 (46947). 4 miles W via Hwy 24. Phone 574/753-2928.* A 500-acre park with waterfall; 100-year-old log cabin at entrance. Swimming beach (Memorial Day-Labor Day), scuba diving, fishing; nature trail; miniature golf (fee); rock-hounding; cross-country skiing (fee), snowmobiling, ice fishing, ice skating. Picnicking (shelters). Primitive and improved camping, camp store. (Daily) **$**

Indiana Beach. *306 Indiana Beach Dr, Monticello. Approximately 20 miles W via Hwy 24. Phone 574/583-4141. www.indianabeach.com.* Rides, games, arcades; beach, swimming; shops. Cottages and camping. Amusement area (mid-May-Labor Day, daily; early May, early Sept, weekends only). **$**

Limited-Service Hotel

★ ★ **HOLIDAY INN.** *3550 E Market St, Logansport (46947). Phone 574/753-6351; fax 574/722-1568. www.holiday-inn.com.* 95 rooms, 2 story. Pets accepted. Check-out noon. Restaurant, bar. Pool. Airport transportation available. **$**

Madison (E-4)

Settled 1809
Population 12,004
Elevation 497 ft
Area Code 812
Zip 47250
Information Madison Area Convention and Visitors Bureau, 301 E Main St; phone 812/265-2956 or toll-free 800/559-2956
Web site www.visitmadison.org

Between the Ohio River and Crooked Creek, the settlement of Madison grew rapidly during the river transport days of the 1850s and was briefly the largest city in Indiana, with a population of 5,000. Many of the town's fine homes reflect the architecture of pre-Civil War days in the South. The 555-acre campus of Hanover College (1827) overlooks the river.

What to See and Do

Clifty Falls State Park. *1501 Green Rd (47250). 1 mile W on Hwy 56. Phone 812/265-1331.* From a high, wooded plateau, this 1,360-acre park offers a view of the Ohio River and its traffic, as well as hills on the Kentucky shore. It also contains waterfalls of Clifty Creek and Little Clifty Creek, bedrock exposures, numerous fossil beds, and a deep boulder-strewn canyon reached by the sun only at high noon; variety of wildlife, regional winter vulture roost. Swimming pool (Memorial Day-Labor Day; fee); tennis; picnicking (shelters, fireplaces), concession, playground. Inn in park has lodgings all year (for reservations, contact PO Box 387, phone 812/265-4135). Primitive and developed camping (fee). Naturalist service, nature center. **$**

Dr. William Hutchings Hospital Museum. *120 W 3rd St. Phone 812/265-2967.* A 19th-century Greek Revival building, which served as office and hospital of a "horse-and-buggy" doctor in the late 1800s. Furnishings, surgical tools, and medical library. (Mid-Apr-Oct, daily) **$**

Jeremiah Sullivan House. *304 W 2nd St. Phone 812/265-2967.* (1818) Federal-style furnished home; pioneer kitchen, smokehouse, bake oven. (Mid-Apr-Oct, daily) **$$** Nearby is

> **Talbot-Hyatt Pioneer Garden.** *Madison.* Frontier garden including many regional plants and flowers. Some plants brought from Virginia. (Daily) **FREE**

Lanier State Historic Site. *511 W 1st St. Between Elm and Vine. Phone 812/265-3526.* Greek Revival mansion completed in 1844 for James F. D. Lanier, a financier who loaned the state of Indiana a total of $1,040,000 when its treasury was in need during the Civil War. Some original possessions. (Tues-Sun; closed holidays) **DONATION**

Madison Train Station Museum. *615 W 1st St (47250). Phone 812/265-2335.* Eight-sided railroad station from the late 19th century features two-story waiting room. Includes various train memorabilia. (Daily) **$$**

Schofield House. *217 W 2nd St. Phone 812/265-4759.* (1809-1814) Two-story, handmade, sun-dried brick tavern-house; early Federal style. (Apr-Oct, Mon-Tues, Thurs-Sun; candlelight tours by appointment) **$$**

Special Events

Madison in Bloom. *615 W 1st St, Madison (47250). Phone 812/265-2335.* Visit several private courtyard gardens throughout the historic downtown during peak spring color. Last weekend in Apr-first weekend in May.

Regatta and Governor's Cup Race. *Madison. Phone 812/265-5000.* Hydroplanes compete on the Ohio River. Late June-early July.

Restaurant

★ **KEY WEST SHRIMP HOUSE.** *117 Ferry St (Hwy 56), Madison (47250). Phone 812/265-2831.* Century-old building; fireplace. Lunch, dinner. Closed Mon. Children's menu. **$**

Marion (B-3)

See also Peru, Wabash

Settled 1826
Population 31,320
Area Code 765
Information Marion/Grant County Convention and Visitors Bureau, 217 S Adams St, 46952; phone 765/668-5435 or toll-free 800/662-9474
Web site www.jamesdeancountry.com

An industrial center and farm trading town, Marion lies on the Mississinewa River. Its principal industrial products are automotive parts, video displays and components, plastics, glass, and paper and wire products. Indiana Wesleyan University (1920) is located here.

What to See and Do

Fairmount, Hometown of James Dean. *203 E Washington (46928). S via I-69, exit 55 then W on Hwy 26. Phone 765/948-4555.* (Screen idol 1950s). In Fairmount are

>**Fairmount Historical Museum.** *203 E Washington St, Fairmount (46928). Phone 765/948-4555. www.jamesdeanartifacts.com.* Contains the most complete collection of articles of James Dean. Also here are exhibits by Jim Davis, creator of the cartoon cat Garfield. (Mar-Nov, Mon-Sat, Sun afternoons; rest of year, by appointment) **$**

>**James Dean Memorial Gallery.** *6508 E Museum Blvd, Marion. Phone 765/998-2080. www.jamesdeangallery.com.* Extensive collection of memorabilia and archives dealing with the career of James Dean. Exhibit includes clothing from his films, high school yearbooks, original movie posters from around the world. (Daily; closed Jan 1, Thanksgiving, Dec 25) **$$**

Matthews Covered Bridge. *3rd and Front sts, Matthews (46957). 5 miles E via Hwy 18, S via I-69 then E on Hwy 26. Phone 765/998-2928.* Cumberland Covered Bridge (1876-1877), 175-foot long, spans the Mississinewa River.

Miami Indian Historical Site. *3750 W County Rd 600 N (46952). 7 miles NW via Hwy 15, then W on 600 N St. Phone 765/668-5435.* Large Native American cemetery with memorials; hiking trails, fishing, hunting. (Daily) **FREE**

Mississinewa Lake. *County Roads 625 E. and 500 S., Peru (46970). 15 miles NW, off Hwy 150 Phone 765/473-5946.* (See PERU)

Special Events

Fairmount Museum Days/Remembering James Dean. *Fairmount Historical Museum, 203 E Washington St, Fairmount (46928). Phone 765/948-4555. www.jamesdeanartifacts.com.* Large car show, including 2,500 classic and custom autos; James Dean look-alike contest; 1950s dance contest; parade; downtown street fair. Last full weekend in Sept.

Marion Easter Pageant. *Marion Coliseum between Washington and Branson sts. 118 N Washington St, Marion (46952). Phone 765/664-3947. www.easterpageant.com.* Cast (2,000). Good Friday evening, Easter Sunday morning.

Mississinewa 1812. *402 S Washington St, Marion (46953). Phone toll-free 800/822-1812.* Battle re-enactment with period food, crafts, and storytelling. Mid-Oct.

Limited-Service Hotels

★ ★ **CLARION HOTEL.** *501 E 4th St, Marion (46952). Phone 765/668-8801; fax 765/662-6827. www.clarion.com.* 121 rooms, 5 story. Check-out noon. Restaurant, bar. Pool. **$**

★ **COMFORT INN.** *1345 N Baldwin Ave, Marion (46952). Phone 765/651-1006; toll-free 800/445-1210; fax 765/651-0145. www.comfortsuites.com.* 62 rooms. Pets accepted, some restrictions; fee. Complimentary continental breakfast. Check-in 3 pm, check-out noon. Fitness room. Indoor pool, outdoor pool, whirlpool. **$**

Merrillville (A-2)

Population 30,560
Elevation 661 ft
Area Code 219
Zip 46410
Information Chamber of Commerce, 255 W 80th Pl; phone 219/769-8180
Web site www.merrillvillecoc.org

Once a thriving stop-off point for the many wagon trains headed west, Merrillville has abandoned its rural beginnings to become a regional center of commerce; it also has established its identity as a leader in commercial-industrial development. Area parks and nearby agricultural lands provide pleasant surroundings.

What to See and Do

Lemon Lake County Park. *5016 W 133rd Ave (46307). 1 mile E via Hwy 30, then S on Hwy 55, SW of Crown Point. Phone 219/769-7275.* Approximately 290 acres of recreation facilities adjacent to Cedar Lake. Park offers fishing, paddleboats; basketball and tennis courts, volleyball, softball fields; hiking/fitness/jogging trails; picnicking (shelters). Arboretum. (Daily) **$$**

Star Plaza Theatre. *8001 Delaware Pl (46410). I-65 and Hwy 30. Phone 219/769-6600. www. starplazatheatre.com.* Theater (3,400 seats) hosts top-name performers. Bill changes weekly and offers a variety of entertainers from comedians to rock 'n' roll, jazz, country, and pop artists. (See RADISSON HOTEL AT STAR PLAZA) **$$$$**

Limited-Service Hotels

★ **FAIRFIELD INN.** *8275 Georgia St, Merrillville (46410). Phone 219/736-0500; toll-free 800/228-2800; fax 219/736-5116. www.fairfieldinn.com.* 132 rooms, 3 story. Complimentary continental breakfast. Check-in 3 pm, check-out noon. Pool. **$**

★ ★ **RADISSON HOTEL AT STAR PLAZA.** *800 E 81st Ave, Merrillville (46410). Phone 219/769-6311; toll-free 800/333-3333; fax 219/769-1462. www. radisson.com.* Just 45 minutes from downtown Chicago, this hotel is a worthy destination in its own right. The waterfall and tropical garden in the atrium will enthrall the kids along with the indoor/outdoor pools. Adults may be more interested in the live entertainment offered in the adjacent Star Plaza Theatre or the in-house Wisecrackers Comedy Club. Just off Interstate 65, the hotel is near a bounty of malls, movie theaters, and restaurants and is convenient to the Indiana Dunes National Lakeshore and Deep River Water Park. 347 rooms, 4 story. Check-in 3 pm, check-out 11 am. High-speed Internet access. Two restaurants, two bars. Children's activity center. Fitness room. Indoor pool, outdoor pool, whirlpool. Business center. **$$**

Restaurant

★ ★ **CAFÉ VENEZIA.** *405 W 81st Ave, Merrillville (46410). Phone 219/736-2203.* Italian menu. Lunch, dinner. Closed Sun. Casual attire. **$$**

Michigan City (A-2)

See also Indiana Dunes National Lakeshore, Indiana Dunes State Park, La Porte

Founded 1833
Population 32,900
Elevation 600 ft
Area Code 219
Zip 46360
Information La Porte County Convention and Visitors Bureau, 1503 S Meer Rd; phone toll-free 800/634-2650. There is a visitor center directly off I-94, exit 40B.
Web site www.harborcountry-in.org

This is Indiana's summer playground on the southeast shore of Lake Michigan. In the center of the famous Indiana sand dunes region, Michigan City offers miles of fine beaches. For fishermen, the lake offers coho salmon (late Mar-Nov), chinook salmon, lake trout, and perch.

What to See and Do

Barker Mansion. *631 Washington St. Phone 219/873-1520.* (1900) A 38-room mansion modeled after an English manor house; marble fireplaces; Tiffany glass; Italian sunken garden. Tours (June-Oct, daily; rest of year, Mon-Fri). **$**

Blue Chip Casino. *2 Easy St (46360). Phone toll-free 888/879-7711. www.bluechip-casino.com.* Located just south of the Michigan-Indiana border and about 60 miles east of Chicago, the Blue Chip Riverboat Casino has more than 1,500 slot machines and 45 gaming tables, including craps, blackjack, roulette, Let It Ride, and Caribbean stud poker. A new poker room hosts games of seven card stud, Omaha, and Texas hold 'em. Due to changes in Indiana law, riverboats are no longer required to cruise, so the ship is dockside, open 8 am-3 am Sunday-Thursday and until 5 am Friday-Saturday. An adjacent pavilion provides the usual restaurants and lounges. Other attractions in the area include a decent outlet mall and, of course, the beautiful Lake Michigan coastline.

You might consider adding in a visit to the Indiana Dunes National Lakeshore (see) or the Michigan Dunes state park, or continue farther up the coastline to the popular resort towns of New Buffalo, Lakeside, and Union Pier. (Daily) **FREE**

John G. Blank Center for the Arts. *312 E 8th St. Phone 219/874-4900.* Paintings, sculptures, and graphic art exhibits of regional, national, and international origin. (Mon-Sat; closed holidays) **DONATION**

Lighthouse Place Outlet Center. *601 Wabash St (46360). Sixth and Wabash sts. Phone 219/879-6506.* More than 135 outlet stores. (Daily)

Washington Park. *115 Lakeshore Dr (46360). N end of Franklin St. Phone 219/873-1506 (park).* Swimming beach, yacht basin, marina, fishing; picnic facilities, concession; tennis courts; observation tower. Zoo (daily). Recreational facilities (daily). Amphitheater Thurs evenings, weekend band concerts (summer). Senior citizens center (Mon-Fri). Some fees (Mar-Dec). **$$** Also here is

> **Old Lighthouse Museum.** *Heisman Rd, Michigan City. In the park. Phone 219/872-6133.* (1858) Marine exhibits, Fresnel lens, shipbuilding tools, local history displays. Site of launching of first submarine on Great Lakes in 1845. (Mar-Dec, Tues-Sun; closed holidays) **$**

Special Events

Lakefront Music Fest. *Washington Park* (see), *115 Lakeshore Dr, Michigan City (46360). Phone 219/873-1506.* Mid-July.

Michigan City Summer Festival. *613 E Garfield St, Michigan City (46360). Citywide. Phone 219/874-9775.* Parades, concerts, fireworks. Early July.

Limited-Service Hotel

★ ★ **BLUE CHIP CASINO & HOTEL.** *2 Easy St, Michigan City (46360). Phone 219/879-7711; toll-free 888/879-7711; fax 219/879-2699. www.bluechip-casino .com.* The sizeable casino offers a full range of gambling opportunities and is connected to the hotel by way of meeting rooms and restaurants, so that you never have to go outside to get from your room to the casino. The hotel, casino, restaurants, and bar all have a fresh, contemporary décor and a very good filtration system—the absence of a heavy tobacco odor is noticeable. 188 rooms, 7 story. Check-in 3 pm, check-out noon. Restaurant, bar. Fitness room. Indoor pool, whirlpool. Business center. Casino. (see BLUE CHIP CASINO) **$**

⬛ ⬛ ⬛ ⬛

Specialty Lodgings

The following lodging establishments are approved by Mobil Travel Guide, but due to their unique and individualized nature have not been given a traditional Mobil Star rating. Included in this listing you may find bed-and-breakfasts, limited-service inns, guest ranches, and other unique hotel properties.

CREEKWOOD INN. *5727 N 600 W, Michigan City (46360). Phone 219/872-8357; toll-free 800/400-1981; fax 219/872-8357. www.creekwoodinn.com.* The feel of a country cottage permeates even the new wing of this hotel set in a 33-acre wooded park filled with flowers and streams. Built in the style of an English cottage, each room boasts unique characteristics—some have a fireplace, others a private patio, and all have charm and distinctive décor. Relax in an overstuffed chair in the conservatory, or get rid of that overstuffed feeling by exercising in the fitness room that overlooks the conservatory. Leisure and business travelers are catered to with nearby attractions and in-house services. 13 rooms, 2 story. Closed early Jan. Complimentary continental breakfast. Check-in 4 pm, check-out noon. Fitness room. Whirlpool. **$$**

⬛

DUNE LAND BEACH INN. *3311 Pottawattomie Trail, Michigan City (46360). Phone 219/874-7729; toll-free 800/423-7729; fax 219/874-0053. www. dunelandbeachinn.com.* Turn-of-the-century inn built in 1892; country atmosphere. 9 rooms, 2 story. Pets accepted. Complimentary continental breakfast. Check-in 3-6 pm, check-out 11 am. Restaurant. Beach. **$**

⬛ ⬛

Restaurant

★ ★ **LUCREZIA.** *428 S Calumet Rd, Chesterton (46304). Phone 219/926-5829.* Italian menu. Lunch, dinner. Bar. Casual attire. Outdoor seating. **$$**

Mishawaka (A-3)

See also Elkhart, Goshen, South Bend

Founded 1832
Population 46,557
Elevation 720 ft
Area Code 574
Information South Bend-Mishawaka Convention and Visitors Bureau, 401 E Colfax Ave, Suite 310, PO Box 1677, South Bend 46634-1677; phone 574/234-0051 or toll-free 800/828-7881
Web site www.livethelegends.org

Directly east of South Bend, Mishawaka is mainly an industrial city. Divided by the St. Joseph River, it was named for a beautiful daughter of Chief Elkhart of the Shawnee, who lived in this region before 1800.

In the southwestern part of the city is a Belgian quarter populated by some 6,000 Flemish-Dutch speaking citizens, most of whom came to Mishawaka following World War I.

What to See and Do

Hannah Lindahl Children's Museum. *1402 S Main St. Phone 574/254-4540.* Hands-on exhibits with Native American and historical items. Also re-created here is a brick street of stores from the 1800s, a traditional Japanese house, and a Survive Alive House that teaches fire prevention. (Sept-May, Tues-Fri; June, Tues-Thurs; closed July-Aug) **$**

Merrifield Park. *1122 Lincoln Way W. Phone 574/258-1664.* This 31-acre park features Shiojiri Niwa Friendship Gardens, a 1 1/2-acre Japanese garden. Also swimming, water slide, fishing, boating (launch); ice skating; playground; picnic area. (Daily) (See SPECIAL EVENT) **$$**

Special Event

Summerfest. *Merrifield Park* (see), *1122 Lincoln Way W, Mishawaka (46544). Phone 574/258-1664.* Food, arts and crafts, entertainment. Fourth Sat in June.

Muncie (C-4)

See also Anderson, New Castle

Founded 1818
Population 67,430
Elevation 950 ft
Area Code 765
Information Muncie-Delaware County Convention and Visitors Bureau, 425 N High St, 47305; phone 765/284-2700 or toll-free 800/568-6862
Web site www.muncievisitorsbureau.org

This area was once the home of the Munsee tribe of the Delaware. The town became an agricultural trading center during the first half of the 19th century; with the construction of railroads and the discovery of natural gas, it developed into an industrial city. Many industrial plants are located here.

Ball Corporation, which for years produced the famous Ball jars, maintains its international headquarters in Muncie. The five Ball brothers took an active part in the city's life and in many philanthropic undertakings. They also supported a number of other industrial enterprises and contributed substantially to Ball State University (see).

Muncie became nationally famous in the 1930s as the subject of Robert and Helen Lynd's sociological studies of a "typical" small city: "Middletown" and "Middletown in Transition."

What to See and Do

Appeal to the Great Spirit. *Walnut St and Granville Ave. N bank of White River. Phone 765/747-4845.* Copy of Cyrus Dallin's famous statue, which stands in front of the Boston Museum of Fine Arts.

Ball State University. *2000 University Ave. Phone 765/285-5683. www.bsu.edu.* (1918) (20,300 students) Purchased by the Ball family and presented to the state of Indiana. Campus has a state-of-the-art telecommunication production facility (phone 765/285-1481); planetarium and observatory (phone 765/285-8871 or 765/285-8862; free). Tours. (Mon-Fri) Also on campus are

Christy Woods. *2000 University Ave, Muncie. Phone 765/285-8839.* A 17-acre biology department laboratory with arboretum, gardens, and greenhouses. Extensive assemblage includes the Wheeler Orchid Collection. Tours (by appointment). **FREE**

Museum of Art. *Fine Arts Building, Riverside Ave and Warwick Rd, Muncie. Phone 765/285-5242.* Collections of 18th- and 19th-century paintings, prints, and drawings; contemporary works; changing exhibits. (Tues-Sun) **FREE**

Minnetrista Cultural Center. *1200 N Minnetrista Pkwy. Phone 765/282-4848.* A 70,000-square-foot facility exhibiting the history, art, and industry of east central Indiana. Changing exhibits feature Native American history, the family, technology, and art. Nationally touring science exhibits offered each spring and fall. Floral gardens, landscaped lawns, and a historic apple orchard surround the center. (Daily; closed Dec 25) **$$**

Muncie Children's Museum. *515 S High St. Phone 765/286-1660.* Exhibits allow visitors to explore the world around them in this completely hands-on museum. Outdoor learning center. Changing exhibits. Gift shop. (Tues-Sun; closed holidays) **$$**

Oakhurst Gardens. *1200 N Minnetrista Pkwy. Phone 765/282-4848; toll-free 800/428-5887.* Six-acre gardens house many naturalized plants. Renovated home (1895) of George, Frances, and Elizabeth Ball has exhibits on gardens and natural history. One-hour guided tours. (Tues-Sun) **$$**

Prairie Creek Reservoir. *7801 S County Rd 560 E, Selma. 6 miles SE on Burlington Dr. Phone 765/747-4776.* A 2,333-acre park with a 1,252-acre lake. Boating (70 mph limit), fishing, swimming (Memorial Day-Labor Day). Picnicking, playground, camping. Some fees.

Special Events

Delaware County Fair. *Fairgrounds, Wheeling Ave, Muncie (47303). Phone 765/284-2700.* Nine days mid-late July.

Muncie Dragway. *7901 E State Rd 28-67, Albany (47320). Phone 765/789-8470.* 5 miles NE on Hwy 67 near Albany. Drag racing. Apr-Oct. Sat.

Limited-Service Hotels

★ ★ **CLUBHOUSE INN.** *420 S High St, Muncie (47305). Phone 765/741-7777; fax 765/741-0067.* Built in 1921, this hotel offers a lot of history and culture along with modern amenities and facilities, including a restaurant, lounge, indoor pool, and more. It is located in downtown Muncie, near many attractions, restaurants, and shops. 130 rooms, 7 story. Pets accepted, some restrictions; fee. Check-out noon. Restaurant, bar. Indoor pool, whirlpool. **$**

★ ★ **RAMADA INN.** *3400 S Madison St, Muncie (47302). Phone 765/288-1911; toll-free 800/272-6232; fax 765/282-9458. www.ramada.com.* 148 rooms, 2 story. Pets accepted, some restrictions; fee. Complimentary continental breakfast. Check-out noon. Restaurant, bar. Pool. **$**

★ **SIGNATURE INN.** *3400 N Chadam Ln, Muncie (47304). Phone 765/284-4200; toll-free 800/822-5252; fax 765/284-4200. www.signatureinn.com.* 101 rooms, 2 story. Complimentary continental breakfast. Check-out noon. Pool. **$**

Nappanee (A-3)

See also Elkhart, Goshen, Warsaw

Founded 1874
Population 6,710
Elevation 878 ft
Area Code 219
Zip 46550
Information Amish Acres Visitor Center, 1600 W Market St; phone 219/773-4188 or toll-free 800/800-4942
Web site www.amishacres.com

Many Amish-run farms dot the countryside surrounding Nappanee. Rich, productive soil makes agricultural crops a major part of the economy; local industry manufactures kitchen cabinets, mobile homes, recreational vehicles, vitreous steel products, and furniture.

What to See and Do

★ **Amish Acres.** *Hwy 6 W (46550). 1 mile W on Hwy 6. Phone 219/773-4188; toll-free 800/800-4942. www. amishacres.com.* Restored Amish homestead and farm. Guided tours, horse-drawn rides, music theater (fees); bakery, restaurant; inns (see); shops. (Daily) (see SPECIAL EVENT) **FREE**

Special Event

Amish Acres Arts & Crafts Festival. *Amish Acres* (see), *252 W Market St, Nappanee (46550). Phone 219/773-4188; toll-free 800/800-4942. www.amishacres.com.* Entries from many states; paintings, ceramics, jewelry; entertainment, dancing, feasts. Mid-Aug.

Limited-Service Hotels

★ ★ **THE INN AT AMISH ACRES.** *1234 W Market St, Nappanee (46550). Phone 219/773-2011; toll-free 800/800-4942; fax 219/773-2078. www. amishacres.com.* 64 rooms, 2 story. Complimentary continental breakfast. Check-out noon. Pool. Airport transportation available. **$**

★ ★ **THE NAPPANEE INN.** *2004 W Market St, Nappanee (46550). Phone 219/773-5999; toll-free 800/800-4942; fax 219/773-5988. www.amishacres.com.* Part of a restored 80-acre farm. 66 rooms, 2 story. Complimentary continental breakfast. Check-out noon. Pool. **$**

Nashville (D-3)

See also Bloomington, Brown County State Park, Columbus

Population 825
Elevation 629 ft
Area Code 812
Zip 47448
Information Brown County Convention and Visitors Bureau, Main and Van Buren sts; phone 812/988-7303 or toll-free 800/753-3255
Web site www.nashville-indiana.com

Driving south from Indianapolis on State Road 135, the scenery quickly evolves from bland to beautiful, as the pavement, at first level and unbending, begins to rise and fall and gently curve. On either side of the road, wide-open farm fields give way to dense forests. Within an hour, travelers arrive at the charming village of Nashville, situated in the heart of Brown County—also known as "The Art Colony of the Midwest," a moniker earned in the early 1900s when the area was one of six art colonies established in the United States. The acclaimed impressionist painter T. C. Steele moved here in 1907, and legend has it that he would rise each day at 4 am and venture out into the woods so that he could capture on canvas the dawn's first glint of light. Steele's homestead, "The House of the Singing Winds," has been preserved as a state historic site (see). Many artists followed Steele's lead and moved to Brown County, and the arts community remains strong today, with the streets of Nashville lined by shops and galleries featuring the works of local artists and craftspeople.

Like the larger city of the same name, Nashville possesses a vibrant country music scene. Two of the more popular venues include The Little Nashville Opry and the Country Time Music Hall. Theater lovers flock to the Brown County Playhouse, which is operated in conjunction with the Indiana University Department of Theatre and Drama; the university is only 18 miles to the west. Nashville has a wide variety of accommodation options, including numerous inns and bed-and-breakfasts, but many visitors to the area seek solitude in cabins nestled deep in the woods. Fishing, hiking, biking, and horseback riding are popular activities, with Brown County State Park (see) offering over 80 miles of trails within 16,000 acres of parkland.

What to See and Do

Bill Monroe Bluegrass Hall of Fame. *5163 State Rd 135 N, Bean Blossom. 5 miles N via Hwy 135. Phone 812/988-6422. www.beanblossom.com.* Museum of memorabilia from bluegrass and country and western performers; log cabin. Special events throughout the summer. (June-Oct, Tues-Sun) **$$$**

Brown County Art Gallery. *1 Artist Dr. Phone 812/988-4609.* Permanent and changing exhibits of Indiana art. (Daily; closed Jan 1, Dec 25) **FREE**

Brown County Art Guild. *48 S Van Buren St. Phone 812/988-6185.* Changing exhibits; Goth estate collection. (Mar-Dec, daily; rest of year, by appointment only) **DONATION**

County Museum. *Artist Dr and E Main St. One block E of courthouse. Phone 812/988-8547.* Weaving and spinning room; antiques; log cabin (circa 1845); county doctor's office and furnishings; blacksmith shop, Old Log Jail (fee). (Sat-Sun; daily by appointment) **$$**

Hoosier National Forest. *811 Constitution Ave. S of town. Phone 812/275-5987.* (See BEDFORD)

Ski World. *2887 State Rd 46 W (47448). 4 miles W via Hwy 46. Phone 812/988-6638.* Two chair lifts, four rope tows; patrol, school, rentals, snowmaking; cafeteria, lounge. Longest run 3,400 feet; vertical drop 325 feet. Dry toboggan slide; summer amusement area. (Apr-Oct, mid-Dec-early Mar, daily) **$$**

T. C. Steele State Historic Site. *Belmont. 8 miles W on Hwy 46 to Belmont, then 1 1/2 miles S on T. C. Steele Rd. Phone 812/988-2785.* Home and studio of American impressionist artist Theodore C. Steele (1847-1926). Site includes 15 acres of gardens, four hiking trails, and exhibits of more than 60 Steele canvases. (Mid-Mar-Dec, Tues-Sun; closed holidays)

Yellowwood State Forest. *772 Yellowwood Lake Rd (47448). 7 miles W on Hwy 46. Phone 812/988-7945.* A 23,326-acre forest with three lakes. Fishing, boating (ramp, rentals). Hiking trails, picnicking (shelter), playground; primitive camping, horseback riders' camp. **FREE**

Special Events

Brown County Playhouse. *800 E 7th St, Bloomington (47405). Phone 812/855-1103.* Presents four theater productions. June-Aug, Wed-Sun; Sept-Oct, Fri-Sun.

Log cabin tour. *10 N Van Buren St, Nashville (47448). Phone 812/988-7303.* Unescorted tours of five log homes in Brown County. Contact the Convention and Visitors Bureau. Early June.

Limited-Service Hotels

★ ★ **BROWN COUNTY INN.** *Hwy 46, Nashville (47448). Phone 812/988-2291; toll-free 800/772-5249; fax 812/988-8312. www.browncountyinn.com.* This country inn offers its guests many recreational facilities, including volleyball and basketball courts,

mini-golf, a pool, and a game room. The property is located within walking distance to shopping and other attractions. 99 rooms, 2 story. Check-out noon. Restaurant (see HARVEST DINING ROOM), bar. Indoor pool, outdoor pool. Tennis. **$**

★ ★ **THE SEASONS LODGE.** *560 Hwy 46 E, Nashville (47448). Phone 812/988-2284; toll-free 800/365-7327.* 80 rooms, 2 story. Check-out noon. Restaurant, bar. Indoor pool, outdoor pool. Adjacent to Brown County State Park (see). **$**

Specialty Lodging

The following lodging establishment is approved by Mobil Travel Guide but, due to its unique and individualized nature has not been given a traditional Mobil Star rating. Included in this listing you may find bed-and-breakfasts, limited-service inns, guest ranches, and other unique hotel properties.

CORNERSTONE INN. *54 E Franklin St, Nashville (47448). Phone 812/988-0300; toll-free 888/383-0300; fax 812/988-0200. www.cornerstoneinn.com.* 20 rooms, 3 story. Complimentary full breakfast. Check-in 3 pm, check-out 11 am. **$**

Restaurants

★ ★ **HARVEST DINING ROOM.** *Hwy 46, Nashville (47448). Phone 812/988-2291; toll-free 800/772-5249; fax 812/988-8312. www. browncountyinn.com.* Breakfast, lunch, dinner, Sun brunch. Bar. Children's menu. Outdoor seating. **$$**

★ **NASHVILLE HOUSE.** *Main St at Van Buren, Nashville (47448). Phone 812/988-4554; fax 812/988-2883.* Limited menu. Lunch, dinner. Closed Tues, except in Oct; also late Dec-early Jan. Children's menu. Bake shop. **$$**

★ **THE ORDINARY.** *Van Buren St, Nashville (47448). Phone 812/988-6166; fax 812/988-2883.* Lunch, dinner. Closed Mon, except in Oct; holidays. Bar. Children's menu. **$$**

New Albany (F-3)

See also Corydon, Jeffersonville, Wyandotte

Founded 1813
Population 37,603
Elevation 450 ft
Area Code 812
Zip 47150
Information Southern Indiana Convention and Tourism Bureau, 315 Southern Indiana Ave, 47130; phone 812/282-6654 or toll-free 800/552-3842
Web site www.sunnysideoflouisville.org

Opposite Louisville, Kentucky, on the Ohio River, New Albany has the first public high school in Indiana, established in 1853. In the last century, this city was famous for its shipyards. Two of the best-known Mississippi and Ohio rivers steamers, the *Robert E. Lee* and the *Eclipse*, were built here. Today, it is a plywood center; other principal products are furniture, machine tools, electronic equipment, frozen food, and fertilizer.

What to See and Do

Blue River Canoe Trips. *Main St, Milltown. Approximately 20 miles W via Hwy 64, at bridge and dam. Phone 812/365-2705.* Canoe trips (7 miles-58 miles), some include camping (2 days-4 days). (Apr-Oct) Contact Cave Country Canoes, PO Box 145, Milltown 47145. **$$$$**

Carnegie Center for Art and History. *201 E Spring St. Phone 812/944-7336.* History and heritage of the area; changing exhibits. Hand-carved animated diorama. Art gallery has works by local and regional artists; lectures, demonstrations, workshops. (Tues-Sat; closed holidays) **FREE**

Culbertson Mansion State Historic Site. *914 E Main St. Phone 812/944-9600.* A 25-room, Second Empire/Victorian residence built in 1869. Period furnishings; cantilevered three-story staircase, hand-painted frescoed ceilings. Serpentine stone walks. Guided tours. (Mar-Dec, Tues-Sun; closed holidays) **$$**

Special Event

Harvest Homecoming. *431 Pearl St, New Albany (47150). Phone 812/944-8572.* Week-long festivities include open house on Mansion Row, parade, hot air balloon race, music. Early Oct.

Specialty Lodging

The following lodging establishment is approved by Mobil Travel Guide but, due to its unique and individualized nature has not been given a traditional Mobil Star rating. Included in this listing you may find bed-and-breakfasts, limited-service inns, guest ranches, and other unique hotel properties.

HONEYMOON MANSION BED & BREAKFAST. *1014 E Main St, New Albany (47150). Phone 812/945-0312; toll-free 800/759-7270; fax 812/ 945-0312. www.bbonline.com/in/honeymoon.* Restored 1850 mansion; Victorian chapel. 6 rooms, 3 story. Children over 12 years only. Complimentary full breakfast. Check-in 3 pm, check-out 11 am. **$**

New Castle (C-4)

See also Muncie, Richmond

Founded 1819
Population 17,780
Elevation 1,055 ft
Area Code 765
Zip 47362
Information Chamber of Commerce, 100 S Main St, Suite 108, PO Box 485; phone 765/529-5210
Web site www.nchcchamber.com

New Castle is a productive city; numerous plants manufacture hundreds of diversified products.

What to See and Do

Henry County Historical Society Museum. *606 S 14th St. Phone 765/529-4028.* (1870) Residence of Civil War general William Grose; houses pioneer and war relics, Wilbur Wright memorabilia, collection of World War I items; genealogical records. (Mon-Sat limited hours; closed holidays) **$**

Henry County Memorial Park. *100 N Sulphur Springs Rd (47362). 1 1/2 miles N on Hwy 3. Phone 765/529-1004.* More than 300 acres; lake, fishing, boats (fee); picnic facilities, concession; playground; 18-hole golf (fee), ball fields; ice skating; open-air theater, auditorium. (Daily) **FREE**

Indiana Basketball Hall of Fame. *1 Hall of Fame Court. Phone 765/529-1891. www.hoopshall.com.* "The home of Hoosier hysteria," a 14,000-square-foot brick and glass museum, honors the spirit of basketball, as well as the game's historical significance and outstanding individuals. An auditorium, library, interactive exhibits, and a video inventory of game films and interviews all help explore what basketball means to Indiana's culture, history, and personality. (Tues-Sun; closed Jan 1, Thanksgiving, Dec 25) **$$**

Summit Lake State Park. *5993 N Messick Rd (47362). 9 miles NE on Hwy 3 to Hwy 36. Phone 765/766-5873.* Approximately 2,550 acres, including 800-acre lake. Swimming, boating; hiking, camping. Naturalist service (summer). (All year) **$$**

New Harmony (F-1)

See also Evansville

Founded 1814
Population 916
Elevation 384 ft
Area Code 812
Zip 47631

During the first half of the 19th century, this was the site of two social experiments in communal living. New Harmony was founded by members of the Harmony Society, under the leadership of George Rapp, who had come with many of his followers from Württemberg, Germany, and settled at Harmony, Pennsylvania. In 1814, the society came to Indiana. The deeply religious members believed in equality, mutual protection, and common ownership of property; practiced celibacy; and prepared for the imminent return of Christ. In a ten-year period, they succeeded in transforming 30,000 acres of dense forest and swampland into farms and a town that was the envy of the surrounding region. In 1825, it was sold to Robert Owen, a Scottish industrialist, social reformer, and communal idealist. Rapp and his followers returned to Pennsylvania.

Owen, supported by his four sons and William Maclure, attempted to organize a new social order, eliminating financial exploitation, poverty, and competition. He tried to establish a model society in New Harmony, with equal opportunities for all, full cooperative effort, and advanced educational facilities

to develop the highest type of human beings. Within a short time, many of the world's most distinguished scientists, educators, scholars, and writers came to New Harmony, which became one of the scientific centers of America. Owen's original experiment was doomed to early failure, mainly because of his absence from the community and rivalry among his followers. But the scientists and educators stayed on. The first United States Geological Survey was done here, and the Smithsonian Institution has its origins in this community.

The town is in a rural area surrounded by rich farmland. Historic New Harmony and the New Harmony State Historic Sites are dedicated to the efforts and contributions made to Indiana's development by the founders and settlers of this community. Many of the buildings and old homes still dominate New Harmony today.

What to See and Do

⭐ **The Atheneum Visitors Center.** *North and Arthur sts. Phone 812/682-4474; toll-free 800/231-2168. www. newharmony.org.* Documentary film. Orientation area in building designed by Richard Meier. All tours begin here; tickets must be purchased here to view sites. (Apr-Oct, daily; Mar, Nov-Dec, call for hours; closed Jan-Feb) Area includes

1830 Owen House. *Tavern and Brewery sts, New Harmony. Phone toll-free 800/231-2168.* Example of English architectural style.

1850 doctor's office. *Church and Brewery sts, New Harmony. Phone toll-free 800/231-2168.* Collection of medical equipment and apothecary workshop from mid- to late 1800s.

David Lenz House. *324 North St, New Harmony. Phone toll-free 800/231-2168.* (1820) Harmonist frame residence furnished with Harmonist artifacts.

Early West Street log structures. *North and West sts, New Harmony. Phone toll-free 800/231-2168.* (1814-1819) Reconstructed buildings establish the character of early Harmonist streetscape.

George Keppler House. *Tavern St, New Harmony. Phone toll-free 800/231-2168.* (1820) This Harmonist frame residence contains the David Dale Owen geological collection.

Harmonist Cemetery. *Church, West, Arthur, and North sts, New Harmony. Phone toll-free 800/ 231-2168.* Members (230) of the Harmony Society are buried here in unmarked graves dating from 1814 to 1824. Site includes several prehistoric Woodland mounds and an apple orchard.

The Labyrinth. *Main St, New Harmony. Phone toll-free 800/231-2168.* Circular maze of shrubbery created to symbolize the twists and choices along life's pathway.

Lichtenberger Building/Maximilian-Bodmer Exhibit. *Tavern and Main sts, New Harmony. Phone toll-free 800/231-2168.* Exhibit of Maximilian-Bodmer expedition (1832-1834) of upper Missouri region, includes original lithographs of field sketches and original prints of life among the Mandan.

Robert Henry Fauntleroy House. *West and Church sts, New Harmony. Phone toll-free 800/231-2168.* (1822-1840) Harmonist family residence. Enlarged and restyled by Robert and Jane Owen Fauntleroy. House museum contains period furniture.

Salomon Wolf House. *Granary and Brewery sts, New Harmony. Phone toll-free 800/231-2168.* (1823) Building houses electronic scale model of New Harmony in 1824. Audiovisual program.

Scholle House. *604 E Tavern, New Harmony. Phone 812/682-4523; toll-free 800/231-2168.* Former Harmonist residence now houses changing exhibits.

Thrall's Opera House. *612 E Church St, New Harmony. Phone 812/682-4503; toll-free 800/231-2168.* Originally Harmonist Dormitory Number 4; later converted to a concert hall by Owen descendants.

Tillich Park. *North St, New Harmony. Phone toll-free 800/231-2168.* (1963) Burial place of German theologian Paul Johannes Tillich. Engraved stones contain selections of Dr. Tillich's writing.

Bendix Woods. *32132 Hwy 2 (46552). 12 miles W on Hwy 2. Phone 574/654-3155.* Nature center. Hiking, picnicking, exercise trail, cross-country skiing. (Daily) **$$**

Community House Number 2. *Granary and Main sts (47631). Phone toll-free 800/231-2168.* (1822) An example of Harmonist brick institutional architecture; houses exhibits on education and printing in old New Harmony.

Harmonie State Park. *Lower New Harmony Rd (47631). 4 miles S on Hwy 69, then 1 mile W on Harmonie Pkwy. Phone 812/682-4821.* Approximately 3,500 acres of open fields and woods on banks of Wabash River. Swimming pool, boating (launch, ramp), fishing. Nature and hiking trails, picnicking (shelters), playground, camping (tent and trailer sites, electrical hookups; cabins). Interpretive, cultural arts programs (summer). (Daily)

Murphy Auditorium. *419 Tavern St (47631). Phone 812/465-1635.* (1913) Facility is used for performing arts, lectures, theater, and local events. Professional summer theater under the direction of University of Southern Indiana. (June-Aug)

Roofless Church. *North and Main sts (47631). Phone toll-free 800/231-2168.* (1959) Interdenominational church, designed by Philip Johnson, commemorates New Harmony's religious heritage. Jacques Lipchitz's sculpture, Descent of the Holy Spirit, is in center. **FREE**

Workingmen's Institute. *407 W Tavern St (47631). Phone 812/682-4806. www.newharmonywmi.lib.in.us.* (1894) One of America's first free public libraries, begun in 1838. Archives of early New Harmony manuscript collections, art gallery, museum, public library. (Tues-Sun; closed holidays) **$**

Limited-Service Hotel

★ ★ **NEW HARMONY INN.** *504 North St, New Harmony (47631). Phone 812/682-4491; toll-free 800/782-8605; fax 812/682-3423. www.redg.com.* Located in a town that was founded in 1814 by a group of Harmonists and later sold to the reformer Robert Owen, this charming inn is a simply designed, contemporary structure complemented by original artwork, a delightful greenhouse-enclosed swimming pool, and a veil of lush gardens. 90 rooms, 3 story. Check-out noon. Restaurant (see RED GERANIUM), bar. Fitness room. Indoor pool, whirlpool. Tennis. **$**

✈ ✗ ☲ ⛷

Restaurant

★ ★ **RED GERANIUM.** *504 North St, New Harmony (47631). Phone 812/682-4431; toll-free 800/782-8605. www.redg.com.* Garden room with painted orchard ceiling. Lunch, dinner. Closed Mon; Jan 1, Dec 25. Bar (see NEW HARMONY INN). **$$**

Peru (B-3)

See also Kokomo, Logansport, Marion, Wabash

Founded 1826
Population 12,994
Elevation 650 ft
Area Code 765
Zip 46970
Information Peru/Miami County Chamber of
Commerce, 13 E Main; phone 765/472-1923
Web site www.miamicochamber.com

Peru is an industrial and agricultural trading community on the banks of the Wabash, near the confluence
of the Mississinewa and Wabash rivers. The surroundings are filled with historic landmarks and
memories of the times when the Miami made their
home here, and the great Tecumseh tried to unite
the various Native American tribes into one nation.
Peru was once the largest circus winter quarters in
the world, home of the famous Hagenbeck-Wallace
circus. Peru also was the hometown of composer Cole
Porter; his birthplace was a large frame house that is
now a duplex apartment at the northeast corner of
Huntington and East 3rd Street.

What to See and Do

Circus Museum. *154 N Broadway (46970). Phone
765/472-3918.* Vast collection of circus memorabilia
and relics, historical items from professional circuses
and the Peru Amateur Circus. (Daily; closed holidays)
(See SPECIAL EVENTS) **DONATION**

Miami County Museum. *51 N Broadway (46970).
Phone 765/473-9183.* Exhibits on the circus, pioneers,
Miami tribe; Victorian rooms and stores; Cole Porter
archive; Art Room. (Tues-Sat; closed holidays)
DONATION

Special Events

Circus City Festival. *Circus Museum (see), 154
N Broadway, Peru (46970). Phone 765/472-3918.*
Amateur circus, museum, displays, performances,
rides, booths; parade (last Sat). Mid-July.

Heritage Days. *Miami County Courthouse Sq, 51
N Broadway, Peru (46970). Phone 765/473-9183.*
Celebrates the county's pioneer heritage. Late Aug.

Plymouth (A-3)

See also South Bend, Tippecanoe River State Park

Founded 1834
Population 9,840
Elevation 799 ft
Area Code 574
Zip 46563
Information Marshall County Convention and Visitors
Bureau, 220 N Center St; phone 574/936-9000 or
toll-free 800/626-5353
Web site www.blueberrycountry.org

Plymouth is a farming and industrial center.
Southwest of the town was the site of the last
Potawatomi village in this area. In 1838, their chief,
Menominee, refused to turn his village over. The
surviving men, women, and children were dispos-
sessed and evacuated by the government to Kansas. So
many members of the tribe died of malaria that fresh
graves were left at every campsite during their long
and tragic journey.

What to See and Do

Chief Menominee Monument. *Peach and 13th rds
(46563). SW of town at Twin Lakes. Phone toll-free
800/626-5353.* A granite memorial with a statue of
Menominee at the site of his original village.

Marshall County Historical Museum. *123 N Michigan
St (46563). Phone 574/936-2306.* Relics pertaining to
local history; Native American artifacts; genealogical
materials. (Tues-Sat; closed holidays) **FREE**

Special Event

Marshall County Blueberry Festival. *1660 N Michigan
St, Plymouth (46563). Phone 574/936-5020.* One of the
Hoosier State's many Labor Day festivals, Plymouth's
Blueberry Festival offers a chance to sample some
of the best fruit in the area. One lucky young lady
is crowned Miss Blueberry, and hundreds of people
race each year in the 15-kilometer Blueberry Stomp.
One of the largest three-day festivals in the state, the
Blueberry Festival also features an annual truck pull,
the Blueberry Challenge, and varieties of blueberry
ice cream, cheesecake, pie, and milkshakes. Labor Day
weekend.

Limited-Service Hotel

★ ★ **RAMADA INN.** *2550 N Michigan St, Plymouth (46563). Phone 574/936-4013; toll-free 800/272-6232; fax 574/936-4553. www.ramada.com.* 108 rooms, 2 story. Pets accepted; fee. Check-out noon. Restaurant, bar. Pool. **$**

Richmond (C-4)

See also New Castle

Settled 1806
Population 39,124
Elevation 980 ft
Area Code 765
Zip 47374
Information Richmond/Wayne County Tourism Bureau, 5701 National Rd E; phone 765/935-8687 or toll-free 800/828-8414
Web site www.visitrichmond.org

Established by Quakers, this city on the Whitewater River is one of Indiana's leading industrial communities; it is the trade and distribution center for agriculturally rich Wayne County.

What to See and Do

Antique Alley. *5701 National Rd E. Phone 765/935-8687.* Over 900 dealers display their treasures within a 33-mile loop. Contact Tourism Bureau for complete listing.

Cardinal Greenway Rail Trail. *Phone 765/287-0399.* Asphalt trail connects Richmond to Muncie. Now completed, the trail is 60 miles long and runs all the way to Marion. Open to walkers, joggers, skaters, horseback riders. (Daily)

Earlham College. *801 National Rd W (47374). W of Whitewater River on Hwy 40. Phone 765/983-1200. www.earlham.edu.* (1847) (1,200 students) Liberal arts. Owns and operates Conner Prairie. On campus are Lilly Library, Stout Memorial Meetinghouse, Runyan Student Center, and

> **Joseph Moore Museum of Natural Science.** *801 National Rd W, Richmond. Phone 765/983-1303.* Birds and mammals in natural settings, fossils, mastodon and allosaurus skeletons. (Academic year, Mon, Wed, Fri, Sun; rest of year, Sun only) **FREE**

Glen Miller Park. *2514 E Main St. Phone 765/983-7285.* A 194-acre park; E. G. Hill Memorial Rose Garden, nine-hole golf (fee), natural springs, picnic shelters, concessions, fishing, paddleboats, playground, tennis courts, and outdoor amphitheatre (summer concerts). **FREE** Also in the park is

> **The German Friendship Garden.** *2500 National Rd E, Richmond.* Features 200 German hybridized roses sent by the German city of Zweibruken from its own rose garden. In bloom May-Oct. **FREE**

Hayes Regional Arboretum. *801 Elks Rd. 2 miles W of jct Hwy 40 and I-70. Phone 765/962-3745.* A 355-acre site with trees, shrubs, and vines native to this region; 40-acre beech-maple forest; auto tour (3 1/2 miles) of site. Fern garden; spring house. Hiking trails; bird sanctuary; nature center with exhibits; gift shop. (Tues-Sun; closed holidays) **FREE**

Huddleston Farmhouse Inn Museum. *838 National Rd, Cambridge City. 1 mile W on Hwy 40, at W edge of town. Phone 765/478-3172.* Restored 1840s farmhouse/inn complex with outbuildings that once served National Road travelers. (May-Aug, Tues-Sat, Sun afternoons; rest of year, Tues-Sat; closed holidays; also Jan) **$**

Indiana Football Hall of Fame. *815 N A St. N 9th and A sts. Phone 765/966-2235.* History of football in Indiana; photos, plaques, memorabilia of more than 300 inductees. High schools, colleges, and universities are represented. (Mon-Fri, also by appointment; closed holidays) **$**

Levi Coffin House State Historic Site. *113 Hwy 27 N, Fountain City. Phone 765/847-2432.* (1839) Federal-style brick home of Quaker abolitionist who helped 2,000 fugitive slaves escape to Canada; period furnishings. Tours. (Tues-Sat afternoons; closed July 4) **$**

Madonna of the Trails. *22nd and E Main sts. Phone 765/983-7200.* One of 12 monuments erected along Old National Road (Hwy 40) in honor of pioneer women.

Middlefork Reservoir. *Hwy 27 and Sylvan Nook Dr (47374). 2 miles N on Hwy 27, just S of I-70. Phone 765/983-7293.* A 405-acre park with 175-acre stream and spring-fed lake. Fishing, boating (dock rental), bait and tackle supplies. Hiking trails, picnicking, playground. **FREE**

Wayne County Historical Museum. *1150 N A St. At 12th St. Phone 765/962-5756.* Pioneer rooms include general store, blacksmith, bakery, cobbler; print, bicycle, apothecary shops; log cabin (1823), loom house; agricultural hall; decorative arts gallery; antique cars and old carriages; Egyptian mummy; collections of the Mediterranean world. (Feb-Dec, Tues-Sun; closed holidays) (See SPECIAL EVENT) **$$**

Special Event

Pioneer Day Festival. *Wayne County Historical Museum (see), 1150 N A St, Richmond (47374). Phone 765/962-5756.* Pioneer crafts, food. Weekend after Labor Day.

Limited-Service Hotel

★ **BEST WESTERN IMPERIAL MOTOR LODGE.** *3020 E Main St, Richmond (47374). Phone 765/966-1505; fax 765/935-1426. www.bestwestern.com.* 44 rooms, 2 story. Complimentary continental breakfast. Check-out noon. Pool. **$**

Restaurants

★ ★ **OLDE RICHMOND INN.** *138 S 5th St, Richmond (47374). Phone 765/962-2247; fax 765/962-9883.* Restored mansion built 1892. American menu. Lunch, dinner. Closed Jan 1, Labor Day, Dec 25. Bar. Children's menu. Outdoor seating. **$$**

★ **TASTE OF THE TOWN.** *1616 E Main St, Richmond (47374). Phone 765/935-5464.* Italian, American menu. Lunch, dinner. Closed Mon; holidays. Bar. Children's menu. Casual attire. **$$**

Rockville (C-2)

See also Terre Haute

Population 2,765
Elevation 711 ft
Area Code 765
Zip 47872
Information Convention and Visitors Bureau, PO Box 165; phone 765/569-5226
Web site www.coveredbridgescountry.com

What to See and Do

⭐ **Historic Billie Creek Village.** *Hwy 36 E (47872). 1 mile E on Hwy 36. Phone 765/569-3430.* Re-created turn-of-the-century village and working farmstead with three covered bridges; more than 30 buildings, includes one-room schoolhouse, country store, blacksmith shop, burr mill, livery; governor's house, log cabin; nature preserve; special events (see SPECIAL EVENTS). Weaving, candle dipping, and many other old-time craft demonstrations (Memorial Day-Halloween, weekends). Self-guided tours (Jan-late Dec, Mon-Fri; free admission). **$$**

Raccoon Lake State Recreation Area. *160 S Raccoon Pkwy (47872). 9 miles E on Hwy 36. Phone 765/344-1412.* Approximately 4,000 acres on reservoir. Swimming, water-skiing, fishing, boating (rentals); campground. **$$**

Special Events

Civil War Days. *Historic Billie Creek Village (see), State Rd 36 E, Rockville (47872). Phone 765/569-3430.* State's largest re-enactment of Civil War battle, costumes, battlefield; ladies tea; dance. Mid-June.

Old-Fashioned Arts & Crafts Christmas. *Historic Billie Creek Village (see), State Rd 36 E, Rockville (47872). Phone 765/569-3430.* Christmas celebration at village. Early Dec.

Parke County Covered Bridge Festival. *401 E Ohio St, Rockville (47872). Phone 765/569-5226.* Arts and crafts, craft demonstrations, food, animals, rides at living museum. Activities countywide. Mid-Oct.

Parke County Maple Fair. *4-H fairgrounds, Hwy 41 N, Rockville (47872). Phone 765/569-5226.* Celebration of maple sugar harvest. Bus and self-guided tours to six maple camps. Arts and crafts. Last weekend in Feb, first weekend in Mar.

Sorghum & Cider Fair. *Historic Billie Creek Village (see), State Rd 36 E, Rockville (47872). Phone 765/569-3430.* Cider made in copper kettles; sorghum cane squeezed by horse-powered press. Early Oct.

Santa Claus (F-2)

See also Lincoln Boyhood National Memorial &
Lincoln State Park

Founded 1846
Population 2,041
Elevation 519 ft
Area Code 812
Zip 47579

This is a small, one-street town with a first-class post office. Its name has made it particularly significant to millions of Americans at Christmastime. At the start of the season, several hundred thousand parcels and a million other pieces of mail arrive at the post office from all over the country, to be remailed with the Santa Claus postmark.

What to See and Do

Holiday World & Splashin' Safari. *Hwy 162 and 245. Phone 812/937-4401; toll-free 877/463-2645. www. holidayworld.com.* Holiday World theme park includes more than 60 rides, games, shows, exhibits, and attractions themed around Christmas, July 4, and Halloween. Live music; high-dive shows; Lincoln-era exhibit; wax museum; antique toy and doll museums; craftspersons at work; petting zoo; and Santa himself! Sidewalk and indoor restaurants. (Mid-May-mid-Aug, daily; early May, mid-Aug-early Oct, weekends) **$$$$**

> **Splashin' Safari Water Park.** *Hwy 162 and 245, Santa Claus. Phone 812/937-4401; toll-free 877/ 463-2645. www.holidayworld.com.* Offers adult and children's water slides, an action river, a children's activity pool, and a sandy beach area. (Mid-May-mid-Aug, daily; mid-Aug-early Sept, weekends; Labor Day)

Limited-Service Hotel

★ **SANTA'S LODGE.** *91 W Christmas Blvd, Santa Claus (47579). Phone 812/937-1902.* 87 rooms, 2 story. Check-out 11 am. Fitness room. Indoor pool. **$**

⏷ 🔲 ⌦

Santa Claus Fun Fact

• Santa Claus, Indiana, receives over a half million letters and requests at Christmastime.

South Bend (A-3)

See also Elkhart, La Porte, Mishawaka, Plymouth

Founded 1823
Population 107,789
Elevation 710 ft
Area Code 574
Information South Bend-Mishawaka Convention and Visitors Bureau, 401 E Colfax Ave, Suite 310, 46617; phone 574/234-0051 or toll-free 800/828-7881
Web site www.livethelegends.com

South Bend is probably most famous, at least in the eyes of football fans, as the home of the Fighting Irish of the University of Notre Dame (see). A visit to the campus, distinguished by the massive golden dome of the Administration Building (see), is worth the trip. Indiana University also has a branch here.

Two Frenchmen, Père Jacques Marquette and Louis Jolliet, who traveled through northern Indiana between 1673 and 1675, were the first Europeans to enter the South Bend area. In 1679, the famous French explorer René-Robert Cavelier proceeded from here with 32 men to the Mississippi River. During a second trip in 1681, Cavelier negotiated a peace treaty between the Miami and Illinois Confederations under an oak tree known as the Council Oak. The first permanent settlers arrived in 1820, when Pierre Freischuetz Navarre set up a trading post for the American Fur Company.

South Bend was founded in 1823 by Alexis Coquillard, who, with his partner Francis Comparet, bought the fur trading agency from John Jacob Astor. Joined by Lathrop Taylor, another trading post agent, Coquillard was instrumental in promoting European settlement of the area and in the construction of ferries, dams, and mills, which began the industrial development of the town.

Industries formerly based in South Bend and contributing to its growth were the Studebaker auto plant and the Oliver Corporation. The St. Joseph River runs at its southernmost bend through the center of the city, which was officially named South Bend by the United States Post Office Department in 1830.

What to See and Do

Century Center. *120 S St. Joseph St (46601). Phone 574/235-9711. www.centurycenter.org.* Multipurpose facility, designed by Philip Johnson and John Burgee, housing a convention center, performing arts and art centers, museum, and park area. General building (daily; closed holidays). **FREE** Within the center is

>   **South Bend Regional Museum of Art.** *120 S St. Joseph St, South Bend. Phone 574/235-9102.* Permanent collection, changing exhibitions. Classes, lecture series. Museum shop. (Tues-Fri, Sat-Sun afternoons) **DONATION**

City Greenhouses and Conservatory. *2105 Mishawaka Ave (46615). Phone 574/235-9442.* Spring and fall flower shows. (Daily; closed holidays) **$**

College Football Hall of Fame. *111 S St. Joseph St (46601). Phone 574/235-9999. www.collegefootball.org.* Sports shrine and museum dedicated to the preservation of college football. The educational and interpretive exhibits bring to life the history, color, and pageantry of the game. (Daily; closed Jan 1, Thanksgiving, Dec 25) (see SPECIAL EVENTS) **$$**

East Race Waterway. *301 S St. Louis Blvd (46617). E side of St. Joseph River at South Bend Dam. Downtown. Phone 574/299-4768.* Only man-made white-water raceway in North America. Recreational, instructional, and competitive canoeing, kayaking, rafting. Lighted sidewalks, foot bridges, seating areas. (June-Aug, Wed-Thurs, Sat-Sun; closed for races) **$$**

Leeper Park. *800 N LaFayette Blvd (46601). Michigan St, on Hwy 31. Phone 574/235-9405.* Tennis center with lighted courts (daily; fee); field for football, soccer, or baseball games; fragrance garden for the visually impaired; Pierre Navarre Cabin (1820), was the home and fur trading post of South Bend's first settler. Playground, picnicking. **$$**

Northern Indiana Center for History. *808 W Washington St (46601). In the W Washington National Historic District. Phone 574/235-9664.* Includes permanent, temporary, and interactive exhibition galleries; research library. Permanent exhibits depict history of the St. Joseph River Valley region of northern Indiana and southern Michigan. (Tues-Sun) On the grounds is

>   **Copshaholm.** *808 W Washington St, South Bend. Phone 574/235-9664.* Built in 1895-1896 by the Oliver family, this 38-room mansion is complete with

original furnishings. The grounds include 2 1/2 acres of historic gardens, a tea house, sunken Italianate gardens, a fountain, and more. The mansion, gardens, and carriage house are on the National Register of Historic Places. Guided tours. (Tues-Sun) **$$$**

Pinhook. *2801 N Riverside Dr (46616). Phone 574/235-9417.* Historical park has lagoon, picnic area; fishing, small boating. **FREE**

Potato Creek State Park. *25601 Hwy 4 (46554). 7 miles S on Hwy 31, then 4 miles W on Hwy 4. Phone 574/656-8186.* Approximately 3,800 acres. Swimming beach (lifeguard), fishing on Lake Worster, boating, canoeing, paddleboats (rentals). Hiking, paved bike trails (rentals), cross-country skiing, picnicking (shelter rentals), camping, horse camping (tie-rail at site), cabins. Nature center, naturalist service (all year). (Daily)

Potawatomi Zoo. *500 Greenlawn (46615). Phone 574/235-9800.* Zoo (daily); conservatories; tropical gardens; concerts; picnic area (fee); swimming (mid-June-late Aug, daily; fee). **$$**

Rum Village. *W Ewing and Gertrude sts (46601). Phone 574/235-9455.* Nature center, picnic area, and hiking and nature trails on 160 acres of woodland. Also contains Safetyville, miniature village teaching youngsters pedestrian, bike, and auto safety. **FREE**

St. Mary's College. *2 miles N on Hwy 33 at IN Toll Rd, exit 77 (46601). Phone 574/284-4626 (ticket and event information). www.saintmarys.edu.* (1844) (1,400 women) Music, theatrical, and art events throughout the year. Campus tours (by appointment).

St. Patrick's Park. *7 miles N near Hwy 31, on the St. Joseph River. Phone 574/277-4828.* Canoeing, boat launch; hiking, cross-country skiing; picnicking. (Daily) (See SPECIAL EVENTS) **$$**

Studebaker National Museum. *525 S Main St (46601). Phone 574/235-9714; toll-free 888/391-5600. www.studebakermuseum.org.* This nostalgiac museum houses and displays Studebaker vehicle collection and artifacts. Exhibits depict the evolution of the industry in the United States from 1852 to 1966, the 114-year span of the company. More than 80 Studebaker wagons, carriages, and motorized vehicles are on display, including the carriages of four United States presidents. (Mon-Sat 9 am-5 pm, Sun noon-5 pm; closed holidays; also Nov-Mar closed Mon) **$$**

★ **University of Notre Dame.** *Juniper and Douglas sts, Notre Dame (46601). N on Hwy 31, 33, and I-80/90. Phone 574/631-5000. www.nd.edu.* (1842) (10,126 students) One of the leading universities in the United States; noted for its biotechnology and vector biology research and studies focusing on radiation, aerodynamics, and social ministry. The school is a major center for constitutional law studies. On campus are

Administrative Building. *Juniper and Douglas sts, Notre Dame. Phone 574/631-5000.* (1879) The "Golden Dome" houses Columbus murals by Luigi Gregori, a former director of the university's art department and portrait painter at the Vatican Museum in the late 1860s.

Basilica of the Sacred Heart. *Juniper and Douglas sts, Notre Dame. Phone 574/631-7329.* (1871) Contains French stained-glass windows and a baroque altar in Our Lady Chapel. Its spire houses the oldest carillon in North America. Contains works by famed Croatian sculptor Ivan Mestrovic.

Eck Visitors Center. *South Bend. Phone 574/ 631-5726.* Offers guided tours of the 1,250-acre campus (academic year, Mon-Fri 11 am, 3pm; summer, Mon-Fri 9 am, 11 am, 1 pm, 3 pm; group tours by appointment).

Grotto of Our Lady of Lourdes. *Juniper and Douglas sts, Notre Dame. Phone 574/631-5000.* Replica of original in the French Pyrenees.

Guided tours. *Notre Dame Ave and Angela St., Notre Dame. Phone 574/631-5726 (Eck Visitors Center).* Tours of the 1,250-acre campus can be arranged at the Eck Visitors Center. (Academic year, Mon-Fri 11 am, 3 pm; summer, Mon-Fri 9 am, 11 am, 1 pm, 3 pm; group tours by appointment; closed holidays) Call the undergraduate admissions office (phone 574/631-7505) for tours for prospective students. **FREE**

Hesburgh Library. *Juniper and Edison sts, Notre Dame. Phone 574/631-6258.* (1963) South wall of 2-million-volume library has ten-story granite mural, "The Word of Life."

Joyce Center. *Juniper and Edison sts, Notre Dame.* (1968) A 10 1/2-acre complex under twin domes for athletic, cultural, and civic events. Includes Sports Heritage Hall, with memorabilia from Notre Dame sports history.

Notre Dame Stadium. *Juniper and Edison sts, Notre Dame. Phone 574/631-5000.* Few stadiums have as much history and tradition behind them as Notre Dame Stadium. From the throngs of fans clad in green and gold to "Touchdown Jesus" painted on the wall of the library just beyond one of the field's end zones, the stadium has played host to several national championship teams and some of the greatest players and coaches in collegiate history. The stadium was expanded in 1997 to hold more than 80,000 fans and is well attended (if not sold out) for almost every regular-season game.

Snite Museum of Art. *Juniper and Douglas sts, South Bend. Phone 574/631-5466.* Contains more than 19,000 works of art representing ancient to contemporary periods. Included are works by Chagall, Picasso, Rodin, and Boucher, as well as 18th- and 19th-century European art. (Tues-Sun; closed holidays) **FREE**

Special Events

Enshrinement Festival. *College Football Hall of Fame* (see), *111 S St. Joseph St, South Bend (46601). Phone 574/235-9999.* Some of college football's all-time greats are inducted into the hall. Includes entertainment, food, events. Aug.

Firefly Festival of the Performing Arts. *St. Patrick's Park* (see), *50651 Laurel Rd, South Bend (46637). Phone 574/288-3472.* Plays, music, and concerts in outdoor amphitheater. Mid-June-early Aug, weekends.

Leeper Park Art Fair. *Leeper Park, 800 N LaFayette Blvd, South Bend (46601). Phone 574/272-8598.* Voted one of the 50 best art fairs in the country by renowned trade magazines. June.

Minor League Baseball. *Stanley Coveleski Regional Baseball Stadium, 501 W South St, South Bend (46601). Phone 574/235-9988.* Baseball stadium (5,000 seats). Home of the South Bend Silver Hawks. Apr-Aug.

South Bend Summer in the City Festival. *301 S St. Louis Blvd, South Bend (46617). Phone 574/299-4768.* Parade, performances; arts and crafts. June.

Limited-Service Hotels

★ ★ **HOLIDAY INN CITY CENTER.** *213 W Washington St, South Bend (46601). Phone 574/232-3941; toll-free 800/465-4329; fax 574/289-3967. www.holiday-inn.com.* 176 rooms, 25 story. Check-in 4 pm, check-out 11 am. Two restaurants, two bars. Fitness room. Indoor pool. Airport transportation available. Business center. **$**

★ ★ **HOLIDAY INN UNIVERSITY AREA.** *515 Dixie Hwy N, South Bend (46637). Phone 574/272-6600; toll-free 800/465-4329; fax 574/272-5553. www.holiday-inn.com.* 229 rooms, 2 story. Pets accepted, some restrictions; fee. Check-in 4 pm, check-out 11 am. Restaurant, bar. Children's activity center. Fitness room. Indoor pool, outdoor pool, children's pool, whirlpool. Airport transportation available. **$**

★ ★ **INN AT SAINT MARY'S.** *53993 Hwy 31/33 N, South Bend (46637). Phone 574/232-4000; toll-free 800/947-8627; fax 574/289-0986. www.innatsaintmarys .com.* 150 rooms, 3 story. Complimentary full breakfast. Check-in 3 pm, check-out noon. High-speed Internet access. Bar. Fitness room. Whirlpool. Airport transportation available. Business center. **$**

★ ★ **MORRIS INN.** *Notre Dame Ave, South Bend (46556). Phone 574/631-2000; fax 574/631-2340. www. morrisinn.com.* 92 rooms, 3 story. Closed ten days during Christmas break. Complimentary full breakfast. Check-in 3 pm, check-out noon. High-speed Internet access. Restaurant (see Sorin's), bar. Fitness room. Business center. **$**

★ **SIGNATURE INN.** *215 Dixie Way S, South Bend (46637). Phone 574/277-3211. www.signatureinn.com.* 123 rooms, 2 story. Pets accepted, some restrictions; fee. Complimentary continental breakfast. Check-in 3 pm, check-out 11 am. Fitness room. Indoor pool, whirlpool. Business center. **$**

Full-Service Hotel

★ ★ ★ **MARRIOTT SOUTH BEND.** *123 N St. Joseph St, South Bend (46601). Phone 574/234-2000; toll-free 800/328-7349; fax 574/234-0077. www. marriott.com.* This hotel is located in historic downtown South Bend and is connected to the Century Center Convention and Civic Complex (see) by a skywalk. The College Football Hall of Fame (see) is across the street. 298 rooms, 9 story. Pets accepted, some restrictions. Check-in 3 pm, check-out noon. High-speed Internet access. Restaurant, bar. Fitness room. Indoor pool, whirlpool. Airport transportation available. Business center. **$**

Specialty Lodgings

The following lodging establishments are approved by Mobil Travel Guide, but due to their unique and individualized nature have not been given a traditional Mobil Star rating. Included in this listing you may find bed-and-breakfasts, limited-service inns, guest ranches, and other unique hotel properties.

OLIVER INN BED & BREAKFAST. *630 W Washington St, South Bend (46601). Phone 574/232-4545; toll-free 888/697-4466; fax 574/288-9788. www.oliverinn.com.* Built in 1886; Victorian décor. 9 rooms, 3 story. Pets accepted, some restrictions; fee. Complimentary continental breakfast. Check-in 4 pm, check-out 11 am. **$**

QUEEN ANNE INN. *420 W Washington St, South Bend (46601). Phone 574/234-5959; toll-free 800/582-2379; fax 574/234-4324. www.queenanneinn.net.* Built in 1893; Victorian décor. 6 rooms, 3 story. Complimentary full breakfast. Check-in 4 pm, check-out 11 am. **$**

Restaurants

★ ★ ★ **THE CARRIAGE HOUSE DINING ROOM.** *24460 Adams Rd, South Bend (46628). Phone 574/272-9220.* For fine dining in South Bend, look no farther than this historic restaurant. With a *Wine Spectator* award-winning wine list for 12 years running, it is sure to please. Outside dining is available in the summer. Restored church (circa 1850); European-style dining. American menu. Dinner. Closed Sun-Mon; holidays; also early Jan. Bar. Outdoor seating. **$$$**

★ ★ **DAMON'S THE PLACE FOR RIBS.**
52885 Hwy 31 Business, South Bend (46637). Phone 574/272-5478; fax 574/271-8799. Dinner. Closed Thanksgiving, Dec 25. Bar. Children's menu. **$$**

★ ★ ★ **LA SALLE GRILL.** *115 W Colfax, South Bend (46601). Phone 574/288-1155. www.lasallegrill .com.* Dinner. Closed Sun; holidays. Bar. **$$$**

★ ★ **SORIN'S.** *Notre Dame Ave, South Bend (46556). Phone 574/631-2000.* Breakfast, lunch, dinner. Closed mid-Dec-early Jan. Bar. Children's menu. Reservations recommended. **$$$**

★ ★ **TIPPECANOE PLACE.** *620 W Washington St, South Bend (46601). Phone 574/234-9077. www.tippe .com.* Former Studebaker mansion (1886-1889); many antiques. Seafood, steak menu. Lunch, dinner, Sun brunch. Bar. **$$**

Spring Mill State Park

See also Bedford, Bloomington

3 miles E of Mitchell on Hwy 60. Phone 812/849-4081.

In this 1,319-acre park, an abandoned pioneer village has been restored in a small valley amid wooded hills. Built around a gristmill, which dates to 1817, are the log shops and homes of a pioneer trading post. The village's main street is flanked by a tavern, distillery, post office, and an apothecary shop. A small stream flowing through the valley turns an overshot waterwheel at the gristmill and furnishes power for a sawmill. The homes of the pioneers have been furnished with household articles from a century ago.

The Virgil I. Grissom Memorial, dedicated to the Indiana astronaut who was the second American in space, is located here. In the building are space exhibits, a slide show, and a visitor center.

In the surrounding forest, which includes 60 acres of woods, are some of the largest oak and tulip trees in Indiana. Some of the many caverns in the park have underground streams with blind fish. In Twin

Caves, boat trips may be taken on an underground stream (Apr-Oct). Park facilities include swimming pool (lifeguard), fishing, boating (rentals, no motors) on a 30-acre artificial lake; hiking trails, picnicking, camping; tennis. Inn has accommodations (phone 812/849-4081). **$$**

Terre Haute (D-1)

See also Brazil, Greencastle, Marshall, Rockville

Founded 1816
Population 59,614
Elevation 507 ft
Area Code 812
Information Terre Haute Convention and Visitors Bureau, 643 Wabash Ave, 47807; phone 812/234-5555 or toll-free 800/366-3043
Web site www.terrehaute.com

Terre Haute was founded as a river town on the lower Wabash River and has become an important industrial, financial, agricultural, educational, and cultural center.

The plateau on which the city is built (27 square miles) was named Terre Haute (high land) by the French, who governed this area until 1763. The dividing line that separated the French provinces of Canada and Louisiana runs through this section. American settlers arrived with the establishment of Fort Harrison in 1811. In later years, it became a terminal for river trade on the Wabash, Ohio, and Mississippi rivers to New Orleans. Many wagon trains with westbound settlers passed through here. The advance of the railroads made large-scale coal operations possible; Terre Haute became a railroad and coal-mining center and developed a highly diversified industrial and manufacturing complex.

Novelist Theodore Dreiser, author of *Sister Carrie* and *An American Tragedy,* and his brother, Paul Dresser, composer of Indiana's state song, "On the Banks of the Wabash," lived here. Eugene V. Debs (see) founded the American Railway Union, the first industrial union in America, in Terre Haute. The city also is the home of Rose-Hulman Institute of Technology (1874).

What to See and Do

Children's Science & Technology Museum. *523 Wabash Ave. Phone 812/235-5548.* Hands-on museum exhibits allow visitors, both young and old, to experience science, explore the world around them, and understand today's ever-changing technology. (Tues-Sat; closed Jan 1, Thanksgiving, Dec 25) **$$**

Deming Park. *E end of Ohio Blvd at Fruitridge Ave (47807). Phone 812/232-2727.* Acres (177) of wooded hills; swimming pool (June-Labor Day; fee), fishing; cross-country skiing (rentals); tennis; picnicking, concession; miniature train rides (weekends, holidays; fee); water slide (fee); 18-hole Frisbee disc course. **FREE**

Dobbs Park & Nature Center. *5170 E Poplar St (47803). 4 miles E via Hwy 42 at jct Hwy 46. Phone 812/877-1095.* Approximately 105 acres. A 25-acre state nature preserve; 2 1/2-acre lake, fishing; 3-acre wetlands area, 4 miles of nature trails, interpretive nature center; butterfly and hummingbird garden (June-Sept). Tree nursery. Picnicking (shelters). (Daily) **FREE** Also here is

Native American Museum. *5170 E Poplar St, Terre Haute. Phone 812/877-6007.* Exhibits include dwellings, clothing, weapons, and music of Eastern Woodland Native American cultures. Hands-on activities. **FREE**

Eugene V. Debs Home. *451 N 8th St. Phone 812/232-2163.* Restored home of the labor and Socialist leader; memorabilia. (Wed-Sun afternoons; also by appointment; closed holidays) **FREE**

Farrington's Grove Historical District. More than 800 residential dwellings in a 70-square-block area; homes dating from 1849.

Fowler Park Pioneer Village. *3000 E Oregon Church Rd. Phone 812/462-3391.* An 1840s pioneer village with 12 log cabins, a general store, schoolhouse, and gristmill. (Summer weekends; also by appointment) **FREE**

Indiana State University. *9th and Sycamore sts #510 (47809). Bounded by 3rd (Hwy 41), 9th, Cherry, and Tippecanoe sts. Phone 812/237-3773. www.indstate.edu.* (1865) (11,000 students) Turman Gallery and the University Gallery in the Center for Performing and Fine Arts have paintings, sculptures, ceramics, and jewelry (Tues-Fri, Sun; free). Cunningham Memorial Library houses the Cordell Collection of rare and early English language dictionaries. Historic Condit House (1860), office of the university president, is an example of Italianate architecture. Campus tours.

Paul Dresser Birthplace State Shrine and Memorial. *Fairbanks Park, 1st and Farrington sts (47802). Phone 812/235-9717.* Restoration of mid-19th-century workingman's home; birthplace of Dresser, author of state song and composer of other popular songs. (May-Sept, Sun; also by appointment) **FREE**

Shakamak State Park. *2 miles W of Jasonville on Hwy 48. Phone 812/665-2158.* More than 1,766 acres with three artificial lakes stocked with game fish. Swimming pool (lifeguard), bathhouse, boating (rentals, no gasoline motors). Picnicking, playground, hiking. Camping, trailer facilities, cabins. Naturalist service (May-Aug), nature center. Per vehicle **$$**

Sheldon Swope Art Museum. *25 S 7th St. Phone 812/238-1676.* Permanent collections of 19th- and 20th-century American art. Special exhibits, films, lectures, classes, and performing arts events. (Daily; closed holidays) **FREE**

Vigo County Historical Museum. *1411 S 6th St (47802). At Washington Ave. Phone 812/235-9717.* Local exhibits in 15 rooms of 1868 house; one-room school, country store, military room, dressmaker's shop. (Tues-Sun; closed holidays)

Special Events

Buffalo Chip Throwing Contest. *Native American Museum, 5170 E Poplar Dr, Terre Haute (47803). Phone 812/877-6007.* Late Sept.

Frontier Day. *Wabash Valley fairgrounds, Terre Haute. 2 miles S on Hwy 41. Phone 217/275-3443.* Horse show, events. July 4.

Maple Sugarin' Days. *Prairie Creek Park, 3364 W French Dr, Terre Haute (47802). Phone 812/462-3391.* Demonstrations of syrup-making process at syrup camp. Actual syrup-making takes place in hand-hewn log house (1852). Early Feb-early Mar.

Pioneer Days. *201 Cherry St, Terre Haute (47807). 7 miles S via Hwy 41. Phone 812/462-3392.* Old-fashioned crafts demonstrated; pioneer exhibits. First weekend in Oct.

Wabash Valley Festival. *Fairbanks Park, 17 Harding Ave, Terre Haute (47807). Phone 812/232-2727.* Flea market, carnival, entertainment. Last week in May.

Limited-Service Hotels

★ **DRURY INN.** *3050 Hwy 41 S, Terre Haute (47802). Phone 812/234-4268; toll-free 800/282-8733; fax 812/234-4268.* 64 rooms, 4 story. Pets accepted, some restrictions. Check-out noon. **$**

★ **FAIRFIELD INN.** *475 E Margaret Ave, Terre Haute (47802). Phone 812/235-2444; fax 812/235-2444. www.fairfieldinn.com.* 62 rooms, 3 story. Complimentary continental breakfast. Check-out noon. Indoor pool, whirlpool. **$**

★ ★ **HOLIDAY INN.** *3300 Hwy 41 S, Terre Haute (47802). Phone 812/232-6081; toll-free 800/465-4329; fax 812/238-9934. www.holiday-inn.com.* 230 rooms, 5 story. Pets accepted, some restrictions. Check-out noon. Restaurant, bar. Fitness room. Indoor pool, whirlpool. **$**

Tippecanoe River State Park (B-2)

See also Plymouth

5 miles N of Winamac on Hwy 35. Phone 574/946-3213.

One of Indiana's larger state parks, its 2,761 acres stretch for more than 7 miles along the Tippecanoe River, on the east side of Highway 35. (The area west of the highway is operated by the Division of Fish and Wildlife as Winamac State Fish and Wildlife Area.)

Tippecanoe is ideal for outdoor enthusiasts, with its oak forests, pine plantations, fields, winding roads, marshes, and occasional sand dune. Fishing, boating (launch); hiking, bridle trails, cross-country skiing; picnicking (shelter); playground; camping (electrical hookups); horseback camping, group camping. Naturalist service (May-Aug). View from fire tower. (Daily) Per vehicle $2-$5 **$$**

Turkey Run State Park (C-2)

See also Marshall

2 miles N of Marshall on Hwy 47. Phone 765/597-2635.

This is a 2,382-acre wooded area. Within the park are deep, rock-walled prehistoric canyons and winding streams that twist through solid rock. Canoeing and fishing in Sugar Creek for bluegill, crappie, and rock bass. Hiking trails (13 1/2 miles) lead through canyons, along cliffs, and into forests. A historic house, built by one of the area's first settlers, is open for tours (seasonal).

Facilities include swimming pool, hiking, saddle barn, tennis, picnicking, concession (summer), trailer and tent camping. Nature center (daily; winter, weekends only), naturalist service; bird observation room. Planetarium. (Daily) Per vehicle $2-$5 **$$**

Valparaiso (A-2)

See also Hammond, La Porte

Founded 1865
Population 27,428
Elevation 738 ft
Area Code 219
Zip 46383
Information Chamber of Commerce, 150 Lincolnway, Suite 1005, 46384; phone 219/462-1105
Web site www.valparaiso.com

Special Events

Popcorn Festival. *204 E Lincolnway, Valparaiso (46383). Downtown. Phone 219/464-8332.* Parade, 5-mile fun run, arts and crafts, entertainment, hot air balloon show. First Sat after Labor Day.

Porter County Fair. *Porter County Expo Center, 215 E Division Rd, Valparaiso (46383). Phone 219/464-0133.* Late July.

Limited-Service Hotels

★ **BEST WESTERN EXPRESSWAY INN.** *760 Morthland Dr, Valparaiso (46385). Phone 219/464-8555; toll-free 800/937-8376; fax 219/477-2492. www.bestwestern.com.* 54 rooms, 4 story. Check-in 3 pm, check-out noon. **$**

★ ★ **COURTYARD BY MARRIOTT.** *2301 E Morthland Dr, Valparaiso (46383). Phone 219/465-1700; fax 219/477-2430. www.courtyard.com.* 111 rooms, 2 story. Check-in 3 pm, check-out noon. Restaurant. Fitness room. Indoor pool, outdoor pool, whirlpool. **$**

★ ★ **INDIAN OAK RESORT & SPA.** *528 Boundary Rd, Chesterton (46304). Phone 219/926-2200; toll-free 800/552-4232; fax 219/921-0864. www.indianoak.com.* 93 rooms, 2 story. Complimentary continental breakfast. Check-in 3 pm, check-out 11 am. Restaurant. Fitness room. Indoor pool, whirlpool. Business center. **$**

Restaurants

★ **BILLY JACK'S CAFÉ & GRILL.** *2904 N Calumet Ave, Valparaiso (46383). Phone 219/477-3797.* Italian, Southwestern menu. Lunch, dinner. Bar. Children's menu. Casual attire. **$$**

★ **BISTRO 157.** *157 Lincolnway, Valparaiso (46383). Phone 219/462-0992.* International/Fusion, French menu. Lunch, dinner. Closed Mon. Casual attire. Outdoor seating. **$$**

★ ★ ★ **CLAYTON'S.** *66 W Lincolnway, Valparaiso (46383). Phone 219/531-0612.* Behind this vintage storefront lies one of the pioneers of northwestern Indiana's fine-dining scene. Self-taught chef William Potts opened Clayton's in the mid-1990s, when words like truffles and foie gras made diners a bit apprehensive. But almost a decade later, things have changed in Valparaiso. The refined American menu, which has included such dishes as foie gras dumplings and wild rice risotto, keeps customers coming back and continues to set the standard for northwestern Indiana dining. American menu. Dinner. Closed Sun-Mon. Casual attire. Outdoor seating. **$$**

★ ★ **DISH RESTAURANT.** *3907 Calumet Ave, Valparaiso (46383). Phone 219/465-9221.* More than just your average local eatery, Dish takes American comfort food to a new level. Utilizing seasonal, locally grown ingredients, chef Erick Staresina gives old favorites like meat loaf and ribs an upscale twist. The concept has quickly become a favorite of locals, who enjoy the extensive wine list, as well as the bright, modern, and unpretentious atmosphere. American menu. Lunch, dinner. Closed Sun. Bar. Casual attire. **$$**

★ **DON QUIXOTE.** *119 E Lincolnway, Valparaiso (46383). Phone 219/462-7976.* Spanish menu. Lunch, dinner. Closed Sun. Children's menu. Casual attire. Reservations recommended. Outdoor seating. **$$**

★ ★ **STRONGBOW INN.** *2405 E Hwy 30, Valparaiso (46383). Phone 219/531-0162.* American menu. Lunch, dinner. Bar. Children's menu. Casual attire. **$$**

Vincennes (E-1)

Founded 1732
Population 18,701
Elevation 429 ft
Area Code 812
Zip 47591
Information Vincennes Area Chamber of Commerce, 102 N 3rd St; phone 812/882-6440 or toll-free 888/895-6622
Web site www.accessknoxcounty.com

This city on the banks of the Wabash River is the oldest town in Indiana. French fur traders roamed through the region as early as 1683, established a trading post, and were soon followed by settlers. Fort Vincennes was built by French troops under Francis Morgamme de Vincennes in 1732. It was turned over to British control in 1763, but many of the French settlers (who frequently intermarried with Native Americans) remained in the area. In 1778, the state of Virginia furnished $12,000 and seven companies of militia to 25-year-old George Rogers Clark (see) and directed him to secure all land northwest of the Ohio River for Virginia. Clark's troops seized Fort Sackville in the summer of 1778, but it fell back into British hands several months later. The second and final capture of Vincennes by Clark the following year opened up the entire Northwest Territory. In 1784, the territory was ceded by Virginia to the United States and became a public domain. Vincennes was, from 1800 to 1813, the capital of the Indiana Territory; between 1808 and 1811, several meetings and negotiations took place here between Governor William H. Harrison and the famous Shawnee Chief Tecumseh and his brother, The Prophet. During the 18th century, the town was almost entirely populated by descendants of the French founders. After 1800, a large number of Easterners and German families settled in Vincennes and advanced farming, local business, and industry. The first newspaper in the Indiana Territory, the *Indiana Gazette,* was published here in 1804.

Today, Vincennes is a Midwest shipping and trading center and the seat of Knox County—notable for its melons and livestock raising. For recreation, the Wabash River offers fishing and boating.

What to See and Do

Fort Knox II. *3 miles N via Fort Knox Rd.* Military post built and garrisoned by new American nation during early 1800s to protect Western frontier prior to Battle of Tippecanoe. As tensions on the frontier increased, additional troops were gathered here, the fort having been hurriedly enlarged and strengthened by Captain Zachary Taylor in 1810. The outline of the fort is marked for self-guided tours. (Daily) **FREE**

George Rogers Clark National Historical Park. *401 S 2nd St (47591). Downtown off Hwy 50 and Hwy 41. Phone 812/882-1776.* Memorial building (daily) commemorates the George Rogers Clark campaign during the American Revolution. Includes the site of Fort Sackville, captured from the British by Clark's forces in 1779. Visitor center with museum, exhibits (daily; closed Jan 1, Thanksgiving, Dec 25); film shown every half hour. **$**

Indiana Military Museum. *2074 N Bruceville Rd. Phone 812/882-8668.* Extensive and varied collection of military memorabilia. Military vehicles, artillery, uniforms, insignia, equipment, and related artifacts spanning the Civil War to Desert Storm. Museum (May-Sept, Mon-Fri afternoons; winter, weekends by appointment; closed Jan 1, Thanksgiving, Dec 25); outdoor display (summer, daily). **$**

Indiana Territory Site. *1 Harrison St (47591). 1st and Harrison sts. Phone 812/882-7422.* From this two-story capitol building, an area consisting of the present states of Indiana, Illinois, Michigan, Wisconsin, and a part of Minnesota was governed in 1811. A replica of the first newspaper printing shop in Indiana is also here, where Elihu Stout first issued the *Indiana Gazette* in 1804. Nearby is Maurice Thompson birthplace, restored 1840 home of author of *Alice of Old Vincennes.* Tours (Apr-Dec, Wed-Sun). **$**

Kimmell Park. *2014 Oliphant Dr (47591). Phone 812/882-1140.* Boating (ramp), fishing; picnicking. (May-Oct)

Log cabin visitor center. *1 Harrison St (47591). Phone 812/882-7422.* (Apr-Dec, Wed-Sun) **FREE**

Michel Brouillet Old French House. *509 1st St (47591). Phone 812/882-7886.* (circa 1806) French Creole house; period furniture. (May-Sept, Thurs-Sun) **$**

The Old Cathedral Minor Basilica. *205 Church St (47591). 2nd and Church sts. Phone 812/882-5638.* (1826) (Daily) **DONATION** Rose Chapel and

Old Cathedral Library and Museum. *207 Church St, Vincennes. Phone 812/882-5638.* (1794) Indiana's oldest library; more than 12,000 documents, books, artworks—some dating from 1400s. (June-Aug, Mon-Fri) **DONATION**

The Old French Cemetery. *205 Church St, Vincennes. Phone 812/882-5638.* William Clark, judge of the Indiana Territory, was buried here in 1802; also local Frenchmen who served in George Rogers Clark's (see) army (1778-1779).

Old State Bank, Indiana State Memorial. *Busseron and 2nd sts (47591). Phone 812/882-7422.* (1838) Operated as a bank until 1877; one of the oldest bank buildings in Indiana. Guided tours (mid-Mar-mid-Dec, Wed-Sun; closed holidays). **$**

Ouabache Trails Park. *3500 N Lower Fort Knox Rd (47591).* Approximately 250 acres of wooded area bordered W by Wabash River. *Phone 812/882-4316.* Two picnicking areas (six shelters), camping (tent and trailer sites, hookups, dump station); interpretive center. Nature and hiking trails. Sand volleyball court, horseshoe pits. Camping (mid-Apr-late Oct). Contact Knox County Parks and Recreation Department, RR 6, Box 227H.

Vincennes University. *1002 N 1st St (47591). 1st and College sts. Phone 812/888-8888; toll-free 800/742-9198. www.vinu.edu.* (1801) (7,000 students) A junior college established as Jefferson Academy; first land-grant college in the Indiana Territory. Tours.

William Henry Harrison Mansion (Grouseland). *3 W Scott St. Opposite Indiana Territorial Capitol. Phone 812/882-2096.* (1803-1804) Residence of the ninth president of the United States while he was governor of the Indiana Territory; first brick building constructed in Indiana; 1803-1812 period furnishings. (Daily; closed holidays) **$$**

Special Events

Indiana State Chili Cook-Off. *102 N 3rd St, Vincennes (47591). Patrick Henry Dr, downtown. Phone 812/ 882-6440.* Chili cooking contest, sanctioned by International Chili Society. Winner advances to national cook-off. One-day event. Sept.

Spirit of Vincennes Rendezvous. *401 S 2nd St, Vincennes (47591). Old French Commons, at Willow St and River Rd. Phone 812/882-6440.* Era (1700-1840) encampment and battle reenactment. Memorial Day weekend.

Wabash (B-3)

See also Huntington, Marion, Peru

Founded 1834
Population 11,743
Elevation 700 ft
Area Code 260
Zip 46992
Information Wabash County Convention and Visitors Bureau, 111 S Wabash; phone 260/563-7171 or toll-free 800/563-1169
Web site www.wabashcountycvb.com

On March 31, 1880, the Wabash courthouse was illuminated by four electric carbon lamps. Wabash thus became the first electrically illuminated city in the world. This is the hometown of Mark C. Honeywell, founder of the Honeywell Corporation, and country singer Crystal Gayle.

The hill from which the town overlooks the Wabash River was, in 1826, the site of the signing of the Paradise Spring Treaty, by which Chief Pierish of the Potawatomi ceded the land between the Wabash and Eel rivers to the United States government for cultivation by white settlers.

In 1835, a section of the Wabash and Erie Canal was dug through this area. Much of the work was done by immigrant Irish laborers who brought with them long-smoldering differences from the old country. On July 12, about 300 men from County Cork and a roughly equal number from the north of Ireland decided to settle old scores by fighting a battle near the present site of Wabash. The first shots had been fired when the state militia arrived and separated the two groups by force.

What to See and Do

Honeywell Center. *275 W Market St. Phone toll-free 800/626-6345.* Historic Art Deco building is a community center with cultural and recreational facilities; gallery; special events, concerts. Fee for some activities. (Daily; closed holidays) **FREE**

Salamonie Reservoir, Dam, and Forest. *7 miles NE on Hwy 24 to Lagro, then 5 miles SE on Hwy 524.* Observation mound and nature center at Army Corps of Engineers project (daily; phone 260/782-2181). Several state recreation areas provide camping on 2,860-acre lake; also fishing, water-skiing, swimming, boating, launching sites (fee) and ramps (Memorial Day-Labor Day); picnicking, hunting, hiking trails. Contact office at Lost Bridge West State Recreation Area, 10 miles northeast via Highway 24, then 8 miles south on Highway 105 (daily); phone 260/468-2125. The state forest offers picnicking, camping, and fishing in Hominy Ridge; 11-acre lake; phone 260/782-2349. Fishing below the Salamonie Dam; phone 260/782-2181 or 260/468-2125.

Wabash County Historical Museum. *1 Market St (46992). Phone 219/563-0661.* Items include records and artifacts from the periods of Native American occupation, pioneer settlement, and the Civil War; research materials include local newspapers dating from 1846. (Tues-Sat; closed holidays) **FREE**

Warsaw (A-3)

See also Nappanee

Population 12,415
Area Code 219
Zip 46580
Information Kosciusko County Convention and Visitors Bureau, 313 S Buffalo St; phone 219/269-6090 or toll-free 800/800-6090
Web site www.wkchamber.com

Warsaw is in the heart of the Indiana lake region and is primarily a vacation resort. Many fine lakes in surrounding Kosciusko County have excellent swimming and boating facilities; fish are plentiful.

Local industry manufactures surgical supplies and movie projection screens; located here is one of the largest rotogravure printing plants in the United States. Kosciusko County also is home to the world's largest duck producer, Maple Leaf Farms. One mile southeast, in Winona Lake, is Grace College (1948) and Seminary (1937).

What to See and Do

Tippecanoe Lake. *6 miles N on Hwy 15, then 4 miles E.* Secluded 4-mile-long lake with recreational facilities. This is Indiana's deepest natural lake.

Special Event

Back to the Days of Kosciuszko. *800 N Park Ave, Warsaw (46580). Phone 219/269-6090.* Re-enactment of the Revolutionary War era. Food of the period, crafts, demonstrations. Participants in period clothing. Late Sept.

Limited-Service Hotel

★ ★ **RAMADA PLAZA.** *2519 E Center St, Warsaw (46580). Phone 574/269-2323; toll-free 800/272-6232; fax 574/269-2432. www.ramada.com.* 156 rooms, 4 story. Pets accepted. Check-out noon. Restaurant, bar. Fitness room. Indoor pool, outdoor pool, whirlpool. **$**

⊠ 🚶 ⛷ ⚓

Wyandotte

See also Corydon, New Albany

Population 50
Elevation 760 ft
Area Code 812
Zip 47179

What to See and Do

Little Wyandotte Cave. *On Hwy 62, 2 miles S of I-64 via Hwy 66 or Hwy 135. Phone 812/738-2782.* Large variety of cave life and formations. Impressively illuminated. Guided tours (30 minutes-45 minutes). (Memorial Day-Labor Day, daily; rest of year, Tues-Sun; closed holidays)

⭐ **Wyandotte Caves.** *7315 S Wyandotte Cave Rd (47137). On Hwy 62, 2 miles S of I-64 via either Hwy 66 or Hwy 135. Phone 812/738-2782. www.wyandottecaves.com.* Approximately 7 miles of mapped passages. Features include Garden of Helictites, a large collection of gravity-defying formations; Rothrock's Cathedral, an underground mountain 105 feet high, 140 feet wide, and 360 feet long; and Pillar of the Constitution, a stalagmite approximately 35 feet high and 71 feet in circumference. The cave was used by prehistoric Native Americans for mining aragonite and is known to have been the source of saltpeter and Epsom salts around 1812. Jacket recommended, cave temperature 52° F. One-hour guided tours (Memorial Day-Labor Day, daily). Two-hour guided tours (Memorial Day-Labor Day, daily; rest of year, Tues-Sun; closed holidays). Two-, three-, five-, and eight-hour tours (Sat-Sun, by reservations only). **$$$$**

If you are looking for a taste of Southern charm and history but are short on time, there are two great side trips to take from southern Indiana or Ohio: Louisville and Mammoth Cave National Park, both in Kentucky. Louisville is just across the Indiana border, and Mammoth Cave is just another hour and a half or so farther down Interstate 65.

Louisville, KY (F-3)

2 hours, 115 miles from Indianapolis, IN

Founded 1778
Population 256,231
Elevation 462 ft
Area Code 502
Information Convention and Visitors Bureau, 400 S First St, 40202; phone 502/584-2121 or toll-free 800/792-5595
Web site www.gotolouisville.com

Louisville is a unique city. It has Southern graces and a determined dedication to music and the arts, but to the world, Louisville is "Derby City" for at least two weeks of every year. Since its first running on May 17, 1875, the Kentucky Derby (see SPECIAL EVENTS) has generated tremendous excitement. Modeled after England's Epsom Derby, it is the oldest race in continuous existence in the United States. The first Saturday in May each year, world attention focuses on Churchill Downs (see) as the classic "run for the roses" is played out against its backdrop of Edwardian towers and antique grandstands.

The highlight of a very social city, Derby festivities are a glamorous mélange of carnival, fashion show, spectacle, and celebration of the horse. From the opening strains of "My Old Kentucky Home," played before the big race, until the final toast of bourbon is made, Louisville takes on a uniquely festive character. Afterward, the center

of thoroughbred racing quickly returns to normalcy—a city Southern in manner, Midwestern in pace.

Situated at the falls of the Ohio River, Louisville is a city long nurtured by river traffic. The Spanish, French, English, Scottish, Irish, and Germans all had roles in its exploration, settlement, and development. George Rogers Clark established the first real settlement, a base for military operations against the British, on a spit of land above the falls, now entirely erased by the river. Named after Louis XVI of France, the settlement became an important portage point around the falls; later a canal bypassed them. Today, the McAlpine Locks and Dam provide modern navigation around the falls of the Ohio River.

Louisville is a top producer of bourbon and a leader in synthetic rubber, paint and varnish, cigarettes, home appliances, and aluminum for home use.

This is a community that takes its culture seriously, with a public subscription Fund for the Arts subsidizing the Tony Award–winning Actors Theater. The city also boasts the Kentucky Center for the Arts (see), home of ballet, opera, art and music groups, and other cultural organizations.

Additional Visitor Information

The Louisville Convention and Visitors Bureau, 400 S First St, 40202, phone 502/582-3732 or toll-free 800/792-5595, provides literature and information. Also available is information about several unique areas of special interest, such as Old Louisville, Butchertown, Phoenix Hill, Cherokee Triangle, and the Main Street Preservation District (see HISTORIC DISTRICTS).

The Convention and Visitors Bureau also operates three visitor information centers that can be found on westbound Interstate 64, in the central lobby of Louisville International Airport, and downtown at 1st and Liberty streets.

For information on parks and courses in the area, call the Metropolitan Park and Recreation Board, phone 502/222-2154.

Public Transportation

Buses (Transit Authority of River City). Phone 502/585-1234

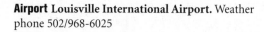

Airport **Louisville International Airport.** Weather phone 502/968-6025

Information Phone 502/367-4636

Lost and found Phone 502/367-4636

What to See and Do

American Printing House for the Blind. *1839 Frankfort Ave. Phone 502/895-2405. www.aph.org.* The largest and oldest (1858) publishing house for the blind. In addition to books and music in Braille, it issues talking books, magazines, large-type textbooks, and educational aids. Tours (Mon-Thurs 10 am-2 pm; closed holidays). **FREE**

Bellarmine University. *2001 Newburg Rd (40205). Phone 502/452-8000. www.bellarmine.edu.* (1950) (2,300 students) A 115-acre campus. Liberal arts and sciences. The campus houses the Thomas Merton Studies Center, with his manuscripts, drawings, tapes, and published works (Tues-Fri by appointment; closed holidays). Guided campus tours (by appointment).

Cave Hill Cemetery. *701 Baxter Ave. At E end of Broadway. Phone 502/451-5630. www.cavehillcemetery .com.* Burial ground of George Rogers Clark. Colonel Harland Sanders, of fried chicken fame, also is buried here. Rare trees, shrubs, and plants; swans, geese, ducks. (Daily)

⭐ **Churchill Downs.** *700 Central Ave. Phone 502/ 636-4400. www.churchilldowns.com.* Founded in 1875, this historic and world-famous thoroughbred race track is the home of the Kentucky Derby (see SPECIAL EVENTS), "the most exciting two minutes in sports." Spring race meet, late Apr-June; fall race meet, late Oct-late Nov; Kentucky Derby, first Sat in May. Adjacent is

🔍 **Kentucky Derby Museum.** *704 Central Ave, Louisville. Phone 502/637-1111. www.derbymuseum.org.* Features exhibits on Thoroughbred racing and the Kentucky Derby. High definition 360-degree show, hands-on exhibits, artifacts, educational programs, tours, and special events. Outdoor paddock area with Thoroughbreds. Tours of Churchill Downs (weather permitting). Gift shop; café serving lunch (weekdays). (Mon-Sat 8 am-5 pm, Sun from noon; closed Dec 25; also Oaks and Derby Days) **$$**

E. P. "Tom" Sawyer State Park. *3000 Freys Hill Rd. Phone 502/426-8950. www.state.ky.us/agencies/parks/ tomsawyr.htm.* Approximately 370 acres with swimming pool. Tennis; archery range; BMX track; ballfields; gymnasium, games area. Picnicking. Some fees.

Farmington Historic Home. *3033 Bardstown Rd N. At jct Watterson Expy (I-264), 6 miles SE on Hwy 31 E. Phone 502/452-9920. www.historicfarmington.org.* (1815) Federal-style house built from plans drawn by Thomas Jefferson. Abraham Lincoln visited here in 1841. Furnished with pre-1820 antiques; hidden stairway, octagonal rooms; museum room; blacksmith shop, stone barn; 19th-century garden. (Tues-Sat 10 am-4:30 pm, Sun from 1:30 pm; closed holidays) **$$**

Filson Historical Society. *1310 S 3rd St. Phone 502/635-5083. www.filsonhistorical.org.* Historical library (fee); manuscript collection, photographs and prints collection. (Mon-Sat 10 am-2 pm; closed holidays) **FREE**

Historic districts. *Old Louisville, between Breckinridge and 9th sts, near Central Park.* Features renovated Victorian housing; West Main Street Historic District is a concentration of cast-iron buildings being renovated on Main Street between 1st and 8th streets; Butchertown is a renovated 19th-century German community between Market Street and Story Avenue; Cherokee Triangle is a well-preserved Victorian neighborhood with diverse architectural details; and Portland is an early settlement and commercial port with Irish and French heritage.

Jefferson County Courthouse. *5th and Jefferson sts (40204). Phone 502/574-5761.* (1835-1860) Designed by Gideon Shryock in Greek Revival style. Cast-iron floor in rotunda supports statue of Henry Clay. Magnificent cast-iron monumental stair and balustrade in 68-foot rotunda. Statues of Thomas Jefferson and Louis XVI, as well as war memorial on grounds. Guided tours (by appointment). (Mon-Fri; closed holidays) **FREE**

Kentucky Center for the Arts. *5 Riverfront Plz. Phone 502/584-7777; toll-free 800/775-7777. www.kca.org.* Three stages present national and international performers showcasing a wide range of music, dance, and drama. Distinctive glass-arched lobby features a collection of 20th-century sculpture and provides a panoramic view of Ohio River and Falls Fountain.

A Slugger of a Tour

Louisville was founded at the falls of the Ohio River in 1788. Today, the city's waterfront around Main Street at 4th Avenue is a great place to start exploring the old downtown area. From the banks, you'll see a view of the river and the floating Louisville Falls Fountain, which periodically lets loose a geyser 375 feet into the air. At night, the display is dramatically lit.

Glance upriver and you'll see the *Belle of Louisville* (see RIVERBOAT EXCURSIONS), docked at the end of 4th Street (phone 502/574-2355). This 1914 steamboat continues to ply the waters for sightseeing cruises. The *Star of Louisville* (phone 502/589-7827) is another sightseeing boat docked a few blocks farther up on the far side of the Highway 31 bridge.

Surrounding the riverfront park is the city's historic district (see) of old warehouses and cast-iron buildings—now restored as restaurants, galleries, and shops. Start exploring around West Main Street at the southwest corner of Riverfront Park. The city's main attractions are conveniently lined up here in a compact row. Proceed west.

At the head of Sixth Street, the Kentucky Center for the Arts (see), 5 Riverfront Plaza (phone 502/584-7777), is home to the city's resident opera, ballet, orchestra, and children's theater. It also has an impressive collection of 20th-century sculpture throughout the dramatic glass-walled center. Free audiotape tours are available. Kentucky's Art and Craft Center at 609 West Main Street displays contemporary pieces by native artists (phone 502/589-0102). Down at 7th and Main streets is the site of Fort Nelson, where the town's original settlement was built in 1782.

Louisville Science Center (see) (727 West Main Street; phone 502/561-6100) contains five stories of hands-on exhibits in a transformed warehouse. Children particularly enjoy the Egyptian mummy and space exhibits, not to mention the IMAX theater.

At the corner of West Main and 8th streets, the landmark 120-foot-high Louisville Slugger—the world's largest baseball bat—marks the site of the Louisville Slugger Museum (see) (phone 502/588-7228). Not only does the museum hold beloved baseball artifacts and memorabilia, but visitors also can watch the bats being made during the factory tour.

Restaurant; gift shop; parking garage. (See SPECIAL EVENTS)

Kentucky Fair and Exposition Center. *937 Phillips Ln (40209). I-65 S at I-264 W. Phone 502/367-5000. www.kyfairexpo.org.* More than 1 million-square-foot complex includes coliseum, exposition halls, stadium, amusement park. More than 1,500 events take place throughout the year, including basketball and Milwaukee Brewers minor league affiliate team games.

Locust Grove. *561 Blankenbaker Ln. 6 miles NE on River Rd, then 1 mile SW. Phone 502/897-9845. www. locustgrove.org.* (circa 1790) Home of General George Rogers Clark from 1809 to 1818. Handsome Georgian mansion on 55 acres; original paneling, staircase; authentic furnishings; garden; eight restored outbuildings. Visitors center features audiovisual program.

(Mon-Sat 10 am-4:30 pm, Sun 1:30-4:30 pm; closed holidays; also Derby Day) **$$**

Louisville Presbyterian Theological Seminary. *1044 Alta Vista Rd. 1/2 mile off Hwy 60 Business, adjacent to Cherokee Park. Phone 502/895-3411. www.lpts.edu.* (1853) (250 students) On 52-acre campus is Gardencourt and a renovated turn-of-the-century mansion. **FREE**

Louisville Science Center & IMAX Theatre. *727 W Main St. Phone 502/561-6100. www.louisvillescience .org.* Hands-on scientific exhibits; aerospace hall; IMAX four-story screen film theater (fee); World We Create interactive exhibit. (Mon-Thurs 9:30 am-5 pm, Fri-Sat to 9 pm, Sun noon-6 pm; closed Thanksgiving, Dec 24-25) **$$**

Louisville Slugger Museum & Bat Factory. *800 W Main St. Phone 502/588-7228. www.sluggermuseum .org.* Manufacturers of Louisville Slugger baseball bats and Power-bilt golf clubs. No cameras. Children over 8 years only; must be accompanied by adult. Tours. (Mon-Sat 9 am-5 pm, also Apr-Nov, Sun noon-5 pm; closed holidays) **$$**

Louisville Zoo. *1100 Trevilian Way. 7 miles SE via I-65, I-264 to Poplar Level Rd N. Phone 502/459-2181. www.louisvillezoo.org.* Modern zoo exhibits more than 1,600 animals in natural settings. In HerpAquarium are simulated water, desert, and rain forest ecosystems. Islands exhibit highlights endangered species and habitats. Camel and elephant rides (summer). (Sept-Mar, daily 10 am-4 pm, rest of year to 5 pm; closed Jan 1, Thanksgiving, Dec 25). **$$**

Otter Creek Park. *850 Otter Creek Park Rd, Brandenburg (40108). 30 miles SW via Hwy 31 W and Hwy 1638, near Fort Knox. Phone 502/574-4583. www. louky.org/fp/ottercreek.* A 3,000-acre park located on the site of Rock Haven, a town destroyed by a 1937 flood. Much of the park that fronts the Ohio River consists of steep cliffs or very wooded banks. Otter Creek is a small, deeply entrenched stream with steep banks. Artifacts found here indicate that many Native American tribes used the Otter Creek area as hunting and fishing grounds. Swimming pools, fishing, boating (ramp). Miniature golf, tennis, basketball, picnic facilities, tent and trailer sites, cabins, lodge, restaurant. Nature center, wildlife area. Park (daily). **FREE**

Riverboat excursions. *Riverfront Plz, 4th St and River Rd (40202). Phone 502/574-2355.* Two-hour afternoon trips on stern-wheelers *Belle of Louisville* and *Spirit of Jefferson* (Memorial Day-Labor Day, Tues-Sun); sunset cruise (Tues, Thurs); dance cruise (Sat).

Six Flags Kentucky Kingdom. *937 Phillips Ln. Adjacent to Kentucky Fair and Exposition Center (see). Phone 502/366-7508. www.sixflags.com.* Amusement and water park with more than 110 rides and attractions, including five roller coasters. (Memorial Day-Labor Day, daily; early Apr-Memorial Day, Fri evenings, Sat-Sun; Labor Day-Oct, Sat-Sun) **$$$$**

Spalding University. *851 S 4th St. Phone 502/585-9911. www.spalding.edu.* (1814) (1,400 students) Liberal arts college. On campus is Whitestone Mansion (1871), a Renaissance Revival house with period furniture (Mon-Fri; closed holidays), art gallery. **FREE**

Thomas Edison House. *729-731 E Washington. Phone 502/585-5247. www.edisonhouse.org.* The restored 1850 cottage where Edison lived while working for Western Union after the Civil War. The bedroom is furnished in the period; four display rooms with Edison memorabilia and inventions: phonographs, records and cylinders, and an early bulb collection. (Tues-Sat 10 am-2 pm; also by appointment) **$**

University of Louisville. *2301 S 3rd St (40292). 3 miles S at 3rd St and Eastern Pkwy. Information centers at 3rd St entrance and at corner of 1st and Brandeis sts. Phone 502/852-6665. www.louisville.edu.* (1798) (23,000 students) On Belknap Campus is the Ekstrom Library with the John Patterson rare book collection, original town charter signed by Thomas Jefferson and the Photo Archives, one of largest collections of photographs in the country. Also here is an enlarged cast of Rodin's sculpture *The Thinker;* a Foucault pendulum more than 73 feet high, demonstrating the Earth's rotation; and the largest concert organ in the Midwest. Two art galleries feature works by students and locals, as well as by national and international artists (Mon-Fri, Sun). The grave of Supreme Court Justice Louis D. Brandeis is located under the School of Law portico. Also on campus are

Rauch Memorial Planetarium. *1st and Brandeis sts, Louisville. Phone 502/852-6665.* Planetarium shows (Sat afternoons). **$$**

Speed Art Museum. *2035 S 3rd St, Louisville. Phone 502/634-2700. www.speedmuseum.org.* Oldest and largest in state. Traditional and modern art, English Renaissance Room, sculpture collection, Kentucky artists; special exhibits. Café, shop, and bookstore. Tours on request. (Tues-Wed, Fri 10:30 am-4 pm, Thurs to 8 pm, Sun noon-5 pm; closed Mon; holidays) **FREE**

Water Tower. *Zorn Ave and River Rd (40207). Phone 502/896-2146.* Restored tower and pumping station built in the classic style in 1860. Tower houses Louisville Visual Art Association, Center for Contemporary Art. Exhibits vary. (Daily; closed holidays) **FREE**

Zachary Taylor National Cemetery. *4701 Brownsboro Rd. 7 miles E on Hwy 42. Phone 502/893-3852.* The 12th president of the United States is buried here, near the site where he lived from infancy to adulthood. The Taylor family plot is surrounded by this national cemetery, established in 1928. (Daily)

Special Events

Corn Island Storytelling Festival. *12019 Donohue Ave, Louisville (40243). Citywide. Phone 502/245-0643. www.cornislandstorytellingfestival.org.* Recaptures bygone days of yarn spinning. Events held at various sites in the city. Programs include ghost stories at night in Long Run Park and storytelling cruises. Third weekend in Sept.

Horse racing. *Churchill Downs* (see), *700 Central St, Louisville (40208).*

Kentucky Derby. *Churchill Downs* (see), *700 Central Ave, Louisville (40208). Phone 502/636-4400. www. kentuckyderby.com.* The first jewel in the Triple Crown. First Sat in May.

Kentucky Derby Festival. *1001 S 3rd St, Louisville (40203). Phone 502/584-6383; toll-free 800/928-3378.* Two-week celebration with Pegasus Parade, Great Steamboat Race (between *Belle of Louisville* (see RIVERBOAT EXCURSIONS) and *Delta Queen*), Great Balloon Race, mini-marathon, concerts, sports tournaments. Held two weeks prior to Kentucky Derby (see).

Kentucky State Fair. *Kentucky Fair and Exposition Center* (see), *937 Phillips Ln, Louisville (40209). Phone 502/367-5002. www.kystatefair.org.* Livestock shows, championship horse show; home and fine arts exhibits; midway, entertainment. Aug.

Performing arts. *300 W Main St, Louisville (40202). Phone 502/583-8738.* Louisville Orchestra (phone 502/587-8681), Kentucky Opera (phone 502/584-4500), Broadway Series (phone 502/561-1003), Louisville Ballet (phone 502/583-2623), Stage One: Louisville's Family Theatre (phone 502/589-5964); all at Kentucky Center for the Arts; (phone 502/584-7777). Actors Theatre, 316 W Main St (phone 502/584-1265). Kentucky Shakespeare Festival, free plays in Central Park, mid-June-late July, Mon-Sat.

Limited-Service Hotels

★ ★ **BEST WESTERN BROWNSBORO INN.** *4805 Brownsboro Rd, Louisville (40207). Phone 502/893-2551; toll-free 800/528-1234; fax 502/895-2417. www.bestwestern.com.* 144 rooms, 2 story. Check-out 11 am. Restaurant, bar. Fitness room. Pool, whirlpool. Airport transportation available. **$**

★ ★ **COURTYARD BY MARRIOTT.** *9608 Blairwood Rd, Louisville (40222). Phone 502/429-0006; fax 502/429-5926. www.courtyard.com.* 151 rooms, 4 story. Check-out noon. Bar. Fitness room. Pool, whirlpool. **$**

★ **FAIRFIELD INN.** *9400 Blairwood Rd, Louisville (40222). Phone 502/339-1900; fax 502/339-2494. www. fairfieldinn.com.* 105 rooms, 3 story. Check-out noon. Pool. **$**

★ ★ **FOUR POINTS BY SHERATON.** *9802 Bunsen Way, Louisville (40299). Phone 502/499-0000; fax 502/493-2905. www.fourpoints.com.* 150 rooms, 5 story. Check-out noon. Restaurant, bar. Fitness room. Indoor pool, whirlpool. Airport transportation available. **$**

★ ★ **GALT HOUSE HOTEL.** *140 N 4th St, Louisville (40202). Phone 502/589-5200; toll-free 800/626-1814; fax 502/589-3444. www.galthouse.com.* 700 rooms, 25 story. Check-out noon. Restaurant, bar. Pool. Overlooks Ohio River. **$$**

★ **HAMPTON INN.** *800 Phillips Ln, Louisville (40209). Phone 502/366-8100; toll-free 800/426-7866; fax 502/366-0700. www.hamptoninn.com.* 130 rooms, 4 story. Complimentary continental breakfast. Check-out noon. Fitness room. Pool. Airport transportation available. **$**

★ ★ **HOLIDAY INN.** *120 W Broadway, Louisville (40202). Phone 502/582-2241; toll-free 800/626-1558; fax 502/584-8591. www.holiday-inn.com.* 289 rooms, 12 story. Pets accepted, some restrictions. Check-out noon. Restaurant, bar. Fitness room. Indoor pool. Airport transportation available. **$**

★ **SIGNATURE INN LOUISVILLE SOUTH.** *6515 Signature Dr, Louisville (40213). Phone 502/968-4100; toll-free 800/822-5252; fax 502/968-6375. www. signatureinn.com.* 123 rooms, 2 story. Complimentary continental breakfast. Check-out noon. Pool. Airport transportation available. Business center. **$**

Full-Service Hotels

★ ★ ★ **THE BROWN HOTEL.** *335 W Broadway, Louisville (40202). Phone 502/583-1234; toll-free 888/888-5252; fax 502/587-7006. www.camberleyhotels.com.* The beautifully restored lobby of this hotel exudes Southern elegance, with intricate plaster moldings, polished woodwork, stained glass, and crystal chandeliers. Built by philanthropist J. Graham Brown in 1923, the property's Georgian Revival-style building remains a cornerstone of Louisville social life. The elegance of the public spaces continues through the rooms and the magnificent mirrored Crystal Ballroom. 292 rooms, 16 story. Check-out 11 am. Restaurant, bar. Fitness room. Airport transportation available. Business center. **$$**

★ ★ ★ **EXECUTIVE INN.** *978 Phillips Ln, Louisville (40209). Phone 502/367-6161; toll-free 800/626-2706; fax 502/363-1880. www.executiveinnhotel .com.* This property has an interesting Tudor-style design with all the charm and warmth of a European hotel. It has richly crafted woodwork and spacious comfortable rooms overlooking a beautiful courtyard and heated pool; surrounded with magnolia trees and waterwheels. 465 rooms, 6 story. Pets accepted; fee. Check-out 1 pm. Restaurant, bar. Fitness room. Indoor pool, outdoor pool, children's pool. Airport transportation available. **$**

★ ★ ★ **HYATT REGENCY LOUISVILLE.** *320 W Jefferson, Louisville (40202). Phone 502/587-3434; fax 502/581-0133. www.hyatt.com.* From this hotel, guests will find views that overlook the Ohio River and the downtown area. The hotel is connected to both the Commonwealth Convention Center and the Louisville Galleria shopping mall. 392 rooms, 18. story. Check-out noon. Restaurant, bar. Fitness room. Indoor pool, whirlpool. Tennis. Business center. **$**

★ ★ ★ **THE SEELBACH HILTON LOUISVILLE.** *500 4th Ave, Louisville (40202). Phone 502/585-3200; toll-free 800/333-3399; fax 502/585-9239. www.hilton.com.* Built in 1905 by brothers Otto and Louis Seelbach, this hotel is on the National Register of Historic Places. From presidents to movie stars to authors (F. Scott Fitzgerald wrote about the hotel in *The Great Gatsby*), everyone seems drawn here. The dramatic entrance, with its muraled ceilings, marble columns, and regal staircase, leads to the impeccable Oakroom restaurant. 321 rooms, 11 story. Pets accepted; fee. Check-out 1 pm. Restaurant, bar. Airport transportation available. Business center. **$$**

Specialty Lodgings

The following lodging establishments are approved by Mobil Travel Guide, but due to their unique and individualized nature have not been given a traditional Mobil Star rating. Included in this listing you may find bed-and-breakfasts, limited-service inns, guest ranches, and other unique hotel properties.

COLUMBINE BED AND BREAKFAST. *1707 S 3rd St, Louisville (40208). Phone 502/635-5000; toll-free 800/635-5010. www.thecolumbine.com.* House built in 1900 with full-length porch. 6 rooms, 3 story. Children over 12 years only. Complimentary full breakfast. Check-in 3 pm, check-out 11 am. **$**

WOODHAVEN BED AND BREAKFAST. *401 S Hubbards Ln, Louisville (40207). Phone 502/895-1011. www.innatwoodhaven.com.* Gothic Revival house built in 1853. 8 rooms, 2 story. Pets accepted, some restrictions. Complimentary full breakfast. Check-in 3 pm, check-out 11:30 am. **$**

Restaurants

★ ★ **ASIATIQUE.** *106 Sears Ave, Louisville (40207). Phone 502/899-3578; fax 502/899-5859. www.asiatique.bigstep.com.* Dinner. Closed holidays. Bar. Children's menu. **$$**

★ ★ ★ **CAFE METRO.** *1700 Bardstown Rd, Louisville (40205). Phone 502/458-4830; fax 502/458-4252.* American menu. Dinner. Closed Sun; holidays. Bar. **$$**

★ **CAFE MIMOSA.** *1216 Bardstown Rd, Louisville (40204). Phone 502-458-2233; fax 502/451-8887.* Chinese, Vietnamese menu. Lunch, dinner, Sun brunch. Children's menu. **$$**

★ ★ ★ **ENGLISH GRILL.** *335 W Broadway, Louisville (40202). Phone 502/583-1234; fax 502/ 587-7006. www.camberleyhotels.com.* This ornate dining room in The Brown Hotel (see) has a decidedly uppercrust English feel and a menu by Joe Castro to match. The sophisticated service and a wine list heavy on Bordeaux complete the experience, considered by many to be the best in town. American menu. Dinner. Closed Sun. Bar. **$$$**

★ ★ ★ **FERD GRISANTI.** *10212 Taylorsville Rd, Louisville (40299). Phone 502/267-0050; fax 502/ 267-0119. www.ferdgrisanti.com.* This restaurant in historic Jeffersontown has been serving up traditional Italian fare on white linen-covered tables for over 25 years. The atmosphere is dressy but not stuffy, and the service is warm and professional. The seafood, eggplant Parmesan, and pasta dishes are sure to please, so don't fill up on the great bread sticks before the entrées arrive. Italian menu. Dinner. Closed Sun. Bar. Children's menu. **$$**

★ ★ **FIFTH QUARTER STEAKHOUSE.** *1241 Durrett Ln, Louisville (40213). Phone 502/361-2363; fax 502/361-3135.* Steak menu. Lunch, dinner. Closed Dec 25. Bar. **$$**

★ **JESSIE'S FAMILY RESTAURANT.** *9609 Dixie Hwy, Louisville (40272). Phone 502/937-6332.* American menu. Breakfast, lunch, dinner. Closed Thanksgiving, Dec 24-26; also July 4 week. **$$**

★ ★ ★ **KUNZ'S FOURTH AND MARKET.** *115 S 4th St, Louisville (40202). Phone 502/585-5555; fax 502/585-5567.* This Louisville institution has been owned and operated by the same family since 1892. Although the original burned down in 1987, and the new building has a little less charm, you can still get great steaks, seafood, and raw bar treats. American menu. Lunch, dinner. Closed Dec 25. Children's menu. **$$$**

★ ★ ★ **LE RELAIS.** *2817 Taylorsville Rd, Louisville (40205). Phone 502/451-9020; fax 502/459-3112. www. lerelaisrestaurant.com.* Formerly a room in an airport administration building. French menu. Dinner. Closed Mon; holidays. Bar. Outdoor seating. **$$**

★ ★ ★ **LILLY'S.** *1147 Bardstown Rd, Louisville (40204). Phone 502/451-0447; fax 502/458-7546. www. lillyslapeche.com.* A brightly colored neon sign marks the window of chef Kathy Cary's innovative dining room, a hint to the Art Deco interior that lies beyond the red brick entrance. Her seasonally changing menu, which in its early days showed more of a Kentucky accent, has an eclectic, urban edge with dishes such as seared scallops in mango-tarragon beurre blanc. Fusion menu. Lunch, dinner. Closed Sun-Mon; Jan 1, Dec 25; also two weeks in Aug. **$$$**

★ ★ **LYNN'S PARADISE CAFE.** *984 Barret Ave, Louisville (40204). Phone 502/583-3447; fax 502/583- 0211. www.lynnsparadisecafe.com.* Fusion menu. Breakfast, lunch, dinner. Closed Mon; Thanksgiving, Dec 25. Bar. Children's menu. Outdoor seating. **$**

★ ★ **MASTERSON'S.** *1830 S 3rd St, Louisville (40208). Phone 502/636-2511; fax 502/636-2515. www.mastersons.com.* Greek, American menu. Lunch, dinner, Sun brunch. Closed holidays. Bar. Children's menu. Outdoor seating. **$$**

★ ★ **SICHUAN GARDEN.** *9850 Linn Station Rd, Louisville (40223). Phone 502/426-6767; fax 502/425-4567.* Frosted glass room dividers. Chinese, Thai menu. Lunch, dinner, Sun brunch. Closed Thanksgiving. Bar. **$$**

★ **THAI SIAM.** *3002-1/2 Bardstown Rd, Louisville (40205). Phone 502/458-6871. www.thaisiamky.com.* Thai menu. Lunch, dinner. Closed holidays. **$$**

★ ★ **TIMOTHY'S.** *826 E Broadway, Louisville (40204). Phone 502/561-0880; fax 502/568-4689.* Italian, American menu. Dinner. Closed Sun; Easter, Thanksgiving, Dec 25. Bar. Outdoor seating. **$$**

★ ★ **UPTOWN CAFE.** *1624 Bardstown Rd, Louisville (40205). Phone 502/458-4212; fax 502/ 458-4252.* Converted storefront. Continental menu. Lunch, dinner. Closed Sun; holidays. Bar. **$$**

★ ★ ★ **VINCENZO'S.** *150 S 5th St, Louisville (40202). Phone 502/580-1350; fax 502/580-1355.* This restaurant is situated in downtown Louisville. Italian menu. Lunch, dinner. Closed Sun; holidays. Valet parking (dinner). **$$$**

★ ★ **WINSTON'S.** *3101 Bardstown Rd, Louisville (40205). Phone 502/456-0980; fax 502/454-4880.* Operated by senior culinary students. Lunch, dinner, Sun brunch. Closed Mon-Thurs; holidays. Bar. Children's menu. **$$$**

Mammoth Cave National Park, KY

3 1/2 hours, 206 miles from Indianapolis, IN

Web site www.nps.gov/maca

On Hwy 70, 10 miles W of Cave City or 8 miles NW of Park City on Hwy 255.

This enormous underground complex of intertwining passages, totaling more than 350 miles in length, was carved by mildly acidic water trickling for thousands of years through limestone. Species of colorless, eyeless fish, crayfish, and other creatures make their home within. The remains of a crude system used to mine 400,000 pounds of nitrate to make gunpowder for use in the War of 1812 are visible. The cave was the scene of an experiment aimed at a cure for tuberculosis. Mushroom growing also was attempted within the cave.

Above ground, the park consists of 52,830 acres with sinkholes, rivers, and 70 miles of hiking trails. Picnicking; lodging. Camping (Mar-Dec, daily; some fees). An orientation movie is offered at the visitor center (daily; closed Dec 25). Evening programs are conducted by park interpreters (summer, daily; spring, fall, weekends).

Ranger-led tours of Mammoth Cave vary greatly in distance and length. Trails are solid and fairly smooth and require stooping or bending in places. Most tours involve steps and extensive walking; many are considered strenuous; proper footwear is recommended (no sandals). A sweater or wrap also is advised, even though it may be a hot day above ground. Tours are conducted by experienced National Park Service interpreters. Contact the Superintendent, PO Box 7, Mammoth Cave 42259, phone 270/758-2328.

What to See and Do

⭐ **Cave tours.** *Phone 270/758-2328; toll-free 800/ 967-2283.* Depart from the visitor center (schedules vary with season; no tours Dec 25). Advance reservations highly recommended. Tickets may be purchased in advance through Destinet Outlets. The following is a partial list of available cave tours:

> **Frozen Niagara.** *Park City. Phone toll-free 800/ 967-2283.* This moderately strenuous tour (two hours) explores huge pits, domes, and decorative dripstone formations. **$$$**

> **Historic cave tour.** *Park City. Phone 270/758-2251.* A 2-mile, two-hour guided tour highlights the cave's rich human history; artifacts of Native Americans, early explorers; ruins of mining operations. **$$**

> **Travertine.** *Park City. Phone toll-free 800/967-2283.* Quarter-mile Travertine (one hour) is considered an easy tour through Drapery Room, Frozen Niagara, and Crystal Lake. Designed for those unable to take many steps. **$$$**

> **Violet City.** *Park City. Phone toll-free 800/967-2283.* A 3-mile lantern-light tour (three hours) of historic features, including tuberculosis hospital huts and some of the cave's largest rooms and passageways. **$$$$**

***Miss Green* riverboat trip.** *511 Grinstead Mill Rd (42259). Phone 270/758-2243.* Round-trip cruise (60 minutes) through scenic and wildlife areas of the park. Advance tickets may be purchased at the visitor center. (Apr-Oct, daily) **$$$**

Limited-Service Hotel

★ **MAMMOTH CAVE HOTEL.** *Hwy 70, Mammoth Cave (42259). Phone 270/758-2225; fax 270/258-2301. www.mammothcavehotel.com.* 62 rooms, 2 story. Check-out noon. Restaurant. Tennis. **$**
🏃

Ohio

Ohio is a combination of rich agricultural farmland and forests, as well as a center for technology, education, industry, and recreation. Its farmland is dotted with major industrial cities and crisscrossed by roads and railways that carry most of the traffic between the East and Midwest. Taking its name from the Iroquois word for "something great," the state has produced its share of great men, including Thomas Edison, astronauts John Glenn and Neil Armstrong, and eight of the nation's presidents—William Harrison, Grant, Hayes, Garfield, Benjamin Harrison, McKinley, Taft, and Harding.

The earliest inhabitants of the area were prehistoric people who built more than 10,000 mounds, many of them effigy mounds of great beauty. The first European to explore the Ohio area was probably the French explorer La Salle, in about 1669. Conflicting French and British claims of the area led to the French and Indian War, which ended in a treaty giving most of France's lands east of the Mississippi to Great Britain.

The Northwest Ordinance of 1787 set up the Northwest Territory, of which the future state of Ohio was a division. New Englanders of the Ohio Company bought land in the Muskingum River Valley and founded Marietta, the first permanent settlement. Other settlements soon sprang up along the Ohio River. The area grew as Revolutionary War veterans received land in payment for their services. Ohio became a state in 1803.

Though Ohioans had mixed feelings about the issue of slavery and the Civil War, about 345,000 men responded to Union calls for volunteers—more than twice the state's quota. Ohio also provided several Union commanders, including Ulysses S. Grant and William T. Sherman.

After the Civil War ended, Ohio's abundant natural resources and its strategic position between two of the country's principal waterways—Lake Erie on the north and the Ohio River on the south—paved the way for rapid industrialization and growth. Today, Ohio has many major metropolitan areas, but its citizens are equally proud of Ohio's excellent park system; its wealth of small, tree-shaded towns; and its "queen city," Cincinnati.

When to Go/Climate

Ohio summers can be hot and humid, especially in the south. The Lake Erie shore areas often experience cooler summer temperatures than elsewhere in the state, but can be subject to harsh winter winds and sudden snowstorms.

Population: 10,847,115
Area: 41,004 square miles
Elevation: 433 feet-1,550 feet
Peak: Campbell Hill (Logan County)
Entered Union: March 1, 1803 (17th state)
Capital: Columbus
Motto: With God, All Things Are Possible
Nickname: Buckeye State
Flower: Scarlet Carnation
Bird: Cardinal
Tree: Ohio Buckeye
Fair: Early August in Columbus
Time Zone: Eastern
Web site: www.ohiotourism.com
Fun Facts:
- The first full-time automobile service station opened in Ohio in 1899.
- Harry M. Stevens created the first hot dog in Ohio in 1900.

Calendar Highlights

JULY

All-American Soap Box Derby (Akron). Derby Downs, Akron Municipal Airport. Phone 330/733-8723. More than 200 boys and girls (9-16 years) from United States and abroad compete with homemade, gravity-powered cars for scholarships, prizes.

Pro Football Hall of Fame Festival (Canton). Pro Football Hall of Fame. Phone 330/456-7253 or toll-free 800/533-4302. Events include parade, induction ceremony, AFC-NFC Hall of Fame Pro Game.

AUGUST

Boat Regatta (Put-in-Bay and Vermilion). Phone 440/967-6634. More than 200 sailboats race to Vermilion.

Ohio State Fair (Columbus). Ohio Expo Center. Phone 614/644-3247 or toll-free 888/646-3976. Agricultural and industrial exposition plus grandstand entertainment, pageants, and horse show.

SEPTEMBER

Riverfest (Cincinnati). Phone 513/532-4000 (Cincinnati Recreation Commission); toll-free 800/246-2987 (Convention and Visitors Bureau). Celebration of Cincinnati's river heritage held along the city's waterfront parks. Festivities include fireworks, three stages of entertainment, food.

OCTOBER

Bob Evans Farm Festival (Gallipolis). Bob Evans Farm. Phone 740/245-5305 or toll-free 800/994-3276. Bluegrass and country entertainment, food, 150 heritage craftspeople and demonstrations; Appalachian clogging, square dancing. Camping.

DECEMBER

Christmas Candle Lightings (Coshocton). Roscoe Village. Phone toll-free 800/877-1830. Tree- and candle-lighting ceremonies; hot-mulled cider, ginger cookies.

Christmas in Zoar (New Philadelphia). Phone 330/874-3011. Tours of private houses, craft show, German food, strolling carolers, and tree-lighting ceremony.

AVERAGE HIGH/LOW TEMPERATURES (° F)

Cleveland

Jan 32/18	**May** 69/47	**Sept** 74/54
Feb 35/19	**June** 78/57	**Oct** 62/44
Mar 46/28	**July** 82/61	**Nov** 50/35
Apr 58/37	**Aug** 81/60	**Dec** 37/25

Columbus

Jan 34/19	**May** 72/50	**Sept** 76/55
Feb 38/21	**June** 80/58	**Oct** 65/43
Mar 51/31	**July** 84/63	**Nov** 51/34
Apr 62/40	**Aug** 82/61	**Dec** 39/25

Parks and Recreation

Water-related activities, hiking, riding, various other sports, picnicking, camping, and visitor centers are available in many of these areas. Camping is permitted all year in 57 parks: $9-$30 each site per night, no reservations. Reservations taken by application beginning March 1 for Rent-A-Camp program (May-Sept) at many parks: $24-$38 each site per night, including all equipment. Reservations taken up to one year in advance for housekeeping cabins at 16 parks (all year-round): $140-$350 per night; June-Aug, by the week only, $285-$900 per week. Resort lodges also are available at eight locations. Pets allowed in designated campsites only. For details, contact Information Center, Ohio Department of Natural Resources, Division of Parks and Recreation, 1952 Belcher Dr, Building C-3, Columbus 43224-1386, phone 614/265-6561 or toll-free 800/282-7275 (reservations only).

FISHING AND HUNTING

Annual fishing license $19, nonresident $40; one-day permit $11; three-day permit $19. Hunting license $19 (resident youth $10), nonresident $125. Special deer and wild turkey permits $24. Fur-taker permit

$15. Wetlands habitat stamp $15. Tourist small game permit $40. Hunting forbidden on Sunday, except for coyote, fox, woodchuck, and waterfowl in season. For latest game and fishing regulations, contact the Department of Natural Resources, Division of Wildlife, 1840 Belcher Dr, Columbus 43224-1329, phone 614/265-6300 or toll-free 800/945-3543.

Driving Information

Safety belts are mandatory for all persons in front seat of vehicle. Children under 4 years or under 40 pounds—anywhere in vehicle—must be in an approved safety seat. For further information, phone 614/466-2550.

INTERSTATE HIGHWAY SYSTEM
The following alphabetical listing of Ohio towns in this book shows that these cities are within 10 miles of the indicated interstate highways. Check a highway map for the nearest exit.

Highway Number	Cities/Towns within 10 Miles
Interstate 70	Cambridge, Columbus, Dayton, Newark, Springfield, St. Clairsville, Vandalia, Zanesville.
Interstate 71	Akron, Cincinnati, Cleveland, Columbus, Delaware, Lebanon, Mansfield, Mason, Mount Gilead, Strongsville, Wilmington.
Interstate 75	Bowling Green, Cincinnati, Dayton, Findlay, Lebanon, Lima, Mason, Miamisburg, Middletown, Piqua, Sidney, Toledo, Vandalia, Wapakoneta.
Interstate 76	Akron, Kent, Youngstown.
Interstate 77	Akron, Brecksville, Cambridge, Canton, Cleveland, Gnadenhutten, Marietta, Massillon, New Philadelphia.
Interstate 90	Ashtabula, Chardon, Cleveland, Geneva-on-the-Lake, Mentor, Painesville.

Additional Visitor Information

For free travel information, contact the Ohio Division of Travel and Tourism, PO Box 1001, Columbus 43216, phone toll-free 800/282-5393. The Ohio Historical Society is a good source for historical information; contact Director, 1982 Velma Ave, Columbus 43211, phone 614/297-2300 or toll-free 800/282-5393.

Travel information centers are located on interstate highways at key roadside rest areas. These centers offer free brochures containing information on Ohio's attractions and events; staff also are on hand to answer any questions.

THE BRIDGES OF ASHTABULA COUNTY

This tour explores Ashtabula County, also known as "Covered Bridge Capital of Ohio" and "Wine Capital of Ohio." Sixty-five percent of Ohio's grapes grow in this county, which is located along 27 miles of Lake Erie shoreline; a collection of family-owned wineries produce excellent award-winning domestic wines. Add 16 covered bridges set in quaint villages, and you have the recipe for a perfect romantic getaway.

This tour can take a few hours, or it can take all day; it all depends on how many of the bridges you plan on visiting, how much time you spend at each one, and how many side trips you make. Keep in mind that road conditions on the route between bridges may vary—a lot of gravel awaits you. Directional signs are up but one or two are missing, so be prepared to backtrack. You can pick up a map outlining several different tour routes from the Ashtabula County Chamber of Commerce.

Jefferson, 10 miles south of Ashtabula, is our starting point for this tour, which includes 11 of the 16 covered bridges in the area. First on our route is Netcher Road Bridge, which crosses Mill Creek. Built in 1998, the Netcher Road Bridge is the newest in this area and features a neo-Victorian design. Head next to nearby South Denmark Bridge, also over Mill Creek. Caine Road Bridge, built to commemorate the 175th anniversary of Ashtabula County, is in Pierpont Township over Ashtabula River, just 6 miles away. Next stop is the Graham Road Bridge, which is no longer in use. You'll find it in a picturesque little park on the south side of the road. Root Road Bridge is just 4 miles away, spanning the Ashtabula River. Middle Road Bridge, State Road Bridge, and Creek Road Bridge (all within a few miles of one another) have the distinct honor of crossing Conneaut Creek, the longest river in eastern Ashtabula County. Middle Road Bridge, originally built in 1868, was rehabilitated in 1984 by a handful of volunteers. State Road Bridge was constructed of over 97,000 feet of southern pine and oak. Continue 2 miles to Benetka Road Bridge, then 3 more miles to Olin Bridge, which is the only Ashtabula County bridge named after a family. The Olin family and their descendants have lived in this area since the bridge was built in 1873. The last bridge on our route is the Giddings Road Bridge, 12 miles away over Mill Creek in Jefferson Township.

To round out your day of covered bridge travels, head north from Jefferson to the Lake Erie shoreline, where you'll have your pick of wineries to visit. The largest concentration of these is in the town of Conneaut. If you're looking for a place to spend the night, look no further than the bed-and-breakfast at Buccia Vineyard. Ferrante Winery & Ristorante is a great place to sample award-winning wines alongside authentic Italian cuisine. Old Firehouse Winery, west of Conneaut in Geneva-on-the-Lake, is a great place to head if you are looking for a more casual eatery. Located in what was originally the village's first firehouse, this winery has the added bonus of a lakefront location. **(Approximately 80 miles)**

Akron (B-4)

See also Alliance, Aurora, Canton, Cleveland, Kent, Massillon, Wooster

Founded 1825
Population 223,019
Elevation 1,027 ft
Area Code 330
Information Akron/Summit Convention and Visitors Bureau, 77 E Mill St, 44308-1401; phone 330/374-7560 or toll-free 800/245-4254
Web site www.visitakron-summit.org

The "rubber capital of the world" is 35 miles south of the St. Lawrence Seaway, on the highest point on the Ohio and Erie Canal, covering an area of approximately 54 square miles. Metropolitan Akron has many manufacturing plants, as well as strong service, trade, and government sectors. Although best known for its rubber factories, housing corporate headquarters of four major rubber companies, Akron also is a center for polymer research.

Akron owes its start to the Ohio and Erie Canal, which was opened to traffic in 1827. General Simon Perkins, commissioner of the Ohio Canal Fund, seeing the trade possibilities, laid out the town two years earlier. The seat of Summit County was already thriving when Dr. Benjamin Franklin Goodrich organized the first rubber plant in 1870. This event aroused little interest, and it took the "horseless carriage" to spark the future of Akron. By 1915, it was a boom town. The major rubber companies maintain large research laboratories and developmental departments. Other products range from fishing tackle to plastics and industrial machine products.

What to See and Do

Akron Civic Theatre. *182 S Main St. Phone 330/535-3179.* (1929) Lavishly designed by Viennese architect John Eberson to resemble a night in a Moorish garden, complete with blinking stars and floating clouds. The theater is one of four atmospheric-type facilities of its size remaining in the country. (Daily)

Akron Zoo. *500 Edgewood Ave. Phone 330/375-2525.* This 26-acre zoo features more than 300 birds, mammals, and reptiles from around the world. Exhibits include the Ohio Farmyard, where children can pet and feed the animals; Tiger Valley, with tigers, lions, and bears; a walk-through aviary; and an underwater viewing window for observing river otters. (Daily; closed holidays) **$$**

Boston Mills. *7100 Riverview Rd, Peninsula. Phone 330/657-2334. www.bmbw.com.* Skiing. Four triple, two double chair lifts, two handle tows; patrol, school, rentals, snowmaking; cafeteria, bar. Longest run 1,800 feet; vertical drop 240 feet. (Dec-mid-Mar, daily) **$$$$**

Brandywine. *7100 Riverview Rd, Peninsula. Phone 330/657-2334. www.bmbw.com.* Skiing. Triple, four quad chair lifts, three handle tows; patrol, school, rentals, snowmaking; cafeteria, bars. Longest run 1,800 feet; vertical drop 240 feet. (Early Dec-mid-Mar, daily) **$$$$**

Cuyahoga River Gorge Reservation. *Main and Market sts. Phone 330/867-5511.* Part of the park system. On the north bank is the cave where Mary Campbell, the first white child in the Western Reserve, was held prisoner by Native Americans.

Cuyahoga Valley National Park. *15610 Vaughn Rd (44141).* Located along 22 miles of the Cuyahoga River just N of Akron. Phone 330/650-4636. On 33,000 acres. Beautiful and varied area with extensive recreational facilities, many historic sites, and entertainment facilities; 20-mile-long, fully accessible Ohio and Erie Canal Towpath Trail. Artistic events, performances, campfire programs, nature walks. Three visitor centers (daily; closed holidays). Park (daily). Fee for some activities. Also here is

> **Dover Lake Waterpark.** *1150 W Highland Rd, Sagamore Hills. Approximately 13 miles N on Hwy 8, then 1 mile W on Hwy 82, then S on Brandywine Rd, then W on Highland (Vaughn) Rd. Phone 330/467-7946. www.doverlake.com.* Beach, wave pool, seven water slides, tube slides, wave pool; video arcade, miniature golf, batting cages, softball fields, chair lift ride; concessions, pavilions, picnic grounds. (Mid-June-late Aug, daily 11 am-7 pm) **$$$$**

Goodyear World of Rubber. *Goodyear Hall, 1201 E Market St. 4th floor; 1 1/2 miles E of Hwy 8, on I-76, at jct Goodyear Blvd. Phone 330/796-7117.* Historic and product displays, including the Goodyear Blimp. A one-hour tour includes movies. (Daily; closed holidays) **FREE**

Hale Farm and Village. *2686 Oak Hill Rd, Bath (44210). Phone 330/666-3711; toll-free 800/589-9703.* Authentic Western Reserve house (circa 1825), other authentic buildings in a village setting depict northeastern Ohio's rural life in the mid-1800s; pioneer implements; craft demonstrations, special events; farming; costumed guides. (May-Oct, Tues-Sat, Sun afternoons) **$$$** Also here is

> **Cuyahoga Valley Scenic Railroad.** *1630 Mill St W, Akron. Phone 330/657-2000; toll-free 800/468-4070.* Scenic railroad trips through the Cuyahoga Valley National Recreation Area between Cleveland and Akron aboard vintage railroad cars pulled by first generation ALCO diesels. Stations include Independence (south of Cleveland), Hale Farm, Akron Valley Business District, NPS Canal Visitor Center, Howard Street, and Quaker Square in Akron. Reservations required. **$$$$**

National Inventors Hall of Fame Museum. *221 S Broadway St. Phone toll-free 800/968-4332.* Dedicated to the creative process; houses interactive exhibit area, national inventors hall of fame. (Tues-Sun) **$$**

Naturealm Visitors Center. *1828 Smith Rd. Phone 330/865-8065.* A 4,000-square-foot "Gateway to Nature" underground exhibit area surrounded by many sights and sounds of nature. (Daily; closed holidays) **FREE**

Portage Lakes State Park. *5031 Manchester Rd (44319). 4 miles S off Hwy 93, 619. Phone 330/644-2220.* Several reservoir lakes totaling 2,520 acres. Swimming, fishing, boating (launch). Hunting, hiking, snowmobiling, picnicking (shelter), camping (campground located 5 miles from park headquarters), pet camping. **FREE**

Portage Princess Cruise. *300 W Turkey Foot Lake Rd (44319). On Hwy 619, 4 miles W of I-77. Phone 330/499-6891.* Cruise the glacier-made lakes on an enclosed riverboat (May-Oct 13, daily). **$$$**

Quaker Square. *135 S Broadway. Phone 330/253-5970.* Shopping, hotel, restaurants, and entertainment center in the original mills and silos of the Quaker Oats Company. Historical displays include famous Quaker Oats advertising memorabilia. (Daily; closed holidays) **FREE**

Stan Hywet Hall and Gardens. *714 N Portage Path. 1 1/2 miles N of jct Hwy 18. Phone 330/836-5533.* Tudor Revival manor house built by F. A. Seiberling, co-founder of Goodyear Tire & Rubber; contains 65 rooms with antiques and art treasures dating from the 14th century. More than 70 acres of grounds and gardens. (Apr-Dec, daily; rest of year, Tues-Sun; closed holidays; also Jan) **$$$**

Summit County Historical Society. *550 Copley Rd. Phone 330/535-1120.* Museums include

> **John Brown Home.** *514 Diagonal Rd, Akron. At Copley Rd.* Remodeled residence where the abolitionist lived from 1844 to 1846. (Wed-Sun afternoons; closed holidays) **$$**

> **Perkins Mansion.** *550 Copley Rd, Akron. At S Portage Path.* (1837) Greek Revival home built of Ohio sandstone by Simon Perkins Jr. on 10 landscaped acres. (Wed-Sun afternoons; closed holidays) **$$**

The University of Akron. *302 Buchtel Mall (44325). Just E of downtown. Phone 330/972-7100. www.uakron .edu.* (1870) (24,300 students) Third-largest four-year university in Ohio; known for its Colleges of Polymer Science, Polymer Engineering, Global Business, and Fine and Applied Arts. Its science and engineering program is ranked in the top five nationally. The E. J. Thomas Performing Arts Hall is home to the Ohio Ballet and Akron Symphony Orchestra (see SPECIAL EVENTS). Bierce Library houses many collections, including the Archives of the History of American Psychology. Campus tours arranged through admissions. Also here is

> **Hower House.** *60 Fir Hill, Akron. Phone 330/ 972-6909.* (1871) A 28-room Victorian mansion, Second Empire Italianate-style architecture, built by John Henry Hower; lavish furnishing from around the world. (Feb-Dec, Wed-Fri, Sun afternoons; closed holidays) **$$**

The Winery at Wolf Creek. *2637 S Cleveland-Massillon Rd, Norton. Approximately 1 1/2 miles N of I-76, at exit 14. Phone 330/666-9285.* Tasting room overlooks the vineyard and lake. (Apr-Dec, daily; Dec-Mar, Thurs-Sun; closed holidays) **FREE**

Special Events

Akron Symphony Orchestra. *University of Akron, E. J. Thomas Hall, 198 Hill St, Akron (44325). Phone 330/535-8131. www.akronsymphony.org.* Sept-May.

All-American Soap Box Derby. *1000 George Washington Blvd, Akron (44312). Derby Downs, Akron Municipal Airport. Phone 330/733-8723.* More than 200 boys and girls (9-16 years) from the United States and abroad compete with homemade, gravity-powered cars for scholarships, prizes. Late July.

Blossom Music Center. *Cuyahoga National Recreation Area, 1145 W Steels Corners Rd, Cuyahoga Falls, Approximately 8 miles N on Hwy 8, then W; Ohio Tpike exits 11, 12. Phone 330/920-8040.* Summer home of Cleveland Orchestra (see); symphony, jazz, pop, rock, and country music concerts. Mid-May-late Sept.

Harvest Festival. *Hale Farm and Western Reserve Village, 146 Wilpark Dr, Akron (44312). Phone 330/666-3711; toll-free 800/589-9703.* Celebrates end of the harvest season. Hands-on 19th-century rural activities include cider pressing, hayrides, crafts; musical entertainment, food. Early Oct.

Ohio Ballet. *University of Akron, E. J. Thomas Hall, 198 Hill St, Akron (44325). Phone 330/375-2835.* Performances in Feb, Apr, July-Sept, and Nov.

Wonderful World of Ohio Mart. *Stan Hywet Hall, 714 N Portage Path, Akron (44303). Phone 330/836-5533.* Renaissance fair with handicrafts, food, entertainment. Early Oct.

Yankee Peddler Festival. *Clay's Park Resort, 13190 Patterson Rd, North Lawrence (44666). 10 miles S on Hwy 21 S, in Canal Fulton. Phone toll-free 800/535-5634.* Arts, crafts, entertainment, costumes, food of pioneer period 1776-1825. Three weekends in Sept.

Limited-Service Hotels

★ ★ **BEST WESTERN EXECUTIVE INN OF AKRON.** *2677 Gilchrist Rd, Akron (44305). Phone 330/794-1050; fax 330/794-8495. www.bestwestern.com.* 112 rooms, 3 story. Check-out 11 am. Restaurant, bar. Fitness room. Pool. **$**

★ ★ **HOLIDAY INN.** *4073 Medina Rd, Akron (44333). Phone 330/666-4131; toll-free 800/465-4329; fax 330/666-7190. www.holiday-inn.com.* 166 rooms, 4 story. Check-out noon. Restaurant. Fitness room. Pool. **$**

★ ★ **RADISSON INN AKRON/FAIRLAWN.** *200 Montrose West Ave, Akron (44321). Phone 330/666-9300; fax 330/668-2270. www.radisson.com.* This hotel features comfortable, oversized guest rooms at affordable rates. Amenities include an indoor pool, health club, and much more. After a long day, relax in front of the fireplace at the Sunken Living Room, the hotel's cozy bar area. 130 rooms, 4 story. Check-out noon. Restaurant, bar. Fitness room. Indoor pool. Airport transportation available. **$**

Full-Service Hotels

★ ★ ★ **CROWNE PLAZA.** *135 S Broadway St, Akron (44308). Phone 330/253-5970; fax 330/253-2574.* Constructed from 19th-century silos and mills—the guest rooms are round—this historic hotel, built in 1932 for the Quaker Oats Company, is a landmark for the business sector of Akron. Also housed here are a large entertainment complex, restaurants, shops, and much more (see QUAKER SQUARE). 196 rooms, 8 story. Check-out noon. Restaurant, bar. Fitness room. Indoor pool. Airport transportation available. Business center. **$**

★ ★ ★ **HILTON AKRON/FAIRLAWN.** *3180 W Market St, Akron (44333). Phone 330/867-5000; fax 330/867-1648. www.hilton.com.* This locally owned hotel has delighted both business travelers and vacationers time and again. Welcoming guests with a total commitment to exceptional service that is both friendly and genuine, this hotel is the preferred destination for guests who expect more from a franchised hotel. 204 rooms, 4 story. Check-out noon. Restaurant, bar. Fitness room. Indoor pool, outdoor pool, whirlpool. Airport transportation available. Business center. **$**

Restaurants

★ ★ **LANNING'S.** *826 N Cleveland-Massillon Rd, Akron (44333). Phone 330/666-1159. www.*

lannings-restaurant.com. On the banks of Yellow Creek, this fine-dining room, offering fresh fish and hand-cut steaks, has been in business for over 25 years. Everything is made in-house, including all dressings, sauces, soups, breads, and desserts. Seafood, steak menu. Dinner. Closed Sun; holidays. Bar. Jacket required. Valet parking. **$$$**

★ ★ ★ **TANGIER.** *532 W Market St, Akron (44303). Phone 330/376-7171; fax 330/376-0165.* This local gem hosts visiting dignitaries, as well as the best of contemporary music. Noted as one of Ohio's most unique locations, enjoy wonderful music by some of the top jazz and light rock artists, as well as an eclectic spin on Middleastern cuisine. Accommodates large parties and catered events. Mediterranean, Middle Eastern menu. Lunch, dinner. Closed Sun; holidays. Bar. Children's menu. **$$**

Alliance (B-5)

See also Akron, Canton, Kent, Massillon, Youngstown

Settled 1805
Population 23,376
Elevation 1,174 ft
Area Code 330
Zip 44601
Information Chamber of Commerce, 210 E Main St; phone 330/823-6260
Web site www.chamber.alliance.oh.us

What to See and Do

Glamorgan Castle. *200 Glamorgan Ave. Phone 330/821-2100.* Historic complex (1904) built by Colonel William H. Morgan. Tours (Mon-Fri afternoons; also by appointment) **$$**

Mabel Hartzell Museum. *840 N Park Ave. Phone 330/823-1677.* Furniture, clothes of 18th and 19th centuries; local historical items; early pewter, glass, china in century-old house. (Afternoons during Carnation Festival; rest of year, by appointment) (see SPECIAL EVENT) **DONATION**

Mount Union College. *1972 Clark Ave. Phone 330/821-5320; toll-free 800/992-6682. www.muc.edu.* (1846) (2,100 students) Liberal arts college. On campus is Crandall Art Gallery (Sept-Apr, Mon-Fri; closed holidays; free). Guided tours.

Special Event

Carnation Festival. *Alliance (44601). Citywide. Phone 330/823-6260 (Chamber of Commerce). www. carnationfestival.com.* Honoring the state flower. Parades, entertainment, food, fireworks, queen pageant, children's activities. Second week in Aug.

Limited-Service Hotel

★ **COMFORT INN.** *2500 W State St, Alliance (44601). Phone 330/821-5555; toll-free 877/424-6423; fax 330/821-4919. www.comfortinn.com.* 113 rooms, 5 story. Pets accepted; fee. Complimentary continental breakfast. Check-out noon. Fitness room. Indoor pool, whirlpool. **$**

⊠ ⊼ ⬟ ⌸

Ashtabula (A-5)

See also Geneva-on-the-Lake, Painesville

Settled 1796
Population 21,633
Elevation 695 ft
Area Code 440
Zip 44004
Information Ashtabula Area Chamber of Commerce, 4536 Main Ave, PO Box 96; phone 440/998-6998

This modern harbor at the mouth of the Ashtabula River is an important shipping center for coal and iron ore. Swimming, fishing, and boating are possible in Lake Erie.

What to See and Do

Conneaut Historical Railroad Museum. *342 Depot St. 12 miles NE on Hwy 20 to Conneaut, just off Broad St. Phone 440/599-7878.* Museum in former New York Central depot; memorabilia of early railroading, model engines. Adjacent are the *Old Iron Horse 755* (retired Nickel Plate Railroad locomotive) and a caboose, which may be boarded. (Memorial Day-Labor Day, daily) Children 11 years and under only with adult. **FREE**

Great Lakes Marine and US Coast Guard Memorial Museum. *1071-1073 Walnut Blvd. Phone 440/964-6847.* In a former lighthouse keeper's home built in 1898. Includes a working scale model of Hulett ore unloading machine, ship's pilot house, marine artifacts, paintings, photos, models, handmade miniature tools.

Guides, tours (by appointment, all year). View of river, harbor, docks; picnicking. (Memorial Day-Oct, Fri-Sun and holidays afternoons) **DONATION**

Special Events

Ashtabula County Fair. *127 N Elm St, Jefferson (44047). Phone 440/576-7626.* Mid-Aug.

Blessing of the Fleet. *Ashtabula. Phone 440/998-6998.* Boat parades on lake; tours, art shows, fireworks. First weekend in June.

Covered Bridge Festival. *Ashtabula County fairgrounds, 127 N Elm St, Jefferson (44047). Phone 440/576-3769.* Second weekend in Oct.

Limited-Service Hotel

★ **COMFORT INN.** *1860 Austinburg Rd, Austinburg (44010). Phone 440/275-2711; toll-free 877/424-6423; fax 440/275-7314. www.comfortinn.com.* 119 rooms, 2 story. Pets accepted, some restrictions; fee. Check-out noon. Restaurant, bar. Pool. **$**

Restaurant

★ ★ **EL GRANDE.** *2145 W Prospect St, Ashtabula (44004). Phone 440/998-2228.* American, Italian menu. Lunch, dinner. Closed Sun-Mon; holidays. **$$**

Athens (D-4)

Founded 1800
Population 21,265
Elevation 723 ft
Area Code 740
Zip 45701
Information Athens County Convention and Visitors Bureau, 667 E State St; phone 740/592-1819 or toll-free 800/878-9767
Web site www.athensohio.com

The establishment of Ohio University (see), oldest college in what was the Northwest Territory, created the town of Athens. It also is the seat of Athens County. A Ranger District office of the Wayne National Forest (see IRONTON) is located here.

What to See and Do

Burr Oak State Park. *Rte 78 E and Hwy 13, Glouster (45732). 3 miles N on Hwy 33, then 14 miles N on Hwy 13, borders Wayne National Forest. Phone 740/767-3570.* More than 2,500 acres. Swimming (lifeguard), bathhouse (Memorial Day-Labor Day), fishing, boating (rentals, ramp). Picnicking, hiking, nearby golf course, cabins, lodge, camping. **FREE**

Lake Hope. *Zaleski State Forest, 27331 Hwy 278, McArthur (45651). 14 miles NW on Hwy 56, then 6 miles S on Hwy 278. Phone 740/596-5253.* Over 3,220 acres. Swimming, bathhouse, fishing, boating (rentals). Hiking, picnicking, camping (pets allowed); 66 cabins, lodge. Nature center with naturalist (May-Labor Day). **FREE**

Ohio University. *Athens campus. Phone 740/593-2097. www.ohio.edu.* (1804) (19,000 students) First university in Northwest Territory. Information and self-guided tours of historic campus available at visitor center, Richland Avenue. Also here is

> **Kennedy Museum of Art.** *Ohio University, Lin Hall, Bypass 682 and Richland Ave, Athens. Phone 740/593-1304.* Permanent collection, traveling exhibits from other institutions. Tours. (Tues-Sun, daily) **FREE**

Strouds Run. *11661 State Park Rd (45701). 5 miles E off Hwy 50. Phone 740/592-2302.* On 161-acre Dow Lake. Swimming (Memorial Day-Labor Day), fishing, boating (rentals); picnicking, hiking, camping, pet camping. (Daily) **FREE**

Wayne National Forest. *219 Columbus Rd (45701). Phone 740/592-6644.* (see IRONTON) Sections west, north, and east.

Special Event

Ohio Valley Summer Theater. *Ohio University, Elizabeth Baker Theater & Forum Theater, Athens. Phone 740/593-4800.* June-July.

Limited-Service Hotels

★ **AMERIHOST INN.** *20 Home St, Athens (45701). Phone 740/594-3000; fax 740/594-5546. www.amerihostinn.com.* 102 rooms, 2 story.

Complimentary continental breakfast. Check-out noon. Fitness room. Indoor pool, whirlpool. **$**

★ ★ OHIO UNIVERSITY INN AND CONFERENCE CENTER. *331 Richland Ave, Athens (45701). Phone 740/593-6661; fax 740/592-5139. www.ouinn.com.* In the foothills of the Appalachian Mountains, this beautiful hotel prides itself on customer service and comfort. With newly renovated rooms and a conference center with a range of services, guests will enjoy hospitality and efficiency here. 139 rooms, 3 story. Pets accepted, some restrictions; fee. Check-out noon. Restaurant, bar. Pool. **$**

Restaurant

★ ★ SEVEN SAUCES. *66 N Court, Athens (45701). Phone 740/592-5555.* International/Fusion menu. Dinner. Closed holidays. Bar. **$$**

Aurora (A-4)

See also Akron, Chardon, Cleveland, Kent, Warren

Population 9,192
Elevation 1,130 ft
Area Code 330
Zip 44202
Information Aurora Chamber of Commerce, 173 S Chillicothe Rd; phone 330/562-3355
Web site www.auroraohiochamber.com

What to See and Do

 Six Flags Worlds of Adventure. *1060 N Aurora Rd (44202). 5 miles N on Rte 43. Phone 330/562-7131. www.sixflags.com.* A 120-acre lake with boardwalk; wave pool, water slides, swimming. Amusement park with rides, including ten roller coasters and historic carousel; Turtle Beach; live musical shows. Marine park includes sea lions, walruses, otters; interactive dolphin show. (Memorial Day-Labor Day, daily; May, Sept-Oct, weekends only) **$$$$**

Limited-Service Hotel

★ ★ THE INN AT SIX FLAGS. *800 N Aurora Rd (Rte 43), Aurora (44202). Phone 330/562-9151; toll-free 800/970-7666; fax 330/562-5701.* A great place to stay when visiting nearby SeaWorld and Six Flags Worlds of Adventure. A tropical atrium welcomes guests upon arrival, and kids will enjoy swimming in the indoor pool year-round. Meeting space is available for business travelers. 144 rooms, 2 story. Check-out 11 am. Restaurant. Fitness room. Indoor pool, whirlpool. **$$**

Full-Service Hotel

★ ★ ★ THE BERTRAM INN AND CONFERENCE CENTER. *600 N Aurora Rd, Aurora (44202). Phone 330/995-0200; fax 330/562-9163. www.thebertraminn.com.* 162 rooms. Check-in 3 pm, check-out noon. High-speed Internet access. Restaurant, bar. Outdoor pool, whirlpool. Airport transportation available. Business center. **$$**

Beachwood

See also Brecksville, Cleveland

Population 10,677
Area Code 216
Zip 44122
Information Beachwood Chamber of Commerce, 24500 Chagrin Blvd, Suite 110; phone 216/831-0003

The suburb of Beachwood is located east of Cleveland.

What to See and Do

Nature Center at Shaker Lakes. *2600 S Park Blvd. Phone 216/321-5935.* This 300-acre tract has nature and hiking trails, bird observation area, two man-made lakes, and six natural habitats. Nature Center facilities include indoor and outdoor classrooms, community meeting room, and gift shop. (Mon-Sat, Sun afternoons) **FREE**

Thistledown Racing Club. *21501 Emery Rd, North Randall (44128). Phone 216/662-8600.* Thoroughbred horse racing; pari-mutuel betting. (Mar-late Dec, Mon, Wed, Fri-Sun) **$$**

Limited-Service Hotels

★ ★ COURTYARD BY MARRIOTT. *3695 Orange Pl, Beachwood (44122). Phone 216/765-1900;*

fax 216/378-1902. www.beachwoodcourtyard.com. 113 rooms, 4 story. Check-in 3 pm, check-out noon. High-speed Internet access. Restaurant, bar. Fitness room. Indoor pool, whirlpool. Business center. **$**

★ ★ **EMBASSY SUITES.** *3775 Park East Dr, Beachwood (44122). Phone 216/765-8066; fax 216/765-0930. www.embassysuitesbeachwood.com.* A tropical garden atrium and waterfalls are the setting at this beautiful hotel with spacious guest suites. Visitors also can take a short drive to enjoy SeaWorld, the Rock and Roll Hall of Fame and Museum, and Jacob's Field. 216 rooms, 4 story, all suites. Complimentary full breakfast. Check-in 3 pm, check-out noon. High-speed Internet access. Restaurant, bar. Fitness room. Indoor pool, whirlpool. Business center. **$$**

★ ★ **HOLIDAY INN.** *3750 Orange Pl, Beachwood (44122). Phone 216/831-3300; fax 216/831-0486. www.holiday-inn.com.* 170 rooms, 4 story. Check-out 11 am. Restaurant, bar. Indoor pool, outdoor pool. **$**

Restaurants

★ ★ **LION & LAMB.** *30519 Pine Tree Rd, Cleveland (44124). Phone 216/831-1213; fax 216/831-8266.* American menu. Lunch, dinner. Closed Sun; holidays. Bar. **$$**

★ ★ ★ **RISTORANTE GIOVANNI.** *25550 Chagrin Blvd, Beachwood (44122). Phone 216/831-8625; fax 216/831-4338. www.giovanniscleveland.com.* Dine in romantic elegance at this restaurant serving the finest in classic Italian dishes and pastas. Enjoy a good cigar with dessert. Italian menu. Lunch, dinner. Closed Sun; holidays. Bar. Jacket required. Reservations recommended. Valet parking. **$$$**

Beavercreek

Restaurant

★ ★ **B R SCOTESE'S.** *1375 N Fairfield Rd, Beavercreek (45432). Phone 937/431-1350; fax*

937/431-1352. Italian menu. Lunch, dinner. Closed Sun; holidays. Bar. Children's menu. **$$**

Bellefontaine (C-2)

See also Lima, Sidney, Springfield, Wapakoneta

Settled 1806
Population 12,142
Elevation 1,251 ft
Area Code 937
Zip 43311
Information Greater Logan County Convention and Tourist Bureau, 100 S Main St; phone 937/599-5121
Web site www.logancountyohio.com

The French name, which means "beautiful fountain," resulted from the natural springs at the site. An industrial town, this area was once a Shawnee village called Blue Jacket's Town, for a white man who was captured by the Shawnee, married the chief's daughter, and became chief of the tribe. The area is rich in Native American lore, Revolutionary history, and scenic and recreational attractions. At Campbell Hill, the elevation is 1,550 feet, the highest point in Ohio.

What to See and Do

Indian Lake State Park. *12774 Hwy 235 (43331). 12 miles NW off Hwy 33. Phone 937/843-2717.* Recreational area and summer resort. Land once belonged to Wyandot, Shawnee, and other tribes. More than 640 acres of land with a 5,800-acre water area. Swimming; fishing for bass, crappie, channel catfish, and bluegill; boating (dock, launch, rentals). Hiking trails, snowmobiling on frozen lake, picnicking, concession, camping. (Daily) **FREE**

Mad River Mountain Ski Resort. *1000 Snow Valley Rd (43311). 5 miles SE on Hwy 33. Phone 937/599-1015. www.skimadriver.com.* Five chair lifts, T-bar, three rope tows; patrol, school, rentals, snowmaking; lodge, cafeteria, bar. Slopes (1,000 feet-3,000 feet). (Dec-Mar, daily)

Ohio Caverns. *2210 E State Rte 245, West Liberty (43357). 8 miles S on Hwy 68 to West Liberty, then 3 miles SE on Hwy 245. Phone 937/465-4017.* Noted for the coloring and white crystal formations; illuminated. Picnicking. One-hour guided tours covering 1 mile. (Daily; closed Thanksgiving, Dec 25) **$$$**

Piatt Castles. *10051 County Rd 47, West Liberty. 7 miles S on Hwy 68 to West Liberty, then 1 mile E on Hwy 245. Phone 937/465-2821.* Castle Mac-A-Cheek (1864-1871) is the Norman-style home of Civil War General Abram Sanders Piatt; original furnishings, firearms, Native American artifacts, patent models, extensive library. Mac-O-Chee (1879-1881) is the Flemish-style home of social critic, writer, editor, and Civil War Colonel Donn Piatt; restored to 1880s style and format. Both castles (Apr-Oct, daily; Mar, weekends). Guided tours. **$$**

Zane Caverns. *7092 Hwy 540 (43311). Phone 937/592-9592.* Illuminated stalactites, stalagmites; display of cave pearls; guided tour. Gift shop. (May-Sept, daily; rest of year, Wed-Sun) **$$$** Also here is

> **Southwind Park.** *7092 Hwy 540, Bellefontaine. Phone 937/592-9592.* Swimming pond. Hiking trails, picnicking, playground, cabins, camping (fee). Pets on leash. Contact Zane Caverns. **$**

Special Event

Logan County Fair. *117 E Columbus Ave, Bellefontaine (43311). Phone 937/599-4227.* Harness racing. Mid-late July.

Limited-Service Hotel

★ **COMFORT INN.** *260 Northview Dr, Bellefontaine (43311). Phone 937/599-5555; toll-free 800/589-3666; fax 937/599-2300. www.comfortinn.com.* 73 rooms, 2 story. Pets accepted; fee. Complimentary continental breakfast. Check-out noon. Bar. Fitness room. Pool. **$**

🏃 🐕 🏊

Bellevue (B-3)

See also Fremont, Milan, Sandusky, Tiffin

Settled 1815
Population 8,146
Elevation 751 ft
Area Code 419
Zip 44811
Information Bellevue Area Tourism and Visitors Bureau, PO Box 63; phone 419/483-5359 or toll-free 800/562-6978
Web site www.bellevuetourism.org

What to See and Do

Historic Lyme Village. *5001 Hwy 4. 2 miles E on Hwy 113. Phone 419/483-4949.* The John Wright Victorian mansion is featured with several other buildings that have been moved here and restored to create a village depicting 19th-century life. (June-Aug, Tues-Sun; May, Sept, weekends only) Several events throughout the year. **$$**

Mad River and NKP Railroad Society Museum. *253 S West St. Phone 419/483-2222.* Display of various old railroad cars, artifacts; gift shop. (Memorial Day-Labor Day, daily; May, Sept-Oct, weekends only) **DONATION**

Seneca Caverns. *15248 Township Rd 178 (44811). 3 miles S on Hwy 269, then 2 miles W on Thompson Township Rd 178. Phone 419/483-6711. www.senecacavernsohio.com.* One of Ohio's largest natural caverns, it is actually a unique "earth crack," created by undetermined geologic forces. Registered Natural Landmark. Eight rooms on seven levels; Old Mist'ry River flows at lowest level (110 feet); electrically lighted. One-hour guided tours; constant temperature of 54° F. Pan for gemstones and minerals (fee). (Memorial Day-Labor Day, daily; May, Sept-mid-Oct, weekends only) **$$**

Limited-Service Hotel

★ ★ **BEST WESTERN BELLEVUE RESORT INN.** *1120 E Main St, Bellevue (44811). Phone 419/483-5740; fax 419/483-5566. www.bestwestern.com.* 83 rooms, 2 story. Check-out 11 am. Restaurant, bar. Indoor pool, outdoor pool, whirlpool. **$**

Restaurant

★ ★ **MCCLAIN'S.** *137 E Main St, Bellevue (44811). Phone 419/483-2727.* Seafood, steak menu. Lunch, dinner. Closed Sun; holidays. Bar. Children's menu. **$$**

Berlin

Specialty Lodging

The following lodging establishment is approved by Mobil Travel Guide, but due to its unique and individualized nature has not been given a traditional Mobil Star rating. Included in this listing you may find bed-and-breakfasts, limited-service inns, guest ranches, and other unique hotel properties.

LAMPLIGHT INN BED & BREAKFAST. *5676 Township Rd 362, Berlin (44610). Phone 330/893-1122; toll-free 866/500-1122.* Located within walking distance of historic downtown Berlin. All rooms have private entrances and baths. 5 rooms, 3 story. **$**

Bowling Green (A-2)

See also Findlay, Fremont, Toledo, Wauseon

Founded 1834
Population 28,176
Elevation 705 ft
Area Code 419
Zip 43402
Information Chamber of Commerce, 163 N Main St, PO Box 31; phone 419/353-7945 or toll-free 800/866-0046
Web site www.visitbgohio.org

Surrounded by rich farmland, Bowling Green is an educational center with diversified industries. It also is the seat of Wood County.

What to See and Do

Bowling Green State University. *1001 E Wooster St (43402). Phone 419/372-2531. www.bgsu.edu.* (1910) (18,000 students) Attractive 1,300-acre campus. Undergraduate colleges of arts and sciences, education, health and human services, music, business administration, and technology; graduate college. A golf course and an all-year ice skating arena are open to the public (fees). Located on campus is

> **The Educational Memorabilia Center.** *900 E Wooster, Bowling Green. Phone 419/372-7405.* (1875) Restored one-room schoolhouse and memorabilia collection; more than 1,500 items

reminiscent of education's past, such as desks, slates, inkwells, McGuffey's Readers, maps, globes; potbellied stove, 100-year-old pump organ. (Sat-Sun afternoons; weekdays, by appointment; closed holidays and school breaks) **FREE**

Mary Jane Thurston State Park. *1466 Hwy 65, McClure (43534). 4 miles NW on Hwy 64, then 8 miles W on Hwy 65, near Napoleon. Phone 419/832-7662.* A 555-acre park. Fishing, boating (unlimited horsepower, dock, launch). Hunting, hiking, sledding, picnicking (shelter), tent camping.

Special Events

National Tractor Pulling Championship. *Wood County fairgrounds, 13800 W Poe Rd, Bowling Green (43402). Phone 419/354-1434.* World's largest outdoor pull. Mid-Aug.

Wood County Fair. *Wood County Fair Speed Office, 13800 W Poe Rd, Bowling Green (43402). County fairgrounds. Phone 419/353-7945.* Agricultural and livestock shows, displays, rides, and concessions. Early Aug.

Limited-Service Hotel

★ **DAYS INN.** *1550 E Wooster St, Bowling Green (43402). Phone 419/352-5211; fax 419/354-8030. www.daysinn.com.* 100 rooms, 2 story. Pets accepted; fee. Complimentary continental breakfast. Check-out 11 am. **$**

Restaurant

★ **JUNCTION.** *110 N Main St, Bowling Green (43402). Phone 419/352-9222. www.junctionbg.com.* American, Mexican menu. Dinner. Closed Easter, Thanksgiving, Dec 25. Bar. Children's menu. **$**

Brecksville

See also Beachwood, Cleveland

Population 11,818
Elevation 900 ft
Area Code 440
Zip 44141
Information Chamber of Commerce, 4450 Oakes Rd; phone 440/526-7350

The suburb Brecksville is located approximately 9 miles south of Cleveland and is adjacent to the Cuyahoga Valley National Recreation Area.

Limited-Service Hotel

★ ★ **CLARION HOTEL.** *5300 Rockside Rd, Independence (44131). Phone 216/524-0700; fax 216/524-6477. www.choicehotels.com.* 179 rooms, 5 story. Check-out 11 am. Restaurant, bar. Indoor pool, outdoor pool, whirlpool. Tennis. Airport transportation available. **$**

Full-Service Hotel

★ ★ ★ **HILTON CLEVELAND SOUTH.** *6200 Quarry Ln, Independence (44131). Phone 216/447-0020; fax 216/447-1300. www.hilton.com.* A contemporary stay in a country setting, this hotel includes an amphitheater, an indoor/outdoor pool, a fitness facility, and Shula's Steak 2 Restaurant. Local attractions such as Six Flags and Jacob's Field are just a short drive away. 195 rooms, 5 story. Check-out noon. Restaurant. Fitness room. Indoor pool, outdoor pool, whirlpool. Tennis. Airport transportation available. **$**

Restaurant

★ ★ **MARCO POLO'S.** *8188 Brecksville Rd, Brecksville (44141). Phone 440/526-6130; fax 440/526-2860.* Former stagecoach stop built in the 1800s. Beamed ceilings with large iron chandeliers. Italian menu. Lunch, dinner. Closed Dec 25. Bar. **$$**

Burton

Restaurant

★ ★ **WELSHFIELD INN.** *14001 Main Market, Burton (44021). Phone 440/834-4164.* Lunch, dinner. Closed Mon. Children's menu. **$$**

Cambridge (C-4)

See also Coshocton, Gnadenhutten, Zanesville

Founded 1806
Population 11,748
Elevation 886 ft
Area Code 740
Zip 43725
Information Visitors and Convention Bureau, 2146 Southgate Pkwy, PO Box 427, phone 740/432-2022 or toll-free 800/933-5480
Web site www.visitguernseycounty.com

Cambridge, an important center for the glassmaking industry, was named by early settlers who came from the English Isle of Guernsey. At one time a center of mining and oil, it is located at the crossroads of three major federal highways.

What to See and Do

Boyd's Crystal Art Glass. *1203 Morton Ave. Phone 740/439-2077.* Glass from molten form to finished product. Tours of glass factory and showroom (Mon-Fri; closed holidays). **FREE**

The Cambridge Glass Museum. *812 Jefferson Ave. Phone 740/432-3045.* More than 5,000 pieces of Cambridge glass and pottery made between 1902 and 1954. (Apr-Oct, Wed-Sun; closed holidays) **$**

Degenhart Paperweight and Glass Museum. *65323 Highland Hills Rd. Phone 740/432-2626.* Large collection of Midwestern pattern glass, Cambridge glass, and Degenhart paperweights. Gift shop. (Apr-Dec, daily; rest of year, Mon-Fri; closed holidays) **$**

Mosser Glass. *9279 Cadiz Rd. Hwy 22 E, 1/2 mile W via I-77 exit 47. Phone 740/439-1827.* Glass making tours; gift shop. (Mon-Fri; closed holidays; also first two weeks in July, last week in Dec) **FREE**

Muskingum Watershed Conservancy District. *Seneca Lake Park, 22172 Park Rd, Senecaville (43780). 9 miles S on I-77, then 7 miles E on Hwy 313, then 2 miles S on Hwy 574 to park entrance. Phone 740/685-6013.* A 3,550-acre lake offers swimming, fishing, boating (299-hp limit), marina; playground; Class A tent and trailer sites at marina and park (daily; hookups). Pets on leash. **$**

Salt Fork State Park. *Hwy 22 E. 9 miles NE off Hwy 22. Phone 740/439-2751 (park); toll-free 800/282-7275 (reservations).* A 20,181-acre park with swimming, fishing, boating (rentals, docks, marina). Hiking trails, golf, picnicking (shelter), concession, tent and trailer sites, cabins (reservations accepted), lodge.

Special Events

The Living Word Outdoor Drama. *6010 College Hill Rd, Cambridge. On S Hwy 209 W, at 6010 College Hill Rd. Phone 740/439-2761.* Ohio's *Passion Play* in outdoor amphitheater retells the life of Jesus Christ. Mid-June-early Sept, Thurs-Sat.

Salt Fork Arts and Crafts Festival. *City Park, 2864 Bloomfield Rd, Cambridge (43725). Phone 740/439-6688.* Early Aug.

Limited-Service Hotels

★ **BEST WESTERN CAMBRIDGE.** *1945 Southgate Pkwy, Cambridge (43725). Phone 740/439-3581; fax 740/439-1824. www.bestwestern.com.* 95 rooms, 2 story. Pets accepted. Check-out 11 am. Bar. Pool. **$**

★ ★ **HOLIDAY INN.** *PO Box 1270, Cambridge (43725). Phone 740/432-7313; fax 740/432-2337. www.holiday-inn.com.* 108 rooms, 2 story. Pets accepted. Check-out noon. Restaurant, bar. Pool. **$**

Restaurant

★ **THEO'S.** *632 Wheeling Ave, Cambridge (43725). Phone 740/432-3878; fax 740/432-3101.* Breakfast, lunch, dinner. Closed Sun; holidays. Bar. Casual attire. **$$**

Canton (B-4)

See also Akron, Alliance, Kent, Massillon, New Philadelphia, Wooster

Settled 1805
Population 84,161
Elevation 1,060 ft
Area Code 330
Information Canton/Stark County Convention and Visitors Bureau, 229 Wells Ave NW, 44703-2642; phone 330/454-1439 or toll-free 800/533-4302
Web site www.visitcantonohio.com

John Saxton, grandfather of Mrs. William McKinley, first published the still-circulating *Ohio Repository* (today *The Repository*) in 1815. In 1867, William McKinley opened a law office in the town and, in 1896, conducted his "front porch campaign" for the presidency. After his assassination, his body was brought back to Canton for burial. Because of his love for the red carnation, it was made the state flower.

This large steel-processing city, important a century ago for farm machinery, is in the middle of rich farmland, on the edge of "steel valley" where the three branches of Nimishillen Creek come together. It is one of the largest producers of specialty steels in the world.

What to See and Do

Canton Classic Car Museum. *555 Market Ave SW (44702). Phone 330/455-3603.* Collection of antique, classic cars; fire pumper; police bandit car; cars of 1950s and 1960s; restoration shop; memorabilia, period fashions, advertising, nostalgia, and popular culture. (Daily; closed Easter, Thanksgiving, Dec 25) **$$$**

The Canton Cultural Center for the Arts. *1001 Market Ave N (44703). Phone 330/627-4096.* Center is the hub of the arts in Canton, including the Canton Ballet, Canton Museum of Art (Tues-Sun), Canton Civic Opera, Canton Symphony Orchestra, and Player's Guild of Canton. (Mon-Fri)

Canton Garden Center. *Stadium Park, 1615 Stadium Park NW. Phone 330/455-6172.* Tulips, daffodils, peonies, chrysanthemums; five senses garden; JFK memorial fountain with continuous flame (daily). Garden Center (Tues-Fri). **FREE**

Harry London Chocolate Factory. *5353 Lauby Rd. Phone 330/494-0833; toll-free 800/321-0444.* Tours (Mon-Sat; closed Sun; holidays). **$**

Hoover Historical Center. *1875 Easton St NW. Phone 330/499-0287.* Hoover farmhouse restored to Victorian era; boyhood home of W. H. Hoover, founder of the Hoover Company. One of the most extensive antique vacuum cleaner collections in the world; memorabilia reflecting the growth and development of the company and the industry; changing exhibits; herb gardens. Tours. (Tues-Sun; closed holidays) **FREE**

McKinley National Memorial. *Unit AA, 800 Market Ave N.* Tomb, statue of McKinley; panoramic view of city. (Daily) Adjacent is

> **McKinley Museum of History, Science, and Industry.** *800 McKinley Monument Dr NW, Canton. Phone 330/455-7043.* (1963) McKinley memorabilia; Discover World, an interactive science center; Historical Hall; Street of Shops. (Daily; planetarium shows Sat-Sun; closed holidays) **$$$**

⭐ **Pro Football Hall of Fame.** *2121 George Halas Dr NW. N of Fawcett Stadium, adjacent to I-77. Phone 330/456-8207.* (1963) Museum, a five-building complex, dedicated to the game and its players; memorabilia; research library; movie theater; museum store. (Daily; closed Dec 25) (See SPECIAL EVENT). **$$$**

Waterworks Park. *2436 30th St NE (44705). Between Tuscarawas St W and 7th St NW. Phone 330/489-3015.* Picnic facilities (tables, cooking stoves, shelter), playground.

Special Event

Pro Football Hall of Fame Festival. *Pro Football Hall of Fame (see), 2121 George Halas Dr NW, Canton (44708). Phone 330/456-8207; toll-free 800/533-4302.* Events include parade, induction ceremony, AFC-NFC Hall of Fame Pro Game. Late July-early Aug.

Limited-Service Hotels

★ ★ **FOUR POINTS BY SHERATON.** *4375 Metro Cir NW, Canton (44720). Phone 330/494-6494; toll-free 877/867-7666; fax 330/494-7129. www.fourpoints.com.* 152 rooms, 6 story. Pets accepted, some restrictions; fee. Check-out noon. Restaurant, bar. Fitness room. Indoor pool, outdoor pool. Airport transportation available. Business center. **$**

★ **HAMPTON INN.** *5335 Broadmoor Cir NW, Canton (44709). Phone 330/492-0151; fax 330/492-7523. www.hamptoninn.com.* 107 rooms, 4 story. Complimentary continental breakfast. Check-out noon. **$**

★ ★ **HOLIDAY INN.** *4520 Everhard Rd NW, Canton (44718). Phone 330/494-2770; fax 330/494-6473. www.holiday-inn.com.* 194 rooms, 3 story. Pets accepted, some restrictions. Check-out noon. Restaurant, bar. Fitness room. Pool. Airport transportation available. **$**

Restaurants

★ **JOHN'S.** *2749 Cleveland Ave, Canton (44709). Phone 330/454-1259. www.johnsgrille.com.* Seafood menu. Breakfast, lunch, dinner. Closed Sun; holidays. Bar. Casual attire. **$**

★ ★ ★ **LOLLI'S.** *4801 NW Dressler Rd, Canton (44178). Phone 330/492-6846; fax 330/492-0836.* This restaurant and banquet center in Belden Village Mall hosts many of the area's special events with space for up to 375 people. For a change from traditional Friday night dinners, try reserving a table at their weekly murder mystery dinner theater. Italian menu. Dinner. Closed Sun-Tues; holidays. Bar. **$$**

Celina (B-1)

See also Van Wert, Wapakoneta

Settled 1834
Population 9,650
Elevation 876 ft
Area Code 419
Zip 45822
Information Celina-Mercer County Chamber of Commerce, 226 N Main St; phone 419/586-2219
Web site www.celinamercer.com

Celina is on Grand Lake, a 17,500-acre man-made lake lined with houses and resorts. The town is a home for metal products, dairying, and wood fabricating industries, and it also attracts anglers and vacationers.

What to See and Do

Grand Lake-St. Marys State Park. *Hwy 703. 7 miles E on Hwy 703, then follow park signs. Phone 419/ 394-2774.* The lake is Ohio's largest inland lake (15,000 acres). Offers swimming, fishing for panfish and bass, boating (marina, rentals, ramps); snowmobiling; picnicking (shelters), concession; camping.

Mercer County Courthouse. *119 W Fulton St. Phone 419/586-3178.* Greek architecture with great bronze doors opening on halls of marble; dome of colored glass has near-perfect acoustics. (Mon-Fri) **FREE**

Mercer County Historical Museum, the Riley Home. *130 E Market St. Phone 419/586-6065.* History of area depicted by 18th- and 19th-century artifacts, including Native American, medical, and farm; also pioneer home furniture displays. (Wed-Fri, Sun) **FREE**

Special Event

Celina Lake Festival. *Hwy 127 and Hwy 29, Celina. Phone 419/586-2219.* Antique car show, parade, triathlon, arts and crafts show, fireworks. Usually late July.

Limited-Service Hotel

★ **COMFORT INN.** *1421 State Rte 703 E, Celina (45822). Phone 419/586-4656; toll-free 800/638-7949; fax 419/586-4152. www.comfortinn.com.* 40 rooms, 2 story. Complimentary continental breakfast. Check-out 11 am. **$**

Chardon (A-5)

See also Aurora, Cleveland, Mentor, Painesville

Population 4,446
Elevation 1,225 ft
Area Code 440
Zip 44024
Information Chardon Area Chamber of Commerce, 112 E Park St; phone 440/285-9050

What to See and Do

Geauga County Historical Society-Century Village. *14653 E Park St. Phone 440/834-1492.* Restored 19th-century Western Reserve village with homes, shops, school, country store. All original with period furnishings (1798-1875). (May-Oct, Tues-Sun; Mar-Apr, Nov-Dec 24, Sat-Sun; closed Easter, Thanksgiving) Museum and country store (Mar-Dec 24). **$$**

Materials Park Geodesic Dome. *9639 Kinsman Rd, Materials Park (44073). 10 miles S on Hwy 44, then 6 miles W on Hwy 87. Phone 440/338-5151.* An 11-story latticework of aluminum tubing designed by R. Buckminster Fuller; world headquarters of ASM International; mineral garden with more than 75 ore specimens. (Daily) **FREE**

Punderson State Park. *1175 Kinsman Rd, Newbury (44065). 10 miles S via Hwy 44, then W 1 mile on Hwy 87. Phone 440/564-2279.* A 990-acre park with a 90-acre lake. Swimming, fishing, boating (rentals); hiking; golf; winter sports area, snowmobiling; camping, cabins, lodge (pool, summer); snack bar. (Daily) **FREE**

Special Event

Geauga County Maple Festival. *Geauga Theater, Chardon Village Sq, 101 Water St, Chardon (44024). Phone 440/286-3007. www.maplefestival.com.* Demonstrations of making syrup, candy, cream, and other maple products; beard and ax-throwing contests; entertainment. Weekend after Easter.

Restaurants

★ ★ **BASS LAKE TAVERNE.** *426 South St, Chardon (44024). Phone 440/285-3100; fax 440/ 285-9393. www.basslaketaverne.com.* Steak menu. Lunch, dinner. Closed holidays. Bar. Casual attire. Outdoor seating. **$$**

★ ★ **THE INN AT FOWLER'S MILL.** *10700 Mayfield Rd, Chardon (44024). Phone 440/286-3111.* American menu. Lunch, dinner. Closed Mon; holidays. Bar. Children's menu. Outdoor seating. **$$$**

Chillicothe (D-3)

Settled 1796
Population 21,923
Elevation 620 ft
Area Code 740
Zip 45601
Information Ross-Chillicothe Convention and Visitors Bureau, 25 E Main St, PO Box 353; phone; 740/702-7677 or toll-free 800/413-4118
Web site www.chillicotheohio.com/rccvb

Chillicothe, first capital of the Northwest Territory, became the first capital of Ohio in 1803. Among the early settlers from Virginia who were active in achieving statehood for Ohio were Edward Tiffin, first state governor, and Thomas Worthington, governor and United States senator. The Greek Revival mansions which today give Paint Street its character were built for the pioneer statesmen.

On the west side of Scioto River Valley, 45 miles south of the present capital, Chillicothe is quite industrialized, though still fringed by wheat fields. Papermaking, begun in the early 1800s, is still an essential industry here. Just east of town is Mount Logan, which is pictured on the State Seal.

What to See and Do

Franklin House. *80 S Paint St. Phone 740/772-1936.* This 1907 Prairie-style home houses museum devoted primarily to the women of Ross County; rotating exhibits of period costumes and accessories, coverlets, quilts and linens, decorative arts. **$**

Hopewell Culture National Historical Park. *16062 State Rte 104 (45601). W bank of Scioto River, 4 miles N on Rte 104. Phone 740/774-1125.* At this site are 23 prehistoric Hopewell burial mounds (200 BC to AD 500), concentrated within a 13-acre area surrounded by an earthwall. Self-guided trails; wayside exhibits. Visitor center with museum exhibits (daily; closed Jan 1, Thanksgiving, Dec 25). **$$**

James M. Thomas Telecommunication Museum. *68 E Main (45601). Phone 740/772-8200.* Collection of documents and equipment depicting evolution of modern phone sytem. (Mon-Fri) **FREE**

Knoles Log House. *39 W 5th St. Phone 740/772-1936.* This simple two-story log home (1800-1825) features open-hearth cooking, kitchen garden, early household utensils and tools; also on-site demonstrations (seasonal). **$** Also here is

Ross County Historical Society Museum. *45 W 5th St, Chillicothe. Phone 740/772-1936. www.rosscountyhistorical.org.* Housed in an 1838 Federal-style home, museum features two floors of exhibits, antiques, furnishings, pioneer crafts, and toys. Includes Ohio's first capital exhibit, Civil War Room, Indian Room, and Camp Sherman Room. Tours; inquire for schedule. (Apr-Dec, Tues-Sun afternoons; Jan-Mar, Fri-Sat afternoons) **$**

Paint Creek State Park. *14265 Hwy 50, Bainbridge (45612). 25 miles W off Hwy 50. Phone 937/365-1401 (park office).* Large lake offers swimming, fishing, boating (ramp, rentals); hiking, bridle trails, cross-country skiing; camping (tent rentals). Paint Creek Pioneer Farm; living history program, summer programs.

Seip Mound State Memorial. *Bainbridge. 14 miles SW of Chillicothe on S side of Hwy 50. Phone 740/297-2630.* Prehistoric burial mound, 250 feet long and 30 feet high, surrounded by smaller mounds and earthworks. This archaeological site is operated by the Ohio Historical Society. Exhibit pavilion; picnicking. (Daily) **FREE**

Seven Caves. *15 miles E of Hillsboro on Hwy 50. Phone 937/365-1283.* A natural attraction of seven caves centered on self-guided walk along trails winding up and down the sides of cliffs, into canyons and gorges; rock formations; wooded park. Picnic area, snack bar. (Daily) **$$$**

Yoctangee Park. *Yoctangee Blvd and Riverside St. Phone 740/702-7677.* Swimming pool (fee), 12-acre lake. Six tennis courts, basketball and volleyball courts, softball diamonds, picnicking facilities, playground. **FREE**

Special Events

Fall Festival of Leaves. *Hwy 50 and N Maple St, Bainbridge (45612). Phone 740/634-2085. 19 miles W on Hwy 50.* Arts and crafts demonstrations, entertainment; scenic self-guided tours. Third weekend in Oct.

Feast of the Flowering Moon. *Chillicothe. Downtown. Phone 740/702-7677.* Native American, frontier, and early American feast featuring Native American demonstrations and encampment, crafts, and parade. Memorial Day weekend.

Tecumseh! *Sugarloaf Mountain Amphitheater, Chillicothe. 5 miles NE off Hwy 23, Hwy 159 N exit. Phone 740/775-0700 (after Mar 1).* Epic outdoor drama depicts the struggle of Tecumseh, the legendary Shawnee warrior who nearly united all the Native American nations. Museum, open-air restaurant, backstage tours. Mid-June-early Sept, Mon-Sat nightly.

Limited-Service Hotels

★ **COMFORT INN.** *20 N Plaza Blvd, Chillicothe (45601). Phone 740/775-3500; toll-free 800/542-7919; fax 740/775-3588. www.comfortinn.com.* 106 rooms, 2 story. Pets accepted. Complimentary continental breakfast. Check-out noon. Bar. Pool. **$**

★ **HAMPTON INN.** *100 N Plaza Blvd, Chillicothe (45601). Phone 740/773-1616; toll-free 800/426-7866; fax 740/773-1770. www.hamptoninn.com.* 71 rooms, 3 story. Complimentary continental breakfast. Check-out noon. Fitness room. Indoor pool, whirlpool. Business center. **$**

Restaurant

★ **DAMON'S.** *10 N Plaza Blvd, Chillicothe (45601). Phone 740/775-8383; fax 740/775-8251. www.damons .com.* Steak menu. Lunch, dinner. Closed holidays. Bar. Children's menu. Casual attire. **$$**

Cincinnati (D-1)

See also Hamilton, Lebanon, Mason, Middletown, Oxford

Settled 1788
Population 364,040
Elevation 683 ft
Area Code 513
Information Greater Cincinnati Convention and Visitors Bureau, 300 W 6th St, 45202; phone toll-free 800/246-2987
Web site www.cincyusa.com

Cincinnati was a bustling frontier riverboat town and one of the largest cities in the nation when poet Henry Wadsworth Longfellow immortalized it as the "queen city of the West." Although other cities farther west have since outstripped it in size, Cincinnati is still the Queen City to its inhabitants and to the many visitors who are rediscovering it. With a wealth of fine restaurants, a redeveloped downtown with skywalk, its own Montmartre (Mount Adams (see)), and the beautiful Ohio River flowing alongside it, Cincinnati has a cosmopolitan flavor uniquely its own.

Early settlers chose the site because it was an important river crossroads used by Native Americans. During 1788-1789, three small settlements—Columbia, North Bend, and Losantiville—were founded. In 1790, Arthur St. Clair, governor of the Northwest Territory, changed the name of Losantiville to Cincinnati in honor of the revolutionary officers' Society of the Cincinnati and made it the seat of Hamilton County. Despite smallpox, insects, floods, and crop failures, approximately 15,000 settlers came in the next five years. They had the protection of General Anthony Wayne, who broke the resistance of the Ohio Native Americans. In the early 1800s, a large influx of immigrants, mostly German, settled in the area.

In the 1840s and 1850s, Cincinnati boomed as a supplier of produce and goods to the cotton-growing South, and great fortunes were accumulated. During the Civil War, the city was generally loyal to the Union, although its location on the Mason-Dixon line and the interruption of its trade from the South caused mixed emotions. After the Civil War, prosperity brought art, music, a new library, and a professional baseball team. A period of municipal corruption in the late 19th century was ended by a victory for reform elements and the establishment of a city manager form of government, which has earned Cincinnati the title of America's best-governed city.

Today, the city is the home of two universities and several other institutions of higher education and has its own symphony orchestra, opera, and ballet. The redevelopment of Cincinnati's downtown area and the renovation of its riverfront into an entertainment and recreation center is appealing to visitors. Major hotels, stores, office complexes, restaurants, entertainment centers, and the Cincinnati Convention Center are now connected by a skywalk system, making the city easily accessible to pedestrians. One can still echo the words of Charles Dickens, who described the city in

1842 as "a place that commends itself . . . favorably and pleasantly to a stranger."

Additional Visitor Information

The Greater Cincinnati Convention and Visitors Bureau, 300 W 6th St, 45202, phone toll-free 800/ 246-2987, has interesting tourist guides and maps. A visitor information center is located at 5th and Vine streets at Fountain Square (see); two others are located off southbound I-71 and I-75.

Public Transportation

Bus (Queen City Metro) Phone 513/621-4455. Information, phone 859/767-3501

Airport Cincinnati/Northern Kentucky International Airport. Weather, phone 513/241-1010; cash machines, Terminal D

Information Phone 859/767-3151

Lost and Found Phone 859/767-3495

Airlines Air France, American Airlines, Continental Airlines, Delta Air Lines, Delta Connection (ComAir), Northwest Airlines, Skyway Airlines, United Airlines, US Airways, USA 3000 Airlines

What to See and Do

Airport Playfield. *Beechmont and Wilmer aves. Phone 513/321-6500.* Baseball fields, 18- and nine-hole golf courses, driving range, miniature golf, tennis courts, paved biking and hiking trails, bike rentals. Land of Make Believe playground with wheelchair-accessible play equipment; jet plane, stagecoach; "Spirit of '76" picnic area. Summer concerts. (May-Sept, daily) Some fees.

BB Riverboats. *1 Madison Ave, Covington, KY (41011). 1 mile SE via I-75 exit 192, foot of Madison, located at Covington (Kentucky) Landing and Newport Dock on Riverboat Row. Phone 859/261-8500.* Variety of cruises include sightseeing, lunch, and dinner cruises (reservations required), all-day. **$$$$**

Bicentennial Commons at Sawyer Point. *801 E Pete Rose Way (45202). Phone 513/352-4000.* Overlooks with different views of the Ohio River; 4-mile Riverwalk has a geologic river timeline. Performance

pavilion and amphitheater. Tennis pavilion with eight courts; skating pavilion; three sand volleyball courts; fitness area with exercise stations. Picnicking, playground. Dining area with umbrella tables. Some fees.

Carew Tower. *441 Vine St (45202). 5th and Vine sts. Phone 513/241-3888.* Cincinnati's tallest building (48 stories). Observation tower (daily; closed holidays). **$**

Cincinnati Bengals (NFL). *1 Paul Brown Stadium (45202). Phone 513/621-3550. www.bengals.com.* Professional football team.

Cincinnati Fire Museum. *315 W Court St. Phone 513/621-5553. www.cincyfiremuseum.com.* Restored firehouse (1907) exhibits firefighting artifacts preserved since 1808; hands-on displays; emphasis on fire prevention. **$**

Cincinnati Reds (MLB). *Cinergy Field, 100 Cinergy Field (45202). Phone 513/421-4510. www.cincinnatireds.com.* Professional baseball team.

Cincinnati Zoo and Botanical Garden. *3400 Vine St (45220). Phone 513/281-4700. www.cincyzoo.org.* Features more than 700 species in a variety of naturalistic habitats, including its world-famous gorillas and white Bengal tigers. The Cat House features 16 species of cats; Insect World is a one-of-a-kind exhibit. The Jungle Trails exhibit is an indoor/outdoor rain forest. Rare okapi, walrus, Komodo dragons, and giant eland also are on display. Participatory children's zoo. Animal shows (summer). Elephant and camel rides. Picnic areas, restaurant. (Gates open daily at 9 am; close at 4 pm in fall and winter, at 5 pm in summer Mon-Fri, and at 6 pm in summer Sat-Sun) **$$$**

City Hall. *801 Plum St. At 8th St. Phone 513/352-3000.* (1888) Houses many departments of city government. The interior includes a grand marble stairway with historical stained-art glass windows at the landings and murals on the ceiling. (Mon-Fri)

Civic Garden Center of Greater Cincinnati. *2715 Reading Rd (45206). Phone 513/221-0981. www.civicgardencenter.org.* Specimen trees; perennials, dwarf evergreens, herbs, raised vegetable gardens; greenhouse; gift shop; library. (Mon-Fri 9 am-4 pm, Sat 9 am-3 pm; closed Sun; holidays) **FREE**

Contemporary Arts Center. *44 E 6th St (45202). Phone 513/721-0390. www.spiral.org.* Changing exhibits and performances of recent art. (Daily; closed holidays) **$$**

Delta Queen and **Mississippi Queen.** *Phone toll-free 800/543-1949. www.deltaqueen.com.* Each paddle wheeler makes three-eight-night cruises on the Ohio, Mississippi, Cumberland, and Tennessee rivers.

East Fork State Park. *3294 Elklick Rd, Bethel. Off Hwy 125, 4 miles SE of Amelia. Phone 513/734-4323.* This 10,580-acre park includes rugged hills, open meadows, and reservoir. Swimming beach, fishing, boating; hiking (overnight hiking areas with permit from park office) and bridle trails, picnicking, camping.

Eden Park. *Gilbert Ave between Elsinore and Morris.* More than 185 acres initially called "the Garden of Eden." Ice skating on Mirror Lake. The Murray Seasongood Pavilion features spring and summer band concerts and other events. Picnicking. Four overlooks with scenic views of the Ohio River, the city, and Kentucky hillsides. Cultural institutions within park include

Cincinnati Art Museum. *953 Eden Park Dr, Cincinnati. Phone 513/721-5204. www. cincinnatiartmuseum.com.* Houses paintings, sculptures, prints, photographs, costumes, decorative and tribal arts, and musical instruments, representing most major civilizations for the past 5,000 years. Also examples of Cincinnati decorative arts, such as art furniture and Rookwood pottery. Continuous schedule of temporary exhibits. Restaurant, gift shop. Tours for the visually impaired (call Education Department for appointment). **FREE**

Cincinnati Playhouse in the Park. *962 Mount Adams Cir, Cincinnati. Phone 513/421-3888; toll-free 800/582-3208. www.cincyplay.com.* Professional regional theater presenting classic and contemporary plays and musicals on two stages: the Robert S. Marx Theater and the Thompson Shelterhouse. (Sept-July, Tues-Sun) Dinner available before each performance.

Krohn Conservatory. *1501 Eden Park Dr, Cincinnati. 1 mile E via Fort Washington Way and Martin St or Gilbert Ave. Phone 513/421-5707.* Floral conservatory of more than 5,000 species of exotic plants, including a five-story-tall indoor rain forest complete with 20-foot waterfall and a major collection of unusual epiphytic plants. Individual

horticultural houses contain palm, desert, orchid, and tropical collections. Themed flower and garden shows six times annually. Guided tours available. Gift shop. (Daily; extended hours for holiday shows) **FREE**

Fountain Square Plaza. *5th St (45202).* Center of downtown activity whose focal point is the Tyler Davidson Fountain, cast in Munich, Germany, and erected in Cincinnati in 1871. The sculpture, whose highest point is the open-armed Genius of Water, symbolizes the many values of water. A bandstand pavilion enables lunch-hour audiences to enjoy outdoor performances. Horse-drawn carriage tours of downtown also begin at the square.

Hamilton County Courthouse. *1000 Main St (45202). Between Court St and Central Pkwy. Phone 513/946-5879.* A good example of adapted Greek Ionic architecture; contains one of America's most complete law libraries. (Mon-Fri; closed holidays)

Harriet Beecher Stowe Memorial. *2950 Gilbert Ave. Phone 513/632-5120.* Author of *Uncle Tom's Cabin* lived here from 1832 to 1836. Completely restored with some original furnishings. (Tues-Thurs) **DONATION**

Hebrew Union College–Jewish Institute of Religion. *3101 Clifton Ave. I-75 Hopple St exit. Phone 513/221-1875. www.huc.edu.* (1875) (120 students) First institution of Jewish higher learning in the United States. Graduate school offers a variety of programs. Klau Library includes Dalsheimer Rare Book Building with rare remnants of Chinese Jewry and collections of Spinoza and Americana. American Jewish Archives Building is dedicated to study and preservation of American Jewish historical records. Archaeological exhibits and Jewish ceremonial objects are in the Skirball Museum Cincinnati Branch. Guided tours (by appointment).

Heritage Village Museum. *11450 Lebanon Rd, Sharonville (45241). Phone 513/563-9484. www. heritagevillagecincinnati.org.* A 30-acre historic village recaptures life in southwestern Ohio prior to 1880. Eleven buildings (1804-1880) reconstructed and authentically restored and refurnished. Special exhibits and events; period craft demonstrations; guided tours. (May-Oct, Wed-Sat noon-4 pm, Sun 1-5 pm; Apr, Nov-Dec, Sat noon-4 pm, Sun 1-5 pm; closed Jan-Mar) **$$**

Historic Loveland Castle. *12025 Shore Dr, Loveland (45140). NW of Cincinnati. Phone 513/683-4686. www. lovelandcastle.com.* A one-fifth scale medieval stone castle built by one man over a period of 50 years. (Sat-Sun 11 am-5 pm; closed Dec 25) **$**

John Hauck House Museum. *812 Dayton St. Phone 513/721-3570.* Ornate 19th-century stonefront town house in historic district. Restored home contains period furnishings, memorabilia, antique children's toys, special displays. (Fri, last two Sun of month, by appointment; special Christmas hours; closed holidays) **$**

Meier's Wine Cellars. *6955 Plainfield Pike, Silverton. NE on Hwy 22 or N on I-71 exit 10 (Stewart Rd), right on Stewart Rd and follow signs. Phone 513/891-2900; toll-free 800/346-2941. www.meierswinecellars.com.* Country wine store, tasting room. Tours (45-minutes) (Mon-Sat 9 am-5 pm; closed Jan 1, Thanksgiving, Dec 25). **FREE**

Mount Adams. *(45202). Area directly SW of Eden Park, on hill overlooking Cincinnati and the Ohio River.* Mount Adams is the Montmartre of Cincinnati: its narrow streets, intimate restaurants, boutiques, and art stores give the area a European flavor.

Mount Airy Forest and Arboretum. *5083 Colerain Ave (45223). 8 miles NW on Hwy 27, off I-75. Phone 513/ 352-4080. www.cincinnati-oh.gov.* Cincinnati's largest park was the first municipal reforestation project in the United States. More than 1,450 acres include 800 acres of conifers and hardwoods, 300 acres of native hardwoods, and 241 acres of grasslands. The 120-acre arboretum (guided tours by appointment, phone 513/541-8176) includes specialty gardens, floral displays, and extensive plant collections. The area is used by students and amateur and professional gardeners as a testing area for observation of growth, habits, and tolerance of plants. Nature trails, picnic areas, lodges; 2 acres reserved for a dog park. (Daily) **FREE**

Paramount's Kings Island. *6300 Kings Island Dr (45034). 20 miles N on I-71. Phone 513/754-5700; toll-free 800/288-0808. www.pki.com.* (See MASON)

Public Landing. *At the foot of Broadway.* Where the first settlers touched the shore and the first log cabin was built. Center of river trade; look for paddle wheelers, Cinergy Field, and six Ohio River bridges to northern Kentucky.

Scenic drives. *On Columbia Pkwy to Ault Park, with views of Ohio River; and on Central Pkwy (Hwy 27) along old Miami-Erie Canal to Mount Airy Forest (see).*

Trailside Nature Center. *3251 Brookline Dr (45220). In Burnet Woods. Phone 513/751-3679.* Discovery center has displays on local birds, mammals, insects, and geology. Weekend nature walks and program (all year). (Tues-Sat, Sun afternoons) **FREE**

★ **Union Terminal.** *1301 Western Ave (45203).* (1933) Famous Art Deco landmark noted for its mosaic murals, Verona marble walls, terrazzo floors, and large-domed rotunda. Three museums on site: Cincinnati History Museum, Museum of Natural History & Science, and Cinergy Children's Museum. Also an Omnimax theater, café, and museum shops. In terminal are

Cincinnati History Museum. *1301 Western Ave, Cincinnati. Phone 513/287-7000. www.cincymuseum .org.* Permanent exhibit on the Public Landing (see) of Cincinnati; temporary exhibits. Library (Mon-Sat; free). (Daily; closed Thanksgiving, Dec 25) **$$$**

Cinergy Children's Museum. *1301 Western Ave, Cincinnati. Phone 513/287-7000; toll-free 800/ 733-2077. www.cincymuseum.org.* Featuring eight different areas, the Cinergy Children's Museum offers a unique opportunity for children and their parents to share an afternoon of discovery and fun. Most of the museum is wheelchair accessible, including a two-story treehouse with a great view from the top. Much of the museum focuses on animals and on mechanical pursuits, but great care has been taken to cater to every kid who attends, especially in the "Children Just Like Me" area of the museum. (Mon-Sat 10 am-5 pm, Sun 11 am-6 pm; closed Thanksgiving, Dec 25) **$$**

Museum of Natural History & Science. *1301 Western Ave, Cincinnati. Phone 513/287-7000. www. cincymuseum.org.* Natural history of Ohio Valley. Wilderness Trail with Ohio flora and fauna and full-scale walk-through replica of a cavern with 32-foot waterfall; Children's Discovery Center. (Daily; closed Thanksgiving, Dec 25) **$$$**

Omnimax theater. *1301 Western Ave, Cincinnati. Phone 513/287-7000. www.cincymuseum.org.* A 260-degree domed screen five stories high and 72 feet wide. Films change every six months. (Daily; closed Thanksgiving, Dec 25) **$$$**

University of Cincinnati. *2624 Clifton Ave. Bounded by Clifton and Jefferson aves, Calhoun St, and Martin Luther King Dr. Phone 513/556-6000. www.uc.edu.* (1819) (37,000 students) Includes 18 colleges and divisions, of which music, law, medicine, and pharmacy are among the oldest west of the Alleghenies. Founded as Cincinnati College; chartered in 1870 as municipal university; became a full state university July 1, 1977. The College-Conservatory of Music has an extensive schedule of performances, phone 513/556-4183. On campus is Tangeman University Center (Mon-Sat; closed holidays).

William Howard Taft National Historic Site. *2038 Auburn Ave. Phone 513/684-3262. www.nps.gov/wiho.* Birthplace and boyhood home of the 27th president and chief justice of the United States. Four rooms with period furnishings; other rooms contain exhibits on Taft's life and careers. (Daily; closed Jan 1, Thanksgiving, Dec 25) **FREE**

Xavier University. *3800 Victory Pkwy. Phone 513/745-3000. www.xu.edu.* (1831) (6,800 students) Campus tours.

Special Events

Cincinnati Ballet. *Aronoff Center, 1555 Central Pkwy, Cincinnati. Phone 513/621-5219. www.cincinnatiballet .com.* Performs five-series program at the Aronoff Center, both contemporary and classical works. Oct-May; also Nutcracker staged at Cincinnati Music Hall during Dec.

Cincinnati Opera. *Cincinnati Music Hall, 1241 Elm St, Cincinnati (45210). Phone 513/241-2742. www.cincinnatiopera.com.* Nation's second-oldest opera company offers a summer season plus special performances throughout the year. Capsulized English translations projected above the stage complement all productions. Mid-June-mid-July.

Cincinnati Symphony Orchestra. *Cincinnati Music Hall, 1241 Elm St, Cincinnati (45210). Phone 513/381-3300. www.cincinnatisymphony.org.* Nation's fifth-oldest orchestra presents symphony and pops programs. Sept-May.

May Festival. *Cincinnati Music Hall, 1241 Elm St, Cincinnati (45210). Phone 513/381-3300. www.mayfestival.com.* Oldest continuous choral festival in the nation; choral and operatic masterworks. Last two weekends in May.

Oktoberfest-Zinzinnati. *Cincinnati. Phone 513/579-3191. www.oktoberfest-zinzinnati.com.* Downtown Cincinnati becomes a German biergarten for this festive weekend. Nonstop German music, singing, dancing, food, and thousands of gallons of beer. Mid-Sept.

River Downs Race Track. *6301 Kellogg Ave, Cincinnati. 10 miles E on Hwy 52. Phone 513/232-8000. www. riverdowns.com.* Thoroughbred racing. Mid-Apr-Labor Day, mid-Oct-mid-Nov, Mon-Wed, Fri-Sun.

Riverfest. *Cincinnati. Phone 513/352-4000 (Cincinnati Recreation Commission); toll-free 800/246-2987 (Convention and Visitors Bureau).* Celebration in honor of Cincinnati's river heritage held along the city's waterfront parks. Festivities include fireworks, three stages of entertainment, food. Labor Day weekend.

Turfway Park Race Course. *7500 Turfway Rd, Florence, KY (41042). 10 miles SW off I-75 via exit 184, on Turfway Pike in Florence, Kentucky. Phone 859/371-0200; toll-free 800/733-0200. www.turfway.com.* Thoroughbred racing. Early Sept-early Oct, late Nov-Mar, Wed-Sun.

Limited-Service Hotels

★ ★ **BEST WESTERN MARIEMONT INN.** *6880 Wooster Pike, Cincinnati (45227). Phone 513/271-2100; fax 513/271-1057. www.bestwestern.com.* 60 rooms, 3 story. Check-out noon. Restaurant, bar. **$**

★ ★ **BEST WESTERN SPRINGDALE HOTEL & CONFERENCE CENTER.** *11911 Sheraton Ln, Springdale (45246). Phone 513/671-6600; fax 513/671-0507. www.bestwestern.com.* 267 rooms, 10 story. Pets accepted; fee. Check-out noon. Restaurant, bar. Fitness room. Indoor pool, whirlpool. **$**

★ **COMFORT INN.** *9011 Fields Ertel Rd, Cincinnati (45249). Phone 513/683-9700; fax 513/683-1284. www.comfortinn.com.* 115 rooms, 3 story. Complimentary continental breakfast. Check-out 11 am. Pool. **$**

★ ★ **COURTYARD BY MARRIOTT.** *4625 Lake Forest Dr, Cincinnati (45242). Phone 513/733-4334; toll-free 800/228-9290; fax 513/733-5711. www. courtyard.com.* 149 rooms, 3 story. Check-in 3 pm, check-out noon. Restaurant. Fitness room. Indoor pool, whirlpool. **$**

★ ★ **EMBASSY SUITES.** *4554 Lake Forest Dr, Blue Ash (45242). Phone 513/733-8900; toll-free 800/ 362-2779; fax 513/733-3720. www.embassysuites.com.* Offering a comfortable stay amid elegant surroundings, this hotel is a welcome oasis to both the business and leisure traveler. It is located just a half mile from the Blue Ash Airport and 8 miles from Paramount's Kings Island amusement park (see MASON). 235 rooms, 5 story, all suites. Complimentary full breakfast. Check-in 3 pm, check-out 1 pm. Restaurant, bar. Fitness room. Indoor pool, whirlpool. **$$**

★ **HAMPTON INN.** *10900 Crowne Point Dr, Cincinnati (45241). Phone 513/771-6888; toll-free 800/426-7866; fax 513/771-5768. www.whihotels.com/ ebrochures/hampcincino.* 130 rooms, 4 story. Pets accepted. Complimentary continental breakfast. Check-in 3 pm, check-out noon. Outdoor pool. **$**

★ ★ **HOLIDAY INN.** *4501 Eastgate Blvd, Cincinnati (45245). Phone 513/752-4400; fax 513/753-3178. www.holiday-inn.com.* 247 rooms, 6 story. Check-out 11 am. Restaurant, bar. Fitness room. Indoor pool, whirlpool. Business center. **$**

★ **QUALITY HOTEL & SUITES.** *4747 Montgomery Rd, Cincinnati (45212). Phone 513/ 351-6000; toll-free 800/292-2079; fax 513/351-0215. www.qualityhotelandsuites.com.* 148 rooms, 8 story. Complimentary full breakfast. Check-out noon. Restaurant, bar. Pool. Business center. **$**

★ ★ **VERNON MANOR HOTEL.** *400 Oak St, Cincinnati (45219). Phone 513/281-3300; toll-free 800/ 543-3999; fax 513/281-8933. www.vernon-manor.com.* 177 rooms, 7 story. Check-out noon. Restaurant, bar. Fitness room. Business center. **$**

Full-Service Hotels

★ ★ ★ ★ **THE CINCINNATIAN HOTEL.** *601 Vine St, Cincinnati (45202). Phone 513/381-3000; toll-free 800/942-9000; fax 513/651-0256. www. cincinnatianhotel.com.* Since 1882, The Cincinnatian Hotel has been a fixture on the local scene. It was one of the first hotels in the world to have elevators and incandescent lighting and now is listed on the National Register of Historic Places. The first luxury hotel in the city, it continues to provide the finest accommodations and highest levels of service to its guests. The accommodations are lovingly maintained and incorporate modern technology, like high-speed Internet access and multi-line telephones. Furnishings lean toward the contemporary, with vivid artwork and fresh flowers adding colorful splashes. Balconies and fireplaces add inviting touches to the gracious, tailored interiors. The eight-story atrium of the Cricket Lounge creates an airy ambience, perfect for whiling away the day. A harpist entertains those partaking in the wonderful afternoon tea, and the mellow notes of a piano entertain diners in the evening. The hotel thoughtfully provides box lunches for guests leaving the hotel for the day, although most are sure to book a table for dinner that evening at The Palace (see). The fine dining and impeccable service make it one of the top tables in town. Located in the heart of downtown, close to upscale shopping and near the convention center, The Cincinnatian Hotel is a wonderful choice for a special-occasion weekend or a business-related stay. 146 rooms, 8 story. Pets accepted, some restrictions. Check-in 3 pm, check-out noon. High-speed Internet access. Restaurant, bar. Fitness room. Indoor pool, whirlpool. **$$**

 ★ ★ ★ **HILTON CINCINNATI NETHERLAND PLAZA.** *35 W 5th St, Cincinnati (45202). Phone 513/421-9100; toll-free 800/445-8667; fax 513/421-4291. www.hilton.com.* The Hilton Cincinnati Netherland Plaza is a showpiece of Art Deco design in the heart of the city. Listed on the National Register of Historic Places, this elegant hotel marries historic character with modern amenities. Its downtown location within the Carew Tower complex is superb, and, with access to the city's skywalk, guests are only a short, climate-controlled distance from the city's major businesses and cultural attractions. The rooms and suites make a striking impression upon visitors with their stylish representation of the Art Deco period. The hotel's restaurant, The Grille at the Palm Court (see), is one of the city's most fashionable dining rooms. 561 rooms, 29 story. Check-in 3 pm, check-out noon. High-speed Internet access. Restaurant, bar. Fitness room. Indoor pool, whirlpool. Business center. **$$**

★ ★ ★ **HYATT REGENCY CINCINNATI.** *151 W 5th St, Cincinnati (45202). Phone 513/579-1234; toll-free 800/233-1234; fax 513/354-4299. www.cincinnati .hyatt.com.* Located in the downtown area, this hotel is across from the Cincinnati Convention Center and is connected to shopping, dining, and entertainment by an enclosed skywalk. It offers an indoor pool, whirlpool, and sundeck along with other amenities. 488 rooms, 22 story. Check-in 3 pm, check-out noon. High-speed Internet access. Two restaurants, bar. Fitness room. Indoor pool, whirlpool. Airport transportation available. Business center. **$**

★ ★ ★ **MARRIOTT CINCINNATI AIRPORT.** *2395 Progress Dr, Hebron (41048). Phone 859/586-0166; fax 859/586-0266. www.marriott.com.* 295 rooms, 8 story. Check-out noon. Restaurant. Fitness room. Indoor pool. Business center. **$$**

★ ★ ★ **MARRIOTT CINCINNATI NORTH-UNION CENTRE.** *6189 Muhlhauser Rd, Cincinnati (45069). Phone 513/874-7335; fax 513/874-7336. www. marriott.com.* 295 rooms, 8 story. Check-out noon. Restaurant. Fitness room. Indoor pool. Business center. **$$**

★ ★ ★ **MILLENNIUM HOTEL CINCINNATI.** *141 W 6th St, Cincinnati (45202). Phone 513/352-2100; toll-free 800/876-2100; fax 513/352-2148. www. millenniumhotels.com.* 422 rooms, 32 story. Pets accepted, some restrictions; fee. Check-in 4 pm, check-out noon. High-speed Internet access. Restaurant, bar. Fitness room. Outdoor pool. Airport transportation available. Business center. **$**

★ ★ ★ **THE WESTIN CINCINNATI.** *21 E 5th St, Cincinnati (45202). Phone 513/621-7700; toll-free 800/ 937-8461; fax 513/852-5670. www.starwood.com/westin.* With a riverside location in the downtown area, this

hotel is near Riverside Park, shopping, restaurants, a theater, and more. It offers a rooftop fitness center and pool along with many other expected amenities. 450 rooms, 17 story. Pets accepted, some restrictions. Check-in 3 pm, check-out noon. Restaurant, bar. Fitness room. Indoor pool, whirlpool. **$$**

Restaurants

★ **AGLAMESIS BROS.** *3046 Madison Rd, Cincinnati (45209). Phone 513/531-5196; fax 513/ 531-5403. www.aglamesis.com.* Old-time ice cream parlor; established 1908. Closed Jan 1, Easter, Dec 25. **$**

★ ★ **BLACK FOREST.** *8675 Cincinnati-Columbus Rd, Pisgah (45069). Phone 513/777-7600; fax 513/ 777-7601. www.theblackforest.com.* German menu. Lunch, dinner. Closed Sun; holidays. Bar. Children's menu. **$$**

★ ★ ★ **CELESTIAL.** *1071 Celestial St, Cincinnati (45202). Phone 513/241-4455; fax 513/241-2095. www.thecelestial.com.* This restaurant's name could just as easily refer to its stunning view of the Ohio River and city as to its street address. Enjoy dining in a clubby atmosphere of carved wood and elegant service. Stop at the Incline Lounge for breathtaking sunsets. Fusion menu. Dinner. Closed Sun-Mon; holidays. Bar. Valet parking. **$$$**

★ **CHENG-1 CUISINE.** *203 W McMillan St, Cincinnati (45219). Phone 513/723-1999; fax 513/723-1999.* Chinese menu. Lunch, dinner. Closed Thanksgiving, Dec 25. **$$**

★ ★ **DESHA'S.** *11320 Montgomery Rd, Cincinnati (45249). Phone 513/247-9933; fax 513/247-2380. www. deshas.com.* Steak menu. Lunch, dinner, Sun brunch. Closed Jan 1, Dec 25. Bar. Children's menu. Outdoor seating. **$$**

★ **THE DINER ON SYCAMORE.** *1203 Sycamore St, Cincinnati (45210). Phone 513/721-1212; fax 513/721-4535.* Lunch, dinner, Sun brunch. Closed Dec 25. Bar. Children's menu. Outdoor seating. **$$**

★ ★ **FERRARI'S LITTLE ITALY.** *7677 Goff Terrace, Cincinnati (45243). Phone 513/272-2220.* Italian menu. Lunch, dinner. Closed Jan 1, Easter, Dec 25. Children's menu. Outdoor seating. **$$**

★ **FORE & AFT.** *7449 Forbes Rd, Cincinnati (45233). Phone 513/941-8400.* Floating barge on Ohio River; nautical memorabilia. Steak menu. Lunch, dinner. Closed Jan 1, Dec 24-25. Bar. Children's menu. Outdoor seating. **$$**

★ ★ **GERMANO'S.** *9415 Montgomery Rd, Cincinnati (45242). Phone 513/794-1155; fax 513/794-1840.* Italian menu. Lunch, dinner. Closed Sun; holidays. **$$$**

★ ★ **GRAND FINALE.** *3 E Sharon Ave, Cincinnati (45246). Phone 513/771-5925. www.grandfinale. info.* This restaurant is located in a remodeled turn-of-the-century saloon, a Victorian landmark. Fresh seafood, hand-trimmed steaks, rack of lamb, frogs' legs, crepes, and homemade breads and pastries are offered. Sunday brunch is beautiful, and the courtyard is opened year-round. Continental menu. Lunch, dinner, Sun brunch. Closed Mon; Dec 25. Bar. Children's menu. Outdoor seating. **$$**

★ ★ **THE GRILLE AT THE PALM COURT.** *35 W 5th St, Cincinnati (45202). Phone 513/421-9100; fax 513/421-4291.* At the Palm Court of the Hilton Cincinnati Netherland Plaza (see), this museum-like dining room offers friendly, accommodating service. The splendid space has a vaulted, muraled ceiling; wood paneling; and brass accents. American menu. Lunch, dinner. Bar. Valet parking. **$$$**

★ **HOUSE OF TAM.** *889 W Galbraith Rd, Cincinnati (45231). Phone 513/729-5566; fax 513/522-5130.* Chinese menu. Lunch, dinner. Closed Sun; holidays. Bar. **$$**

★ ★ **IRON HORSE INN.** *40 Village Sq, Cincinnati (45246). Phone 513/771-4787; fax 513/771-8708. www.ironhorseinn.net.* Lunch, dinner, Sun brunch. Bar. Children's menu. Valet parking. Outdoor seating. **$$**

★ ★ **LA NORMANDIE.** *118 E 6th St, Cincinnati (45202). Phone 513/721-2761; fax 513/287-7785.* Lunch, dinner. Closed Sun; holidays. Bar. Valet parking. **$$$**

★ **LE BOX CAFE.** *819 Vine St, Cincinnati (45202). Phone 513/721-5638; fax 513/562-2032.* American menu. Lunch. Closed Sat-Sun; holidays. Children's menu. Casual attire. **$**

★ **LENHARDT'S AND CHRISTY'S.** *151 W McMillan St, Cincinnati (45219). Phone 513/281-3600. www.lenhardtsandchristys.com.* German, Hungarian menu. Lunch, dinner. Closed Sun-Mon; July 4; also first two weeks in Aug, two weeks at Christmas. Bar. **$$**

★ ★ ★ ★ **MAISONETTE.** *114 E 6th St, Cincinnati (45202). Phone 513/721-2260; fax 513/287-7785. www.maisonette.com.* When you have been serving haute French cuisine with gracious warmth since 1949, you might lose your edge. This is not the case at Maisonette, however, where age is worn well. Bathed in classic French charm, with original oil paintings adorning the walls, loveseat-styled banquettes for cozy dining for two, and elegant table settings, this is the Casablanca of restaurants: a classic that never goes out of style. The menu makes a case for authentic, elegant French food all over again. The kitchen prepares light, flavorful, and luxurious meals from shimmering seasonal produce, dressed up with garnishes chosen with as much care as the main ingredients. Medallions of veal wrapped in country bacon with Spanish pepper and chorizo risotto and roasted domestic rack of lamb with tomato crust and chickpea crepes are house specialties, but there truly isn't a dish on the menu that won't inspire a tear or two . . . of joy, of course. French menu. Lunch, dinner. Closed Sun; holidays. Bar. Jacket required. Valet parking (dinner). **$$$$**

★ **MECKLENBURG GARDENS.** *302 E University, Cincinnati (45219). Phone 513/221-5353; fax 513/221-5383. www.mecklenburg.com.* German menu. Lunch, dinner. Closed holidays. Bar. Casual attire. Valet parking Fri-Sat. Outdoor seating. **$$**

★ ★ **MONTGOMERY INN.** *9440 Montgomery Rd, Cincinnati (45242). Phone 513/791-3482. www. montgomeryinn.com.* Lunch, dinner. Closed holidays. Bar. Children's menu. **$$**

★ ★ **MONTGOMERY INN AT THE BOATHOUSE.** *925 Eastern Ave, Cincinnati (45202). Phone 513/721-7427; fax 513/345-3712. www. montgomeryinn.com.* Barbecue menu. Lunch, dinner. Closed holidays. Bar. Children's menu. Valet parking. Outdoor seating. **$$**

★ ★ **NATIONAL EXEMPLAR.** *6880 Wooster Pike, Cincinnati (45227). Phone 513/271-2103; fax 513/271-8443.* Steak menu. Breakfast, lunch, dinner. Closed Dec 25. Bar. Children's menu. Casual attire. **$$**

★ ★ **NICOLA'S.** *1420 Sycamore St, Cincinnati (45210). Phone 513/721-6200; fax 513/721-1777. www.nicolasrestaurant.com.* Italian menu. Lunch, dinner. Closed Sun; holidays. Bar. Valet parking. Outdoor seating. **$$**

🔍 ★ ★ **PACIFIC MOON CAFE.** *8300 Market Place Ln, Cincinnati (45242). Phone 513/891-0091; fax 513/891-8824. www.pacificmooncafe.com.* Asian menu. Lunch, dinner, brunch. Closed Thanksgiving. Bar. Outdoor seating. **$$**

★ ★ ★ **THE PALACE.** *601 Vine St, Cincinnati (45202). Phone 513/381-6006. www.palacecincinnati .com.* Every expectation will be met, from the food to the service. The regional American cuisine changes seasonally to ensure only the freshest ingredients available grace the tables. The wine list boasts 350 choices, one sure to be perfect for any meal. American menu. Breakfast, lunch, dinner. Bar. Valet parking. **$$$**

★ ★ ★ **THE PHOENIX.** *812 Race St, Cincinnati (45202). Phone 513/721-8901; fax 513/721-1475.* Built in 1893; white marble staircase, 12 German stained-glass windows from the 1880s. Dinner is served in the President's Room, which is adorned with two elegant chandeliers. The historical east wall showcases a magnificent hand-carved library breakfront, and the menu consists of steaks and cuisine with American, Asian, German, and Caribbean influences. Dinner. Closed Sun-Tue; holidays. Valet parking. **$$**

★ ★ ★ **PRECINCT.** *311 Delta Ave, Cincinnati (45226). Phone 513/321-5454; toll-free 877/321-5454. www.jeffruby.com.* This 1890s police precinct offers the best in steakhouses—from aged angus beef to the perfect "eye," broiled to perfection and seasoned with a secret spice mix, this is a steakhouse like no other. Steak menu. Dinner. Closed holidays. Bar. Valet parking. **$$$**

🅳

★ ★ ★ **PRIMAVISTA.** *810 Matson Pl, Cincinnati (45204). Phone 513/251-6467. www.pvista.com.* Italian menu. Dinner. Closed holidays. Bar. **$$**

★ **ROOKWOOD POTTERY.** *1077 Celestial St, Cincinnati (45202). Phone 513/721-5456; fax 513/721-5403. www.rookwoodbistro.com.* Originally housed production of Rookwood pottery; some seating in former pottery kilns. Collection of Rookwood pottery. Seafood menu. Lunch, dinner. Closed Memorial Day, Thanksgiving, Dec 25. Bar. Children's menu. **$$**

★ **TEAK.** *1049 St. Gregory St, Cincinnati (45202). Phone 513/665-9800.* Thai menu. Lunch, dinner. Closed holidays. Bar. Outdoor seating. **$$**

Cleveland (A-4)

See also Akron, Aurora, Beachwood, Brecksville, Chardon, Elyria, Kent, Lorian, Mentor, Oberlin, Painesville, Strongsville

Founded 1796
Population 505,616
Elevation 680 ft
Area Code 216, 440
Information Convention and Visitors Bureau of Greater Cleveland, 3100 Terminal Tower, 50 Public Sq, 44113; phone 216/621-4110 or toll-free 800/321-1001
Web site www.travelcleveland.com
Suburbs Beachwood, Brecksville, Mentor, Strongsville. (See individual alphabetical listings)

Ohio's second-largest city extends 50 miles east and north along the shore of Lake Erie and 25 miles south inland. It is a combination of industrial flats, spacious suburbs, wide principal streets, and an informality due partially to its diverse population. Many nationalities have contributed to its growth—Poles, Italians, Croats, Slovenes, Serbs, Lithuanians, Germans, Irish, Romanians, Russians, and Greeks. Formerly, the various national groups divided regionally, but this is less true today.

Cleveland has more than 600 churches, 11 colleges, one metropolitan newspaper, and several suburban weeklies, as well as a progressive independent mayor-council form of government. A transportation crossroads and a big steel, electrical, and machine tool center, the city also serves as home to the famed Cleveland Clinic.

Cleveland's history has been peppered with industrial giants—John D. Rockefeller, the Mathers of iron and shipping, Mark Hanna of steel and political fame, the Van Sweringens, and others. The village, founded by Moses Cleaveland, profited from the combination of Great Lakes transportation and fertile country. At the time, northern Ohio was still almost entirely unoccupied; growth was slow. Not until 1827, when the Ohio Canal was opened to join Lake Erie with the Ohio River, did the town start to expand. Incoming supplies of coal and iron ore led to the manufacture of locomotives and iron castings. Before the Civil War, the city had surpassed Columbus in population to become the second largest in the state and was changing from a commercial to an industrial center. The boom era after World War I saw the birth of Shaker Heights, one of the more affluent suburbs; the Terminal Tower Group of buildings downtown; and the Group Plan, with civic buildings surrounding the central mall.

The layout of the city is systematic. All the main avenues lead to the Public Square (Tower City Center (see)), where the Terminal Tower is located. The east-west dividing line is Ontario Street, which runs north and south through the square. The north and south streets are numbered; the east and west thoroughfares are avenues, with a few roads and boulevards. Euclid Avenue is the main business street running through Cleveland and many of its suburbs. Many of the early buildings have been razed and replaced by planned urban architecture, while other buildings are being restored. "Millionaire's Row" and the magnificent mansions on Euclid Avenue are all but gone. The Cuyahoga River Valley, where refineries, oil tanks, and steel mills once made many fortunes, now is known for its entertainment and dining area. The 39 city parks and 17,500 acres of metropolitan parks are still a tribute to what was once called "forest city." Cleveland also is home to many universities, including Case Western Reserve, John Carroll (see), and Cleveland State (see).

Additional Visitor Information

Cleveland Magazine and *Northern Ohio Live*, at newsstands, have up-to-date information on cultural events and articles of interest to visitors.

Tourist information may be obtained from the Convention and Visitors Bureau of Greater Cleveland, 3100 Terminal Tower, 50 Public Square, 44113, phone 216/621-4110 or toll-free 800/321-1001. Information

booths are located in the Terminal Tower Building on Public Square, at Hopkins International Airport, and at Powerhouse and Nautica Boardwalk in The Flats.

Public Transportation

Buses and trains (RTA) Phone 216/621-9500. Information, phone 216/265-6030

Airport Hopkins International Airport. Weather, phone 216/931-1212

Information Phone 216/265-6030

Lost and Found Phone 216/265-6030

Airlines Air Canada, America West, American Airlines, American Trans Air, Continental Airlines, Continental Express, Delta Air Lines, Northwest Airlines, Southwest Airlines, United Airlines, US Airways, USA 3000

What to See and Do

Alpine Valley Ski Area. *10620 Mayfield Rd, Chesterland. 30 miles E on Hwy 322. Phone 440/285-2211.* Area has quad, double chair lifts; J-bar, two rope tows; patrol, school, rentals, snowmaking; cafeteria, lounge. Longest run 1/3 mile; vertical drop 240 feet. (Early Dec-early Mar) **$$$$**

Beck Center for the Arts. *17801 Detroit Ave, Lakewood (44107). Phone 216/521-2540.* (Sept-June; reduced schedule July-Aug)

Brookside Park. *Denison Ave and Fulton Pkwy. 4 miles SW of Public Sq (downtown) on I-71. Phone 216/621-3300.* A 157-acre park with tennis courts, athletic fields, and picnic areas. Also here is

Cleveland Metroparks Zoo. *3900 Wildlife Way, Cleveland. Phone 216/661-6500. www.clemetzoo.com.* Seventh-oldest zoo in the country, with more than 3,300 animals occupying 165 acres. Includes mammals, land and water birds; animals displayed in naturalized settings. More than 600 animals and 7,000 plants are featured in the 2-acre Rain Forest exhibit. (Daily; closed Jan 1, Dec 25) **$$$**

The Cleveland Arcade. *401 Euclid Ave. Between Superior and Euclid at E 4th St. Downtown. Phone 216/776-4461.* (1890) This five-story enclosed shopping mall, one of the world's first, features more than 80 shops and restaurants. (Mon-Sat)

Cleveland Browns (NFL). *Cleveland Browns Stadium, 1085 W 3rd St (44114). Phone 440/891-5001. www. clevelandbrowns.com.* Professional football team.

Cleveland Cavaliers (NBA). *Gund Arena, 1 Center Court (44115). Phone 216/420-2287. www.nba.com/cavs.* Professional basketball team.

Cleveland Hopkins International Airport. *5300 Riverside Dr. 12 miles SW of Public Sq (downtown).* Municipally owned; 1,800 acres. Observation deck for ticketed passengers only (May-Nov, weather permitting; free). Adjacent is

> **NASA Lewis Visitor Center.** *21000 Brookpark Rd, Cleveland. Phone 216/433-2001.* The display and exhibit area features the Space Shuttle, space station, aeronautics and propulsion, planets and space exploration; also Skylab 3, an Apollo capsule, and communications satellites. (Daily; closed holidays) **FREE**

Cleveland Indians (MLB). *Jacobs Field, 2401 Ontario St (44115). Phone 216/420-4200. www.cleveland.indians .mlb.com.* Professional baseball team.

Cleveland Institute of Art. *11141 East Blvd. Also 11610 Euclid Ave in University Cir. Phone 216/421-7000. www/cia.edu.* (1882) (460 students) Professional education in the visual arts. Professional and student exhibition gallery (daily; closed holidays).

Cleveland Institute of Music. *11021 East Blvd (44106). Phone 216/791-5000. www.cim.edu.* (1920) (Students: conservatory, 370; preparatory, 1,700) A leading international conservatory that is distinguished by an exceptional degree of collaboration between students and teachers. This same stimulating environment extends to the institute's community education programs, which help students realize their musical potential. Free public concerts and recitals. Tours.

Cleveland Metroparks. *3395 Scranton Rd (44109). Phone 216/351-6300. www.clevemetparks.com.* Established in 1917, the system today consists of more than 20,000 acres of land in 14 reservations, their connecting parkways, and Cleveland Metroparks Zoo (see). Swimming, boating, and fishing; more than 100 miles of parkways provide scenic drives, picnic areas, and play fields; wildlife management areas and waterfowl sanctuaries; hiking and bridle trails, stables; golf courses; tobogganing, sledding, skating, and

cross-country skiing areas; eight outdoor education facilities offering nature exhibits and programs.

⭐ **The Cleveland Museum of Art.** *11150 East Blvd. At University Cir. Phone 216/421-7340. www. clemusart.com.* Extensive collections of approximately 30,000 works of art represent a wide range of history and culture; included are arts of the Islamic Near East, the pre-Columbian Americas, and European and Asian art; also African, Indian, American, ancient Roman, and Egyptian art. Concerts, lectures, special exhibitions, films; café. Museum entrance from East Boulevard. (Tues-Sun; closed holidays) Parking (fee). **FREE**

Cleveland Museum of Natural History. *1 Wade Oval, University Cir (44106). Phone 216/231-4600. www. cmnh.org.* Dinosaurs, mammals, birds, geological specimens, gems; exhibits on prehistoric Ohio, North American native cultures, ecology; Woods Garden, live animals; library. (Daily; closed holidays) **$$$** Also here is

> **Shafran Planetarium.** *1 Wade Oval Dr, Cleveland. Phone 216/231-4600.* Shows (daily). Observatory (Sept-May, cloudless Wed nights; planetarium program on cloudy nights). Children's programs. **$$**

The Cleveland Orchestra. *1154 Steels Corners Rd, Cuyahoga Falls. Phone 216/231-1111. www. clevelandorchestra.com.* One of the world's finest orchestras. International soloists and guest conductors. (Mid-Sept-mid-May, Tues, Thurs-Sun) During summer months, orchestra performs at Blossom Music Center, approximately 28 miles south via Highway 71.

Cleveland Play House. *8500 Euclid Ave. Phone 216/ 795-7000; toll-free 800/278-1274. www.clevelandplayhouse .com.* America's oldest regional professional Equity theater presents traditional American classics and premiere productions of new works in five performance spaces; organized in 1915. (Sept-June, Tues-Sat evenings, also weekend matinees)

Cleveland Rockers (WNBA). *Gund Arena, 1 Center Court (44115). Phone 216/263-7625. www.wnba.com/ rockers.* Women's professional basketball team.

Cleveland State University. *1983 E 24th St (44115). Euclid Ave and E 24th St. Phone 216/687-2000. www. csuohio.edu.* (1964) (16,000 students) James J. Nance College of Business Administration, Fenn College of Engineering, Cleveland-Marshall College of Law,

Maxine Goodman Levin College of Urban Affairs, graduate studies, education, arts and sciences. Campus tours.

Cuyahoga Valley Line Steam Railroad. *315 Clark Ave (44113). Phone 330/657-2000.* Scenic railroad trips between Independence (south of Cleveland) and Akron aboard vintage train.

Dittrick Museum of Medical History. *Allen Memorial Medical Library, 11000 Euclid Ave, third floor. University Cir area. Phone 216/368-3648.* Collection of objects relating to history of medicine, dentistry, pharmacy, nursing; doctor's offices of 1880 and 1930; exhibits on development of medical concepts in the Western Reserve to the present. Also history of the X-ray and microscopes. (Mon-Fri; closed holidays; also Fri after Thanksgiving) **FREE**

Dunham Tavern Museum. *6709 Euclid Ave. East Side. Phone 216/431-1060.* Restoration of early stagecoach stop (1824) between Buffalo and Detroit; historic museum with changing exhibits; period furnishings. (Wed and Sun afternoons; closed holidays) **$**

Edgewater Park. *7600 W Memorial Shore Way (44108). West Blvd and Cleveland Memorial Shoreway; unit of Cleveland Lakefront State Park on Lake Erie. Phone 216/881-8141.* A 119-acre park with swimming beach, fishing, boating (ramps, marina); biking; fitness course; picnic grounds (pavilions); concessions; playground. Scenic overlook. (Daily) **FREE**

Euclid Beach Park. *16300 Lakeshore Blvd. Unit of Cleveland Lakefront State Park on Lake Erie. Phone 216/881-8141.* A 51-acre park with swimming beach, fishing access; picnic grounds, concession. **FREE**

Goodtime III boat cruise. *Phone 216/861-5110.* Two-hour sightseeing and dance cruises on Cuyahoga River, lake, and harbor. Leaves pier at East 9th Street. (Mid-June-Sept, daily; limited schedule rest of year) **$$$$**

Gordon Park. *6516 Detroit Ave (44102). E 72nd St and Cleveland Memorial Shoreway; unit of Cleveland Lakefront State Park on Lake Erie. Phone 216/881-8141.* A 117-acre park with fishing piers, boat ramp; picnic area, playground. (Daily) **FREE**

Great Lakes Science Center. *601 Erieside Ave. Phone 216/694-2000. www.greatscience.com.* More than

350 hands-on exhibits explain scientific principles and topics specifically relating to the Great Lakes region. Also features an Omnimax domed theater. (Daily; closed holidays) **$$$**

Hanna Fountain Mall. *Lakeside Ave and E Mall Dr.* Rectangular section in the heart of downtown, with a plaza, fountains, and a memorial to World War II veterans. Surrounding the mall are the following governmental and municipal buildings:

> **City Hall.** *12650 Detroit Ave, Cleveland. Lakeside Ave and E 6th St, overlooking Lake Erie.*

> **County Court House and Administration Building.** *Justice Center, 1 W Lake St, Cleveland. Ontario and Lakeside aves.*

> **Federal buildings.** *E 6th St and Lakeside Ave, Cleveland. (Old) at Superior Ave and Public Sq and (new) at E 6th St and Lakeside Ave.* Courts, customs, passport bureau.

> **Public Auditorium and Convention Center.** *1220 E 6th St, Cleveland. St. Clair Ave, E 6th St, and Lakeside Ave.* Seats 10,000; includes ballroom, music hall, small theater, and 375,000 square feet of usable space. Space for 28 events at one time.

> **Public Library.** *325 Superior Ave, Cleveland. Near Public Sq. Phone 216/623-2800.* Business and Science Building adjoining, separated by a reading garden; special exhibits. (Daily; closed holidays)

Health Museum of Cleveland. *8911 Euclid Ave. East Side. Phone 216/231-5010. www.healthmuseum.org.* More than 200 participatory exhibits and displays on the human body, including Juno, the transparent talking woman, and Wonder of New Life. Events and educational programs, including Corporate Wellness, Distance Learning, and school programs. (Daily; closed holidays) **$$**

High-level bridges. *Main Avenue Bridge, Lorain Carnegie Bridge, Innerbelt Freeway Bridge, all spanning Cuyahoga River Valley.*

John Carroll University. *20700 N Park Blvd, University Heights (44118). Warrensville Center and Fairmount Blvd. Phone 216/397-1886. www.jcu.edu.* (1886) (4,500 students) Arts and sciences, business, and graduate schools in 21 Gothic-style buildings on 60-acre campus. Large collection of G. K. Chesterton works.

Karamu House and Theater. *2355 E 89th St. Phone 216/795-7070. www.karamu.com.* Multicultural center for the arts. Classes/workshops in music, creative writing, dance, drama, and visual arts; dance, music, and theatrical performances (Sept-June); two theaters, art galleries. Fee for some activities.

Lake Erie Nature and Science Center. *28728 Wolf Rd. 14 miles W on Hwy 6 or I-90 to Bay Village, in Metropark Huntington. West Side. Phone 440/871-2900.* Features animals, marine tanks, nature displays, wildlife/teaching garden; planetarium show (fee). Science Center (daily; closed holidays). **FREE**

Lake View Cemetery. *12316 Euclid Ave. At E 123rd St. East Side. Phone 216/421-2665.* Graves of President James A. Garfield, Mark Hanna, John Hay, John D. Rockefeller. Garfield Monument (Apr-mid-Nov, daily). Cemetery (daily).

***Nautica Queen* boat cruise.** *Phone 216/696-8888.* Lunch, brunch, and dinner cruises. For details, contact East 9th Street Pier, North Coast Harbor, 44113.

Oldest Stone House Museum. *14710 Lake Ave, Lakewood. 5 miles W, One block N of Hwy 6. Phone 216/221-7343.* (1838) Authentically restored and furnished with early 19th-century artifacts; herb garden. Guided tour by costumed hostess. (Feb-Nov, Wed and Sun afternoons; closed holidays) **DONATION**

Playhouse Square Center. *1501 Euclid Ave. Phone 216/241-6000; toll-free 800/766-6048.* Five restored theaters form the nation's second-largest performing arts and entertainment center. Performances include legitimate theater, Broadway productions, popular and classical music, ballet, opera, children's theater, and concerts.

⭐ **Rock and Roll Hall of Fame and Museum.** *North Coast Harbor, E 9th St Pier, 1 Key Plz (44114). Phone 216/781-7625; toll-free 888/764-7625. www.rockhall.com.* A striking composition of geometric shapes, this building is now the permanent home of the hall of fame. More than 50,000 square feet of exhibition areas explore rock's ongoing evolution and its impact on culture. Interactive database of rock and roll songs; videos; working studio with DJs conducting live broadcasts; exhibits on rhythm and blues, soul, country, folk, and blues music. (Daily; closed Jan 1, Thanksgiving, Dec 25) **$$$$**

Rockefeller Park. *750 E 88th St (44108). Phone 216/881-8141.* Connects Wade Park and Gordon Park. A 296-acre park with lagoon area, playground, tennis courts, picnic facilities. Also here are

> **Cultural Gardens.** *22701 Lake Shore Blvd, Cleveland. Along East and Martin Luther King Jr. blvds.* Chain of gardens combining landscape architecture and sculptures of 24 nationalities. (Daily) **FREE**

> **Rockefeller Greenhouse.** *750 E 88th St, Cleveland. Phone 216/664-3103.* Japanese, Latin American, and peace gardens; garden for the visually impaired; seasonal displays. (Daily) **FREE**

Steamship William G. Mather Museum. *1001 E 9th St Pier, Cleveland. Phone 216/574-6262.* Former flagship of the Cleveland Cliffs Iron Company, this 618-foot steamship is now a floating discovery center. Built in 1925 to carry iron ore, coal, grain, and stone throughout the Great Lakes, she now houses exhibits and displays focusing on the heritage of the "Iron Boats." Her forward cargo hold is an exhibit hall and also houses a theater and gift shop. Guided and self-guided tours of the vessels are available (depending on the time of year); visitors can see the pilot house, crew's and guests' quarters, galley, guests' and officers' dining room, and the four-story engine room. (June-Aug, daily; May, Sept-Oct, Fri-Sun) **$$**

Temple Museum of Religious Art. *1855 Ansel Rd. University Cir area. Phone 216/831-3233.* Jewish ceremonial objects; antiquities of the Holy Land region. (Daily, by appointment; closed Jewish holidays) **FREE**

Tower City Center. *50 Public Sq (44113). Downtown.* A former railroad station and terminal, built in the 1920s. "The Avenue," a three-level marble, glass, and brass complex of dining, entertainment, and retail establishments, has an 80-foot high skylight, a 55-foot glass dome, 26 escalators and elevators, and a 40-foot-long fountain. An underground walkway connects Tower City to the Gateway Complex containing Jacobs Field and Gund Arena. Terminal Tower (circa 1930) was reborn again in the 1990s as the nucleus of Tower City Center. On the 42nd floor of this 52-story building is an observation deck (Sat-Sun). For further information, check Terminal Tower Lobby. **$**

Trolley Tours of Cleveland. *2000 Sycamore St (44113). Phone 216/771-4484; toll-free 800/848-0173.* One- and two-hour tours leave from Powerhouse at Nautica Complex. Advance reservations requested. **$$$$**

USS *COD*. *9th St and N Marginal Rd.* Docked at N Marginal Rd, between E 9th St and Burke Lakefront Airport. *Phone 216/566-8770. www.usscod.org.* World War II submarine credited with seven successful war patrols that sank more than 27,000 tons of Imperial Japanese shipping. Tours include all major compartments of this completely restored Gato-class submarine. (May-Sept, daily)

Wade Park. *Euclid Ave and 107th St. At University Cir. Phone 216/621-4110.* More than 80 acres; lake; rose and herb gardens. **FREE** Also here is

Cleveland Botanical Garden. *11030 East Blvd, Cleveland. Phone 216/721-1600.* Herb, rose, perennial, wildflower, Japanese, and reading gardens. Grounds (Apr-Oct, daily). **FREE**

Western Reserve Historical Society Museum and Library. *10825 East Blvd. In University Cir. Phone 216/721-5722. www.wrhs.org.* Changing exhibits; special programs; genealogy department; costume collection; American decorative arts. (Daily; closed holidays) **$$$** Also here and included in admission is

Frederick C. Crawford Auto-Aviation Collection. *Magnolia Dr and E 108th, Cleveland.* Antique cars and planes; 20th-century motorcycles and bicycles; National Air Racing exhibit; Main Street, Ohio, 1890. (Daily; closed holidays)

Wildwood Park. *16975 Neff Rd. Unit of Cleveland Lakefront State Park on Lake Erie. Phone 216/881-8141.* An 80-acre park with fishing, boating (ramps); picnic grounds, concession; playground. **FREE**

Special Events

Cleveland National Air Show. *Burke Lakefront Airport, 1501 N Marginal Rd #166, Cleveland (44114). Phone 216/781-0747.* Labor Day weekend.

Cuyahoga County Fair. *Cuyahoga County/Berea fairgrounds. 164 Eastland Road, Berea (44017). Phone 440/243-0090.* One of the largest fairs in the state. Early or mid-Aug.

Slavic Village Harvest Festival. *Slavic Village, Fleet Ave at 55th St, Cleveland. Phone 216/429-1182.* Mid-Aug.

Tri-City JazzFest. *700 Carnegie Ave, Cleveland (44115). Phone 216/987-4400.* Early Apr.

Limited-Service Hotels

★ ★ **CLARION HOTEL.** *17000 Bagley Rd, Middleburg Heights (44130). Phone 440/243-5200; toll-free 800/321-2323; fax 440/243-5244. www.choicehotels.com.* 223 rooms, 2 story. Pets accepted, some restrictions; fee. Check-out 11 am. Restaurant, bar. Indoor pool, outdoor pool, children's pool. Airport transportation available. **$**

★ **COMFORT INN.** *17550 Rosbough Dr, Middleburg Heights (44130). Phone 440/234-3131; fax 440/234-6111. www.comfortinn.com.* 136 rooms, 3 story. Pets accepted, some restrictions; fee. Complimentary continental breakfast. Check-out noon. Pool. Airport transportation available. Business center. **$**

★ **FAIRFIELD INN.** *16644 Snow Rd, Brook Park (44142). Phone 216/676-5200; toll-free 800/228-2800; fax 216/676-5200. www.fairfieldinn.com.* 135 rooms, 3 story. Complimentary continental breakfast. Check-out noon. Pool. **$**

★ **HAMPTON INN.** *1460 E 9th St, Cleveland (44114). Phone 216/241-6600; fax 216/241-8811. www.hamptoninn.com.* 192 rooms. Check-in 3 pm, check-out noon. Fitness room. **$**

★ ★ **HILTON GARDEN INN.** *1100 Carnegie Ave, Cleveland (44115). Phone 216/658-6400; fax 216/658-6405. www.hiltongardeninn.com.* 240 rooms. Check-in 3 pm, check-out noon. Restaurant, bar. Fitness room. Indoor pool, whirlpool. Business center. **$**

★ ★ **RADISSON HOTEL CLEVELAND AIRPORT.** *25070 Country Club Blvd, North Olmsted (44070). Phone 440/734-5060; toll-free 800/333-3333; fax 440/734-5471. www.radisson.com.* This hotel understands the art of business and pleasure and makes for a truly enjoyable stay, whether traveling for business or pleasure. With a staff well versed in ensuring a guest's pleasures, along with first-class amenities, this hotel not only meets guests' needs, it surpasses them. 140 rooms, 6 story. Check-out noon. Restaurant, bar. Fitness room. Indoor pool, whirlpool. Airport transportation available. **$**

Full-Service Hotels

★ ★ ★ CLEVELAND AIRPORT MARRIOTT.

4277 W 150th St, Cleveland (44135). Phone 216/252-5333; toll-free 800/228-9290; fax 216/251-1508. www.marriott.com. Located only 2 miles from the Cleveland Hopkins Airport and 10 miles from downtown, this hotel offers, a restaurant, lounge, indoor pool, health club, and more. It is near tennis courts, golf courses, and attractions. 375 rooms, 9 story. Pets accepted; fee. Check-out noon. Restaurant, bar. Fitness room. Indoor pool, whirlpool. Airport transportation available. **$$**

★ ★ ★ EMBASSY SUITES. *1701 E 12th St, Cleveland (44114). Phone 216/523-8000; fax 216/523-1698. www.embassysuites.com.* Perched amid Cleveland's thriving downtown district, guests are welcomed to this elegantly appointed hotel by a friendly and attentive staff ready to ensure each trip is a memorable one. Located two blocks away is the Galleria and Playhouse Square (see), and just seven blocks away is the Rock and Roll Hall of Fame and Museum (see), a must-see while visiting the Cleveland area. 268 rooms, 13 story, all suites. Complimentary full breakfast. Check-in 3 pm, check-out noon. High-speed Internet access. Restaurant, bar. Fitness room. Indoor pool. Business center. **$$**

★ ★ ★ HYATT REGENCY CLEVELAND AT THE ARCADE. *420 Superior, Cleveland (44114). Phone 216/575-1234; fax 216/575-1690. www.cleveland.hyatt.com.* 293 rooms, 9 story. Check-in 3 pm, check-out noon. High-speed Internet access. Two restaurants, bar. Fitness room. Business center. **$**

★ ★ ★ INTERCONTINENTAL HOTEL & CONFERENCE CENTER. *9801 Carnegie Ave, Cleveland (44106). Phone 216/707-4100; toll-free 877/707-8999; fax 216/707-4101. www.intercontinental.com.* 299 rooms. Check-in 2 pm, check-out noon.

High-speed Internet access. Three restaurants, two bars. Fitness room. Airport transportation available. Business center. **$$$**

★ ★ ★ ★ THE RITZ-CARLTON, CLEVELAND.

1515 W 3rd St, Cleveland (44113). Phone 216/623-1300; toll-free 800/241-3333; fax 216/623-1485. www.ritzcarlton.com. The Ritz-Carlton is Cleveland's premier destination. This hotel enjoys a coveted downtown location with views of Lake Erie and the Cuyahoga River, and all of the city's attractions and businesses are within walking distance. Adjacent is Tower City Center (see), an upscale multilevel shopping mall with indoor access to the Cleveland Indians' Jacobs Field; the lower level of Tower City is the train/subway station, providing easy access to the airport. Visitors are hosted in grand style here, where the usual Ritz-Carlton opulence reigns and thoughtful service grants every wish. The guest rooms, with commanding city and water views, are luxury defined to the last detail. The marble bathrooms are sumptuous, and guests are graciously provided with every imaginable service. Even pets are pampered here, with cookies upon check-in, a personalized water bowl, and a room-service menu just for pets. Walking service is available for a fee. All-day dining at the Century Restaurant & Bar is always a delight, its clean, modern design providing a soothing alternative to urban life. Seafood is a specialty here, and the sushi bar is an ever-popular choice. By day, the Lobby Lounge is ideal for traditional afternoon tea, while in the evening, its live entertainment attracts hotel guests and local residents alike. 208 rooms, 7 story. Pets accepted; fee. Check-in 4 pm, check-out noon. High-speed Internet access. Restaurant, two bars. Fitness room, spa. Indoor pool, whirlpool. Airport transportation available. Business center. **$$**

★ ★ ★ SHERATON CLEVELAND CITY CENTRE HOTEL. *777 St. Clair Ave, Cleveland (44114). Phone 216/771-7600; toll-free 800/321-1090; fax 216/771-5129. www.sheratoncleveland.com.* This hotel offers 470 rooms and 45 suites, a restaurant, two bars, a fitness center, and more, all located downtown overlooking Lake Erie. The property is adjacent to the Galleria Shopping and near Tower City Center (see), Municipal Stadium, and other attractions. 515 rooms, 22 story. Pets accepted, some restrictions. Check-in 3 pm, check-out noon. High-speed Internet access.

Restaurant, two bars. Fitness room. Airport transportation available. Business center. **$$**

★ ★ ★ WYNDHAM CLEVELAND AT PLAYHOUSE SQUARE. *1260 Euclid Ave, Cleveland (44115). Phone 216/615-7500; fax 216/615-3335. www.wyndhamcleveland.com.* 205 rooms, 14 story. Check-in 3 pm, check-out noon. Restaurant, bar. Fitness room. Indoor pool, whirlpool. Airport transportation available. **$**

Full-Service Inns

★ ★ ★ BARICELLI INN. *2203 Cornell Rd, Cleveland (44106). Phone 216/791-6500; fax 216/791-9131. www.baricelli.com.* This charming brownstone (1896) with individually decorated rooms is known for its wonderful restaurant (see). With a seasonal menu, the chef combines American cuisine with European flare. Just a few of the favorites here are seafood risotto, Maine lobster and crab ravioli, and cassoulet of duck. 7 rooms, 3 story. Complimentary continental breakfast. Check-in 2 pm, check-out 11 am. Restaurant. **$$**

★ ★ ★ GLIDDEN HOUSE INN. *1901 Ford Dr, Cleveland (44106). Phone 216/231-8900; toll-free 800/759-8358; fax 216/231-2130. www.gliddenhouse.com.* 52 rooms. Check-in 3 pm, check-out noon. High-speed Internet access. Restaurant, bar. Fitness room. Airport transportation available. Business center. **$**

Restaurants

★ ★ ★ BARICELLI INN. *2203 Cornell Rd, Cleveland (44106). Phone 216/791-6500. www.baricelli.com.* Adjacent to University Circle, this inn (see) and Italian restaurant are perched on a bluff in a large, turn-of-the-century brownstone mansion. The Little Italy location has romantic, old-world charm, and the seasonal menu features thoughtful preparations of local ingredients. Continental menu. Dinner. Closed Sun; holidays. Outdoor seating. **$$**

★ CABIN CLUB. *30651 Detroit Rd, Westlake (44145). Phone 440/899-7111.* Seafood, steak menu.

Lunch, dinner. Closed holidays. Bar. Children's menu. **$$$**

★ CAFE SAUSALITO. *1301 E 9th St, Cleveland (44114). Phone 216/696-2233; fax 216/696-8040.* Seafood menu. Lunch, dinner. Closed Sun; Thanksgiving, Dec 25. Valet parking. **$$**

★ ★ DON'S LIGHTHOUSE GRILLE. *8905 Lake Ave, Cleveland (44102). Phone 216/961-6700; fax 216/961-1966. www.donslighthouse.com.* American menu. Lunch, dinner. Closed Thanksgiving, Dec 25. Bar. Valet parking. **$$**

★ GREAT LAKES BREWING CO. *2516 Market Ave, Cleveland (44113). Phone 216/771-4404. www.greatlakesbrewing.com.* Seafood menu. Lunch, dinner. Closed holidays. Bar. Children's menu. Outdoor seating. **$$**

★ GUARINO'S. *12309 Mayfield Rd, Cleveland (44106). Phone 216/231-3100; fax 216/721-6289.* Oldest restaurant in Cleveland. Italian, American menu. Lunch, dinner. Closed holidays. Bar. Children's menu. Reservations recommended. Valet parking. Outdoor seating. **$$**

★ JOHN Q'S STEAKHOUSE. *55 Public Sq, Cleveland (44113). Phone 216/861-0900; fax 216/861-1237.* Steak menu. Lunch, dinner. Closed holidays. Bar. Children's menu. Valet parking Sat. Outdoor seating. **$$$**

★ ★ ★ JOHNNY'S BAR. *3164 Fulton Rd, Cleveland (44109). Phone 216/281-0055; fax 216/631-6890.* Former neighborhood grocery. Italian menu. Lunch, dinner. Closed Sun; holidays. Bar. Reservations recommended. **$$$**

★ ★ ★ MORTON'S OF CHICAGO. *1600 W 2nd, Cleveland (44113). Phone 216/621-6200; fax 216/621-7745. www.mortons.com.* The epitome of an all-American steakhouse. The food is always plentiful and of the highest quality. This chain also promises fine dining with attentive and animated service. Steak menu. Lunch, dinner. Closed holidays. Bar. **$$$**

★ ★ ★ PARKER'S. *2801 Bridge Ave, Cleveland (44113). Phone 216/771-7130; fax 216/771-8130.*

Dining at this restaurant on the near West Side is a dress-up occasion. Chef/owner Parker Bosley's seasonal menu is a testament to his avid support of local organic produce and farm-fed meats. American, French menu. Dinner. Closed Sun; holidays. Bar. **$$$**

★ ★ ★ **SANS SOUCI.** *24 Public Sq, Cleveland (44113). Phone 216/696-5600; fax 216/696-0432.* Fine cuisine is served in this comfortable dining room of exposed beams, lush greens, and a stone hearth. The Renaissance Hotel space is sectioned into intimate rooms where diners feast on the specialties. Mediterranean menu. Lunch, dinner. Closed holidays. Bar. **$$$**

Cleveland Heights (A-4)

Restaurant

★ **LEMON GRASS.** *2179 Lee Rd, Cleveland Heights (44118). Phone 216/321-0210; fax 216/321-2180.* Thai menu. Lunch, dinner. Closed Sun; holidays. Bar. Outdoor seating. **$$**

Columbus (C-3)

See also Delaware, Lancaster, Newark, Springfield

Founded 1812
Population 632,910
Elevation 780 ft
Area Code 614
Information Greater Columbus Convention and Visitors Bureau, 90 N High St, 43215-3014; phone 614/221-6623 or toll-free 800/345-4386
Web site www.columbuscvb.org

Columbus was created and laid out to be the capital of Ohio; it is attractive, with broad, tree-lined streets, parks, Ohio State University (see), and a handsome Greek Revival capitol. Both Chillicothe and Zanesville had previously been capitals, but, in 1812, two tracts were selected on the banks of the Scioto River, one for the capitol, the other for a state penitentiary, and construction began immediately. The legislature first met here in 1816.

By 1831, the new National Road reached Columbus, and stagecoach travel stimulated its growth. The first railroad reached Columbus in 1850 and, from then on, the city grew rapidly. Floods in 1913 made it necessary to widen the channel of the Scioto River. Levees, fine arched bridges, and the Civic Center were built.

Transportation equipment, machinery, fabricated and primary metals, food, printing, and publishing are among the principal industries, but education and government are the most important functions of Columbus. Its people are civic-minded, sports-minded, and cultured. The city has more than 1,130 churches and congregations and 12 colleges and universities.

Additional Visitor Information

Tourist brochures and a quarterly calendar of events may be obtained at the visitor center/gift shop in the Convention and Visitors Bureau, 90 North High Street, or on the second level of Columbus City Center, South High Street and South Third Street at Rich Street, phone toll-free 800/345-4386. A third visitor information center is located at the Columbus International Airport, I-670 E, I-270.

Public Transportation

Information Phone 614/239-4000

Lost and Found Phone 614/239-5035

Airlines Air Canada Jazz, America West, America West Express, American Airlines, American Express, Continental Airlines, Continental Express, Delta Air Lines, Delta Connection, Midwest Express, Northwest Airlines, Northwest Airlink, Skyway, Southwest Airlines, United Airlines, United Express, US Airways, US Airways Express

What to See and Do

Camp Chase Confederate Cemetery. *Sullivant and Powell aves.* Burial ground for Confederate soldiers who were prisoners in the camp.

City Hall. *N Front, W Gay, and W Broad sts and Marconi Blvd.* Occupies an entire block in the Civic Center. Greco-Roman style. Municipal departments and city council chamber.

Columbus Blue Jackets (NHL). *Nationwide Arena, 200 W Nationwide Blvd (43228). Phone 614/431-3600. www.bluejackets.com.* Professional hockey team.

Columbus Crew (MLS). *Columbus Crew Stadium, 2121 Velma Ave (43211). Phone 614/221-2739. www.thecrew .com.* Professional soccer team.

Columbus Museum of Art. *480 E Broad St. At Washington Ave. Phone 614/221-6801.* Collections focus on 19th- and 20th-century European and American paintings, sculptures, works on paper, and decorative arts; contemporary sculpture; 16th- and 17th-century Dutch and Flemish Masters. Galleries arranged chronologically. Museum shop; indoor atrium; Sculpture Garden; café. (Tues-Sun; closed holidays) **$$$**

Columbus Symphony Orchestra. *55 E State St. Phone 614/228-8600.* Performances at Ohio Theatre.

COSI Columbus, Ohio's Center of Science & Industry. *333 W Broad St. Phone 614/228-2674.* Hands-on museum includes exhibits, programs, and demonstrations. Battelle Planetarium shows (daily). Coal Mine, Hi-Tech Showcase, Free Enterprise Area, Foucault pendulum, Solar Front Exhibit Area, Computer Experience, Street of Yesteryear, Weather Station, KIDSPACE, and FAMILIESPACE. (Daily) **$$$**

Federal Building. *200 N High St.* Federal offices.

German Village. *588 S 3rd St. S of Downtown, bounded by Livingston Ave, Blackberry Alley, Nursery Ln, Pearl Alley. Phone 614/221-8888. www.germanvillage.org.* Historic district restored as old-world village with shops, old homes, gardens; authentic foods. Bus tour available; inquire. (Daily) **FREE**

Hoover Reservoir Area. *7600 Sunbury Rd, Westerville (43081). 12 miles NE on Sunbury Rd. Phone 614/ 645-1721.* Fishing, boating; nature trails, picnicking. (Daily) **FREE**

Martha Kinney Cooper Ohioana Library. *274 E 1st Ave. Phone 614/466-3831.* Reference library of books on Ohio and by Ohioans. (Mon-Fri; closed holidays) **FREE**

McKinley Memorial. *W Broad and N High sts. W entrance to capitol grounds.* Statue of President McKinley delivering his last address.

⭐ **Ohio Historical Center.** *1982 Velma Ave (43211). 17th Ave at I-71. Phone 614/297-2300.* (1970) Modern architectural design contrasts with the age-old themes of Ohio's prehistoric culture, natural history, and history. Exhibits include an archaeology mall with computer interactive displays and life-sized dioramas; a natural history mall with a mastodon skeleton and a demonstration laboratory; and a history mall with transportation, communication, and lifestyle exhibits. Ohio archives and historical library (Tues-Sat). Museum (daily; closed Jan 1, Thanksgiving, Dec 25). **$$$** Also here and included in admission is

Ohio Village. *1982 Velama Ave, Columbus.* (1974) Reconstruction of a rural, 1860s Ohio community, with one-room schoolhouse, town hall, general store, hotel, farmhouse, barn, doctor's house, and office. Costumed guides. (Memorial Day-Oct, Sat-Sun)

Ohio State Capitol. *High and Broad sts. In a 10-acre park bounded by High, Broad, State, and 3rd sts, on Hwy 23, 40. Phone 614/728-2695.* Fine building that has at its northwest corner a group of bronze statues by Levi T. Scofield. The sculpture depicts Ohio soldiers and statesmen under Roman matron Cornelia. Her words, "These are my jewels," refer to Grant, Sherman, Sheridan, Stanton, Garfield, Hayes, and Chase, who stand below her. Rotunda; observation window on 40th floor of State Office Tower Building, across from rotunda. (Daily) **FREE**

Ohio State University. *190 N Oval Mall (43219). N High St and 15th Ave. Phone 614/292-6446. www. osu.edu.* (1870) (55,000 students) One of largest universities in the country with 19 colleges, a graduate school, and more than 100 departments; medical center. Libraries have more than 4 million volumes. Tours. Also on campus are

Chadwick Arboretum. *2120 Fyffe Rd, Columbus.* (Apr-Oct) **FREE**

Wexner Center for the Arts. *1871 N High St, Columbus. Phone 614/292-0330.* Contemporary art. Film, video, performing arts, and educational programs and exhibits. Gallery tours during exhibitions (free). (Tues-Sun; closed holidays)

⭐ **Ohio's Prehistoric Native American Mounds.** Driving tour of approximately 244 miles for a visit to several of these areas. There are more than 10,000 Native American mounds in Ohio, many of which, like the famous Serpent Mound, were built in complex and fascinating forms, such as birds, snakes, and other animals. Ohio State University (see) has been responsible for the excavation and exploration of Ohio's earliest history. The Ohio Historical Center (see), 17th Avenue at Interstate 71, is a good place to start; here the entire prehistory is made clear in exhibits. After taking in these exhibits, take Highway 23 approximately 46 miles south to junction Highway 35, head 1 mile west to Highway 104/207, and then turn right (north) to.

Hopewell Culture National Historical Park. *16062 Hwy 104, Columbus.* (See CHILLICOTHE) Thirteen acres of Hopewell mounds; pottery and relics in museum. Return south on Highway 104, 4 miles to Chillicothe. Here drop in at the

Ross County Historical Society Museum. *45 W 5th St, Chillicothe.* (See CHILLICOTHE) See more exhibits on the lives of the earliest dwellers in Ohio. Then, take Highway 50 approximately 17 miles southwest to

Seip Mound State Memorial. *7078 Hwy 50, Bainbridge.* (See CHILLICOTHE)

O'Shaughnessy Reservoir. *16 miles N on Riverside Dr, Hwy 257.* Water-skiing, fishing, boating; picnicking. **FREE** At reservoir dam is

Columbus Zoo. *9990 Riverside Dr, Columbus. Phone 614/645-3550. www.colszoo.org.* More than 11,000 birds, mammals, fish, and reptiles; children's zoo. Picnic areas. (Daily)

Wyandot Lake Amusement & Water Park. *10101 Riverside Dr, Columbus. Phone 614/889-9283. www.wyandotlake.com.* Over 60 rides and attractions, including a wooden roller coaster, a 55-foot-tall Ferris wheel, water slides, wave pool, and a five-story aquatic treehouse. (Daily) **$$$$**

Park of Roses. *Whetstone Park, Acton and High sts. 5 1/2 miles N.* Contains over 10,000 rose bushes representing 350 varieties. Picnic facilities. Rose festival (early June). Musical programs (summer; Sun evenings). (Daily) **FREE**

Santa Maria Replica. *Battelle Riverfront Park, Marconi Blvd and Broad St. Phone 614/645-8760.* A full-scale, museum-quality replica of Christopher Columbus's flagship, the *Santa Maria.* Costumed guides offer tours of upper and lower decks. Visitors learn of life as a sailor on voyages in the late 1400s. (Apr-Jan, Tues-Sun; closed holidays)

Special Events

Actors Theater. *1000 City Park Ave, Columbus (43206). Schiller Park in German Village. Phone 614/444-6888.* Two Shakespearean productions, one American musical. June-Aug.

BalletMet. *Ohio Theatre, 322 Mt Vernon Ave, Columbus. Phone 614/229-4848.* Sept-mid-Apr.

Greater Columbus Arts Festival. *Columbus. Downtown riverfront area. Phone toll-free 800/345-4386.* Exhibits, music, dancing. Early June.

Harness racing. Scioto Downs. *6000 S High St, Lockbourne (43137). 3 miles S of I-270. Phone 614/491-7674.* Restaurants. Early May-mid-Sept, Mon-Sat, nightly.

Ohio State Fair. *Ohio Expo Center, 717 E 17th Ave, Columbus (43211). Phone 614/644-3247; toll-free 888/646-3976.* Agricultural and industrial exposition plus grandstand entertainment, pageants, and horse show. Early-mid-Aug.

Opera/Columbus. *Palace Theatre, 117 Naghten, Columbus. Phone 614/461-0022.* English translation projected onto screen above stage. Oct-May.

Thoroughbred racing. Beulah Park Jockey Club. *3664 Grant Ave, Grove City (43123). At Southwest Blvd. Phone 614/871-9600.* Jan-May.

Limited-Service Hotels

★ **BEST WESTERN FRANKLIN PARK SUITES-POLARIS.** *2045 Polaris Pkwy, Columbus (43240). Phone 614/396-5100; toll-free 800/780-7234; fax 614/396-5101. www.bestwestern.com.* 64 rooms. Check-in 3 pm, check-out 11 am. Indoor pool, whirlpool. **$**

★ **BEST WESTERN SUITES.** *1133 Evans Way Court, Columbus (43228). Phone 614/870-2378; toll-free 800/780-7234; fax 614/870-9919. www.bestwestern.com.* 66 rooms, 2 story. Complimentary continental breakfast. Check-out noon. Fitness room. Indoor pool, whirlpool. **$**

★ **COMFORT INN.** *4270 Sawyer Rd, Columbus (43219). Phone 614/237-5847; fax 614/231-5926. www. comfortsuites.com.* 67 rooms, 2 story. Complimentary continental breakfast. Check-out noon. Pool. Airport transportation available. **$**

★ ★ **COURTYARD COLUMBUS DOWNTOWN.** *35 W Spring St, Columbus (43215). Phone 614/228-3200; toll-free 800/228-9290; fax 614/228-6752. www.courtyard.com/cmhcy.* 149 rooms, 5 story. Check-out noon. High-speed Internet access. Restaurant, bar. Fitness room. Indoor pool, whirlpool. **$**

★ ★ **DOUBLETREE HOTEL.** *50 S Front St, Columbus (43215). Phone 614/228-4600; fax 614/228-0297. www.doubletree.com.* Located in the heart of scenic downtown Columbus, this hotel boasts spacious guest rooms, some offering spectacular views of the Scioto River. 194 rooms, 10 story, all suites. Pets accepted, some restrictions; fee. Check-out noon. Restaurant, bar. Opposite the river. **$$**

★ ★ **EMBASSY SUITES.** *2700 Corporate Exchange Dr, Columbus (43231). Phone 614/890-8600; fax 614/890-8626. www.embassysuites.com.* This hotel, with a beautiful atrium setting, is perfect for guests who want extra space and comfort. With its two-room suites, guests also can enjoy a complimentary breakfast, an evening reception to unwind, and much more. 221 rooms, 8 story, all suites. Complimentary full breakfast. Check-out noon. Restaurant, bar. Fitness room. Indoor pool, outdoor pool, whirlpool. Airport transportation available. Business center. **$**

★ **FAIRFIELD INN AND SUITES COLUMBUS/OSU.** *3031 Olentangy River Rd, Columbus (43202). Phone 614/267-1111; fax 614/267-0904. www.fairfieldinn.com.* 200 rooms. Complimentary continental breakfast. Check-in 3 pm, check-out noon. Restaurant, bar. **$**

★ **SIGNATURE INN COLUMBUS.** *6767 Schrock Hill Court, Columbus (43229). Phone 614/890-8111; toll-free 800/822-5252; fax 614/890-8111. www. signatureinn.com.* 125 rooms, 2 story. Complimentary

continental breakfast. Check-out noon. Pool. Business center. **$**

Full-Service Hotels

★ ★ ★ **THE BLACKWELL.** *2110 Tuttle Park Pl, Columbus (43210). Phone 614/247-4000; toll-free 800/556-4638; fax 614/247-4040. www.theblackwell.com.* 151 rooms. Check-in 3 pm, check-out noon. High-speed Internet access. Restaurant, bar. Airport transportation available. Business center. **$$**

★ ★ ★ **COLUMBUS MARRIOTT NORTH.** *6500 Doubletree Ave, Columbus (43229). Phone 614/885-1885; toll-free 800/228-9290; fax 614/885-7222. www. marriott.com.* This property is conveniently located to such area attractions as the Polaris Amphitheater, Columbus Zoo, and Center of Science and Industry. 300 rooms, 9 story. Pets accepted; fee. Check-out noon. Restaurant, bar. Fitness room. Indoor pool, outdoor pool, whirlpool. Airport transportation available. Business center. **$**

★ ★ ★ **CROWNE PLAZA.** *33 Nationwide Blvd, Columbus (43215). Phone 614/461-4100; fax 614/224-1502. www.crowneplaza.com.* Connected to the Columbus Convention Center, this hotel is perfectly located near all that Columbus has to offer. With a convenient shuttle service, guests are just minutes away from downtown. The hotel also has three restaurants, fitness facility, and more. 378 rooms, 12 story. Check-out noon. Restaurant, bar. Fitness room. Indoor pool. **$**

★ ★ ★ **HYATT ON CAPITOL SQUARE.** *75 E State St, Columbus (43215). Phone 614/228-1234; fax 614/469-9664. www.hyatt.com.* This hotel is located in the downtown area across from Capitol Park and connected to the Columbus City Center shopping and historic Ohio Theater. The property offers 400 rooms and a health club that overlooks the State Capitol. 400 rooms, 21 story. Check-out noon. Restaurant, bar. Fitness room. Business center. **$$**

★ ★ ★ **HYATT REGENCY COLUMBUS.** *350 N High St, Columbus (43215). Phone 614/463-1234; fax 614/280-3034. www.hyatt.com.* Connected to

German Village

German Village is a neighborhood to its roots. Uneven brick streets hand-laid in a herringbone pattern are lined with trees and the plain, simple brick cottages of German brewery workers. Boxlike brick houses feature carved limestone lintels and steps, slate roofs, and miniscule, well-kept yards. The village offers weekend zither concerts, a huge Oktoberfest, a clutch of German restaurants, and genuine old-world charm. There is a noticeable absence of neon. In fact, the entire historic district is listed on the National Register of Historic Places. Start at the German Village Meeting Haus (588 S 3rd St), where an 11-minute video tells the story of the settlement. An exhibit includes a timeline of German Village and items from the Wagner Brewery collection. Head south to the Golden Hobby Shop (630 S 3rd St). This 125-year-old former schoolhouse is chock-full of items crafted by local seniors. Included are handmade quilts, Afghans, ceramics, jewelry, stained glass, woodcrafts, and holiday decorations—all at great prices. The Boot Loft (631 S 3rd St) is a city-block long with 32 rooms of bargain paperbacks and hardcovers, many 50 percent-90 percent off original prices. One of the nation's largest independents, this rambling bookstore stocks more than 1 million items. It is contained (barely) in pre-Civil War era buildings that once housed general stores, a saloon, and a nickelodeon cinema. The courtyard provides a great space to sit, relax, and people-watch. Next door is Cup O' Joe (627 S 3rd St), where comfy couches and chairs make it a favorite hangout for locals and visitors. Grab a cup of house blend or a latte and indulge from an irresistible assortment of pastries, cheesecake, scones, and muffins. Hausfrau Haven (769 S 3rd St) is a whimsical general store with an eclectic stock of wine, beer, outrageous greeting cards, political put-down T-shirts, and a scrump-

tious local confection known as buckeyes: rich peanut butter-filled chocolates resembling the horse chestnuts that give Ohio its nickname. Turn left to Kossuth Street and Helen Winnemore's Contemporary Craft Gallery (150 E Kossuth St), one of the nation's oldest, continuously operating fine crafts shops, with jewelry and works of clay, metal, and wood. Housed in a charming brick cottage, it is the ultimate customer-friendly shop. Visitors are greeted with coffee or tea and invited not only to browse items on display, but also to check out drawers of jewelry and other items.

Mohawk dead-ends into Schiller Park, a beautiful 23-acre urban park named after German poet-philosopher Frederick Schiller. Actors Summer Theatre stages Shakespeare productions and musicals in the amphitheater. The park, containing a large statue of the eponymous Schiller, is ringed by large homes built by German brewery owners in the early and mid-19th century. Stroll north down City Park Avenue, arguably the prettiest street in the village. It's a great place to enjoy beautiful landscaping, peek into backyard gardens, and greet a few neighborhood dogs. Quilts & Stuff (911 City Park Ave) has been selling quilted items at this location for many years. Continue north, make a left on Beck, a right on 3rd, and end your tour at Katzinger's Delicatessen (475 S 3rd St) (see). Sandwich #59, a hot corned beef and Swiss on pumpernickel, was renamed "Bill's Day at the Deli" after former President Clinton enjoyed one. Other eateries include Schmidt's Sausage Haus (240 E Kossuth St) (see), a historic landmark specializing in German/American foods. At Juergen's German Village Backerei & Konditorei (525 S 4th St), proprietor Rosemarie Keidel serves up German pastries and foods in a former boarding house where waitresses wear traditional dirndls.

the Columbus Convention Center, this hotel is conveniently located for both business and leisure travelers. Luxurious guest suites are spacious, and, it also houses an indoor pool, health club, deli, café,

and 63,000 square feet of meeting space. 631 rooms, 20 story. Check-out noon. Restaurant, bar. Fitness room. Indoor pool. Business center. **$$**

★ ★ ★ **THE LOFTS HOTEL.** *55 E Nationwide Blvd, Columbus (43215). Phone 614/461-2663; toll-free 800/735-6387; fax 614/461-2630. www.55lofts.com.* For a departure from the ordinary, travelers check into The Lofts. Located in the heart of downtown Columbus, with the thriving cultural scene at its doorstep, this hotel is the city's coolest address. Guests are treated to a singular experience here, where a 100-year-old warehouse has been infused with contemporary design. The public spaces are industrial chic, with exposed brick and wood beams. The soaring ceilings and floor-to-ceiling windows of the accommodations introduce guests to the best of loft living. Clean, simple lines and furnishings are used to create an uncluttered décor, while patterned carpets add a dazzling element to the guest rooms. Stylish and unique, this hotel delights guests seeking a change without forsaking the luxuries of Frette linens and attentive service. 44 rooms, 4 story. Complimentary continental breakfast. Check-out noon. Restaurant, bar. Fitness room. Indoor pool. **$$**

★ ★ ★ **MARRIOTT COLUMBUS NORTHWEST.** *5605 Paul G Blazer Memorial Pkwy, Dublin (43017). Phone 614/791-1000; fax 614/791-1001. www.marriottnorthwest.com.* This hotel is located in one of Columbus's fastest growing entertainment and business districts. Just minutes from all the delights this elegant city has to offer, this hotel invites guests to relax and enjoy the graciously elegant guest rooms, as well as the pampering of a friendly and attentive staff. Nearby attractions include Columbus Zoo, Murfield Village and Golf Club, and Anheuser Busch Brewery. 303 rooms, 7 story. Pets accepted, some restrictions; fee. Check-out noon. Restaurant, bar. Fitness room. Indoor pool. Business center. **$**

★ ★ ★ **SHERATON SUITES COLUMBUS.** *201 Hutchinson Ave, Columbus (43235). Phone 614/436-0004; fax 614/436-0926. www.sheraton.com.* With over 250 guest suites, each with modern, comfortable appointments, this hotel provides a homestyle feel, as you take advantage of many of the nearby attractions including the university, zoo, and fairgrounds. 260 rooms, 9 story, all-suites. Check-out 1 pm. Restaurant, bar. Fitness room. Indoor pool, outdoor pool, whirlpool. **$**

Full-Service Inn

★ ★ ★ **THE WORTHINGTON INN.** *649 High St, Worthington (43085). Phone 614/885-2600; fax 614/885-1283. www.worthingtoninn.com.* Renovated Victorian inn. 26 rooms, 3 story. Complimentary full breakfast. Check-in 3 pm, check-out noon. Restaurant (see SEVEN STARS), bar. **$$**

Specialty Lodgings

The following lodging establishments are approved by Mobil Travel Guide, but due to their unique and individualized nature have not been given a traditional Mobil Star rating. Included in this listing you may find bed-and-breakfasts, limited-service inns, guest ranches, and other unique hotel properties.

50 LINCOLN INN. *50 E Lincoln St, Columbus (43215). Phone 614/299-5050; toll-free 888/299-5051; fax 614/291-4924. www.50lincoln.com.* 8 rooms. Complimentary full breakfast. Check-in 4 pm, check-out 11 am. **$$**

HARRISON HOUSE B&B. *313 5th Ave, Columbus (43201). Phone 614/421-2202; toll-free 800/827-4203. www.columbus-bed-breakfast.com.* 4 rooms. Complimentary full breakfast. Check-in 4 pm, check-out 11 am. **$**

Restaurants

★ ★ ★ **ALEX'S BISTRO.** *4681 Reed Rd, Columbus (43220). Phone 614/457-8887.* A surprisingly charming dining room accented with dark wood and brass is found at this suburban strip-mall location. The menu highlights chef Alex Gosetto's Italian and French heritage, with classic preparations of rich, baked crepes and various veal, fish, and pasta dishes. French, Italian menu. Dinner. Closed Sun; holidays. Bar. **$$**

★ ★ **BEXLEY'S MONK.** *2232 E Main St, Columbus (43209). Phone 614/239-6665; fax 614/239-7861. www.bexleymonk.com.* Fusion menu. Dinner. Closed holidays. Bar. **$$$**

★ ★ **BRAVO! ITALIAN KITCHEN.** *3000 Hayden Rd, Columbus (43235). Phone 614/791-1245. www. bestitalianusa.com.* Italian menu. Lunch, dinner. Closed holidays. Bar. Valet parking. Outdoor seating. **$$**

★ **CAP CITY DINER-GRANDVIEW.** *1299 Olentangy River Rd, Columbus (43212). Phone 614/ 291-3663; fax 614/443-3212.* Upscale diner. American menu. Lunch, dinner. Closed holidays. Bar. Children's menu. Outdoor seating. **$$**

★ **CLARMONT.** *684 S High St, Columbus (43215). Phone 614/443-1125; fax 614/443-3212.* Seafood, steak menu. Breakfast, lunch, dinner. Closed holidays. Bar. **$$**

★ ★ ★ **HANDKE'S CUISINE.** *520 S Front St, Columbus (43215). Phone 614/621-2500; fax 614/ 621-2626. www.chefhandke.com.* Located in the brewery district, this restaurant has global cuisine with world-class appeal. Set in a former 19th-century brewery, openly spacious with three dining rooms, vaulted ceilings, and exquisite décor. The second dining room offers a more intimate atmosphere. International menu. Dinner. Closed Sun; Dec 25. Valet parking. **$$**
🅓

★ ★ **HUNAN HOUSE.** *2350 E Dublin-Granville Rd, Columbus (43229). Phone 614/895-3330; fax 614/895-3073.* Chinese menu. Lunch, dinner. Closed Thanksgiving. Bar. **$$**

★ ★ **HUNAN LION.** *2038 Bethel Rd, Columbus (43220). Phone 614/459-3933; fax 614/459-9675.* Chinese, Thai menu. Lunch, dinner. Bar. **$$**

★ **KATZINGER'S DELICATESSEN.** *475 S 3rd St, Columbus (43215). Phone 614/228-3354. www.katzingers .com.* Deli menu. Dinner. Closed Easter, Thanksgiving, Dec 25. Children's menu. Outdoor seating. **$$**

★ ★ ★ **L'ANTIBES.** *772 N High St, #106, Columbus (43215). Phone 614/291-1666. www.lantibes .com.* Exceptionally sophisticated French fare in a quiet, calm, and unpretentious atmosphere. The small restaurant allows chef Dale Gussett to personally oversee a diner's meal. The sweetbreads are the talk of the town. French menu. Dinner. Closed Sun-Mon; Thanksgiving, Dec 25. **$$$**

★ ★ **LINDEY'S.** *169 E Beck St, Columbus (43206). Phone 614/228-4343; fax 614/288-8920.* Restored

building (1888) in German Village. German menu. Lunch, dinner, Sun jazz brunch. Closed holidays. Bar. Valet parking. Outdoor seating. **$$**

★ ★ ★ **MORTON'S OF CHICAGO.** *2 Nationwide Plz, Columbus (43215). Phone 614/464-4442; fax 614/ 464-2940. www.mortons.com.* For the freshest lobster and steaks, put Morton's on your list. Professional service and clublike setting offer a truly professional dining experience. Steak menu. Dinner. Closed holidays. Bar. Valet parking. **$$$**

★ ★ ★ **REFECTORY.** *1092 Bethel Rd, Columbus (43220). Phone 614/451-9774; fax 614/451-4434.* Residing in a historic church, this fine French restaurant is known as one of the area's most romantic, special-occasion destinations. For a great deal, try chef Richard Blondin's three-course bistro menu served Monday through Thursday in the lounge or outdoor patio. French menu. Dinner. Closed Sun; holidays. Bar. Outdoor seating. **$$$**
🅓

★ ★ **RIGSBY'S CUISINE VOLATILE.** *698 N High St, Columbus (43215). Phone 614/461-7888; fax 614/461-0741.* Mediterranean menu. Lunch, dinner. Closed Sun. Bar. Valet parking. Outdoor seating. **$$**

★ ★ **RJ SNAPPERS.** *700 N High St, Columbus (43215). Phone 614/280-1070; fax 614/280-1090.* Seafood menu. Dinner. Closed holidays. Bar. Children's menu. Valet parking. **$$**

★ **SCHMIDT'S SAUSAGE HAUS.** *240 E Kossuth St, Columbus (43204). Phone 614/444-6808; fax 614/ 444-1446.* American, German menu. Lunch, dinner. Closed Easter, Thanksgiving, Dec 25. Bar. Children's menu. **$$**

★ ★ ★ **SEVEN STARS.** *649 High St, Columbus (43085). Phone 614/885-2600; fax 614/885-1283. www. worthingtoninn.com.* This acclaimed restaurant has an enlightened American menu, on-premise baking, and an extensive wine list. Meals served in the dining room, in the pub, or outside in the brick courtyard are often accompanied by live music. American menu. Breakfast, lunch, dinner, Sun brunch. Closed holidays. Bar. Outdoor seating. (See THE WORTHINGTON INN.) **$$$**
🅓

★ ★ **TAPATIO.** *491 N Park St, Columbus (43215). Phone 614/221-1085; fax 614/221-7432.* Modern contemporary bistro. Fusion menu. Lunch, dinner. Closed Thanksgiving, Dec 25. Bar. Outdoor seating. **$$**

★ ★ **TONY'S.** *16 W Beck St, Columbus (43215). Phone 614/224-8669; fax 614/224-0159.* Italian menu. Lunch, dinner. Closed Sun; holidays. Bar. Outdoor seating. **$$**

Coshocton (C-4)

See also Cambridge, Gnadenhutten, New Philadelphia, Newark, Zanesville

Founded 1802
Population 12,193
Elevation 775 ft
Information Coshocton County Convention and Visitors Bureau, PO Box 905; phone 740/622-4877 or toll-free 800/338-4724

This unusual name was derived from travelers' spellings of Native American words meaning either "river crossing" or "place of the black bear." The settlement was first known as Tuscarawa. Coshocton is on the banks of the Muskingum River at the junction of the Tuscarawas and Walhonding rivers; Johnny Appleseed planted some of his orchards here. Specialty advertising originated in Coshocton, which has a variety of other industries, including leather goods, iron pipe, plastics, pottery, appliances, rubber products, stainless steel, and baskets.

What to See and Do

⭐ **Roscoe Village.** *381 Hill St (43812). NW edge of town on Hwy 16. Phone 740/622-9310; toll-free 800/877-1830. www.roscoevillage.com.* Visitor center has information on canal era and historic attractions in the area; displays and continuous slide presentations. Roscoe Village creates a quaint living museum as an 1830s Ohio and Erie Canal town, with pocket gardens, old-time shops, exhibits, and crafts; lodging and dining available. Many special events throughout the year. (Daily; closed Jan 1, Thanksgiving, Dec 25) **FREE** Also in the village are

Boat trips. *23253 Hwy 83, Coshocton. Phone 740/622-7528.* One-mile horse-drawn boat trips (35 minutes) on the Ohio and Erie Canal aboard *Monticello III.* (Memorial Day-Labor Day, daily; rest of May, after Labor Day-late Oct, weekends) **$$$**

Johnson-Humrickhouse Museum. *300 N Whitewoman St, Coshocton. Phone 740/622-8710. www.jhm.lib.oh.us.* Houses four permanent galleries: Native American and Eskimo collection ranging from Stone Age to the present, Oriental Room with Chinese and Japanese collections, Early American gallery that has a pioneer room display, Decorative Arts has some European pieces. Museum also has traveling exhibits. (May-Oct, afternoons; rest of year, Tues-Sun afternoons; closed holidays) **$**

Village Exhibit Tour. *381 Hill St, Coshocton. Phone 740/622-9310; toll-free 800/877-1830.* Exhibit buildings include Township Hall (1880), with one-room school exhibit; blacksmith's shop; 19th-century print shop; Craft and Learning Center, with 1800s craft demonstrations; the Dr. Maro Johnson Home (1833), furnished with antiques (1690-1840); the Toll House, with model locks and canal artifacts; and the Craftsman's House, an 1825 workingman's house where the art of broom making is revived. Self-guided tour of exhibit buildings (daily; closed Jan 1, Thanksgiving, Dec 25); guided tours (Jan-Mar). **$$$**

Special Events

Apple Butter Stirrin'. *Roscoe Village, Coshocton. Phone toll-free 800/877-1830.* Third weekend in Oct.

Christmas Candle Lightings. *381 Hill St, Coshocton (43812). Roscoe Village. Phone toll-free 800/877-1830.* Tree- and candle-lighting ceremonies; hot-mulled cider, ginger cookies. First three Sat in Dec.

Coshocton Canal Festival. *600-699 N Whitewoman St, Coshocton (43812). Roscoe Village. Phone toll-free 800/877-1830.* Celebrates arrival of first boat from Cleveland in 1830. Art exhibits, parades, old-time crafts, costume promenade, musical events, food. Third weekend in Aug.

Dulcimer Days. *23253 Hwy 83 N, Coshocton (43812). Roscoe Village. Phone toll-free 800/877-1830.* Displays, jam sessions, workshops. Third weekend in May.

Hot Air Balloon Festival. *Coshocton County fairgrounds, 707 Kenilworth Ave, Coshocton (43812). Phone 740/622-5411.* Hot air balloon launches, family entertainment. First weekend in June.

Olde Time Music Fest. *381 Hill St, Coshocton (43812). Roscoe Village. Phone toll-free 800/877-1830.* Banjo and barbershop music. Mid-June.

Limited-Service Hotel

★ ★ **THE INN AT ROSCOE VILLAGE.** *200 N Whitewoman St, Coshocton (43812). Phone 740/ 622-2222; toll-free 800/237-7397; fax 740/623-6568. www.roscoevillage.com.* Open year-round, this resort has many offerings for the whole family. The inn is just steps away from an interactive village where costumed artisans demonstrate their crafts, providing a clean, fun place for the family to laugh and learn. 50 rooms, 4 story. Check-out noon. Restaurant, bar. **$**

Restaurant

★ ★ **OLD WAREHOUSE.** *400 N Whitewoman St, Coshocton (43812). Phone 740/622-4001; fax 740/ 623-6532. www.roscoevillage.com.* In converted warehouse (1831) in Roscoe Village. Lunch, dinner. Closed Mon; Jan 1, Dec 25. Children's menu. **$**

Dayton (D-1)

See also Lebanon, Mason, Miamisburg, Middletown, Piqua, Springfield, Vandalia, Wilmington

Founded 1796
Population 182,044
Elevation 757 ft
Area Code 937
Information Dayton/Montgomery County Convention and Visitors Bureau, Chamber Plaza, 1 Chamber Plaza, Suite A, 45402-2400; phone 937/226-8211 or toll-free 800/221-8235
Web site www.daytoncvb.com

Dayton is situated at the fork of the Great Miami River. The river curves through the city from the northeast, uniting with the Stillwater River half a mile above Main Street Bridge. Mad River from the east and Wolf Creek from the west join the others four blocks from there. Dayton has 28 bridges crossing these rivers.

The first flood, in 1805, started a progression of higher levees. In 1913, the most disastrous flood took 361 lives and property worth $100 million and inspired a flood-control plan effective to date.

Here, between 1870 and 1910, James Ritty invented a "mechanical money drawer" (which only amused people at first); John Patterson, promoting this cash register, opened the first daylight factory with 80 percent glass walls; Barney Oldfield, in his "Old 999" pioneer racing car, won a local exhibition match; the Wright brothers experimented with kites and gliders, built a wind tunnel, and developed the aileron; and Charles Kettering sold a big order of automobile self-starters to the Cadillac Motor Company. During and after World War I, the city added Frigidaire and Wright-Patterson Air Force Base (see) to its economic base. Today, Dayton is a well-planned, well-run industrial city with a council-manager form of government.

What to See and Do

Aullwood Audubon Center and Farm. *1000 Aullwood Rd. 10 miles NW on Hwy 48 to jct Hwy 40, at Englewood Dam. Phone 937/890-7360.* A 350-acre environmental educational center and working educational farm. Interpretive museum, nature trails, exhibits. Working farm has seasonal programs. (Daily; closed holidays, holiday weekends) **$$**

Benjamin Wegerzyn Horticultural Center. *1301 E Siebenthaler. Phone 937/277-6545.* Stillwater Gardens and wetland woods; horticultural library; Gift Gallery. Grounds (daily). **FREE**

Boonshoft Museum of Discovery. *2600 DeWeese Pkwy. Phone 937/275-7431.* Natural history exhibits include live animals common to Ohio; Philips Space Theater shows (daily). Bieser Discovery Center and the Dayton Science Center feature hands-on interactive exhibits and activities. (Daily) **$$$**

Carillon Park. *1000 Carillon Blvd. 2 miles S via I-75 to exit 51. Phone 937/293-2841.* Collections depict history of transportation and early pioneer life in the area, including original early railroad depot and section of the Miami and Erie Canal fitted with an original lock; Dayton-built motor vehicles; Wright brothers' 1905 plane; 1912 steam locomotive and tender. In 23 buildings and structures on 65 acres. (May-Oct, Tues-Sun, Mon holidays) Concerts (May-Oct, Sun; June-Aug, Sat). **$$** Also in park is

Newcom Tavern. *2001 S Patterson Blvd, Dayton. Phone 937/226-8211.* Oldest preserved house in the city; miraculously withstood the 1913 Dayton flood. Collection of pioneer, early Dayton relics.

The Dayton Art Institute. *456 Belmonte Park N (45405). Riverview and Forest aves. Phone 937/223-5277. www.daytonartinstitute.org.* European and American paintings and sculptures; Asian Gallery; pre-Columbian arts, prints, and decorative arts; changing exhibits; Experiencenter participatory gallery; reference library. Concerts. (Daily) **FREE**

Eastwood Lake. *Hwy 4 and Harshman Rd (45431). Phone 937/275-7275.* A 185-acre lake designed for most water sports: motor boating, fishing boats, and water-skiing (even calendar days); sailboards, personal water craft, sailing, fishing boats at idle speed (odd calendar days). 35-mph speed limit and 40-power boat capacity. (Daily) **FREE**

Masonic Temple. *525 W Riverview Ave. At Belmonte Park N. Phone 937/224-9795.* Modern adaptation of Greek Ionic architecture; considered one of the most beautiful Masonic buildings in the country. (Daily) **FREE**

Paul Laurence Dunbar House State Memorial. *219 Paul Laurence Dunbar St. Phone 937/224-7061.* The Dayton-born black poet and novelist lived here from 1903 until his death at age 34 in 1906. (Memorial Day-Labor Day, Wed-Sun; Sept-Oct, weekends; Nov-May, Mon-Fri) **$$**

SunWatch Prehistoric Indian Village and Archaeological Park. *2301 W River Rd. S off I-75. Phone 937/268-8199.* Reconstructed village. Planting and harvesting of Native American gardens, house construction, demonstrations, and hands-on activities available throughout the year. Visitor information center houses audiovisual program, exhibits, and life-size dioramas. Tours. (Tues-Sun; closed Thanksgiving, Dec 25) **$$**

University of Dayton. *300 College Park Ave. SE part of city. Phone 937/229-4114. www.udayton.edu.* (1850) (6,700 students) Engineering, liberal arts, arts and science, law, business, and education. On campus is Kennedy Union Art Gallery (academic year, daily; free). Campus tours.

Woodland Cemetery and Arboretum. *118 Woodland Ave. Phone 937/228-2581. www.woodlandarboretum .org.* Graves of Orville and Wilbur Wright, Charles F. Kettering, Deeds, Cox, and Patterson. Maps available. (Daily)

Wright Brothers Memorial. *Kauffman Rd off Hwy 444 (45433). E on Hwy 444 at jct old Hwy 4. Phone 937/226-8211.* A monolith dedicated to the "fathers" of aviation; overlooks Huffman Prairie, where the Wrights practiced flying.

Wright Cycle Shop. *22 S Williams St.* Replica of the shop where Wright brothers performed some of their experiments; turn-of-the-century bicycles. (Sat-Sun; also by appointment) **FREE**

Wright-Patterson Air Force Base. *4771 Lahm Cir, WPAFB (45433). 10 miles NE on Hwy 444. Phone 937/257-7826.* Center of research and aerospace logistics for United States Air Force; also site of Air Force Institute of Technology. On the grounds is

> **United States Air Force Museum.** *1100 Spaaz St, Dayton. Area B, Springfield and Harshman rds. Phone 937/255-3284.* One of the world's most comprehensive military aviation museums; more than 200 major historic aircraft and missiles; exhibits span period from Wright brothers to space age. IMAX theater (fee). (Daily; closed holidays) **FREE**

Wright State University. *3640 Allyn Hall. 8 miles E on Colonel Glenn Hwy (E 3rd St). Phone 937/775-5700 (admissions); toll-free 800/589-9703 (public relations). www.wright.edu.* (1967) (15,000 students) Library contains one of the largest collections of Wright brothers memorabilia. Biological preserve with walking trails. The Creative Art Center is home to The Dayton Art Institute Museum of Contemporary Art.

Special Events

City Folk Festival. *125 N Main St, Dayton (45402). Phone 937/461-5149.* Third weekend in June.

Dayton Air Show. **Dayton International Airport**, *3600 Terminal Rd, Vandalia (45377). Phone 937/898-5901.* Features approximately 100 outdoor exhibits; flight teams. Third weekend in July.

The Dayton Art Institute Concert Series. *456 Belmonte Park N, Dayton (45405). Phone 937/ 223-5277.* Summer concerts in cloistered garden. June-mid-Aug, Thurs evenings.

Montgomery County Fair. *Montgomery County fairgrounds, 1043 S Main St, Dayton. Phone 937/ 224-1619.* Labor Day weekend.

Limited-Service Hotels

★ **COMFORT INN.** *7907 Brandt Pike, Huber Heights (45424). Phone 937/237-7477; toll-free 800/ 228-5150; fax 937/237-5187. www.comfortinn.com.* 53 rooms, 2 story. Complimentary continental breakfast. Check-out 11 am. Fitness room. **$**

★ **DAYS INN.** *100 Parkview Dr, Brookville (45309). Phone 937/833-4003; fax 937/833-4681. www.daysinn .com.* 62 rooms, 2 story. Pets accepted, some restrictions; fee. Complimentary continental breakfast. Check-out 11 am. Pool. **$**

★ ★ **DOUBLETREE GUEST SUITES DAYTON/MIAMISBURG.** *300 Prestige Pl, Dayton (45342). Phone 937/436-2400; toll-free 800/222-8733; fax 937/436-2886. www.doubletree.com.* Located minutes from the downtown business district, this hotel offers a wealth of services to both the casual and business traveler alike. Each room comes with a private balcony area, coffee maker, dataport for Internet service, and many nice personal touches. 137 rooms, 3 story, all suites. Check-in 3 pm, check-out noon. High-speed Internet access (some suites). Restaurant, bar. Fitness room. Indoor pool, outdoor pool, whirlpool. **$**

★ **FAIRFIELD INN.** *6960 Miller Ln, Dayton (45414). Phone 937/898-1120; toll-free 800/228-2800; fax 937/898-1120. www.fairfieldinn.com.* 135 rooms, 3 story. Complimentary continental breakfast. Check-out noon. Pool. **$**

★ **HAMPTON INN.** *2550 Paramount Pl, Fairborn (45324). Phone 937/429-5505; fax 937/429-6828. www. hamptoninn.com.* 63 rooms, 3 story. Complimentary continental breakfast. Check-out 11 am. Indoor pool, whirlpool. **$**

Full-Service Hotels

★ ★ ★ **CROWNE PLAZA.** *33 E 5th St; 5th and Jefferson sts, Dayton (45402). Phone 937/224-0800; fax 937/224-3913. www.crowneplaza.com.* In the heart of the business district, this hotel is adjacent to the convention center and near many local attractions. Enjoy dining with a view served every evening in the rooftop restaurant. Airport shuttle service is available. 283 rooms, 14 story. Check-out noon. Restaurant, bar. Fitness room. Pool. **$**

★ ★ ★ **MARRIOTT DAYTON.** *1414 S Patterson Blvd, Dayton (45409). Phone 937/223-1000; fax 937/ 223-7853. www.marriott.com.* Whether one is taking work with them or taking the family along, this hotel offers a variety of services to ease one's travels. Concierge services are available to assist guests with plans, and babysitter service is available to help with the family. 399 rooms, 6 story. Pets accepted, some restrictions; fee. Check-out noon. Restaurant, bar. Fitness room. Indoor pool, outdoor pool, whirlpool. Business center. **$**

Restaurants

★ **AMBER ROSE.** *1400 Valley St, Dayton (45404). Phone 937/228-2511; fax 937/228-0479.* Victorian-style residence (1906); pressed-tin ceilings; original wood flooring; stained-glass windows with rose motif. American, European menu. Lunch, dinner. Closed Sun; holidays. Bar. **$$**

★ **BARNSIDER.** *5202 N Main St, Dayton (45415). Phone 937/277-1332.* Steak menu. Dinner. Closed holidays. Bar. Children's menu. **$$**

★ ★ **BRAVO! ITALIAN KITCHEN.** *2148 Centerville Rd, Dayton (45459). Phone 937/439-1294; fax 937/439-9370. www.bestitalianusa.com.* Upscale family dining. Italian menu. Lunch, dinner. Closed Thanksgiving, Dec 25. Bar. Children's menu. **$$**

★ **CHINA COTTAGE.** *6290 Far Hills Ave (Hwy 48), Dayton (45459). Phone 937/434-2622; fax 937/438-5899.* Chinese menu. Lunch, dinner. Closed Thanksgiving, Dec 25. Bar. **$$**

★ ★ **EL MESON.** *903 E Dixie Dr, West Carrolltown (45449). Phone 937/859-8220; fax 937/859-8220.* Latin American, Spanish menu. Cuisine of different countries on weekends. Lunch, dinner. Closed Sun-Mon; holidays; also first three weeks in Jan. Bar. Reservations recommended. Outdoor seating. **$$**

★ ★ **J. ALEXANDER'S.** *7970 Washington Village Dr, Centerville (45459). Phone 937/435-4441; fax 937/435-7723. www.jalexanders.com.* This fast-growing chain serves generous portions of contemporary American fare. Steaks are the house specialty, with daily-changing fish selections, hearty salads and soups, and piled-high sandwiches rounding out the menu. The atmosphere is clubby, the staff clad in all black. American menu. Lunch, dinner. Closed Thanksgiving, Dec 25. Bar. Children's menu. Casual attire. **$$**

★ ★ **JAY'S.** *225 E 6th St, Dayton (45402). Phone 937/222-2892; fax 937/222-7547. www.jays.com.* This premier seafood restaurant has fresh fish flown in from all over the East Coast. Top-quality beef is cut on premises. All meals are accompanied by freshly baked breads, an extensive wine list, and handmade desserts to die for. Seafood menu. Dinner. Closed holidays. Bar. Children's menu. **$$$**
🄳

★ ★ **LINCOLN PARK GRILLE.** *580 Lincoln Park Blvd, Dayton (45429). Phone 937/293-6293.* Lunch, dinner. Closed Jan 1, Thanksgiving, Dec 25. Bar. Outdoor seating. **$$**

★ ★ **PINE CLUB.** *1926 Brown St, Dayton (45409). Phone 937/228-7463. www.thepineclub.com.* Casual atmosphere; collection of Toby mugs and beer steins. Steak menu. Dinner. Closed Sun; Jan 1, Thanksgiving, Dec 25. Bar. Children's menu. **$$**

★ ★ **THOMATO'S.** *110 N Main St, Dayton (45402). Phone 937/228-3333; fax 937/228-0277.* Seafood menu. Lunch, dinner. Closed Sun; holidays. Bar. **$$**

★ **WELTON'S.** *4614 Wilmington Pike, Dayton (45440). Phone 937/293-2233; fax 937/293-2294.* American menu. Dinner. Closed Sun; holidays. Bar. **$$**

Defiance (B-1)

Population 16,768
Elevation 691 ft
Area Code 419
Zip 43512
Information The Greater Defiance Area Tourism and Visitors Bureau, 415 2nd St; phone 419/782-0864 or toll-free 800/686-4382
Web site www.defiance-online.com

Defiance was named for Fort Defiance (1794), which was constructed during Major General "Mad Anthony" Wayne's vigorous campaign against the Native Americans. The fort was so named after Wayne said "I defy the English, the Indians, and all the devils in hell to take it." Defiance also was the site of a major Native American council in 1793 and is the birthplace of Chief Pontiac. Johnny Appleseed lived in Defiance during 1811-1828 while growing his pioneer apple orchards.

What to See and Do

Au Glaize Village. *Krouse Rd. 3 miles SW off Hwy 24. Phone 419/784-0107.* Over 110 acres. Replicas and restored late-19th-century buildings, including Kieffer log cabin, Kinner log house; cider, sorghum, and saw mills; blacksmith shop; railroad station and rolling stock; church, school, post office, gas station, dental and doctor offices; four museum buildings; black powder range. (June-Sept, weekends) Special events throughout the season. **$$**

Independence Dam State Park. *3 miles E on Hwy 424. Phone 419/784-3263.* A 604-acre park on the Maumee River. Fishing, boating (marina); hiking, picnicking (shelter), camping.

Special Event

Fort Defiance Days. *Defiance. Phone 419/782-7946.* Riverboat cruises, hot air balloon races. Early Aug.

Limited-Service Hotel

★ **DAYS INN.** *1835 N Clinton St, Defiance (43512). Phone 419/782-5555; toll-free 800/329-7466; fax 419/782-8085. www.daysinn.com.* 121 rooms, 2 story. Check-out noon. Restaurant, bar. Indoor pool. **$**

🏊

Delaware (C-2)

See also Columbus, Marion, Mount Gilead, Mount Vernon

Founded 1808
Population 20,030
Elevation 880 ft
Area Code 740
Zip 43015
Information Delaware County Convention and Visitors Bureau, 44 E Winter St; phone 740/368-4748 or toll-free 888-335-6446
Web site www.visitdelohio.com

Delaware, on the Olentangy River, derives its name and heritage from New England. Now a college town, trading center for farmers, and site of diversified industry, the area was chosen by Native Americans as a campsite because of its mineral springs. The Mansion House (a famous sulphur-spring resort built in 1833) is now Elliot Hall, the first building of Ohio Wesleyan University (see). There is a legend that President Rutherford B. Hayes (a native of Delaware) proposed to his bride-to-be, Lucy Webb (one of the school's first coeds), at the sulphur spring.

What to See and Do

Alum Creek State Park. *3615 Old State Rd (43015). 6 miles E on Hwy 36, 37. Phone 740/548-4631.* On 8,600 acres. Versatile topography and character of lake provide for abundance of activities. Swimming, water-skiing, fishing, boating; hunting, hiking and bridle trails, snowmobiling, camping (rentals; fee). Nature programs. (Daily) **FREE**

Delaware County Historical Society Museum. *157 E William St. Phone 740/369-3831.* Relics tracing area's history from 1800. Genealogy library. (Mar-mid-Nov, Sun and Wed afternoons; also by appointment; closed holidays) **FREE**

Delaware State Park. *5202 Hwy 23 (43015). Phone 740/369-2761.* Park (1,815 acres) with 1,330-acre lake. Swimming, bathhouse, fishing, boating (rentals, ramp); hiking, picnicking, concession, camping. (Daily) **FREE**

Ohio Wesleyan University. *61 S Sandusky St (43015). Phone 740/368-2000. www.owu.edu.* (1842) (2,000 students) Sandusky Street passes through historic 200-acre campus. Liberal arts educational institution. Mayhew Gallery, Humphreys Art Hall (Sept-May, Mon-Sat). Gray Chapel houses one of three Klais organs in the United States. Campus tours.

Olentangy Indian Caverns and Ohio Frontierland. *1779 Home Rd. 7 miles S, off Hwy 23. Phone 740/548-7917.* Natural limestone cave; 55 feet-105 feet below ground on three levels are various rock strata and fossils; once refuge for the Wyandot. Tours (35 minutes) guided and self-guided (Apr-Oct). Also re-creation of Ohio frontierland and Native American village (Memorial Day-Labor Day). **$$$**

Perkins Observatory. *(43015). 4 miles S on Hwy 23. Phone 740/363-1257. www.perkins-observatory.org.* Operated by Ohio Wesleyan University (see). Thirty-two-inch reflecting telescope. (Mon-Fri; closed holidays) Stargazing programs (Fri-Sat evenings; closed holidays; also second Sat each month, first two weeks in June). Daytime tours and programs (by appointment). Lectures. Special events. Tickets required; reservations recommended. **FREE**

Special Event

Delaware County Fair. *Delaware County fairgrounds, 236 Pennsylvania Ave, Delaware. Phone 740/362-3851.* Grand Circuit harness racing, Little Brown Jug harness race for pacers. Usually third week in Sept.

Limited-Service Hotel

★ **DAYS INN.** *16510 Square Dr, Marysville (43040). Phone 937/644-8821; toll-free 877/644-8821; fax 937/644-8821. www.daysinn.com.* 74 rooms, 2 story. Pets accepted; fee. Complimentary continental breakfast. Check-out noon. Business center. **$**

🚶 🐾

Specialty Lodging

The following lodging establishment is approved by Mobil Travel Guide, but due to its unique and individualized nature has not been given a traditional Mobil Star rating. Included in this listing you may find bed-and-breakfasts, limited-service inns, guest ranches, and other unique hotel properties.

WELCOME HOME INN. *6400 Home Rd, Delaware (43015). Phone 740/881-6588; toll-free 800/381-0364. www.welcomehomeinn.com.* 5 rooms. Complimentary full breakfast. Check-in 2 pm, check-out noon. **$**

Restaurants

★ **BRANDING IRON.** *1400 Stratford Rd, Delaware (43015). Phone 740/363-1846.* Barbecue, steak menu. Dinner. Closed Mon; Jan 1, Dec 24-25; also first two weeks in Aug. Bar. Children's menu. **$$**

★ **BUN'S OF DELAWARE.** *6 W Winter St, Delaware (43015). Phone 740/363-3731; fax 740/ 369-9284.* Breakfast, lunch, dinner. Closed Mon; holidays. Bar. Children's menu. **$$**

★ ★ **MICHAEL OLIVER'S.** *351 S Sandusky St, Delaware (43015). Phone 740/363-1262.* Italian menu. Dinner. Bar. Casual attire. **$$**

Dublin (C-2)

Limited-Service Hotels

★ ★ **EMBASSY SUITES COLUMBUS- DUBLIN.** *5100 Upper Metro Pl, Dublin (43017). Phone 614/790-9000; fax 614/790-9001. www.embassy-suites.com.* 284 rooms, all suites. Check-in 3 pm, check-out noon. High-speed Internet access. Restaurant, bar. Indoor pool, whirlpool. Business center. **$**

★ ★ **WYNDHAM DUBLIN HOTEL.** *600 Metro Pl N, Dublin (43017). Phone 614/764-2200; fax 614/ 764-1213. www.wyndhamdublin.com.* 217 rooms, 3 story. Pets accepted; fee. Check-out 1 pm. Restaurant, bar. Fitness room. Indoor pool. **$**

East Liverpool (B-5)

See also Steubenville

Settled 1798
Population 13,654
Elevation 689 ft
Area Code 330
Zip 43920
Information East Liverpool Chamber of Commerce, 529 Market St; phone 330/385-0845
Web site www.elchamber.com

Located where Ohio, Pennsylvania, and West Virginia meet on the Ohio River, East Liverpool was called Fawcett's Town (after its first settler) until 1860. Its clay deposits determined its destiny as a pottery center; everything from dinnerware to brick is produced here.

What to See and Do

Beaver Creek State Park. *12021 Echi Dell Rd (43920). 8 miles NW off Hwy 7. Phone 330/385-3091.* There are many streams in this 3,038-acre forested area that contains the ruins of the Sandy and Beaver Canal and one well-preserved lock. Gaston's Mill (circa 1837) has been restored. Fishing, canoeing; hunting, hiking, bridle trails, picnicking, primitive camping. (Daily) **FREE**

Museum of Ceramics. *400 E 5th St. Phone 330/ 386-6001.* History museum contains collection of regional pottery and porcelain; bone china; life-size dioramas; multimedia presentation. (Mar-Apr, weekends; May-Nov, Wed-Sun; closed Thanksgiving) (See SPECIAL EVENT) **$$**

Pottery tours. *Hall China Company, 10 Anna St (43920). Phone 330/385-2900.* (Mon-Fri mornings) *Pioneer Pottery, 761 Dresden Ave. Phone 330/385-4293.* Tours (by appointment).

Special Event

Tri-State Pottery Festival. *Museum of Ceramics (see), 400 E 5th St, East Liverpool (43920). Phone 330/385- 0845.* Pottery industry displays, plant tours, pottery olympics; art and antique show, rose show; rides. Third weekend in June.

Specialty Lodging

The following lodging establishment is approved by Mobil Travel Guide, but due to its unique and individualized nature has not been given a traditional Mobil Star rating. Included in this listing you may find bed-and-breakfasts, limited-service inns, guest ranches, and other unique hotel properties.

THE STURGIS HOUSE. *122 W 5th St, East Liverpool (43920). Phone 330/382-0194. www. sturgishouse.com.* Located in a restored Victorian mansion. Private baths. 6 rooms, 2 story. Complimentary continental breakfast. **$**

Elyria (A-4)

See also Cleveland, Lorain, Oberlin, Sandusky, Strongsville, Vermilion

Settled 1817
Population 56,746
Elevation 730 ft
Area Code 440
Zip 44035
Information Lorain County Visitors Bureau, 611 Broadway, 44052; phone 440/245-5282 or toll-free 800/334-1673
Web site www.lcvb.org

This retailing and industrial city, at the junction of the east and west branches of the Black River, is the seat of Lorain County. The novelist Sherwood Anderson managed a paint factory here before his literary career began. Now, the city has more than 130 industries manufacturing automotive parts, golf balls, air-conditioning and home-heating units, aircraft parts, and pumps and metal castings. Surrounding greenhouses and farms contribute poultry, fruits, vegetables, and dairy products to the city's economy.

What to See and Do

Cascade & Elywood parks. *Washington Ave and W River Rd (44035). Phone 440/322-0926.* Picnic areas, playground; trails, sledding hill; waterfalls, views of rock cliffs.

The Hickories Museum. *509 Washington Ave. Phone 440/322-3341.* (1894) Shingle-style mansion of industrialist Arthur Lovett Garford. Changing exhibits on Lorain County. Hicks Memorial Research Library. **$$**

Special Event

Apple Festival. *Elyria. Phone 440/245-5282.* Third weekend in Sept.

Limited-Service Hotels

★ **COMFORT INN.** *739 Leona St, Elyria (44035). Phone 440/324-7676; fax 440/324-4046. www. comfortinn.com.* 66 rooms, 2 story. Pets accepted; fee. Complimentary continental breakfast. Check-out 11 am. **$**

★ ★ **HOLIDAY INN.** *1825 Lorain Blvd (Rte 57), Elyria (44035). Phone 440/324-5411; toll-free 800/321-7333; fax 440/324-2785. www.holiday-inn.com.* 250 rooms, 6 story. Check-out noon. Restaurant, bar. Pool. Airport transportation available. **$**

Findlay (B-2)

See also Bowling Green, Lima, Tiffin

Founded 1821
Population 35,703
Elevation 780 ft
Area Code 419
Zip 45840
Information Hancock County Convention and Visitors Bureau, 123 East Main Cross St; phone 419/422-3315 or toll-free 800/424-3315
Web site www.findlayhancockchamber.com

In 1860, the editor of the *Findlay Jeffersonian*, in letters signed "Petroleum V. Nasby," attacked slavery. In the previous decade, the "grapevine telegraph" and Underground Railroad, piloting runaway slaves to safety, were active in Findlay. Named for Fort Findlay, one of the outposts of the War of 1812, it is the seat of Hancock County, 45 miles south of Toledo in the state's rich farm area. Congress designated Findlay as Flag City, USA, in 1974.

Tell Taylor, educated in Findlay, was inspired to write the song "Down by the Old Mill Stream" while fishing along the Blanchard River. Marilyn Miller, Russell Crouse, Dr. Howard T. Ricketts, and Dr. Norman Vincent Peale also came from Findlay.

What to See and Do

Hancock Historical Museum. *422 W Sandusky St. Phone 419/423-4433.* Exhibits depicting history of the county. Exhibits of glass, include examples produced in Findlay during the great gas boom of the 1880s; Pendleton art glass collection. (Wed-Fri afternoons) Tours (Sun afternoons by appointment). **DONATION**

Mazza Museum, International Art from Picture Books. *1000 N Main St. In the Virginia B. Gardner Fine Arts Pavilion on the campus of the University of Findlay. Phone 419/424-4777.* Exhibited here is the Mazza Collection; original art created by illustrators of children's books. More than 2,000 works of distinguished illustrators are displayed, including those of Ezra Jack Keats, Maurice Sendak, and other Caldecott Medal winners. (Wed-Fri, Sun afternoons; closed holidays) **FREE**

Limited-Service Hotels

★ **FAIRFIELD INN.** *2000 Tiffin Ave, Findlay (45839). Phone 419/424-9940; fax 419/424-9940. www.fairfieldinn .com.* 57 rooms, 3 story. Complimentary continental breakfast. Check-out noon. Indoor pool, whirlpool. **$**

★ ★ **FINDLAY INN & CONFERENCE CENTER.** *200 E Main Cross St, Findlay (45840). Phone 419/422-5682; toll-free 800/825-1455; fax 419/ 422-5581. www.findlayinn.com.* The three-story atrium lobby of this 64-room, 16-suite hotel is a pleasant, no-frills space catering to corporate clientele. The 56,000-square-foot property has an in-house restaurant, various meeting rooms, an auditorium,

and a fitness center with an indoor pool. 80 rooms, 3 story. Complimentary continental breakfast. Check-out noon. Restaurant, bar. Fitness room. Indoor pool, whirlpool. **$**

Fort Ancient State Memorial

See also Lebanon

7 miles SE of Lebanon on Hwy 350. Phone 513/932-4421.

Fort Ancient is one of the largest and most impressive prehistoric earthworks of its kind in the United States. The Fort Ancient earthworks were built by the Hopewell people between 100 BC-AD 500. This site occupies an elevated plateau overlooking the Little Miami River Valley. Its massive earthen walls, more than 23 feet high in places, enclose an area of 100 acres; within this area are earth mounds once used as calendar of events markers and other archaeological features. Relics from the site and the nearby prehistoric Native American village are displayed in Fort Ancient Museum. Hiking trails, picnic facilities. (Mar-Nov, daily) $2-$5 **$$**

Fort Hill State Memorial (D-2)

3614 Fort Hill Rd, Hillsboro (45133). 5 miles N of Sinking Spring off Hwy 41; SW of Chillicothe via Hwy 50, Hwy 41. Phone 937/588-3221; toll-free 800/283-8905.

This is the site of a prehistoric Native American hilltop earth and stone enclosure. The identity of its builders has not been determined, but implements found in the vicinity point to the Hopewell people. There is a 2,000-foot trail that leads to ancient earthworks. Picnic area and shelterhouse. (Daily) **FREE**

Fostoria (B-2)

Restaurant

★ **BLACK CAT.** *820 Sandusky St, Fostoria (44830). Phone 419/435-2685.* Over 575 black cat figurines on display. Seafood, steak menu. Lunch, dinner. Closed holidays; also mid-June-Labor Day Sun. Bar. Children's menu. **$$**

🄳

Fremont (A-2)

See also Bellevue, Bowling Green, Port Clinton, Tiffin

Founded 1820
Population 17,648
Elevation 601 ft
Area Code 419
Zip 43420
Information Sandusky County Convention and Visitors Bureau, 1510 E State St, PO Box 643; phone 419/332-4470 or toll-free 800/255-8070
Web site www.sanduskycounty.org

Wyandot settled here as early as 1650; scouts and settlers came in the late 1700s. Fort Stephenson was built and defended in the War of 1812. Earlier known as Lower Sandusky, the town became Fremont in 1849. Rutherford B. Hayes, 19th United States president, lived in Fremont and is buried here. Seat of Sandusky County, 20 miles from Lake Erie on the Sandusky River, Fremont is an industrial town known for cutlery, food processing, and tools and dyes. It also is an agricultural area.

What to See and Do

Library Park. *423 Croghan St. Between Arch and High sts. Phone 419/334-7101.* Scene of 1813 Fort Stephenson battle; "Old Betsy," only cannon used to defend the fort; Soldiers Monument. (Mon-Sat) **FREE**

Rutherford B. Hayes Presidential Center. *Spiegel Grove estate, 1337 Hayes Ave. Hayes and Buckland aves. Phone 419/332-2081; toll-free 800/998-7737. www. rbhayes.org.* Rutherford B. Hayes Library, museum and home; Hayes memorabilia, period and community exhibits. Graves of the president and Mrs. Hayes. (Daily; closed Jan 1, Thanksgiving, Dec 25) Library (Mon-Sat; closed holidays). Tours of the residence and museum (daily). **$$**

Special Events

Civil War Encampment & President Hayes Birthday Reunion. *Rutherford B. Hayes Presidential Center* (see), *1337 Hayes Ave, Fremont. Phone 419/332-2081; toll-free 800/998-7737.* First full weekend in Oct.

Haunted Hydro. *Haunted Hydro Dark Attraction Park, 1313 Tiffin St, Fremont. Phone 419/334-2451.* Late Oct.

Gallipolis (E-3)

See also Ironton

Settled 1790
Population 4,831
Area Code 740
Zip 45631
Information Ohio Valley Visitors Center, 45 State St; phone 740/446-6882 or toll-free 800/765-6482

Gallipolis, "the old French city" along the Ohio River, was the second permanent settlement in Ohio. The columnist O. O. McIntyre lived in Gallipolis, often wrote about it, and is buried here. The district library has an extensive collection of his work.

What to See and Do

Bob Evans Farm. *10854 State Rte 588, Rio Grande (45674). 12 miles W; just off Hwy 35, on Rte 588. Phone 740/245-5305; toll-free 800/994-3276.* A 1,100-acre farm. Canoeing (fee); hiking, horseback riding (fee); special weekend events (fee); craft barn; farm museum; craft demonstrations; domestic animals, farm crops. (Memorial Day weekend-Labor Day weekend, daily; Sept, weekends; call for schedule) **FREE**

French Art Colony. *530 1st Ave. Phone 740/446-3834.* Monthly exhibits. (Tues-Sun; closed holidays) **FREE**

Our House State Memorial. *434 1st St. Phone 740/ 446-0586 (museum).* Built as a tavern in 1819; restored. Lafayette stayed here. (Memorial Day-Labor Day, Tues-Sun) **$$**

Special Event

Bob Evans Farm Festival. *Bob Evans Farm, 10854 State Rte 588, Rio Grande (45674). Phone 740/245-5305; toll-free 800/994-3276.* Bluegrass and country entertainment, food, 150 heritage craftspeople and demonstrations; Appalachian clogging, square dancing. Camping. Mid-Oct.

Limited-Service Hotel

★ ★ **HOLIDAY INN.** *577 Hwy 7 N, Gallipolis (45631). Phone 740/446-0090; fax 740/446-0090. www.holiday-inn.com.* 100 rooms, 2 story. Pets accepted, some restrictions. Check-out noon. Restaurant, bar. Pool, children's pool. **$**

Geneva-on-the-Lake (A-5)

See also Ashtabula, Mentor, Painesville

Founded 1869
Population 1,626
Elevation 605 ft
Area Code 440
Zip 44041
Information Convention and Visitors Bureau, 5536 Lake Rd; phone 440/466-8600 or toll-free 800/862-9948
Web site www.ncweb.com/gol

Geneva-on-the-Lake is Ohio's first summer resort. Its 129-year-old entertainment "strip" has a wide variety of nightlife, while Lake Erie offers boating, fishing, and beaches.

What to See and Do

Ashtabula County History Museum, Jennie Munger Gregory Memorial. *5685 Lake Rd (44041). Lake Rd (Hwy 534) between Putnam and Grandview drs. Phone 440/466-7337.* (1823-1826) One of the first frame houses built on Lake Erie's southern shore. Victorian furnishings, clothing, quilts, and artifacts. (June-Sept, Wed and Sun afternoons) **DONATION**

Erieview Park. *5483 Lake Rd. Phone 440/466-8650.* Amusement park with adult and kiddie rides, water slides; train ride; arcade. Nightclub; lodging;

restaurant, picnicking. (May-Sept, daily; early and late season hours vary) **$$$$**

Geneva State Park. *Padanarum Rd, Geneva. Off Hwy 534. Phone 440/466-8400.* This 698-acre park offers swimming, fishing, boating, 383-slip marina with six-lane ramp; hunting; hiking; snowmobile and cross-country ski trails; picnicking (shelter), concession; camping, pet camping, cabins. (Apr-Nov; daily) **FREE**

Special Event

Geneva Grape Jamboree. *81 E Main St, Geneva-on-the-Lake (44041). Downtown. Phone 440/466-5262.* Festival marks the grape harvesting season. Grape products, grape stomping; parades, entertainment, exhibits, contests, winery tours. Last full weekend in Sept.

Gnadenhutten (C-4)

See also Cambridge, Coshocton, New Philadelphia

Settled 1772
Population 1,226
Elevation 835 ft
Area Code 614
Zip 44629
Information Gnadenhutten Chamber of Commerce, PO Box 830; phone 614/254-4314

Gnadenhutten (ja-NA-den-hut-ten) is a rural center in Tuscarawas County in the Muskingum Conservancy District.

What to See and Do

Clendening Lake Marina. *79100 Bose Rd, Freeport. 7 miles E on Hwy 36 to Dennison, then 12 miles S, off Hwy 800. Phone 614/658-3691.* Fishing, boating (ramp); lodgings, tent and trailer sites. Pets on leash. (Apr-Oct, daily; Mar, Nov, weekends)

Gnadenhutten Historical Park and Museum. *352 S Cherry St. 1 mile S. Phone 614/254-4756.* Monument to 90 Christian Native Americans who were massacred here in 1782. Native American burial mound. Reconstructed log church and cooper's cabin. Museum. Oldest tombstone in Ohio. (Memorial Day-early Sept, daily; early Sept-Oct, weekends; rest of year, by appointment) **DONATION**

Tappan Lake Park. *84000 Mallernee Rd, Deersville (44693). 7 miles E on Hwy 36, 15 miles SE on Hwy 250, W on County 55, 3 miles to park entrance. Phone 614/922-3649.* Swimming, fishing, boating (ramp), marina; playground; tent and trailer sites (showers, flush toilets), cabins. Pets on leash. (Daily) **$$**

Granville

Restaurant

★ ★ ★ **BUXTON INN DINING ROOM.** *313 E Broadway, Granville (43023). Phone 740/587-0001; fax 740/587-1460.* Period décor produces a warm and comfortable atmosphere at this restaurant, which serves fine American and French cuisine. Enjoy lighter fare Monday through Sunday in the tavern. Dining and meeting space accommodate up to sixty. American, French menu. Dinner, Sun brunch. Closed Sun-Mon; Jan 1, Dec 25. Bar. **$$**

Hamilton (D-1)

See also Cincinnati, Mason, Middletown, Oxford

Founded 1791
Population 61,368
Elevation 580 ft
Area Code 513
Information Greater Hamilton Convention and Visitors Bureau, 201 Dayton St, 45011; phone 513/844-1500 or toll-free 800/311-5353
Web site www.hamilton-ohio.com

Originally Fort Hamilton, an outpost of the Northwest Territory, the city became an industrial center in the 1850s with the completion of the Miami and Erie Canal. It continues as such today. Much of Hamilton's rich 19th-century heritage is preserved in the large number and variety of restored homes in several historic districts.

What to See and Do

Dayton Lane Historic Area Walking Tour. *Dayton and 10th sts (45011). From the railroad tracks on the W to Hwy 4 on the E; from Buckeye St on the N to High St on the S. Phone toll-free 800/311-5353.* Many examples of restored Victorian and turn-of-the-century architecture, mostly homes. Allow an hour.

German Village Walking Tour. *Dayton and 3rd sts (45011). Phone toll-free 800/311-5353.* Nine-block area just north of the business district. German Village was part of the original city plan of 1796, with the first courts, school, newspaper, and many early businesses. Allow at least one hour; 2 miles. Within the district are

Butler County Historical Museum (Benninghofen House). *327 N 2nd St, Hamilton. Phone 513/896-9930.* (1861) Historical museum housed in Victorian Italianate mansion. Period furnishings; antique clothing, toys; doll collection; 19th-century dentist's office; local memorabilia. (Tues-Sun; closed holidays) **$**

Lane-Hooven House. *319 N 3rd St, Hamilton. Phone 513/863-1389.* (1863) Unusual octagonal home in the Gothic Revival style; octagonal turret, Tudor front door, cast-iron balconies, jigsaw bargeboard-decorated eaves. Exterior and interior fully restored. Home of Hamilton Community Foundation. (Mon-Fri; closed holidays) **FREE**

Rossville Walking Tour. *D and Main sts (45013). Phone toll-free 800/311-5353.* Eleven-block area on the west side of the Great Miami River. Until 1855, this was the separate town of Rossville, which was laid out in 1804 as a mercantile community. More buildings survived here, because it was less susceptible to flooding than the east bank. Wide range of styles from 1830 to 1920. Allow at least one hour; over 2 miles; level ground except for Millikin Street. Before crossing to Rossville, visit Monument Park with the 1804 Log Cabin and

Soldiers, Sailors, and Pioneers Monument. *High and Monument sts, Hamilton. Phone 513/867-5823.* (1902) Permanent memorial to the pioneer settlers and those of the area who fought in conflicts from the Indian Wars to the Spanish-American War. Displays inside building. (Mon-Sat)

Special Events

Antique Car Parade. *Butler County Courthouse Sq, 315 High St, Hamilton (45011). Phone 513/844-8080.* Three hundred cars in one of nation's oldest antique car parades. Fourth Sat in July.

Butler County Fair. *Butler County fairgrounds, Rte 4 and Fair Ave, Hamilton (45011). Phone 513/892-1423.* Last full week in July.

Dam Fest. *Neilan Blvd and Knight's Bridge, Hamilton. Phone 513/867-2281.* Two-day festival centered on the Great Miami River and Miami campus; features world champion water-skiers in doubles and freestyle competition; booths, games, entertainment. Weekend after Labor Day.

Limited-Service Hotel

★ ★ **HAMILTONIAN HOTEL.** *1 Riverfront Plz, Hamilton (45011). Phone 513/896-6200; toll-free 800/ 522-5570; fax 513/896-9463.* 120 rooms, 6 story. Pets accepted; fee. Check-out noon. Restaurant, bar. Pool. On river. **$**

Hocking Hills State Park

12 miles SW of Logan via Rte 374, 664; or SE of Lancaster via Hwy 33, SW on Rte 664

What to See and Do

Ash Cave. *19852 Rte 664 S, Logan (43138). Phone 740/385-6841. www.hockinghillspark.com.* Natural rock shelter with 90-foot waterfall in spring and winter. Ashes from Native American campfires were found here. Picnicking, shelter, hiking; a 1/4-mile wheelchair-accessible trail to Ash Cave. (Daily) **FREE**

Cantwell Cliffs, Cedar Falls, Conkie's Hollow. *Logan. Phone 740/385-6841. www.hockinghillspark.com.* Features cliffs, good trails, rare plants, and picnicking. (Daily) **FREE**

Old Man's Cave. *Logan. Phone 740/385-6841. www. hockinghillspark.com.* The most popular and highly developed area. Waterfalls, gorges, and caves. A hermit who lived in the main cave after the Civil War gave the cave its name. Fishing; hiking; picnicking, shelter, concession, restaurant; cabins, camping. Park naturalist in summer. (Daily) **FREE**

Rock House. *Logan. Phone 740/385-6841. www. hockinghillspark.com.* Unusual "house" formation in the sandstone cliff. Picnicking, hiking. **FREE**

Ironton (E-3)

See also Gallipolis, Portsmouth

Founded 1848
Population 12,751
Elevation 558 ft
Area Code 740
Zip 45638
Information Greater Lawrence County Convention and Visitors Bureau, PO Box 488, South Point 45680; phone 740/377-4550 or 740/532-9991
Web site www.lawrencecountyohio.org

Extensive ore pockets in the district once gave Ironton a thriving iron industry; the first charcoal furnace north of the Ohio River started producing pig iron here in 1826. The town was founded by one of the first ironmasters. Ironton was the southern terminus for the Detroit, Toledo, and Ironton (DT&I) Railroad. The Chesapeake and Ohio and the Norfolk and Southern railroads still serve the area.

Ironton is now an important industrial city and home to the large plants of many companies.

What to See and Do

Lake Vesuvius. *6518 Hwy 93, Ironton. 10 miles N off Hwy 93. Phone 740/534-6500.* The stack of Vesuvius (1833), one of the earliest iron blast furnaces, still remains. Swimming, fishing, boating (dock; May-Sept); hiking, picnicking, camping. (Daily) **$$$**

Lawrence County Museum. *506 S 6th St. Phone 740/532-1222.* Changing exhibits in Italian-style villa (1870). (Early Apr-mid-Dec, Fri-Sun afternoons) **DONATION**

Wayne National Forest. *13700 Hwy 33, Nelsonville (45764). Phone 740/753-0101.* Three sections make up this 202,967-acre area of southeast Ohio. Private lands are interspersed within the federal land. One section is the east side of Ohio, northeast of Marietta (see); the second is northeast of Athens (see); and the third is in the southern tip of the state, southwest of Gallipolis (see). The forest lies in the foothills of the

Appalachian Mountains. It's characterized by rugged hills covered with diverse stands of hardwoods, pines, and cedars; lakes, rivers, and streams; springs, rock shelters, covered bridges, trails, and campgrounds are located in the forest. A Ranger District office of the forest also is located here. (Daily) **FREE**

Special Events

Festival of the Hills. *1804 Liberty Ave, Ironton. Phone 740/532-5285.* Celebrates cultural heritage of Lawrence County; musical entertainment, demonstrations, displays. Mid-Sept.

Lawrence County Fair. *Rtes 7 and 243, Ironton (45669). E on Hwy 52, at fairgrounds in Proctorville. Phone 740/532-9195.* Mid-July.

Kelleys Island (A-3)

See also Port Clinton, Put-in-Bay, Sandusky

Founded 1833
Population 172
Elevation 598 ft
Area Code 419
Zip 43438
Information Chamber of Commerce, PO Box 783; phone 419/746-2360
Web site www.kelleysisland.com

Kelleys Island, one of the largest of 20 islands in Lake Erie, is 5 miles across at the widest point. This is a vacation spot with auto and passenger service available from Marblehead on Neuman Boat Line or Kelleys Island Ferry Boat Line. Island hopping cruises are available from Port Clinton (see) and Sandusky (see).

What to See and Do

Glacial Grooves State Memorial. *Kelley's Island. On the N side of Kelleys Island, W of dock, on W shore. Phone 419/797-4530.* Limestone with unusually long, smooth grooves made by glacial action. The largest easily accessible such grooves in North America, they were scoured into solid limestone bedrock approximately 30,000 years ago by glaciers of the great ice sheet that covered part of North America. Outdoor exhibits. (Daily) **FREE**

Inscription Rock State Memorial. *On the S shore, E of dock. Phone 419/797-4530.* Inscription Rock is marked

with prehistoric Native American pictographs. The flat-topped limestone slab displays carvings of human figures smoking pipes and wearing headdresses, as well as various animal forms. (Daily) **FREE**

Kelleys Island State Park. *733 Division St (43438). N shore. Phone 419/797-4530.* This 661-acre park offers swimming, fishing, boating (launch); hunting, hiking, picnicking (shelter), camping.

Kent (B-4)

See also Akron, Alliance, Aurora, Canton, Cleveland, Warren

Population 28,835
Elevation 1,097 ft
Area Code 330
Zip 44240
Information Kent Area Chamber of Commerce, 155 E Main St; phone 330/673-9855
Web site www.kentbiz.com

What to See and Do

Kent State University. *E Main and S Lincoln sts. Phone 330/672-2727. www.kent.edu.* (1910) (33,000 students) Twenty schools and colleges. Nonacademic campus tours arranged by University News and Information Office. On campus are the Kent State University Museum, with more than 10,000 costumes and treasures (Wed-Sat, Sun afternoons; donation); Gallery of the School of Art in the Art Building and the Student Center Gallery (academic year, Mon-Fri); Planetarium (by appointment); and the May 4 Memorial, next to Taylor Hall.

West Branch State Park. *5708 Esworthy Rd, Ravenna (44266). 12 miles E on Hwy 5. Phone 330/296-3239.* An 8,002-acre park with swimming, fishing, boating (launch, rentals); hiking, bridle, and snowmobiling trails; picnicking (shelter), concession; camping. (Daily) **FREE**

Limited-Service Hotels

★ ★ **HOLIDAY INN.** *4643 Hwy 43, Kent (44240). Phone 330/678-0101; toll-free 800/240-1881; fax 330/677-5001. www.holiday-inn.com.* 152 rooms, 2 story. Pets accepted; fee. Check-out noon. Restaurant, bar. Fitness room. Pool. **$**

★ ★ **UNIVERSITY INN.** *540 S Water St, Kent (44240). Phone 330/678-0123; fax 330/678-7356. www. kentuniversityinn.com.* 107 rooms, 7 story. Check-out 11 am. Restaurant. Pool. **$**

Restaurant

★ ★ **PUFFERBELLY LTD.** *152 Franklin Ave, Kent (44240). Phone 330/673-1771; fax 330/673-5407.* Historic railroad depot (1875); museum. American menu. Lunch, dinner, Sun brunch. Closed holidays. Bar. Children's menu. **$$**

Kettering (D-1)

Restaurant

★ ★ ★ **L'AUBERGE.** *4120 Far Hills Ave, Kettering (45419). Phone 937/299-5536; fax 937/299-9129. www. laubergedayton.com.* For more than 20 years, serious lovers of classic French fare have flocked to L'Auberge. Drawing them to this charming place is owner Josef Reif, who has succeeded in fashioning a hospitable and elegant restaurant for both special occasions and general indulgence. The entire dining room is dressed to the nines, complete with staff in tuxedoes. It is filled with giant floral arrangements, silk draperies, European paintings, and tables set with large floral centerpieces, colorful matched china, and oversized stemware. The cuisine is as opulent as the room. It is rich and valuable. The kitchen focuses on seasonal ingredients of the region, preparing them with a light, classic French hand. L'Auberge is the perfect choice for those in search of a night away from the real world. The restaurant is simply charming. An evening here is sure to leave you feeling rested, rejuvenated, and completely satisfied. French, seafood menu. Dinner. Closed Sun; holidays. Bar. Jacket required. Outdoor seating. **$$$**

Lakewood

Restaurant

★ **PLAYERS ON MADISON.** *14523 Madison Ave, Lakewood (44107). Phone 216/226-5200. www. playersonmadison.com.* Italian menu. Dinner. Closed holidays. Bar. **$$**

Lancaster (D-3)

See also Columbus, Newark

Founded 1800
Population 34,507
Elevation 860 ft
Area Code 740
Zip 43130
Information Fairfield County Visitors and Convention Bureau, 1 N Broad, PO Box 2450; phone 740/653-8251 or toll-free 800/626-1296
Web site www.lancoc.org

What to See and Do

The Georgian. *105 E Wheeling St. Phone 740/654-9923.* (1833) Two-story brick house reflects Federal and Regency styles. Headquarters of the Fairfield Heritage Association. (Apr-mid-Dec, Tues-Sun afternoons; closed holidays)

Mount Pleasant. *963 Prestige Blvd (43130). In Rising Park, N High St and Fair Ave.* A 250-foot rock outcropping overlooking the city; was a favorite Native American lookout. Trails wind to the top.

Square 13. *Main and Broad sts (43130). Phone 740/653-8251.* Here are 19 historic buildings; a free pamphlet describing these buildings may be obtained from the Fairfield County Visitors and Convention Bureau or from the Fairfield Heritage Association, 105 E Wheeling Street; also inquire about walking tour tape rentals (free with refundable deposit). Also here is

Mumaugh Memorial. *162 E Main St, Lancaster. Phone 740/654-8451.* (1805-1824) First and second floors have restored rooms. (By appointment only) **FREE**

Sherman House Museum. *137 E Main St, Lancaster. Phone 740/654-9923.* (1811) Birthplace of General William Tecumseh Sherman and Senator John Sherman (Sherman Anti-Trust Act). Civil War Museum. (Apr-mid-Dec, Tues-Sun afternoons; closed holidays)

Stanbery-Rising. *131 N High St, Lancaster.* (1834) Educational building for First United Methodist Church. (Not open to the public)

Special Events

Christmas Candlelight Tour. *The Georgian (see), 105 E Wheeling St, Lancaster (43130). Phone 740/654-9923.* Tour of downtown area churches; musical presentations. Tickets at The Georgian. Second Sat in Dec.

Fairfield County Fair. *Fairfield County fairgrounds, 157 E Fair Ave, Lancaster (43130). Phone 740/653-3041.* Harness racing, exhibits, amusements. Mid-Oct.

Lancaster Festival. *Lancaster Festival office, 127 W Wheeling St, Lancaster (43130). Phone 740/687-4808.* Throughout town. Features dance, musical, and theatrical performances; special art and museum exhibits; children's events. Ten days mid-late July.

Lancaster Old Car Club Spring Festival. *Fairfield County fairgrounds, 157 E Fair Ave, Lancaster (43130). Phone 740/862-8233.* Antique automobiles, steam engines, old farm equipment, car parts; swap meet. First weekend in June.

Pilgrimage. *Lancaster. Phone 614/837-4765.* Tours of mid-19th-century-modern houses and museums. First weekend in May.

Zane Square Arts & Crafts Festival. *203 E Fair Ave, Lancaster (43130). Corner of Broad and Main sts.Phone 740/687-6651.* More than 125 craftsmen display and sell handcrafted items; entertainment, street dancing. Weekend mid-Aug.

Limited-Service Hotels

★ **AMERIHOST INN.** *1721 River Valley Cir N, Lancaster (43130). Phone 740/654-5111; fax 740/654-5108. www.amerihostinn.com.* 60 rooms, 2 story. Complimentary continental breakfast. Check-out noon. Fitness room. Indoor pool, whirlpool. **$**

★ ★ **BEST WESTERN LANCASTER INN.** *1858 N Memorial Dr, Lancaster (43130). Phone 740/653-3040; toll-free 800/780-7234; fax 740/653-1172. www.bestwestern.com.* 168 rooms, 2 story. Pets accepted, some restrictions; fee. Check-out noon. Restaurant, bar. Pool. **$**

Full-Service Inn

★ ★ ★ **GLENLAUREL.** *14940 Mount Olive Rd, Rockbridge (43149). Phone 740/385-4070; toll-free 800/809-7378; fax 740/385-9669. www.glenlaurel.com.* Turning guests into friends who return year after year, this utterly charming Scottish country inn offers guests a magnificent stay. Located on a 140-acre estate, this delightful inn enchants guests with its magnificent scenery, including a series of waterfalls, a private gorge, and 50-foot rock cliffs, as well as with its elegant retreat feel and luxurious accommodations. 16 rooms, 2 story. Children over 16 years only. Complimentary full breakfast. Check-in 3 pm, check-out noon. Restaurant. **$$$**

Restaurant

★ ★ ★ **SHAW'S.** *123 N Broad St, Lancaster (43130). Phone 740/654-1842; fax 740/654-7032. www.shawsinn .com.* This charming restaurant is located in historic Lancaster. The menu features regional-themed chef specials from Southwestern to country French. Wonderfully fresh fish flown in from Boston, tangy ribs, and steaks are cooked to perfection. Seafood menu. Dinner. Closed Jan 1-2, Dec 25. Bar. Outdoor seating. **$$**

Lebanon (D-1)

See also Cincinnati, Dayton, Fort Ancient State Memorial, Mason, Middletown, Wilmington

Settled 1796
Population 10,453
Elevation 769 ft
Area Code 513
Zip 45036
Information Chamber of Commerce, 25 W Mulberry, phone 513/932-1100

Some of the early settlers around Lebanon were Shakers who contributed much to the town's culture and economy. Though their community, Union Village, was sold over 50 years ago and is now a retirement home, local interest in the Shakers still thrives.

What to See and Do

Glendower State Memorial Museum. *105 Cincinnati Ave. Hwy 42. Phone 513/932-1817.* (1836) Period furnishings, relics of area in Greek Revival mansion. (June-Aug, Wed-Sun; Sept-Oct, Sat-Sun) **$$$**

Turtlecreek Valley Railway. *198 S Broadway St (45036). Phone 513/398-8584; toll-free 800/488-7246.* Scenic train excursion. (May-Dec, Sat-Sun) **$$$**

Valley Vineyards Winery. *2276 Hwy 22 E, Morrow (45152). 4 miles S on Hwy 48 from I-71, then 3 miles NE on Hwy 22. Phone 513/899-2485.* Tours of winery, wine tastings. (Daily; closed holidays) **FREE**

Warren County Historical Society Museum. *105 S Broadway. Phone 513/932-1817.* Historical museum portrays Warren County history from prehistoric times to present; exhibits of fossils and Native American artifacts; pioneer and period rooms; large indoor village green depicting 19th-century shops; extensive Shaker collection; library of historical, genealogical, and Shaker material. (Tues-Sun; closed holidays) **$$**

Special Events

Applefest. *Lebanon. Phone 513/934-5252.* Farmers' market; crafts; entertainment; food. Fourth Sat in Sept.

Lebanon Raceway. *Warren County fairgrounds, 665 N Broadway St, Lebanon (45036). Hwy 48 N. Phone 513/932-4936.* Night harness racing. Sept-May.

Warren County Fair. *Fairgrounds, 655 N Broadway St, Lebanon (45036). Phone 513/932-1100.* Mid-July.

Full-Service Inn

★ ★ ★ **THE GOLDEN LAMB.** *27 S Broadway, Lebanon (45036). Phone 513/932-5065. www.goldenlamb .com.* This national historic inn, built in 1803, boasts an outstanding collection of authentic Shaker antiques, many of which are used daily during meal service. 18 rooms, 4 story. Complimentary continental breakfast. Check-out 10 am. Restaurant (see THE GOLDEN LAMB RESTAURANT), bar. **$**

Restaurant

★ ★ **THE GOLDEN LAMB RESTAURANT.** *27 S Broadway, Lebanon (45036). Phone 513/621-8373. www.goldenlamb.com.* Lunch, dinner. Closed Dec 25. Bar. Children's menu. **$$**

Lima (B-1)

See also Bellefontaine, Findlay, Van Wert, Wapakoneta

Founded 1831
Population 45,549
Elevation 880 ft
Area Code 419
Information Lima/Allen County Convention and Visitors Bureau, 147 N Main St, 45801; phone 419/222-6075 or toll-free 888/222-6075
Web site www.allencvb.lima.oh.us

Lima is an industrial, agri-business, and retail center.

What to See and Do

Allen County Museum. *620 W Market St. Phone 419/222-9426.* Pioneer and Native American relics; displays of fossils and minerals; railroad and street railway history; separate children's museum. Scale model of George Washington's home, Mount Vernon, in separate room. (Tues-Sun; closed holidays) **FREE**

Lincoln Park Railway Exhibit. *E Elm and Shawnee sts (45801). Lincoln Park. Phone 419/222-9426.* DT&I Railroad depot; last steam locomotive built by the Lima works of Baldwin-Lima Hamilton; 1883 private car and 1882 caboose. (All year, lighted at night) **FREE**

MacDonell House. *632 W Market St. Phone 419/ 222-9426.* Restored Victorian mansion, completely furnished in the style of the 1890s; listed in the National Register of Historical Places. (Tues-Sun; closed holidays) **$**

Special Event

Allen County Fair. *Allen County fairgrounds, 2750 Harding Hwy, Lima (45804). Phone 419/228-7141.* Rides, games, livestock shows, entertainment, grandstand shows, night harness racing, displays, and exhibits. Late Aug.

Limited-Service Hotel

★ ★ **HOLIDAY INN.** *1920 Roschman Ave, Lima (45804). Phone 419/222-0004; fax 419/222-2176. www.holiday-inn.com.* 150 rooms, 4 story. Pets accepted. Check-out noon. Restaurant, bar. Fitness room. Indoor pool, whirlpool. **$**

Restaurant

★ ★ **MILANO CAFE.** *2383 Elida Rd, Lima (45805). Phone 419/331-2220; fax 419/331-2834.* Dinner. Closed Jan 1, July 4. Bar. Children's menu. **$$**

Lorain (A-4)

See also Cleveland, Elyria, Oberlin, Sandusky, Vermilion

Settled 1807
Population 71,245
Elevation 608 ft
Area Code 440
Information Lorain County Visitors Bureau, 611 Broadway, 44052; phone 440/245-5282 or toll-free 800/334-1673
Web site www.lcvb.org

This industrial city, on Lake Erie's south shore at the mouth of the Black River, has a fine harbor and nine major public parks. Struck by a devastating tornado in 1924, the city was rebuilt. Lorain is the birthplace of Admiral Ernest J. King, of World War II fame.

What to See and Do

Lakeview Park. *W Erie Ave and Lakeview Dr. Phone 440/244-9000.* A 50-acre park along lake shore. Large beach, bathhouse; boardwalk. Colored-light fountain; garden with 3,000 roses of 40 varieties; tennis, baseball, basketball, volleyball, lawn bowling, ice skating; picnicking, concessions; playground. (Daily) **FREE**

Lorain Harbor. Innovative ore transfer facility regularly brings giant ore vessels to port. Several excellent vantage points for viewing (Lake Erie shipping season only).

Municipal Pier. *110 Alabama Ave (44052). Phone 440/204-2269.* Pier fishing, boating (launch), supplies (fuel, bait); concession.

Special Event

International Festival Week. *Sheffield Shopping Center, 1220 W 38th, Lorain (44053). Phone 440/245-5282.* Three-day celebration of Lorain's ethnic diversity. Song, dance, crafts, and foods of many nations; entertainers in ethnic costumes. Three days in late June.

Mansfield (B-3)

See also Mount Gilead, Mount Vernon, Wooster

Founded 1808
Population 50,627
Elevation 1,230 ft
Area Code 419
Information Mansfield/Richland County Convention and Visitors Bureau, 124 N Main St, 44902; phone 419/525-1300 or toll-free 800/642-8282
Web site www.mansfieldtourism.org

A pioneer log blockhouse, built as protection against the Native Americans in the War of 1812, still stands in South Park in the city's western section. Named for Jared Mansfield, United States Surveyor General, it is a diversified industrial center, 75 miles southwest of Cleveland. John Chapman, better known as Johnny Appleseed, lived and traveled in Richland County for many years. Pulitzer Prize–winning novelist Louis Bromfield was born here and later returned to conduct agricultural research at his 914-acre Malabar Farm.

What to See and Do

Clear Fork Reservoir. *7 miles S on Hwy 42, then W on Hwy 97. Phone 419/884-0166 (marina and camping information).* Fishing, boating (docks); picnicking; camping (Mar-Nov; fee). (Daily) **FREE**

Clear Fork Ski Area. *341 Resort Dr, Butler. 12 miles S on Hwy 13, then 7 miles SE on Hwy 97, then N on Hwy 95. Phone 419/883-2000; toll-free 800/237-5673 (snow conditions). www.skiclearfork.com.* Area has quad, triple, double chair lifts, J-bar, two handle bars; patrol, school, rentals; snowmaking; cafeteria, bar. Longest run 2,460 feet; vertical drop 300 feet. (Nov-Mar, daily) **$$$$**

Kingwood Center and Gardens. *900 Park Ave W. Phone 419/522-0211. www.kingwoodcenter.org.* Center has 47 acres of landscaped gardens, greenhouses, and wooded property. French Provincial mansion with horticultural library (Easter-Nov 1, Tues-Sat, Sun afternoon; rest of year, Tues-Sat; closed holidays).

Greenhouses and gardens (daily). Flower and art shows, special lectures, workshops throughout the year. **FREE**

Malabar Farm State Park. *4050 Bromfield Rd. 10 miles SE on Hwy 39, then S on Hwy 603 to Pleasant Valley Rd. Phone 419/892-2784.* Louis Bromfield's farm and house are within this 914-acre park. Fishing; hiking; bridle trails, equestrian camp, picnicking. Tractor-drawn wagon tour of farm; house tour. (Memorial Day-Labor Day, daily; Nov-Apr, call for hours; closed holidays) (See SPECIAL EVENTS) **$**

Muskingum Watershed Conservancy District. *Charles Mill Lake Park, 1271 State Rte 430 (44903). 9 miles E on Rte 430. Phone 419/368-6885.* On 1,350-acre lake. Boating (10-hp limit). **$$**

Oak Hill Cottage. *310 Springmill St. Phone 419/524-1765.* (1847) With seven gables, five double chimneys, and seven marble fireplaces, as well as all original period furnishings of the 1800s, this restored house is considered one of the most perfect Gothic houses in the nation. (Apr-Dec, Sun afternoons; closed holidays) **$$**

Ohio State Reformatory. *Near intersection of Hwy 545 and Hwy 30. Phone 419/522-2644.* Site was used as a prison in such films as *The Shawshank Redemption* and *Air Force One.* Tours (May-Oct, Sun; reservations necessary). **$$$**

Richland Carrousel Park. *75 N Main. 4th and Main sts. Phone 419/522-4223.* Features a wooden, hand-carved, hand-painted, turn-of-the-century–style carousel with 52 animals and two chariots. (Daily; closed holidays; may be closed for private functions) **$** Also here is

> **Carrousel Magic!** *44 W 4th St, Mansfield. Phone 419/526-4009.* Visitors can watch the carrousel figures get carved here. (Apr-Dec, Tues-Sat) **$$**

Richland County Museum. *51 W Church St, Lexington. 7 miles SW on Hwy 42. Phone 419/884-2230.* Remodeled schoolhouse (circa 1847), two period rooms; local memorabilia, artifacts. (May-Oct, Sat-Sun) **DONATION**

Snow Trails. *3100 Possum Run Rd, 5 miles S near jct Hwy 13, I-71. Phone 419/774-9818; toll-free 800/644-6754. www.snowtrails.com.* Six chair lifts; patrol, school, rentals; snowmaking; cafeteria, bar. (Dec-mid-Mar, daily) Cross-country and night skiing. **$$$$**

Special Events

Auto racing. *Mid-Ohio Sports Car Course, 7721 Lexington Steam Corners Rd, Lexington (44904). 6 miles S on Hwy 42, then W on Hwy 97 to Steam Corners Rd. Phone 419/884-4000; toll-free 800/643-6446.* A 2 1/4-mile track. Usually June-Sept.

Ohio Heritage Days. *Malabar Farm State Park (see), 4050 Bromfield Rd, Lucas (44843). Phone 419/892-2784.* Celebration of the pioneer era with participants dressed in period clothing; apple butter-making, horse-drawn wagon rides, crafts displays, demonstrations; tour Louis Bromfield's house and farm. Sept.

Ohio Winter Ski Carnival. *Snow Trails Ski Resort (see), 3100 Possum Run Rd, Mansfield (44903). Phone 419/756-7768.* Costumes, queen contest, races, dance. Late Feb.

Richland County Fair. *Fairgrounds, 750 N Home Rd, Mansfield. Phone 419/747-3717.* Flea market; circus; hardware and auto shows. Early Aug.

Limited-Service Hotels

★ **COMFORT INN.** *500 N Trimble Rd, Mansfield (44906). Phone 419/529-1000; toll-free 800/918-9189; fax 419/529-2953. www.comfortinn.com.* 114 rooms, 2 story. Pets accepted; fee. Complimentary continental breakfast. Check-out noon. Bar. Indoor pool. **$**

★ ★ **HOLIDAY INN.** *116 Park Ave W, Mansfield (44902). Phone 419/525-6000; toll-free 800/521-6744; fax 419/525-0197. www.holiday-inn.com.* 149 rooms, 7 story. Check-out 11 am. Restaurant, bar. Fitness room. Indoor pool, whirlpool. **$**

Marietta (D-4)

Founded 1788
Population 15,026
Elevation 616 ft
Area Code 740
Zip 45750
Information Tourist and Convention Bureau, 316 3rd St; phone 740/373-5176 or toll-free 800/288-2577
Web site www.marietta-ohio.com/chamber

General Rufus Putnam's New England flotilla, arriving at the junction of the Muskingum and Ohio rivers for western land–buying purposes, founded Marietta, the oldest settlement in Ohio. Its name is a tribute to Queen Marie Antoinette for French assistance to the American Revolution. Most of the landmarks are along the east side of the Muskingum River. Front Street is approximately the eastern boundary of the first stockade, which was called Picketed Point. Later, the fortification called Campus Martius was erected and housed General Putnam, Governor Arthur St. Clair, and other public officials.

One of the most important Ohio River ports in steamboat days, Marietta, today, is a beautiful tree-filled town and the home of Marietta College and manufacturers producing oil, plastics, rubber, paints, glass, dolls, safes, and concrete. Information for Wayne National Forest (see IRONTON) may be obtained from the National Forest Service office in Marietta.

What to See and Do

Campus Martius, Museum of the Northwest Territory. *601 2nd St. At Washington St. Phone 740/ 373-3750.* Rufus Putnam's home, which was part of the original Campus Martius Fort (1788); furnished with pioneer articles. On grounds is the Ohio Company Land Office (1788); restored and furnished. (Mar-Apr, Oct-Nov, Sat-Sun; May-Sept, Wed-Sun; closed Thanksgiving) **$$**

Fenton Art Glass Company. *420 Caroline Ave, Williamstown (26187). Across the Ohio River in Williamstown, West Virginia; off I-77, exit 185. Phone 304/375-7772. www.fentonartglass.com.* Handmade pressed and blown glassware. Free 30-minute guided tours (Mon-Fri; closed holidays; also first two weeks in July). Must wear shoes; no children under 2. Gift shop and outlet on the premises; also a museum with a film of the tour (daily; closed holidays).

Mound Cemetery. *5th and Scammel sts.* A 30-foot-high conical mound stands in the cemetery where 24 Revolutionary War officers are buried. Also here is

> **Sacra Via Street.** *3rd and Sacra Via, Marietta. Extends from Muskingum River to Elevated Sq. Phone 740/373-5178.* Built originally by Mound Builders as "sacred way" to Muskingum River.

Muskingum Park. *Putnam and Front sts (45750). Between Front St and the Muskingum River, N of Putnam St. Phone 740/373-5178.* Riverfront common where Arthur St. Clair was inaugurated first governor of the Northwest Territory in 1788; monument to westward migration sculpted by Gutzon Borglum.

Ohio River Museum State Memorial. *601 2nd St (45750). Front and St. Clair sts. Phone 740/373-3717.* Exhibits on history and development of inland waterways (May-Sept, daily; Mar-Apr, Oct-Nov, Wed-Sun; closed Thanksgiving). Steamboat *W. P. Snyder, Jr.,* (1918) is moored on Muskingum River; guided tours (Apr-Oct). **$$**

Rossi Pasta. *114 Greene St. At Front St. Phone 740/373-5155; toll-free 800/227-6774.* Pasta makers for many fine stores offer opportunity (limited) to watch the process in factory. (Mon-Sat, Sun afternoons; closed holidays) Also retail outlet. **FREE**

Trolley tours. *127 Ohio St. Phone 740/374-2233.* One-hour narrated tours of Marietta aboard turn-of-the-century–style trolley. (July-Aug, Tues-Sun; mid-late June, Wed-Sun; May-mid June, Thurs-Sun; Sept-Oct, weekends) **$$$**

Valley Gem stern-wheeler. *Phone 740/373-7862.* Excursions on the Ohio and Muskingum rivers aboard stern-wheeler *Valley Gem.* Fall foliage trips in Oct. (June-Aug, Tues-Sun; May, Sept-Oct, weekends only)

Special Events

Autumn Leaves Craft Festival. *Washington County fairgrounds, 901 Front St, Marietta. Phone 740/ 374-3708.* Displays and demonstrations of new and traditional crafts and artwork; musicians; food; children's activities. Late Sept.

Ohio River Stern-Wheel Festival. *Ohio Riverfront Park, 316 3rd St, Marietta (45750). Phone 740/373-5178.* Stern-wheel races, fireworks, entertainment on riverfront; several stern-wheel boats from across the nation. Weekend after Labor Day.

Showboat *Becky Thatcher*. *237 Front St, Marietta. Phone 740/373-6033.* Permanently docked stern-wheeler presents showboat melodrama on its first deck. Restaurant and lounge occupy the second and third decks. Theater season may vary; call for schedule. Late June-late Aug.

Limited-Service Hotels

★ **COMFORT INN.** *700 Pike St, Marietta (45750).
Phone 740/374-8190; toll-free 800/537-6858; fax 740/
374-3649. www.comfortinn.com.* 120 rooms, 4 story.
Complimentary continental breakfast. Check-out
11 am. Restaurant, bar. Fitness room. Indoor pool.
Airport transportation available. **$**

★ ★ **HOLIDAY INN.** *701 Pike St, Marietta
(45750). Phone 740/374-9660; fax 740/373-1762. www.
holiday-inn.com.* 109 rooms, 2 story. Check-out noon.
Restaurant, bar. Pool, children's pool. **$**

★ ★ **THE LAFAYETTE HOTEL.** *101 Front St,
Marietta (45750). Phone 740/373-5522; toll-free 800/
331-9336; fax 740/373-4684. www.lafayettehotel.com.*
78 rooms, 5 story. Pets accepted; fee. Check-out noon.
Restaurant (see), bar. Airport transportation available.
On Ohio River. **$**

Restaurant

★ ★ ★ **THE GUN ROOM.** *101 Front St, Marietta
(45750). Phone 740/373-5522. www.lafayettehotel.com.*
The traditional American menu at this Lafayette
Hotel (see) restaurant is as much a draw as the room's
ornate, 19th-century riverboat décor and antique gun
collection. The adjacent Riverview Lounge offers great
Ohio River views. American, seafood menu. Breakfast,
lunch, dinner, Sun brunch. Bar. Children's menu. **$$$**

Marion (B-2)

See also Delaware, Mount Gilead

Settled 1820
Population 34,075
Elevation 956 ft
Area Code 740
Zip 43302
Information Marion Area Convention and Visitors
Bureau, 1952 Marion-Mount Gilead Rd, Suite 121;
phone 740/389-9770 or toll-free 800/371-6688
Web site www.marion.net

Marion's beginnings are due to Jake Foos, a chainman
on a party surveying the territory for a proposed

road in 1808. Thirsty after a meal of salt bacon, he
discovered a spring. From then on, the area became
a stopping place for travelers. Originally named
Jacob's Well for this reason, it was renamed for
General Francis Marion, the "Swamp Fox" of the
Revolutionary War.

Both agricultural and industrial, Marion's growth
was largely influenced by the Huber Manufacturing
Company, which introduced the steam shovel (1874),
and Marion Power Shovels, now known as Dresser
Industries. Marion also is the center of a major
popcorn-producing area in the United States. Its best-
known citizen was Warren G. Harding, owner and
publisher of the *Star*. Later, he became a state senator,
lieutenant governor, and 29th president of the United
States.

What to See and Do

Carousel Concepts. *2209 Marion-Waldo Rd. Phone
740/389-9755.* Working museum; view woodworkers
carving carousel horses. (Daily) **$$**

Harding Memorial. *Delaware Ave and Vernon Heights
Blvd (43302). Phone 740/387-9630.* A 10-acre area
with rows of maple trees that create the shape of a
Latin cross. The circular monument is made of white
Georgia marble and contains the stone coffins of
Harding and his wife. Grounds (daily). **FREE**

President Harding's Home and Museum. *380 Mt.
Vernon Ave (43302). Phone 740/387-9630; toll-free
800/600-6894.* Built during Harding's courtship with
Florence Mabel Kling and where they were married in
1891. Harding administered much of his 1920 "front
porch campaign" for presidency from the front of the
house; the museum, at the rear of the house, was once
used as the campaign's press headquarters. (Memorial
Day weekend-Labor Day weekend, Wed-Sun; Apr-May,
by appointment; after Labor Day-Oct, Sat-Sun) **$**

Stengel True Museum. *504 S State St. Phone 740/
387-6140.* Displays include Native American artifacts;
china and glassware; firearms; antique watches, clocks;
toys; utensils. Under age 12 only with adult. (Sat-Sun
afternoons; other times by appointment; closed Easter,
Dec 25) **FREE**

Special Events

Marion County Fair. *220 E Fairground St, Marion
(43302). Phone 740/382-2558.* Late June-early July.

Popcorn Festival. *Marion City Hall, 233 W Center St, Marion (43302). Phone 740/387-3378.* Tours, food, entertainment. First weekend after Labor Day.

US Open Drum and Bugle Corps Competition. *Harding High School Stadium, 420 Presidential Dr, Marion (43302). Phone 740/387-6736.* Aug.

Limited-Service Hotel

★ **COMFORT INN.** *256 James Way, Marion (43302). Phone 740/389-5552; fax 740/389-5552. www.comfortinn.com.* 56 rooms, 2 story. Pets accepted; fee. Complimentary continental breakfast. Check-out 11 am. Indoor pool, whirlpool. **$**

Mason

See also Cincinnati, Dayton, Hamilton, Lebanon, Middletown, Oxford, Wilmington

Population 11,452
Elevation 800 ft
Area Code 513
Zip 45040
Information Mason Area Chamber of Commerce, 316 W Main St; phone 513/336-0125
Web site www.mlkchamber.org

What to See and Do

The Beach Waterpark. *2590 Waterpark Dr. W of I-71 at Kings Mills Rd exit 25, opposite Paramount's Kings Island (see). Phone 513/398-7946; toll-free 800/886-7946. www.thebeachwaterpark.com.* Offers 30 water slides and attractions on 35 acres, including The Aztec Adventure water coaster; Thunder Beach, a 750,000-gallon wave pool; and Lazy Miami, a meandering river slowly winding through the park. Two sand volleyball courts. A children's activity area with pools, slides, and mini-waterfall. Picnic area, restaurants. (Memorial Day weekend-Labor Day, daily) **$$$$**

The Golf Center at Kings Island. *6042 Fairway Dr. Phone 513/398-7700 (tee reservations). www.thegolfcenter.com.* Two golf courses designed by Jack Nicklaus and architect Desmond Muirhead (fee). Grizzly Course features the famed 546-yard 18th hole. The 18-hole Bruin Course, a mid-length version of the Grizzly, features six par-four holes. Also includes a tennis stadium that seats 10,500 for the Tennis

Masters Championship. Restaurant, lounge, pro shop, driving range (fee). (Daily, weather permitting)

⭐ **Paramount's Kings Island.** *6300 Kings Island Dr (45034). I-71 to Kings Mills Rd exit. Phone 513/574-5700; toll-free 800/288-0808. www.pki.com.* Premier seasonal family theme park. Facility (350 acres) with more than 100 rides and attractions. Includes The Outer Limits thrill ride and Flight of Fear, an indoor roller coaster. (Late May-early Sept, daily; mid-Apr-late May, weekends; early Sept-Oct, selected weekends) **$$$$**

Limited-Service Hotel

★ **COMFORT INN.** *5457 Kings Center Dr, Mason (45040). Phone 513/336-9000; toll-free 800/228-5150; fax 513/336-9007. www.comfortsuites.com.* 78 rooms, 3 story. Complimentary continental breakfast. Check-out 11 am. Indoor pool. **$**

Full-Service Hotel

★ ★ ★ **MARRIOTT CINCINNATI NORTHEAST.** *9664 Mason-Montgomery Rd, Mason (45040). Phone 513/459-9800; fax 513/459-9808. www.marriott.com.* Graciously welcoming guests with well-appointed accommodations, this hotel is a delight for both the busy executive and the adventure traveler. Nearby attractions include The Beach Waterpark, Paramount's Kings Island, and The Golf Center at Kings Island (see all). 302 rooms, 6 story. Check-out noon. Restaurant, bar. Fitness room. Indoor pool, outdoor pool. Business center. **$**

Full-Service Resort

★ ★ ★ **KINGS ISLAND RESORT & CONFERENCE CENTER.** *5691 Kings Island Dr, Mason (45034). Phone 513/398-0115; toll-free 800/727-3050; fax 513/398-1095. www.kingsislandresort.com.* Across the street from Paramount's Kings Island theme park, this 288-room resort offers 13,000 square feet of meeting space and various recreational facilities, including an indoor pool and an outdoor pool. Visit The Main Street Grill for the weekend prime rib buffet. 288 rooms, 2 story. Check-out 11 am. Restaurant, bar. Fitness room. Indoor pool, outdoor pool, whirlpool. Tennis. **$**

Restaurant

★ ★ **HOUSTON INN.** *4026 Hwy 42, Mason (45040). Phone 513/398-7377.* Seafood, steak menu. Dinner. Closed Mon; holidays. Bar. **$$**

Massillon (B-4)

See also Akron, Alliance, Canton, New Philadelphia, Wooster

Founded 1826
Population 31,007
Elevation 1,015 ft
Area Code 330
Zip 44646
Information Chamber of Commerce, 137 Lincoln Way E; phone 330/833-3146
Web site www.massillonchamber.com

Massillon is an industrial center on the Tuscarawas River in northeastern Ohio.

What to See and Do

Canal Fulton and Museum. *103 Tuscarawas St (44616). 6 miles NW on Hwy 21, then 1 mile NE on Hwy 93. Phone 330/854-3808; toll-free 800/435-3623.* St. Helena III, a replica of mule-drawn canal boat of the mid-19th century, takes 45-minute trip on the Ohio and Erie Canal. Leaves Canal Fulton Park (June-Aug, daily; mid-May-late May, early Sept-mid-Sept, weekends only). **$$**

Massillon Museum. *121 Lincoln Way E. Phone 330/833-4061.* Historical and art exhibits. (Tues-Sat, Sun afternoons; closed holidays) **FREE**

Spring Hill. *1401 Spring Hill Ln NE. Hwy 241. Phone 330/833-6749. www.massillonproud.com/springhill.* (1821) Historic 19th-century home, including basement kitchen and dining room, secret stairway, original furnishings; on grounds are springhouse, smokehouse, woolhouse, and milkhouse; picnicking. (June-Aug, Wed-Sun; Apr-May, Sept-Oct, by appointment) **$**

The Wilderness Center. *9877 Alabama Ave SW, Wilmot. 5 miles S on Hwy 21, then 8 miles SW on Hwy 62 to Wilmot, then 1 mile NW on Hwy 250. Phone 330/359-5235.* Nature center on 573 acres includes six nature trails, 7 1/2-acre lake, 23-foot observation platform; picnicking. Interpretive building (Tues-Sun; closed holidays). Grounds (daily). **DONATION**

Mentor (A-4)

See also Chardon, Cleveland, Geneva-on-the-Lake, Painesville

Founded 1797
Population 47,358
Elevation 690 ft
Area Code 440
Zip 44060
Information Mentor Area Chamber of Commerce, 7547 Mentor Ave, Room 302; phone 440/946-2625; and City of Mentor, 8500 Civic Center Blvd; phone 440/225-1100
Web site www.mentorchamber.org

Site of the first Lake County settlement, Mentor was once an agricultural center. James A. Garfield resided here before his election as United States president. Mentor serves as a retail trade center.

What to See and Do

Headlands Beach State Park. *600 Headlands Rd (44060). Hwy 44 N, to Lake Erie. Phone 440/257-1330.* A 125-acre park with 1-mile-long beach on shore of Lake Erie. Swimming, lifeguard (Memorial Day-Labor Day, Fri-Sun), fishing; picnicking, concessions. **$**

⭐ **Lawnfield (James A. Garfield National Historic Site).** *8095 Mentor Ave (44060). Phone 440/255-8722. www.nps.gov/jaga.* Garfield's last house before the White House. Two floors of original furnishings; memorial library contains Garfield's books, desk. On grounds are campaign office, carriage house, and picnic area. (Sat-Sun; closed holidays) **$$**

Wildwood Cultural Center. *7645 Little Mountain Rd. Phone 440/974-5735.* English Tudor Revival manor house listed on National Register of Historic Places. (Mon-Fri; closed holidays) **FREE**

Limited-Service Hotel

★ ★ **RADISSON HOTEL & SUITES CLEVELAND EASTLAKE.** *35000 Curtis Blvd, Eastlake (44095). Phone 440/953-8000; fax 440/953-1706. www.radisson.com.* This hotel offers 126 rooms, a full business center, a restaurant and lounge with a fireplace, an indoor pool, and an exercise room. It is located only 8 miles from the Great Lakes Mall and 15 miles from downtown Cleveland.

126 rooms, 5 story. Check-out noon. Restaurant, bar. Fitness room. Indoor pool. Business center. **$**

Restaurant

★ ★ **MOLINARI'S.** *8900 Mentor Ave (Hwy 20), Mentor (44060). Phone 440/974-2750. www.molinaris .com.* Italian menu. Lunch, dinner. Closed Sun; holidays. Bar. **$$**

Miamisburg (D-1)

See also Dayton

Population 17,834
Elevation 690 ft
Area Code 937
Zip 45342
Information South Metro Chamber of Commerce, 1410 B Miamisburg Centerville Rd, Centerville, 45459; phone 937/433-2032
Web site www.smcoc.org

Limited-Service Hotels

★ ★ **COURTYARD BY MARRIOTT.** *100 Prestige Pl, Miamisburg (45342). Phone 937/433-3131; toll-free 800/321-2211; fax 937/433-0285. www.courtyard.com.* 146 rooms, 3 story. Check-out noon. Restaurant, bar. Fitness room. Indoor pool, whirlpool. **$**

★ ★ **HOLIDAY INN.** *31 Prestige Plz Dr, Miamisburg (45342). Phone 937/434-8030; fax 937/434-6452. www. holiday-inn.com.* 195 rooms, 3 story. Pets accepted, some restrictions; fee. Check-out 11 am. Restaurant, bar. Fitness room. Indoor pool, outdoor pool, children's pool. **$**

Restaurants

★ **ALEX'S.** *125 Monarch Ln, Miamisburg (45342). Phone 937/866-2266.* Steak menu. Dinner. Closed Sun; holidays. Bar. Children's menu. **$$**

★ **BULLWINKLE'S TOP HAT BISTRO.** *19 N Main St, Miamisburg (45342). Phone 937/859-7677; fax 937/859-9967.* Patrons may grill own entrée. American menu. Lunch, dinner. Closed Sun; holidays. Bar. Children's menu. **$$**

Middletown (D-1)

See also Cincinnati, Dayton, Hamilton, Lebanon, Mason, Oxford

Population 46,022
Elevation 650 ft
Area Code 513
Zip 45042
Information Middletown Convention and Visitors Bureau, 1504 Central Ave; phone 513/422-3030 or toll-free 888/664-3353
Web site www.visitmiddletown.org

What to See and Do

Americana Amusement Park. *5757 Middletown-Hamilton Rd, Middletown (Butler County). Phone 513/539-2193.* Over 100 rides, shows, and attractions, including two roller coasters and log flume; also pony rides, petting zoo; swimming. (June-Aug, daily; Apr-May, Sept, weekends only) **$$$$**

Sorg Opera Company. *63 S Main St, Middletown (Butler County). Phone 513/425-0180.* Annually produces three major operas, fully staged with orchestra. **$$$$**

Special Event

MiddFest. *1 City Centre Plz, Middletown (Butler County) (45042). Phone 513/425-7707.* Celebrates international arts, history, culture, sports, and food. First weekend in Oct.

Limited-Service Hotels

★ **FAIRFIELD INN.** *6750 Roosevelt Pkwy, Middletown (45044). Phone 513/424-5444; toll-free 800/228-2800; fax 513/424-5444. www.fairfieldinn.com.* 57 rooms, 3 story. Complimentary continental breakfast. Check-out noon. Indoor pool, whirlpool. **$**

★ **HOLIDAY INN EXPRESS.** *6575 Terhune Dr, Middletown (45044). Phone 513/727-8440; toll-free 800/ 270-5272; fax 513/727-8440. www.holiday-inn.com.* 64 rooms, 3 story. Complimentary continental breakfast. Check-out 11 am. Indoor pool, whirlpool. **$**

Restaurant

★ **DAMON'S.** *4750 Roosevelt Blvd, Middletown (45044). Phone 513/423-8805; fax 513/423-8865.* Seafood menu. Lunch, dinner. Closed holidays. Bar. Children's menu. **$$**

Milan (A-3)

See also Bellevue, Oberlin, Sandusky, Vermilion

Founded 1817
Population 1,464
Elevation 602 ft
Area Code 419
Zip 44846
Information Chamber of Commerce, PO Box 544; phone 419/499-2001
Web site www.milanohio.com

Milan was founded by settlers from Connecticut, and many homes here bear the mark of New England architecture. A canal connecting the town with Lake Erie was built in 1839, making Milan one of the largest shipping centers in the Midwest at that time.

What to See and Do

Galpin Wildlife and Bird Sanctuary. *Edison Dr and Berlin Rd (44846). 1/2 mile SE on Edison Dr. Phone 419/499-4909.* Woodland with many varieties of trees, wildflowers, and birds; nature trail. (Daily) **FREE**

Milan Historical Museum. *10 Edison Dr. Phone 419/499-2968.* Seven-building complex includes House of Dr. Lehman Galpin, Edison family doctor. Contains nationally known glass collection; doll and toy houses; Native American artifacts; gun room, blacksmith shop, general store. (Apr-Oct, Tues-Sun) **$$** Nearby are

Newton Memorial Arts Building. *10 Edison Dr, Milan. Phone 419/499-2968.* Displays include collections of antiques, fine arts, needlepoint and laces, and netsukes (ornamental buttons or figures of ivory or wood, used to attach a purse or other article to a sash).

Sayles House. *10 Edison Dr, Milan. At Front St. Phone 419/499-2968.* Restoration of mid-19th century home.

Thomas A. Edison Birthplace Museum. *9 Edison Dr. 3 miles S of OH Tpike exit 7. Phone 419/499-2135.* Two-story red brick house where the inventor spent his first seven years; contains some original furnishings, inventions, and memorabilia. Guided tours. (June 2-Labor Day, Tues-Sat, Sun afternoons; Feb-June 1, after Labor Day-Nov, Tue-Sat afternoons; closed Thanksgiving) **$$**

Limited-Service Hotel

★ **COMFORT INN.** *11020 Milan Rd, Milan (44846). Phone 419/499-4681; fax 419/499-3159. www.comfortinn.com.* 102 rooms, 2 story. Check-out noon. Indoor pool, outdoor pool, whirlpool. **$**

Restaurant

★ ★ **HOMESTEAD INN.** *12018 Hwy 250 N, Milan (44846). Phone 419/499-4271.* Victorian house (1883). American menu. Breakfast, lunch, dinner. Closed holidays. Bar; closed Sun. Children's menu. **$$**

Millersburg (C-4)

Specialty Lodgings

The following lodging establishments are approved by Mobil Travel Guide, but due to their unique and individualized nature have not been given a traditional Mobil Star rating. Included in this listing you may find bed-and-breakfasts, limited-service inns, guest ranches, and other unique hotel properties.

THE BARN INN BED & BREAKFAST. *6838 County Road 203, Millersburg (44654). Phone 330/674-7600; toll-free 877/674-7600. www.bbonline.com/oh/thebarn.* Located in the picturesque Honey Run Valley, this bed-and-breakfast was once home to a dairy farm and has been restored to its former splendor. 7 rooms, 2 story. **$$**

BIGHAM HOUSE BED & BREAKFAST. *151 S Washington St, Millersburg (44654). Phone toll-free 866/689-6950.* Located in the heart of Amish country. Private bath and TV in every room. 5 rooms, 3 story. **$$**

Restaurant

★ ★ **CHALET IN THE VALLEY.** *5060 Hwy 557, Millersburg (44654). Phone 330/893-2550. www.chaletinthevalley.com.* Beautiful farm setting serving traditional Viennese dishes. Austrian menu. Lunch, dinner. Closed Mon. **$**

Mount Gilead (C-3)

See also Delaware, Mansfield, Marion, Mount Vernon

Population 2,846
Elevation 1,130 ft
Area Code 419
Zip 43338
Information Morrow County Chamber of Commerce, 17 1/2 W High St; phone 419/946-2821
Web site www.morrowcochamber.com

What to See and Do

Mount Gilead State Park. *1 mile E on Hwy 95. Phone 419/946-1961.* More than 170 acres. Fishing, boating (electric motors only); hiking, picnicking (shelter), camping. (Daily)

Mount Vernon (C-3)

See also Delaware, Mansfield, Mount Gilead, Newark

Founded 1805
Population 14,550
Elevation 990 ft
Area Code 740
Zip 43050
Information Knox County Convention and Visitors Bureau, 236 S Main St; phone 740/392-6102 or toll-free 800/837-5282
Web site www.knox.net/visitor

Descendants of the first settlers from Virginia, Maryland, New Jersey, and Pennsylvania still live in this manufacturing and trading center. Seat of Knox County, it is in a rich agricultural, sandstone, and oil- and gas-producing area. It is in the largest sheep-raising county east of the Mississippi.

Johnny Appleseed owned two lots in the original village plot at the south end of Main Street. Daniel Decatur Emmett, author and composer of "Dixie,"

was born here. The offices of the state headquarters of the Ohio Conference of Seventh-Day Adventists are here. Colonial-style architecture has been used for many public buildings and residences.

Limited-Service Hotel

★ ★ **HISTORIC CURTIS INN ON THE SQUARE.** *6-12 Public Sq, Mount Vernon (43050). Phone 740/397-4334; toll-free 800/934-6835; fax 740/397-4334.* 72 rooms, 2 story. Pets accepted, some restrictions; fee. Check-out noon. Restaurant, bar. **$**

Full-Service Inn

★ ★ ★ **WHITE OAK INN.** *29683 Walhonding Rd, Danville (43014). Phone 740/599-6107. www.whiteoakinn.com.* Enjoy the peace-and-quiet feel at this inn close to everything. Turn-of-the-century farmhouse with original white oak woodwork. Relaxed dining with creative breakfast and dinner offerings are available daily. 10 rooms, 2 story. Children over 12 years only. Complimentary full breakfast. Check-in 3 pm, check-out 11 am. **$$**

Munroe Falls

Restaurant

★ ★ **TRIPLE CROWN.** *335 S Main, Munroe Falls (44262). Phone 330/633-5325; fax 330/633-1816. www.triplecrownrestaurant.com.* Steak menu. Lunch, dinner, Sun brunch. Closed holidays. Bar. Children's menu. Horse racing memorabilia. **$$**

New Philadelphia (C-4)

See also Canton, Coshocton, Gnadenhutten, Massillon

Founded 1804
Population 15,698
Elevation 910 ft
Area Code 330
Zip 44663
Information Tuscarawas County Convention and Visitors Bureau, 125 McDonald's Dr, SW; phone 330/339-5453 or toll-free 800/527-3387
Web site www.neohiotravel.com

New Philadelphia, seat of Tuscarawas County, and its neighbor, Dover, still reflect the early influences of the German-Swiss who came from Pennsylvania. Some of the earliest town lots in New Philadelphia were set aside for German schools.

What to See and Do

Fort Laurens State Memorial. *11067 Fort Laurens Rd NW, Bolivar. 14 miles N via Hwy 39, I-77, Hwy 212 to Bolivar, then 1/2 mile S. Phone 330/874-2059.* An 82-acre site of the only American fort in Ohio during the Revolutionary War. Named in honor of Henry Laurens, Continental Congress president. Built in 1778 as a defense against the British and Native Americans. Picnicking. Museum has artifacts and multimedia program on American Revolution. (Memorial Day-Labor Day, Wed-Sun; after Labor Day-Oct, weekends only) **$**

Muskingum Watershed Conservancy District. *1319 3rd St NW. Phone 330/343-6647.* A Muskingum River flood control and recreation project. The district maintains a total of ten lakes, five lake parks, ten marinas, and ten campgrounds. (Daily) **$$**

Atwood Lake Park. *4956 Shop Rd NE, Mineral City. 12 miles E on Hwy 39, then N off Hwy 212. Phone 330/343-6780.* A 1,540-acre lake with swimming, fishing, boating (25-hp limit), marinas; golf; tent and trailer sites (showers, flush toilets). Restaurant, cottages, resort. Pets on leash only. (Daily) **$$**

Leesville Lake. *4131 Deer Rd SW, Bowerston. 12 miles E on Hwy 39, then S off Hwy 212. Southfork Marina, on SW shore, off Hwy 212. Petersburg Marina, on N shore, off Hwy 332 (phone 330/627-4270). Phone 740/269-5371.* Fishing and boating on 1,000-acre lake (10-hp limit); tent and trailer sites (Apr-Oct).

Schoenbrunn Village State Memorial. *1984 E High Ave. 3 miles SE off Hwy 250 on Hwy 259. Phone 330/339-3636; toll-free 800/752-2711.* Partial reconstruction of the first Ohio town built by Christian Native Americans under the leadership of Moravian missionaries; one of six villages constructed between 1772-1798. Picnicking. Museum. (Memorial Day-Labor Day, daily; after Labor Day-Oct, weekends only) **$**

Tuscora Park. *161 Tuscora Ave (44663). Phone 330/343-4644.* Swimming (fee); tennis, shuffleboard; picnicking, concession; amusement rides (fee per ride), includes 100-year-old carousel. (Late May-Labor Day, daily) **FREE**

Warther Museum. *331 Karl Ave, Dover. 1/2 mile E of I-77. Phone 330/343-7513. www.warthers.com.* Collection of miniature locomotives by master carver Ernest Warther, carved of ebony, pearl, ivory, and walnut; largest model has 10,000 parts; collection of buttons in quilt patterns and arrow points. On landscaped grounds are telegraph station, operating hand car, and caboose. Tour of cutlery shop. (Daily; closed holidays) **$$**

Zoar State Memorial. *221 W 3rd St, Zoar. I-77 exit 93; 2 1/2 miles SE on Hwy 212. Phone 330/874-3011.* A quaint village where the German religious Separatists found refuge from persecution (1817); an experiment in communal living that lasted for 80 years. Number One House on Main Street houses the historical museum and has Zoar Society pottery and furniture. Zoar Garden, in the center of the village, follows the description of New Jerusalem in the Bible. Restoration includes the garden house, blacksmith shop, bakery, tinshop, wagon shop, kitchen, magazine shop, and dairy. (Memorial Day-Labor Day, Wed-Sat, Sun and holiday afternoons; Apr-May, after Labor Day-Oct, weekends) **$$**

Special Events

Christmas in Zoar. *Historic Zoar Church, 142 E 5th, New Philadelphia (44697). Phone 330/874-3011.* Tours of private houses, craft show, German food, strolling carolers, and tree-lighting ceremony. Early Dec.

Swiss Festival. *106 Main St, New Philadelphia (44681). 8 miles W on Hwy 39, in Sugarcreek. Phone 330/852-4113.* Swiss cheese from more than 13 factories in the area. Swiss musicians, costumes, polka bands. Steinstossen (stone-throwing), Schwingfest (Swiss wrestling); parade each afternoon. Fourth Fri-Sat after Labor Day.

Trumpet in the Land. *Schoenbrunn Amphitheatre, New Philadelphia. Off Hwy 250 on University Dr. Phone 330/339-1132.* Outdoor musical drama by Paul Green takes you back to a time when Ohio was the Western frontier of America to witness the founding of Ohio's first settlement, Schoenbrunn, in 1772. Mid-June-late Aug, Mon-Sat.

Zoar Harvest Festival. *Historic Zoar Church, 142 E 5th, New Philadelphia (44697). In Zoar. Phone 330/874-2646.* Antique show; 1850s craft demonstrations; music in 1853 church; museum tours; horse-drawn wagon rides. Early Aug.

Limited-Service Hotel

★ ★ **HOLIDAY INN.** *131 Bluebell Dr SW, New Philadelphia (44663). Phone 330/339-7731; fax 330/339-1565. www.holiday-inn.com.* 107 rooms, 2 story. Check-out 11 am. Restaurant, bar. Fitness room. Indoor pool, outdoor pool, whirlpool. **$**

Full-Service Resort

★ ★ ★ **ATWOOD.** *2650 Lodge Rd, New Philadelphia (46620). Phone 330/735-2211; fax 330/735-2562.* This hilltop resort overlooking the lake provides a unique retreat spot with each room offering either a view of the lake or lovely countryside. Boat rentals are available through the hotel, and harbor cruises are available through the nearby marina. 104 rooms, 2 story. Check-in 4 pm, check-out 1 pm. Restaurant, bar. Children's activity center. Fitness room. Indoor pool, outdoor pool, whirlpool. Golf, 9-hole par-3, 18-hole par-70, pro shop, driving range, putting green. Tennis. Airport transportation available. Private airstrip, heliport. A Muskingum Watershed Conservancy District facility. **$**

Newark (C-3)

See also Columbus, Coshocton, Lancaster, Mount Vernon, Zanesville

Founded 1802
Population 44,389
Elevation 829 ft
Area Code 740
Zip 43055
Information Licking County Convention and Visitors Bureau, 50 W Locust St, PO Box 702; phone 740/345-8224 or toll-free 800/589-8224
Web site www.lccvb.com

This industrial city on the Licking River attracts many visitors because of its large group of prehistoric mounds. Construction of the Ohio and Erie Canal began here on July 4, 1825, with Governor DeWitt Clinton of New York as the official groundbreaker and speaker. The Ohio Canal was then built north to Lake Erie and south to the Ohio River.

What to See and Do

Blackhand Gorge. *9 miles E of Newark, S of Hwy 146. Phone 740/763-4411.* On 970 wooden acres; bike trails, hiking, bird-watching, canoeing. **FREE**

Buckeye Central Scenic Railroad. *5475 National Rd SE (43025). Hwy 40. Phone 740/366-2029.* A 90-minute scenic rail trip through Licking County. (Memorial Day weekend-Oct, weekends, holidays). Also special holiday-themed trains available (Oct, Dec). **$$$**

Buckeye Lake State Park. *76 Jefferson St. 11 miles S on Hwy 79, on Buckeye Lake (3,300 acres water and 200 acres land). Phone 740/467-2690.* Swimming, water-skiing, fishing, boating (ramp); picnicking (shelter). (Daily)

Dawes Arboretum. *7770 Jacksontown Rd SE. Phone 740/323-2355.* Over 2,000 species of woody plants on 355 acres; 3-acre Japanese Garden; Cypress Swamp; All Seasons Garden; nature trails; picnic areas and shelter; special programs. (Daily; closed Jan 1, Thanksgiving, Dec 25) **FREE**

Flint Ridge State Memorial. *7091 Brownsville Rd SE (43799). 5 miles E on Hwy 16, then 5 miles S on County 668. Phone 740/787-2476.* Prehistoric Native American flint quarry; trails for the disabled and the visually impaired; picnic area. Museum (Memorial Day-Labor Day, Wed-Sun; after Labor Day-Oct, weekends only). Park (Apr-Oct). **$$**

Gallery Shop. *50 S 2nd St. Phone 740/349-8031.* Bimonthly exhibits by regional and local artists. (Mon-Sat, daily; closed holidays) **FREE**

Licking County Historical Society Museum. *Veterans Park, 6 N 6th St. Phone 740/345-4898.* Restored Sherwood-Davidson House (circa 1815) with period furnishings. Adjacent is restored Buckingham Meeting House (circa 1835). Guided tours (Apr-Dec, daily, except Mon). **DONATION** The society also maintains

Robbins-Hunter Museum in the Avery Downer House. *221 E Broadway, Granville. Phone 740/587-0430.* Outstanding Greek Revival house (1842). Period furnishings; decorative and fine arts. Guided tours. (Wed-Sun afternoons; also by appointment) **DONATION**

Webb House Museum. *303 Granville St, Newark. Phone 740/345-8540.* Home (1908) of lumber executive includes family heirloom furnishings and wooden interior features. Guided tours. (Apr-Dec, Thurs-Fri, Sun afternoons; also by appointment) **FREE**

National Heisey Glass Museum. *169 W Church St. At 6th St. Phone 740/345-2932.* Displays of Heiseyware manufactured in the area from 1896 to 1957. (Tues-Sat afternoons; closed holidays) **$**

⭐ **Newark Earthworks.** *S 21st St and Hwy 79 (43055). Phone toll-free 800/600-7174.* The group of earthworks here was originally one of the most extensive of its kind in the country, covering an area of more than 4 square miles. The Hopewell used their geometric enclosures for social, religious, and ceremonial purposes. Remaining portions of the Newark group are Octagon Earthworks and Wright Earthworks, with many artifacts of pottery, beadwork, copper, bone, and shell exhibited at the nearby Moundbuilders Museum.

Moundbuilders State Memorial. *65 Messimer Dr, unit 2, Newark. SW on Hwy 79, at S 21st St and Cooper. Phone toll-free 800/600-7174.* The Great Circle, 66 acres, has walls from 8 feet to 14 feet high with burial mounds in the center; picnic facilities. Museum containing Hopewell artifacts (Memorial Day-Labor Day, Wed-Sun; after Labor Day-Oct, weekends only). Park (Apr-Oct). **$**

Octagon Earthworks. *N 30th St and Parkview, Newark. Phone toll-free 800/600-7174.* The octagon-shaped enclosure encircles 50 acres that include small mounds and is joined by parallel walls to a circular embankment enclosing 20 acres. **FREE**

Wright Earthworks. *James and Waldo sts, Newark. 1/4 mile NE of Great Cir. Phone toll-free 800/600-7174.* One-acre area has a 100-foot wall remnant, an important part of original Newark group. **FREE**

Ye Olde Mill. *11324 Mount Vernon Rd, Utica. Hwy 13, 10 miles N of Newark. Phone 740/892-3921.* Museum of milling history; gift shop; ice cream parlor. Picnic areas. (May-Oct, daily) **FREE**

Limited-Service Hotel

⭐⭐ **CHERRY VALLEY LODGE.** *2299 Cherry Valley Rd, Newark (43055). Phone 740/788-1200; toll-free 800/788-8008; fax 740/788-8800. www.cherryvalleylodge.com.* Specializing in all-inclusive packages and customized group outings, this resort is located on 18 acres, 45 minutes outside of Columbus. 120 rooms, 2 story. Check-out noon. Restaurant, bar. Fitness room. Indoor pool, outdoor pool, whirlpool. **$$**

Full-Service Inn

⭐⭐⭐ **BUXTON INN.** *313 E Broadway, Granville (43023). Phone 740/587-0001; fax 740/587-1460.* Built in 1812, this charming landmark is considered to be one of Ohio's oldest inns. Listed on the National Register of Historic Places, this inn successfully combines the gentility of a time long past with modern amenities to make for a delightful stay. Relax on the sprawling veranda, which offers views of the lush, well-maintained gardens and soothing fountains, and take in the history of a bygone era. 26 rooms (in two houses), 2 story. Complimentary continental breakfast. Check-in 2 pm, check-out noon. Restaurant. **$**

Restaurants

⭐⭐ **CHERRY VALLEY LODGE DINING ROOM.** *2299 Cherry Valley Rd, Newark (43055). Phone 740/788-1336. www.cherryvalleylodge.com.* American menu. Breakfast, lunch, dinner, brunch. Bar. Children's menu. **$$$**

⭐ **DAMON'S.** *1486 Granville Rd, Newark (43055). Phone 740/349-7427; fax 740/344-7808.* Lunch, dinner. Closed Dec 25. Bar. Children's menu. Casual attire. **$$**

⭐ **NATOMA.** *10 N Park, Newark (43055). Phone 740/345-7260.* American menu. Lunch, dinner. Closed Sun; holidays. Bar. **$$**

Niles (B-5)

Restaurant

⭐⭐⭐ **ALBERINI'S.** *1201 Youngstown-Warren Rd, Niles (44446). Phone 330/652-5895; fax 330/652-7041. www.alberinis.com.* Husband-wife team Richard and Gilda Alberini preside over this popular Italian restaurant on an energetic downtown street.

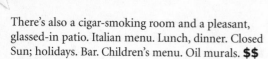

There's also a cigar-smoking room and a pleasant, glassed-in patio. Italian menu. Lunch, dinner. Closed Sun; holidays. Bar. Children's menu. Oil murals. **$$**

Oakwood (B-3)

Restaurant

★ ★ **OAKWOOD CLUB.** *2414 Far Hills Ave, Oakwood (45419). Phone 937/293-6973; fax 937/293-8438.* Seafood, steak menu. Dinner. Closed Sun; holidays. Bar. Neiman originals on walls. **$$**

Oberlin (A-3)

See also Cleveland, Elyria, Lorain, Milan, Strongsville, Vermilion

Founded 1833
Population 8,191
Elevation 800 ft
Area Code 440
Zip 44074
Information Lorain County Visitors Bureau, 611 Broadway, 44052; phone 440/245-5282 or toll-free 800/334-1673
Web site www.lcvb.org

Oberlin College (see) and the town were founded together. Oberlin was the first college to offer equal degrees to men and women and the first in the United States to adopt a policy against discrimination because of race. The central portion of the campus forms a 6-acre public square, called Tappan Square, in the center of the town.

Charles Martin Hall, a young Oberlin graduate, discovered the electrolytic process of making aluminum in Oberlin. The Federal Aviation Agency maintains an Air Traffic Control Center here.

What to See and Do

Oberlin College. *135 W Lorain St (44074). At jct Hwy 511, 58. Phone 440/775-8121. www.oberlin.edu.* (1833) (2,750 students) College of Arts and Sciences and Conservatory of Music (1867). Campus tours from admissions office, Carnegie Building. On campus are

Allen Memorial Art Museum. *87 N Main, Oberlin. Phone 440/775-8665.* Major collection of more than 14,000 works, including 17th-century Dutch paintings, 19th- and 20th-century European works, Japanese woodcuts, and contemporary works. (Tues-Sun; closed holidays) **FREE**

Conservatory of Music. *77 W College St, Oberlin.* Complex of buildings (1964) by architect Minoru Yamasaki; includes 667-seat Warner Concert Hall, a teaching and classroom building, rehearsal and library unit, and Robertson Hall, which houses practice facilities.

Hall Auditorium. *67 N Main St, Oberlin. Phone 440/775-8121.* Dramatic arts center.

Seeley G. Mudd Center. *148 W College St, Oberlin.* Library with more than 1 million volumes; also houses archives, audiovisual center.

Oberlin Heritage Center tour. *73 1/2 S Professer St (44074). Phone 440/774-1700. www.oberlinheritage.org.* Oberlin Heritage Center tour includes James Monroe House (1866), Little Red Schoolhouse (1836), and Jewett House (1884). **$**

Limited-Service Hotel

★ ★ **OBERLIN INN.** *7 N Main St, Oberlin (44074). Phone 440/775-1111; toll-free 800/376-4173; fax 440/775-0676. www.oberlininn.com.* 76 rooms, 3 story. Check-out noon. Restaurant. Airport transportation available. **$**

✈

Oxford (D-1)

See also Cincinnati, Hamilton, Mason, Middletown

Founded 1810
Population 18,937
Elevation 972 ft
Area Code 513
Zip 45056
Information Visitors and Convention Bureau, 30 W Park; phone 513/523-8687
Web site www.oxfordchamber.org

Situated in the rolling hills of southwestern Ohio, this small town has many brick streets and unique shops and is home to Miami University (see).

What to See and Do

Hueston Woods State Park. *Doty and Brown rds (45056). 5 miles N on Hwy 732. Phone 513/523-6347 (park office).* A 3,596-acre park with swimming, bathhouse, boating (launch, rentals); nature, hiking, and bridle trails; 18-hole golf; picnicking, concession; lodge, camping, cabins. Nature center, naturalist. (Daily) **FREE** At the south entrance is

> **Pioneer Farm & House Museum.** *Doty and Brown rds, Oxford. Phone 513/523-8005.* Farmhouse (1835) has period furniture, clothing, toys. Barn (circa 1850) has early farm implements, tools. Arts and crafts fair (first weekend in June). Apple butter-making demonstrations (second weekend in Oct). (Memorial Day-Oct, call for hours) **$**

Miami University. *500 E High St. Phone 513/529-1809. www.muohio.edu.* (1809) (16,000 students) On campus are the Miami University Art Museum (Tues-Sun) and two other art galleries; zoology, geology, and anthropology museums; entomological collections; Turrell Herbarium. Campus tours. Also on campus is

> **McGuffey Museum.** *410 E Spring St, Oxford. Spring and Oak sts. Phone 513/529-2232.* Restored home of William Holmes McGuffey, who compiled the McGuffey Eclectic Readers while a member of the faculty here; memorabilia; collection of his books. (Call for schedule) **FREE**

Special Events

Outdoor Summer Music Festival. *High and Main sts, Oxford (45056). Phone 513/523-8687. Uptown Oxford at Martin Luther King Park.* June-July, every Thurs.

Red Brick Rally Car Show. *High and Main sts, Oxford (45056). Phone 513/523-8687. Uptown.* Second Sun in Oct.

Limited-Service Hotels

★ **BEST WESTERN SYCAMORE INN.** *6 E Sycamore St, Oxford (45056). Phone 513/523-0000; toll-free 800/523-4678; fax 513/523-2093. www.bestwestern.com.* 61 rooms, 2 story. Complimentary continental breakfast. Check-out noon. Fitness room. Indoor pool, whirlpool. **$**

🛉 🖭 🖼

★ **HAMPTON INN.** *5056 College Corner Pike, Oxford (45056). Phone 513/524-0114; fax 513/524-1147. www.hamptoninn.com.* 66 rooms, 3 story. Complimentary continental breakfast. Check-out 11 am. Fitness room. Indoor pool, whirlpool. **$**

🛉 🖼

★ ★ **HUESTON WOODS RESORT.** *5201 Lodge Rd, College Corner (45003). Phone 513/523-6381; toll-free 800/282-7275; fax 513/523-1522. www.huestonwoodsresort.com.* Indian motif. 92 rooms, 3 story. Check-out noon. Restaurant, bar. Children's activity center. Fitness room. Indoor pool, outdoor pool, children's pool. Golf, 18 holes. Tennis. All facilities of state park available. **$**

🛉 🏌 🖼 ⛵

Painesville (A-5)

See also Ashtabula, Chardon, Cleveland, Geneva-on-the-Lake, Mentor

Population 15,699
Elevation 677 ft
Area Code 440
Zip 44077
Information Lake County Visitors Bureau, 1610 Mentor Ave; phone 440/354-2424 or toll-free 800/368-5253
Web site www.lakevisit.com

What to See and Do

Fairport Harbor Lighthouse and Marine Museum. *129 2nd St, Fairport Harbor. 2 miles N off Hwy 2. Phone 440/354-4825.* Lighthouse, lighthouse keeper's dwelling (museum) with attached ship's pilothouse. (Memorial Day weekend-second weekend in Sept, Wed, Sat-Sun, holidays) **$**

Special Event

Lake County Fair. *Lake County fairgrounds, 1301 Mentor Ave, Painesville (44077). Phone 440/354-3339.* Late Aug.

Full-Service Resort

★ ★ ★ **RENAISSANCE QUAIL HOLLOW
RESORT.** *11080 Concord Hambden Rd, Concord
(44077).* Phone 440/497-1100; toll-free 800/792-0258;
fax 440/497-1111. www.marriott.com. Convenient to
the city but promoting a sense of remoteness, this
resort is a nice getaway with 36 holes of golf, a spa,
and many other recreational facilities on-site. Enjoy
elegant dining in the dining room, which features
many classically prepared dishes. 180 rooms, 4 story.
Check-in 4 pm, check-out 11 am. Restaurant, bar.
Fitness room. Indoor pool, outdoor pool, whirlpool.
Golf, 36 holes. Tennis. Business center. **$**

Specialty Lodging

The following lodging establishment is approved
by Mobil Travel Guide, but due to its unique and
individualized nature has not been given a traditional
Mobil Star rating. Included in this listing you may
find bed-and-breakfasts, limited-service inns, guest
ranches, and other unique hotel properties.

RIDERS 1812. *792 Mentor Ave, Painesville
(44077).* Phone 440/942-2742. www.ridersinn.com.
Original stagecoach stop (1812); historic stop on
the Underground Railroad; some original antiques.
10 rooms, 2 story. Pets accepted, some restrictions.
Complimentary full breakfast. Restaurant (see).
Airport transportation available. **$**

Restaurants

★ **DINNER BELL DINER.** *1155 Bank St,
Painesville (44077).* Phone 440/354-3708. American
menu. Breakfast, lunch, dinner. Closed July 4,
Thanksgiving, Dec 25. **$**

★ ★ **RIDER'S INN.** *792 Mentor Ave, Painesville
(44077).* Phone 440/942-2742. www.ridersinn.com.
Features fare from original 19th-century recipes.
Lunch, dinner, Sun brunch. Closed Dec 25. Bar.
Children's menu. Outdoor seating. (See SPECIALTY
LODGING) **$$**

Piqua (C-1)

See also Dayton, Sidney, Vandalia

Population 20,612
Elevation 869 ft
Area Code 937
Zip 45356
Information Piqua Area Chamber of Commerce,
326 N Main, PO Box 1142; phone 937/773-2765

What to See and Do

⭐ **Piqua Historical Area.** *9845 Hardin Rd (45356).*
3 1/2 miles NW on Hwy 66. Phone 937/773-2522. More
than 170 acres in Great Miami River valley, near cross-
roads used by prehistoric people, French and English fur
traders, and soldiers of General "Mad Anthony" Wayne.
(Memorial Day-Labor Day, Wed-Sun; after Labor Day-
Oct, weekends only) **$$** Area and fee include

Historic Indian Museum. *9845 N Hardin Rd,
Piqua.* Phone 937/773-2522. Has artifacts from the
17th century-19th century.

John Johnston Home. *9845 N Hardin Rd, Piqua.*
Phone 937/773-2522. (1810) Restored Dutch
colonial-style farmhouse built by Ohio Indian
agent and businessman. Other buildings include
double pen log barn, springhouse, fruit kiln, and
ciderhouse; craft demonstrations.

Miami and Erie Canal. *Piqua.* (1825-1845) Rides
on *Gen'l Harrison*, replica of a mid-19th-century
canal boat.

Special Event

Heritage Festival. *525 N Main St, Piqua (45356).*
Phone 937/773-2765. Piqua heritage re-created. Native
American and square dancing; demonstrations,
including long rifle, blacksmith, wood carving, dulcimer, soap making, weaving; contests; food; canal boat
rides. Labor Day weekend.

Limited-Service Hotel

★ **COMFORT INN.** *987 E Ash St and Miami Valley
Centre, Piqua (45356).* Phone 937/778-8100; fax 937/
778-9573. www.comfortinn.com. 124 rooms, 5 story.
Pets accepted; fee. Complimentary continental breakfast. Check-out noon. Fitness room. Indoor pool,
whirlpool. **$**

Port Clinton (A-3)

See also Fremont, Kelleys Island, Put-in-Bay, Sandusky, Toledo

Founded 1828
Population 7,106
Elevation 592 ft
Area Code 419
Zip 43452
Information Chamber of Commerce, 304 Madison St, Suite C; phone 419/734-5503; or the Ottawa County Visitors Bureau, 109 Madison St, Suite E; phone 419/734-4386
Web site www.portclintonchamber.com

What to See and Do

African Safari Wildlife Park. *267 S Lighter Rd (43452). 4 miles E to Lightner Rd, off Hwy 2 bypass.* Phone 419/732-3606. Visitors may drive their own cars through game preserve to see lions, ostriches, giraffes, zebras, and other animals roaming freely in natural setting. Camel rides available. (Mid-May-Labor Day, daily; Sept, weekends if weather permits) **$$$$**

Camp Perry Military Reservation. *1000 N Lawrence Dr (43452). 5 miles W on Hwy 2.* Phone toll-free 888/ 889-7010. Largest military camp on the Great Lakes. (Daily) **FREE**

Catawba Island State Park. *4049 E Mooresdock Rd (43452). 4 miles E on Hwy 163, then N on Hwy 53.* Phone 419/797-4530. Fishing (perch, catfish, bluegill, bass, crappie), boating on Lake Erie (ramps); picnicking. (Daily) **FREE**

East Harbor State Park. *1169 N Buck Rd, Lackside Marblehead (43440). 7 miles E on Hwy 163, then N on Hwy 269.* Phone 419/734-4424 (park). Swimming beach (lifeguard), bathhouse (Memorial Day-Labor Day), fishing, boating, marina, docks; hiking, snowmobiling; concession; camping. (Daily) **FREE**

Ottawa County Historical Museum. *126 W 3rd St (43452).* Phone 419/732-2237. Guns, dolls; Native American and county relics; 1813 Battle of Lake Erie exhibit. (Mon-Fri afternoons; also by appointment; closed holidays) **FREE**

Perry's Victory and International Peace Memorial. *911 N Camp Rd (43452). 12 miles by ferry to Put-in-Bay* (see).

Special Event

National matches. *Camp Perry-Small Arms Firing Schools, 600 Lawrence Rd, Port Clinton (43452).* Phone 419/635-0101. Held since 1907. Hundreds of competitors each in outdoor pistol, small-bore, and high-power rifle championships. Early July-mid-Aug.

Limited-Service Hotel

★ **FAIRFIELD INN.** *3760 E State Rd, Port Clinton (43452).* Phone 419/732-2434; toll-free 800/228-2800; fax 419/732-2434. www.fairfieldinn.com. 64 rooms, 2 story. Complimentary continental breakfast. Check-out noon. Indoor pool. **$**

Restaurant

★ ★ **GARDEN AT THE LIGHTHOUSE.** *226 E Perry St (Hwy 163), Port Clinton (43452).* Phone 419/732-2151. In former lighthouse keeper's building; glassed-in porch overlooking gardens. American menu. Lunch, dinner. Closed Sun (Sept-May); holidays. Bar. Children's menu. Outdoor seating. **$$**

Portsmouth (E-3)

See also Ironton

Founded 1803
Population 22,676
Elevation 533 ft
Area Code 740
Zip 45662
Information Convention and Visitors Bureau, 324 Chillicothe St, PO Box 509; phone 740/353-1116
Web site www.portsmouthcvb.org

Portsmouth is the leading firebrick and shoelace center of southern Ohio. At the confluence of the Ohio and Scioto rivers, 100 miles east of Cincinnati, it is connected to South Portsmouth, Kentucky, by bridge. The Boneyfiddle Historic District in downtown Portsmouth includes many antique and specialty shops.

Portsmouth was the childhood home of cowboy movie star Roy Rogers and baseball's Branch Rickey.

What to See and Do

The 1810 House. *1926 Waller St. Phone 740/354-3760.* Original homestead built by hand. Nine rooms with period furniture. Guided tours. (May-Dec, Sat-Sun afternoons; weekdays by appointment) **DONATION**

Brewery Arcade. *224 2nd St. In the historic Boneyfiddle District.* (1842) A former brewery, restored.

Floodwall Murals Project. *Front St (45662). At Ohio River. Phone 740/353-1116.* Thirty-four murals depicting area history completed by Robert Dafford. (Daily) **FREE**

Shawnee State Forest. *13291 Hwy 52, West Portsmouth (45663). 7 miles SW on Hwy 52, then W on State Rte 125. Phone 740/858-6685.* A 63,000-acre forest with six lakes. Hunting in season. Bridle trail. (Daily) (See SPECIAL EVENTS) **FREE** In the forest is

  Shawnee State Park. *940 2nd St, Portsmouth. Phone 740/858-4561.* Swimming, fishing, boating (ramps, dock) on 68-acre lake; 18-hole golf; picnicking (shelter); lodge, camping, teepees, cabins. Nature center. (Daily) **FREE**

Southern Ohio Museum and Cultural Center. *825 Gallia St. Phone 740/354-5629.* Changing exhibits in visual arts; performing arts; workshops; guided tours. (Tues-Sun; closed holidays; also Jan, Aug) Free admission Fri. **$**

Special Events

Fall foliage hikes and tours. *Shawnee State Park and Forest (see), 4404 State Rte 125, West Portsmouth (45663). Phone 740/858-6621.* Guided hikes; hoedowns;, camp-outs; auto tours. Third weekend in Oct.

River Days Festival. *Downtown Portsmouth. Phone 740/355-6622.* Labor Day weekend.

Roy Rogers Festival. *Downtown Portsmouth. Phone 740/353-0900.* Old-time Western stars, memorabilia, staged gunfights. First weekend in June.

Scioto County Fair. *Fairgrounds, Hwy 348 and Hwy 23, Portsmouth (45662). Phone 740/353-3698.* Second week in Aug.

Trout Derby. *Shawnee State Park (see), 4404 State Rte 125, Put-in-Bay (45663). Phone 740/858-6652.* Last weekend in Apr.

Limited-Service Hotels

★ ★ **DAYS INN.** *3762 Hwy 23, Portsmouth (45662). Phone 740/354-2851; fax 740/353-6107.* 100 rooms, 2 story. Pets accepted; fee. Check-out noon. Restaurant, bar. Pool. **$**

★ ★ **RAMADA.** *711 2nd St, Portsmouth (45662). Phone 740/354-7711; fax 740/353-1539. www.ramada .com.* 119 rooms, 5 story. Pets accepted. Complimentary continental breakfast. Check-out noon. Restaurant. Fitness room. Indoor pool, children's pool, whirlpool. **$**

Put-in-Bay

See also Kelleys Island, Port Clinton, Sandusky

Settled 1811
Population 141
Elevation 570 ft
Area Code 419
Zip 43456
Information Put-in-Bay Chamber of Commerce, PO Box 250; phone 419/285-2832
Web site www.put-in-bay.com

On South Bass Island in Lake Erie, this village is an all-year resort that can be reached by ferry from Port Clinton (inquire as to times and seasons, phone toll-free 800/245-1538) and Catawba Point (inquire as to times and seasons, phone 419/285-2421) or by plane from Sandusky (phone toll-free 800/368-3743). The area claims the best smallmouth black bass fishing in America in spring; good walleye fishing in June-August; and ice fishing for perch and walleye in winter. Boating, swimming, bicycling, picnic grounds, yachting facilities, golf, and water-skiing are available. Wine is produced in the area.

What to See and Do

Crystal Cave. *978 Catawba Ave. Phone 419/285-2811.* Unusual deposit of strontium sulphate crystals; the largest is 18 inches long. Heineman Winery is located on the grounds; winery tour and tasting is included in cave tour. (Mid-May-mid-Sept, daily) **$$**

Lake Erie Island State Park. *441 Catawba Ave. S shore. Phone 419/797-4530.* Includes South Bass Island, Kelleys Island, and Catawba parks. Water-skiing, fishing, boating (ramps); hiking trail; picnicking (shelter); camping (fee), cabins (fee).

Perry's Cave. *Catawba Ave. Phone 419/285-2405.* Commodore Perry is rumored to have stored supplies here before the Battle of Lake Erie in 1813; later, prisoners were kept here for a short time. The cave is 52 feet below the surface and is 208 feet by 165 feet; the temperature is 50° F. It has an underground stream that rises and falls with the level of Lake Erie. Picnic area available (no water). Mini-golf (fee), rock climbing (fee). Twenty-minute guided tour. (June-Labor Day, daily; spring and fall, weekends; rest of year, by appointment) **$$$**

Perry's Victory and International Peace Memorial. *2 Bay View Ave, Put-in-Bay. Phone 419/285-2184.* Greek Doric granite column (352 feet high) commemorates Commodore Oliver Hazard Perry's victory over the British naval squadron at the Battle of Lake Erie, near Put-in-Bay, in 1813. The United States gained control of the lake, preventing a British invasion. Observation platform in monument (317 feet above lake) provides views of the battle site and neighboring islands on a clear day. The 3,986-mile United States–Canadian boundary is the longest unfortified border in the world. Children under 16 only with adult. (May-late Oct, daily) **$$**

Put-in-Bay Tour Train. *2071 Langram Rd. Phone 419/285-4855.* Departs from downtown depot and Jet Express dock. A one-hour tour of the island (May-mid-Sept, daily). **$$$**

Special Event

Boat Regatta. *Put-in-Bay. Phone 419/285-2832.* More than 200 sailboats race to Vermilion (see). Early Aug.

Sandusky (A-3)

See also Bellevue, Elyria, Kelleys Island, Lorain, Milan, Port Clinton, Put-in-Bay, Vermilion

Settled 1816
Population 29,764
Elevation 600 ft
Area Code 419
Zip 44870
Information Sandusky/Erie County Visitor and Convention Bureau, 4424 Milan Rd, Suite A; phone 419/625-2984 or toll-free 800/255-3743
Web site www.buckeyenorth.com

On a flat slope facing 18-mile-long Sandusky Bay, this town stretches for more than 6 miles along the waterfront. Originally explored by the French, named by the Wyandot "Sandouske," meaning "at the cold water," it is the second largest coal-shipping port on the Great Lakes. It became a tourist center in 1882; automotive parts industry and manufacturing also are important to the economy.

What to See and Do

Battery Park. *701 E Water. Phone 419/625-6142.* Piers, marina, sailing club; lighted tennis; picnicking (shelter), playground. Restaurant. **FREE**

Cedar Point. *1 Cedar Point Dr. SE on Hwy 6 to Causeway Dr, then N over Causeway (look for Cedar Point signs in town). Phone 419/627-2350.* Swimming beach, marina; RV campground, resort hotels on Lake Erie. Amusement park has more than 50 rides, live shows, crafts area, restaurants, concessions. Also here is Challenge Park, including Soak City water park, Challenge Golf miniature-golf course, and the Cedar Point Grand Prix go-kart race track (additional fee). (Early May-Labor Day, daily; after Labor Day-Oct, weekends only) Price includes unlimited rides and attractions, except Challenge Park. **$$$$**

Merry-Go-Round Museum. *301 Jackson St (44870). Phone 419/626-6111. www.merrygoroundmuseum.org.* Housed in a circular rotunda, this museum brings all the childhood charms of merry-go-rounds together in one place. The actual merry-go-round housed inside the museum was built by renowned designer Allan Herschel more than 60 years ago, and, since it came with no figurines attached to it, the museum attached some of its own collection to the motor. Tours of the museum are given daily and are free with admission to the building, as are rides on the carousel itself. (Memorial Day-Labor Day, Mon-Sat 11 am-5 pm, Sun noon-5 pm; Jan-Feb, weekends only; other months, Wed-Sun only; closed holidays) **$**

MV City of Sandusky. *226 W Shorline Dr. Phone 419/627-0198; toll-free 800/426-6286.* Three hundred-passenger excursion boat from Downtown. (Memorial Day-Labor Day, daily; Sept, weekends)

MV Pelee Islander. *Foot of Jackson St. Phone 519/724-2115.* (Reservations necessary for autos) Ferry transportation in summer to Leamington and Kingsville, Ontario (for Border Crossing Regulations, see MAKING THE MOST OF YOUR TRIP). (Mid-June-Labor Day)

Old Woman Creek National Estuarine Research Reserve. *2514 Cleveland Rd E, Huron (44839). Approximately 12 miles E on Hwy 6 (2 miles E of Huron). Phone 419/433-4601.* Old Woman Creek is protected as a National Estuarine Research Reserve and State Nature Preserve. It is one of Ohio's best remaining examples of a natural estuary and serves as a field laboratory for the study of estuarine ecology. Ohio Center for Coastal Wetlands Studies has a visitors center and reference library. Trails (daily). Visitors center (Apr-Dec, Wed-Sun afternoons; rest of year, Mon-Fri; closed holidays). **FREE**

Special Events

Erie County Fair. *Fairgrounds, 3110 Columbus Ave, Sandusky (44870). Phone 419/626-1020.* Livestock show, rides, entertainment. Early Aug.

Tour of homes. *Sandusky. Phone 419/627-0640.* Tour historic homes decorated for the holidays. Early Dec.

Limited-Service Hotels

★ ★ **BEST WESTERN CEDAR POINT AREA.** *1530 Cleveland Rd, Sandusky (44870). Phone 419/625-9234; fax 419/625-9971. www.bestwestern.com.* 106 rooms, 2 story. Check-out 11 am. Restaurant. Pool. **$**
⌕

★ **FAIRFIELD INN.** *6220 Milan Rd, Sandusky (44870). Phone 419/621-9500; fax 419/621-9500. www.fairfieldinn.com.* 63 rooms, 2 story. Complimentary continental breakfast. Indoor pool. **$**
⌕

★ ★ **HOLIDAY INN.** *5513 Milan Rd, Sandusky (44870). Phone 419/626-6671; fax 419/626-9780.* 175 rooms, 2 story. Check-out 11 am. Restaurant, bar. Fitness room. Indoor pool, outdoor pool. Miniature golf. **$**
⌕ ⌕

★ ★ **RADISSON HARBOUR INN AT CEDAR POINT.** *2001 Cleveland Rd, Sandusky (44870). Phone 419/627-2500; toll-free 800/333-3333; fax 419/627-0745. www.radisson.com.* With each room offering a stunning view overlooking the harbor, this hotel is a full-service resort. Choose from a variety of recreational and fitness services provided to put one's mind at ease and body in play. 237 rooms, 4 story. Check-out noon. Restaurant, bar. Children's activity center. Fitness room. Indoor pool, whirlpool. Airport transportation available. Business center. **$**
⌖ ⌕ ⌕ ⌕

★ ★ **RIVERS EDGE INN.** *132 N Main St, Huron (44839). Phone 419/433-8000; toll-free 800/947-3400; fax 419/433-8552.* 65 rooms, 3 story. Complimentary continental breakfast. Check-out 11 am. Restaurant, bar. Fitness room. Indoor pool, whirlpool. **$**
⌕ ⌕

Restaurant

★ ★ **BAY HARBOR INN.** *1 Causeway Dr, Sandusky (44870). Phone 419/625-6373; fax 419/627-2130.* Dinner. Closed Sun (Oct-Apr); holidays. Bar. Children's menu. **$$**

Serpent Mound State Memorial (E-2)

3850 State Rte 73, Columbus (45660). 4 miles NW of Locust Grove on State Rte 73. Phone 937/587-2796.

The largest and most remarkable serpent effigy earthworks in North America. Built between 800 BC-AD 100 of stone and yellow clay, it curls like an enormous snake for 1,335 feet. An oval earthwall represents the serpent's open mouth. In the 61-acre area are an observation tower, a scenic gorge, a museum, and picnicking facilities. Park (all year, daily 10 am-5 pm); museum (Apr-Oct, daily; Nov-Mar, hours vary, phone ahead). **$$**

Sidney (C-1)

See also Bellefontaine, Piqua, Wapakoneta

Population 18,710
Elevation 956 ft
Area Code 937
Zip 45365
Information Sidney-Shelby County Chamber of Commerce, 100 S Main, Suite 201; phone 937/492-9122
Web site www.accesswestohio.com

Special Event

Country Concert at Hickory Hill Lakes. *Sidney. Phone 937/295-3000.* Mid-July.

Limited-Service Hotel

★ ★ **HOLIDAY INN.** *400 Folkerth Ave, Sidney (45365). Phone 937/492-1131; fax 937/498-4655. www. holiday-inn.com.* 134 rooms, 2 story. Pets accepted, some restrictions; fee. Check-out noon. Restaurant, bar. Fitness room. Pool. **$**

Springfield (C-2)

See also Bellefontaine, Columbus, Dayton, Vandalia

Founded 1801
Population 70,487
Elevation 980 ft
Area Code 937
Information Convention and Visitors Bureau, 333 N Limestone St, Suite 201, 45503; phone 937/325-7621
Web site www.springfieldnet.com

Indian Scout Simon Kenton, an early settler, set up a gristmill and sawmill on the present site of the Navistar International plant. His wife gave the village its name. When the National Pike came in 1839, Springfield came to be known as the "town at the end of the National Pike."

Agricultural machinery gave Springfield its next boost. A farm journal, *Farm and Fireside*, published in the 1880s by P. J. Mast, a cultivator-manufacturer, was the start of the Crowell-Collier Publishing Company. The 4-H movement started here in 1902 by A. B. Graham, and hybrid corn grown by George H. Shull had its beginning in Springfield. A center for some 200 diversified industries, Springfield is in the rich agricultural valley of west central Ohio.

What to See and Do

Antioch College. *795 Livermore St, Yellow Springs (45387). 9 1/2 miles S on Hwy 68, E Center College St. Phone 937/767-7331. www.antioch-college.edu.* (1852) (800 students) Liberal arts and sciences. Horace Mann, first president, aimed to establish a school free of sectarianism. Known for the cooperative educational plan under which students alternate periods of study and work.

Buck Creek State Park. *1901 Buck Creek Ln (45502). 4 miles NE on Hwy 4; exit 62 off Hwy 70. Phone 937/322-5284.* A 4,030-acre park with swimming (lifeguard), bathhouse (Memorial Day-Labor Day), fishing, boating (launch, ramp); hiking, snowmobile trails; picnicking, concession; camping, cabins. (Daily) **FREE** On grounds is

> **David Crabill House.** *818 N Fountain Ave, Springfield. Phone 937/399-1245 for schedule.* (1826) Built by Clark County pioneer David Crabill; restored. Period rooms; log barn; smokehouse. Maintained by Clark County Historical Society. (Tues-Fri) **$**

John Bryan State Park. *3790 Hwy 370 (45387). 9 1/2 miles S of I-70 on Hwy 68, then 3 miles SE via Hwy 343, 370, near Yellow Springs. Phone 937/767-1274.* A 750-acre park with fishing; hiking; picnic area; camping. (Daily) **FREE**

Pennsylvania House. *1311 W Main St. Phone 937/322-7668.* (1824) Built as tavern and stagecoach stop on National Pike; period furnishings, pioneer artifacts; button, quilt, and doll collections. (First Sun afternoon of each month; also by appointment; closed Easter; also late Dec-Feb) **$$**

Springfield Museum of Art. *107 Cliff Park Rd. Phone 937/325-4673.* Loaned exhibits change monthly; permanent collection includes 19th- and 20th-century

American and French art; fine arts school; library; docent tours. (Tues-Sun; closed holidays; also week of Dec 25) **FREE**

Wittenberg University. *200 W Ward St (45504). Phone toll-free 800/677-7558. www.wittenberg.edu.* (1845) (2,000 students) Liberal arts and sciences. Private school affiliated with the Evangelical Lutheran Church in America.

Special Events

Clark County Fair. *Fairgrounds, 4401 S Charleston Pike, Springfield (45502). Phone 937/325-7621.* Horse shows, rodeos, tractor pulls. Mid-July.

Fair at New Boston. *George Rogers Clark Park (Hwy 4), 930 S Tecumseh Rd, Springfield (45506). W of Springfield. Phone 937/882-6000.* Recreation of a 1790-1810 trade fair; period demonstrations, food, and displays. Late Aug.

Springfield Arts Festival. *Veterans Memorial Park amphitheater, area auditoriums, Cliff Pk Rd and N Plum St, Springfield (45503). Phone 937/324-2712.* Six-week series of free performances; music, dance, visual arts, drama. June-mid-July.

Limited-Service Hotel

★ ★ **SPRINGFIELD INN.** *100 S Fountain Ave, Springfield (45502). Phone 937/322-3600; toll-free 800/359-5672; fax 937/322-0462.* Located across the street from the Marketplace shops, this hotel offers guests personal and attentive service along with well-appointed guest rooms to ensure a relaxing stay. 124 rooms, 6 story. Check-out noon. Restaurant, bar. **$**

Restaurants

★ ★ **CASEY'S.** *2205 Park Rd, Springfield (45504). Phone 937/322-0397; fax 937/322-0177.* American menu. Dinner. Closed Sun; holidays. Bar. **$$**

★ ★ **KLOSTERMAN'S DERR ROAD INN.** *4343 Derr Rd, Springfield (45503). Phone 937/399-0822.* American menu. Lunch, dinner. Closed holidays. Bar. Children's menu. **$$**

St. Clairsville (C-5)

See also Steubenville

Population 5,162
Elevation 1,284 ft
Area Code 740
Zip 43950
Information St. Clairsville Area Chamber of Commerce, 116 W Main St; phone 740/695-9623
Web site www.stclairsville.com

This charming tree-shaded town has been the seat of Belmont County since 1804.

Special Event

Jamboree in the Hills. *St. Clairsville. 4 miles W off I-70 exit 208 or 213. Phone toll-free 800/624-5456.* A four-day country music festival featuring more than 30 hours of music; top country stars. Camping available. Third weekend in July.

Limited-Service Hotel

★ **DAYS INN.** *52601 Holiday Dr, Saint Clairsville (43950). Phone 740/695-0100; toll-free 800/551-0106; fax 740/695-4135. www.daysinn.com.* 137 rooms, 2 story. Complimentary continental breakfast. Check-in 3 pm, check-out 11 am. Outdoor pool. **$**

Steubenville (C-5)

See also East Liverpool, St. Clairsville

Settled 1797
Population 22,125
Elevation 715 ft
Area Code 740
Zip 43952
Information Jefferson County Chamber of Commerce, 630 Market St, PO Box 278; phone 740/282-6226
Web site www.jeffersoncountychamber.com

Although its early industries were pottery, coal, woolen cloth, glass, and shipbuilding, the rolling mills of Wheeling-Pittsburgh Steel and Weirton Steel started Steubenville's economic growth.

The town's location was selected by the government as a fort in 1786. Fort Steuben (destroyed by fire in 1790) and the town were named for the Prussian Baron Frederick William von Steuben, who aided the colonies in the Revolutionary War. It is the seat of Jefferson County.

What to See and Do

Creegan Company. *510 Washington St. Phone 740/283-3708.* Country's largest designer and manufacturer of animations, costume characters, and décor offers guided tours (approximately one hour) through its three-story factory and showroom. (Daily) **$**

Jefferson County Courthouse. *301 Market St. Phone 740/283-4111.* Contains first county deed record, signed by George Washington, and portraits of Steubenville personalities. Statue of Edwin Stanton, Lincoln's secretary of war, is on the lawn. (Mon-Fri; closed holidays) **FREE**

Jefferson County Historical Association Museum and Genealogical Library. *426 Franklin Ave. Phone 740/283-1133.* Tudor-style mansion with collection of historic memorabilia and genealogical materials; guided tours. (Mid-Apr-Dec, Tues-Sat; closed holidays) **$**

Union Cemetery. *1720 W Sunset Blvd. Phone 740/283-3384.* Contains many Civil War graves, including the "fighting McCook" plot, where members of a family that sent 13 men to fight in the Union Army are buried. (Daily)

Limited-Service Hotel

★ ★ **HOLIDAY INN.** *1401 University Blvd, Steubenville (43952). Phone 740/282-0901; fax 740/282-9540. www.holiday-inn.com.* 120 rooms, 2 story. Check-out noon. Restaurant, bar. Pool. **$**

Strongsville (A-4)

See also Cleveland, Elyria, Oberlin

Population 35,308
Elevation 932 ft
Area Code 440
Zip 44136
Information Chamber of Commerce, 18829 Royalton Rd; phone 440/238-3366
Web site www.strongsvillecofc.com

First settled in 1816, Strongsville is the largest suburban community in Cuyahoga County.

What to See and Do

Gardenview Horticultural Park. *16711 Pearl Rd (44136). On Hwy 42, 1 1/2 miles S of Hwy 82. Phone 440/238-6653.* English-style cottage gardens devoted to collecting uncommon and unusual plants. Sixteen acres, including 6 acres of gardens with seasonal plantings and a 10-acre arboretum; 2,000 flowering crab apples bloom first two weeks in May. (Early Apr-mid-Oct, Sat-Sun afternoons) **$**

Tiffin (B-2)

See also Bellevue, Findlay, Fremont

Founded 1817
Population 18,604
Elevation 758 ft
Area Code 419
Zip 44883
Information Seneca County Convention and Visitors Bureau, 114 S Washington; phone 419/447-5866 or toll-free 888/736-3221
Web site www.senecacounty.com/visitor

Tiffin is a quiet, tree-shaded town on the Sandusky River; it has diversified industries that include pottery, glassware, electric motor, heavy machinery, and conveyor manufacturing.

What to See and Do

Crystal Traditions. *145 Madison St. Phone 419/448-4286.* Glassblowing and glass engraving. Free factory tours. Showroom (Mon-Sat; closed holidays).

Glass Heritage Gallery. *109 N Main St, Fostoria. 14 miles W via Hwy 18. Phone 419/435-5077.* Museum houses a collection of glass made in Fostoria plants from 1887 to 1920; examples include lamps, crystal bowls, mosaic art glass, novelty glass. (Tues-Sat; closed holidays) **FREE**

King's Glass Engraving. *181 S Washington St. Phone 419/447-0232.* Demonstrations. (Mon-Sat; closed holidays) **FREE**

Seneca County Museum. *28 Clay St. Phone 419/447-5955.* Historic house (circa 1853) museum contains extensive collection of Tiffin glass; drawing room furnished with early Victorian pieces; porcelain collection; research library; kitchen with original built-in stove. Second floor has music room with a pianola and a 200-year-old harp and bedrooms with a rope bed and trundle bed. The third floor has collection of Native American artifacts, toy and doll collection. Tours (June-Aug, Tues-Thurs, Sun afternoons; rest of year, Wed and Sun afternoons; also by appointment). **DONATION**

Special Events

Glass Heritage Festival. *Fostoria. Phone 419/435-0486.* Glass festival features glass shows, tours, entertainment, arts and crafts. Third weekend in July.

Tiffin-Seneca Heritage Festival. *Tiffin. Phone 419/447-5866.* Entertainment, crafts, living history village, ethnic foods, parade. Third weekend in Sept.

Toledo (A-2)

See also Bowling Green, Monroe, Port Clinton, Wauseon

Settled 1817
Population 332,943
Elevation 587 ft
Area Code 419
Information Greater Toledo Convention and Visitors Bureau, 401 Jefferson, 43604; phone 419/321-6404 or toll-free 800/243-4667
Web site www.toledocvb.com

The French first explored the Toledo area, situated at the mouth of the Maumee River on Lake Erie, in 1615. Probably named after Toledo, Spain, the present city began as a group of small villages along the river. During 1835-1836, it was claimed by both Michigan and Ohio in the Toledo War, which resulted in Toledo becoming part of Ohio and the Northern Peninsula going to Michigan.

Toledo's large, excellent natural harbor makes it an important port. Numerous railroads move coal and ore to the South, East, and North; grain from the Southwest; steel from Cleveland and Pittsburgh; and automobile parts and accessories to and from Detroit.

Edward Libbey introduced the glass industry to Toledo in 1888, with high-grade crystal and lamp globes. Michael Owens, a glassblower, joined him and invented a machine that turned molten glass into bottles by the thousands. Today, Owens-Illinois, Inc.; Libbey-Owens-Ford Company; Owens-Corning Fiberglas Corporation; and Johns-Manville Fiber Glass, Inc., manufacture a variety of glass products. Metropolitan Toledo has more than 1,000 manufacturing plants producing Jeeps, spark plugs, chemicals, and other products.

What to See and Do

COSI Toledo. *1 Discovery Way. Corner of Summit and Adams sts. Phone 419/244-2674. www.cositoledo.org.* Firsthand science learning is available here through hands-on experiments, demonstrations, and eight Exhibition Worlds. These include Kidspace, Babyspace, and an outdoors Science Park. Restaurant. (Mon-Sat, Sun afternoons; closed holidays) **$$**

Crane Creek State Park. *13531 Rte 2 W, Oak Harbor (43449). 18 miles E off Rte 2, SE of Bono. Phone 419/898-2495.* A 79-acre park with swimming (lifeguard; Memorial Day-Labor Day), fishing, ice fishing; hiking; picnicking; trail for bird-watching. (Daily) **FREE**

Detwiler/Bay View Park. *4001 N Summit St. At Manhattan Blvd.* Pool (early May-Sept), boating (launch; fee), marina; picnicking, concessions; playgrounds on 219 acres; two golf courses (fee), tennis. Lighted ball field; view of port. (Daily) **FREE**

Fort Meigs State Memorial. *2900 W River Rd, Perrysburg. Take I-475 to exit 2, turn N onto Hwy 65. Phone 419/874-4121.* Reconstruction of fort built under supervision of William Henry Harrison in 1813; used during War of 1812. Blockhouses with exhibits; demonstrations of military life. (Memorial Day-Labor Day, Wed-Sun; after Labor Day-Oct, weekend, holidays) Picnicking in area. **$**

Maumee Bay State Park. *1400 State Park Rd, Oregon (43618). 8 miles E on Rte 2, then N on Curtice Rd. Phone 419/836-7758 (park administration); toll-free 800/282-7275 (lodge and cabin reservations).* The wet woods and marshes of this 1,860-acre shoreline park are havens to wildlife and are good for bird-watching. Beaches, fishing, boat rentals; hiking; 18-hole golf; camping (tent rentals available), 24 cabins, lodge. Amphitheater. Nature center. (Daily) **FREE**

Ottawa Park. *4100 W Central Ave (43606). Bancroft at Parkside St.* Picnicking on 305 acres, concessions; playgrounds; 18-hole golf course (fee), tennis; jogging and nature trails, cross-country ski trails (fee). Nature center; artificial skating rink (fee).

Port of Toledo. *3319 St. Lawrence Dr (43605). Lower 7 miles of Maumee River. Phone 419/243-8251.* In total tonnage, this is one of the 25 largest ports in the United States and one of the world's largest shippers of soft coal and grain. More than 1,000 vessels call at the port each year.

SS *Willis B. Boyer* Museum Ship. *26 Main St. Moored across from Downtown, on the E side of the Maumee River, in International Park. Phone 419/936-3070.* This 600-foot freighter, launched in 1911, has been authentically restored and houses memoribilia, photos, and nautical artifacts. Tours (45 minutes-one hour). (May-Sept, daily; rest of year, Tues-Sat)

Toledo Botanical Garden. *5403 Elmer Dr. 6 miles W near I-475 W Central exit. Phone 419/936-2986. www.toledogarden.org.* Seasonal floral displays; herb, rhododendron, and azalea gardens, perennial garden, rose garden, fragrance garden for the visually and physically impaired. Pioneer Homestead (1837); art galleries, glassblowing studios. Gift shops. Special musical and crafts programs throughout year. Arts festival (fee). (Daily) (See SPECIAL EVENTS) **FREE**

The Toledo Museum of Art. *2445 Monroe St. At Scottwood, one block off I-75. Phone 419/255-8000. www.toledomuseum.com.* Considered to be one of the finest art museums in the country; collections range from ancient Egypt, Greece, and Rome through the Middle Ages and the Renaissance to European and American arts of the present; includes glass collections, paintings, sculptures, decorative and graphic arts; Egyptian mummy, medieval cloister, French château room, African sculpture, Asian art, and Southeast Asian and Native American art. Art reference library; café; museum store. (Tues-Sun; closed holidays) **FREE**

The Toledo Symphony. *1838 Parkwood Ave, #310 (43624). Phone 419/246-8000; toll-free 800/348-1253. www.toledosymphony.com.* Presents classical, pops, casual, chamber, and all-Mozart concerts. Performances at different locations. (Mid-Sept-May) Facilities for hearing and visually impaired.

The Toledo Zoo. *2700 Broadway. 3 miles S of Downtown on Hwy 25. Phone 419/385-5721. www.toledozoo.org.* On exhibit are nearly 2,000 specimens of 400 species. On its 30 acres are fresh and saltwater aquariums, large mammal collection, reptiles, birds, a Children's Zoo, botanical gardens and greenhouse, Museum of Science and the Diversity of Life hands-on exhibit; Hippoquarium offers filtered underwater viewing of hippopotamus. (Daily; closed Jan 1, Thanksgiving, Dec 25) **$$**

University of Toledo. *2801 W Bancroft St (43606). W Bancroft St, 4 miles W. Phone 419/530-4636. www.utoledo.edu.* (1872) (21,000 students) The 250-acre main campus has eight colleges, continuing education division, graduate school; several other campuses; 47-acre arboretum by Sylvania Avenue and Corey Road; Seagate Centre campus downtown at Jefferson Avenue. Lake Erie Center is an environmental research facility. Campus tours. Planetarium presents several shows and educational programs (Oct-June). Savage Hall has frequent concerts and sporting events. Music and theater departments have concerts and shows. Obtain free parking permit at transportation center.

Wolcott Museum Complex. *1031 River Rd, Maumee. SW via I-75, I-475 Anthony Wayne Trail exit. Phone 419/893-9602.* Museum complex includes early 19-century home, log house, Greek Revival village house, saltbox farmhouse, and depot furnished with period artifacts. (Apr-Dec, Wed-Sun; closed holidays) **$$**

Special Events

Crosby Festival of the Arts. *Toledo Botanical Garden, 5403 Elmer Dr, Toledo (43615). Phone 419/936-2986.* Fine arts and crafts, music, dance, and drama. Last full weekend in June.

Horse racing. Toledo Raceway Park. *5700 Telegraph Rd, Toledo. 5 miles N on Hwy 24 or 2 miles W of I-75, exit Alexis Rd. Phone 419/476-7751.* Harness racing. Mar-late Nov, Wed, Fri-Sun.

Northwest Ohio Rib-Off. *Toledo. Phone 419/321-6404. www.uhs-toledo.org/rib-off/ribinfo.htm.* Centered around an eating competition where the winner is crowned Biggest Pig, the Northwest Ohio Rib-Off has spent more than 20 years making some of the best baby back ribs in the state. Held at beautiful Promenade

Park near the banks of Lake Erie, the festival donates all its proceeds to United Health Services to help families beset by disabilities. Early Aug.

Limited-Service Hotels

★ ★ **CLARION HOTEL.** *3536 Secor Rd, Toledo (43606). Phone 419/535-7070; fax 419/536-4836. www. clarionhotel.com.* 305 rooms, 3 story. Check-out noon. Restaurant, bar. Fitness room. Indoor pool, whirlpool. Business center. Landscaped enclosed courtyard. **$**

★ ★ **COURTYARD BY MARRIOTT.** *1435 E Mall Dr, Holland (43528). Phone 419/866-1001; fax 419/866-9869. www.marriott.com.* 149 rooms, 3 story. Check-out noon. Restaurant, bar. Fitness room. Indoor pool, whirlpool. Airport transportation available. **$**

★ **DAYS INN.** *150 Dussel Dr, Maumee (43537). Phone 419/893-9960; toll-free 800/431-2574; fax 419/893-9559. www.daysinn.com.* 120 rooms, 2 story. Pets accepted, some restrictions; fee. Complimentary continental breakfast. Check-out noon. Pool. **$**

★ ★ **HOLIDAY INN.** *2340 S Reynolds Rd, Toledo (43614). Phone 419/865-1361; fax 419/865-6177. www. holiday-inn.com.* 218 rooms, 11 story. Check-out noon. Restaurant, bar. Fitness room. Indoor pool. Airport transportation available. **$**

Full-Service Hotels

★ ★ ★ **HILTON TOLEDO.** *3100 Glendale Ave, Toledo (43614). Phone 419/381-6800; fax 419/389-9716. www.hilton.com.* Situated on the campus of the Medical College of Ohio, this hotel offers easy access to nearby attractions. A fitness center, tennis courts, a pool, and a jogging track are available to guests. 213 rooms, 6 story. Check-out noon. Restaurant, bar. Fitness room. Indoor pool, whirlpool. Tennis. Airport transportation available. **$**

★ ★ ★ **WYNDHAM TOLEDO HOTEL.** *2 Summit St, Toledo (43604). Phone 419/241-1411; fax 419/241-8161. www.wyndham.com.* 241 rooms, 14 story. Check-out noon. Restaurant, bar. Fitness room. Indoor pool, whirlpool. Business center. On river. **$**

Restaurants

★ ★ ★ **FIFI'S.** *1423 Bernath Pkwy, Toledo (43615). Phone 419/866-6777. www.fifisrestaurant .com.* Fifi's cuisine offers a wide array of regional and traditional dishes with a creative flair. House specialties not to miss are the soups, which range from traditional vichyssoise to gourmet fruit soups; a refreshing, delicious way to begin your meal. French menu. Dinner. Closed Sun; holidays. Bar. **$$$**

★ ★ **MANCY'S.** *953 Phillips Ave, Toledo (43612). Phone 419/476-4154. www.mancys.com.* Lunch, dinner. Closed Sun; holidays. Bar. Children's menu. **$$**

★ **TONY PACKO'S CAFE.** *1902 Front St, Toledo (43605). Phone 419/691-6054; fax 419/691-6054. www. tonypackos.com.* Hungarian menu. Lunch, dinner. Closed holidays. Bar. Children's menu. **$$**

Van Wert (B-1)

See also Celina, Lima, Wapakoneta

Founded 1835
Population 10,891
Elevation 780 ft
Area Code 419
Zip 45891
Information Van Wert County Chamber of Commerce, 118 W Main St; phone 419/238-4390
Web site www.vanwert.com

What to See and Do

Van Wert County Historical Society Museum. *602 N Washington St. At 3rd St. Phone 419/238-5297.* Restored Victorian mansion (1890) houses farm room, fabric room, children's room; early town artifacts; research center. Annex built in 1985 houses war memorabilia; country store, cobbler's shop, and barbershop. One-room school building and caboose also on grounds. (Sun afternoons; also by appointment; closed holidays; also last week in Dec) **FREE**

Special Events

Peony Festival & Parade. *Van Wert. Downtown. Phone 419/238-4390.* First weekend in June.

Van Wert County Fair. *Fairgrounds, 1055 S Washington St, Van Wert (45891). Fox Rd off S Washington St. Phone 419/238-9270.* Begins Wed before Labor Day.

Vandalia (C-1)

See also Dayton, Piqua, Springfield

Settled 1838
Population 13,882
Elevation 994 ft
Area Code 937
Zip 45377
Information Chamber of Commerce, 76 Fordway Dr, PO Box 224; phone 937/898-5351
Web site www.vandaliabutlerchamber.com

What to See and Do

Trapshooting Hall of Fame and Museum. *601 W National Rd. Phone 937/898-1945.* Exhibits depict highlights of this sport. (Mon-Fri; closed holidays) **FREE**

Special Events

Air Show Parade. *Vandalia. Phone 937/898-5901.* Kick-off event for international air show. Involves over 150 parade units. Third Fri in July.

Grand American World Trapshooting Championship of the Amateur Trapshooting Association of America. *Trapshooting Hall of Fame and Museum (see). Vandalia. Phone 937/898-4638.* Grand American Shoot; membership and shooting fee. Ten days in mid-Aug.

US Air & Trade Show. *Dayton International Airport, 3600 Terminal Rd, Vandalia (45377). Phone 937/898-5901.* Features approximately 100 outdoor exhibits; flight teams. Late July.

Limited-Service Hotel

★ **SUPER 8.** *550 E National Rd, Vandalia (45377). Phone 937/898-7636; fax 937/898-0630. www.super8.com.* 94 rooms, 3 story. Check-out noon. Pool. **$**
🔲 🛏

Vermilion (A-3)

See also Elyria, Lorain, Milan, Oberlin, Sandusky

Settled 1808
Population 11,127
Elevation 600 ft
Area Code 440
Zip 44089
Information Chamber of Commerce, 5495 Liberty Ave; phone 440/967-4477
Web site www.vermilionohio.com

What to See and Do

Inland Seas Maritime Museum. *480 Main St (Hwy 6). On lakeshore. Phone 440/967-3467.* Maritime museum containing Great Lakes ship models, paintings, photographs, artifacts. Audiovisual displays. (Daily; closed Dec 25) **$$**

Special Events

Festival of the Fish. *Vermilion. Phone 440/967-4477.* Entertainment, exhibits, sports events, parade, contests, crazy craft race, lighted boat parade. Father's Day weekend.

Woolly Bear Festival. *Victory Park, Vermilion (44089). Phone 440/967-4477.* Races, children's games, crafts, entertainment. Mid-Oct.

Restaurant

★ ★ ★ **CHEZ FRANCOIS.** *555 Main St, Vermilion (44089). Phone 440/967-0630. www.chezfrancois.com.* Located in a small, Lake Erie harbor town, this French restaurant has a formal dining room and a more casual, outdoor dining area with a view of the Vermilion River. French menu. Dinner. Closed Mon; also Jan-mid-Mar. Jacket required. Outdoor seating. **$$$**
🔲

Wapakoneta (B-1)

See also Bellefontaine, Celina, Lima, Sidney, Van Wert

Population 9,214
Elevation 895 ft
Area Code 419
Zip 45895
Information Wapakoneta Chamber of Commerce, 16 E Auglaize St, PO Box 208; phone 419/738-2911
Web site www.wapakoneta.com

What to See and Do

Neil Armstrong Air and Space Museum. *500 S Apollo Dr. Phone 419/738-8811.* A few aircraft, from early planes to spacecraft, showing aerospace accomplishments; audiovisual presentation, other exhibits. (Daily) **$$**

Limited-Service Hotel

★ ★ **BEST WESTERN WAPAKONETA.** *1510 Saturn Dr, Wapakoneta (45895). Phone 419/738-8181; toll-free 877/738-8181; fax 419/738-6478. www. bestwestern.com/wapakoneta.* 94 rooms, 4 story. Pets accepted; fee. Complimentary continental breakfast. Check-out noon. Restaurant, bar. Fitness room. Pool. Neil Armstrong Museum (see) is adjacent. **$**

Warren (B-5)

See also Aurora, Kent, Youngstown

Founded 1799
Population 50,793
Elevation 893 ft
Area Code 330
Information Youngstown/Warren Regional Chamber, 160 E Market, Suite 225, 44481; phone 330/393-2565
Web site www.regionalchamber.com

In 1800, Warren became the seat of the Western Reserve and then the seat of newly formed Trumbull County. At one of its stagecoach inns, the Austin House, Stephen Collins Foster is said to have begun writing "Jeannie with the Light Brown Hair," and, according to local history, while walking along the Mahoning River, he found the inspiration for "My Old Kentucky Home."

What to See and Do

John Stark Edwards House. *303 Monroe St NW. Phone 330/394-4653.* (1807) Oldest house in the Western Reserve, now maintained by Trumbull County Historical Society. (Sun afternoons limited hours; closed holidays) Children must be accompanied by adult. **$**

Mosquito Lake State Park. *1439 Hwy 305 (44410). 7 miles NE on Hwy 5, then 1 mile W on Hwy 305 to park entrance. Phone 330/637-2856.* An 11,811-acre park with 7,850-acre lake and 40 miles of lakeshore. Swimming, fishing, boating (launch, rentals); hunting; hiking, bridle trails, snowmobiling, picnicking; camping (showers; 218 sites with electric hookup). (Daily) **FREE**

Limited-Service Hotel

★ **COMFORT INN.** *136 N Park Ave, Warren (44483). Phone 330/393-1200; fax 330/399-2875.* Restored brick hotel (1887). 55 rooms, 4 story. Pets accepted; fee. Check-out noon. Restaurant, bar. Airport transportation available. **$**

Full-Service Resort

★ ★ ★ **AVALON INN AND RESORT.** *9519 E Market St, Warren (44484). Phone 330/856-1900; toll-free 800/828-2566; fax 330/856-2248. www.avaloninn .com.* Guests will find many of the rooms here dressed in a lovely colonial style, with appointments in dark wood and brass abounding. The resort offers 36 holes of golf, an olympic-sized pool, and modern tennis, racquetball, and volleyball courts. 144 rooms, 2 story. Check-out noon. Restaurant, bar. Fitness room. Indoor pool, whirlpool. Golf, 36 holes. Tennis. **$**

Restaurant

★ ★ **ABRUZZI'S CAFE 422.** *4422 SE Youngstown Rd, Warren (44484). Phone 330/369-2422; fax 330/ 369-6431. www.cafe422.com.* Italian menu. Lunch, dinner. Closed Dec 25. Bar. Children's menu. **$$**

Wauseon (A-1)

See also Bowling Green, Toledo

Population 6,322
Elevation 757 ft
Area Code 419
Zip 43567
Information Wauseon Chamber of Commerce, 115 N Fulton St, PO Box 217; phone 419/335-9966
Web site www.wauseonchamber.com

What to See and Do

Sauder Village. *22799 State Rte 2, Archbold (43502). 9 miles W via Rte 2, near Archbold.* Phone 419/446-2541. *www.saudervillage.com.* Three areas: farmstead has furnished a turn-of-the-century farmhouse with summer kitchen and barnyard, pioneer village has craft demonstrations, museum building has antique implements and household items; costumed guides. Restaurant, lodging. Campground. (Late Apr-Oct, daily) **$$$**

Limited-Service Hotel

★ ★ **BEST WESTERN DEL MAR.** *8319 Hwy 108, Wauseon (43567).* Phone 419/335-1565; toll-free 800/647-2260; fax 419/335-1828. *www.bestwestern.com.* 48 rooms. Pets accepted; fee. Complimentary continental breakfast. Check-out 11 am. Pool. **$**

Wilmington (D-2)

See also Dayton, Lebanon, Mason

Population 11,199
Elevation 1,022 ft
Area Code 937
Zip 45177
Information Wilmington-Clinton County Chamber of Commerce, 40 N South St; phone 937/382-2737
Web site www.wccchamber.com

What to See and Do

Caesar Creek State Park. *8570 Hwy 73 E, Waynesville (45068). 11 miles NW on Hwy 73.* Phone 937/897-3055. A 10,771-acre park. Crystal blue lake waters have smallmouth and largemouth bass, crappie, cat-fish, bluegill, and walleye. Swimming, fishing, boating (ramps); hiking, bridle trails; picnic areas. Campground has 287 sites (35 open in winter), 30-site horsemen's camp. Nature preserve, visitor center, and complex near dam. A focal point of the park is Pioneer Village, with many restored examples of early log architecture. (Daily) **FREE**

Cowan Lake State Park. *729 Beechwood Rd (45177). 6 miles S via Hwy 68, then W on Hwy 350.* Phone 937/289-2105. A 1,775-acre park with swimming, fishing, boating (launch, rentals) on 700-acre lake; hiking; picnicking, concession; camping, cabins. (Daily) **FREE**

Little Miami Scenic State Park. *8570 Hwy 73 E, Waynesville (45068). 15 miles NW on Hwy 73.* Phone 937/897-3055. This 452-acre park offers 45 miles of hiking and bridle trails, 22 miles of paved bicycle trails. Canoeing, access points at Corwin, Morrow, and Loveland. (Daily) **FREE**

Rombach Place–Museum of Clinton County Historical Society. *149 E Locust St (45177).* Phone 937/382-4684. Home of General James W. Denver, for whom Denver, Colorado, was named. Antique furniture; Quaker clothing; tools, implements, and kitchenware of pioneer days. Bronze animal sculptures and paintings by Eli Harvey, Quaker artist from Ohio. Photographs of Native American chieftains made in early 1900s by Karl Moon, a native of Wilmington. (Mar-Dec, Wed-Fri afternoons; closed holidays)

Wilmington College. *Fife Ave. E on Hwy 22.* Phone 937/382-6661; toll-free 800/341-9318. *www.wilmington.edu.* (1870) (1,000 students) Liberal arts school. On campus is the Simon Goodman Memorial Carillon. Campus tours.

Special Event

Banana Split Festival. *Wilmington.* Phone 937/382-1965. Commemorates the invention of the banana split. Second weekend in June.

Limited-Service Hotels

★ **AMERIHOST INN.** *201 Carrie Dr, Wilmington (45177).* Phone 937/383-3950; fax 937/383-1693. *www.amerihostinn.com.* 61 rooms, 2 story. Complimentary continental breakfast. Check-out noon. Fitness room. Indoor pool, whirlpool. **$**

★ **HOLIDAY INN EXPRESS.** *155 Holiday Dr, Wilmington (45177). Phone 937/382-5858; fax 937/ 382-0457. www.holiday-inn.com.* 61 rooms, 3 story. Pets accepted, some restrictions; fee. Complimentary continental breakfast. Check-out noon. Fitness room. Indoor pool, whirlpool. **$**

🚶 🐾 🏊

★ **WILMINGTON INN.** *909 Fife Ave, Wilmington (45177). Phone 937/382-6000; toll-free 877/363-3614; fax 937/382-6655. www.wilmingtoninn.com.* 51 rooms, 2 story. Complimentary continental breakfast. Check-out 11 am. **$**

Restaurant

★ **DAMON'S.** *1045 Eastside Dr, Wilmington (45177). Phone 937/383-1400; fax 937/383-1488. www. damons.com.* American menu. Lunch, dinner. Closed Thanksgiving, Dec 25. Bar. Children's menu. **$**

Wilmot

Restaurant

★ **ALPINE ALPA.** *1504 Hwy 62, Wilmot (44689). Phone 330/359-5454. www.alpine-alpa.com.* Beautiful Swiss chalet on the Amish Country Byway. Serves traditional specialties. Swiss menu. Lunch, dinner. **$**

Wooster (B-4)

See also Akron, Canton, Mansfield, Massillon

Settled 1807
Population 22,191
Elevation 897 ft
Area Code 330
Zip 44691
Information Wayne County Convention and Visitor Bureau, 428 W Liberty St; phone 330/264-1800 or toll-free 800/362-6474
Web site www.wooster-wayne.com/wccvb

Wooster claims to have had one of the first Christmas trees in America, introduced in 1847 by August Imgard, a young German immigrant. Disappointed with American Christmas, he cut down and decorated

a spruce tree, which so pleased his neighbors that the custom spread throughout Ohio and the nation.

The town is in very productive farm country, with wheat, corn, potatoes, and many dairy farms. It also produces brass, paper, aluminum, roller bearings, brushes, rubber products, furniture, and other products.

What to See and Do

College of Wooster. *1189 Beall Ave (44691). E University St and Beall Ave, 1 mile N. Phone 330/ 263-2000. www.wooster.edu.* (1866) (1,865 students) Liberal arts, sciences. Campus tours; art museum. Home of Ohio Light Opera Company, performing Gilbert & Sullivan and light opera classics with orchestra. (Mid-June–mid-Aug)

Ohio Agricultural Research and Development Center. *Ohio State University, 1680 Madison Ave (44691). 1 mile S on Madison Ave. Phone 330/263-3701.www. oardc.ohio-state.edu.* (1882) Research on livestock, fruits, vegetables, ornamentals, field crops, environmental and energy conservation, pesticides; greenhouses, orchards, Secrest Arboretum, rhododendron and rose gardens. (Mon-Fri; closed holidays; grounds open daily, tours by appointment) **FREE**

Wayne County Historical Society Museum. *546 E Bowman St. Phone 330/264-8856.* Pioneer relics, paintings, lusterware, Native American artifacts, mounted animals and birds; log cabin and country schoolhouse on grounds. Kister Building has carriage house, blacksmith and carpenter shops. (Tues-Sun; also by appointment; closed holidays) **$$**

Special Event

Wayne County Fair. *Fairgrounds, 199 Vanover St, Wooster (44691). W on Hwy 30A. Phone 330/262-8001.* Five days, beginning weekend after Labor Day.

Full-Service Inn

★ ★ ★ **WOOSTER INN.** *801 E Wayne Ave, Wooster (44691). Phone 330/263-2660; fax 330/263-2661. www. wooster.edu.* This quaint country inn offers comfortable rooms and elegant dining experiences. Enjoy American-style fare served in the restaurant or a night cap in the billiard parlor over a game of pool on the vintage table. 16 rooms, 2 story. Closed Jan 2-9, Dec 25-26. Pets accepted; fee. Check-out noon. Restaurant (see). Golf, nine holes, putting green, driving range. Colonial décor. Owned and operated by College of Wooster (see); on campus. **$$**

Specialty Lodging

The following lodging establishment is approved by Mobil Travel Guide, but due to its unique and individualized nature has not been given a traditional Mobil Star rating. Included in this listing you may find bed-and-breakfasts, limited-service inns, guest ranches, and other unique hotel properties.

INN AT HONEY RUN. *6920 County Rd 203, Millersburg (44654). Phone 330/674-0011; toll-free 800/ 468-6639; fax 330/674-2623. www.innathoneyrun.com.* 39 rooms, 3 story. Check-in 4:30 pm, check-out noon. **$$**

Restaurants

★ ★ **TJ'S.** *359 W Liberty St, Wooster (44691). Phone 330/264-6263; fax 330/262-5741.* American menu. Lunch, dinner. Closed Sun; holidays. Children's menu. **$$**

★ ★ ★ **WOOSTER INN.** *801 E Wayne Ave, Wooster (44691). Phone 330/263-2660; fax 330/ 263-2661. www.wooster.edu.* Nestled in peaceful Amish country, this inn (see) offers itself as an intimate dining option. The 14-room property serves dinner in the main dining room, which overlooks a nine-hole golf course and driving range. In the summer, enjoy the local opera company and return in the fall for the guest chef's series. Lunch, dinner. Closed Jan 2-9, Dec 25-26. **$$**

Youngstown (B-5)

See also Alliance, Warren

Settled 1797
Population 95,732
Elevation 861 ft
Area Code 330
Information Youngstown/Mahoning County Convention and Visitors Bureau, 100 Federal Plz E, Suite 101, 44503; phone 330/747-8200 or toll-free 800/447-8201
Web site www.youngstowncvb.com

Youngstown, 5 miles from the Pennsylvania line, covers an area of 35 square miles in the eastern coal province, which has nine-tenths of the country's high-grade coal. It is the seat of Mahoning County.

Youngstown's steel history started in 1803, with a crude-iron smelter; the first coal mine began operating in the valley in 1826; in 1892, the first valley steel plant, Union Iron and Steel Company, opened. Youngstown industry has become more diversified in recent years, with products such as rubber goods, electric light bulbs, aluminum and paper goods, office equipment, clothes, rolling-mill equipment, vans, automobiles and parts, paint, electronic equipment, and plastics.

What to See and Do

The Arms Family Museum of Local History. *648 Wick Ave. Phone 330/743-2589.* Major arts and crafts house with original furnishings; local historical items; B. F. Wirt collection of paintings, books, and antiques; period costumes; pioneer and Native American artifacts. Guided tours. (Tues-Sun 1-5 pm; closed holidays) **$**

The Butler Institute of American Art. *524 Wick Ave. Phone 330/743-1711.* Specializes in American art; collections include works on Native Americans, clipper ships; antique glass bells. (Tues-Sun; closed holidays) **FREE**

Mill Creek Park. *7574 Columbiana Canfield Rd, Canfield. Located in the SW part of city, bounded by Mahoning Ave, Hwy 224, Lockwood, and Mill Creek Blvd. Phone 330/702-3000.* Park has more than 3,200 acres of gorges, ravines, and rolling hills from the Mahoning River to south of Highway 224. A Western Reserve pioneer woolen mill (1821) is now the Pioneer Pavilion used for picnics and dancing. Lanternman's Mill (phone 330/740-7115) (circa 1846), a working gristmill; tours. (May-Oct, Tues-Sun; Apr, Nov, weekends) The Fellows Riverside Gardens has 6 acres of formal gardens, including rose, chrysanthemum, lily, tulip, and annual flower displays. Area includes Garden Center and a large stone terrace overlooking the city. The James L. Wick Jr. Recreation Area has lighted tennis, horseshoe courts, par-three golf course, supervised playground, ball diamonds, volleyball court, picnic facilities, ice skating, and shelter house; on Old Furnace Road is Ford Nature Education Center (daily; closed Jan 1, Thanksgiving, Dec 25; phone 330/740-7107).

Walter Scholl Recreation Area and Volney Rogers Field have supervised playgrounds, picnic facilities, softball diamonds, tennis courts, shelter house. Two of the lakes provide fishing (May-Nov). Boat rides and rentals available at Newport and Glacier lakes. Park (daily); facilities (in season; fees for some).

Stambaugh Auditorium. *1000 5th Ave. Phone 330/747-5175.* Seats 2,800. Local events, concerts, and Monday Musical Club.

Youngstown Historical Center of Industry & Labor. *151 W Wood St. Phone 330/743-5934.* Chronicles the rise and fall of the steel industry in Youngstown and its region; exhibit combines artifacts, videotaped interviews with steelworkers and executives, and full scale re-creation of the places the steelworkers lived and labored. (Wed-Sat, Sun afternoons; closed Jan 1, Thanksgiving, Dec 25) **$$**

Youngstown Playhouse. *600 Playhouse Ln (44511). Off 2000 block of Glenwood Ave, 1 1/2 miles S of I-680. Phone 330/788-8739.* (Sept-June, weekends; additional summer productions)

Youngstown State University. *1 University Plz. Phone 330/742-3000; toll-free 877/468-6978. www.ysu.edu.* (1908) (12,500 students) Planetarium on campus (by reservations only, phone 330/742-3616); also here is McDonough Museum of Art (phone 330/742-1400). Campus tours.

Youngstown Symphony Center. *260 Federal Plz W. Phone 330/744-4269.* Seats 2,303. Presents concerts, symphony, ballet, and other cultural events.

Limited-Service Hotels

★ ★ **BEST WESTERN MEANDER INN.** *870 N Canfield Niles Rd, Youngstown (44515). Phone 330/544-2378; toll-free 800/780-7234; fax 330/544-7926. www.bestwestern.com.* 57 rooms, 2 story. Pets accepted; fee. Complimentary continental breakfast. Check-out noon. Restaurant, bar. Pool. **$**

★ **QUALITY INN.** *4055 Belmont Ave, Youngstown (44505). Phone 330/759-3180; fax 330/759-7713. www.comfortinn.com.* 144 rooms, 6 story. Complimentary continental breakfast. Check-out noon. Restaurant, bar. Indoor pool. Airport transportation available. **$**

Zanesville (C-4)

See also Cambridge, Coshocton, Newark

Settled 1797
Population 26,778
Elevation 705 ft
Area Code 740
Zip 43701
Information Visitors and Convention Bureau, 205 N 5th St; phone 740/455-8282 or toll-free 800/743-2303
Web site www.zanesville-ohio.com

Ebenezer Zane, surveyor of Zane's Trace through the dense Ohio forests and great-great-grandfather of Zane Grey, writer of Western novels, selected the Zanesville site because the valley was at the junction of the Muskingum and Licking rivers. First called Westbourne, it was the state capital from 1810 to 1812.

Today, beautiful pottery is made here, as well as transformers, electrical steel sheets, and automobile components. The "Y" Bridge, which a person can cross and still remain on the same side of the river from which he started, divides the city into three parts.

What to See and Do

Blue Rock State Park. *7924 Cutler Lake Rd (43720). 12 miles SE off Hwy 60, adjacent Blue Rock State Forest. Phone 740/674-4794.* A 350-acre park with swimming, fishing, boating (launch, electric motors only); hiking, trails; picnicking, concession; camping. (Daily) **FREE**

Dillon State Park. *5265 Dillon Hills Dr (43830). 8 miles NW on Hwy 146. Phone 740/453-4377 (daytime).* A 7,690-acre park with swimming, boating (ramps, rentals); picnicking (shelter), concession; camping, cabins (by reservation). (Daily) **FREE**

⭐ **National Road-Zane Grey Museum.** *8850 E Pike (43767). On Hwy 22/40, 10 miles E via I-70 exit 164, near Norwich. Phone 740/872-3143.* A 136-foot diorama traces history of Old National Road (Cumberland, Maryland, to Vandalia, Illinois); display of vehicles that once traveled the road; Zane Grey memorabilia; reconstructed craft shops, antique art pottery exhibit. (Mar-Apr, Oct-Nov, Wed-Sun; May-Sept, daily) **$$**

Ohio Ceramic Center. *7327 Ceramic Rd, Roseville (43777). On Hwy 93, 12 miles S via Hwy 22, near Roseville. Phone 740/697-7021.* Extensive displays of pottery housed in five buildings. Exhibits include primitive stoneware; area pottery. (Daily) Demonstrations of pottery making during pottery festival (weekend in mid-July). **$**

Robinson-Ransbottom Pottery Company. *5545 3rd St, Roseville. 12 miles S via Hwy 22, Hwy 93. Phone 740/697-7355.* A 15-minute-20-minute self-guided tour of pottery factory; inquire for hours. (Mon-Fri; closed holidays) **FREE**

Stern-Wheeler *The Lorena*. *Phone 740/455-8883.* Named for the Civil War love song. One-hour trips on the Muskingum River. (May-Sept)

The Wilds. *14000 International Rd, Cumberland (43732). Phone 740/638-5030.* A 9,154-acre conservation center dedicated to increasing the population of endangered species. (May-Oct, daily) **$$$**

Zane Grey Birthplace. *705 Convers Ave.* The author's first story was written here. (Private residence)

Zanesville Art Center. *620 Military Rd. 2 miles N on Hwy 60. Phone 740/452-0741.* American, European, and Asian art; children's art; early Midwestern glass and ceramics; photographs; special programs; gallery tours. (Tues-Sun; closed holidays) **FREE**

Special Events

Muskingum County Fair. *1300 Pershing Rd, Zanesville (43701). Phone 740/872-3912.* Mid-Aug.

Pottery Lovers Celebration. *Zanesville. Phone 740/697-0075.* A week of activities featuring collectible antiques and art pottery. Mid-July.

Zane's Trace Commemoration. *Zanesville.* Commemorates Pioneer Heritage. Fine arts, crafts, parades, flea market. Three days in mid-June.

Limited-Service Hotels

★ **COMFORT INN.** *500 Monroe St, Zanesville (43701). Phone 740/454-4144; fax 740/454-4144. www.comfortinn.com.* 81 rooms, 2 story. Pets accepted, some restrictions; fee. Complimentary continental breakfast. Check-out noon. Fitness room. Indoor pool, whirlpool. **$**

★ ★ **HOLIDAY INN.** *4645 E Pike, Zanesville (43701). Phone 740/453-0771; fax 740/588-6617. www. holiday-inn.com.* 130 rooms, 2 story. Pets accepted, some restrictions. Check-out noon. Restaurant, bar. Fitness room. Indoor pool, whirlpool. **$**

Restaurant

★ ★ **MARIA ADORNETTO.** *953 Market St, Zanesville (43702). Phone 740/453-0643.* Contemporary dining room in converted home. Italian menu. Lunch, dinner. Closed Sun; holidays. Bar. **$$**

In a little over two hours from Cleveland, you can explore a new, vibrant Pittsburgh. The sooty mill town has transformed itself into a viable and inviting destination spot. Pittsburgh now boasts 25 parks, 45 "parklets," 60 recreation centers, and 27 public swimming pools. The city also has a ballet company, a symphony orchestra, and tons of museums to wander.

Pittsburgh, PA

2 hours 15 minutes, 132 miles from Cleveland, OH

Settled 1758
Population 334,563
Elevation 760 ft
Area Code 412
Information Greater Pittsburgh Convention and Visitors Bureau, 425 6th Ave 30th floor 15219; phone 412/281-7711 or toll-free 800/366-0093
Web site www.visitpittsburgh.com

Pittsburgh has had a remarkable renaissance to become one of the most spectacular civic redevelopments in America, with modern buildings, clean parks, and community pride. In fact, it has been named "all-American city" by the National Civic League. The new Pittsburgh is a result of a rare combination of capital-labor cooperation, public and private support, enlightened political leadership, and imaginative, venturesome community planning. Its $1 billion international airport was designed to be the most user-friendly in the country.

After massive war production, Pittsburgh labored to eliminate the 1930s image of an unsophisticated mill town. During the 1950s and 1960s, Renaissance I began, a $500 million program to clean the city's air and develop new structures such as Gateway Center (see), the Civic Arena, and Point State Park (see). The late 1970s and early 1980s ushered in Renaissance II, a $3 billion expansion program reflecting the movement away from industry and toward high technology.

Today, Pittsburgh has completed this dramatic shift from industry to a diversified base including high technology, health care, finance, and education and continues its transition to a services-oriented city.

Pittsburgh's cultural personality is expressed by the Pittsburgh Symphony Orchestra, Pittsburgh Opera, Pittsburgh Ballet, Phipps Conservatory (see SCHENLEY PARK), and The Carnegie Museums of Pittsburgh (see), which include the Museum of Natural History and the Museum of Art. The city has 25 parks, 45 "parklets," 60 recreation centers, and 27 public swimming pools.

Born of frontier warfare in the shadow of Fort Pitt, the city is named after the elder William Pitt, the great British statesman. Its strategic military position was an important commercial asset, and Pittsburgh soon became a busy river port and transit point for the western flow of pioneers.

Industry grew out of the West's need for manufactured goods; foundries and rolling mills were soon producing nails, axes, frying pans, and shovels. The Civil War added tremendous impetus to industry, and, by the end of the war, Pittsburgh was producing half the steel and one-third of the glass made in the country. Such captains of industry and finance as

Thomas Mellon, Andrew Carnegie, and Henry Clay Frick built their industrial empires in Pittsburgh. The American Federation of Labor was born here (1881); the city has been the scene of historic clashes between labor and management.

World War I brought a fresh boom to the city, as well as changes in its industrial character. It was a vast arsenal for the Allies during World War II.

Additional Visitor Information

For additional information about Pittsburgh, contact the Greater Pittsburgh Convention and Visitors Bureau, 425 6th Ave, 30th floor, 15219 (Mon-Fri), phone 412/281-7711 or toll-free 800/366-0093. A visitor information center is along Liberty Avenue, adjacent to 4 Gateway Center (Mar-Dec, daily; rest of year, Mon-Sat). Other centers can be found in the Carnegie Library's Mount Washington branch and on the University of Pittsburgh's (see) campus, Log Cabin, Forbes Avenue. For a schedule of events in Pittsburgh, 24-hour visitor information, phone toll-free 800/366-0093.

Public Transportation

Subway and Surface Trains, Buses (Port Authority of Allegheny County). Phone 412/442-2000.

What to See and Do

Alcoa Building. *425 6th Ave.* Pioneer in aluminum for skyscraper construction, exterior work was done from inside; no scaffolding was required. Draped in aluminum waffle, 30 stories high; considered to be one of the country's most daring experiments in skyscraper design.

Allegheny County Courthouse. *Grant St and 5th Ave.* One of the country's outstanding Romanesque buildings, the two-square-city-block structure was designed by Henry Hobson Richardson in 1884. (Mon-Fri; closed holidays) **FREE**

Andy Warhol Museum. *117 Sandusky St (15212). Phone 412/237-8300. www.warhol.org.* The most comprehensive single-artist museum in the world. More than 500 works. (Tues-Sun 10 am-5 pm) **$$**

Benedum Center for the Performing Arts. *719 Liberty Ave. Phone 412/456-6666.* Expansion and restoration of the Stanley Theater, a movie palace built in 1928. Gilded plasterwork, 500,000-piece crystal chandelier, and a nine-story addition to backstage area make this an exceptional auditorium, with one of the largest stages in the country. The center is home to the Pittsburgh Ballet Theatre, the Pittsburgh Dance Council, the Pittsburgh Opera, and Civic Light Opera. Free guided tours (by appointment).

Boyce Park Ski Area. *Plum. 18 miles E on I-376 to Plum exit (16B); follow signs to park. Phone 724/733-4656.* Beginner-intermediate slopes; two double chair lifts, two surface lifts; patrol, school, rentals, snowmaking; cafeteria. Longest run, 1/4 mile; vertical drop 160 feet. Night skiing. (Dec-Mar, daily) **$$$$**

Carnegie Mellon University. *5000 Forbes Ave (15213). Adjacent to Schenley Park (see). Phone 412/268-2000. www.cmu.edu.* (1900) (7,900 students) Founded by Andrew Carnegie. Composed of seven colleges. Tours of campus.

⭐ **The Carnegie Museums of Pittsburgh.** *4400 Forbes Ave. Phone 412/622-3360. www.carnegiemuseums .org.* Public complex built by industrialist Andrew Carnegie. (Daily, except Mon; closed holidays) **$$** Includes

Carnegie Museum of Art. Possibly America's first modern art museum, as Carnegie urged the gallery to exhibit works dated after 1896. Collection of impressionist and post-impressionist paintings; Hall of Sculpture; Hall of Architecture; films, videos.

Carnegie Museum of Natural History. Houses one of the most complete collections of dinosaur fossils. Exhibits include Dinosaur Hall, Polar World, Hillman Hall of Minerals and Gems, the Walton Hall of Ancient Egypt; changing exhibits.

Library of Pittsburgh. Central branch contains more than 4 1/2 million books. Houses first department of science and technology established in a United States public library.

Music Hall. Home to Mendelssohn Choir, Pittsburgh Chamber Music Society, and River City Brass Band. Elaborate gilt and marble foyer; walls of French eschallion, 24 pillars made of green stone and a gold baroque ceiling.

The Carnegie Science Center. *1 Allegheny Ave. On Ohio River. Phone 412/237-3400.* Learning and entertainment complex has over 40,000 square feet of exhibit galleries that demonstrate how human activities are affected by science and technology. USS *Requin*, moored in front of the center, is a World War II diesel-electric submarine; tours (40 minutes) demonstrate the electronic, visual, and voice communication devices on board. Henry Buhl Jr. Planetarium and Observatory is a technologically sophisticated interactive planetarium with control panels at every seat. Also here are the 350-seat Omnimax Theater and the Health Sciences Amphitheater. Restaurant; gift shop. (Daily; closed Dec 25) **$$$$**

County parks. *South Park. 12 miles S on Hwy 88.* **North Park,** *14 miles N on Hwy 19.* **Boyce Park,** *14 miles E on I-376, Hwy 22.* **Settler's Cabin Park,** *9 miles W on I-279, Hwy 22. Phone 412/350-2455 (county park information and permits).* Swimming, fishing, boating. Bicycling (rentals); ball fields, golf, tennis. Cross-country skiing, ice skating (winter, daily). Picnicking. Parks open daily. Fees for activities. Attractions for each park vary.

⭐ **Fallingwater.** *Hwy 381, Mill Run. 27 miles S on Hwy 51, 10 miles E on Hwy 201 to Connellsville, 8 miles E on Hwy 711, then 8 miles S on Hwy 381, near Mill Run.* One of the most famous structures of the 20th century, Fallingwater, designed by Frank Lloyd Wright in 1936, is cantilevered on three levels over a waterfall; interior features Wright-designed furniture, textiles, and lighting, as well as sculpture by modern masters; extensive grounds are heavily wooded and planted with rhododendron, which blooms in early July. Visitor center with self-guided orientation program; concession; gift shop. Guided tours (mid-Mar-Thanksgiving: Tues-Sun 10 am-4 pm; winter: Sat-Sun 10 am-3 pm). No children under age 6; child-care center. No pets. Reservations required. **$$$**

⭐ **The Frick Art and Historical Center.** *7227 Reynolds St. Phone 412/371-0600. www.frickart.org.* Museum complex built on grounds of estate once belonging to industrialist Henry Clay Frick; gardens, carriage house museum, greenhouse, café (see), and restored children's playhouse that now serves as a visitors center. (Tues-Sun; closed holidays) **FREE** Also on the grounds are

Clayton, the Henry Clay Frick Home. *7227 Reynolds St, Pittsburgh.* A restored four-story Victorian mansion with 23 rooms; only remaining house of area in East End once known as

"Millionaire's Row." Some original décor and personal mementos of the Fricks. Tours; reservation recommended. **$$$**

The Frick Art Museum. *7227 Reynolds St, Pittsburgh. Phone 412/371-0600.* Collection of Helen Clay Frick, daughter of Henry Clay Frick, includes Italian Renaissance, Flemish, and French 18th-century paintings and decorative arts. Italian and French furniture, Renaissance bronzes, tapestries, Chinese porcelains. Also changing exhibits; concerts, lectures. **FREE**

Frick Park. *Beechwood Blvd and English Ln. Phone 412/422-6536.* Covers 476 acres, largely in natural state; nature trails wind through ravines and over hills; nature center (2005 Beechwood Blvd); tennis courts; picnic areas, playgrounds. Park (daily). **FREE**

Gateway Center. *420 Fort Duquesne Blvd (15222). Covers 23 acres adjacent to Point State Park (see). Phone 412/392-6000.* Complex includes four skyscrapers of Trizec Properties, Inc. Gateway Center Plaza, a 2-acre open-air garden over underground parking garage, has lovely walks, three fountains, more than 90 types of trees, and 100 varieties of shrubs and seasonal flowers. (Mon-Fri; closed holidays) (See SPECIAL EVENTS)

Guided bus and walking tours. *1 Station Sq, Suite 450 (15219). Phone 412/471-5808. www.phlf.org.* Offered through the Pittsburgh History and Landmarks Foundation. **$$**

Hartwood. *215 Saxonburg Blvd. 12 miles N via Hwy 8. Phone 412/767-9200.* (1929). A 629-acre re-creation of English country estate; Tudor mansion with many antiques; formal gardens, stables. Tours (Tues-Sun; closed holidays). Also music and theater events during summer. **$$**

⭐ **Inclines.** (Hill-climbing trolleys). Travel to the top of Mount Washington for an excellent view of Golden Triangle, where the Allegheny and Monongahela rivers join to form the Ohio River.

Duquesne Incline. *1220 Grandview Ave, Pittsburgh. Lower station, W Carson St, opposite the fountain, SW of Fort Pitt Bridge; upper station, in restaurant area. Phone 412/381-1665.* Built 1877; restored and run by community effort; observation deck. (Daily) Free parking at lower station. **$**

Monongahela Incline. *Pittsburgh. Station on W Carson St near Station Sq and Smithfield Street Bridge. Phone 412/442-2000.* Panoramic views from observation deck. (Daily) **$**

James L. Kelso Bible Lands Museum. *616 N Highland. On grounds of Pittsburgh Theological Seminary. Phone 412/362-5610.* Artifacts and displays from the ancient Near East, especially Palestine. (Call for hours) **FREE**

Kennywood Park. *4800 Kennywood Blvd, West Mifflin. 8 miles SE on Hwy 837. Phone 412/461-0500. www.kennywood.com.* Combines modern rides with rides from traditional streetcar parks, popular at the turn of the 20th century. Lost Kennywood, with lagoon, Victorian-era buildings, shopping. Gardens, picnic groves. (Mid-May-Labor Day, daily) **$$$$**

Mellon Arena. *66 Mario Lemieux Pl. www.mellonarena.com.* This $22 million all-weather amphitheater accommodates 17,500 people. Retractable roof can fold up within 2 1/2 minutes.

Museum of Photographic History. *531 E Ohio. Phone 412/231-7881.* Photo gallery and museum. Selections from 100,000 antique photographic images. (Mon-Sat; closed holidays) **$$**

National Aviary. *Allegheny Commons West (15212). Approximately 1 mile W of Downtown. Phone 412/323-7235.* The aviary is home to one of the world's premier bird collections and is the only indoor bird facility independent of a larger zoo in North America. A veritable jungle of colorful, amusing, and exotic birds. (Daily; closed Dec 25) **$$**

Pittsburgh Children's Museum. *10 Children's Way. Phone 412/322-5058. www.pittsburghkids.org.* Hands-on exhibits. Hands-on silkscreen studio; storytelling; regularly scheduled puppet shows; live performances; two-story climber. (Memorial Day-Labor Day, daily; rest of year, Tues-Sat, Sun afternoons) **$$**

Pittsburgh Penguins (NHL). *Mellon Arena, 66 Mario Lemieux Pl. Phone 412/323-1919. www.pittsburghpenguins.com.* Professional hockey team.

Pittsburgh Pirates (MLB). *PNC Park, 115 Federal St. Phone 412/323-5000. www.pittsburgh.pirates.mlb.com.* Professional baseball team.

Oakland, the City Beautiful

Once known as the "Forge of the Universe," industrial Pittsburgh was a smoky, pulsating mill town that fed the fortunes of such corporate giants as Carnegie, Westinghouse, and Mellon. Since then, the city has cleansed its air and its reputation to rank as one of America's most delightful big cities. Before this renaissance, Pittsburgh's 19th-century elite created a second city just 3 miles east of Downtown called Oakland. A sparkling cultural and educational center, it was an antidote to the blue-collar grime from which many of them profited. Under the patronage of Andrew Carnegie and others, Oakland became, as historians have described it, "the City Beautiful," a lavish fantasy of parks and monumental structures housing museums and universities. This one-hour, 1-mile tour is an introduction to this rich heritage bequeathed to the public. To explore it fully might take days. Begin on the steps of The Carnegie (see) at 4400 Forbes Avenue. An immense gray building, it is shared by the Museum of Art and the Museum of Natural History. Born to a poor family in Scotland in 1835, founder Carnegie came to the United States with his parents at age 12. Starting his career as a telegraph messenger, he went on to make a fortune in steel. A generous man, he gave The Carnegie to the city. For the Museum of Art, he sought contemporary artworks, thus creating what is considered the first museum of modern art in America. It boasts a fine collection of impressionists. Acquiring Jurassic Age fossils, Carnegie put the Museum of Natural History in the paleontology business. The Dinosaur Hall is particularly impressive. Across Forbes Avenue is the Foster Memorial, where composer Stephen Collins Foster is cited for the "beautiful ideals" given voice in his enduring music. Soaring above the memorial is the University of Pittsburgh's 42-story Cathedral of Learning (see), one of the largest academic buildings in the world. It was built in the early 1930s as a symbol of power and achievement. A ten-minute walk away in adjacent Schenley Park is Phipps Conservatory (see) on Frank Curto Drive (west from The Carnegie), an elegant Beaux-Art greenhouse that is believed to be the largest in the country. When it opened in 1893, it was one of the nation's first large-scale enclosed botanical gardens. Conclude your tour by strolling among its many exhibits, from tropical flowers to a major assortment of bonsai.

Pittsburgh Steelers (NFL). *Heinz Field, 600 Stadium Cir. Phone 412/432-7800. www.steelers.com.* Professional football team.

The Pittsburgh Zoo. *1 Wild Pl (15260). NE on Highland Ave in Highland Park area. Phone 412/665-3639.* Over 70 acres containing over 6,000 animals, children's farm (late May-Oct), discovery pavilion, reptile house, tropical and Asian forests, African savanna, and aqua zoo. Merry-go-round and train rides (fee). Highland Park covers 75 acres and has tennis courts, picnic grounds, shelters (some require permit), twin reservoirs, swimming pool (fee). (Daily; closed Dec 25) **$$$**

Point State Park. *Fort Duquesne and Fort Pitt blvds. Phone 412/471-0235.* Point where the Allegheny and Monongahela rivers meet to form the Ohio; 36 acres. A 150-foot fountain symbolizes the joining of the rivers. There are military drills with fifes and drums, muskets and cannon (May-Labor Day; some Sun afternoons). (See SPECIAL EVENTS) In the park are

Block House of Fort Pitt. *Fort Duquesne and Fort Pitt blvds, Pittsburgh.* Last remaining building of original fort (1767). (Wed-Sun) **FREE**

Fort Pitt Museum. *101 Commonwealth Pl, Pittsburgh. Phone 412/281-9284.* Built on part of original fort. Exhibits on early Pittsburgh and Fort Pitt; military struggles between France and Britain for western Pennsylvania and the Old Northwest Territory. (Wed-Sun; closed holidays) **$$**

PPG Place. *Market Sq.* Designed by Philip Johnson, this is Pittsburgh's most popular Renaissance II building. PPG Place consists of six separate buildings designed in a postmodern, Gothic skyscraper style. Shopping and a food court can be found in 2 PPG Place. (See SPECIAL EVENTS)

Riverview Park. *2 miles N on Hwy 19.* Covers 251 acres. Swimming pool (mid-June-Labor Day, daily; fee); tennis courts (Apr-Nov, daily); picnic shelter

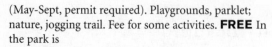

(May-Sept, permit required). Playgrounds, parklet; nature, jogging trail. Fee for some activities. **FREE** In the park is

Allegheny Observatory. *159 Riverview Ave, Pittsburgh. Phone 412/321-2400.* Slides, tour of building. Maintained by University of Pittsburgh (see). Children under 12 years only with adult. Reservation required. (Apr-Oct, Thurs-Fri; closed holidays) **FREE**

Rodef Shalom Biblical Botanical Garden. *4905 5th Ave. Phone 412/621-6566. www.rodefshalom.org.* The natural world of ancient Israel is re-created here in settings that specialize in plants of the Bible. A waterfall, desert, and stream all help simulate the areas of Jordan, Lake Kineret, and the Dead Sea. Tours (by appointment). Special programs and exhibits. (June-mid-Sept, Mon-Thurs, Sat-Sun; Sat hours limited) **FREE**

Sandcastle Water Park. *1000 Sandcastle Dr (15120). Approximately 5 miles SE of Downtown via I-376 and Hwy 837. Phone 412/462-6666. www.sandcastlewaterpark.com.* The city's down-by-the-riverside water park has 15 slides, adult and kiddie pools; boardwalk; food. (First Sat June-Labor Day, daily; closed holidays) **$$$$**

Schenley Park. *5000 Forbes Ave (15217). Adjacent Carnegie Mellon University* (see). *Phone 412/687-1800.* Covers 456 acres; picnic areas; 18-hole golf course, lighted tennis courts; swimming pool; ice skating (winter); softball fields, running track; nature trails; bandstand (summer; free). Fee for some activities. (Daily) **FREE** Also in park is

Phipps Conservatory. *1 Schenley Park (Frank Curto Dr), Pittsburgh. Phone 412/622-6914. www.phipps.conservatory.org.* Constantly changing array of flowers; tropical gardens; outstanding orchid collection. Children's Discovery Garden with interactive learning opportunities. Seasonal flower shows (see SPECIAL EVENTS). (Tues-Sun) **$$$**

The Senator John Heinz Regional History Center. *1212 Smallman St. Phone 412/454-6000. In Chatauqua Ice Warehouse (1898).* Preserves 300 years of region's history with artifacts and extensive collection of archives, photos. Houses the Historical Society of Western Pennsylvania. Library (Tues-Sat). (Daily; closed Jan 1, Thanksgiving, Dec 25) **$$$**

Sightseeing USA/Lenzner Coach USA. *110 Lenzner Court, Sewickley (15143). Phone 412/741-2720; toll-free 800/342-2349.* Bus tours.

Soldiers and Sailors Memorial Hall and Military History Museum. *4141 5th Ave at Bigelow Blvd. Phone 412/621-4253.* Auditorium has Lincoln's Gettysburg Address inscribed above stage; flags, weapons, uniforms, memorabilia from United States wars. (Tues-Fri, Sat-Sun afternoons; closed holidays) **$$**

Station Square. *450 Landmarks Bldg, 1 Station Sq. Along Monongahela River across from Downtown, via Smithfield Street Bridge. Phone 412/471-5808. www.stationsquare.com.* This 40-acre area features shopping, dining, and entertainment in and among the historic buildings of the P&LE Railroad. Shopping in warehouses that once held loaded railroad boxcars. (Daily; closed holidays)

Tour-Ed Mine and Museum. *748 Bull Creek Rd (15084). 20 miles NW via Hwy 28 (Allegheny Valley Expy) to Tarentum, then 1/4 mile W via Red Belt W. Phone 724/224-4720. www.tour-edmine.com.* Complete underground coal mining operation; sawmill; furnished log house (1789); old company store; historical mine museum; shelters; playground. (May-Labor Day week, daily 1-4 pm) **$$$**

Two Mellon Bank Center. *Grant St and 5th Ave.* Formerly the Union Trust Building, its Flemish-Gothic style was modeled after a library in Louvain, Belgium. Interior has a glass rotunda.

University of Pittsburgh. *5th Ave and Bigelow Blvd. Phone 412/624-4141. www.pitt.edu.* (1787) (33,000 students) Tours of nationality rooms in Cathedral of Learning (weekends; fee). Campus of 70 buildings on 125 acres. Buildings include

Cathedral of Learning. *4200 5th Ave, Pittsburgh. Phone 412/624-6000.* (1935) Unique skyscraper of classrooms, stretching its Gothic-Moderne architecture 42 floors high (535 feet); vantage point on 36th floor. Surrounding a three-story Gothic commons room are an Early American Room and 24 nationality rooms, each reflecting the distinctive culture of the ethnic group that created and furnished it. Tours (daily; closed holidays). **$$**

Heinz Chapel. *5th and Bellefield aves, Pittsburgh. E of Cathedral of Learning. Phone 412/624-4157.* Tall stained-glass windows; French Gothic architecture. (Mon-Thurs, Sat-Sun; closed holidays) **FREE**

Henry Clay Frick Fine Arts Building. *104 Frick Fine Arts, Pittsburgh. Schenley Plz. Phone 412/ 648-2400.* Glass-enclosed cloister; changing exhibits; art reference library. (Sept-mid-June, daily; rest of year, Mon-Fri; closed university holidays; also Dec 24-Jan 2) **FREE**

Stephen Foster Memorial. *4301 Forbes Ave, Pittsburgh. Phone 412/624-4100.* Auditorium/ theater. Collection of the Pittsburgh-born composer's music and memorabilia. Said to be one of the most elaborate memorials ever built for a musician. (Mon-Sat, Sun afternoons; closed holidays)

USX Tower. *Grant St and 7th Ave (15219).* Once known as the US Steel Building, it is 64 stories high and the tallest building in Pittsburgh. Ten exposed triangular columns and an exterior paneling of steel make up its construction. (See SPECIAL EVENTS)

Special Events

Folk Festival. *Pittsburgh Expo Mart, 105 Mall Blvd, Monroeville (15146). Phone 412/856-8100.* Food of many nations; arts and crafts; folk music, dancing. Memorial Day weekend.

Phipps Conservatory Flower Shows. *Schenley Park (see), 1 Schenley Park (Frank Curto Dr), Pittsburgh. Phone 412/622-6914.* Spring, summer, fall, and holidays.

Pittsburgh Irish Festival. *I. C. Light Amphitheatre, 1 Station Sq, Pittsburgh (15219). Phone 412/422-1113. www.pghirishfest.org.* Irish foods, dances, and entertainment. Early or mid-Sept.

Pittsburgh Public Theater. *621 Penn Ave, Pittsburgh. Phone 412/316-1600.* City's largest resident professional company. Sept-June.

Pittsburgh/Shop 'N Save Three Rivers Regatta. *Point State Park, Pittsburgh. www.pghregatta.com.* Water, land, and air events; water shows and speedboat races. Last weekend in July, first weekend in Aug.

Pittsburgh Symphony Orchestra. *600 Penn Ave, Pittsburgh. Phone 412/392-4900.* Classical, pop, and family concerts. Heinz Hall for the Performing Arts. Sept-May.

Three Rivers Arts Festival. *707 Penn Ave, Pittsburgh. At Point State Park, Gateway Center, USX Tower, and PPG Place (see all). Phone 412/281-8723.* Juried,

original works of local and national artists: paintings, photography, sculpture, crafts, and videos; artists' market in outdoor plazas. Ongoing performances include music, dance, and performance art. Special art projects; film festival; food; children's activities. Early-mid-June.

Limited-Service Hotels

★ **HAWTHORN SUITES.** *700 Mansfield Ave, Pittsburgh (15205). Phone 412/279-6300; toll-free 800/331-3131; fax 412/279-4993. www. hawthornsuitespittsburgh.com.* Chalet-style buildings. 151 rooms, 2 story, all suites. Pets accepted; fee. Complimentary full breakfast. Check-out noon. Pool, whirlpool. Airport transportation available. **$**

★ ★ **HOLIDAY INN.** *2750 Mosside Blvd, Monroeville (15146). Phone 412/372-1022; toll-free 800/465-4329; fax 412/373-4065. www.holiday-inn.com.* 188 rooms, 4 story. Pets accepted, some restrictions. Check-out noon. Restaurant, bar. Fitness room. Pool. **$**

★ ★ **RAMADA PLAZA SUITES.** *1 Bigelow Sq, Pittsburgh (15219). Phone 412/281-5800; toll-free 800/225-5858; fax 412/281-4208. www.plazasuites.com.* 311 rooms, 20 story, all suites. Complimentary continental breakfast. Check-out noon. Restaurant, bar. Fitness room. Indoor pool. **$**

Full-Service Hotels

★ ★ ★ **HILTON PITTSBURGH.** *600 Commonwealth Pl, Pittsburgh (15222). Phone 412/391-4600; fax 412/594-5161. www.hilton.com.* 713 rooms, 24 story. Check-out noon. Restaurant, bar. Fitness room. Airport transportation available. Business center. **$**

★ ★ ★ **MARRIOTT PITTSBURGH CITY CENTER.** *112 Washington Pl, Pittsburgh (15219). Phone 412/471-4000; fax 412/281-4797. www.marriott .com.* 402 rooms, 11 story. Check-in 3 pm, check-out noon. Restaurant, bar. Fitness room. Indoor pool. Business center. **$$**

★ ★ ★ **OMNI WILLIAM PENN HOTEL.**
530 William Penn Pl, Pittsburgh (15219). Phone 412/281-7100; fax 412/553-5252. www.omnihotels.com. Relive the grandeur of a bygone era at the Omni William Penn. This hotel, built in 1916, fuses historic charm with modern luxury in the heart of downtown Pittsburgh. The sumptuous public spaces invite daydreaming, while the rooms and suites are tastefully and elegantly appointed with a distinguished style. Executives on the go appreciate the hotel's complete business and fitness centers; families adore the Omni Kids Program; and leisure visitors enjoy the spa and salon services and proximity to the city's leading stores. The hotel offers a variety of convenient and tempting dining choices, from Starbucks and Brueggers Bagels for quick bites and snacks to pub food at the Palm Court and Tap Room and fine dining at the Terrace Room. 596 rooms, 24 story. Check-in 3 pm, check-out noon. Wireless Internet access. Restaurants, bar. Fitness room, spa. Airport transportation available. Business center. **$$**

★ ★ ★ **RENAISSANCE PITTSBURGH HOTEL.** *107 6th St, Pittsburgh (15222). Phone 412/562-1200; fax 412/562-1644. www.renaissancehotels.com.* 300 rooms, 14 story. Check-in 4 pm, check-out 1 pm. Restaurant, bar. Fitness room. Whirlpool. Business center. **$$**

★ ★ ★ **SHERATON STATION SQUARE HOTEL.** *7 Station Square Dr, Pittsburgh (15219). Phone 412/261-2000; toll-free 800/255-7488; fax 412/261-2932. www.sheraton.com.* 292 rooms, 15 story. Check-out noon. Restaurant, bar. Fitness room. Indoor pool, whirlpool. Business center. On riverfront. **$$**

★ ★ ★ **THE WESTIN CONVENTION CENTER PITTSBURGH.** *1000 Penn Ave, Pittsburgh (15222). Phone 412/281-3700; fax 412/227-4500. www.westin.com.* 616 rooms, 26 story. Pets accepted, some restrictions; fee. Check-in 3 pm, check-out noon. Restaurant, bar. Fitness room, spa. Indoor pool, whirlpool. Business center. **$$**

Full-Service Inns

★ ★ ★ **INN AT OAKMONT.** *300 Rte 909, Oakmont (15139). Phone 412/828-0410; fax 412/828-1358. www.pittsburghbnb.com.* 8 rooms, 2 story. Complimentary full breakfast. Check-in 2 pm, check-out 11 am. Fitness room. **$**

★ ★ ★ **PRIORY INN.** *614 Pressley St, Pittsburgh (15212). Phone 412/231-3338; fax 412/231-4838. www.thepriory.com.* European-style inn with fountain and floral arrangements in courtyard. Previously a haven for Benedictine monks (1888). 24 rooms, 3 story. Complimentary continental breakfast. Check-in 3 pm, check-out 11 am, weekends noon. **$**

Specialty Lodging

The following lodging establishment is approved by Mobil Travel Guide, but due to its unique and individualized nature has not been given a traditional Mobil Star rating. Included in this listing you may find bed-and-breakfasts, limited-service inns, guest ranches, and other unique hotel properties.

APPLETREE BED AND BREAKFAST. *703 S Negley Ave, Pittsburgh (15232). Phone 412/661-0631; fax 412/661-7525. www.appletreeb-b.com.* Historic building (1884). 8 rooms, 3 story. Children over 12 years only. Complimentary full breakfast. Check-in 3-6 pm, check-out 11 am. **$$**

Restaurants

★ ★ **1902 LANDMARK TAVERN.** *24 Market Sq, Pittsburgh (15222). Phone 412/471-1902.* Restored tavern (1902); ornate tin ceiling, original tiles. Italian, American menu. Lunch, dinner. Closed Sun; holidays. Bar. **$$**

★ **ABRUZZI'S RESTAURANT.** *52 S 10th St, Pittsburgh (15203). Phone 412/431-4511.* Italian menu. Dinner. Bar. Casual attire. **$$**

★ ★ ★ **CAFE ALLEGRO.** *51 S 12th St, Pittsburgh (15203). Phone 412/481-7788; fax 412/481-4520.* The romantic ambience of several intimate dining areas draws crowds to this South Side Mediterranean restaurant. Try uncomplicated dishes like fish cooked in papillote and pastas. Italian menu. Dinner. Closed holidays. Bar. Valet parking. **$$**

★ ★ **CAFE AT THE FRICK.** *7227 Reynolds St, Pittsburgh (15208). Phone 412/371-0600; fax 412/371-6030. www.frickart.org.* Lunch. Closed Mon; holidays. Outdoor seating. **$**

★ ★ ★ **CARLTON.** *500 Grant St, Pittsburgh (15219). Phone 412/391-4099; fax 412/391-4240. www.thecarltonrestaurant.com.* American menu. Lunch, dinner. Closed Sun; holidays. Bar. Children's menu. **$$$**

★ ★ **CASBAH.** *229 S Highland Ave, Pittsburgh (15206). Phone 412/661-5656; fax 412/661-0616. www.bigburrito.com.* Mediterranean menu. Lunch, dinner. Closed holidays. Bar. Casual attire. Outdoor seating. **$$**

★ ★ **CHEESE CELLAR CAFE & BAR.** *25 Station Sq, Pittsburgh (15219). Phone 412/471-3355; fax 412/281-0549.* International menu. Breakfast, lunch, dinner. Closed Thanksgiving, Dec 25. Bar. Children's menu. Outdoor seating. **$$**

★ ★ **CHINA PALACE.** *5440 Walnut St, Pittsburgh (15232). Phone 412/687-7423; fax 412/687-5555.* Chinese menu. Lunch, dinner. Closed July 4, Labor Day, Thanksgiving. Bar. Casual attire. **$$**

★ ★ **THE CHURCH BREW WORKS.** *3525 Liberty Ave, Pittsburgh (15201). Phone 412/688-8200; fax 412/688-8201. www.churchbrew.com.* Brew pub in 1902 church; vaulted ceiling, stained-glass windows. American menu. Dinner. Closed Thanksgiving, Dec 25. Bar. Outdoor seating. **$$**

★ ★ ★ **CLIFFSIDE.** *1208 Grandview Ave, Pittsburgh (15211). Phone 412/431-6996.* American menu. Dinner. Closed holidays. Bar. Valet parking. **$$**

★ ★ ★ **COMMON PLEA.** *308 Ross St, Pittsburgh (15219). Phone 412/281-5140; fax 412/281-6856. www.commonplea.citysearch.com.* With its dark paneling, glass wall, and subdued lighting, this restaurant caters to the legal crowd. Seafood menu. Lunch, dinner. Closed holidays. Bar. Valet parking (dinner). **$$**

★ ★ **COZUMEL.** *5507 Walnut St, Pittsburgh (15232). Phone 412/621-5100.* Mexican menu. Lunch, dinner. Bar. Children's menu. Casual attire. **$**

⊙ ★ **DAVE AND ANDY'S ICE CREAM PARLOR.** *207 Atwood St, Pittsburgh (15213). Phone 412/681-9906.* 1930s look; some counters. Closed holidays. **$**

★ ★ **DEJAVU LOUNGE.** *2106 Penn Ave, Pittsburgh (15222). Phone 412/434-1144.* American, pan-Asian menu. Lunch, dinner, late-night. Closed Sun. Bar. Casual attire. Outdoor seating. **$$**

★ ★ ★ **D'IMPERIO'S.** *3412 William Penn Hwy, Pittsburgh (15235). Phone 412/823-4800; fax 412/823-4804.* Reserve ahead for Friday night al fresco dining in summer. Otherwise, go for traditional Italian favorites accompanied by opera and Italian crooners. American, Italian menu. Lunch, dinner. Closed Sun; holidays. Bar. Children's menu. **$$$**

★ ★ **GEORGETOWN INN.** *1230 Grandview Ave, Pittsburgh (15211). Phone 412/481-4424.* Seafood, steak menu. Lunch, dinner. Closed holidays. Bar. **$$$**

★ ★ ★ **GRAND CONCOURSE.** *1 Station Sq, Pittsburgh (15219). Phone 412/261-1717; fax 412/261-6041. www.muer.com.* Converted railroad station. American menu. Lunch, dinner, Sun brunch. Closed Dec 25. Bar. Children's menu. Outdoor seating. **$$$**

★ ★ **INDIA GARDEN.** *328 Atwood St, Pittsburgh (15213). Phone 412/682-3000; fax 412/682-3130. www.indiagarden.net.* Indian menu. Lunch, dinner. **$**

★ ★ **KAYA.** *2000 Smallman St, Pittsburgh (15222). Phone 412/261-6565; fax 412/261-1526. www.bigburrito.com.* Caribbean menu. Dinner. Closed holidays. Bar. Outdoor seating. **$$$**

★ **KENNY B'S EATERY.** *123 6th St, Pittsburgh (15222). Phone 412/201-1626.* American, Cuban menu. Breakfast, lunch, dinner. Casual attire. **$**

★ ★ **LE MONT.** *1114 Grandview Ave, Pittsburgh (15211). Phone 412/431-3100; fax 412/431-1204. www.lemontpittsburgh.com.* American menu. Dinner. Closed holidays. Bar. Valet parking. **$$$**

★ ★ ★ **LE POMMIER.** *2104 E Carson St, Pittsburgh (15203). Phone 412/431-1901. www. lepommier.com.* Located in oldest storefront in area (1863). French menu. Lunch, dinner. Closed Sun; holidays. Bar. Valet parking Fri-Sat. Outdoor seating. **$$**

★ ★ **MAX'S ALLEGHENY TAVERN.** *537 Suismon St, Pittsburgh (15212). Phone 412/231-1899; fax 412/231-5099. www.maxsalleghenytavern.com.* German menu. Lunch, dinner. Closed holidays. Bar. **$$**

★ ★ **MEZZANOTTE CAFE.** *4621 Liberty Ave, Pittsburgh (15224). Phone 412/688-8070. www.mezza-nottecafe.com.* Modern Italian, Mediterranean menu. Lunch, dinner. Closed Sun; holidays. Bar. Casual attire. **$$**

★ ★ **MONTEREY BAY FISH GROTTO.** *1411 Grandview Ave, Pittsburgh (15211). Phone 412/481-4414; fax 412/481-4448. www.montereybayfishgrotto.com.* Lunch, dinner. Children's menu. **$$$**

★ ★ **OLD EUROPE.** *1209 E Carson St, Pittsburgh (15203). Phone 412/488-1700.* Eastern European menu. Dinner. Bar. Casual attire. **$$**

★ ★ **PASTA PIATTO.** *736 Bellefonte St, Pittsburgh (15232). Phone 412/621-5547; fax 412/621-2164.* Italian menu. Lunch, dinner. Closed holidays. Bar. Children's menu. **$$**

★ ★ **PENN BREWERY.** *800 Vinial St, Troy Hill, Pittsburgh (15212). Phone 412/237-9402; fax 412/237-9406. www.pennbrew.com.* Restored 19th-century brewery, German beer hall-style communal dining. German menu. Lunch, dinner. Closed Sun; holidays. Bar. Children's menu. Outdoor seating. **$$**

★ ★ ★ **PICCOLO MONDO.** *661 Andersen Dr, Pittsburgh (15220). Phone 412/922-0920; fax 412/922-0921. www.piccolo-mondo.com.* Italian menu. Lunch, dinner. Closed Sun except Mother's Day; holidays. Bar. Children's menu. Jacket required. **$$**

★ ★ **POLI.** *2607 Murray Ave, Pittsburgh (15217). Phone 412/521-6400. www.polisince1921.com.* The Poli family has been operating this Italian seafood restaurant for three generations and prides itself on serving the freshest fish possible. Seafood, Italian menu. Lunch, dinner. Closed Mon; Thanksgiving, Dec 25. Bar. Children's menu. Casual attire. Valet parking. **$$**

★ **PRIMANTI BROTHERS.** *46 18th St, Pittsburgh (15222). Phone 412/263-2142. www.primantibros.com.* American, Italian menu. Dinner. Closed holidays. **$**

★ ★ ★ **RICO'S.** *1 Rico Ln, Pittsburgh (15237). Phone 412/931-1989; fax 412/931-2293. www.ricosrestaurant.com.* Italian, American menu. Lunch, dinner. Closed Sun; holidays. Bar. Jacket required. Valet parking. **$$$**

★ ★ **SOBA.** *5847 Ellsworth Ave, Pittsburgh (15232). Phone 412/362-5656; fax 412/361-4318. www.bigburrito .com.* Pan-Asian menu. Dinner. Bar. Outdoor seating. **$$$**

★ ★ ★ **STEELHEAD GRILL.** *112 Washington Pl, Pittsburgh (15219). Phone 412/394-3474; fax 412/394-1017. www.steelheadgrill.com.* Lunch, dinner. Children's menu. **$$$**

★ ★ **SUSHI TWO.** *2122 E Carson St, Pittsburgh (15203). Phone 412/431-7874; fax 412/431-7864. www.sushi2-too.com.* Japanese menu. Lunch, dinner. Closed Thanksgiving. Bar. **$$$**

★ ★ ★ **TAMBELLINI.** *860 Saw Mill Run Blvd, Pittsburgh (15226). Phone 412/481-1118; fax 412/481-7565. www.tambellini.com.* Guests should come hungry when visiting Louis Tambellini's place just outside of Pittsburgh. Prime steaks, veal chops, pastas, and seafood dishes await eager diners; vegetarian dishes also are available. Continental menu. Lunch, dinner. Closed Sun; Jan 1, Thanksgiving, Dec 25. Bar. Children's menu. Valet parking (dinner). **$$**

★ ★ **TESSARO'S.** *4601 Liberty Ave, Pittsburgh (15224). Phone 412/682-6809.* Casual décor has pressed tin ceiling (circa early 1900s), paddle ceiling fans, fireplaces. American, Mexican menu. Lunch, dinner. Closed Sun; holidays. Bar. **$$**

★ ★ **THAI PLACE.** *5528 Walnut St, Pittsburgh (15232). Phone 412/687-8586; fax 412/687-7970.* Thai menu. Lunch, dinner. Bar. Casual attire. **$$**

★ ★ ★ **TIN ANGEL.** *1200 Grandview Ave, Pittsburgh (15211). Phone 412/381-1919; fax 412/381-6270.* Located in a prime spot on Grandview Avenue, Tin Angel boasts wonderful views of downtown Pittsburgh in a candlelit setting. Seafood, steak menu. Closed Sun; holidays. Bar. **$$$**

Index

Flanagan House (Peoria, IL), *131*
Flanagan's (Fort Wayne, IN), *179*
Flint Ridge State Memorial (Newark, OH), *300*
Flo (Chicago, IL), *66*
Floodwall Murals Project (Portsmouth, OH), *306*
Foellinger Theatre (Fort Wayne, IN), *179*
Foellinger-Freimann Botanical Conservatory (Fort Wayne, IN), *178*
Fogo de Chão (Chicago, IL), *66*
Folk Festival (Pittsburgh, PA), *327*
Fond De La Tour (Oak Brook, IL), *125–126*
Forbes, Stephen A., State Park (Salem, IL), *138–139*
Ford Center for the Performing Arts Oriental Theater (Chicago, IL), *29*
Fore & Aft (Cincinnati, OH), *257*
Forest City Queen (Rockford, IL), *136*
Forest Glen Preserve (Collinsville, IL), *85*
Forest Park (Brazil, IN), *171*
Forest Park (St. Louis, MO), *152*
Forest Park Nature Center (Peoria, IL), *130*
Forks of the Wabash (Huntington, IN), *183*
Forks of the Wabash Pioneer Festival (Huntington, IN), *184*
Fort Ancient State Memorial, OH, *281*
Fort Dearborn (Chicago, IL), *21*
Fort Defiance Days (Defiance, OH), *277*
Fort Defiance State Park (Cairo, IL), *14*
Fort Hill State Memorial, OH, *281*
Fort Kaskaskia State Historic Site, IL, *96*
Fort Knox II (Vincennes, IN), *221*
Fort Laurens State Memorial (New Philadelphia, OH), *299*
Fort Meigs State Memorial (Toledo, OH), *312*
Fort Nelson (Louisville, KY), *226*
Fort Ouiatenon (Lafayette, IN), *196*
Fort Pitt Museum (Pittsburgh, PA), *325*
Fort Wayne, IN, *178–179*
Fort Wayne Children's Zoo (Fort Wayne, IN), *178*
Fort Wayne Museum of Art (Fort Wayne, IN), *178*
Foster, Stephen, Memorial (Pittsburgh, PA), *327*
Foster, Stephen Collins, *325*

Foster Memorial (Pittsburgh, PA), *325*
Fostoria, OH, *282*
Fountain Square Plaza (Cincinnati, OH), *252*
Four Points by Sheraton (Canton, OH), *247*
Four Points by Sheraton (Louisville, KY), *228*
Four Seasons, The (Chicago, IL), *35*
Four Seasons Hotel Chicago (Chicago, IL), *50–51*
Fourth Presbyterian Church (Chicago, IL), *29*
Fourth Street Art Fair (Bloomington, IN), *170*
Fourwinds Resort (Bloomington, IN), *170*
Fowler Park Pioneer Village (Terre Haute, IN), *218*
Fox Ridge State Park (Charleston, IL), *18*
Fox River Trolley Museum (Elgin, IL), *91*
Fox River Valley Trail (St. Charles, IL), *144*
France Park (Logansport, IN), *198*
Frances E. Willard Home/National Woman's Christian Temperance Union (WCTU) (Evanston, IL), *93*
Francesco's Hole in the Wall (Northbrook, IL), *124*
Francis Stupey Log Cabin (Highland Park, IL), *104*
Frank Lloyd Wright Home and Studio (Oak Park, IL), *127*
Franklin House (Chillicothe, OH), *249*
Frazer's Traveling Brown Bag (St. Louis, MO), *158*
Frederick C. Crawford Auto-Aviation Collection (Cleveland, OH), *263*
Freeport, IL, *96*
Freeport Arts Center (Freeport, IL), *96*
Fremont, OH, *282*
French Art Colony (Gallipolis, OH), *282*
French Lick, IN, *180*
French Lick Springs Resort & Spa (French Lick, IN), *180*
Frick, Henry Clay, *322*
Frick, Henry Clay, Fine Arts Building (Pittsburgh, PA), *327*
Frick Art and Historical Center (Pittsburgh, PA), *323*
Frick Art Museum, The (Pittsburgh, PA), *324*
Frick Park (Pittsburgh, PA), *324*
Fried Green Tomatoes (Galena, IL), *99*

Friends Creek Regional Park (Decatur, IL), *86*
Froggy's (Highwood, IL), *106*
Frontera Grill (Chicago, IL), *66*
Frontier Day (Terre Haute, IN), *218*
Frozen Niagara (Mammoth Cave National Park, KY), *231*
Fullersburg Woods Environmental Center (Oak Brook, IL), *125*
Funk Prairie Home (Bloomington-Normal, IL), *12*

G
Gabriel's (Highwood, IL), *106*
Gale Street Inn (Libertyville, IL), *112*
Galena, IL, *5, 97–99*
Galena Arts Festival (Galena, IL), *98*
Galena Cellars Winery (Galena, IL), *5*
Galena Country Fair (Galena, IL), *98*
Galena Post Office and Customs House (Galena, IL), *97*
Galena/Jo Daviess County History Museum (Galena, IL), *5, 97*
Galesburg, IL, *99–100*
Gallery Shop (Newark, OH), *300*
Gallipolis, OH, *282–283*
Galpin Wildlife and Bird Sanctuary (Milan, OH), *297*
Galt House Hotel (Louisville, KY), *228*
Garden at the Lighthouse (Port Clinton, OH), *305*
Gardenview Horticultural Park (Strongsville, OH), *311*
Garfield, James A., *232*
Garfield Farm Museum (Geneva, IL), *101*
Garfield Park and Conservatory (Chicago, IL), *29*
Garfield Park and Conservatory (Indianapolis, IN), *187–188*
Garland Building (Chicago, IL), *21*
Gary, IN, *164, 180*
Gateway Center (Pittsburgh, PA), *324*
Gateway Riverboat Cruises (St. Louis, MO), *152–153*
Gaylord Building (Lockport, IL), *114*
Geauga County Historical Society-Century Village (Chardon, OH), *248*
Geauga County Maple Festival (Chardon, OH), *248*
Gebhard Woods State Park (Morris, IL), *119*
Geja's Cafe (Chicago, IL), *66*
Gene & Georgetti (Chicago, IL), *67*
Gene Stratton Porter Historic Site (Auburn, IN), *166*

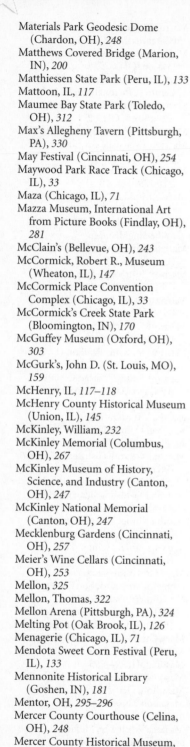

Notes

Notes

Notes

Notes

Notes

Notes